(*From an original miniature on copper, circa 1702, in the possession of Charles Dalton, Esq.*)

GEORGE THE FIRST'S ARMY
1714–1727

CHARLES DALTON, F.R.G.S.

IN TWO VOLUMES
• VOLUME 1 •

The Naval & Military Press Ltd

Reproduced by kind permission of the Central Library,
Royal Military Academy, Sandhurst

Published by
The Naval & Military Press Ltd
Unit 10, Ridgewood Industrial Park,
Uckfield, East Sussex,
TN22 5QE England
Tel: +44 (0) 1825 749494
Fax: +44 (0) 1825 765701
www.naval-military-press.com

© The Naval & Military Press Ltd 2005

In reprinting in facsimile from the original, any imperfections are inevitably reproduced and the quality may fall short of modern type and cartographic standards.

Dedicated

BY GRACIOUS PERMISSION

TO

HIS MAJESTY

KING GEORGE THE FIFTH

PREFACE.

WHEN I brought out, in 1904, the sixth and last volume of my *English Army Lists and Commission Registers*, 1661–1714, I was asked if I intended to continue the series. It was suggested that I should carry on the work from 1714 to 1740, the year that the first official *Army List* since the birth of England's Standing Army in 1661 made its tardy appearance. After fourteen years' hard labour spent over the aforesaid book of reference, I did not feel inclined at that time to turn my attention to the early Georgian Army. Historic proportion seemed to demand that the Standing Armies of Scotland and Ireland, from the Restoration to the Revolution, ought not to be further neglected. Three splendid Scottish regiments (the Scots Greys, the Scots Guards, and the Scots Fusiliers) date from the period when Scotland had an army of her own, while the Irish Army of Charles II.'s reign is represented by the Royal Irish Regiment of Foot. In 1905 I set to work on *Irish Army Lists*, 1661–1685, which appeared in January, 1907. The Irish Lists were only brought down to the accession of James II., because the Earl of Tyrconnell's remodelling of the Irish Army practically eliminated Protestant officers, who, to use an old English expression, were sent packing. *The Scots Army, 1661–1688, with Memoirs of the Commanders-in-Chief (Illustrated)* was finished by Christmas, 1908. When this work was published I prospected among the early Georgian State Papers at the Public Record Office. Pending re-arrangement, these documents are tied up in bundles according to their dates. Here I found a rich and varied store of letters and memorials relating to the Jacobite Rising of 1715. There were also touching appeals from widows and orphans on the brink of starvation; from Jacobites, belonging to good families, who petitioned the

Prince of Wales, when he was acting as Guardian of the Realm in 1716, that they might be removed from their particular cells in Newgate and the Fleet, being in company with prisoners suffering from "malignant spotted fevers." In another bundle I turned up a witty epigram by Lady Mary Wortley-Montague, which was found pinned to the portrait of a well-known English colonel in the latter's house. Silently laughing over this, I next read a badly-spelt, and worse-written, epistle to one of the highest ladies in St. James's Palace, who is informed by an anonymous female correspondent of a Jacobite plot to assassinate George I. Before this letter was fully digested, I found myself perusing a most touching and beautiful hymn penned in Newgate by a would-be regicide, a Jacobite youth of eighteen, who was hanged at Tyburn in 1718. Side by side with this poetic effusion was the defiant and unrepentant speech of the aforesaid young fanatic on the scaffold, which was printed at the time to the great indignation and displeasure of the Government. Passing on to a faded document without date, I came face to face with the lacquey of the Chief of Clanranald, in "The humble petition of Donald McMurray, running footman to ye Captt. of Clanranald for ye space of 15 yeares." The petitioner stated that "when in search of my Master, who was killd at ye battle of Dumblain, I was taken prisoner and keept in prison for 9 weekes." In order to gain his freedom McMurray turned King's evidence, and was sent up to London, where he gave important information before both Houses of Parliament. "Being in no respect further servisable to ye Government," writes this traitor, "and having a poor wife and children which are ruind upon ye account of my serving ye Government, and I have 500 millis (*sic*) fra home, [I] ask for freedom as a servant and a consideration to carry me to my poor wife and starving children."

After a week or two's research among these early eighteenth-century State Papers, I made up my mind to bring out a book, in two volumes, on *George the First's Army*, 1714–1727, devoting one-third of each volume to a series of memoirs of distinguished soldiers, whose lives were spent in the service of their country;

and in place of the usual Introduction to give a chapter on "The Early Georgian Era."

The present volume covers the period from George I.'s Accession to the declaration of war with Spain, the end of December, 1718. The Regimental Lists and Commission Registers, on the British Establishment, embrace the last four months of 1714 and the momentous years 1715–1718; while full lists of regiments serving in Ireland during the year 1715 are added, with supplementary commissions to the end of that red-letter year. This volume closes with a unique List of his Majesty's Train of Artillery in Ireland, 1716.

I am much indebted to the Council of the Royal United Service Institution for kindly permitting me to incorporate, in my present volume, the papers on "The Great Duke of Argyll's Military Career," "The Premier Field-Marshal of England," and "Field-Marshal Viscount Molesworth," formerly contributed by me to the *R.U.S.I. Journal*. I am equally indebted to the Council of the Royal Artillery Institution for allowing me to reprint my paper on "The Marquis de Montandre, a British Field-Marshal, 1739," printed some years since in the *R. A. Journal*. My best thanks are also due to Major Ferrar, Editor of *The Green Howards' Gazette*, for similar permission in connection with my article on "Lieut.-General Richard Sutton." I also wish to gratefully acknowledge items of information, chiefly biographical, from the following, viz., Mrs. Palmer-Douglas of Cavers; Sir James Balfour Paul, the Lord Lyon; my brother Major-General J. C. Dalton; Colonel W. O. Cavenagh; Lt.-Colonel G. H. Johnston of Kilmore, Co. Armagh; Major M. L. Ferrar; Mr. David Gemmell of Carley Bank, Bothwell, N.B.; Mr. J. R. Anderson of Albert Drive, Crosshill, Glasgow; Mr. G. T. Longley of the British Museum. And I wish to record my appreciation of the help and courtesy I have invariably received, when working at the Public Record Office, London, from Mr. Salisbury and Mr. Ratcliff; also from the Deputy Keeper and other officials of the Record Office of Ireland, Dublin, when making researches there.

As regards the illustrations, I may state that the portrait of the Premier Field-Marshal of England (the first Earl of Orkney) is taken from the original picture (three-quarters), which the late Earl of Orkney allowed me to have photographed. He also kindly had this large portrait taken down from the wall that I might inspect the long list of battles, sieges, and actions inscribed on the back of the canvas. The record of these war-services adds greatly to the interest attached to this historical portrait. I am indebted to my uncle, Captain Tancred, of Weens House, Roxburghshire, for the photo of the rare Molesworth medal facing page 85.

The design on the cover of this book needs a few words of explanation. It is from a photo of George the First's marble statue now in the Museum of the Public Record Office. There has been some correspondence lately in *Notes and Queries* on the subject of George I.'s statues in London. The statement was made, in above periodical, that "of the four statues of George I., in London, only one remains—that on St. George's steeple, Bloomsbury." So far as I know this assertion has not been contradicted. The statue in the R. O. Museum represents George I. in the costume of an ancient Roman. "It formerly occupied a niche over the judicial bench of the court in Rolls House, now demolished. On its present pedestal is a leaden tablet, from the foundation stone of that building, bearing the royal arms and inscribed—'G.R., 1717.'" (*Official Catalogue*).

I have received great assistance with the Index from Mr. G. T. Longley of the MS. Department, British Museum. The unfettered orthography of the early 18th century has added considerably to the labour of preparing a comprehensive *Index Nominum*.

CHARLES DALTON.

Union Club,
    London, S.W.
        1st December, 1910.

CONTENTS

	PAGE
PREFACE	v
THE EARLY GEORGIAN ERA, PART I.	xv
CHAPTER I.—The Great Duke of Argyll's Military Career, 1694–1742	1–9
CHAPTER II.—The Duke of Argyll's Letter to William Stuart, Esq., M.P.	10–16
CHAPTER III.—Colonel Charles Douglas, Anti-Jacobite Conspirator, 1715	17–34
CHAPTER IV.—The Premier Field-Marshal of England	35–38
CHAPTER V.—François de la Rochefoucauld, Marquis de Montandre	39–47
CHAPTER VI.—Major-General Joseph Wightman	48–54
CHAPTER VII.—Lieut.-General Richard Sutton, 1674–1738	55–58
CHAPTER VIII.—General Sir Charles Wills, K.B., 1661–1741	59–70
CHAPTER IX.—General the Right Hon. William Steuart, 1658?–1726	71–80
CHAPTER X.—Archibald, Earl of Forfar, Acting Brigadier-General at Sheriffmuir	81–84
CHAPTER XI.—Field-Marshal Viscount Molesworth	85–86
CHAPTER XII.—George Keith, Hereditary Earl Marshal of Scotland	87–90
Lists of Officers in the Regiments on the British Establishment, 1715	91–182
Military Commissions and Notifications, 1714–1718	183–217
(Prepared by Mr. James Craggs, Secretary-at-War.)	
Biographical Illustrations to Mr. Craggs's aforesaid List	218–224
Non-Regimental Commissions on the British Establishment, 1714–1715	225–255
Including :—	
Companies of Invalids, 1715	232–234
Establishment for Chelsea Hospital, 1715	235
General and Staff Officers in Scotland, 1714–1715	235–236
Castles and Forts with their Garrisons in Scotland, 1715	236
Three Independent Companies in the Highlands, 1715	236–237
Officers of the Scottish Field Train at Edinburgh Castle, 1715	237
Officers of the Gibraltar Garrison, 1714–1715	237–238
Officers of the Minorca Garrison, 1714–1715	238
Artillery Officers at Gibraltar, 1715	238–239
Artillery Officers at Port Mahon, 1715	239

CONTENTS

	PAGE
Non-Regimental Commissions on the British Establishment, &c.—*cont.*	
Garrison at Annapolis Royal, Nova Scotia, 1715	239–240
Artillery Officers at do., 1715	240
Four Independent Companies at Placentia, Newfoundland, 1715	241
The Placentia Garrison, 1715	241
Artillery Officers at do., 1715	241
Four Independent Companies in the Province of New York, 1715	242
Independent Companies in Jamaica, 1715	242–243
Independent Company in Bermuda, 1715	243
Biographical Illustrations to Non-Regimental Commissions	243–245
List of the General Officers upon the Establishment of Guards and Garrisons, 1716	246
Officers appointed to a newly-raised Independent Company in the Bahamas, 1717	250
Non-Regimental Commissions, 1716–1719, including England, Scotland, and the Colonies	247–252
Biographical Illustrations to Non-Regimental Commissions	253–255
Supplementary Commissions in Cavalry Regiments on the British Establishment, 1715–1719	257–280
Officers of the English Train of Artillery in May, 1715	281–282
Artillery Train for Service in Scotland, Nov. 1715	283–284
Ordnance List, 1715	285
Two Companies of Artillery, raised by Royal Warrant of May 26th, 1716	287–288
Supplementary Commissions in Infantry Regiments on the British Establishment, 1715–1719	289–319
Including :—	
List of Officers in Viscount Shannon's Regt. of Foot, 3rd September, 1717	307–308
List of Officers in Col. Richard Philipps's newly-raised Regt. of Foot, August 25th, 1717	312–313
Lists of Officers in the Regiments on the Irish Establishment, 1715	321–366
His Majesty's Train of Artillery in Ireland, 1716	367–372
INDEX	373–407

ILLUSTRATIONS

John, Duke of Marlborough		*Frontispiece*
Medal struck in Commemoration of George I.'s Accession	*page*	xvi
John, Duke of Argyll and Greenwich	*Facing* ,,	8
Letter from Colonel Charles Douglas to General James Stanhope	*Between pages*	24–25
The Premier Field-Marshal of England	*Facing page*	35
The Sheriffmuir Medal	,, ,,	49
Plan of the Town of Preston when Besieged in November 1715	,, ,,	63
General Sir Charles Wills, K.B.	,, ,,	64
Medal struck in honour of Captain Richard Molesworth, afterwards Field-Marshal Viscount Molesworth	,, ,,	85
John, Duke of Montagu	,, ,,	96
Richard, Earl of Scarborough	,, ,,	99
General Sir Philip Honywood, K.B.	,, ,,	115
Lord Cadogan	,, ,,	128
Charles, Lord Cathcart	,, ,,	224
Lieut.-General Borgard	,, ,,	283
General Thomas Erle	,, ,,	285
Monument to Field-Marshal Viscount Shannon, and Statue to ditto on his Monument	*Between pages*	308–309
Lord Hinchinbroke	*Facing page*	321
General Joseph Sabine	,, ,,	347
General William Barrell	,, ,,	353

KEY TO REFERENCE LETTERS

MSS. AT PUBLIC RECORD OFFICE, LONDON.

a = War Office Commission Entry Book, 1714–1716.
b =   ,,   ,,   ,,   1717–1718.
c =   ,,   ,,   ,,   1718–1723.
d = War Office MS. Army List, 1715.
e =   ,,   ,,   1717.
f = War Office MS. Gradation List, 1730.
g = Ordnance Treasury Ledgers, 1714–1715, 1715–1716.

MSS. AT PUBLIC RECORD OFFICE, DUBLIN.

h = Commission Entry Book, 1709–1716.
i =   ,,   ,,   1715–1717.
j =   ,,   ,,   1716–1720.
k = Martial Affairs, 1717–1719.
l = Ordnance Establishment for 1717.

PRINTED BOOKS.

m = *London Gazettes.*
n = *Historical Register,* 1715, &c.
o = *Half-Pay List,* 1739.

ABBREVIATIONS

Cy. = Company.
Comn. = Commission.
Tp. = Troop.
Gds. = Guards.
Dns. = Dragoons.
Capt.-Lt. = Captain-Lieutenant.
C. in C. = Commander-in-Chief.
Qr.-Mr. = Quartermaster
Indep. Cy. = Independent Company.
M.I. = Monumental Inscription.

ERRATA

Page 109, note 1, line 14, *for* "Commander-in-Chief in Scotland, 1718–1719" *read* "Commander-in-Chief in Scotland, 1716–1724."

„ 140, *for* "Ensign Maximilian Vannarsen" *read* "Ensign Maximilian Vannamen."

„ 166, *for* "Captain George Dawson" *read* "Captain George Lawson."

„ 168, *for* "Ensign Maynard de Querin" *read* "Ensign Maynard de Guerin."

„ 201, *for* "William Krant" (four lines from the bottom) *read* "Wm. Kraut."

„ 203, *for* "[Jarves] Eyton" (thirteen lines from the bottom) *read* "[James] Eyton."

„ 298, *for* "Patrick McAva" *read* "Patrick McAra."

OMISSIONS.

Page 172, John Gilby, Ensign.
„ 182, Jerome Bellingham, Ensign.

THE EARLY GEORGIAN ERA

PART I

The Accession of George I. on 1st August, 1714, is celebrated every anniversary by a boat race between six watermen from London Bridge to Chelsea. The prize is a waterman's coat and silver badge, known as "Doggett's Coat and Badge." Thomas Doggett, a London actor of some note, was so attached to the Hanoverian succession that, in the year after George I. came to the Throne, he instituted the above race on the first day of August, and continued it till his death in 1722. In his will Doggett "bequeathed a certain sum of money, the interest of which was to be appropriated annually, for ever, for the purchase of a like coat and badge to be rowed for in honour of the day by six young watermen whose apprenticeships had expired the year before."* The coat was of orange colour, in honour of William III., and the silver badge had a horse on it with the motto "Liberty." The equine emblem deserves more than passing mention, as it is a greatly prized badge of some distinguished British regiments. The "White Horse on a red field" was the armorial bearing of Wittekend, the last Saxon King, and has for centuries been borne by the House of Brunswick. Tradition has it that the banner of Wittekend bore a black horse, "which, on his conversion to Christianity by Charlemagne, was altered to white, as the emblem of the pure faith he had embraced." † The story is a beautiful one, and ought to be perpetuated.

After the Jacobite Rising of 1715 was successfully crushed, George I. bestowed the Royal badge of the White Horse on certain cavalry and infantry regiments which had taken an active part in suppressing the rebellion in Scotland. The first infantry corps to obtain the coveted distinction of the "White Horse" was

---

* Hone's *Every-Day Book*, Vol. II., p. 1062.
† *Hist. Record of The King's Regiment of Foot*, 2nd Edit. 1883, p. 39, note 1.

the 8th Regiment of the Line, known as "The Queen's," during Queen Anne's reign. There being no Queen Consort when George I. ascended the throne, "The Queen's" was, in 1717, given the title of "The King's," the facings being changed from yellow to blue, and the regiment authorised to bear the White Horse as a badge.* The motto which invariably goes with the White Horse, viz., "Nec Aspera Terrent," was, by some strange oversight, left out at the date in question, and the authorisation for its use only granted in 1840, "when it appears on the colours for the first time." † "The 8th," says the late Mr. S. M. Milne, "still has the distinction of being the only infantry regiment which bears the 'White Horse' as the principal badge in the centre of its colours." ‡

Whilst on the subject of this historic horse, it may be mentioned that a medal was struck in 1714 to commemorate George Lewis's accession to the British Throne. The reverse of this medal has the White Horse.

Medal of George I.

Obv.: GEORG LVD . D . G . M . BRIT . FR . et HIB REX DVX B & L. S. R . I . ELEC. Bust, laureate, to right. Rev.: ACCEDENS DIGNVs DIVIsos ORBE BRITANNOS. The horse of Brunswick, running across the map of the north-west of Europe. Below, vnvs non svfficit orbis.

The horse in this case has been also described as "leaping from Hanover to England." § But the white steed on the colours of many old British regiments is represented going at a hand gallop, which recalls Virgil's cantering hexameter:

"Quadrupedante putrem sonitu quatit ungula campum."

* *Hist. Record of The King's Regiment of Foot*, 2nd Edit. 1883, p. 39, note 1.
† Milne's *Standards and Colours of the Army*, 1661–1881, p. 93. ‡ *Ibid.*
§ Official Catalogue, Department of Coins and Medals, Brit. Mus.

The "Black Cockade" now worn in the hat by coachmen and livery servants of persons serving under the Crown was introduced into the British Army by George I., it having been "originally the distinctive badge of the House of Hanover, as the white cockade was of the House of Stuart."* The rosette of black leather was well known in the German wars during the 17th century, and in Scotland rosettes of coloured ribbons were occasionally used by Covenanters on the "cock of their hats" when "marching as to war." † It is an interesting fact that during the '15 British soldiers wore the black rosettes in their shakos, as recorded in an old Scots ditty describing the battle of Sheriffmuir :

"The red-coat lads wi' black cockades."

It is also worthy of record that the Jacobites did not always sport the pure white cockade, the Stuart badge, at the period in question, either in Scotland or England. This assertion is amply proved by a trustworthy contemporary chronicle, wherein it is stated that on the march of the Scottish Highlanders under Brigadier Mackintosh, of Borlum, and "General" Forster's Northumberland Jacobites, from Kelso, across the Borders, the insurgent forces passed the night of 29th October, 1715, at Hawick, "where a quantity of cockades, consisting of blue and white ribbons, was made for the Scotch, to distinguish them from the English insurgents, who wore red and white cockades." ‡

In the Clothing Regulations for British regiments issued 1st July, 1751, "The King's" and "The Queen's Dragoons" (the present 3rd and 7th Hussars) were ordered to wear black cockades in their hats. The shakos of other British regiments were similarly ornamented.

After the French Revolution the regiments of *émigrés* (refugees from France) in the Austrian, British, and Dutch pay, "were obliged to wear the black cockade, an emblem common

---

* *The New English Dictionary.*
† The Rev. James Kirkton's *Church of Scotland*, p. 439.
‡ *Faithful Register of the late Rebellion*, p. 127.

to the British and Austrian troops alike."* It thus happened that the British troops under the Duke of York which joined the Allied Forces in the Low Countries in 1793, wore *la cocarde noire*, introduced into the English Army by George I.

Returning to George I.'s accession, seven weeks elapsed before the King arrived in England. It has been truly said that "it was not George who wanted England but England who wanted George." He had not, however, been forgetful of the great English soldier who had been in voluntary exile at The Hague since 1712. By a stroke of his pen at Hanover the King restored Marlborough to the post of Captain-General of the British Army. The illustrious Duke landed at Dover on 1st August, and received a great ovation when he entered London; but Marlborough's *amour propre* was grievously wounded by his name having been omitted from the number of the Lords Justices of the Kingdom.

On 18th September George I. landed at Greenwich, and made his public entry into London two days later.

The Coronation took place on 22nd October. The Countess Cowper, wife of the Lord Chancellor and Lady of the Bedchamber to the Princess of Wales, has left a graphic account of what she saw and heard at this great function in her charming *Diary*. She tells how Lord Bolingbroke did homage to the King, and how his Majesty, who had not seen this quasi-Jacobite peer before, asked his name, "and he (Lord B.) hearing it as he went down the steps from the Throne, turned round and bowed three times down to the very ground."† Referring to the Jacobites present at the Coronation Service, Lady Cowper records that "they were all there looking as cheerful as they could, but very peevish with everybody that spoke to them. My Lady Dorchester stood underneath me, and when the Archbishop went round the Throne demanding the consent of the people, she turned about to me and said, 'Does the old

---

* See paper on "The Black Cockade" in the *Cornhill Magazine*, May, 1910, p. 719.

† *Diary of Mary, Countess Cowper*, Edit. 1864, p. 5.

fool think that anybody here will say no to his question when there are so many drawn swords?'"

A little later the King went in State, accompanied by the Prince and Princess of Wales, to the Guildhall, it being Lord Mayor's Day. The troops added to the brilliancy of the "show." Lady Cowper writes:—

> "I thought I should have lost the use of my ears with the continual noise of huzzas, music, and drums. . . My poor Lady Humphreys made a sad figure in her black velvet, and did make a most violent bawling to her page to hold up her train before the Princess, being loath to lose the privilege of her Mayoralty. But the greatest jest was that the King and the Princess both had been told that my Lord Mayor had borrowed her for that day only, so I had much ado to convince them of the contrary, though he by marriage is a sort of relation of my Lord's first wife. At last they did agree that if he had borrowed a wife it would have been another sort of one than she was." *

Without doubt Lady Cowper thoroughly believed that the "Lady Mayoress" who masqueraded before the Princess and the Royalties was the Lord Mayor's wife. But it is difficult to imagine that on this, the King's first State visit to the Guildhall, anyone should have wilfully deceived both his Majesty and the Princess by telling them that the Lord Mayor had borrowed the Lady Mayoress for that day only!

Hidden away in a bundle of State Papers for the reign of George I., at the Public Record Office, is an undated document which has never hitherto seen the light of print. It is as follows:

> "To His Grace the Lord Archbishop of York, Lord High Almoner.
> "The humble petition of Lady Humphrys, Widow.
>> "Sheweth that your Petitioner has been a creditable Housekeeper, but now reduced to great necessity, being left with a child and no subsistence but what she receives by charity. Your Petitioner therefore humbly prays that your Grace will make her a partaker of his Majesty's Royal Maunday at the ensuing occasion, and your Petitioner as in duty bound shall ever pray, etc.
>> "LADY HUMPHREY."

Now there are two remarkable things about this petition. The first is that her "Ladyship" does not inform the Archbishop

---

* *Diary of Mary, Countess Cowper*, Edit. 1864, p. 11.

who her deceased husband was. And secondly, she signs the petition (the body of which is in a clerkly hand) as "Lady Humphrey," which does not look as if she were either a lady by birth or the widow of a knight or baronet. Who shall say that she was not the person whom Sir William Humphreys,* the Lord Mayor of London, "borrowed for the day only," on 29th October (O.S.), 1714?

When Queen Anne died the total strength of the Army in Great Britain was 7,813,† and about 5,000 on the Irish establishment. The three British infantry regiments in Flanders (which did not return to England till the autumn of 1715) had a total strength of 1,895.‡ The regiments and independent companies in the colonies need not be taken into account here, as they were not available for home service in 1715. It is a matter of history why the Harley and Bolingbroke Ministry, at the close of Queen Anne's reign, disbanded whole regiments of cavalry and infantry,§ and reduced all the others to a "Peace" strength.

The British public in general, and their representatives in Parliament, highly approved at the time of the dismemberment of the Standing Army. But the new King was a soldier of wide experience, and quickly grasped that Great Britain was entirely unprepared to resist a foreign invasion or cope with an internal rebellion. George I. had made up his mind to stay in England whatever happened, and with this fixed resolve he restored,

---

* Created a baronet by George I. 30 Nov. 1714. He was twice married, and had a son and heir by his first wife, who succeeded as 2nd Bt. in 1735. According to G.E.C.'s *Baronetage*, Sir Wm. Humphreys re-married in 1705, but had no issue of his second wife, who predeceased her husband by three years, and whose will was proved in 1734.

† *A Particular of the Numbers of the Troops and Regiments of Horse, Foot, and Dragoons in Great Britain and in Flanders on the 5th day of April*, 1715, *by a Member of Parliament.* The numbers given in the text are exclusive of "Ker's Dragoons" restored by George I. in Jan. 1715.

‡ *Ibid.*

§ Ker's and Pepper's Regts. of Dragoons (present 7th and 8th Hussars); Handasyde's Regt. (22nd Foot); Lord Mark Kerr's (29th Foot); three Regts. of Marines (the present 30th, 31st, and 32nd Regts. of Foot); Wade's Regt. (33rd Foot); Chudleigh's Regt. (34th Foot).

between 31st January and 31st July, 1715, all the old regiments mentioned on a former page as having been "broke" at the close of Queen Anne's reign. But the three Regiments of Marines became respectively the 30th, 31st, and 32nd Regiments of the Line, thus losing their former individuality as sea-going battalions. The King compelled some general officers who commanded regiments, and were suspected of Jacobite leanings, to sell their commissions. Among these were Generals Webb, Echlin, William Steuart, Hans Hamilton, the Earls of Arran and Strafford; also Colonel Sir Henry Goring, Bt. With the exception of General Steuart, all of these experienced veterans openly, or secretly, aided and abetted the Chevalier St. George during the '15. Some high-minded officers in George I.'s Army voluntarily resigned their commissions to join the Jacobite Cause. Among these was George Keith, 10th Earl Marischal. And when the Chevalier landed in Scotland, Captain Arthur Elphinstone, of Lord Shannon's Regiment, threw up his commission, bade good-bye to his brother officers, and openly left his garrison at Dunfermline to join James Stuart.* This conscientious young Scotsman succeeded as 6th Lord Balmerinoch, 5th January, 1746, and was beheaded on Tower Hill the 18th August following for his share in the '45.

It has been remarked by more than one historian that though Marlborough was restored to his high military commands his power with regard to military matters was merely nominal. It has been suggested that George I. owed the Duke a grudge because the latter, when commanding the British Forces and their Allies on the Continent, had declined to unfold his plan of campaign in 1708 to George Lewis, who had taken the field in command of the Imperial Troops on the Upper Rhine. This refusal on the Duke's part certainly gave the Elector (as he then was) deep offence at the time, for the latter, like William III., had been a soldier from boyhood, and his fitness for command had

* The writer of an Edinburgh "Newsletter" of 3 Feb. 1716 says Capt. Elphinstone "had been suspended and deserted." The anecdote quoted in the text is taken from a very reliable source, viz., *The Records of the King's Own Borderers*, by Lt.-Col. Higgins, p. 31.

been proved on several closely-contested battle-fields. Take, for instance, that of Neerwinden (generally called Landen by English writers), on the fatal 19th July, 1693. This was, after Steinkirk (in 1692), the most sanguinary battle in Flanders during the latter half of the 17th century; William III. and George Lewis were among the last to leave the field. In the retreat "everyone," as Corporal Trim used to say, "was left to shift for himself." King William and the Electoral Prince of Hanover narrowly escaped capture; the former, it is said, owed his safety to a gallant English officer (Hatton Compton), and the latter was rescued by Baron Hamerstein. George I. and his Ministers were at one in their desire to limit Marlborough's power during the critical period of 1715 and subsequent years, well knowing the Duke's real feelings towards the son of James II. Hence it was that General Stanhope and Lord Townshend (the Secretaries of State) acted as War Ministers to the King, whom they consulted on military matters,* as well as in affairs of state; while William Pulteney (afterwards Earl of Bath) had the onerous post of Secretary-at-War, which at the period in question was equivalent to Under Secretary of State in later times.

In the early summer of 1715 it became generally known that there would not only be a Jacobite rising in Scotland, but that the Chevalier St. George would attempt a landing on the British coast, and that he would not come with merely a handful of his own followers, but be accompanied by French officers and men supplied by Louis XIV. When George I. landed in England, Parliament added a clause to a money bill, offering a reward of "£100,000 to such as should seize the Pretender dead or alive if he landed on British soil." A new Parliament assembled at Westminster on 19th March, 1715. On 13th July the King attended in the House of Lords and informed both Houses "that a rebellion had actually begun at home, and that an invasion was threatened from abroad, and he therefore solicited the Commons to enable him to provide for the defence of the Kingdom."

---

* See p. 16, note 1.

Parliament gave a ready assent. Thirteen regiments of Dragoons (each with six troops) were raised without delay. The first was Major-General Pepper's (8th), which had been "broke" by Queen Anne's Government; it was now restored by George I. and given its old precedence. Eight Regiments of Foot (each containing ten companies) were also raised. The commissions of the officers were dated 22nd July, 1715, and duly signed by the King. Most of the officers in the new levies were taken from the Half-pay Lists. On 1st August the Secretary-at-War (William Pulteney) wrote to Lord Townshend's secretaries to the effect that His Majesty directed Ker's Dragoons (7th) to be styled "Her Royal Highness the Prince of Wales's Own Royal Regiment of Dragoons." * On the above date the Princess was appointed Honorary Colonel of Thomas Pitt's Regiment of Horse † (now the 2nd D.G.), and also of Kirk's Regiment of Foot (now The Queen's). George, Prince of Wales, had been appointed Colonel of the Regiment of Horse (now known as the 4th D.G.),‡ and also of the present Royal Welsh Fusiliers.§ The King changed the title of "The Queen's Regiment of Horse" (now the first D.G.) into "The King's Regiment of Horse," and ordered "The Queen's Own Regiment of Foot" (which was in garrison at Windsor during the latter half of 1715) to be henceforth styled "The King's Own," which title it still bears. By way of paying a compliment to the Churchill family, George I. gave one of the new Dragoon regiments to Colonel Charles Churchill, and honoured this corps by appointing the Prince of Wales Honorary Colonel.

Colonel Charles Churchill was the illegitimate son of General Charles Churchill, brother to Marlborough. Of the younger Charles Churchill it may be said that though he was a brave officer, who had seen considerable service, he is best remembered as the paramour of the celebrated actress, Anne Oldfield, by whom he had a son. Among the MSS. relating to the early Georgian

---

* Cannon's *Records of the 7th Hussars*, p. 26.
† See p. 326.
‡ See p. 327 and note.
§ See p. 347.

era, at the Public Record Office, are some lines by the talented Lady Mary Wortley Montagu :—

"Verses by Lady M—— W——ly, pinned upon the picture of Charles Churchill at Van Loes :—

"Still hovring round the Fair at fifty four,
Unfit to love, unable to give o'er,
A flash fly, that just flutters on the wing,
Awake to buzz, but not alive to sting.
Brisk, when he cannot, backward when he can,
A teazing Ghost of the departed man."

In addition to the twenty-one new regiments, **thirty men were added to each of the twenty-eight companies in the 1st Foot Guards and four new companies to the Coldstream Guards,** while the 3rd Foot Guards was augmented by strengthening the eighteen companies. Each troop in existing Cavalry Regiments was increased by ten men, and two additional companies of fifty men to each Infantry Corps on the Home Establishment. The last-named augmentation was exclusive of ten men added to the existing companies. Here is the form of oath required in George I.'s Army :—

"THE OATH OF FIDELITY.*

"I swear to be true to our Sovereign Lord King George and to serve him honestly and faithfully in defence of his Person, Crown, and Dignity against all his Enemies and opressors (*sic*) ; and to observe and obey his Majesties orders, and the orders of the Generals and Officers set over me by his Majesty. So help me God."

One of the many romantic incidents of the '15 took place on 2nd August, when that double-dyed traitor John, Earl of Mar, embarked at Gravesend, disguised as a collier, on a vessel bound for Newcastle, accompanied by Lieut.-General George Hamilton and Colonel Hay, also disguised. From Newcastle these three Jacobite plotters reshipped for the Firth of Forth. General Hamilton had served many years with distinction † in the Scots Brigade in Holland, and commanded a regiment which was placed on British half-pay in 1714. From time immemorial

---

* *S. P. Dom. George I.*, Bundle 66.
† *English Army Lists and Commission Registers*, 1661–1714, Vol. VI., p. 302, note 8.

the officers in the Scots and English brigades, in the Dutch service, were required to take an oath of allegiance to the English Sovereign on taking up their military appointments, as well as to their High Mightinesses the States-General.

On 6th September Lord Mar raised the Chevalier's standard at Kirkmichael, in Braemar, in presence of a force of about 2,000 men, most of whom were horse.* The ceremony is described in an old Scots ditty:—

> "But when the standard was set up,
> Right fierce the wind did blaw, Willie,
> The royal nit upon the tap
> Down to the ground did fa', Willie."

The fall of the ball from the top of the pole was looked upon as a sad omen by the superstitious Highlanders:—

> "Then second-sighted Sandy said,
> We'd do nae guid at a', Willie."

The death of Louis XIV. on 1st September, 1715, considerably delayed the Chevalier's departure for Scotland; but the Jacobites in that kingdom had gone too far to withdraw and "mark time" until the arrival of James VIII. Events indeed moved rapidly. On the night of 8th September a well-planned attempt to seize Edinburgh Castle was made and nearly succeeded. Colonel James Stewart, the Deputy-Governor, commanded the Castle garrison. He had been warned of the projected design, but made light of it and took no precautions. "Had it not been for [Lieut.] Lindsie (*sic*) quho contrair to the Colonel's advice," says a contemporary writer, "was very vigilant, the Castle had that night been surprised."† Stewart was superseded in his post by Brigadier George Preston; but as there was no conclusive proof of his guilt he was placed on half-pay. His military career, however, was finished.

The attempt on Edinburgh Castle hastened the Duke of Argyll's journey north from Boroughbridge, where the news reached him. A full account of his doings from the time he left

---

* *Annals of 2nd year of George I.*, p. 28.
† *News Letters* of 1715–16, pp. 33, 34.

London, to within two (?) days of the battle of Sheriffmuir, is given in the Duke's long and interesting, though forcible, letter to a Scottish M.P. (pp. 10–16), which epistle, so far as can be ascertained, has not been previously printed. The battle of Dumblane, as the engagement at Sheriffmuir was sometimes termed, has been described by a Scottish humorist in satirical verse (p. 8); but there is a soldierly narrative (Appendix in Vol. II.) of the battle from Major-General Wightman who commanded the centre of the Royalist army on the memorable 13th November, 1715. It was only to be expected that Major-General Whetham (p. 164), who was in command of the defeated wing of Argyll's army, should fall under the lash of Jacobite writers and verse-makers. Such an opportunity was not to be lost. Under date of 15th November, 1715, Argyll writes to the Ministry concerning rumours to Whetham's discredit:—

> "I have enquired exactly into this matter, that I might be able to do justice to Mr. Whetham, who by experience I know to be . . . a good officer and as brave a man as any serves his Majesty." *

And in his dispatch to Lord Townshend on 6th December Argyll declares:—

> "I do most sincerely think that what happened was Mr. Whetham's misfortune and not his fault." †

The butcher's bill at Sheriffmuir was very heavy as regards Royalist officers. Moryson's regiment (8th Foot) suffered most. Eight officers were killed (p. 196). The Earl of Forfar, who acted as a brigadier and charged at the head of aforesaid corps, was wounded and taken prisoner. His barbarous treatment by the Highlanders, as he lay helpless on the field, is fully narrated in a letter to the said Earl's aunt written on the third day after the battle (pp. 82–83). In the *Records of The King's Regiment* the name of Ensign Glenkennely appears as having been wounded at Sheriffmuir. ‡ There was no officer of this name in the British army at the period in question; but it so happened that a

---

* *Home Office MSS. Scotland,* Bundle 10.
† *Ibid.*
‡ P. 38.

Scottish gentleman, Patrick Strachan of Glenkindie, served as a volunteer in Argyll's army, and being attached to Moryson's corps at Sheriffmuir was taken prisoner by the rebels.

In his petition, at a later date, to George I. for repayment of moneys he had expended while employed on military service in Scotland, Glenkindie records that—

> "Being the only gentleman in his part of the country who remained loyal to the King, he was treated with great barbarity by the Earl of Mar, being confined in a most nauseous dungeon [14 weeks], till the Pretender fled from Scotland, when he was released. His Majesty's Generals, then in Scotland, employed petitioner in several marches to the Highlands with their troops. He has expended considerable sums of money of his own, has been a great sufferer in his private fortune, and to this day has received no reimbursement. Prays payment and a reward for services." *

On the very day that Argyll and Mar tried conclusions on the field of Sheriffmuir, Preston, in Lancashire, surrendered to Generals Wills and Carpenter after a few days' siege (pp. 67-68). In the first attack on the town, Brigadier Preston's Regiment of Foot (the Cameronians), under command of Lord Forester, suffered heavily, losing between 60 and 70 in killed and wounded. Captain Robert Preston of this Corps, who was taken prisoner, owed his life on this occasion to the gallantry of a Jacobite officer, Captain Nicholas Wogan, who saved Preston from being cut to pieces.†

During the winter of 1715-16, Newgate was crowded to overflowing with Jacobite prisoners; while Carlisle Castle was similarly honoured. The Scottish peers taken at Preston were sent to the Tower. Every student of history is well acquainted with the Countess of Nithsdale's thrilling story of her Lord's escape, the night before his intended execution, by her instrumentality. This brave lady's narrative, in the form of a letter to her sister, Lady Lucy Herbert, written from Rome 26th April, 1718, is still extant; but this invaluable MS. is defaced by the

---

* Petition endorsed "16th July, 1718." *Treasury Papers*, Vol. ccxiii., No. 64. Patrick Strachan of Glenkindie was knighted in 1717 and d. at Aberdeen, 2 Jan. 1726. See account of this gentleman in Colonel Allardyce's *The Strachans of Glenkindie*, pp. 27-28.

† Rapin's *Hist. of England*, 2nd Edit. 1751, Vol. IV., p. 451, note 1.

Countess's signature having been cut off.* The narrative caused so much interest at the time, that more than one copy was sent to intimate friends; and a well-known historian of the 19th century printed it.† Among the Georgian State Papers at the Public Record Office is a single quarto sheet of paper closely written over, on both sides, in a lady's small running hand. The sheet is numbered "4." A slip is pinned on to it containing a memorandum to the effect that the paper was found at Greenwich Hospital, and relates to Lord Nithsdale's escape from the Tower of London. Unfortunately the remaining sheets have never been found; and there is nothing to show who wrote it or to whom it was originally sent. But from the fact of this MS. having been found among the documents at Greenwich Hospital, which institution was enriched by the rents from the forfeited Derwentwater Estates, it is within the bounds of possibility that this sheet formed part of a contemporary copy of Lady Nithsdale celebrated narrative, sent from Rome to the widowed Lady Derwentwater, at whose death, or her son's attainder, papers relating to the Radcliffe family may have found their way to Greenwich.

Among the Scottish prisoners in Carlisle Castle was a certain Captain William Hay. He had been arraigned for high treason and had pleaded "guilty." The Mayor of Carlisle had given the head gaoler directions to "be very circumspect in looking after the said Hay in particular." ‡ Accordingly, the gaoler "locked the said Hay up in the high Castle." On the night of Sunday, 9th February, 1716, a certain Ensign Wm. White, of General Wills's Regiment (The Buffs), was "Captain of the Guard." It was this officer's duty to get a list of the prisoners from the head gaoler, then proceed to the "high Castle" and personally see that each captive answered to his name; he also had to make certain that they were all safe behind locked and barred doors. The Ensign went his rounds, called out the names, and found the

---

* Sir Wm. Fraser's *The Book of Carlaverock*, Vol. II., pp. 222-234.

† Earl Stanhope in his *Hist. of England*, 1713-1783, 5th Edition, Vol. II. Appendix, pp. iv.–xi.

‡ Major Duquerry's evidence, under oath, relative to Capt. Hay's escape from Carlisle Castle, given 18th Feb. 1716. *S. P. Dom. George I.*

number of prisoners tallied with the gaoler's list. Having seen all the doors locked and bolted, the "Captain of the Guard" retired for the rest of the night to the guard-room. Early next morning the gaoler came in great trepidation to Major Duquerry (p. 110), the Commandant, and reported that—

> "Mr. Wm. Hay, one of the rebell prisoners, had made his escape out of the Castle; upon which the Major gave him some hard language . . . . the gaoler replied that he had taken all the care he could and had locked him the said Hay up in the high Castle the night before amongst the other prisoners there." *

On examining the list of prisoners given to Ensign White by the gaoler on the previous night, it was discovered that "only one Mr. Hay was mentioned [thereon], though there were, or ought to have been, two of that surname." The Mayor of Carlisle held a searching inquiry in the Castle relative to Wm. Hay's escape. It came out in White's evidence that "he had seen Mr. Hay walking on the terrace of the said Castle, in the daytime, without any company with him or being under any restraint." † Nothing relative to the escape was discovered; but the natural inference is that the gaoler never locked up Wm. Hay at all on the night of February 9th, and helped him to escape in the same way that St. Paul's friends adopted at Damascus! Advantage was taken of the young officer's inexperience to purposely leave out the escaped prisoner's name from the list when the former went his rounds.

There is reason to believe that this Wm. Hay was the Jacobite officer of this name who subsequently held a high post in the Chevalier's household.

The escape from Newgate of "General" Forster encouraged Brigadier Mackintosh, his son John, Charles Wogan, James Talbot, and a dozen other prisoners, to make a dash for freedom. Having knocked down the turnkeys and disarmed the sentinels, these Jacobites broke out of Newgate between 11 and 12 at night on 3rd May, 1716, which was the day before the trial of Mackintosh and some other rebels was fixed to take place at

---

* *S. P. Dom. George I.*

† Affidavit of Ensign Wm. White of General Wills's Regt. before the Mayor of Carlisle in Feb. 1716. *S. P. Dom. George I.*

Westminster. Brigadier Mackintosh and seven of his companions got clear away. Seven others, being unacquainted with the streets, ran into Warwick Court, a *cul de sac*, and fell into the hands of their pursuers. "James Talbot, one of the fugitives, was retaken in a house in Windmill St., Piccadilly, and sent back to Newgate."* Among the Georgian State Papers is "The humble petition of James Talbott to Lord Townshend," which

> "sheweth that the prison being very full and infected with the spotted feaver, and other distempers, and your Petitioner in a very ill state of health, was advised to petition His Royal Highness to be removed into the custody of a messenger, for the benefit of his health. Prays Lord Townshend to present his petition to H.R.H."

In the same bundle of documents is the petition of Robert Talbott concerning "his being confined in a most loathsome and stinking place"; and "John Thornton, Esq., who surrendered himself at Preston, and had been confined in the Fleet and Newgate," petitions the Prince of Wales, in July, 1716, to this effect:

> "That about two months ago your Petitioner had a violent spotted feaver which, together with his close confinement, hath so much impaired his health . . . that without the benefit of the fresh air he can never hope to recover . . . he pleaded guilty to his indictment, and by your Royal Highness's mercy and goodness is now reprieved for six weeks."

This petition is certified as follows by the learned Sir Samuel Garth (p. 227), Physician-General to the Army: "The contents of this petition is the real truth.—S. Garth, M.D."

Whilst Jacobite captives had suffered for their loyalty to the Chevalier St. George, either on the scaffold or by transportation to the American Plantations and the West Indies,† or by weary months of imprisonment in English and Scottish dungeons, their titular monarch had paid his brief winter visit to Scotland, and returned to France with the Earl of Mar and some of his principal officers. The story of James Stuart's journey to

---

* Rapin's *Hist. of England*, Vol. IV., p. 496.

† "Thirty of the Preston Rebels having been put on board a ship to be transported, affidavits were made before the Mayor of Liverpool, that they had mastered the ship's crew, and carried the vessel to France. One hundred of the same prisoners, who had been confined in the Savoy, were shipped off for the West Indies." Rapin's *Hist. of England*, Vol. IV., p. 504, note 1.

St. Malo and Dunkirk, from Lorraine, in November, 1715, is fully told in this volume (pp. 22–25), and the attempt to kidnap the Chevalier St. George, on his way to the French coast, is thoroughly thrashed out (*Ibid.*). When it is remembered that the Earl of Berkeley, First Lord of the Admiralty, offered to kidnap George, Prince of Wales, transport him to America, and keep him there, at the time when the strained relations between George I. and his son had reached fever heat, it is not difficult to realise that the Earl of Stair, British Envoy in Paris, had planned, with the help of Colonel Charles Douglas and other spies, to seize James Stuart on his historic journey and transport him as far as possible from the French coast. The often-repeated story of attempted assassination is, so far as the Earl of Stair and Colonel Charles Douglas are concerned, purely imaginary.

The Standing Army was further increased, in February, 1716, by five regiments of dragoons and eight of infantry, which were raised for the Irish Establishment.* The *raison d'être* for these levies was because Pitt's Horse (2nd D. G.), Evans's Dragoons (4th), Moryson's Foot (8th), Clayton's (14th), Wightman's (17th), Sabine's (23rd), Preston's (26th), Egerton's (36th), and Fane's (37th) had been sent to Great Britain from Ireland, during the previous summer and autumn, to serve against the rebels.

By the terms of an existing treaty with the States-General, Dutch troops to the number of 6,000 were sent to England late in the year 1715 and were dispatched to Scotland in December, to augment Argyll's force and strengthen certain weak garrisons. A small Swiss contingent, also in British pay, made its appearance in Scotland. The Dutch troops were under the command of Lieut.-General Vanderbeck. Things were very topsy-turvy in Scotland when a Dutch officer held the post of

---

* Full lists of officers appointed to the five regiments of dragoons and eight of infantry will be given in Vol. II., under "Irish Establishment, 1716." Millan in his *Succession of Colonels*, published 1742, erroneously gives "22 July, 1715" as the date of all the Colonels' Commissions to above 13 regiments. The correct date was, in each case, 16 Feb. 1716.

Commandant at Blair Castle and assisted Lord Edward Murray (p. 133), Governor of this stronghold, to disarm Highlanders, and receive their submission to his Majesty King George.*

After Sheriffmuir, Argyll's Army had to mark time for many weeks until the arrival of additional British troops and Dutch auxiliaries. An Artillery train (p. 283) was ordered to be sent by sea from London to Leith, in November. Owing to unavoidable delay the train was not embarked before the end of December; and a succession of head winds prevented the arrival of the Artillery at Leith till 26th January. Colonel Albert Borgard (p. 283), the "hero of a hundred fights," was in command of the train, and his first orders were to join Argyll, with his "people" and guns, at Stirling. The Duke has been adversely criticised, by a military historian, for the contrary orders he sent to Borgard relative to the train in question, and for marching to Perth without it. Argyll was in no way to blame. The following Edinburgh newsletter admirably explains the situation:—

"January 27, 1716

"SIR,

"Owr train of artillery from London came up Thursday, January 26, but the armie as I told yow dispairing of there (sic) being here in time is provided from Bervick [Berwick] and the Castle here. There came up one of the train shipes abowt 10 days agon with bomb shells and ball quhich have been forwarded by land cariage to Stirling. There were some of the shells to the number of 20 stolen the first night. The cairts stoped at Carsterfin, but Cadugan [General Cadogan] threatned the vilage with military execution and they have been since restord. All the use these covetows people proposed I supose was to break there coals with them. The shipes last come up ar abowt eight. They were by stres contrary winds sometime detained at the Boi a nore (sic), afterward at Harwich, and then by stress of wether put into Hull. Our armie has taken possession by there advance gwairds of Dumblain." †

---

* "I Lord Edward Murray, Deputy Lieut. of Perthshire and Governor of Blair Castle, and Baron Leckop (?), Capt. in the Regiment of Lieut.-General Baron Van Palant, commanding officer at Blair Castle, doe hereby certifie that Patrick Auchmoutie in Blair, in Perthshire, has delyvered to us his armes and submitted himself to his Majesty King George his mercie and obedience, etc.

"Signed at Blair Castell the fourteen day of March, seventeen hundred and sixteen years, EDWARD MURRAY."—*S.P. Dom. George I.*

† *News Letters of* 1715-16, edited by A. Francis Steuart, 1910, p. 109.

Argyll's "forward movement" from Stirling began on 29th January. Owing to the late heavy fall of snow the march to Perth, 34 miles, occupied three days! On arrival, the "Fair City" was found to have been evacuated by the Jacobite forces the previous day.* On 4th February, James VIII. quitted Scotland for ever. The march of the Royalist Army from Perth to Aberdeen was practically a triumphal progress. A sidelight is thrown on the labour and expense of procuring draught horses for artillery, and stores, to accompany Argyll's troops from Perth to the North, by a memorial, in 1717, to the Lords of the Treasury from Gabriel Napier, Commissary for the Horses, whose services seem to have been left unrewarded :—

> "The Petitioner was Commissary for the Horses employed in the train of artillery at the battle of Sheriffmuir, where there were several horses killed and others lost . . . was continued Commissary for the Horses set out by the shires of Stirling, Clackmannan, and a part of Perthshire in the expedition to the north, where there were several horses and furniture lost. Was also employed by the Duke of Argyle to raise and receive 700 horses that were demanded from the shires of Ayr, Lanark, Renfrew, Dumbarton, and town of Glasgow, for which he had no reward. Prays inquiry and an order for payment." †

The ill-success which attended the Chevalier St. George's affairs in Scotland, during his sojourn there, did not damp the ardour of several prominent Jacobite plotters in England. On 7th April, 1716, Ezekiel Hamilton wrote from Paris to the titular Duke of Mar, then a wanderer on the Continent like his Stuart chief, as follows :—

> "I will endeavour to give your Grace an exact account of the steps which have been taken at London with regard to the memorial which Mr. Gare brought over. As soon as Sir Redman Everard received it, he carried it to the Bishop of R[ochester] and sent an express to bring Lord Arran to London. At the same time an express was sent to Sir Henry Goring in Sussex ; this occasioned a delay of three days, for the Bishop judged it proper to make the first approach to Mr. Web[b], and Lord Arran was of the same opinion, that though Mr. Web[b] does not need a spur such a compliment would be well taken, and Sir Harry, who

---

* A letter from Lord Townshend to the Lords of the Treasury, dated 13th Feb. 1716, contains this order for payment : "The King has given £500 to Major James Stewart, who came express from the Duke of Argyll with the news that the rebels had abandoned Perth."—*Treasury Papers*.

† *Treasury Papers*, Vol. ccxi, No. 19.

is his intimate follower, was employed to communicate the memorial to him. They were further induced to take this method because, a few days before the receipt of the memorial, Mr. Web[b] had declared his opinion to Sir Constantine Phipps that if he had 6,000 regular troops he would undertake to beat all the forces which could on a sudden be brought together in England. . . . After three days he [Webb] agreed to Sir Harry's sentiments, and said that by the blessing of God he would meet them. He desired timely notice when and where the descent will be made that he might draw his money out of the funds, and bring a good purse with him to the field."*

It is almost needless to say that the "Mr. Webb" named in above letter was the redoubtable Lieut.-General John Richmond Webb, the ex-Colonel of the 8th (The King's) Regt. of Foot. Webb was one of Marlborough's best Generals, and for his victory over the French at Wynendael, near Lille, in 1708, had received the personal thanks of Queen Anne, and of Parliament. The late Queen had also settled £1,000 upon Webb in 1709. These honours somewhat turned this General's head. He had quarrelled with Marlborough for not giving him the full share of praise which the former expected. To make up for Marlborough's backwardness in this matter, Webb sounded his own trumpet on every possible occasion. The story goes that, being in the Duke of Argyll's company, on one occasion, General Webb began to talk about his victory over the French at Wynendael, and mentioned that he had been wounded in this battle. Argyll, who could say very cutting things when he chose, replied: "I would to God you had been wounded in your tongue, and then I could have heard about your victory at Wynendael from someone else!"

The Scriptural *dictum* that "a little leaven leaveneth the whole lump" was fully exemplified at the city of Oxford, in 1716. Charles, Earl of Arran, had succeeded his brother the Duke of Ormonde as Chancellor in September 1715. Lord Arran was a strong Jacobite, and his views were well known to Oxford residents. He was in close touch with Colonel Hugh Owen, a Roman Catholic, who had been given a Company in the 1st Foot Guards, at the close of Queen Anne's reign, by the Tory Ministry for reasons of their own. In December 1715 Owen was

* *Stuart Papers*, Vol. II. pp. 67-68.

forced to sell his commission in the Guards (p. 185). He came to reside in Oxford some months later, and soon became an open Jacobite leader. "It is well known," wrote an Oxford diarist, "that Owen the rebel and his companions were entertain'd publicly by most of the heads of colleges, that they walk'd about the streets, at noonday, with the mob at their heels, huzzaing 'King James and the Duke of Ormond for ever, and no usurpers,' in defiance of the Government and the friends of the Government."* Major-General Pepper (p. 112) received orders to proceed with his regiment to Oxford and take that city by surprise. One of his officers was sent there in disguise to find out who were the chief instigators of the Jacobite movement; and when Pepper with his Dragoons entered Oxford, very early on 5th October, 1716, he surrounded the houses of several ill-affected persons whom he made prisoners. "But Colonel Owen escaped from the Greyhound Inn in his night-gown and climbed over the wall into Magdalen College Gardens, where he was not pursued. The Vice-Chancellor and Mayor thought it well to concur with Pepper's demands, and assisted him, and his officers, to arrest certain Jacobites." †

During 1716 many riots took place in different parts of England on George I.'s Accession anniversary and on the birthday of the Prince of Wales. These tumults had to be quelled by the military forces. At Ashbourne, in Derbyshire, the 29th of May (the anniversary of the Restoration of Charles II and that monarch's birthday) was celebrated by the citizens with illuminations, bonfires, and ringing of bells. But 1st August—King George's Accession anniversary—would have passed over disregarded if it had not been for the loyalty of Major Richard Roberts of the Prince of Wales's Own Dragoons (p. 120) and some of his officers. Here is Roberts's account of what occurred:—

> "Ashburn, 1 August, at 9 at night. Some friends observing how little regard the town had to the Day in omitting to send up lights &c., the Company and myself went to the market place and found a bonfire just beginning to be lighted. I ordered wine thither, and with drums beating we drank his Majesty's health,

---

* *Reminiscences of Oxford by Oxford Men*, 1559–1850, p. 70.
† Rapin's *Hist. of England*, Vol. IV. p. 443.

and then ordered them, with a file of men to prevent mischief, to go about the town and give notice to put up lights as they had done 29 May, and then went to bed. When the mob was tumultuous, which I believe was occasioned by that horrid distinction in the different celebration of the 2 days, and hearing that disorders had hapned, I ordered some officers and men who were then out of their quarters in arrest. . . . That the 29 of May was celebrated in the manner above mentioned, and the 1st of August passed over with all imaginable disrespect to his Majesty, I can make appear by affidavit. Notwithstanding the contempt the town shewed to that day the officers prevented several windows being broke." *

On the Prince of Wales's birthday (1st November) there was a serious riot at Oxford † which was subsequently the subject of a debate in Parliament.

An important addition was made to the British Standing Army in 1716. This was two permanent Companies of Artillery (the present Royal Regiment of Artillery), which was to take the place of the spasmodic and ephemeral "Trains" that had from time immemorial been raised in time of war and rebellion. It was by the advice of the Duke of Marlborough, Master-General of the Ordnance, that George I. directed by Royal Warrant the aforesaid two Companies of Artillery to be added to the Military Establishment. "It was on the 26th day of May, 1716, that the Regimental Baby was born," writes the late Colonel Duncan, the able historian of the Royal Artillery. "It was smaller than had been expected; but it has proved a healthy and long-lived child, and, as its nurse might have said, it has grown out of all knowledge. Only two companies—without any staff—were given at first at an annual cost of £4,891. . . . Ere many years had passed, the whole of the scheme recommended by the Duke of Marlborough was at work; in 1722 a Colonel was given to the Regiment; and in 1727 we find a Lieut.-Colonel and a Major, as well as four complete Companies." ‡

Among the Scottish nobles who materially assisted General Cadogan (the Duke of Argyll's successor) and Major-General

---

* Letter from Major Roberts to the Duke of Marlborough, *S. P. Dom. George I.* Bundle 7.

† Letter from Major O'Farrell to Lord Townshend, 2nd November, 1716. *S. P. Dom. George I.*

‡ *History of the Royal Regiment of Artillery*, by Major Francis Duncan, R.A. Third Edition, Vol. I. pp. 81–82.

Wightman in "settling" the Highlands, the Earl of Sutherland and Lord Lovat stand out in bold relief during 1716. The former had proved himself an active commander against the rebels during the critical period of the Rebellion. For his services he had been made a Lieut.-General, 16th November, 1715 (p. 235); and Lord Lovat, a proscribed outlaw, had been pardoned by George I. for his past heinous offences, when he wrested Inverness from the Jacobite Governor, Sir John Mackenzie of Coul. For this and later services Lovat was made Governor of Inverness and Captain of an Independent Company (p. 248). "I have my two Commissions in my pocket," wrote Lord Lovat, jubilantly, to Duncan Forbes of Culloden, from London, 28th June, 1716; "and the Prince [of Wales] told me last night he was glad they were expeded."*

On 9th July, 1716, George I. left London for Hanover. The Prince of Wales was constituted Guardian of the Kingdom during the King's absence from England. The latter hoped to have been Regent; but this was not to be. Among the restrictions imposed on the Prince by his Majesty were several that related to military appointments. "You will not dispose of any government," wrote George I. to his son on 5th July, 1716, "as well in the Kingdom as in any of the Plantations abroad, without my express consent, nor of any commission of lieutenant or superior rank in my Horse Guards; of major or above in my Foot Guards, nor of Colonel or above in the Army. In the same manner I reserve to myself the power of cashiering and reforming the body of the Army which is now on foot."

Those who have searched and made extracts from the Commission Entry Books for the reign of George I. at the Public Record Offices of London and Dublin, can testify to the regularity with which the King filled up Army vacancies and signed new commissions. Former British monarchs had almost invariably left the appointments to regiments on the Irish Establishment to the Lord Lieutenant or Lords Justices of Ireland: but

---

* *Culloden Papers*, p. 56. These two original parchment commissions are now among the Stuart Papers at Windsor Castle.

George I. signed a great number of the Irish commissions himself, and kept a watchful eye, so to speak, over the appointments in the sister kingdom as well as in Great Britain. During the several periods of the King's residence abroad, the Secretaries of State kept his Majesty *au fait* as to military matters, great and small. In fact the military coach proceeded on its course with the same well-oiled wheels when George I. was abroad as when he was at home. And yet the Princess of Wales told the King, early in 1716, that he was grown lazy. "He laughed and said he was busy from morning to night. She said, 'Sir, I tell you they say the Ministry does everything, and you nothing.' He smiled, and said, 'This is all the thanks I get for all the pains I take.'" *

In May, 1717, the King gave his consent to a reduction of 10,000 men in the Standing Army. Popular clamour necessitated this act on the part of George I. It was the old story over again which is plainly told in the lines—

> "When danger approaches and the battle is nigh,
> 'God and the soldier' is the cry;
> When the war is over and everything righted,
> God is forgotten, the soldier slighted."

The Army reductions in the summer of 1717 included the five regiments of dragoons and the eight of infantry—all on the Irish Establishment—which had been raised in February, 1716. And in Scotland the "Independent Companies raised for the protection of the Highlands" (one of which was Lord Lovat's Company) were broke. In England some of the "Companies of Invalids" were taken off the Establishment and transferred to Chelsea Hospital.† The remaining Invalid Companies were formed, in March, 1719, into a regiment which still exists—the Forty-first of the Line—and is now known as "The Welsh Regiment." And there is yet another gallant corps in the British Army of to-day which owes its existence to George I. This is the old 40th Foot, now styled

---

* *Diary of Mary, Countess Cowper, Lady of the Bedchamber to the Princess of Wales,* 1714–20. Edit. 1864, p. 79.

† From "A speech by Sir T—— H——, Bt., spoken the 7th Dec. 1717 in the House of Commons."

"The 1st Batt. Prince of Wales's Volunteers," which was formed (p. 312) in August, 1717, from the Independent Companies in garrison at Annapolis, Nova Scotia, and Placentia, Newfoundland.

The great reductions in the small Standing Army only whetted the appetites of certain Members of Parliament, who found a ready leader and spokesman in the person of William Shippen. This ill-advised M.P. (known as "Downright" Shippen) not only advocated a further sweeping reduction in the Army, but showed an utter lack of respect for the King by his speech in Parliament on 4th December, 1717, against continuing the Army. Alluding to his Majesty's speech, this demagogue said :—

> "But we are to consider that speech as the composition and advice of his Ministry, and are therefore at liberty to debate every proposition in it; especially those which seem rather calculated for the meridian of Germany, than of Great Britain." *

For this and other remarks about the King, Shippen was sent to the Tower the same day. In the Tower registers is this entry :—

> "4 Dec. 1717. William Shippen Esq, 'for speaking words highly dishonorable to, and unjustly reflecting on, his Majesty's person and government,' committed by order of the House of Commons.
>
> (signed) "H. COMPTON,
> "Speaker."

Much has been said by Jacobite writers about plots to assassinate the Chevalier St. George; but little has been written about similar designs on the life of George I. Among the State Papers at the Public Record Office, London, is a letter written to Mme. Kielmansegge, then resident at St. James's Palace, by an anonymous female correspondent who tells the following story :—

> "WORTHY LADY,
>
> "May it please your Ladyship, altho' a stranger to you I have pitched upon you, as the worthiest person in the Kingdom, to imparte the greatest of secrets which I have kept to myself this five weeks; misfortune, Madam, has forst me to comply outwardly with the Romish errours whereby I have got so far into a

---

* "A speech against continuing the Army as it was spoken the 4th Day of December, 1717, in the House of Commons by W—— S——, Esq."

priests favour, as Dalliah (*sic*) did by Sampson, that he has discovered one of the greatest secrets to me, being no less than an intended murder of his present sacred Majesty ethier (*sic*) by poison or pistol this summer; but withall he mad me swear not to divldge (*sic*) him, for he said I should be killed which makes me conceal who I am, not Madam but I would freely discover the person and every circumstance if his Majesty will be pleased in his royal bounty [to] protect me from the malice of the papists, and likewise grant me the life of the priest for he has kept me from starving, but my conscience would not let me keep it. They have engaged themselves under an oath of damnation never to discover the least thing; but if his Majesty pleases to issue out a proclamation, or order it to be put in the news [letter] to require the person to appear that writ to your ladyship, I shall be very free provided I don't endanger my own life. Pray, madam, think not lightly of this . . . so wishing his Majesty prosperity and long to reighn (*sic*), I rest his obedient subject and your ladyship's most humble servant to command.

"To the right honorable lady Kilmansacks att Saint James house, London."

Hard things have been said of Madame Kielmansegge by past and present writers. She has been handed down to posterity as one of George I.'s German mistresses whose greed for gold and titles made her Royal lover ennoble her with an English peerage and a lucrative pension on the Irish Civil List. It was definitely proved by Carlyle that this much-traduced lady was "*half-sister* by blood to George I., being the illegitimate daughter of Lewis Augustus, Elector of Hanover, by the Countess Platten." *

In December, 1716, a murderous attack was made on the Prince of Wales, in his box at Drury Lane Theatre, by a ruffian armed with a pistol. In the encounter the guard in attendance on the Prince was killed before the assailant could be secured. It is recorded that the Prince showed great coolness.

George I. was often warned that his life was in danger, London being full of Jacobites and disaffected malcontents, in the early years of the new reign. But the King took little heed of his personal safety. "All the king-killers are on my side," was the joking retort of his Majesty when urged to be careful. In January, 1717–18, a young apprentice to a London coachmaker formed a wild scheme to assassinate King George in St. James's Palace. This youth, for he was barely eighteen, was named

---

* Carlyle's *Frederick the Great*, Book V. Chap. I.; see also *The First George in England and Hanover*, by Lewis Melville, Vol. II. p. 24.

James Shepheard, and being half crazy with fanatical valour for the "King over the water," wrote to a non-juring clergyman named Leake and unfolded his project, "at the same time expressing his desire to receive the Holy Sacrament daily from a clergyman who was unaware of his (Shepheard's) design, till it had been effected."* Leake thought it his duty to acquaint the Government with Shepheard's murderous intent. The youth was arrested forthwith. Shepheard openly admitted his guilt on his trial, and was sentenced to be hanged on 17th March, 1718. The sentence was carried out at Tyburn. A non-juring clergyman, named Orme, attended Shepheard in his last moments and "absolved" him on the gallows. While in Newgate this poor deluded fanatic wrote some beautiful lines, in blank verse, which were found by his mother the morning of his execution. The hymn, for such it was, was printed on a folio sheet of paper and sold in the London Streets, apparently. A printed copy of the remarkable lines in question has been preserved among the Georgian State Papers at the Public Record Office, and well deserves being reprinted after the lapse of nearly two centuries.

AN HYMN TO THE HOLY AND UNDIVIDED TRINITY.

BY

JAMES SHEPHEARD

Newgate, 17th March 1717-18.

"All Creating Father, all sustaining
God, living Sonne of Love, raise in my Soul
Diffusive Charity, and Love like Thine
Extensive; a Love both of friends and foes,
But first of Thee, a Love divinely great,
A Love my Will to Thee uniting.
So when an earthly Judge shall me condemn
To death most shameful, if this be Thy Will,
No terror shall dismay my ravish'd Soul;
No malice, or hate, by Thee forbidden,
Or evil thought disturb my constant calm;
But every passion shall subside in Love."

---

* Shepheard's letter to Mr. John Leake is given in full by Rapin in his *Hist. of England*, Vol. IV. pp. 555, 556; also in the *Historical Register* for 1718.

Thirty years after, the Earl of Chesterfield, writing to his son, says:—

> "I remember that I saw . . . . . the execution of Shepheard, a boy of eighteen years old, who intended to shoot the late King, and who would have been pardoned if he had expressed the least sorrow for his intended crime; but, on the contrary, he declared that if he was pardoned he would attempt it again; that he thought it a duty which he owed his country, and that he died with pleasure for having endeavoured to perform it." *

The deadly feud that existed between the Scottish Jacobites and Royalists during the '15, and for some years subsequent to the Rising, is plainly set forth in the sad petition given below, which document is preserved at the Public Record Office:—

"THE HUMBLE PETITION OF ELIZABETH CAMERON, WIDDOW, TO THE KING'S MOST EXCELLENT MAJESTY.

> "Sheweth that your petitioner is the widdow of Major Daniel (*sic*) † Cameron deceased, son of Sir Evan (*sic*) ‡ Cameron of Lochiel, in the North of Scotland, who served first in Colonel Clayton's Regiment and afterwards in Lieut.-General Murray's, now Colonel Cunningham's Regiment in the service of the States General. That the said Major having been a person of great loyalty, and zeal for your Majesty's interest, procured leave to come home to Scotland, in the beginning of the late Rebellion, in hopes to have prevented by his endeavours his elder brother and other relations from embarking into so unnatural a design; and though his endeavours had not the desired effect, as to his brother [Lochiel] and some others, yet he had the honour of doing that great piece of service in prevailing with many of his numerous and powerful Clan to desist from it; and by encouraging others, whom he knew to be well affected to your Majesty, by furnishing them with arms at his own expense for the suppressing and bringing in of the Rebells. His great loyalty and zeal was the cause of his death, for having broke his constitution with the fatigues and hardships of that service, and in bad weather, he dyed the 26th of March, 1718, in the Highlands. All which facts are certified under the hands of the R. Hon. the Earls of Sunderland (*sic*), Lauderdale, Terphichen, Brigadier Preston, Col. Blackader, and other persons of note and distinction . . . That your Petitioner's insuperable loss, attended with circumstances very inhuman and uncommon, for while your Petitioner's husband lay a dying in one room, and your Petitioner in labour in another; the house was surprised by a party of the rebell brothers friends, and [they] strip'd her not only of all her goods but likewise of the writings and other papers belonging to her; and to compleat the scene of cruelty a set of bagpipes and

---

* Letter quoted in Jesse's *Memoirs of the Court of England from* 1688-1760, Vol. II. pp. 304-305.
† *Donald.*
‡ *Ewen.*

drums were ordered to play upon us day and night for some time. And forasmuch as your petitioner and two children being reduced to the utmost extremity, and destitute of all relief, they humbly throw themselves at your Majesty's feet and hope you will deem them proper objects of your Royal Bounty . . . And your Petitioner shall ever pray, &c."*

This petition was laid before the King, 17th February, 1723, and he referred it to the Lords Commissioners of the Treasury, who were desired to "report their opinion as to what his Majesty may fitly do therein." The endorsement by the Lords of the Treasury on the petition in question was short and heartless: "Nothing can be done in this."

It has been said, and with some truth, that George I.'s reign was one of the most pacific in English history; but during the first few years of the Georgian era Great Britain was threatened by a Swedish invasion and by a Spanish armada. Peter the Great tried to get a foothold in North Germany and sent a Russian army to assist at the taking of Wismar, a Swedish possession on the Baltic, then besieged by the Prussians, Hanoverians, and Danes, which he wished to obtain for the Duke of Mecklenberg-Schwerin who had married the Czar's niece. George I. was equally determined that the Czar should have no finger in the Wismar pie, and the Russian forces had to return from whence they came. This rebuff made Peter the Great England's enemy. Those who have read *George I. and the Northern War*† know how Admiral Norris circumvented Charles XII. in this monarch's attempt to keep British ships out of the Baltic and cripple the English Navy, which depended largely on timber from the northern ports; while the projected Swedish invasion, in favour of the exiled Stuart prince, was disclosed through the arrest, by Major-General George Wade, of Count Gyllenberg, the Swedish Ambassador in London, 29th January, 1717, eleven days after the return of George I. from Hanover. The correspondence found in Gyllenberg's house revealed a Jacobite conspiracy concocted by Baron Gortz, Swedish Minister at The Hague, for the invasion of Scotland with 12,000 Swedish soldiers. It was clearly proved

---

* *Treasury Papers*, ccxliii. No. 17.
† By Mr. Chance. Published in 1909.

that Gyllenberg and the Swedish Ambassador in Paris were in league with Gortz. Putting aside the privileges belonging to ambassadors from foreign Courts, George I. had the Swedish Count's correspondence published, and sent Gyllenberg to Plymouth Citadel under charge of Lieut.-Colonel Wm. Hanmer (p. 292) of the Coldstream Guards. The King also demanded the arrest of Baron Gortz, to which the States General acceded. The inscrutable Charles XII kept his own counsel and merely retaliated by imprisoning Mr. Robert Jackson, the British Envoy at Stockholm. Gyllenberg was kept prisoner till August, 1717, when he was sent to Sweden on board a British frigate, and Mr. Jackson was released.

Europe breathed more freely when news reached the Great Powers that the heroic King of Sweden—the lion of the north—had met a soldier's death at the siege of Frederikshald on 11th December (N.S.) 1717. This event was well defined in after years by Dr. Samuel Johnson:—

> "His fall was destined to a barren strand,
> A petty fortress, and a dubious hand;
> He left the name at which the world grew pale,
> To point a moral or adorn a tale."

The Quadruple Alliance of England, France, Austria, and Holland, ratified in the summer of 1718, which had for its ostensible object the preservation of the peace of Europe, helped to safeguard Great Britain against the proposed coalition of Spain and Russia in favour of the Stuart cause. England had hardly entered upon the Alliance before she had to send a fleet under Sir George Byng to the Mediterranean, Spain having seized Sardinia and threatened Sicily. Byng had orders to embark the infantry regiments of James Otway (9th Foot), Andrew Bisset (30th Foot), and Charles Otway (35th Foot), from the Isle of Wight. These three regiments had been sent from Ireland for service on board the fleet. There were no marine regiments in George I.'s Navy as there had been in the reigns of William III. and Queen Anne—hence the employment of land soldiers. Byng had been used, in the late reign, to veteran and experienced sea-soldiers. He was not much pleased with the appearance of the rank and file he found waiting to be embarked at St. Helens. "I find," he writes in an official letter, "a great many of them miserable creatures and not fit to serve. The best of them I shall pick out to endeavour to complete our complements, and the best of what shall be left I will put on board fire frigates in the harbour and discharge the remainder."* It is true that Bisset's Regiment had been a Marine Corps (Wills's) in the late reign; but when disbanded in December, 1713, the men had returned to their respective homes. When George I. restored Wills's Regiment in the spring of 1715 it was as an infantry corps for land service; the officers were mostly the same as in the old regiment, but the men were undoubtedly raw and young. Byng sailed on 3rd June and on arrival at Minorca he landed some of his troops and embarked some others. One of the regiments now taken on board the Fleet was the Royal Fusiliers, commanded by Colonel James O'Hara;† the other corps to sail with Byng was Sankey's (39th Foot). On 31st July the British Fleet anchored in the Bay of Naples. On the next day the troops were sent off to garrison the fort and citadel of Messina, where they arrived on 9th August. Two days later Admiral Byng, with twenty ships of the line, attacked the Spanish fleet and destroyed a number of their ships off Cape Passaro.

As there had been no declaration of war between England and Spain, Admiral Byng's attack on the Spanish fleet off the coast of Sicily may seem unjustifiable. But it was not so. Spain, then governed by Cardinal Alberoni, had been officially warned, some weeks earlier, that England and France were guarantors of the neutrality of Italy. Every diplomatic effort had been made to induce Spain to settle her outstanding differences with Austria and not to violate Italy's neutrality. George I. even went so far as to offer to cede Gibraltar to Spain by way of a sop to keep the rulers of that country from disturbing the peace of Europe. Curious to say, the offer was declined. When the Spanish troops invaded Sicily, took Palermo, and threatened

* "The Expedition to Sicily, 1718, under Sir George Byng." *Rl. U. S. Institution Journal* for Sept. 1909.
† Afterwards Field-Marshal Lord Tyrawly.

Messina, Sir George Byng carried out his orders with the result already narrated.

The system of purchasing and selling commissions was greatly disapproved of by George I.* He did his best to stop the practice; but the Board of General Officers, to whom the King had to refer this weighty matter, was too strong for him.† Purchase continued in the British Army till 1870, when it was abolished as "a hoary abuse." It is to George I.'s credit that he regulated the prices to be given for commissions and so helped poor officers in many instances to gain their coveted promotion. There were not a few subalterns in George I.'s Army who served twenty years before they attained the rank of Captain; and in some cases were still lieutenants after twenty-one years' service. Take for instance Lieut. Roger Sterne (father of Laurence Sterne) of the 34th Foot; he received his commission as Ensign in aforesaid Corps 1st July, 1710, and saw some active service in Flanders. Sixteen months later Chudleigh's Regt. (34th) was reduced and Ensign Sterne placed on half-pay. In July, 1715, Chudleigh's was re-formed and Sterne rejoined in Dublin. After constant change of garrisons the regiment was sent to the Isle of Wight, early in 1719, and embarked with the expedition to Vigo that summer. On return from Spain, Sterne accompanied his corps to Ireland. He served with the same at the defence of Gibraltar in 1727. While stationed on the "Rock" he had a duel with Captain Christopher Phillips of the same corps and was run through the body. Sterne survived, but with impaired health. He was able to accompany his regiment to the West Indies, and died of fever, and a worn-out constitution, at Port Antonio, Jamaica, in March, 1731, with the rank of Lieutenant.‡

Parliament decreed, early in 1718, a considerable reduction of the Standing Army. The Dragoon Regiments commanded by Sir C. Hotham, Col. Tyrrell, Brigadier Crofts, Col. Molesworth, and Col. Stanhope were "broke" in November, 1718; and the

---

* *Hist. of the British Army*, by the Hon. J. W. Fortescue, Vol. II. p. 29.
† *Ibid.* p. 30.
‡ Laurence Sterne's "Fragment of Autobiography" in Preface to Lydia Sterne's edition of *Sterne's Letters*.

Foot Regiments of Brigadier Ferrers, Col. Nassau, Brigadier Pocock, Col. Hales,* Major-Gen. Armstrong, and Brigadier Dubourgay, were disbanded before the close of 1718 and the officers placed on half-pay. Hardly had these regiments ceased to exist when the tocsin of war sounded throughout the British Isles. For months past it had been a foregone conclusion that there must be a war with Spain, and that a Spanish armada was to be dispatched to Scotland to co-operate with the Jacobites. And yet the Army in Great Britain (exclusive of regiments in Ireland) had been pruned down to a total strength of 16,347 officers and men!

PROCLAMATION OF WAR WITH SPAIN BY THE LORDS JUSTICES OF IRELAND.

"These are to will and request you this present Friday, being the 26th of this instant December, between the hours of Twelve and Two of the Clock in your Coats of Arms to read and publish his Majesty's Declaration of War against Spain, herewith sent you, according to the manner in such cases accustomed, in the most public places within the City of Dublin wherein you are to be accompanied by the Lord Mayor, Aldermen, and Sheriffs, of the said City. And for so doing this shall be a sufficient Warrant. Given at his Majesty's Castle of Dublin the 26th day of December, 1718.

"CHA. MADDOCKS.

"To Our Trusty and Welbeloved Wm. Hawkins, Esq., Ulster King of Arms, and to Philip Ridgate, Esq., Athlone, Pursuivant of Arms."

---

* This regiment must have survived till March, 1718–19, as commissions were signed up to that date (see p. 319); but the Half-pay Lists give the date of [November] 1718 for all the corps named above.

GEORGE THE FIRST'S ARMY

1714—1727

CHAPTER I

THE GREAT DUKE OF ARGYLL'S MILITARY CAREER

1694–1742 [1]

> "Two men wish to have the command of the Army, the King and Argyll, but by God neither of them shall have it."—
>
> SIR ROBERT WALPOLE.

"JOHN LORD LORNE to be Colonel of the regiment of foot whereof Archibald, Earl of Argyll, was late Colonel, and likewise to be Captain of a Company in the same regiment. Dated at Whitehall, 7th April, 1694."

So runs the commission appointing a youth of $15\frac{1}{2}$ years [2] to the command of the Highland regiment then serving in Flanders. The juvenile Colonel did not take up the command of this corps, which his father made over to him by permission of William III., but continued for a short time his studies, which we are told showed a strong military bent. After the peace of Ryswick, Lord Lorne's regiment was disbanded, with many others, and the officers, including the Colonel, were placed on half-pay.[3]

On the breaking out of the war of the Spanish Succession, Lord Lorne was appointed Colonel of a Scots regiment of foot, in the service of the States of Holland, and commanded the same at the siege of Keyserwaert, a town situated on the Waal, which was invested on 16th April, 1702, by the allied army. At this successful siege, which lasted two months, Lorne behaved himself with much gallantry, evincing that recklessness of danger for which he was afterwards celebrated. On 20th June, 1702, the Earl of Marlborough took over the command of the allied army; and on 18th August the town of Venlo was invested, which stood a siege of four weeks before capitulating. When the fighting Lord Cutts led the victorious assault on Fort St. Michael (an outwork of Venlo) Lorne served

---

[1] This memoir, by Charles Dalton, appeared in the *Journal of the Royal United Service Institution*, June, 1898.

[2] According to his biographer, Robert Campbell, he was born 10th October, 1678.

[3] *Journals of the House of Commons*, 1698.

as a volunteer. In September, 1703, he succeeded his father as 2nd Duke of Argyll, and was appointed by Queen Anne to the colonelcy of the 4th (Scots) troop of Life Guards. State affairs prevented Argyll from returning to the seat of war until the spring of 1706. In the interim he had been appointed a Brigadier-General in the British Army—a rank which he likewise held in the Dutch forces.[1] In this capacity Argyll commanded the Scots Brigade on his return to Flanders. At Ramillies we are told that Argyll gave signal proofs of his valour and conduct.[2] Lord Stair, writing to Lord Mar, in September, 1706, thus refers to Argyll:—" The Duke of Marlborough seems resolved to do everything to gratify the Duke of Argyll, who has indeed acquired a great deal of honour in this campaign. He seems resolved to gratify him in his pretensions of being Major-General, and having the first English regiment." Argyll's "pretensions" grew apace, as we shall presently see.

In June, 1706, Argyll commanded the five British regiments, and the Dutch troops, detached from the main army to besiege Ostend, and gained fresh laurels by the surrender of that town. He likewise distinguished himself at the siege of Menin, this same year, being one of the leaders of the storming party which captured the counterscarp after an obstinate fight. The loss on the side of the allies on this occasion was 1,000 killed and wounded. Argyll appears to have been among the latter, as a report reached London that he had been killed.[3] For his services Argyll was promoted Major-General, his commission being ante-dated to 1st June, 1706; and in February, 1707, he was appointed Colonel of the 3rd Foot (Buffs).

At the battle of Oudenarde, in 1708, Argyll commanded 20 battalions of infantry, which were the first foot regiments to engage the enemy. It is recorded that Argyll's personal bravery excited a spirit of emulation in the troops under his orders, which paved the way to victory. At the siege of Lille he was slightly wounded.[4] The capture of Lille was followed by the siege and capture of Ghent, which was taken possession of by Argyll with his own and five other regiments, 3rd January, 1709. In the following April, Argyll was promoted Lieut.-General, and in this capacity commanded at the attacks on the citadel of Tournay, although suffering from a wound received during the siege of this town. The taking of Tournay was followed by the battle of Malplaquet, on which bloody field Argyll displayed extraordinary valour and coolness. To him fell the critical undertaking of dislodging the French from the wood of Sart, and it was almost entirely due to Argyll's valour and leadership that the French were dislodged and routed, thereby contributing to the ultimate success of the most hardly-contested battle of the whole war. An able historian, in his graphic account of this battle, says:—" The Duke of Argyll, who fought also on the right, exposed his person in such a manner that he had several musket shots through his wig and through his clothes, not from an over-heated valour which runs into all places of danger merely to show a contempt of it, but that he might animate the troops to imitate his example and to perform those miracles which, from their being

---

[1] " During the War of the Succession three newly-raised Scotch regiments were added to the Scots brigade, and the whole commanded by John, Duke of Argyll, whose commission as Brigadier was from the States-General."—*Historical Accounts of the Scots Brigade*, p. 76.
[2] Memoir of Argyll in *British Military Biography*.
[3] Luttrell's *Brief Relation of State Affairs*, Vol. VI, p. 76.
[4] *Ibid.*, Vol. VI., p. 351.

put upon such an attack, seems to have been expected from them."[1] The soldiers who served under Argyll idolised him, and were ready to follow him to the cannon's mouth. His popularity in the ranks and growing influence in Marlborough's camp turned the head of so young a commander whose ambition was as boundless as his independence. Never having served in a subordinate position in the Army, but having been jumped into a colonelcy at an age when most boys are at school, he had none of the self-discipline which all commanding officers ought to possess. Neither had he the patience with his juniors, the respect for his seniors and equals, nor the experience of an old commander, which are the necessary qualifications for a commander-in-chief. And yet, there is no doubt whatever that this last-named post was what this ambitious young nobleman coveted, and, in the plenitude of his self-reliance, thought himself fitted to hold.

For some years past there had been a more than ordinary coolness between Marlborough and Argyll. So far back as May, 1707, we find Marlborough writing to his own wife in this strain:—"The character you have given me of the Duke of Argyll is but too true, so that I shall be on my guard as much as possible." Dean Swift tells us that when Marlborough wrote to Queen Anne after Malplaquet, asking that he might be appointed Captain-General for life, the Queen consulted Argyll and two or three other lords in the matter. She asked if there would be any danger in her refusing to make such an appointment; upon which Argyll is said to have offered to arrest Marlborough at the head of his troops, and bring him prisoner to London alive or dead. If this be true, it is not surprising that when Marlborough arrived in London, the end of December, 1709, and some of his friends in the House of Lords moved for the thanks of that House, the motion was opposed by Argyll and fell through. The feud between the two Dukes grew stronger, and on 25th March, 1710, Marlborough confides to his beloved Sarah:—"I cannot have a worse opinion of anybody than the Duke of Argyll." And again, two months later:—"I have so resented the behaviour of the Duke of Argyll, that nobody converses with him but such as are angry with me." Marlborough had every reason to be displeased; Argyll had openly asserted that Marlborough wished to prolong the war for his own individual advantage. No good reason has ever been assigned for Argyll's rooted antipathy to Marlborough, excepting that of jealousy; but it is only fair to a really great man to point out what it seems strange has never before been suggested, the patent fact that the death of General Tollemache,[2] who was mortally wounded at the attack on Brest, in 1694, was laid at Marlborough's door by the Tollemache family, he (Marlborough) having treacherously informed James II., the close ally of Louis XIV., of the projected attack. Tollemache was Argyll's maternal uncle, and it is only natural to suppose that the deceased general's relatives never felt friendly to Marlborough after this sad event. Minor causes than this have raised worse family feuds.

During the campaign of 1710, in Flanders, Argyll aspired to be made General of the Foot, but there were other Generals senior to him, and of

---

[1] Narrative of the battle of Malplaquet in *Military History of Marlborough and Prince Eugene*.
[2] His monument in Helmingham Church, Suffolk, has these lines inscribed thereon:—
"Thus fell the brave man, not without the suspicion of being made a sacrifice in the desperate attempt through the envy of his pretended friends."

equal ability; nor could he expect any favour from Marlborough, in whose hands all military appointments were vested. The Earl of Orkney was named for this appointment, and it is said that Lord Sunderland, Marlborough's son-in-law, the out-going minister, wittily remarked that he wished Lord Orkney was made General of the Foot, as he believed it would make the Duke of Argyll shoot himself through the head! In September, 1710, Queen Anne summoned Argyll to England, and he left Flanders the same month.[1] The Whig Ministry having fallen, the Tories showed their appreciation of Argyll's open hostility to Marlborough by recommending him to the Queen for the Garter, and, in December, 1710, Argyll was installed a Knight of this Order. In February following, Argyll was appointed Commander-in-Chief of the British Forces in Spain and Ambassador Extraordinary to Charles III. Parliament voted a supply of £1,500,000 for the Spanish Service, and Argyll received £1,500 for his equipage; his pay as Ambassador being settled at £50 per week. Queen Anne also settled a pension on him (grant dated 22nd January, 1711) out of the revenue of the Post Office "for the term of 99 years, if Her Majesty so long live." In addition to the above, Argyll was to receive pay in Spain as Commander-in-Chief. He was allowed to sell the colonelcy of his regiment (Buffs), which was to remain in Flanders, and he disposed of it to Colonel John Selwyn for £7,000. Argyll left England for Barcelona the last week in March, 1711, and stayed a day or two at the Hague, where he had sufficient time to call on the British Ambassador and the General Pensionary, but was too hurried to pay his respects to Marlborough, who was there preparing for his last campaign.

Argyll had long sighed for a "separate" command where he might be his own master. He had got it. Let his own letters,[2] which are now for the first time printed, bear witness to how he appreciated the responsible situation in which he was now placed. Argyll was to discover, at an early age, that there is such a thing as the curse of a granted prayer.

ARGYLL to QUEEN ANNE.

"Genoa, May 14th (N.S.), 1711. Miserable state of the Spanish Army. Encloses General Pepper's report on same. Requests to be allowed to return to England and someone else appointed in his (Argyll's) place."

The large sums of money voted by the British Parliament for the Spanish Service were never sent.

ARGYLL to LORD RABY.

"Genoa, May 16th. How Mons. Staremberg and I shall be able to persuade the troops to serve without pay I know not. Since the battle of Saragossa there has been but about £40,000 sent to Spain, and I have now neither money nor credit to subsist these poor starving people who have so well deserved better treatment."

---

[1] It was about time, as Argyll had been confined to his tent by Marlborough for striking Mr. Cardonnel. Letter from Lord Barnard to a friend, dated "Raby, August 22nd, 1710."—*Bagot Papers* at Levens, Westmorland, printed by the *Hist. MSS. Commission*, in 1885.

[2] Extracted from *State Papers, Spain*, Public Record Office.

The Tory Government being anxious to patch up a peace with France, delayed sending money and troops to Spain. Argyll was obliged to raise £10,000 on his plate, and personal credit, to meet current expenses.

ARGYLL to LORD DARTMOUTH.

"Barcelona, June 3rd. States the difficulties of his situation and reports that if he finds any faults with the heads of the departments they reply that 'they serve better than they are paid.'"

ARGYLL to LORD RABY.

"Barcelona, June 6th. The number of troops we have here amount to 32 battalions and 33 squadrons, most of which are very much weaker than they appear to be by their returns, and very ill-armed. Our towns are in a worse condition than can be expressed, the fortifications being bad and quite out of repair; there is also a great deficiency in spare arms, powder, and ordnance stores. As to money, in last six months only £71,000 has been sent here from England, which sum does not clear this establishment for one month. Judge then in what a condition we must be! The privates have hitherto been subsisted by what money could be borrowed up and down this town and in the villages where they are quartered. The officers have been reduced to the extremest misery, having scarcely clothes to their backs, and neither tents nor horses, all their equipages being lost at the battle of Villa Viciosa."

Argyll's repeated requests to the home authorities for "money" were answered by the "We will see what we can do" style of official letters, which nearly drove him wild.

ARGYLL to LORD DARTMOUTH.

"Barcelona, July —. I am sure your Lordship cannot believe that an army which has been nine months, in a manner, without pay, can, after all, be fed with hopes. Promises, my Lord, is a diet that these people have been made to subsist upon too long, and which they are now weary of. The condition of everybody is to be pitied, but, I think, my own most of all. For everybody has recourse to me, everybody makes their complaints to me, and everybody is uneasy that I don't relieve them, so that while I am here I am to be torn to pieces from morning till night for what I can't remedy."

In a letter to Lord Raby, dated June 6th, 1711, Argyll says, in reference to his application to return to England:—

"I am so much in earnest that the Captain-Generalship of Her Majesty's Army would not prevail with me to continue in this post."

One fertile cause of Argyll's discontent was the opposition he met with in military matters from the Imperial commander, Marshal Count Staremberg, whose command was a larger one than Argyll's, which was a source of constant friction. "I believe there is not a man here," writes Argyll to Dartmouth, in July, 1711, "who serves Her Majesty in Fleet or Army who does not think that the Spaniards have an aversion to all Germans in general."

In August, 1711, the allied forces in Spain took the field. Argyll commanded the Army, for a short time, in the absence of Count Staremberg, and defeated a body of French cavalry at Prato del Rey, in September, killing about 80 men and taking several prisoners. The Duke of Vendôme had boasted that he would dislodge the allies out of all their posts in Catalonia before Christmas; but he could not draw them from their position at Prato del Rey, and he had to raise the siege of Cardona, which was relieved by Staremberg in October. Before this took place, Argyll had to leave the army, being taken dangerously ill.

Argyll to Lord Dartmouth.

"Barcelona, November 20th. I had, my Lord, the misfortune, the 12th of last month, to be seized with a very dangerous fever; I continued notwithstanding four or five days in the camp, though I was obliged to lie in a tent, but proving worse and worse it was judged proper to remove me to Ygualada, where for two or three days I was a little better, but then grew infinitely worse, upon which they removed me to this town. For several days I have been free from fever, but am so very weak as not to be able to apply myself to anything. My physicians are of opinion that nothing could contribute so much to the entire re-establishment of my health as being for some time in my native air."

Whilst awaiting the Queen's tardy consent to his returning home, Argyll set himself to redress several abuses in his little army. One of these was stopping the granting of commissions to children, which abuse he inveighed against as "the ruin of the Service."[1] Another irregularity was the flying Spanish colours in Minorca, which island had been taken by the British in 1708. Also the fact of the lieutenant-governor (Colonel Petit) and garrison at Port Mahon having accepted commissions from Charles III. and taken the oaths to this titular monarch whilst owing allegiance to Queen Anne.[2] These manifest irregularities were brought to Lord Dartmouth's notice, and resulted in Argyll being appointed Governor of Minorca and the town and garrison of Port Mahon, etc., 7th June, 1712.

In March, 1712, Argyll was back in London, and in recognition of his services Queen Anne appointed him Commander-in-Chief in Scotland and Constable of Edinburgh Castle. These appointments he was allowed to hold by deputy, being ordered to take up his command in Spain, and was likewise given the Governorship of Minorca. On August 11th this same year, a cessation of hostilities for four months between the British and French forces was proclaimed. Argyll's orders to proceed to Catalonia were cancelled, but he was despatched early in September to Port Mahon. On his arrival at Minorca, Argyll immediately ordered the Spanish colours to be taken down and the British flag hoisted on the several forts in the island. British troops were brought from Spain, and all Spaniards holding office in Minorca were obliged to take the oath of fidelity to Queen Anne or else leave the island.[3] The fortifications were repaired, new defences set in hand, and British rule established on a firm footing. Argyll now returned to England, *via* France, leaving the island in charge of Colonel Kane, the lieutenant-governor. The Duke's reception at the French court was very flattering, and is recorded by the Duke of Newcastle in a letter to the Earl of Middleton from St. Germains, dated January 4th (n.s.), 1713:— "I was yesterday at Versailles, where I saw

---

[1] Letter from Colonel Wm. Stanhope (afterwards Earl of Harrington) to his brother Charles Stanhope, Secretary of the Treasury, dated December 31st, 1711.
[2] Letters from Argyll to Dartmouth.—*State Papers, Spain.*
[3] Argyll's "Declaration to the Inhabitants of Minorca, December 5th, 1712."—*State Papers, Spain.*

the Duke of Argyll . . . he had two marshals of France and a captain of the Guards attending him . . . a crowd of other courtiers following him as if they would carry him on their shoulders."

Soon after his return to England, Argyll fell foul of the Harley Ministry, whom he thoroughly despised. He was, accordingly, deprived of his military commands, which were bestowed elsewhere.[1]

George I. owed his undisputed accession to the British Crown in a large measure to Argyll and the Lords of the Regency. The King appointed Argyll to the command in Scotland, and gave him the colonelcy of the Blues. He was also restored, in October, 1714, to the Governorship of Minorca.

On the breaking out of the rebellion in Scotland, September, 1715, Argyll proceeded there with all the despatch possible, and assumed the command of the Royal troops, who only numbered 1,000 foot and 300 cavalry. The situation was extremely critical. There was no enthusiasm for the Hanoverian cause north of the Tyne, and whereas large numbers flocked to the standard raised by the Earl of Mar, who had proclaimed James VIII., the Royalist force depended almost entirely on succours from England and Ireland, which Argyll had in the first instance asked for in vain.[2]

The rebels held Perth, a position of great strength. Had Argyll, with the mere handful of troops under his command, attempted to attack Mar in this stronghold a defeat as disastrous as befell Mackay in the Pass of Killiecrankie might have overtaken the Royal troops. Argyll well knew that Highland irregulars were more easily led to battle than induced to bear the fatigues of a campaign. He, therefore, concentrated on Stirling and adopted Fabian tactics. On September 26th, the regiments of Carpenter and Kerr (3rd and 7th Hussars) arrived from England, but being below their strength only added a total of 300 to the Royal army. In the following month, Brigadier McIntosh and a party of 2,000 rebels were detached from Mar's army to cross the Firth of Forth and attack Argyll in the rear. This expedition was fraught with great danger, as three English men-of-war guarded the Firth; but for all that, about 1,600 men, under the adventurous McIntosh, crossed the channel in boats and effected their landing at North Berwick. News reaching McIntosh, on his arrival at Haddington, of the panic that their landing had caused in Edinburgh, the brigadier determined to make a dash for such a prize as the capital. But the provost had sent an express to Argyll, who marched to the relief of the city with 300 dragoons and 200 infantry mounted on country horses. "I arrived at the Town in the nick [of time]," wrote Argyll to Wm. Stuart, M.P., "for the Rebells were within 2 miles of it, and the people were in so extream a consternation that it certainly would not have been defended." McIntosh and his party now turned aside from Edinburgh, and marching to Leith took possession of this citadel. He took eight pieces of cannon from vessels in the harbour to mount upon the ramparts, and helped himself to large stores of provisions which he removed from the Custom House. The citadel gates were strengthened by barricades, as if in expectation of a siege. Next morning,

---

[1] Lord Dundonald was appointed Colonel of the Scots Troop of Life Guards, and Lord Peterborough was made Governor of Minorca.

[2] Argyll to Wm. Stuart, M.P. Letter written shortly before the battle of Sheriffmuir. *Add. MS.* 35,838, fol. 390, British Museum. *See* Chapter II.

Argyll appeared before the citadel at the head of 1,200[1] men, and summoned the rebels to surrender. A scornful reply was given from the ramparts, and a siege seemed inevitable.

Argyll had no artillery nearer than Edinburgh, and consequently had to return thither for the same. Before retracing his steps he dismounted and deliberately walked round the citadel, surveying it both on the land and sea side. That night McIntosh evacuated Leith citadel and marched with his men to Seton House, near Musselburgh, which was strongly fortified. Thence he shortly marched southwards to join the Northumbrian rebels at Kelso. Mar had meanwhile received intelligence of Argyll's being in Edinburgh, and determined to march upon Stirling, which was ill-defended. He left Perth at the head of 8,000 men, on October 16th, and got within six miles of the Royalist camp when news reached him that Argyll, apprised of Mar's advance, had hastily fallen back on Stirling with all his troops. Had Mar been a soldier at heart, he would, despite his lack of generalship, have attacked Argyll without further delay, and not retreated to Perth, which was the timid course he pursued. It was not till four weeks later that Mar, at the head of 9,000 men, again advanced on Stirling and met Argyll, whose force now numbered 3,500, on the field of Sheriffmuir. This one-sided victory, as it has been termed owing to Argyll's right wing defeating Mar's left wing, and Mar's right wing defeating Argyll's left wing, showed no skill or strategy on either side, but was a very sanguinary contest, and effectually stemmed the rebellion in Scotland until large succours reached Argyll's camp. The humorous Jacobite song[2] on Sheriffmuir gives perhaps as true an account of this strange battle as is to be found in any contemporary work:—

I.

"There's some say that we wan,
Some say that they wan,
And some say that nane wan at a', man;
But one thing I'm sure,
That at Sherramuir,
A battle there was, that I saw, man,
And we ran, and they ran,
And they ran, and we ran,
And we ran, and they ran awa', man

II.

Argyll and Belhaven,
Not frighted like Leven,
Which Rothes and Haddington saw, man;
For they all, with Wightman,
Advanc'd on the right, man,
While others took flight, being raw, man.
And we ran, and they ran,
And they ran, and we ran,
And we ran, and they ran awa', man."

On December 22nd, 1715, the Chevalier, known in history as the Old Pretender, landed at Peterhead, and on January 8th arrived at Scone Palace. Argyll was now obliged to prepare for a march northwards. His

---

[1] More than half this force was local militia.
[2] Hogg's *Jacobite Songs*.

JOHN, DUKE OF ARGYLL AND GREENWICH.

little army had been increased by 6,000 Dutch troops under Lieut.-General Vanderbeck; and Lieut.-General William Cadogan had been sent to Stirling, it not being deemed advisable for the Dutch general to be second in command. A train of artillery under Colonel Albert Borgard was on its way from London to Leith, by sea, but owing to its tardy arrival a detachment of troops under Cadogan was sent to Berwick to hurry up such artillery as could be procured. On the arrival of the ordnance from Berwick the forward movement began. Argyll had previously given orders for clearing away the snow on the roads by the country people. The rebels at Perth feeling their inability to defend the "fair city" quitted it on January 30th, and retreated to Dundee. Twelve hours after the evacuation of Perth the vanguard of the Royal army, with Argyll at their head, marched in. After a day's rest Argyll followed in pursuit of the rebels. On February 4th the Chevalier, deeming his cause hopeless, secretly embarked at Montrose on board a small French vessel with the Earl of Mar, and quitted Scotland for ever.

The rebellion was now practically over, and Argyll returned by the King's permission to London the end of February.[1]

Argyll's active military career had now practically come to an end. His exertions on behalf of the Scottish prisoners were displeasing to the King and his advisers. Early in 1717, Argyll was deprived of all posts he held in the army and at court. He had foreseen this for some time, and in November, 1715, had thus expressed himself in a letter to a Scotch M.P.:— "But for my places I have not the least concern in nature." In 1718, Argyll was restored to Royal favour and created Duke of Greenwich; Master-General of the Ordnance (1725); Colonel of the 2nd Dragoon Guards (1726); Colonel of the Horse Guards (1733); Field-Marshal (1736). In May, 1740, Argyll, who had aspired to the chief command of the army, was once more deprived of all his posts on account of his opposition to the Walpole Ministry; but on the fall of Walpole was restored for the second time to the colonelcy of the Blues and appointed Commander-in-Chief in South Britain (February 24th, 1742). A fortnight later, viz., on March 10th, 1742, Argyll voluntarily resigned all his appointments and retired into private life.

On October 4th, 1743, the Duke of Argyll's chequered career terminated. He died of a paralytic disorder, and received honourable burial in Westminster Abbey, where there is a monument to his memory, bearing this inscription from the pen of Sir Thomas Fermor, Bart.:—

> "In Memory of an Honest Man, a Constant Friend,
> John, the Great Duke of Argyll and Greenwich,
> A General and Orator exceeded by
> None in the age he lived."

[1] Argyll was not superseded by General Cadogan as Earl Stanhope and one or two other writers have erroneously stated. So far back as December, 1715, Argyll had requested leave from the King to return to London on private affairs, and Lord Townshend sent Argyll the King's permission early in January, 1716. See Report on the *Townshend MSS.* published by the *Hist. MSS. Commission*, 11th Rept. Appx. Pt. IV. p. 182.

CHAPTER II.

THE DUKE OF ARGYLL'S LETTER TO WILLIAM STUART, ESQ., M.P.[1]

MR. STUART,

I am very much surpriz'd to find by the accounts I have from my few friends in London that my conduct is found fault with, and am sorry that to the rest of my troubles I must add that of defending actions, which I flatterd my self, would have obtain'd me the good opinion even of those who entertain'd ill thoughts of me before; but I find we are in so much on a worse foot even than Turkish Generals, that we are not only to serve without being gott the better of by the Enemy, but we must absolutely destroy them to save our good name, let our circumstances be never so bad, let our numbers be never so small, and those of the Enemy never so great, and let never so many impossibilities stand in the way to Victory. One would think, my friend, that people had either never heard of what has happen'd in other Rebellions, or that they were determined to make no judgment of this by any other; if they would be pleas'd to call to mind that the Rebells in Hungary very lately employ'd above forty thousand of the Emperors troops, with some of his best officers, for some years together, and that the Camisars forc'd the King of France to send three different Marshals against them with considerable numbers of troops, Monsieur Villars and the Duke of Berwick being of the number, & Monsieur Villars ended that Rebellion at last by a Treaty. I hope it will not be said that Rebellion is to be compared with this, either in regard to the numbers of Rebells or the considerableness of their heads, I will only putt them in mind of one more, which is Dundees in this Country. No man can say that half so many persons of distinction were concerned in that; that the numbers were half of what we have to deal with, or that there were not many more troops for three years employed, before that Rebellion was suppressed, with, at last, the help of money.

But since, 'tis plain, no comparisons are to be made for my justification, I'l tell you my story as well as I can in a few words for it is not worth many; before I left London[2] I took all the pains I could to perswade . . . both by arguments and ent[r]eaties, those who are at the helm of affairs, to send more troops to Scotland, and told them plainly that it was impossible to save this Country without a considerable number of troops, but all in vain, so by his Majesty's commands, I set out from London, & was not got farther than Burrowbridge when I received letters from Scotland with the news of the attempt upon the Castle of Edinburgh, and some Horse of the Rebells being gott together, I then repeated my intreatys for more

---

[1] *Add. MS.* 35,838, fol. 390. *Brit. Mus.* This letter (a copy of the original) is undated: but it was evidently written about two days before the battle of Sheriffmuir. Wm. *Stewart*, M.P. for Inverness burghs 1713-15, was 3rd son of James, 2nd Earl of Galloway.

[2] On the 9th September.

troops, by a letter to Lord Townshend,[1] which had no more effect than my former applications. When I arriv'd at Edinburgh I found all the friends of the Government in the last consternation, and all its enemys in the greatest hopes, a number of the Rebells already in arms, the rest all over the Kingdom ready to rise, nobody in arms for his Majesty, and only about thirteen hundred men encamp'd at Stirling, which, by my advise, had been assembled to guard that Pass, which, criminal as I now am, I think sav'd, at least, Scotland. I lost not a moments time in having five hundred arms delivered out of the Castle of Edinburgh with ammunition which were that night sent to Leith, to be put into the hands of the fencible men of Fife, that they might march into Perth to secure that place; how that project failed, why those men did not march to Perth? I presume I am not to be accountable for; before I went to bed, I likewise writt letters to Glasgow, & to many other places, from whom I expected assistance, and sent to Stirlingshire orders for the spoiling the fords upon the Forth, and directed arms and ammunition to be delivered to the people for keeping guards at those places.

Next day I writt a long letter to Lord Townshend, containing the state of affairs,[2] and repeating my instances for a speedy Reinforcement, and gave proper directions for the security of the Castle and Town of Edinburgh, resolving to sett out next morning for Stirling, which accordingly I did, but just as I was getting on horseback, the news arrived of the Rebells having gott into Perth[3] and our people in Fife having separated; upon which, I writt to Lord Townshend again, and ordered a thousand arms to be sent to Argylshire, and so came to Stirling, where I found the vast number of troops before mentioned, and where I took all the pains I could to prepare every thing to inable me to prevent the Rebells passing this river; which all mankind, whose prejudice or stupidity will permit them to judge must allow, was the only thing I had to think of, and was every day entertain'd with the news of numbers joining the Rebells even from behind me. One detachment of which I had intelligence were to pass at Bridge of Doun, and I march'd a detachment to apprehend them, but found they had taken the way through the mountains and so shunn'd us. I still continu'd to press for reinforcements, and delivered out great quantitys of arms to the country, which proved of little or no use, for where ever the Rebells sent the least detachments, our people from all hands sent to me for troops, as they continue still to do. The 26th of September the 2 Regiments of Carpenter and Kerr were all arriv'd, which made an addition of 300 Dragoons; but at that time the Enemy were grown very strong, and to make their passage the more difficult, as I had some time before, I press'd the Militia to take possession of three strong castles on the other side of this river, which at the same time served to

---

[1] "Lord Townshend to Argyll, 15th Sept., 1715. I had yesterday the honour of your Grace's letter from Burrowbridge of the 12th .... which brought us an account of the attempt made to surprise the Castle of Edinburgh .... I have laid your Grace's letter before the King, and his Majesty is very much dissatisfied with the slow motions of the Regiments of Carpenter and Kerr .... The Secretary at War has received directions to hasten their march with all possible expedition."—*Townshend Papers*, p. 173.

[2] "Townshend to Argyll, 24 Sept., 1715. I am now to acquaint your Grace that whatever you have writ hath been faithfully and punctually communicated to his Majesty .... and it is with very great pleasure I obey his Majesty's orders, in assuring your Grace that he is entirely satisfied with your Grace's conduct and with every step you have made." *Ibid.* p. 174.

[3] On the 16th September.

prevent any single people or small numbers from joining them from this side, and might make their correspondence with their friends in the south, and in England, more difficult; but 'twas with a good deal of time and infinite strugling that I at last persuaded them to comply with that request, tho' among other conveniencies those garrisons prevented the Rebells from sending small partys over to plunder, they every day threatening to leave those houses and return home, some of them deserting every day, and will certainly not stay in them long. I beg pardon for this digressional observation. The first detachment the Rebells made of any consequence was, the one that took Lord Southerlands arms, for which I hear I am blamed, and more unjustly than ever man was, the history of that affair being this.—So soon as Lord Southerland arrived at Edinburgh, he writt to me to let him have arms and ammunition, in answer to which I sent him an order to receive 300 arms and ammunition proportionable; two days after, he lett me know he had received the arms, but said that if I had ordered him as many thousands as I had done hundreds, he could put them in honest hands to serve the Government. This I took to be prepar'd as a charge against me, and therefore, tho' I did not beleive his Lordship, I immediately sent him an order for 300 more, which he thought fitt to leave behind him to be sent on board a ship of his son's that went into the Enemys hands, and we knew nothing of his arms being taken till three days after they were lost; the party[1] that took them march'd out of Perth after dinner, and I receiv'd intelligence of their march about 4 next morning, at which time they were upon their return. I was told that the party was composed of 300 Foot and 200 Horse, and that they were to march to Burnt Island to fetch some arms which their friends had lodged there for them, and I easily considered that they must needs be returned, before a detachment from hence could possibly reach any part of the way they were to march, being every step of it towards 20 miles off. I could say more on this point, but that I think what I have said is sufficient.

The next objection that I am told is modestly made to my conduct is, the Rebells passing about fifteen hundred men over the Frith into Lothian.[2] As to that, I answer, that I gave about ten orders to have all the boats ships and other vessels sent over to the Lothian side, but they were not obeyed, and indeed the number of boats upon the Frith is so extreamly great, that it was next to impossible to obey the order strictly; in the next place, they pass'd those people about 38 miles from hence, and will any mortal be so void of justice as to say, that I could with about seventeen hundred men, two thousand even with Grants Regiment, guard forty miles on each hand of me, besides there were at that time 3 Ships of Warr in the Frith, and 2 or 3 arm'd Sloops. Will not this satisfy? This leads me to the affair of the Citadell, which is the next ground of complaint; so soon as the Rebells were landed at North Berwick, I received letter upon letter from the Town of Edinburgh, full of consternation and fright, and begging me to send both Horse and Foot to their assistance; the first day I made them answer, that they had walls about their Town, and about

---

[1] Commanded by the Master of Sinclair. "One of the very few successful enterprises performed during that ill-fated insurrection was the seizure by the Master of a vessel loaded with arms which was lying in the harbour of Burntisland."—*The Spottiswoode Miscellany*, Vol. II., p. 434.

[2] On the nights of 12th and 13th October.

fifteen hundred arm'd men of one kind or other; that they had but to shutt their gates, and the Enemy could not possibly hurt them; that I had good reason to believe their main body would advance at the same time that they heard of their detachments being landed, so that if I should by separating the very few troops I had here, let their main body force their way to Glasgow, and so to England, the whole would be lost, which must be my chief care; however, to do all I could on all hands, I sent 200 Dragoons to Linlithgow, where I thought they might be pretty well at hand to serve either here or there, as they should be most needfull, and orderd 200 country horses to be ready in order to transport some Foot in case of necessity; next day about noon I received another letter from Edinburgh, by which I plainly saw that the Town would be delivered up, if the Enemy came to it, that the Rebells were come to Haddingtoun; so I immediately ordered 100 Dragoons more, and clapp'd 200 Foot on the country horses, and march'd with them my self to Edinburgh, leaving orders behind me to send out spies, and to advertise me frequently of what could be learnt of the motions of the main body of the Rebells, which I took for granted would move forwards; however, I was in hopes by next day at noon, with the help of some of the Edinburgh people, to attack the Rebells if I found them in ground that my horse could come at them; as it chanced I arriv'd at the Town in the nick, for the Rebells were within 2 miles of it, and the people were in so extream a consternation that it certainly would not have been defended, which the honestest and boldest men in the Town will I'm sure confess; I was no sooner in the Abby with my detachm^t, but many people of fashion with the Magistrates of the Town came to me and told me, spys were sent out to learn where the Rebells were, what were their numbers, and what they were doing, and I desir'd all the Militia and Volunteers that I could have, might be ready against break of day. All night we could have no tolerable account of the Rebells, but at day light, we were inform'd that they were in the Citadell, and had been working all night; I endeavoured to have a description of the place, and was told and positively assur'd by some noblemen and gentlemen present, that they must needs lye intirely expos'd, nay might be come at even with Horse, this they asserting so extream positively, was the reason of my not reconnoitring the place, which I should otherwise have done, before I march'd the Troops, and what made me hasten to invest it was, a persons coming to me in all haste, who belonged I think to the Customs, and telling me he himself had seen them marching out of the Citadel along the strand to the westward, as he said to seize the boats at the Queens Ferry and transport themselves back to Fife; so without loss of time I invested them with my Cavalry,[1] and march'd the Foot down to the strand, where they told me was a plain easy access, and so much did I beleive it, that I ordered a squadron of Dragoons to come to the rear of the Foot to march in after and sustain the Foot, but when I took a near view of the place, I found in the first place that all along the beach there were great numbers of large stones grown over with sea weed, which you know makes them very slippery; next that, we were to march about five hundred yards under a flank fire; and thirdly, I found a garden wall flank'd us, when within the place; so I thought the only thing to be done was to retire the Troops, who had been extreamly fatigu'd, and the weather so extreamly bad, that

---

[1] On the 15th October.

there was no pretending to make them lye fourteen or sixteen hours longer upon their arms, which was as soon as I could gett materials ready to sett the houses on fire about the Rebells, and bombard them, the only method to drive them out, and accordingly march'd to Edinburgh; some people say, I should have putt the Troops in North Lieth; would they have put the Dragoons in the Town? then they became no better than so many Foot, and with the Foot would have made but five hundred, who must have been at their arms the whole time or else they might have been surpris'd; for I suppose people would not have had me trusted to the Militia, of whose use, the very night before was enough to satisfy us; besides, I was expecting every moment to be oblig'd by Mar's marching from Perth, to return with most part of my detachment, and if that happened, 'twould I thought be better they were farther off than in Lieth, and if they continued there, and Mar gave me the next day, there was hopes of forcing them out, as well as if I had invested them all night. About 2 in the morning I was informed that th· Rebells were actually marching out of the Citadell, upon which I ordered Colonel Dubourg [ay][1] with a detachment of Foot and Horse, to march and try if any thing could be done, who took about 35 men, part of their baggage, and two barrells of gunpowder. I went down in the morning and found every thing, as to the strength of the post, as I took it to be, with this addition, that the houses within, are dispos'd as if they had been contriv'd on purpose for defence, and on the backside all gardens with good walls, so that to my mind, four thousand men would suffer very much in forcing a thousand so posted; while I was there, I received information of the Rebells being retir'd to Seaton House, the history of which place is pritty strange; the Marquess of Twedal, as he retir'd from Hadingtoun upon the Rebells landing, took out the garrison which I had put into it with three half-pay officers, judging it of consequence to have possession of that house, which it seems others did not. While I was at Lieth, I sent to one of the captains of the ships, who had larger gunns than any we had in order, and prevailed with him to fall down near Seaton House, to be ready when I should come before the house next day, to give me out half a dozen, with which and some mortars, I gave orders to prepare in the Castle of Edinburgh. I would have destroyed them If I had had time; but receiving that night one express, and the next morning another, with news of Marr's being march'd past Artererduck,[2] and that he had all his baggage and 7 peices of cannon with him, I thought it absolutely necessary, and that the whole depended upon it, that I should march with two hundred and fifty of my detachment to rejoin the Troops here, being forc'd to save the Town, to leave an hundred Dragoons, and one hundred and fifty Foot behind me, the Town continuing still in their unaccountable panick; by that time I arriv'd at Stirling about ten at night I found the Rebells were actually at Dumblain, and I prepar'd everything accordingly, but by next day at twelve, I found upon their hearing of my return, they march'd back that morning to Actererduck, and the day after returned to Perth; and the Clanns who had been some time at Strafillin, march'd to Invarary, where I heard about two days after that they were arriv'd, as also that the Rebells at Seaton House were march'd to Dunse, and were there

---

[1] Quarter-Master General in Scotland.

[2] The Earl of Mar's troops were quartered at and near Auchterarder from the 9th to 11th November. On the 12th Mar advanced south and on the 13th gave battle to Argyll.

join'd by the Northumberland Horse and our South Country Rebells. At this time it is, that it seems Monsieur Robethon and some other people at London are pleas'd to think I should have advanc'd to Perth. I'l trouble you only with a very few Words to shew the reasonableness of that project. If I had advancd to Perth, what had hindered the Clanns at Inverary to march to Glasgow, and what could have hindered the Rebells in the South either to have join'd them there or farther to the Southward; Mr. Carpenter[1] I fancy would not have been able to have attack'd those two bodies joined, and what could I have done at Perth? Could I have attack'd the body with Marr in the Town, which has either a wall or very good ditch all round it; and could I have pretended to make a formal seige with the Troops I had, or have now, 3 Batallions[2] of which, and 2 Troops of Dragoons[3] were not then come over; about the time that Mr. Carpenter came to Kelso, the Clanns were returned to Strafillin, and march'd imediately to Actererduck, and a few days after, Seaforth was within a days March of Perth, and the 2d of this month I heard at the same time, that 2 of the Regiments from Ireland would be that night at Glasgow, and one at Kilsyth, and that the Rebells in the South having differed among themselves, their Horse with part of the Foot was marched into England, and the rest were returning Westward to try to force their way by the head of this river, upon this I judg'd it for the Service to stop the 2 Regiments at Glasgow,[4] and that at Killsyth, with which I join'd 2 Troops of Evans's Dragoons, the rest and a detachment being posted at Falkirk, and sent them all orders to be alert and intercept those Rebells, which has had the good effect of 350 of them having surrendered themselves to the country people—upon hearing of the Troops being posted to intercept them. And every moment I expect to hear of the remainder of them who took the same routs having had the same fate. Thus much for what is past; as to the future, I think we are in no danger of the Rebells gaining upon us, and if they advance, I think we may give a good account of them; but if they content themselves with remaining about Perth, neither the numbers of our Troops, nor the season of the year will in my poor judgment permit of their being dislodg'd. We are now as appears by the returns, out of which you have an abstract, a very little above 3000 Horse and Foot, and they, by all the accounts We can gett, are about seven thousand; the season of the year you know such as makes it impossible to keep the feild; and even here at Stirling, where we are incamp'd on the very dryest spot of ground in the whole country, having plenty of coals, and the Town to be in sixteen hours in the 24, our men begin to fall sick, and depend upon it, every Officer here is of opinion that 'twill ruin the Troops if we do not very soon cantoon them, which I find may be done with safety.

If any thing could be done by an expedition of 2 or 3 or 4 days, and then return to warm quarters, the men could bear it; but that (if my judgment and that of the other General Officers be not the worst in the world) is by no means our case; for if we should march to them, what should hinder them to defend the Earn, or if they should be so wonderfully

---

[1] Lieut.-General George Carpenter.
[2] Clayton's Regt. (14th Foot); Moryson's (8th Foot); and Egerton's (36th Foot) sent over to Scotland from Ireland.
[3] These two troops belonged to Evans's (4th) Dragoons. Two squadrons of this corps were engaged at Sheriffmuir.
[4] The reinforcements from Ireland joined Argyll on 11th, or 12th, November.

stupid or fearfull to abandon that good post with their great numbers, may not they then put as many men as they please into Perth, and march the rest round by Crief through the mountains and fall in on the head of the river, and must we not then come back like fools, after having lost not a few men by the fatigue of such a movement. I desire only to add to these difficultys, those of bread, provisions, and forrage, and is it in nature to make me an answer; after all, my friend, I know too well the effects of this war's lingering, which tho' I cannot help, and would have prevented if my advise had been heard; yet, since the people must needs complain, and consequently somebody must be blam'd, I know upon whose shoulders the load will be put, and I think tis very plain by a letter I received last night sign'd by both Lord Townshend and Mr. Stanhope, in which they are pleas'd to fall upon me[1] for complaining of the measures that have been taken, that I am not to be longer in the Service than there is use for me, and also, *that* I shall be extreamly concern'd, if the King or my Master are made to think ill of me, and shall be sorry that the Ministry should be offended. But for my places, I have not the least concern in nature, so much on the contrary, that had I twice as many as I have, I would think my being reliev'd from this damn'd post, where I have quiet neither night nor day, worth them all, and the best news I could possibly hear would be, that I were at liberty, which I hope in God will be soon the fate of your most faithful servant, who will afterwards do every thing in nature to perswade the King & my beloved Master, that it was not the profit or honour of places that ingag'd me in their interest; believe me in the state of the damned till I escape from hence.

Yours

after you have con'd this confus'd account, writ in a hurry, you may read it to those who you believe my friends—among the rest to ... to whom I am much oblig'd, but pray let nobody look upon it, 'tis a dreadfull scrawl.

[Endorsed] "Copy of a Letter from John Duke of Argyll to William Stuart Esqr. Member of Parliam^t.

Written from Scotland in 1715 a little before the Battle of Dunblane."

---

[1] "Lord Townshend and Secretary Stanhope to Argyll, Nov. 2nd 1715. The same Express having brought to each of us a letter from your Grace, the one of the 18th & the other of the 19th inst., you will allow us to answer them together in one letter.

"We did immediately on receipt of them get them translated into French for His Majesty's perusal and we are commanded by His Majesty to tell your Grace very plainly, that he was not a little surprised at some expressions in them . . . . His Majesty is surprised to find that you treat these orders as bills on Terra Incognita; how becoming your Graces's reflections touching the necessary precautions, which have been taken to prevent a rebellion in England, are, your Grace upon reflection will yourself best judge. His Majesty hath had and has good reasons for all the resolutions he has taken, which a very little time may possibly demonstrate, and however your Grace may be pleased to treat his Ministers, certainly some respect is due to the resolutions of the King . . . . We hope my Lord that the Irish Regiments will have joined you before now, that Mr. Carpenter will likewise be in Scotland . . . ." *Hist. MSS. Comn.*, Report XI. Appx., Part IV., p. 176.

CHAPTER III

COLONEL CHARLES DOUGLAS

ANTI-JACOBITE CONSPIRATOR, 1715

Past and present writers have branded a certain Colonel Douglas as the would-be assassin of that unfortunate prince who was known to his adherents as James VIII. of Scotland and III. of England. The writers in question have mostly founded their charge against Douglas on the graphic narrative told by the Duc de Saint-Simon in his *Mémoires*. This French nobleman was a *raconteur* of the first order, but in some respects his reminiscences, written long after the events which he narrates took place, may be likened to those of Sir Nathaniel Wraxall, who had a happy facility for misquoting, misplacing, misstating, and misdating.

The depositions[1] made by the postmistress and others at Nonancourt, in November, 1715, tell a plain unvarnished tale of the attempt to waylay James Stuart when on his way to St. Malo to embark for Scotland. But so far as Douglas was himself concerned there is no conclusive evidence to show that he had planned the assassination of the illustrious Stuart exile. Douglas was one of Lord Stair's principal spies, and took his orders direct from this nobleman. We shall see later on what gave rise to the report that Colonel Douglas and his party meant to murder the titular King of Great Britain in the vicinity of Nonancourt.

Saint-Simon owns that Colonel Douglas had the reputation of distinguished valour; but he erroneously describes him as a reformed officer of the Irish Brigade in French pay. Within recent years two well-known authors[2] have blindly endorsed Saint-Simon's random statement about the Irish Brigade; while neither of them has taken the trouble to inquire into the antecedents, or even give the Christian name, of this same Colonel Douglas. It is our object to show that the above officer had served with credit in the British Army, and came of a family which had rendered splendid service to three Stuart monarchs. We also wish to prove that Douglas was only speaking the bare truth when he declared "he was incapable of the crime attributed to him."[3]

Lewis Charles Douglas was the only surviving child of Major-General Sir William Douglas, Knt., who in a memorial to the Scottish Parliament, about 1704, described himself as "a soldier of fortune."[4] Sir William's

---

[1] Printed in the *Pièces Justificatives* of *Histoire de la Régence et de la Minorité de Louis XV.*, by P. E. Le Montey (Paris 1832).
[2] Mr. Andrew Lang, author of *The King over the Water*; and writer of a paper in the *Cornhill Magazine* for June, 1909, entitled "Anti-Jacobite Conspiracies," wherein Colonel Douglas is three times spoken of as an ex-officer of Irish in the French Service. The other author is Mr. Murray Graham, who wrote *Annals of the Viscount and 1st and 2nd Earls of Stair*.
[3] See letter from Douglas to the Regent, given on p. 25.
[4] Information given by Sir Balfour Paul, the Lord Lyon.

early services were with the old Douglas Regiment (the present Royal Scots) in the pay of France. So far back as the Commonwealth we find Cromwell granting a pass, dated 21st August, 1655, to "Captain Archibald Douglas and his brother William to go to France."[1] Eleven years later the Douglas Regiment was recalled to England by Charles II., and rendered valuable service during the Anglo-Dutch War. Here we must make a slight digression in favour of William Douglas's elder brother Archibald, whose name and heroic death ought to have a prominent place in every Scottish biographical dictionary instead of being generally ignored and forgotten. Captain Archibald Douglas, of Lord George Douglas's Regiment, was sent on board the *Royal Oak*, lying off Chatham, with part of his company, on the fatal 12th June, 1667, when De Ruyter's fleet sailed up the Medway; this ship was set on fire by the Dutch, but Archibald Douglas, who was conducting the defence, refused to retire, though advised to do so, saying: "It shall never be told that a Douglas quitted his post without orders." David Hume, Lediard, Campbell, and Charnock[2] tell how the heroic Douglas perished in the flames of the ship he so nobly defended. Charles II. granted £100, 18th October, 1667, to "the relict of Captain A. Douglas, slain by the Dutch at Chatham."[3] This lady was Frances, daughter, by a third marriage, of Andrew, 7th Baron Gray in the peerage of Scotland. She married, secondly, Captain Mackenzie, son of the Bishop of Moray.

Returning to Sir William Douglas, we find that he was knighted about 1678, when his corps was recalled from France, and sent to Ireland in March, 1679. Sir William left the army shortly afterwards, on his marriage to a Huguenot heiress—the Lady Anne de Bey, daughter of the Baron Antoine de Bey de Batilly, "Major-General to Louis XIV. and Governor of New Château in Lorraine."[4] This lady had two estates in Alsace, at one of which Sir William and Lady Douglas resided until 1685, when Louis XIV. thought fit to revoke the Edict of Nantes. In consequence of the Douglas couple refusing to abjure the Protestant faith, their Alsatian estates were seized by the French Government. Sir William being a British subject was at liberty to return to England, but not so his wife, who had then one child—presumably Lewis Charles, who in early childhood was a playfellow of the Duke of Lorraine's little son.[5]

On 9th December, 1685, Sir William Trumbull, British Ambassador at the French Court, wrote to the Earl of Sunderland: "I acquainted M. de Croissey with Sir William Douglas's petition for leave for his wife and child to go into England with him; but this he plainly told me the King had refused."[6]

When and how Lady Douglas escaped out of France, with her child, does not appear; but at the Revolution Sir William Douglas offered his services to the Prince of Orange, who honoured this Scottish veteran soon afterwards by preferring him to the vacant lieut.-colonelcy of the Scots

---

[1] *Cal. S.P. Dom.*

[2] Charnock shrewdly suggests that Captain A. Douglas was "a land officer sent from the shore to defend the *Royal Oak* with a detachment of soldiers."

[3] *Cal. S.P. Dom.*

[4] Inscription on memorial tablet to Lady Douglas in St. James's Church, Piccadilly. Sir William Douglas's arms, as given on said tablet, are: "Ermine, a heart gules royally crowned, on a chief azure, three stars of the second. Crest, an arm arg. holding a heart gules royally crowned."

[5] See letter from Douglas to the Duke of Newcastle given on p. 32.

[6] *Protestant Exiles from France*, by David Agnew, p. 153.

Dragoons (Greys), 16th July, 1689.[1] Five years later, Sir William was given the command of a newly-raised infantry corps in Scotland. We have now to deal with Sir William Douglas's son, Lewis Charles. For obvious reasons his parents had lost their affection for the name of Louis, even in its Anglican form. It therefore came to pass that their son's first name was entirely dropped, and he figures simply as "Charles Douglas" in all British military records and official documents. Owing to the fact that there were two or three young officers in William III.'s Army bearing the name of Charles Douglas, it is difficult to say when Sir William's young son first obtained his Commission. He may be identical with the Charles Douglas appointed Ensign in the Earl of Argyll's Regiment of Scots Foot, 1st August, 1693; but he certainly is the Charles Douglas who appears as a Captain in the list of Sir William Douglas's Regiment of Foot in 1696.[2] This corps was reduced in 1697. William III. caused to be inserted in the Treaty of Ryswick, under the head of "Scotland," this clause:—"Also the restoration to Sir William Douglas of the lands held by him in his wife's right at Dankelsheim and Ketelsheim in Alsace and elsewhere in France."[3] And when the French Government evaded carrying out the restitution of the forfeited Alsatian estates, King William, in consequence of the "Memorial" addressed to him by Sir William Douglas in July, 1699, sent orders to the British Ambassador (the Earl of Manchester) in Paris, to bring the matter to Louis XIV.'s personal notice. We are told that our Ambassador represented the Douglas case to the French King, who said that "as it was a matter triable by law he would recommend it to the Chief President of Alsace."[4] Time rolled on and no restitution was made. On 29th January, 1704, Captain Charles Douglas joined Major-General George Maccartney's Regiment of Scots Foot as Capt.-Lieutenant.[5] With this corps Douglas served at the siege of Ostend, in 1706, and when that town was taken Maccartney's Regiment was sent to Spain. Promotion was rapid. At the fatal battle of Almanza, in April, 1707, Lieut.-Colonel Charles Douglas succeeded Colonel John Ramsay, who was killed, in command of this corps, Maccartney having a Brigade. It is on record that twenty officers, including Lieut.-Colonel Douglas, of Maccartney's, were taken prisoners and five killed.[6] This corps temporarily ceased to exist. Douglas was kept a prisoner in France.[7]

There is no record to show when he returned to England. Colonel Douglas does not appear to have been at the siege of Douay, in 1710, where Maccartney's reconstituted corps, under new field officers, earned distinction.

On 31st January, 1706, Queen Anne, by the recommendation of the Scottish Parliament, granted a pension of "£1 *per diem* to Major-General Sir William Douglas in consequence of his long and faithful service to Our Royal predecessor and of the loss of his estate in France."[8] In addition to this grant of £1 *per diem*, Sir William

---

[1] *English Army Lists and Commission Registers*, 1661–1714, Vol. III., p. 30.
[2] *Ibid.*, Vol. IV., p. 157.
[3] Marquis of Bath's MSS. at Longleat, Vol. III. Printed by the Hist. MSS. Comn.
[4] *Protestant Exiles from France*, p. 154.
[5] *English Army Lists* as before, Vol. V., p. 224.
[6] *Ibid.*, Vol. VI., p. 370.
[7] Colonel Douglas mentions his imprisonment in France, after Almanza, in a petition to the Lords of the Treasury, dated "Lammas, 1713, concerning arrears of pay due to his late father." *Treasury Papers*, Vol. 171, No. 16.
[8] *Warrant Book for Scotland*, Vol. XXI.

Douglas already received a pension of 10s. a day, making a total of £547 10s. *per annum*.

Lady Douglas, wife of Sir William Douglas, died in London on 20th March, 1709, and was interred three days later in the vaults under St. James's Church, Piccadilly.[1] The memorial tablet to this lady states that she had four children by Sir William Douglas, "Charles only surviving, now Colonel of Her Majesty's Forces."[2] In 1710, Sir William Douglas died in Scotland, and on 27th September, same year, the Duke of Queensberry, Secretary for Scotland, in a letter to the Secretary for War, writes: "Her Majesty desires a Warrant to be prepared to transfer a yearly pension of £547 10s. enjoyed by Sir William Douglas to his son Colonel Charles Douglas."[3] Queen Anne showed her appreciation of the service and loyalty of Colonel Douglas and his late father by ordering her ministers to insert in the Treaty of Utrecht, under Article 22, that the estates in France of which the Duke of Richmond, the Duke of Hamilton, and Colonel Charles Douglas were the rightful owners must be restored.[4] On the strength of his pension, and the expectation of recovering his late mother's estates, Douglas sold his commission and was succeeded in the lieut.-colonelcy of his corps, 2nd April, 1712, by Lieut.-Colonel James Douglas, of Major-General Owen Wynne's Regiment of Foot. When it was too late he repented of having left the Army, and applied in March, 1713, through the Earl of Radnor, to Lord Dartmouth, one of the principal Secretaries of State, for "the Governorship of one of the Plantations in the West Indies."[5] Douglas's wish was not gratified, and he soon afterwards experienced an unexpected misfortune. This was the cancelling of his pension of £547 10s. from Queen Anne. The *raison d'être* for withdrawing the annual payment is very clear. The pension had been, in the first instance, bestowed on Sir William Douglas in consequence of "the loss of his estate in France." But when the Treaty of Utrecht was signed, 31st March, 1713, the English Government naturally concluded that Louis XIV. would restore the forfeited French estates to Colonel Charles Douglas, in accordance with the terms of Article 22 of said Treaty; hence the cancelling of the aforesaid pension. Le Grand Monarque fulfilled part of the said Article 22 by restoring the estates of Aubigny and Chatelherault to the Dukes of Richmond and Hamilton. But Douglas's mother having been a proscribed Huguenot exile, Louis foresaw that if he restored the Alsatian estates to Colonel Douglas it would establish a dangerous precedent in the case of other forfeited Huguenot lands; so the King of France quietly ignored Douglas's rights as he had done by the claimant's parents after the signing of the Treaty of Ryswick.

Douglas repaired to Paris in the year 1713 to prosecute his claims. It was about this time, probably, that he married a French lady who was a native of Metz. Of her hereafter.

Two months after the accession of George I., the Earl of Stair was appointed Envoy to France, and he proceeded to Paris in January, 1715. Colonel Douglas lost no time in making himself and his claims known to

---

[1] *Parish Register.*

[2] It is evident that Charles Douglas was Brevet-Colonel, though the register of his Commission as such is not forthcoming. Having command of his corps at the close of the battle of Almanza entitled him to aforesaid Brevet.

[3] *Treasury Papers* under date of 27th September, 1710.

[4] See letter from George I. to the Regent of France given on p. 27.

[5] *Lord Dartmouth's MSS.* Printed by the *Hist. MSS. Commission*, Vol. II., p. 495.

the new British Envoy. He was, in fact, a frequent caller at the Embassy. The Jacobites in Paris attributed evil motives to Douglas's conferences with Lord Stair, knowing that his lordship employed several British ex-officers to watch the movements of the Pretender, then at Bar-le-Duc. Sinister reports found their way to London, and account for the following information contained in an anonymous letter still extant among the *Stuart Papers*:—

> "London, 1715 . . . Mr. Elliot now in France under the protection of the Earl of Stair, and in his house, has undertaken to assassinate, or kill, by some means or other, the Pretender wherever he finds him. Mr Douglas (commonly called Count), son to Sir William Douglas, is engaged on the same account."[1]

The above-named Mr. Douglas was Colonel Douglas, and when in France he appears to have adopted the title of Count, to which his rightful estates in Alsace entitled him. As for Mr. Elliot he had not come to Lord Stair with any murderous scheme in his head; nor does his name appear as a spy in any contemporary documents or letters. It is recorded in a letter from Mr. Crawford, Secretary to the British Embassy in Paris, that Mr. Elliot was anxious for his son to be appointed an assistant-secretary at the Embassy in question.[2] Douglas had undertaken to watch the Chevalier St. George's movements and report thereon to Lord Stair. The *rôle* of a spy is certainly not the calling of a gentleman; but it must be remembered that when Douglas entered on this detective work, the Chevalier, who called himself King of Great Britain, was meditating an expedition to Scotland, and, practically speaking, was the prime mover of the Rebellion that was then hatching. Add to this, Douglas was terribly in need of funds.

About the 1st August, 1715, Douglas left Paris for Metz, where his wife resided. He went by way of Bar-le-Duc. His visit to that town is thus recorded in a letter of 6th August from the Chevalier to Lord Bolingbroke:[3]—

> "There was one Mr Douglas here on Thursday who left Paris on Tuesday; if he be a spy he cann certainly know nothing however for the curiosity I will when he returns from Metz get a *fausse confidence* made to him to see what will come of it. This Douglas professes loyalty as you may believe, but he has no acquaintance here and what common civilities he has on occasion met with here was less on his own account than on Mr Walters'[4] whose relation I hear he is."

Bolingbroke replied to this letter as follows:—

> "Aug. 14, 1715. I know nothing of Douglas than what I once writ to your Majesty, except that I remember 17, 6, 22 (Mar) once corresponded with him as (to) the business of 13, 25, 16 (Hull). I believe it might have succeeded had the Governor remained in and had your Majesty been able to begin your enterprise with some *éclat*."[5]

From this letter it is evident that the Earl of Mar had tried to win over Douglas to the Stuart Cause but had failed in the attempt.

[1] Vol. I., p. 481.
[2] Thomas Crawford to Paul Methuen from Paris, 7th December, 1715, *S.P. Foreign, France*, Vol. 160.
[3] *Stuart Papers*, Vol. I., p. 386.
[4] John Walters (sometimes called Waters) was banker to the Chevalier St. George. His name is frequently to be met with in Jacobite correspondence. He may or may not have been related to Colonel Douglas. [5] *Ibid.*

On 1st September, 1715, Louis XIV. died. "He was," says Bolingbroke, "the best friend the Chevalier had." The Regent Orleans was but a feeble prop to the exiled Stuart Prince. The former had outwardly to discountenance any attempt of the latter to export arms and ammunition, or to embark from any French seaport, either with or without followers. The Earl of Mar having cut the Gordian knot by raising the standard of the Chevalier in the Scottish Highlands, on 6th September (old style), the Chevalier had to make plans for reaching Scotland. We are told that "dogged by Stair's spies, James failed in his first attempt to reach Nantes, where lay a swift vessel provided for him by Mr., afterwards Lord, Walsh, a wealthy shipowner."[1] The Chevalier now left Bar on 28th October (new style), for Château Thierry, his first stopping-place. When Lord Stair represented this to the Regent on 8th November, and asked him to stop the Pretender at the above-named place, "His Highness directed the Duke de Guiche to give order to Major-General (de) Contades *to carry the Pretender back to Lorraine, and for that end to use force if necessary*."[2] On his arrival at Château Thierry De Contades found the Chevalier gone. The latter arrived safely at Chaillot, where he stayed a day with his mother, and then made a fresh start for the Normandy coast by way of Alençon. The Chevalier travelled in a chaise with two attendants. Lord Stair's spies had been watching James Stuart's movements for months past. From Stair's own "Account of the Particulars of the Article of Money given to Persons sent to several Parts and Places in France"[3] (which account has not been previously printed), we get at the names of the spies his lordship employed during November and December, 1715, and the sums paid them:—

		£	s.
"Novbr. 1. To Colel Douglass 200 Livers (sic)		18	
,, 2. To M. Delapoitrine, his journey to Bar 50 Louis d'or		57	
More sent him into Normandy 25½ Louis d'or		29	5
,, 5. To Colel Douglass 400 Livers		36	
To do, his journey to Caen 100 Louis d'or		114	5
,, 10. To Mr. Moore his journeys and expenses to Havre de Grace and Rouen, 30 Louis d'or		34	5
,, 17. To Delaune his journey to Evreux, 12 Louis d'or		14	
,, 20. To Verdun Colel Douglass' man sent express to his master at Caen, 6 Louis d'or		7	
Dec. 3. Given Colel Douglass 500 Livers		45	
,, 10. To Verdun his servant sent express to Verneuil, Louis d'or 7½		9	
,, 28. To Colel Douglass 100 Livers		9"	

It is noticeable in the above list that the name of Captain Macdonald, a well-known spy employed by Lord Stair, is not to be found. And yet a writer in the *Cornhill Magazine*, when referring to Colonel Douglas, says:—"He turns up now and again in the *Stuart MSS*. always as a spy, and in company with one Macdonald another spy of Stair."[4] The writer of the paper in question has inadvertently taken the obscure

---

[1] *James Francis Edward, the Old Chevalier*, by Martin Haile, p. 191.
[2] Letter from Lord Townshend to Argyll, 4th Nov. (old style), *Townshend Papers*, printed by the *Hist. MSS. Commission*, p. 177.
[3] *S. P. Foreign, France*, Vol. 160, fol. 171. This document is signed by the Earl of Stair.
[4] "Anti-Jacobite Conspiracies," by Andrew Lang. See *Cornhill Magazine*, June, 1909.

allusion to Colonel Maclean,[1] in a letter among the *Stuart MSS.*,[2] as referring to Colonel Douglas. There is no documentary evidence to prove that Douglas and Macdonald ever were employed together as spies. They had different beats.

Stair's directions to the spies sent on the Chevalier's track were to turn him back at Evreux and prevent him from reaching any French seaport. Colonel Douglas's plan was to kidnap the Pretender on the road and carry him off, by force if necessary, as far from the coast as was possible under the circumstances. As the son of an exiled Huguenot lady, Douglas knew how, in 1705, one of Louis XVI.'s ministers had sent one of his agents to the Low Countries to kidnap, and bring back to Paris, a Huguenot banker, a millionaire, whose fortune le Grand Monarque coveted. The banker in question was kidnapped and carried off in a closed chaise; but by a lucky accident, at the Flemish frontier, the hapless millionaire was discovered at the bottom of the chariot, where he lay gagged and bound, and was released.[3] The affair made a great sensation in England, as the kidnapped millionaire fled to London, and subsequently established himself in Scotland, where he became a naturalised British subject 24th March, 1707.[4]

Saint-Simon tells us that Colonel Douglas left Paris in a postchaise, accompanied by two armed men on horseback. The trio arrived at Nonancourt, a small place nine leagues from Paris, on 10th November, at noon, and stopped at the post-house for refreshment. What next happened has been graphically narrated by Saint-Simon, but his account is a fancy sketch in some essential respects. We can, however, safely rely on the deposition made before a magistrate, 18th November, 1715, by the postmistress[5] at Nonancourt. From her evidence we learn that Douglas inquired as to whether another Englishman—a long lean man whose face was marked with smallpox—had passed in a chaise. Whilst prosecuting his inquiries, another mounted traveller arrived and came into the post-house. Soon after this, Douglas, who had been consulting a map (*Routes de France*), which he said had been given him by the Marquis de Torcy, ordered three fresh horses and drove off in the chaise with one of his companions, leaving the other behind. The traveller, who had arrived shortly before Douglas's departure, stopped the night at the post-house. Before retiring he begged the landlady to warn him directly a chaise arrived containing an Englishman. Between six and seven next morning the postmistress roused the sleeping guest with the announcement that other travellers had just arrived. The stranger got up at once and looked out of his window, but seeing that the new-comers were on horseback he remarked that he only wanted a traveller in a chaise. A moment after,

---

[1] He betrayed the Duke of Ormond's English expedition in 1715.

[2] Letter dated 13th Aug. 1716, from J. Menzies to L. Inese. The writer refers to Captain Alex. Macdonald, and goes on to say:—"Mr. Polton (Duke of Ormond) believes him still to be an honest man and a true friend to Jeremy (James III.) . . . but when this was first whispered about, and then his going along with that Colonel known, many friends were alarmed."—*Stuart Papers*, Vol. II., p. 344.

[3] See paper on "The Huguenot Huguetans," by Charles Dalton, F.R.G.S., in Vol. VII. of *Proceedings of the Huguenot Society of London* (1905). The kidnapping of the French millionaire banker (J. H. Huguetan) is also narrated in the *Gentleman's Magazine* for 1791. The Messieurs Haag, in *La France Protestante*, briefly refer to Huguetan being kidnapped in these words:—"Le gouvernement français le fit enlever et qu'il ne recouvra la liberté qu'à la frontière où un heureux hasard le fit reconnaître."

[4] *Acts of the Parliament of Scotland.*

[5] Madame de l'Hôpital.

a carriage drove up in which was an Englishman, and the postmistress shouted, from the bottom of the staircase, that the expected gentleman had just arrived. Down came the stranger from his bedroom in his stockinged feet, and closely scrutinised the man in the chaise. Making an irrelevant remark, the former re-entered the house, and ascended to his room, where he unloaded a jointed gun and immediately primed and reloaded it. This man then came downstairs, and having again scrutinised the Englishman, who was having a drink in the "salle," he went out and ordered a horse, saying he wished to leave with the last arrival. He then told the postmistress that if the two travellers who had left in a chaise the day before returned, after his departure, she was to say he would come back in the evening if he could; if not he would go to the appointed place. The stranger's behaviour aroused the postmistress's suspicions, and she took advice from a kinsman who was a near neighbour. The latter told her she must warn the gentleman in the chaise. She did so, and the Chevalier St. George replied :—"I owe my life to you; these people mean to kill me. There are four of them." Here we must digress for a moment to remark that considering the Chevalier had, at the battle of Malplaquet, "charged no less than twelve times, at the head of 1,200 horse, with a valiant intrepidity which won the admiration of friend and foe,"[1] he and his mounted escort of two men[2] showed a somewhat craven spirit by allowing themselves to be surreptitiously taken to a neighbouring house and concealed three or four days, in order to escape from the "man with a musket," and another man, who is not stated to have been armed. It would be ridiculous to suppose that the Chevalier and his companions were travelling unarmed when engaged on such a great enterprise. And surely these three men might, when they had given the slip to the "brigands" at the post-house, have faced the two kidnappers—Colonel Douglas and his man—who were said to be waiting in the vicinity with the chaise. Forgetting his own soldiering experience, the Chevalier asked the magistrate at Nonancourt for an escort. A private in the Guards was found who was known to be honest. After the man with a musket, and his companion at the post-house, had been arrested by order of M. Ronjault, the chief magistrate at Rouen, the Chevalier and his party, with the soldier as a mounted escort, departed *en route* to St. Malo. The Chevalier wore the dress of an Abbé—a *rôle* to which he was in all respects admirably fitted—while the soldier, by his own desire, borrowed the dress of a civilian.

It is interesting to have an eyewitness's report of his meeting the Chevalier in his chaise, near Evreux, a few days after the Nonancourt incident. A copy of the said report, which is undated, was sent by Lord Stair to Secretary Stanhope. It bears this endorsement :—"In the Earl of Stair's, November 12th (old style), 1715," and runs as follows :—

> "Il y eut samedi dernier huit jours qu'un particulier rencontra le Pretendant entre neuf et dix du matin à trois lieux d'Evreux allant du coste de la basse Normandie, ayant seulement avec luy le nommé St. Paul qui est fils d'une

---

[1] *James Francis Edward, the Old Chevalier*, by Martin Haile, p. 99.
[2] See pages 24-25. Mr. Lang, in his article on "Anti-Jacobite Conspiracies," states that "James . . . travelled with but a doctor valet, a Scottish surgeon, and a servant." It will be seen from Lord Stair's "circular" of 12th Nov. (new style) given in the text that the Pretender travelled with *two* attendants.

Monsieur

J'epris la liberté il y a quinze jours de vous supplier de remontrer au Roy que mon zèle pour la cause de Sa Majesté m'avoit attiré des mauvaises affaires Icy, c'est ce que j'ay encore l'honneur de vous Réiterer, vous faisant savoir que Monsieur de Torcy mon Allié, m'a chargé d'Infames Calomnies voulant faire croire dans le monde que j'avois de concert avec le Comte de Stair entrepris d'assassiner le Pretendant, la quelle fable n'étoit d'abord forgée que pour couvrir plusieures grossières fautes que luy et les ministres avoient Commis au sujet de l'Evasion du Pretendant hors de France, Mais pour me faire d'autant plus passer pour coupable en france, Ils ont eu recours a l'artifice d'Insinüer a monsieur le Regent des choses qui ont porté Son Altesse Royale (avec Laquelle j'ay toujours eu l'honneur d'être très bien) a me refuser les Entrées de la Cour Comme a un Espion de ces Actions et des Leurs, Et pour d'autant mieux marquer ma disgrace on m'a depuis quelques jours ôté le pouvoir

LETTER FROM COL. CHARLES DOUGLAS TO GENERAL JAMES STANHOPE.

(See page 26.)

de me servir des Permissions qui m'avoient étés
accordées a la sollicitation meme du Duc d'Orléans
des quelles J'ay l'honneur de vous envoyer les Copies
cy Jointes, Permettez Monsieur que je vous fasse
remarquer que les permissions M'étoient tres
considerables, par raport a mes Interets, aussy bien
qu'aux Negotians de la Grande Bretagne, Comme
on le peut remarquer par la Teneur desdites
permissions. Faites Moy l'honneur de Juger si J'ay
lieu d'être fort Content des Ministres de Cette Cour
qui veulent me déshonnorer et me Ruiner, et si Je
n'ay pas quelque Raison de vous Représenter mes
griefs dans l'Esperance que J'ay, que vous auray
la bonté d'en parler au Roy, pour que sa Majesté
ne M'abandonne pas a la malice et a la furie de
Messieurs les Ministres de france,

Quoy que Je ne me donne pas pour avoir beaucoup
d'esprit, cependant ayant apris a Obeir, J'ose dire
Que si sa Majesté trouvoit bon de m'Employer a

quelque Chose pour Son Service, Quelle ne trouveroit
pas un Sujet plus disposé que Moy, a executer
Ses ordres de point en point selon una Capacité
c'est de qúoy Monsieur vous pouvez en toutte assurance
Asseurer Sa Majesté, vous Suppliant tres humblement de m'affaires
de le faire, comme Aussy la grace de Croire que Jay
L'honneur d'être avec beaucoups de respect

Monsieur

Votre tres humble &
tres Obeissant serviteur
J. Douglas

A paris ce 14. decembre
1715

Mr Hanbye

francaise et un Anglois qui est a son service depuis longtemps en qualité de son valet-de-chambre et de Chirurgien et un autre homme pour faire tenir tous prest les chevaux de poste. Le dit St. Paul qui estoit de sa connaissance l'embrassa à cheval, et voyant que le Pretendant et luy etoient reconnu par le dit particulier, qui demeure ordinairement à St. Germains ou il retournoit de Normandie, prie le partie de luy recommander le secret et le pria qu'aussitot qu'il seroit arrivé à St. Germains de dire à la Reine en particulier, qu'il les avoit trouvé en bonne santé.

"Le Particulier . . . a dit que la chaise de poste dans laquelle etoit le Pretendant parassoit assez mauvaise, et qu'il n'y avoit point de place aux cotes.

"Le Pretendant etoit habillé au Evesque de campagne ayant un sourtout (sic) violet avec des boutons d'or, une petite peruque Abacialle et un petit collet, une petite croix d'or Abacialle ou Episcopale, et le chapeau sans retrousse." [1]

Colonel Douglas and his companion escaped arrest,[2] and proceeded to Caen. As for the two men captured at the Nonancourt post-house, the one who had loaded his musket so carefully gave the name of Thomas Deane—an Englishman;[3] the other was a young Frenchman named Louis Verdun.[4] These two men produced passports from Lord Stair; but Mr. Ronjault detained them in custody when he heard that they had taken circuitous routes from Paris to Nonancourt. They were, however, liberated by order of the Regent, to whom Lord Stair complained of the treatment to which his domestics had been subjected.[5]

The Chevalier's adherents in Paris, in order to divert public attention from their chief's political designs, raised the report that Lord Stair had hired brigands to assassinate the Pretender. In consequence of this fable Colonel Douglas was excluded from Court circles on his return to the French capital; hence the following letter to the Regent:—

"MONSEIGNEUR,

Une imprudence que j'ai commise m'a justement attiré le courroux de votre Altesse Royale; je la supplie pourtant de me permettre de lui representer qu'à tous péchés il y a misericorde, et que même il y va de sa justice et de son equité de ne pas me perdre dans le monde, puisque je sais que V.A.R. me rend assez de justice pour ne me point croire capable des crimes énormes dont on m'accuse très injustement avec beaucoup de malice. Si V.A.R. n'a pas la bonté de me permettre de l'approcher comme autre fois, j'aurai beau être innocent et le paraitre à V.A.R. je passerai toujours pour coupable. Je m'étais flatté que my Lord Stair m'aurait procuré le bonheur de me mener chez V.A.R. pour avoir lieu de me justifier en présence d'une partie de mon imprudence; mais le malheur a voulu que depuis cinq jours il n'ait pas pu trouver l'occasion d'en demander la permission à V.A.R. dont je ressens une très vive douleur . . .

(Signé) "L. C. DOUGLASS,"
"ce 4 Decembre 1715." [6]

---

[1] *S.P. Foreign, France*, Vol. 160, fol. 135.

[2] Mr. Martin Haile, in his life of *The Old Chevalier*, has misread the letter (to which he refers on p. 192) from Marshal d'Uxelles to the French Ambassador in London, dated 9th Dec., 1715, regarding the Nonancourt incident and the arrest of the two men at the posthouse. Douglas was *not* arrested, nor was he the man with the loaded gun whose conduct aroused the postmistress's suspicions, as Mr. Haile has inadvertently stated.

[3] Letter from Marshal d'Uxelles as above, printed in the *Pièces Justificatives* of *Histoire de la Régence*.

[4] Douglas's servant. See p. 22.

[5] Stair to the Duke of Orleans, 16th Nov. 1715. *S.P. Foreign, France*, Vol. 160.

[6] Printed in *Pièces Justificatives* of *Histoire de la Régence*, by P. E. le Montey, Vol. II. p. 382.

The writer of the above letter does not specify the nature of the "imprudence" which he had committed. Presumably, it was having left the "man with the musket" at the Nonancourt posthouse; the suspicious conduct of said individual had spoilt the preconcerted plan for kidnapping the Chevalier. We feel convinced that neither Lord Stair nor Colonel Douglas ever countenanced or suggested any attempt being made on the Pretender's life. The orders sent by the Regent to General de Coutades on 8th November "to carry the Pretender back to Lorraine and to use force if necessary," were practically the same directions that Stair gave to Douglas. Yet, the Duke of Orleans—that shivering and dastardly Duke, as an able Scottish writer describes the Regent—affected to believe in the so-called assassination plot and acted accordingly. Douglas's letter to Secretary Stanhope, from Paris, 14th December, 1714, contains a telling accusation against the French Ministry:

"Monsieur de Torcy,[1] my ally, has charged me with infamous calumnies, wishing people to believe that I had planned, with the Earl of Stair, an enterprize to assassinate the Pretender. Which fable was only forged, in the first instance, to cover several shameful faults which he, and the ministers, had committed on the subject of the flight of the Pretender out of France."[2]

Lord Stanhope, in his *History of England,* tells us that "James's partisans circulated a shameful rumour that Lord Stair had formed a plan for his assassination on the road." Lord Stair's biographer dismisses the charge against the former in a few contemptuous lines:—"It is unnecessary to notice the base insinuation, in the Memoirs of the Duke of Saint-Simon, of Stair having planned the assassination of the Pretender when on his journey from Bar . . . the insinuation, for it is no more, is as malicious as it is entirely unconfirmed."[3] The historian (Le Montey) of the *Regency and the Minority of Louis XV.,* referring to the Nonancourt incident, says:— "The Earl of Stair did not hesitate to reclaim the two men who carried his passports, and exposed himself by this proceeding to the suspicion of having himself armed them. But all those who knew his character have exonerated him of this infamous conspiracy.[4] And lastly we have Lord Stair's own indignant refutation given in his letter to Robethon (George I.'s Minister), 28th November, 1715:—

". . . . tous les mauvais bruits qu'on a fait courir sur mon chapitre comme si j'avois ici des gens en campagne pour assassiner le pretendant n'ont pas laissé de me chagriner, quoy que ces bruits sont d'une nature à se detruire bientot, car la verité a une force naturelle à la quelle on a de la peine à resister : je suis le Prime (*sic*) de toute L'Europe le moins capable de donner de tels ordres, et je n'ay pas donné lieu à ne faire soupconner d'être propre a des pareilles entreprises, mais il falloit trouver des pretextes pour couvrir les violence qu'on a exercé en mettant plusieurs de mes dometics (*sic*) en prison quoyque ils avoient mon passeport, en ouvrant mes Lettres, en même temps qu'on a laissé passer librement le Duc d'Ormonde et le Pretend[t] . . . ."[5]

---

[1] Jean Baptiste Colbert, Marquis de Torcy, Louis XIV.'s favourite Minister during the King's last years, was deprived of his posts soon after 1715.
[2] See facsimile given as illustration in this volume.
[3] *Annals of the Viscount and 1st and 2nd Earls of Stair,* by John Murray Graham Vol. II., p. 297, note.
[4] Vol. I, p. 95.
[5] *Stowe MSS.,* Brit. Mus. 228, fol. 182b.

Stair had an assured position; but Douglas only had his claims to certain estates in France and had nearly come to the end of his money. The former stood Douglas's friend and did his best to help him. On 25th May (new style) Stair wrote to Robethon as follows:—

" . . . . cette lettre vous sera rendue par Monsr. Douglas qui perdre les esperances en France par son attachment au service du Roy je le recommande à votre protection. Vous aurez la bonté de parler pour luy à Monsr. de Bernsdorf et Monsr. de Bothmaer dont je vous seray bien obligé.[1]

This letter resulted in an order on the Treasury in Douglas's favour, for £200:—

"SECRETARY STANHOPE to the LORDS of H.M.'s TREASURY.

"Whitehall.

"MY LORD, "26th May (Old Style) 1716.

"Colonel Charles Douglas having been employed by His Majesty's Minister at the Court of France in several things relating to His Majesty's Service there, I am commanded to signify to you His Majesty's pleasure that in consideration thereof you cause to be paid to the said Colonel Douglas, or his order, the summe of two hundred pounds.

(Signed) "JAMES STANHOPE."[2]

Presumably Douglas was in very straitened cicumstances when this £200 was paid over to him, and also much in debt. On 27th June (New Style) we find Lord Stair again writing to M. Robethon on Douglas's behalf:—

" . . . . Je vous prie Monsr. dites un mot pour pauvre Douglas, il a servi le Roy on ne doit pas le laisser mourir de faim, Adieu . . . ."[3]

George I. did the wisest thing possible under the circumstances, and wrote an autograph letter to the Duke of Orleans in Douglas's favour:—

"MON FRERE ET COUSIN,

"Le Sieur Douglas estant prêt à retour en France, je profite avec plaisir de cette occasion pour vous renouveller le desir sincere que j'ay de cultiver de plus en plus une parfaite Correspondance, et une etroite amitié avec Vous. Et comme ledit Sieur de Douglas a des Pretensions à la Cour de mon Frere et Cousin le Roy T. C., entre autres pour des Terres en Alsace qui luy devoient etre rendues en vertu du Traité de Paix d'Utretcht, je le recommande a l'honeur de votre Protection, en luy faisant rendues en vertu du Traité de Paix d'Utrecht je le recommande à l'honneur de vôtre Protection, en luy faisant rendre une prompte et bonne Justice sur ses Pretensions, et comme il m'a informé, que par vos bons Offices, il avoit obtenu sous le Regne du feu Roy certaines Permissions tres avantageuses, qui luy ont estées [privées] depuis peu, j'espere que Vous les luy ferez rendre d'autant plus volontiers, que pendant son Séjour ici il a tenu une conduite que m'est tout à fait agreable, tant par l'Affection qu'il a toujours temoignée pour ma Maison, que pour les Sentimens de Veneration, de respect, et de zéle qu'il a marqué avoir pour les Interêts particuliers de vôtre personne dans toutes les occasions. Je suis au reste avec beaucoup de Passion et de verité, Mon Frere et Cousin, Vostre bien bon Frere et Cousin,

"GEORGE R.

"A St. James le 2nde Juillet, 1716."[4]

---

[1] *Stowe MSS.*, Brit. Mus. 228, fol. 244.
[2] *Treasury Papers*, Vol. 204, No. 68.
[3] *Stowe MSS.* 288, fol. 296b.
[4] *King's Letters, France*, 1714-16, Vol II., No. 14, Public Record Office.

An untoward event now happened. Douglas was arrested for debt and detained in the King's Bench Prison, which was "for debtors, bankrupts, and such like."

Mr. T. Crawford, Secretary to the British Embassy in Paris, writing to Mr. Pringle at the Foreign Office, London, on 15th August, 1716, says :—

> "I recommend to you the inclosed to Monsr. Douglas whose wife here is in very great affliction about him not having heard from him these six weeks. It will be charity to send it by some of the messengers of the Office to the King's Bench prison where I hear he is at present."[1]

Some friend in need either paid Douglas's debts, or helped him to compound with his creditors, as early in September, 1716, we find him on his way to Paris as recorded in a letter from a Capuchin to the titular Duke of Mar :—

> "ARCHANGEL GRÆME to the DUKE of MAR.
>
> "Calais, 19th September, 1716.
>
> ".... if I be not very much mistaken Douglas, who undertook to murder the King, arrived here yesterday by the packet boat and went straight towards Paris."[2]

Saint-Simon's statement that Douglas was excluded from the French Court is only partly true. After the Regent had received George I.'s letter, Douglas was not only re-admitted to the Duke of Orleans's presence, but he received many marks of H.R.H.'s good will, for which George I. thanked the Regent by letter in 1719, as will presently appear.

In September, 1716, Captain Alexander Macdonald, who had been employed by Lord Stair in several secret-service affairs, came to London with a letter of recommendation from the British Envoy to the Prince of Wales, then acting as Guardian of the Kingdom, who received this ex-officer at Hampton Court and granted him a Captain's pension on the Half-Pay List.[3] On 3rd October in the same year, Lord Stair wrote to Mr. Methuen, Secretary of State in General Stanhope's absence, and asked the Secretary to bring Colonel Douglas's case to the notice of the Prince of Wales. Mr. Methuen did so, but the Prince said he could do nothing at present in this matter, and advised Lord Stair to write to the King.[4] Before the close of the year, George I. granted a pension of £400 per annum to Colonel Charles Douglas.[5] In the spring of the following year, the King sent Colonel Douglas abroad on some secret-service employment the nature of which is not recorded. We have it on Douglas's own authority that "he was employed by His Majesty George I. with success."[6] These last two words give the lie to the Jacobite reports, circulated in 1717, that Colonel Douglas was sent to Italy to assassinate the Pretender.

---

[1] *S.P. Foreign, France*, Vol. 160, fol. 323, Public Record Office.

[2] *Stuart Papers*, Vol. II., p. 449.

[3] P. Methuen to Lord Stair, Whitehall, 24 Sept. 1716. *S.P. France*, Vol. 29 (*Secretaries' Letter Book*), Public Record Office.

[4] Do. to do., 2nd Oct., 1716, *Ibid.*

[5] *Treasury Accounts Revenue Quarterly.* "To Charles Douglas, Esq., on his pension of £400 per annum, one quarter due Lady Day, 1717."

[6] See Douglas's letter to the Duke of Newcastle on p. 33.

On 23rd August (New Style), 1717, General Dillon, of Irish Brigade renown, wrote to Earl Marischal on the report of a design on the Chevalier's life :—

"Several letters from friends .... having confirmed the danger of not taking due measures to prevent the ill design they believed Prescott (Peterborough) had, and affirming at the same time that the noble Count Douglas was dispatcht beforehand to Italy in order, as they presume, to be aiding and assisting to Prescott in his vile undertaking; those advertisements reiterated tho' perhaps grounded on suspicion and I believe hearsay." [1]

Jacobite spies in London who had to send information of some kind to their employers, in order to earn their money, repeated any cock-and-bull story that came their way; and when there was a dearth of news the spies in question started rumours of their own manufacture. Here is a specimen of another "warning" sent to Earl Marischal by a certain James Wilson :—

"Paris, 29 Aug. 1717.

"I've had two letters by last post from Herr Boome .... In the second he says .... 'tis whispered among the first rank a black design the Earl of Peterborrow has taken in hand; that he was remarkably carest at Court for his intelligence while abroad, and is now gone with a resolution to serve them effectually by employing his emissaries to assassinate the Chevalier. And (Boome) further says that those who know his lordship of a very long time, affirm there's none redier (*sic*) to undertake such a work; that the Court has settled £1,000 per annum on Count Douglas who, it seems, is gone to Italy on the same Conigsmark errand." [2]

Rodomontade of this kind was poured in the ears of the Chevalier's mother at St. Germains. This lonely and sad lady had grown as nervous about her son as the mother of Oliver Cromwell was during the last year of the Protectorate, of which latter lady it is recorded that she never heard a shot fired in the London streets without thinking Oliver had been killed. Queen Mary Beatrice sent a special express to her son at Urbino, warning him against the design on his life.[3] It is needless to say that neither Peterborough nor Douglas had any murderous intentions against that mild, unreliable, good-tempered, pliable Prince, of the melancholy countenance, who had found a safe resting-place in the Papal Dominions. And at the very time that George I. was supposed to be sending emissaries to Italy to assassinate the Chevalier, the former, according to Lord Stanhope's confidential statement at Madrid to M. Blondel (afterwards French Minister at Turin), sent the Pretender an anonymous £1,000 *per annum*.[4] George I. felt safe on the English throne so long as there was a rival Pretender to the British crown who, being a Papist, was unacceptable, at any price, to the bulk of the English nation. What George and his Minister wished to guard against was, that none of the Courts of Europe should receive the Pretender, or help him with troops and money in any projected invasion of the British Isles. Peterborough was arrested at Bologna by Cardinal

---

[1] *MSS. of Eliot Hodgkin, Esq.*, printed by the *Hist. MSS. Commission*, Report XV., Part II., pp. 229–230.
[2] *Ibid.* p. 230.
[3] General Dillon in above letter to Earl Marischal of 23rd Aug., 1717, continues: "Andrew [Queen Mary Beatrice] determined to send an express to Patrick [The Chevalier] with full information on this score."—*Stuart Papers*.
[4] Quoted in Haile's *Life of the Old Chevalier*, p. 241 note.

Origo " at the request of James III." This nobleman was imprisoned at Fort Urbano. Nothing suspicious was found in his papers, and after a month's detention Peterborough was released. The insult to a peer of the realm greatly offended the British Government, and Pope Clement XI., in order to avert reprisals, got the Chevalier to take the onus of Peterborough's arrest on his own shoulders. Queen Mary Beatrice, at her son's urgent request, begged the Regent to intervene with George I. in this matter. The Duke of Orleans did so and the incident ended.

When Lord Peterborough was arrested at Bologna, on or about 10th September, 1717, a report was spread that Count Douglas (as he was styled) was at Venice. An officious Italian, Signor Belloni, who resided at Bologna, and was in constant correspondence with Sir David Nairne, the Chevalier's trusted Secretary, undertook a search for Douglas. With this intent, Belloni sent a spy to Venice with a description of Colonel Douglas, whose arrest had been decreed at Urbino, where King James was holding his Court. Belloni's letters to Nairne, referring to Douglas, are still in existence. In his despatch of 29th September he informs Nairne :—

> "My man who ought to have returned yesterday from Venice has not yet come back; this makes me think he has found Count Douglas and that he does not wish to leave him before having discovered his design. It appears he seeks to bring him (Douglas) into the Ecclesiastical State, in which case it will be better to make the arrest here." [1]

The worthy Belloni's next letter, dated 2nd October, is not quite so hopeful :—

> "My man returned from Venice but he has not been able to find anything about Count Douglas after all his enquiries. Mr. Smide (Smith) an Englishman has no knowledge of him (Douglas) .... I have left a message with my man's brother in Venice in order that he may let me know if Douglas turns up, in which case he will tell me and I will report immediately." [2]

On 9th October Belloni reports :—

> "I have heard from a Cardinal that six weeks ago Count Douglas was in Venice, and a Venetian nobleman said this was the man who attempted to assassinate the King. But he was called by another name. This is all talk although the facts agree in a good many things with the description given in the first letters. If he (Douglas) is still there it is probable that he may still come into the Ecclesiastical State." [3]

And on 13th October Belloni writes :—

> "From your Honour's note of the 8th inst. I hear that the King is well satisfied with my poor endeavours in this matter by sending me a competent sum .... If Douglas should be in Venice we should know it with the description of his stature which has been sent." [4]

The Royal exile at Urbino spent his money in a vain quest after Douglas. When Peterborough was arrested, John Paterson, one of the

---

[1] *Gualterio Papers*, Add. MS. 20312, fol. 50.
[2] *Ibid.* fol. 79
[3] *Ibid.* 83b.
[4] *Ibid.* 84b. The following description of Colonel Douglas appears in the deposition made 18th Nov. 1715, by Nicholas de L'Hôpital, Sieur de Lacunelle, controller at Nonancourt :— "Un gros homme beau de visage et belle physionomie." Printed in Le Montey's *Histoire de la Régence*, &c.

Secretaries at Urbino, wrote to John Carney at Rome to tell him the good news; and Carney replied that he meant to start next day for Florence "to look out for Colonel Douglas."[1] The Intelligence Department at James III.'s Court seems to have been badly organised.

For nearly two years we lose trace of Douglas. In the summer of 1719 he turns up at Hanover, where George I. was then sojourning. Douglas was the bearer of a letter to the King from the Duke of Orleans. This epistle is not forthcoming; but a copy of George's reply to the Regent is still extant and runs as follows:—

"MON FRERE ET COUSIN,

"Le Col. Douglas m'a bien remis la lettre dont vous l'avez chargé pour moy. Comme il ne s'offre presentement aucune occasion de L'employer, et qu'il retourne à Paris, je n'ay pas voulu manquer de vous remerciez des Bontez que vous avez eues pour luy, et de vos egards obligeans pour mes recommendations. Il me semble qu'il ai lieu d'en esperer encore une nouvelle marque par rapport aux Villages de Dankelsheim, et de Kitelsheim, qui ont esté réunis au Grand Bailliage de Haguenau, et qu'il est fonde à en demander un Dedommagement; et comme il s'agit à cet egard de l'execution de l'Article 22e du Traité d'Utrecht lequel il n'y a esté inseré qu'apres qu'on en produit les titres sur lesquels Son Droit est appuyé, il y avoit lieu de croire que la Couronne de France se chargeroit du Dedommagement susdit pour satisfaire au Traité, au lieu de renvoyer cette affaire par devant des Commissaires ce que ne peut manquer d'engager le Col. Douglas dans de longs Procez contre des Parties beaucoup plus puissantes que luy. C'est a quoy il vous sera facile d'apporter remede en continuant au dit Col. l'honneur de votre protection, dont je vous serez fort obligé. Je demeure avec sinceritè, &c., &c.,

"GEORGE R."

"à Herrenhausen
le 25 d'Aout
1719
"À Mon Frere et Cousin le Duc d'Orleans."[2]

Lord Stanhope, in reply to a letter from Lord Stair, writes to the latter on 26th August, 1719, from Hanover, and encloses a copy of the King's letter to the Regent. Stanhope goes on to say:—

"You will see, by enclosed copy, that the interests of Col. Douglas are recommended to the Regent in the strongest manner possible; and if your Excellency will support these interests, by your personal representations to His Royal Highness, there is no reason to doubt that the said Col. Douglas will receive a favourable answer about his claims."[3]

There is no record to show that the French Government gave Douglas any compensation whatever for the loss of his estates. But the Regent stood Douglas's friend and gave him a letter of recommendation to the Duke of Lorraine, at whose Court he "Received great honour and favour."[4] These facts entirely disprove Saint-Simon's statement that after the Nonancourt incident, in November 1715, Colonel Douglas was a social outcast in French society.

---

[1] Quoted in Haile's *Life of the Old Chevalier*, p. 245
[2] *S.P. Dom. Entry Book* 269, fols. 166-7
[3] *Ibid.*, fol. 167.
[4] Douglas to the Duke of Newcastle, see p. 32.

On the accession of George II. Colonel Douglas again visited London. His letters to the Duke of Newcastle very clearly explain why he came. The first is dated "May the 9th, 1728":—

"MY LORD DUKE,

"Not having had the honour to see your Grace last Tuesday att your Office as I expected, I send your Grace this little proposal, as being very much assured it is more in my power to be servicable to his Majesty, and the Ministry, in Lorraine than any other of his Majesty's subjects.

"I allsoe send your Grace a petition which I humbly begg your Grace to have the goodness and charity to present to the King that I may have something ordered me to subsist; I am persuaded none in the Ministry will be against his Majesty's providing one who has rendered so many services to the present Government. I have received such favour from your Grace that I hope you will assist me still in this who am with great submission and respect, My Lord Duke, your Grace's most humble and most obedient servant

"L. C. DOUGLASS.

"I'll wait on your Grace att Court."[1]

(Enclosure.)

"PROPOSAL TO HIS GRACE THE DUKE OF NEWCASTLE.

"To be sent to the Court of Lorraine being very well acquainted with the principals there, and having received great honour and favour from both their R.H.'s upon the late Duke of Orleans recommendation when I went last to that Court, and particularly because her R.H. remembered that I had the honour to be very well known to her when both very young, and then a play fellow of her brother the said Duke.

"My wife and her family being much considered att that Court and wee having a part of our estate in Lorraine, it would be easyer for me to goe about my affaire, or to find out any thing his Majesty or the Ministry would be desirous to know from that Court than any other of his Majesty's subjects. And lastly, iff his late Majesty in the years 1719 or 1720 had resolved to have sent any body to Lorraine I was told by the late Earl Stanhope att Hanover his Majesty designed to employ me, and as there is two ways of goeing about that affair viz. privately or with a Caracter, I offer to your Grace to goe as you'll think, to the best effect.

"L. C. DOUGLASS.

"As I have been employed by his late Majesty with success I hope to be as happy in this negotiation."[2]

It is not surprising that Douglas's "proposal" brought him no employment. On 20th May following, he again memorialised the Duke of Newcastle, and this time he showed very good reasons for George II. helping him to prosecute his claims in France:—

"MY LORD DUKE,

"Since I am told your Grace dont think proper to move the King upon my pension as being a money matter belonging to Sr. Robert Walpole, I then shall only beg your Grace's favour, soe far as to recommend me to him; but as to what regards my pretensions in France, stipulated by the late Queen's specifique demands and the 22nd Article of the Treaty of Utrecht, it totally depends on your Grace to move the King upon it as Secretary of State. And that your

---

[1] *S.P. Dom.* George II, Bundle VI, 91.
[2] *Ibid.*

Grace may be the better able to give the King a perfect account of it, I send your Grace herewith, to be left at Mr. Delafaye's, Letters, Instructions, demands and papers of consequence to me by which your Grace will soon be able to know how much reason I have to complain of the injustice done me, and how I may by your Grace's means, and His Majesty's authority, be rectifyed and at last obtain satisfaction and right. I beg your Grace to read my Lord Dartmouth's and the Earl of Marr's letters and [it] will appear clearly the reason why I lost a pension of £547 10s. p. annum (granted to my late Father and me by a recommendation of Parliament for our Loyalty to our Country and as having lost an estate in France for the Nation's Cause), and by the same Letters your Grace will be pleased to observe why I did not get satisfaction for my Claim in France as well as the Dukes of Richmond and Hamilton for theirs, when we were all three comprehended in the same 22nd Article of the Treaty.

"The late King's Letters, his Instructions to his Ministers, the Duke of Orleans' letters, the Duke d'Aumont's, and the other papers prove, 1st, my unquestionable Right to my pretensions in France, and 2ndly my service to the late King and present Government in many occasions, all which being true matter of fact, and considered by your Grace, I am hopeful you will be incouraged not only to recommend me to Sir Robert Walpole but allsoe to procure me the Justice that is due to any of His Majesty's best and loyal subjects; and lastly as the late Queen Anne, and particularly his late Majesty, and both their Ministers had some regard and value for me, and designed to see me righted in France, I have with submission as much right to expect his present Majesty, after your Grace has represented him my case, will do me justice in every respect, since I am deprived of my estate in France, and am under great straits and oppression for only haveing been thought in France too zealous for the Illustrious house of Hanover (soe help me God). I beg pardon for this long epistle and with submission and respect remain my Lord Duke,

&c., &c.,

"L. C. DOUGLASS."[1]

Whilst waiting for an answer to his Memorial the unfortunate Douglas suffered a severe illness which kept him laid up for months, as he states in this piteous letter to the Duke of Newcastle:—

"MY LORD DUKE,

"The great sickness I have had these three months past hath reduced me sadly, and now that I am pretty well, and should goe to France with his Majesty's letter to get either my Grandfather's estate, or an equivalent, I can't appear abroad as I should haveing sold everything to subsist till now, besides being considerably indebted haveing had my pension discontinued and the arrears due thereon not payed me. I beg your Grace and for God sake to move the King to consider that haveing rendred the present Government great service, it's not reasonable I should now starve in not being put in the capacity of getting to France, to recover what I have been deprived of these many years for haveing been ever against the Pretender's interest, and for the Protestant Succession.

"I send your Grace a petition for the King and most humbly begg your Grace to protect me, and let me have a favourable answer. I am with submission and respect, My Lord Duke,

&c., &c.,

"L. C. DOUGLASS.

"Be pleased to remember you have promised to doe me service, now is the time.

"The 6th 9 ber. 1728."[2]

[1] S.P. Dom. George II. Bundle VI. 100.
[2] S.P. Dom. George II. Bundle IX. 56.

Six weary months of debt and difficulty rolled away before Col. Douglas was able to return to France. When he did so he was the bearer of an autograph letter from George II. to Louis XV. A copy of this letter is still extant :—

"MONSIEUR MON FRÈRE,

"Le Colonel Douglas s'en retournant en France pour soliciter ses prétensions à votre Cour, Je le recommande à votre protection, vous priant d'ordonner qu'on luy fasse droit, selon ce qui est stipulé par la Traité d'Utrecht sur les terres en fonds qu'il reclame. Je recevray comme une marque de votre amitié pour moy cette justice que vous luy rendres, et Je vous prie d'être persuadé que Je me serviray toujours avec plaisir des occasions de vous donner des preuves de l'éstime et de l'affection avec laquelle je suis,
"Monsieur mon Frère
"Votre bon Frère
"GEORGE R.

"À St James le 15e. de Mai, 1729."[1]

The most Christian King's reply to his "good brother"[1] is not forthcoming. But we know that Colonel Douglas's estate was not restored to him, and St. Simon tells us that Douglas died beyond the sea (delà la mer);[2] and that when the Abbé St. Simon went to Metz, from Noyon, he found Douglas's widow "*fort miserable.*" Such was the end of a life that had begun with great promise, but the latter half of which was labour and sorrow. Whatever his faults may have been, he had a large share of the tenacity of purpose which has distinguished Scotchmen bearing the name of Douglas in all parts of the world. Charles Douglas was the plaything of Fortune. Four British monarchs in succession tried to wring from successive French Governments the estates which France had agreed, in two separate Treaties, to restore to the Douglas family. Yet, despite unfulfilled expectations, Colonel Douglas was true to the motto :—

"SPERO MELIORA."

---

[1] *Townshend Papers*, printed by the *Hist. MSS. Commission*, Report XI., Appx. Pb. IV. p. 121.

[2] As a result of my exhaustive researches into Col. Charles Douglas's career, I find that I was mistaken in thinking him to be identical with the Col. Charles Douglas to whom George II. gave a Regt. of Marines in Nov. 1739, with which corps he served at the siege of Carthagena in 1741, and had his head taken off by a cannon-ball. I take this opportunity of correcting the statement I made about Sir Wm. Douglas's son, Col. Charles Douglas, in *Notes and Queries*, 10th Series, Vol. X., p. 182.

C. D.

THE PREMIER FIELD-MARSHAL OF ENGLAND.

CHAPTER IV

THE PREMIER FIELD-MARSHAL OF ENGLAND[1]

"An honest, good-natured gentleman, who has much distinguished himself as a soldier."—DEAN SWIFT.

LORD GEORGE HAMILTON, fifth son of Anne, Duchess of Hamilton, and William, Duke of Hamilton (so created in 1660), was born at Hamilton Palace, Lanark, and baptised there on 9th February, 1666. On 9th May, 1684, Lord George was appointed captain in the Royal Scots Regiment of Foot, then commanded by his paternal uncle, the Earl of Dumbarton. At the Revolution, George Hamilton joined the Standard of William of Orange, and on 1st March, 1690, succeeded to the command of an Enniskillen Regiment of Infantry, lately commanded by Colonel Thomas Lloyd, whose dash, bravery, and success in the field had earned for him the *sobriquet* of "the little Cromwell." At the battle of the Boyne Hamilton earned his first laurels. The successful crossing of the Boyne by the Williamite forces was chiefly due to some Irish officers of Lord George Hamilton's corps, who had been specially brought to the King's notice by their colonel, on the eve of the battle, as guides who knew the fords of the river. Lord George commanded his regiment at the siege of Athlone; also in the sharply contested battle of Aughrim, where Hamilton's Enniskilleners were in the first line of attack and suffered heavily, he himself being wounded; he was also present at the capture of Galway and Limerick. On the reduction of his regiment, at the close of the campaign in Ireland, Hamilton was appointed by William III., in January, 1692, Colonel of the Royal Fusiliers. He commanded this regiment at the defence of Namur in May and June, 1692, during which siege "the besieged behaved themselves with great gallantry, and the French lost a great many men."[2] At the disastrous battle of Steinkirk, Lord George Hamilton gained fresh distinction and was rewarded with the colonelcy of the 1st Battalion of his old regiment—the Royal Scots. In the closely contested battle of Landen, 19th July, 1693, the Royal Scots bore the brunt of the enemy's attack and suffered heavily. They were also actively engaged during the siege of Namur, where Lord George Hamilton was wounded, though not severely. Whilst the siege was in progress Lord George was promoted to the rank of Brigadier-General (10th July, 1695), but commanded his regiment in person until the fall of Namur. On the 25th November, 1695, he married Elizabeth Villiers, eldest daughter of Sir Edward Villiers, Knight Marischal, sister of Edward, first Earl of Jersey. This lady had held the post for some years of maid of honour to Queen Mary when Princess of Orange, and was a great favourite with King William. Indeed there is no doubt that she was a

---

[1] This memoir, by Charles Dalton, appeared in the *Journal of the Royal United Service Institution* for March, 1901.
[2] *London Gazette.*

"favourite" in every sense of the word, and that her intimacy with the King caused much unhappiness to Queen Mary. If it be true, as Macaulay tells us, that it took all Kneller's art to make King William's "only English mistress" presentable on canvas, it must be undoubtedly true that she was a most fascinating woman and possessed, as Macaulay allows, of mental powers which qualified her to partake the cares and guide the counsels of statesmen and politicians. Dean Swift described her as the "wisest woman he ever knew." She certainly was clever enough to retain the King's friendship long after any unlawful intimacy had ceased to exist between them, and he bestowed upon her by Royal grant, dated 30th March, 1695, all the private estates of the late King James in Ireland (except a small part in grant to Lord Athlone), containing 95,649 acres, valued, or rather over-valued, at £25,995 per annum. Historians have been unduly severe in aspersing the character of Lord George Hamilton for marrying Elizabeth Villiers. He has been accused of a base desire to curry favour in his Sovereign's eyes by taking a mistress off his master's hands, and to advance his own fortune and position. It is very unlikely that this was the case. His birth, position, and rank were all assured, and at the age of twenty-nine love was more likely to be the one predominant feeling in his breast than any base or sordid motive. All the writers who refer to this marriage have, seemingly, been unaware of the fact that the lady in question was a distant cousin to her husband, whose maternal great-grandmother was a Villiers. Whatever may be said, or thought, of this marriage, it turned out a very happy one, and was in no way shadowed by the forfeiture, by Act of Parliament, of the Irish estates, which only brought in about a sixth of their nominal value and were saddled by two annuities amounting to £3,000, payable to two of King James' former mistresses! On 3rd January, 1696, Lord George Hamilton was created Earl of Orkney with remainder to the heirs of his body whatsoever. In March, 1702, he was made a Major-General, and served at the siege of Stevensvaert this year. In January, 1704, Orkney was advanced to the rank of Lieut.-General, and, a month later, was made a Knight of the Thistle, which noble Order Queen Anne re-established in December, 1703. On 13th August, 1704, Lord Orkney was at the battle of Blenheim, where he commanded a brigade of infantry, and he made prisoners of war a great body of French troops which had been posted in the village of Blenheim. In June, 1705, he commanded a detachment of 12,000 men sent to prevent a conjunction of two large bodies of French troops near Liege, and he used such expedition that he seasonably reinforced the Dutch and prevented Marshal Villeroy taking the citadel at Liege, about which his troops were then formed. At the battle of Ramillies, on 23rd May, 1706, Lord Orkney, at the head of a large body of cavalry, was instrumental in defeating the French, who, after a hard-fought battle, were driven from their position, and obliged to fly in frightful confusion. "The British Horse under Lord Orkney," writes Sir A. Alison, "did not draw bridle from the pursuit till they reached the neighbourhood of Louvain, having, besides fighting the battle, ridden full 25 miles that day." In July, 1706, Orkney assisted at the siege of Menin; and on the 12th February, 1707, was elected one of the sixteen representative peers for Scotland to sit in the first Parliament of Great Britan after the Union. This same year Orkney served again under Marlborough in Flanders, and at the head of seven battalions of foot kept the communication open from Meldert to Louvain as long as the Allied Army lay at the former place. And when they decamped to Nivelle, within two leagues of the French Army, and a battle was expected, the Earl with twelve battalions of foot and thirty squadrons of horse, and all the grenadiers of the army, advanced and charged their rear in their retreat for about four miles and killed and dispersed about 4,000 of the enemy. On the 11th July, 1708, the allies under Marlborough crossed the Scheldt, near Oudenarde, and attacked the French with the greatest bravery. After several hours of stubborn resistance the French were overpowered and forced to retreat. If night had not supervened their whole army would have been annihilated. Lord Orkney was one of Marlborough's generals who on this occasion advocated an immediate advance on Paris, but the great commander saw too many obstacles in the way to attempt it. This is the only occasion on which we find any serious disagreement between Marlborough and Orkney, and it is probable that the former's enemies at home made the most of what Orkney wrote to a friend in Scotland in the heat of the moment.[1] He assisted in covering the siege of Lille, and in November, 1708, commanded the van of the army at the passing of the Scheldt, serving at the siege of Tournay the following June, and taking the forts of St. Amand and St. Martin. On the 31st August (N.S.), Marlborough, anticipating the surrender of Tournay, despatched Lord Orkney with all the grenadiers of the army, and twenty squadrons to surprise St. Ghislain and secure the passage of the Heine. On 3rd September, the Prince of Hesse Cassel was sent after him with 4,000 foot and twenty squadrons. On arriving at the banks of the Heine, Orkney found the passage so strongly guarded that he did not deem it prudent to alarm the enemy or reveal the real point of attack by attempting to force it. The Prince of Hesse was more fortunate, as he surprised the passage near Obourg early on the 6th and entered the French lines of the Trouille unopposed, the enemy retreating with precipitation. By a master-stroke of military genius the Prince of Hesse turned the enemy's lines and invested Mons on the side of France. Marlborough rapidly followed the Prince of Hesse with the main body and was joined by Orkney with his detachment. On 11th September was fought the most bloody action of this war. The French army commanded by Marshals Villars and Boufflers, occupied a position near Malplaquet, made formidable by treble intrenchments and other works, and covered by thick woods. The allies under Marlborough and Eugene were encamped on the open ground in front of the enemy's position. Lord Orkney at the head of 15 battalions and supported by cavalry on each flank was ordered to advance and force the enemy's intrenchments in the centre. "Lord Orkney then made the attack with such vigour that the intrenchments were at once carried, and the horse following rapidly on the traces of the foot soldiers broke through at the openings between the works and spread themselves over the plain, cutting down the fugitives in every direction."[2] The right and left wings of the allied army were equally successful, but the victory was dearly bought, costing the allies about 18,350 men—a number much in excess of the French loss. In 1710, Lord Orkney was sworn a member of the Privy Council. He was present at the siege of Douay in 1710, and commanded 20 battalions of infantry at the siege of Bouchain. Although one of the

---

[1] *Hist. MSS. Comn.*, Report VIII., Part I. (letter from Defoe to Godolphin, 3rd August, 1708).
[2] Sir A. Alison's *Life of Marlborough*, Vol. II.

Duke of Marlborough's favourite generals, Orkney was so essentially free from all party bias and rancour of political hostility, that the Duke of Ormonde, who superseded Marlborough as Captain-General of Queen Anne's forces at home and abroad, obtained for Orkney the appointment of General of the Foot in Flanders, and he accompanied Ormonde to the Netherlands in 1712, and continued with the allied army until the close of the campaign. As a further reward for his eminent war services, Lord Orkney was appointed Colonel of the 2nd Battalion of the 1st Foot, so that he had the exceptional honour of being Colonel-Commandant of both battalions of the regiment he had so often led to victory. On the 28th October, 1714, he was appointed Gentleman Extraordinary of the Bed-Chamber to George I., and, on the 17th December following, Governor of Virginia. Orkney was afterwards made Constable, Governor and Captain of Edinburgh Castle, Lord-Lieutenant of Lanark, and on 12th January, 1736, was appointed Field-Marshal of all His Majesty's forces—his commission to this high rank, then first introduced into England, being dated two days prior to the Duke of Argyll's appointment to this rank.

Beyond the bare record of his war services, the Earl of Orkney has left few memoirs of his career behind him. As a general he was fitter to command a wing of an army than an army itself. He was no strategist, and was much below Marlborough in military genius. At the same time, his military talents were much beyond the average, and as a second-in-command he was a most dependable and successful commander. He saw an immense deal of active service, and he won his high rank and position by his sterling qualities and personal bravery. William III. had the most perfect confidence in him, and when Marlborough was detected in shameless "trimming," the King sent Orkney to Marlborough to formally acquaint him that "His Majesty had no further need for his services." Marlborough's Fusilier Regiment was, at the same time (January, 1692), bestowed on Orkney.

Lord Orkney died at his house in Albemarle Street on 29th January, 1737, and by his special request, named in his will, was buried at Taplow, Buckingham, without any funeral ostentation whatever. By his Countess (died 19th April, 1733, and buried at Taplow) he had three daughters, viz., Lady Anne, married to William O'Brien, Earl of Inchiquin, who succeeded as Countess of Orkney; Lady Frances, married to Sir Thomas Lumley-Sanderson, Earl of Scarborough; and Lady Harriet, who married John Boyle, Earl of Orrery, and predeceased her parents. From the eldest daughter descends the present Earl of Orkney.

A touching anecdote is told of the second Countess of Orkney in her own right, who married her first cousin, Murrough, Earl of Inchiquin (subsequently created Marquis Thomond):—

"This lady was deaf and dumb. Shortly after the birth of her first child the nurse saw her cautiously approach the cradle in which the infant was asleep, and fling down a large stone, with all her force upon the floor. The noise it made awoke the child, who cried. The Countess fell on her knees in a transport of joy. She had discovered that her child possessed the sense which was wanting in herself."

CHAPTER V

FRANÇOIS DE LA ROCHEFOUCAULD, MARQUIS DE MONTANDRE,[1]

MASTER-GENERAL OF THE ORDNANCE IN IRELAND AND A BRITISH FIELD-MARSHAL, 1739

" He was esteemed by all the princes under whom he had the honour to serve, and well beloved by everybody that knew him."—*London Daily Post*, August 16th, 1739.

SPECIAL interest attaches to this Field-Marshal from the fact of his being a Frenchman by birth and descent. Of ancient lineage—a scion of a house whose nobility dates from the 10th century—honourable character, and endowed with military ardour, François de la Rochefoucauld was well fitted to hold high rank in the French Army; but the short-sighted policy of " Le Grand Monarque " drove the subject of this memoir, with many brave compatriots, into the service of France's most bitter foe, William III., King of England.

Francis, 1st Count de la Rochefoucauld, was Prince of Marsillac, Lord of Barbezieux, of Mount Guyon, of Montandre, and Chamberlain of King Charles VIII and Louis XII. He died in 1516 or 1517, leaving a younger son, Louis Seigneur de Montandre, who was great-great-grandfather of our Field Marshal who was born in September, 1672. " He appears," says Colonel Chester, " to have been bred a Canon in the Abbey of St. Victor at Paris, but fled to England on account of the change in his religious sentiments." The young Huguenot refugee probably served as a volunteer in King William's army in Ireland [2] prior to his being appointed Captain and Brevet-Lieut.-Colonel in Colonel François du Cambon's Regiment of Foot. His first two commissions are thus officially entered in the War Office MS. Commission Books :—

"Francis de Montandre, Esq. to be Captain of a company whereof Lieut.-Colonel James Montant was Captain in Colonel Francis de Cambon's Regiment of Foot, dated 15th February, 169$\frac{2}{3}$."

"Brevet for Francis de Montandre, Esq. to command and take his rank as Lieut.-Colonel of Foot, dated Kensington, 15th February, 169$\frac{2}{3}$."

---

[1] This *Memoir* by Charles Dalton appeared in Vol. *XXIII.* of *Royal Artillery Proceedings*. A very full memoir of the Marquis de Montandre is to be found in Mr. Agnew's *Protestant Exiles from France* (three vols.), published in 1871-4; biographical notices in La Haag's *La France Protestante*, and Colonel Chester's *Westminster Abbey Registers*. Letters and MS. references in *Treasury Papers*, and *State Papers* at Public Record Office; newspapers and contemporary diaries, etc.; Boyer's *Annals of Reign of Queen Anne;* Captain George Carleton's *Memoirs;* Walpole's *Letters;* Cannon's *Regimental Records; The Marlborough Despatches;* Walpole's *Letters to Miss Berry* (edited by Lady Theresa Lewis), Vol. I; Parnell's *War of the Succession in Spain*.

[2] An obituary notice of the Marquis de Montandre in the *London Daily Post*, August 16th, 1739, says: " He made all the campaigns in Ireland and Flanders under William III."

It would seem from these commissions that the future Field Marshal dropped his surname of Rochefoucauld on entering the British army and adopted in its place the name of his father's marquisate. In 1702, on the death of his elder brother, Isaac Charles, third Marquis, he assumed the title of Marquis de Montandre, by which he was henceforth known.

In August, 1692, Cambon's regiment, which had done good service in Ireland, sailed for Flanders with fourteen other regiments and arrived at Ostend 1st September. On the death of Colonel Cambon in this year the regiment was given to Count Marton, afterwards created Earl of Lifford, and served with King William in all his campaigns in Flanders until the Peace of Ryswick. We have no record of Montandre's services during this period, but from the following curious notices in several contemporary London newspapers it appears that sixteen French Protestant officers, and six men of Colonel Cambon's Regiment were taken prisoners by a French ship when on their way to England and carried to Dunkirk, where they suffered great privations.

> *Post-Boy*, March 18th-20th, 1697. "I am credibly informed that Sir Wm. Jennings,[1] who is now with King James in France, has writ a letter to a Person that is in a considerable position in the Government offering for Mr. Jennings, his son, who has been a long time in Newgate under sentence of death, to discharge 16 French Protestant officers and six soldiers of Colonel Cambon's Regiment, who were taken on their voyage from Flanders to England and carried to Dunkirk, and I hear the same was readily agreed to and that Mr. Jennings was to be sent over to France forthwith in exchange for these prisoners."
>
> *Post-Man*, January 30th.—"There is advice that the French Protestant officers who are prisoners in Dunkirk have been forced to cast lots who should go to the gallies, the French King having ordered it so to gratify the vengeance of a certain abdicated Prince."

In 1698, Lord Lifford's, late Cambon's Regiment, was quartered in Ireland, and from a list of the regiments in that year, still extant, we find that François de Montandre was the acting Lieut.-Colonel. Four years later we find him receiving a pension of £200 a year upon the Irish Establishment.

In 1703, Portugal joined the "Grand Alliance" against France. An Anglo-Dutch force was sent to Lisbon commanded by the Duke of Schomberg, whose father had liberated Portugal from the Spanish yoke; but the Duke was superseded in the following spring by the Earl of Galway, who, like Cincinnatus of old, left his retirement and the planting of cabbages to fight the battles of his adopted country. Some months prior to this command being thrust upon the gallant veteran, Henry Massue de Ruvigny, Earl of Galway, we find this nobleman soliciting some appointment for the Marquis de Montandre at the hands of the great Marlborough. The latter commander had not the power just then to accede to Galway's request, but he expressed his esteem for Colonel de Montandre[2] One of the first officers chosen by Galway to serve on his own staff, when he was selected for the Portuguese command, was our Huguenot Marquis,

---

[1] A captain in the navy who accompanied James II. into France. His son was captured on board a French privateer fighting against his own countrymen, was brought to England, tried, and condemned to death. We read in the *Post-Boy* of July 22nd, 1699, that "Mr. Jennings having obtained His Majesty's most gracious pardon, pleaded the same at Doctors Commons according to custom."

[2] Murray's *Marlborough Dispatches*, Vol. I., p. 183.

who was promoted Brigadier-General on the British Establishment. The military operations in Portugal in the autumn of 1704 are not worth detailing. In the following spring the allies under Lord Galway, Count Fagel and the Comte de Corzana marched to the frontier and laid siege to Valencia de Alcantara. "In all our march," wrote an officer in Galway's army from the camp before Valencia, May 2nd, 1705, "we met nobody in arms, nor can we learn what has become of the Spanish cavalry—a feint my Lord Galway made by sending to view Badajoz has, 'tis said, drawn them that way. I suppose 'twill not be long before we hear of them, for if they let Alcantara fall into our hands, if we can get provisions, nothing can hinder our piercing much further into Spain. My Lord Galway, who is not perfectly recovered of his late sickness yet, is the soul of this matter here, and if he does not do the work on this side, any other man will find it impossible." Valencia surrendered and the towns of Salvaterra and Albuquerque were successfully besieged and taken. After these slight successes the allies went into summer quarters. In October they again took the field. *The London Gazette* of October 18th, 1705, gives the following official account of the siege of Badajoz where the Marquis de Montandre did good service :—

"The confederate forces being all joined on the 1st inst. near the Caya, the Earl of Galway marched with them, the next day passed that river, the Xevera, and the Guardiana, and encamped before Badajoz, where the forces lay all night upon their arms. The 3rd they took post before the town. The 4th, at night, the trenches were opened and the Marquis de Montandre, who commanded as Major-General that week, did very good service and they are already carried forward within less than 100 paces of the town which has no outworks."

The siege was carried on with great vigour until Lord Galway was severely wounded—his hand being struck off by a cannon-ball which necessitated the amputation of his right arm. The leading spirit of the army being incapacitated from serving for some time, the entire command devolved on Count Fagel, General of the Dutch troops, and the Marquis des Minas, General of the Portuguese and Generalissimo of the allied forces. They were outgeneralled and outmanoeuvred by the French Marshal, Tessé, who succeeded in throwing 1,000 men into Badajoz. The siege was raised, and on October 17th the allies began their retreat. Marshal Tessé followed them with part of his army, "but the march of the confederate forces being covered by the Marquis de Montandre with six battalions and eight squadrons, they drew off in very good order without any loss . . . . On arrival at Elvas the army separated and went into winter quarters."

The following spring found the veteran Earl of Galway once more in the field and eager to march with the allied troops into Spain, and join forces with the Earl of Peterborough. But, as before, his actions were hampered by the vacillating councils of the Portuguese Generals who were in favour of a defensive war in their own country rather than an offensive campaign in Spain. The old saying, that "every cock crows on his own dunghill" was strongly exemplified in the case of the Portuguese officers, whether taken as a body or individually. They were willing, and more than willing, to serve with the British and Dutch troops, for had not England and Holland engaged themselves by treaty to pay 13,000 Portuguese soldiers while the war lasted, and were not England and Holland better paymasters than His Majesty the King of Portugal? But they hoped to acquire a maximum of glory at a minimum of risk, and also at a minimum of discomfort. After several councils of war had been held it was decided to march to the frontier and besiege Alcantara. The allies arrived in front of this place early in April, and on the first night of their arrival 800 sappers were employed in raising earthworks and digging a trench deep enough to cover the troops. "The Marquis de Montandre," we are told, "sustained the workmen with five battalions of foot and 200 horse. The French kept up a brisk fire all night and next day made a vigorous sally. Being repulsed with loss, the enemy surrendered the town on April 14th and the allies were left in possession.

Lord Galway took advantage of this success to again press the question of a march to Madrid. Lord Peterborough sent pressing messages. "Come over and help us," was the continual cry from the Carlists and their allies in Spain. Barcelona was besieged by a large French army under Marshal Tessé and invested on the seaboard by a fleet of 30 French ships. Peterborough had his hands full in Catalonia. Charles III. was shut up in the beleaguered town. Never was there more need of a "war of diversion," and never was there a better opportunity for it. The road to Madrid from Alcantara lay open to the Portuguese army, who outnumbered four to one the force under the Duke of Berwick—Philip the Fifth's best General. Madrid could not offer any prolonged resistance. The capital, once gained, might be held until Barcelona was relieved by the expected English fleet, when Peterborough's army could bring Charles III in triumph to his capital. So eager were Galway and the English officers to march on Madrid that the former agreed to the Portuguese troops taking the right on all occasions in Spain, which before had only been acceded to them when in their own country. This important concession, for which Galway was afterwards blamed by the House of Lords, induced the Portuguese Generals to march into Spain. On ariving at Almaraz, half way between the frontier and Toledo, these half-hearted allies determined to proceed no further eastward until more reassuring news was received from Barcelona. The invading army turned northward and laid siege to Ciudad Rodrigo, capturing two Spanish towns on the march thither. It is recorded by Boyer that "these two towns declared for King Charles because communication with their ice-houses was cut off!" When the allies arrived before Ciudad Rodrigo Montandre was commanded, with five battalions and some cavalry, to possess himself of the mountain pass called Robredillo and so prevent a relieving force being thrown into the invested town, which capitulated in seven days. The very day that this happened news arrived that Barcelona was relieved. Once more did Galway press the necessity of the march upon Madrid, and, on 3rd June, the allies began their march to the capital, which they reached on June 29th, a few days after Philip, titular King of Spain, had fled from it. The allies wasted a whole month at Madrid in inaction. Well might Lord Peterborough say that this halt was as fatal as Hannibal at Capua.

The Marquis de Montandre was despatched by Lord Galway from Spain to give a relation to Queen Anne of the affairs that had taken place in that country. While in England he wrote a memorial to the Lord High Treasurer of England to the effect that, as he had a Major-General's command in Portugal, he begged to be promoted to that rank in the British Army. In this memorial he thanks for the promise that had been made him of the Colonelcy of the first English regiment that might become vacant. As a reward for his eminent services in Portugal and Spain he was promoted Major-General, his commission being ante-dated to June 1st, 1706. In November of this year Montandre left London for Spain to rejoin Lord Galway. He received a handsome present from Queen Anne and was instructed to urge upon Lord Galway to continue in his high command in Spain.

On 8th November, Viscount Dungannon, Colonel of an English regiment, died at Alicante, and on the news reaching London the Marquis de Montandre was given the vacant regiment, his commission as Colonel being dated 23rd November, 1706.

Captain Carleton in his graphic memoirs, says :—

> The Marquis de Montandre lost the regiment before he had possession, by an action as odd as it was scandalous.[1] That regiment had received orders to march to the Lord Galway's camp under the command of their Lieut.-Colonel, Bateman, a person before reputed a good officer, tho' his conduct here gave people, not invidious, too much reason to call it in question. On this march he was so very careless and negligent . . . . that his soldiers marched with their muskets slung at their backs and went one after another (as necessity had forced us to do in Scotland), himself at the head of them in his chaise, riding a considerable way before."
>
> "It happened there was a Captain with three score dragoons, detached from the Duke of Berwick's camp, with a design to intercept some cash that was ordered to be sent to Lord Galway's army from Alicant. This detachment, missing of that intended prize, was returning very disconsolately, *re infecta*, when their Captain, observing that careless and disorderly march of the English, resolved, boldly enough, to attack them in the wood. To this purpose he secreted his little party behind a great barn, and so soon as they were half passed by he fell upon them in the centre with his dragoons, cutting and slashing at such a violent rate that he soon dispersed the whole regiment, leaving many dead and wounded on the spot. The three colours were taken and the gallant Lieut-Colonel taken out of his chaise and carried away prisoner with many others ; only one officer, who was an ensign and so bold as to do his duty, was killed."

The narrator of this inglorious episode goes on to say that the Duke of Berwick turned pale when he was told that a whole British regiment had been taken prisoners by a troop of Spanish cavalry. He declined to see the colours which were being exhibited in his camp, and when Colonel Bateman was brought before him the Duke, who was at heart a Briton, tho' in arms against his own countrymen, merely said : "You seem to have been very strangely taken, sir," and then took no further notice of the crestfallen commander. There is such a thing as "the curse of a granted prayer," and the Marquis de Montandre must have felt this when he heard of what had befallen his new regiment which he was not destined to see for several years.

Although Montandre rejoined the Earl of Galway in Spain, he does not appear to have been present at the fatal battle of Almanza. It is probable that after delivering Queen Anne's instructions and wishes to Lord Galway the Marquis was despatched to Portugal, to take up his divisional command there. We find him at Lisbon the first week in June, 1707, when four British infantry regiments landed there from Ireland and marched under his command to the frontier. This timely reinforcement revived the drooping spirits of the Portuguese and gave a check to the enemy who had marched into Portugal with a view to besiege Olivenza, or oblige the Portuguese to give them battle.

---

[1] Carleton's story is entirely corroborated by the account given in the *Post-Man* of April 29th, 1707.

The reduced condition of the allied forces in Portugal, owing to the fact of the veteran troops being in Spain with Lord Galway, did not allow of any offensive operations on the part of our forces, but in March, 1708, Galway returned to Lisbon and by his representations Queen Anne determined to increase the strength of the allied forces in Portugal. Six dragoon regiments were ordered to be raised and equipped in Portugal at Her Majesty's expense who reserved the right of appointing the officers to the said regiments. It was decided to appoint Huguenot officers to these cavalry regiments, and the Marquis de Montandre was one of the first officers chosen for command of a regiment. A MS. list of Montandre's regiment, dated July, 14th, 1708, is still extant; but owing to many delays, partly caused by the King of Portugal objecting to have any of his regiments commanded by French Protestant officers, these new regiments were not embodied until the following summer, when we find this notice in a London chronicle:—

> "*Post-Boy*, April 9th, 1709.—"The French officers and others who are to serve in the five (*sic*) Portuguese regiments in Her Majesty's pay that are raising in Portugal, having received four months' pay, began yesterday, according to their orders, to set out for Portsmouth in order to embark there. Four of the Colonels are to be Portuguese, the fifth the Marquis de Montandre."

In the spring of 1709, viz. on May 7th, was fought the battle of the Caya. For once in their lives the Portuguese were anxious to bring on a general action and try their strength with the Franco-Spanish force commanded by the Marquis de Bay. Lord Galway, knowing the instability of his Portuguese allies, was averse to their opening the ball, and advised a defensive, rather than an offensive, course. But the Marquis de Fronteira, who commanded as Generalissimo, persisted in the contrary resolution. Accordingly, the Portuguese cavalry and artillery, with a British infantry brigade, consisting of the 5th, 20th, 39th, and Lord Paston's regiments, commanded by the Marquis de Montandre, crossed the River Caya, and gaining the opposite heights opened fire on the enemy. The Marquis de Bay, who commanded the Spanish army, being very advantageously posted, lost no time in leading a cavalry charge against Fronteira's right wing, composed of Portuguese horse. These latter wheeled round and fled *ventres à terre* without waiting to be attacked, leaving their artillery to be captured. Montandre's brigade was then attacked, but this General made a most determined stand and repulsed three charges. Galway lost no time in coming to Montandre's assistance with the remaining British infantry brigade, commanded by Major-General Sankey, and supported by the Portuguese cavalry of Fronteira's left wing. Sankey's brigade (Barrymore's, Stanwix's, and Galway's regiments) retook the captured guns with a rush, but meanwhile the cavalry of the left wing had followed the example of the right and had bolted. Sankey's brigade being far in advance were isolated and cut off from the other British regiments; and being surrounded by Bay's cavalry had to surrender as prisoners of war.[1] Montandre retreated in square, and though exposed to the enemy's fire on both flanks, as well as in front, he made such bold stands and charges that the whole of the Portuguese infantry, who had never come to the front at all, were able to secure

---

[1] General Sankey, Brigadiers Pearce and Lord Barrymore, and Colonel Meredith, of Stanwix's Regiment, were among the prisoners.

their retreat to Arronches. Montandre lost only 150 men and inflicted a heavy loss on the Spaniards.

The *Monthly Mercury* for May, 1709, gives a glowing description of the bravery shown by Montandre's little band in their retreat—"exhibiting one of the most noble spectacles of war." Galway had a horse shot under him and barely escaped capture. The allies encamped that night at Arronches and next day reached Elvas, where they took up a strong position which Bay was wise enough not to try and force. So ended the spring campaign—the last in which Montandre took a part. On September 29th, 1709, he arrived in London to give the Queen a report of affairs in Portugal, and, for reasons which are not specified, Montandre relinquished his command.

On April 21st, 1710, Montandre was married at St. James's, Westminster, to Mary Anne, daughter, and only surviving child, of Ezekiel Baron Spanheim, Prussian Ambassador at the Court of St. James.[1] On the 9th May following he was promoted a Lieut.-General in Her Majesty's service. At the close of this year, or early in 1711, the shattered remnants of Montandre's English regiment, which had been taken prisoners in the spring of 1707 by the Spaniards, arrived at Portsmouth, where it was recruited. Not only had the Marquis gained no advantage by the Colonelcy of this regiment, but he was a considerable loser thereby. The regiment had to be reclothed and the colonel, whose business it was to provide the money for this, out of his own allowances, had not received the "wherewithal" from the Government. "Out of sight out of mind" is a true saying, and Montandre's, late Dungannon's, regiment, having been three and a half years imprisoned, had not received much notice from the authorities at home. Hence there were great arrears due to both officers and men when they arrived in England. There are several letters and petitions from Montandre regarding his regiment and the arrears due him and his officers, among the Treasury papers. In 1713 this unlucky regiment was disbanded and there was an end to it.[2] But the arrears were not settled, and petitions to the Lord High Treasurer of England setting forth the grievances of the Colonel and his late regiment went on for some time after, until much importunity partly opened the Treasury purse and a settlement of some sort was effected. As to Montandre's Dragoon Regiment in Portugal, it does not appear to have been embodied until the autumn or winter of 1709, as we find Lord Galway in the October of that year representing to the King of Portugal that his army could not act offensively until the men for the six dragoon regiments, in the pay of Great Britain, had been raised. Montandre was colonel of the last of these six regiments and his name appears as colonel in a list of the regiment under date of 23rd December, 1709. On his relinquishing his command in Portugal, Lieut.-Colonel Sarlande was appointed Colonel in Montandre's place.[3] These dragoon regiments were

---

[1] *Post-Man*, April 22nd, 1710.—" Yesterday the Marquis de Montandre of the family of the Duke de Rochefoucauld and chief of one of the branches thereof, and Major-General in Her Majesty's service, was married to Mademoiselle de Spanheim, only daughter to His Excellency, the Baron de Spanheim, Ambassador Extraordinary of His Majesty the King of Prussia."

[2] *The Daily Courant*, April 22nd, 1713.—" Letters from Dublin of the 13th advise that four regiments on the Irish Establishment are to be broke on the 1st May, Pearce's, Morris's Dragoons, Deloraine's, and Montandre's Foot."

[3] Mr. Agnew makes no mention of Montandre's Portuguese regiment.

disbanded in 1711. His long connection with the British army made Montandre anxious to have, and to hold, the Colonelcy of a British regiment which would bear his name and place a certain amount of military patronage in his hands. As we have already seen, his own regiment was reduced after the peace of Utrecht. On February 16th, 1716, we find the Marquis de Montandre appointed Colonel of a newly-raised regiment on the Irish Establishment, but, in 1718, this corps was reduced and the Marquis had once again to urge his claims for a regiment.[1] In 1719 we find him writing two letters to General Stanhope, Secretary of War, dated respectively 3rd June and 12th July, begging that General's interest in obtaining for him a regiment which had just become vacant by the death of its Colonel.[2] But *the* wish of Montandre's latter years remained ungratified. Other high honours were, however, in store for him, and he found a friend in George II. On 16th January, 1728, Montandre was appointed Master-General of the Ordnance in Ireland[3] and was allowed in his latter years to discharge this office by deputy. On October 27th, 1735, Montandre was promoted to the rank of General and three years later was appointed Governor of Guernsey with a salary of £1,500 per annum. This latter appointment was also a "non-resident" one and allowed the Marquis to reside at his house in Brook Street, London. On the death of the Earl of Orkney, in 1737, it was announced in one or two of the London papers that Montandre had been raised to the Marshalate. That there was some ground for this rumour we may readily believe from the following extract out of a letter to the Duke of Ormonde, from his friend Mr. Ezekiel Hamilton:—

> Leyden, June 2nd, 1737.—"I hear that the Marquis de Montandre is to be made Field-Marshal, in the room of the late Earl of Orkney, which is not agreeable to many of the English General officers, who were disgusted that fourteen foreigners were amongst the list of the last promotion of General officers in England."

It was not till July 2nd, 1739, that the *London Gazette* contained the formal notice of Montandre's promotion to the Marshalate. The gallant veteran only lived until the 8th of the following month. His death and burial are thus chronicled in two contemporary London journals:—

> Saturday, August 11th, 1739.—"Wednesday about 4 o'clock in the afternoon, aged near 70, of a complication of distempers, at his house in Great Brook Street, Grosvenor Square, the Marquis de Montandre, Field-Marshal of England, Governor of Guernsey, Master of the Ordnance in Ireland and General of Foot. He was a Peer of France and came over here on account of his religion. He married the daughter of Baron Spanheim formerly Envoy from the King of Prussia, by whom he had no issue. His corpse is to be interred in a grand manner in Westminster by that of his father-in-law."[4]
>
> Saturday, August 18th, 1739.—"Wednesday the corpse of the Marquis de Montandre, after lying in state in the Jerusalem Chamber, was carried from thence and interred in great funeral pomp and solemnity with the remains of

---

[1] It is curious to read in Mr. Agnew's memoir of Montandre's services that "he maintained his regiment through the various administations."

[2] The vacancies occurred by the deaths of Generals Meredith and Davenport, both of whom were Colonels of Regiments on the Irish Establishment.—*Stanhope Correspondence*, Record Office.

[3] The seal used by Montandre as Master General of the Ordnance in Ireland is in the possession of the Des Voeux family.

[4] *Read's Weekly Journal.*

Baron Spanheim and his lady in a vault near King Henry VII chapel, Westminster Abbey. The whole choir attended at the ceremony. The Right Hon. Sir Paul Methuen, Knight of the Bath, walked as chief mourner."[1]

The Marquis left no issue by his wife, who survived him many years. She was a well-known figure in London society and on more than one occasion entertained royalty. The Marquis having only enjoyed the emolument from his Governorship of the island of Guernsey for one year, George II. was pleased to allow the Marquise to remain in possession of the salary from Guernsey for one year more. Various anecdotes concerning this lady will be found in the diaries and correspondence of the period. One of these anecdotes is worthy of being re-told. "I remember," wrote Walpole to Miss Berry, from Strawberry Hill, July 4th, 1791, "an old French refugee here, the Marquise de Montandre (the Mademoiselle Spanheim of the *Spectator*) who, on the strength of her pinchbeck Marquisate,[2] pretended to supersede our sterling countesses; but being sure of its not being allowed she thus entered her claim. When at a visit, tea was brought in; before the groom of the chambers could offer it to anybody, she called out, 'I would not have any tea;' and then, when she had thus saved her dignity, she said to him, after others had been served, 'I have bethought myself, I think I will have one cup.'"

The witty, but sceptical, Lord Hervey makes passing mention of the Marquis de Mondandre and his wife in his poetical epistle, written in 1736 and addressed to the Queen:—

> "Who ev'ry Wednesday hear Montandre prate
> Of politics and maxims out of date,
> And with old fringes furbelow the State.
> As well that Ever Green his wife might boast
> The long fled bloom of a last century toast."

Being himself an unbeliever, Lord Hervey despised all Huguenot refugees whom he stigmatised as "having more religion than sense," and he never lost an opportunity of sneering at them.

The Right Hon. Mary Ann, Marchioness of Montandre, died at her house in Lower Brook Street on February 5th, 1772, aged 89, and was buried on February 18th in Westminster Abbey.

---

[1] *Read's Weekly Journal*. Sir Paul Methuen was for some years British Ambassador at Lisbon.
[2] This remark was not so ill-natured as it would appear at first reading. By French law a title reverts on the death of the eldest son without issue male to his youngest brother. On the death of Isaac Charles Marquis de Montandre, in 1702, the heir, by French law, was not Francis de Montandre, but his younger brother.

CHAPTER VI

MAJOR-GENERAL JOSEPH WIGHTMAN
ACTING COMMANDER-IN-CHIEF IN SCOTLAND, 1712-1714

THE name of Wightman is not uncommon in England and is to be found in Scotland. The English Wightmans were settled in Leicestershire early in Queen Elizabeth's reign. From them branched off the Weightmans or Wightmans who held landed property in Kent. The subject of this memoir is not specially mentioned in the pedigree of Wightman of Peckleton given in Nichols' *History of Leicestershire*.[1] He might possibly be the Joseph Wightman, 3rd son of a John Wightman of Peckleton; the latter died in 1666. It is a curious coincidence that from 1707 to the time of his death in 1722 General Wightman was Colonel of the regiment subsequently known as the Leicestershire Regiment.

On 29th December, 1690, Joseph Wightman began his military career as Ensign to Sir Francis Wheeler's Company in the 1st Foot Guards and was promoted Lieutenant 7th August, 1693, to Lieut.-Col. Thos. Hopsons's Company with the additional rank of Captain. It is a remarkable fact that young Wightman should have been successively appointed to companies nominally commanded by distinguished admirals. It may well be that the deeds of these two brave commanders stimulated Joseph Wightman's ambition to rise in the army and not to lose any chance of active service. At this distance of time it is impossible to state in which of William III.'s campaigns Wightman took part; but it is believed that he served at the siege of Namur. In the following year (8 December, 1696) he was promoted Captain and Lieut.-Colonel and served under Marlborough in the campaigns of 1702-3. In the autumn of 1703 several British regiments serving in Flanders were sent to Portsmouth, being part of the force destined for the expedition to Portugal under the Earl of Galway. One of the regiments selected was Blood's, afterwards known as the 17th Leicestershire Regiment of Foot. This corps had volunteered for service in Portugal, and as Colonel Blood was unable to accompany it, having the responsible command of the British Train of Artillery in Flanders, Marlborough placed a capable officer temporarily at the head of the corps in question. This officer was Lieut.-Colonel Joseph Wightman of the Guards, who was made a Brevet Colonel.[2] "I daresay the service will not suffer by Colonel Blood's absence," wrote Marlborough to the Earl of Nottingham from the camp at St. Trou in October, 1703; "Colonel Wightman who is at the head (of this regiment) with a commission of colonel being a very careful and diligent officer."[3]

Sir George Rooke was unable to accommodate all the troops on board his fleet which sailed from Portsmouth to Lisbon in February, 1704, and

---

[1] Vol. IV, p. 876.
[2] "List of all the Brevets granted by my Lord Duke of Marlborough [prior to] 1st August, 1704."—*English Army Lists and Commission Registers*, 1661-1714, Vol. V., p. 111.
[3] *Marlborough Dispatches*, Vol. I., p. 192.]

THE SHERIFFMUIR MEDAL.

Wightman was selected to command the troops that had been left behind. "I must desire you," wrote Major-General Lord Cutts to Colonel Wightman, from the Hague, on 30th December, 1703, "to take upon you the chief command of any troops left behind, and to be responsible for them until some general officer shall join you; and hereby require and direct all officers of the said expedition who are still on this side the water punctually to obey your orders as they will answer the same to her Majesty."[1]

In May, 1704, Colonel Wightman with his adopted corps embarked on board Sir Cloudesley Shovell's fleet for Lisbon. The military operations in Portugal were of minor importance in 1704; but in 1705 Galway's campaign commenced in earnest. Wightman served at the siege and capture of Valencia di Alcantara, in May, 1705, and accompanied Galway and the allied troops in their march to Madrid in the following spring. On 1st January, 1707, Wightman was appointed a Brigadier-General by Queen Anne. At the fatal battle of Almanza, fought on Easter Sunday, 1707, Wightman's corps suffered heavily. Three of the senior officers were killed, several officers wounded, and sixteen others taken prisoners. In the autumn following, news reached Galway's camp that Brigadier Blood had died at Brussels, on 19th August, and Brigadier Wightman was given the Colonelcy of the corps he had virtually commanded since August, 1703. In consequence of the great loss in officers and men, suffered at Almanza, some of the British regiments practically ceased to exist and had to be re-formed in England. Wightman's corps had no less than thirty new officers appointed thereto *en second* by commissions dated at Kensington, 5th March, 1708. Recruits were raised at the same time and this temporary battalion was then shipped to Spain. One of Wightman's new ensigns deserves special mention as he became a man of some note in his latter years, and as a Lieut.-Colonel, on the Unattached List, he accompanied Lord Anson round the world in 1741-44. A curious anecdote is told of this officer:—"Mordaunt Cracherode went out to make his fortune as a Commander of the Marines in Lord Anson's ship. He returned, in consequence of his share of prize money, a wealthy man. It was said he returned from this Ansonian circumnavigation in the identical buckskins which he wore on leaving England, they having been the object of his exclusive attachment during the whole voyage! It is said that there is one particular volume in the Cracherode collection which is bound in a piece of the identical buckskins."[2]

Wightman was actively employed in Catalonia during the years 1708-1709 and was promoted Major-General 1st January of the last-named year, when he returned to England.

On 13th June, 1712, General Wightman was appointed Commander-in-Chief in Scotland "during the absence of the Duke of Argyle and Major-General Thos. Whetham." While holding this responsible appointment Wightman "received no more than the pay of a Brigadier although he was actually a Major General at the time he was first employed."[3] In August, 1716, he memorialised the Prince of Wales (then Guardian of the Kingdom) for the amount owing to him, and explained that "his personal pay had been chiefly expended in supporting the interest of his present Majesty." Wightman's petition not bringing the desired result he had to lay his case before the House of Commons in 1718.[4]

---

[1] *Hist. MSS. Comn.* Report on MSS. at Chequers Court, pp. 157-158.
[2] Davy's *Suffolk Collections.*
[3] *Treasury Papers.*
[4] *Journals of the House of Commons*, Vol. XIX, 9th March, 1718.

When news reached England of Queen Anne's death, General Wightman lost no time in forwarding the Protestant Succession. We find him writing to the Duke of Montrose from "Edinburgh, 10 August, 1714," informing that nobleman how he (Wightman) had sent some persons into the Highlands "to feall the puls of those lads"; and he had also summoned all the half-pay officers to Edinburgh to take their oaths to King George and to give an account of their residence."[1]

At Sheriffmuir, Wightman commanded the centre of the Royal Army. Argyll's right wing, led by the Duke in person, signally defeated the Jacobite left. But by a strange concatenation of circumstances Argyll's left wing, under General Whetham, was routed with heavy loss by the Earl of Mar's right. Thus the honours of the engagement were divided. Part of the centre of Argyll's Army gave way with their left wing; but Wightman drew off three regiments of foot and rejoined Argyll. This timely support prevented Mar from renewing the contest. Wightman's account[2] of the battle has been severely criticised, and in our opinion unjustly, by Argyll's biographer.[3] By far the best account of Sheriffmuir is to be found in a 20th century historical work.[4]

Wightman accompanied the Duke of Argyll in the latter's march to, and occupation of, Perth, and was actively employed during February and March, 1716, in the Highlands. On 18th February (O.S.), 1716, we find the Marquis of Huntly writing to Lord Seaforth as follows:—

> "General Wightman, Brigadier Grant his brother, and some horse and foot arrived to-day at Gordon Castle. The General sends me word if I surrender to him he will only put two sentries on me in my house."

But the astute Marquis, whose supineness at Sheriffmuir has been handed down in the humorous old song which avers that—

> "Huntly and Sinclair
> They baith played the tinkler
> With consciences black as a craw, man,"

had already, on 10th February, written to the Earl of Sutherland and submitted himself, his followers and friends, to his Majesty's mercy.[5]

Late in February, 1716, General Cadogan succeeded the Duke of Argyll in command of the Royal forces in Scotland. Among the Scottish nobles who now showed themselves zealous for the King's service was Simon Fraser, Lord Lovat. On March 10th (O.S.) we find this Highland chief writing to General Cadogan from Inverness on military matters:—

> "In obedience to your commands I have presumed to give my advice to Major-General Wightman and offered to concur with him to execute your commands; and certainly he is very active and laborious since he came here, and designs a little expedition to Lord Seaforth's country, in a day or two, and I have the honour to accompany him."[6]

By way of helping the Royal Exchequer heavy contributions were levied on the disaffected nobility, and gentry, in the West of Scotland and

---

[1] *Hist. MSS. Comn.* Report on the Duke of Montrose's MSS.
[2] See Appendix.
[3] *Life of John Duke of Argyll and Greenwich*, by Robert Campbell, 1745, p. 198.
[4] *A Military History of Perthshire*, edited by the Marchioness of Tullibardine.
[5] *Stuart Papers*, Vol. I., p. 516.
[6] *Culloden Papers*, p. 36.

other parts. Wightman issued an order on March 26th (O.S.) to the Lord Lieutenant and Deputy Lieutenants of Nairn "to cause the inhabitants of the shire to bring into Inverness 100 horses with crook saddles and sacks, and one man to every three horses for the King's service."[1] The General did not come away empty-handed from his visit to the Earl of Seaforth's stronghold, as we learn from Mr. Robert Baillie's letter to Forbes of Culloden, dated at Inverness, March 30th, 1716:—

"General Wightman hath taken six Coach horses, with Coach and Shaes (*sic*) from Seafort [h]; the Coach is sent on board one of the Ships."[2]

The Dowager Countess of Seaforth was very irate at the loss of her son's coach and six horses. She wrote to General Cadogan on the subject and said her daughter[3] was unable to undertake her journey to London. She also complained of soldiers being left at Brahan. General Cadogan's reply was most courteous:—

"Inverness
"6th April, 1716.

"I am very sorry her [Ladyship's] coach and horses were taken away and mine are at her ladyship's service. There is an indispensable necessity for leaving a garrison at Brahan till my Lord Seaforth comes in and his people give up their arms as their neighbours have done: and indeed it appears unaccountable that his Lordship, who was one of the first to submit, should be one of the last to do it."[4]

Lord Lovat also wrote to the Dowager Countess under same date:—

"I obtained a passport for my lady, your daughter, to go South and the General is to write to Court in her favour. He was very angry that the General Wightman took your coach and horses, but they are lost by the not taking my advice."[5]

Wightman had only acted according to standing orders; but he did his best to pacify old Lady Seaforth and help her son's wife to accomplish her projected journey:—

"Inverness
"April 10th, 1716.

"MADAM,
"I have sent two or three messengers to acquaint your Ladyship that it would be very convenient for the young lady to be in this town today, for I had found out an expedient to conduct her Ladyship in a chariot with six horses to Edinburgh. I shall leave this place tomorrow in order for Fort William with General Cadogan and, if I am absent, fear things wont be so well managed for the young lady's advantage, and perhaps miss the opportunity of the chariot. I am Madam, your Ladyship's most obedient humble servant

"J. WIGHTMAN."

"Pray let me have your Ladyship's answer by express."[6]

The coach and horses' incident was soon ended by General Cadogan giving a "Protection" to the Dowager Lady Seaforth which secured "any goods, cattle, or corn in the house or on the estate of Brahan, or any other belonging to the Countess Dowager of Seaforth," from being taken away by officers and soldiers of his Majesty's Army in North Britain.[7]

---

[1] *Culloden Papers*, pp. 65–66.
[2] *Ibid.*
[3] Daughter-in-law. She was Mary, only dau. and heir of Nicholas Kennet of Coxhow, Northumberland, and md. 22nd April, 1715, the 5th Earl of Seaforth.
[4] *Notes and Queries*, 2nd Series, Vol. VIII., p. 445.
[5] *Ibid.* p. 446.   [6] *Ibid.*   [7] *Ibid.*

On 5th June, 1719, we find General Wightman marching from Inverness with 1,800 regulars (including three troops of the North British Dragoons under Major Robinson), a few score Highlanders of the Mackay and Munro clans, also a battery of four Cohorn mortars. These Royalist troops had orders to seek out and engage the mixed force of Jacobites, and Spaniards, lately landed on the west coast of Scotland under the command of Earl Marischal and the Earl of Tullibardine. The Earl of Seaforth, Lord George Murray, and the Hon. James Keith (the future Prussian Field-Marshal) had also accompanied the expedition "from beyond seas." According to one historian the Jacobite force numbered 2,000 men on the day of action; be this as it may we may take it that Wightman's force [1] was very little inferior in numbers.

Wightman's victory at Glenshief, on 10th June, reflected great credit on him and his troops, as the insurgents occupied a very strong position which they might have held much longer had they not been shelled out of it by the effective fire from the four mortars. The Highlanders and their leaders made good their retreat; but the Spaniards who were strangers to the country and kept together had to surrender. Wightman dispatched Ensign Hugh Mackay [2] to London with an account of the victory and the King was pleased to bestow £100 bounty on this officer. The day after the action Wightman wrote to Secretary Craggs:—

"SIR,

"I beg leave to congratulate you on the success of his Majesty's troops under my command. The rebel camp being fortified by art as well as nature at the Brae of Glenshiell, I attacked them yesterday at 5 o'clock at night and by 8 beat them out . . . . There is a vacancy in Colonel Montague's regiment, by the death of Captain Downs; therefore I beg leave to recommend to your favour Captain Abercrombie, who is a half-pay officer on the English establishment, he coming a volunteer into that day's service, and was very ill wounded in the head charging with that regiment." [3]

Two subalterns of Montague's were also killed at Glenshiel, and Captains Moor and Heighington of Clayton's were wounded.[4] In addition, eighteen Royalist soldiers were killed and one hundred and twenty wounded.[5]

For some reason, which does not appear, General Wightman did not send any account of the late action at Glenshiel to Lord Carpenter, the Commander-in-Chief in Scotland, until June 17th. This tardiness on Wightman's part caused great offence to his lordship, who lost no time in bringing the matter to the notice of the English Lords Justices who were acting as Regents of the Kingdom during the absence of George I. at

---

[1] In a letter from Mr. Johnson in London to Admiral Thos. Gordon in Russia, dated 22nd June, 1719, Wightman's force is stated to have consisted of: "General Stuffles' Regt., four companies of Amarony's (*sic*), Clayton's and Montagu's Regts., 200 of Harrison's Regt., from Inverlochy, 150 dragoons, 90 of the Monroes and one hunder (*sic*) of Sutherland's men—1,800 men."—*Stirling-Home-Drummond-Moray's Papers.*

[2] On the half-pay list of Brigadier James Douglas' Regt. in the Dutch Scots Brigade. Appointed Ens. in Col. H. Harrison's Foot 29th July, 1719. Capt. in Col. Jas. Oglethorpe's Regt. 23rd Aug. 1737. This corps, known as "The Georgia Rangers," was raised by Oglethorpe in 1737. Part of the Regt. was in England on the outbreak of the '45 and was attached to Marshal Wade's Army.

[3] Letter printed in *Annals of the Earls of Stair*, Vol. I., pp. 119-120.

[4] Provost Hossack to the Laird of Culloden from Inverness, "13th June, 1719."—*Culloden Papers.*

[5] Lord Mahon's *Hist. of England.*

Hanover. The Lords Justices when announcing Wightman's victory to Earl Stanhope, then with the King in Germany, thought fit to refer to Lord Carpenter's complaint, and on 3rd July, 1719, we find the aforesaid Secretary of State writing as follows to Mr. Delafaye in London:—

> "The letter of thanks their Excellencys ordered you to write to Major-General Wightman his Majesty thinks was very proper, and seasonable, he being well pleased with his behaviour in the late Action and which may be an encouragement to him to use his utmost diligence in annoying and distressing the Rebels. And his Majesty is likewise of opinion that the caution you have given him of being more subordinate and respectful to his superior officers was very requisite and necessary."[1]

The belated letter from Wightman to Lord Carpenter, Commander-in-Chief in Scotland, written from the camp at Aderhanon (*sic*), on June 17th, contained the following news:—

> "I have the Spaniards prisoners with me; the whole number, officers included, is 274, and am taking a tour through all the difficult parts of Seaforth's country to terrify the Rebels by burning the houses of the guilty and preserving those of the honest .... There are no parties of the Rebels together, unless stealing parties in scores, up and down the mountains. Seaforth, Tullibardine, Marischal, &c., are gone off to the Lewes Islands, as is given out, but we rather apprehend to the Orkneys, and no numbers with them, and 'tis believed they will go to Spain as soon as they can; they passed through this camp the day after the battle."[2]

Glenshiel was Wightman's last service in the field. About 1720 he was appointed a Major-General on the Irish Establishment. When Lord Shannon was Commander-in-Chief in Ireland (1721), the post of Lieut.-General in Ireland was absorbed and the Commander-in-Chief's pay increased by £260; but Wightman's pay as Major-General appears to have remained the same.[3]

General Joseph Wightman died suddenly at Bath, late in September, 1722.[4] "I hear," wrote an anonymous correspondent to Viscount Bolingbroke (then in France) 6th October, 1722, "poor Jo. Whiteman is dead suddenly of an apoplex at the Bath."[5]

He left a widow and daughter almost totally unprovided for. The former survived her husband only a few months; the latter then petitioned King George in the touching document of which the following is a copy:—

> "La tres humble suppliant Eliz. Wightman fille de feu Majr.-Gen. Joseph Wightman cy devant Colonel d'un Regiment d'Infanterie represente avec un tres profond respect a Votre Majesté:
>
> "Que par la mort subite de feu son dit pere, sa mère et elle furent laissez dans un tres triste et deplorable etat, manquant même des choses les plus necessaires a la vie, et depuis la mére de la suppliante est aussy decedée qui la laisse orpheline sans amis ny parens pour luy aider; n'ayant pas dequoy acheptez (*sic*) du pain ny aucunes autres choses, et outre cela tres infirme.

---

[1] *S.P. Regencies*, Vol. II., Public Record Office.
[2] *London Gazette*, No., 5759.
[3] *Treasury Papers* under date of 5th Oct., 1721.
[4] One writer in the past has stated that General Joseph Wightman was present as a spectator at the battle of Preston Pans in 1745. The error was due to the fact that a Robert Wightman was at the battle in question.—*Culloden Papers*.
[5] *Hist. MSS. Comn.* Report XI., Appx., Pt. IV., p. 191.

"Que feu sa mère et elle presenterent à Votre Majesté il y a quelque temps une tres humble requête dans laquelle elles informaient tres humblement votre Majesté de leurs tristes circonstances, a quoy Votre Majesté eut la bonté de repondre qu'il donnerait order (*sic*) qu'elles peussent secourires par pension ou autrement . . . .

"Et elle priera sans cesse pour Votre Majesté."

This petition is endorsed by the Lords of the Treasury:—"May, 21, 1723. £100 bounty."[1]

And that was all—at first. Some years later a pension of £50 *per annum* was bestowed on Elizabeth Wightman. This was paid quarterly and the lady in question was drawing it in 1740[2]

---

[1] *Treasury Papers*, May, 1723.
[2] *Cal. Treasury Books and Papers*, 1739–40, p. 246.

CHAPTER VII.

LIEUT.-GENERAL RICHARD SUTTON, 1674–1738.[1]

RICHARD SUTTON was born in 1674. He was second son of Robert Sutton (nephew of the first Lord Lexington), whose family had long been settled in Nottinghamshire. In 1690 Richard Sutton was appointed ensign in Viscount Castleton's regiment. This corps had been raised in Yorkshire and Lincolnshire in March, 1689, by the fifth Viscount Castleton, a far-away kinsman of the present Earl of Scarborough. In December, 1691, Castleton's was ordered on active service, and embarked at Portsmouth for Holland. This corps and the Royal Fusiliers formed part of the garrison of Namur, which fortress was besieged in May, 1692, by a French army of 40,000 men; the siege being covered by another of 60,000 men, under the celebrated Marshal Luxembourg. It was at this siege that young Sutton learnt his first lesson in the art of war, and it was a disappointing experience, as, after much heavy fighting from time to time, and a brave defence, the town capitulated on 28th May, 1692. The Castle of Namur, and the new fort, called Fort William, still held out. It is computed that during the fortnight's siege of Fort William the French loss amounted to not less than 6,000 men, and when this fort was carried by assault on the 13th June, the Castle garrison kept an overwhelming force at bay for a week longer. In recognition of their stubborn defence, the besieged were allowed to march out of the place with muskets loaded and matches lighted, with drums beating and colours flying, to Louvain, where the two English regiments joined King William's army.

There is no record of Castleton's regiment being engaged at the battle of Steinkirk on 24th July, 1692. The probability is that this corps, being comparatively new, was left at Halle as a baggage guard. Be this so or not, Castleton's escaped the terrible slaughter inflicted on the British infantry in the above fatal battle, which, for the numbers engaged, was one of the most bloody on record.

On the 1st June, 1693, Richard Sutton was promoted Captain, his commission being signed by King William at Parck Camp. On the 8th July following, Castleton's formed part of the division under the Duke of Wurtemburg, which took part in the attack on the French fortified lines between the rivers Scheldt and Lys. This service was gallantly performed on the 9th July, at D'Ottignies, when the enemy's works were carried by assault, and the French driven from their entrenchments with great loss. It is recorded that Castleton's, which led the right attack on Beau Verd redoubt, gained great honour in this business, and lost many lives. The victory was marred and stained by the excesses of the soldiers. "The very men," writes Colonel Clifford Walton, in his admirable *History of the British Standing Army*, "who in the morning would have risked their lives for a comrade, who would have endured all and dared all for a point

---

[1] This memoir, by Charles Dalton, appeared in the *The Green Howards' Gazette*, January, 1903.

of honour, were in the evening plundering inoffensive cottagers, insulting helpless women, and wantonly destroying property unprotected except by females and children, or at the most by unarmed men . . . Alas, that among these soldiers drenched with wine, and glutted with such brutalities, were to be seen, mingled with the foreign troops, the red coats of Argyll's Scotchmen, the purple-faced grey[1] of Castleton's men, and the blue coats of the Tenth."

Saunderson's, late Castleton's, regiment played a leading part at the siege and capture of Namur in the summer of 1695. It was at this famous siege, so glorious to the troops of the allies under William III., that Richard Sutton earned the goodwill and confidence of the fighting Lord Cutts,—that heaven-born leader of forlorn hopes and storming parties, who loved to fight in the deadly breach, with any weapon that came to his hand, and whose immunity under the hottest fire had earned for him in the British Army the name of the "Salamander." It happened that at midnight on the 18th August the French made a sortie from the Castle of Namur with 200 mounted dragoons and 500 grenadiers. Half this force made an attack on the advanced guard of the British right, while the remainder tried to rush the advanced guard of the British left. Count de Rivers and Lord Cutts, who had just posted the advanced guards to cover the workmen in the trenches, beat back the attacking party on the right. While they were doing this, 100 dragoons charged the advance guard to the left, which consisted of about 40 soldiers under Captain Sutton. This officer told his men to keep their ground, and not to fire until he gave the order. When the dragoons were within a few yards of Sutton, he gave the order to fire, and during the confusion that followed the discharge, he marched his men quietly towards the British main body. But the dragoons pressing again upon him, he directed those of his men who had reserved their fire to give the enemy another volley. "The French," says the historian who relates the foregoing incident, "received the volley undauntedly, pressed on, and, if their grenadiers had charged at the same time, would doubtless have caused a great confusion in the trenches; but the Spanish and Bavarian horse, who were near, fell upon the enemy with so much vigour, that they drove them to the very palisades of the Castle, killing some and taking others prisoners.[2]

At the Peace of Ryswick, in 1697, many British regiments, including Saunderson's, were disbanded. Sutton was placed on half-pay, and remained unemployed till 14th April, 1701, when he was appointed Major of the Princess Anne of Denmark's Regiment of Foot, the present King's (Liverpool) Regiment. This corps embarked at the Cove of Cork on 15th June, 1701, for Holland. The end of August, 1702, Marlborough detached a considerable body of troops from the main army to besiege Venloo, a strong fortress in Guelderland. Sutton's corps (styled the Queen's after the accession of Queen Anne) formed part of the force under Lord Cutts which besieged Fort St. Michael, situated on the west side of the Meuse, and connected with Venloo by a bridge of boats. The siege and storming of Fort St. Michael under the eye of the intrepid Cutts (whose motto was "With labour and blood") are matters of history, and glorious history

---

[1] Oliver Cromwell ordered and enforced the wearing of red in his new model army, but this rule was temporarily departed from in the case of a few infantry regiments raised by James II. and William III.

[2] Tindall's *Hist. of England*. The historian erroneously calls Sutton a Lieut.-Colonel in his narrative.

too. So also are the taking of Ruremond, and the storming of the citadel of Liege, in which services the Queen's took part. On 10th December, 1702, Sutton was promoted Lieut.-Colonel of his regiment, and on 1st January, 1704, when Colonel Richmond Webb was appointed a Brigadier, the command of the Queen's devolved on Lieut.-Col. Sutton, who led his corps to victory at the glorious battles of Schellenberg and Blenheim. Sutton commanded the Queen's in 1705, when the formidable French lines near the Gheet river were forced, and the enemy driven, with heavy loss, to Louvain. On the 1st January, 1706, Sutton was made a Brevet Colonel, with rank from 13th August, 1704, in consideration of his services at Blenheim.

A number of regiments were ordered to be raised in the spring of 1706, and Sutton applied for the colonelcy of a new corps. His application to Marlborough was backed by General the Earl of Orkney, whose recommendation, preserved in a War Office MS., states that "his lordship knew Colonel Sutton, all the last war and this, to behave himself well, and believes him very capable to raise a regiment and to maintain it in good condition." Sutton's hope of a regiment was to remain unfulfilled for three years, and in the interim he commanded Brigadier Webb's regiment (the Queen's) on several notable occasions, viz., at the battle of Ramillies, at the siege of Menin (a fortress of great strength), and at the siege of Aeth.

Early in 1708 that unfortunate Prince, known in history as the Old Pretender, put to sea from Dunkirk with 5,000 men, for the purpose of invading England. The Queen's, under Colonel Sutton, was one of the thirteen corps ordered to return home to repel the invaders. The British force left Ostend on 17th March, and did not reach Tynemouth, their first place of call, till 21st of the same month! After waiting ten days off Tynemouth for orders, the transports, escorted by Admiral Baker's convoy, set sail for Leith Roads. On arrival at Leith, it was found that Admiral Byng had chased the Jacobite fleet from the British coast, capturing a cruiser with some of their leaders. The scare was over. The run on the Bank of England stopped, and the military preparations throughout the kingdom ceased. The little-known journal of John Deane, a private in the 1st Foot Guards, who served with this *corps élite* in the above "voyage," gives a graphic description in quaint language of the sufferings of the troops on board the over-crowded and ill-victualled ships, for a whole month, during part of which time the transports were beating it out in the North Sea:—

"While we lay on board," writes Private Deane, "we had continual destruction in the fore-top; the small-pox above board; the plague between decks; hell in the forecastle; and the devil at the helm: so that we may easily judge what course we steered; and amongst all other plagues, one of the greatest was, which way to confound our allowance, which was so sparingly distributed amongst us that the purser was daily blessed with the soldiers' prayers, being grown as fat as whipping posts . . . and such sharp weather that for one while I shall not care for any more voyages to the northward. Thus, having weathered the main point, and safely arrived at our desired haven (Ghent), we bid adieu to the wooden world, being translated from Purgatory to Paradise, and from pinch gut to whole allowance . . . . caused us to forget the old grievance, though it was, if rightly understood, a fatigue for the devil."

Colonel Sutton commanded the Queen's at the Battle of Oudenarde, and his corps led the attack on the village of Eyne, which was held by seven battalions of Swiss. After a brave defence, Eyne was carried sword in hand, and three entire Swiss battalions were taken prisoners, and Sutton received their colours. Shortly after this event, Lille was besieged, and the Queen's formed part of the covering army under Marlborough.

On 23rd March, 1709, Sutton was given the colonelcy of a foot regiment, which was disbanded at the Peace of Utrecht; and on 1st January, 1710, was appointed Brigadier-General in Marlborough's army. His preferment prevented him from commanding his regiment at the siege and capture of Douay, where this corps suffered severely, losing many officers and men. Sutton commanded a brigade at the forcing of the French lines at Arleux in August, 1711, and had the honour of bringing home Marlborough's despatch announcing this important victory. He was appointed Governor (non-resident) of Hull the same summer, and on 3rd April, 1712, purchased the colonelcy of the 19th Foot from Brigadier Freake. Sutton commanded a brigade in Flanders, under the Duke of Ormonde, in 1712, and on 3rd October, 1713, was appointed by Queen Anne Commander-in-Chief of the troops in garrison at Bruges. In 1714, Sutton brought home the British troops from Flanders.

In August, 1715, Brigadier Sutton resigned the colonelcy of the 19th Foot. Political motives caused this step. It was not till the last year of the reign of George I. that Richard Sutton came to the front again. In March, 1727, he was promoted Major-General, and sent as Envoy to the Landgrave of Hesse Cassel. On 4th July, 1727, General Sutton reviewed at Rinteln the Hessian troops which had entered into the pay of George I. on 1st April, 1727. In 1729 Sutton was sent Envoy Extraordinary to the King of Prussia; and on 27th October of same year he was restored to the colonelcy of his old corps—the 19th Foot. It was Sir Robert Walpole, the Prime Minister, who brought Sutton back to public life, recognising his fitness for employment. Horace Walpole, in one of his letters to the Hon. Henry Conway (a future Field-Marshal) gives the following amusing anecdote, illustrative of Sutton's friendship for Sir Robert Walpole:—

"General Sutton was one day sitting by my father at his dressing. Sir Robert said to Jones, who was shaving him, 'John, you cut me,'—presently afterwards, 'John, you cut me,'—and, again, with the same patience, 'John, you cut me.' Sutton started up and cried, 'My God! if he can bear it, I can't. If you cut him once more, d—n my blood if I don't knock you down!'"

It is not recorded whether this threat steadied the barber's hand.

On 27th October, 1735, Sutton was promoted Lieut.-General. In 1736 he lost his wife (*née* de Tolmer), and two years later he followed her to the grave. He was succeeded in the colonelcy of the 19th Foot by the Hon. Charles Howard, on 1st November, 1738, from which time dates the regimental *sobriquet*, "The Green Howards."

General Sutton enjoyed the friendship of Lord Cutts, and at Chequers Court, Bucks, is preserved a letter from the former to the latter on military matters. He is said to have been a favourite of Henry St. John (Bolingbroke), Secretary at War; and was very intimate with Dean Swift, who mentions Sutton in his Journal. Sutton was many years M.P. for Newark, and owned the estate of Scofton, Notts., which was inherited by his son Robert. There is, or was, a portrait of the General at Kelham Hall, Notts., which was named among the heirlooms left by the will of the second Baron Lexington in 1723,

CHAPTER VIII

GENERAL SIR CHARLES WILLS, K.B. 1661-1741 [1]

THIS distinguished soldier, son of Anthony Wills of St. Gorran, Cornwall, by "Jenofer" (Guinevere) his wife, was baptised at St. Gorran on 23rd October, 1666.[2] His father farmed his own land, and having encumbered his estate with debts, quitted the same at the Revolution, and offered his services, and those of six of his sons, to the Prince of Orange, who it is said, gave them all commissions.[3] Charles Wills appears to have been appointed a subaltern in Colonel Thomas Erle's Regiment of Foot (disbanded in 1697) with which corps he served in the Irish Campaign.

On 1st July, 1691, he was appointed Captain in the regiment known subsequently as the 19th Foot, the colonelcy of which had been bestowed on Colonel Erle, 1st January, 1691. On 6th November, 1694, he was appointed Major to Colonel Thomas Saunderson's Regiment of Foot and served at the siege of Namur the following year. Promoted Lieut.-Colonel 1st May, 1697. A few months later Saunderson's was disbanded and the officers placed on half-pay.

By a Royal Warrant, dated 28th June, 1701, William, Viscount Charlemont was authorised to raise an infantry regiment in Ireland, which was afterwards numbered the Thirty Sixth. Wills was given the lieut.-colonelcy of this corps and, in the following spring, embarked with it for Cadiz, an expedition against which port and Spain's possessions in the West Indies, having been planned by William III. some months before his death.

On 4th May, 1702, war was declared against France and Spain, and in the following month Sir George Rooke sailed from Spithead with a large fleet, on board of which were 10,000 soldiers under the command of the Duke of Ormonde. From a MS. among the Harleian Manuscripts, we find that Colonel Lord Charlemont, Lieut.-Colonel Wills, and some of the senior officers of this regiment, embarked on board the *Grey* transport, and sailed with the fleet to Cadiz. The chief object of this expedition was the reduction of Cadiz. But as on previous occasions, this town was found so well protected by the strong fort of Matagorda, which stands at the mouth of the harbour, that the 4,000 English and Dutch troops sent to attack the fort were obliged to retire, after many lives had been lost, as the Spanish ships within the harbour poured such a destructive fire upon our troops whilst raising batteries on the low marshy ground, destitute of cover. To atone for this repulse another body of troops took and occupied the adjacent towns of Rota and Port St. Mary. The latter was a wealthy town, and full of loot. "Scarce a man but got something," says a

---

[1] The greater part of this revised memoir was written by myself, in 1888, for *The Preston Herald*, and appeared in said journal on 23rd June same year under the title of "General Wills & Preston." I am also responsible for the article on General Wills in the *Dict. of Nat. Biog.*—C.D.

[2] *Parish Register.*

[3] *Parochial Hist. of Cornwall*, pp. 11, 101.

contemporary writer, "for Port St. Mary was so thoroughly plundered that the very iron about the houses was brought away." The capture of Cadiz being found impracticable, the troops were reimbarked. Following out the Queen's instructions, Sir George Rooke despatched Captain Hovenden Walker with a dozen ships, on 24th September, to the West Indies. Four regiments, one of them being Viscount Charlemont's, sailed with Captain Walker on this expedition. The four regiments arrived in the West Indies at an opportune moment. Admiral Benbow, who had been sent to the West Indies by William III., had just died of his wounds at Port Royal, Jamaica, received when engaging the French squadron of seven ships (under Du Casse) *single-handed*, in August. Cheated out of victory by the base desertion of five captains, who kept their ships astern during the fight, which continued several days, the gallant Benbow's death was inexpressibly sad. Such a lasting disgrace to the British flag did an infinity of harm, which even the summary execution of the two chief offenders, and the cashiering of the others, did not efface.

General Christopher Codrington, commanding the British forces in the Leeward Islands, organised an expedition against the French Island of Guadaloupe in the winter of 1702–1703. On the arrival at Antigua, of Captain Walker with the four regiments, and some recruits taken on board at Barbadoes, Codrington joined Walker with all the soldiers that could be spared from the Antigua garrison, and the little fleet sailed for Guadaloupe. Walker's squadron arrived off Guadaloupe on 7th March, and anchored opposite a French settlement called Les Petits Habitants. Most of the troops under Codrington were landed. The French gave them such a warm reception, that several British officers and men were killed and wounded. H.M.S. *Chichester*, which was nearest the shore, brought her guns to bear upon the French batteries, which lay between our troops and the town, with such good effect, that the enemy retired precipitately, leaving our troops in possession. The next morning the rest of the soldiers and 400 seamen were landed in a bay to the northward of the town of La Bayliffe. Here the British met with a most vigorous resistance from all the French troops, posted in very strong and advantageous breastworks, who kept up a galling fire while our troops were landing. Notwithstanding, our men bravely marched up to the French entrenchments, with their muskets shouldered, without firing a shot, until they could lay the muzzles of their pieces upon the top of the enemies' breastworks. Then the first breastwork was carried with a volley and rush, in which three officers on our side were killed. In the *London Gazette* of 10th May, 1703, we find special mention of Colonel Charles Wills's bravery in this assault: "Colonel Wills signalised himself with great bravery in this action. In a word, both officers and men fought with all the courage and resolution imaginable." The official report in this paper goes on to say:—" By noon we were masters of the enemy's outworks; in an hour after of the town called the Bayliffe, of the Jacobin's church which they had fortified, and of ten pieces of their cannon. At two o'clock we took a platform where they had planted three pieces of cannon, and a redoubt with one. At night a detachment of 400 men and the regiment of marines attacked the Jacobin's plantation and the breastwork along the Jacobin's river, which is, perhaps the strongest and most advantageous in all the Indies."

The day after these successful operations the troops marched to the large town of Basseterre, which was surrendered, the French retiring to a large fort and castle, which commanded part of the town. Some cannon and ammunition having been brought on shore, batteries were raised to bombard the fort and castle, which the French held until 2nd April, when they blew them both up and retreated to the woods and mountains. Parties of soldiers were now sent out to burn and destroy the enemy's houses, works, sugar plantations, and stores, also to collect provisions and plunder. But little was to be found in the way of food, and the English were chiefly dependent on their own ships for provisions. Sickness broke out among our soldiers. By the end of April, General Codrington and Colonel Whetham, the two senior officers, were both obliged by illness to leave Guadaloupe. The former sailed for Nevis, and the latter in H.M.S. *Burford*, to Antigua. "Colonel Wills," says Mr. Burchett in his able naval chronicle of this expedition, "now succeeded to the command on shore."

After burning and destroying the French towns and fortifications along the coast he embarked his troops on board the squadron on 7th May, bringing away all the captured French guns, and the little fleet sailed for St. Christopher's. The retreat was well-timed, as the French had sent a relieving force from Martinique, who arrived just too late. Wills did not lose a single man whilst embarking his troops, but the loss in the engagements with the French, and by sickness, were very heavy, viz.: one major, two captains, and six subalterns killed, two colonels, seven captains, and nine lieutenants wounded, two colonels, four lieutenants, and three ensigns died, 154 soldiers were killed, 211 wounded, 72 died, 59 deserted, and twelve were taken prisoners. Whilst Guadaloupe was being devastated by our soldiers a squadron was on its way to the West Indies, under the command of Vice-Admiral Graydon. This naval commander is described by a contemporary writer as "a man of brutal character" and deservedly unpopular.

One regiment of foot was ordered to the West Indies to reinforce the little British force there. The regiment selected was Columbine's (now 6th or Warwickshire Regiment of Foot), and for the first time in its long record of military service a mutiny broke out in its ranks at Tilbury, on the eve of embarkation, and part of the regiment deserted *en masse*, refusing to go on board the transports. It was given out that the mutiny was due to the amount of "sea pay" to which the regiment was entitled (being one of the six infantry regiments chosen for sea service at the beginning of the war) not being deemed enough, but there were doubtless other reasons of which that "sea dog," Admiral Graydon, was one, for this mutiny. The deserters having been brought back and safely shipped, the fleet set sail for the West Indies on the 13th March. Graydon had orders to collect all the forces that were scattered throughout the plantations and then attempt the capture of Placentia, driving the French out of the Newfoundland trade. It is said that when Admiral Graydon came to the plantations that he acted in so strange a manner that it seemed as if he had been sent to terrify rather than protect them. Obnoxious to his superiors, insolent to his equals, and a bully to his inferiors, no commander could well have been worse chosen. Having collected the four shattered regiments, of which Lord Charlemont's (now 36th Foot) was one, on board his fleet, he sailed in the middle of summer for Placentia. Arrived off the south-eastern coast of Newfoundland, a terrible fog, so common even in summer off the "banks," set in, and navigation became impossible. "This fog," says Secretary Burchett, the naval chronicler of this expedition, "was a fog to admiration, lasting thirty days." After the sweltering heat of the "Indies" the sudden change to damp and cold had a baneful effect on our poor soldiers. "They were," says Burchett, "benumbed in their limbs, and subject to fluxes and scurvies." The five regiments on board the fleet were reduced to a total strength of 1,038. Many officers were also dead, amongst them being Colonel Columbine, of the 6th Foot. When this fog at last "lifted" it was decided by a council of war, at which the senior military officer was Lieut.-Colonel Rivers, of the 6th, that an attack on Placentia was impracticable, it having been ascertained that the French, expecting an attack, had sent a strong force to defend this place. Nothing remained, therefore, in Graydon's opinion, but to return to England. The fleet set sail on September 24th, and the first week in November Lord Charlemont, Lieut.-Colonel Wills, and the "remains" of their regiment were landed at an Irish port. In April, 1705, Charlemont's regiment was sent to England, and in May embarked on board the fleet under the command of the Earl of Peterborough, who was sent to Spain with an expeditionary force of 5,000 men to help the Archduke Charles of Austria to win and wear the Spanish crown. In consideration of his West Indian services, Charles Wills was appointed Quartermaster General to the forces under Peterborough, and in this capacity shared in the reduction of Fort Montjuich, a fortress which was of such immense strength as to be deemed impregnable, and the subsequent capture of the rich town of Barcelona. This was followed by the submission of nearly all Catalonia. On the 13th October, nine days after Barcelona surrendered, Colonel Wills was promoted to the colonelcy of a marine regiment (now 30th Foot) then serving in Spain under Peterborough. Major (afterwards Colonel) Burston of Wills' Marines has left a detailed narrative of the operations in which his corps was engaged during the winter of 1705-6. The following curtailed account is extracted from Burston's book.[1]

"Whilst Peterborough was reducing the province of Valencia, the marine regiments, under the command of Colonel Wills, were garrisoning Gerona, Lerida, and other Catalonian towns. In January, 1706, Major-General Cunningham commanded the British troops in the district of Lerida, and Colonel Wills, with the local rank of brigadier, was second in command. On the 23rd of this month General Cunningham, having intelligence that a body of French troops then lying at Balbastro had a design to attack our dragoons at Tamarette, ordered Brigadier Wills to march there with 300 fusiliers and as many marines. The next day this detachment with half a troop of dragoons continued their march to a village named St. Estevan. On the following afternoon nine troops of French cavalry appeared in a little plain about half a mile from the village among the mountains. A narrow lane led from the village, between two hills, to the plain where the enemy were, and half way up this lane was a small cottage and garden. Brigadier Wills immediately ordered one hundred foot to occupy the cottage and garden, and defend the passage. The dragoons were likewise ordered to march up the lane and 'discover' the French troops. At the same time six companies of marines were ordered to march up the hill, on the right side of the lane, in six columns, and to beat the 'Grenadiers' March' when in sight of the enemy. These orders were so well executed that at the same moment our dragoons entered the plain, killing the enemy's advanced sentinel, our infantry showed themselves and beat the 'Grenadiers' March' upon the

[1] *The Case of Colonel George Burston*, printed in London, 1720, pp. 7-10.

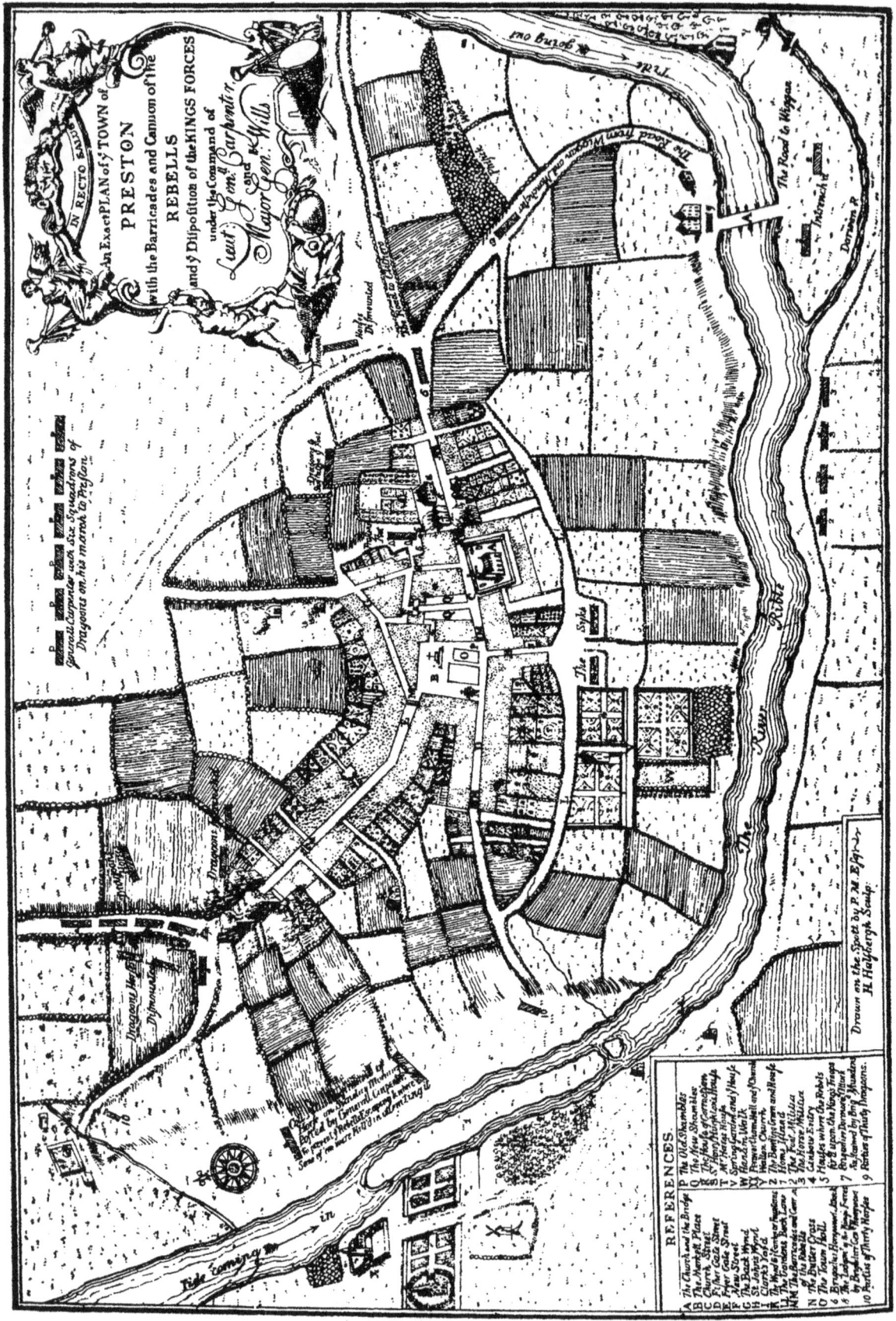

hills. The enemy being unused to the uniform of marines, mistook the six companies of Wills' marines for six companies of grenadiers, as the marines wore *grenadier caps*, and knowing there was only one company of grenadiers in each British foot regiment, they naturally thought that there was a regiment of foot to every company of grenadiers, and that we had six regiments in the background ready to attack them. Brigadier Wills had laid this trap for them, and his stratagem succeeded so well that the French cavalry immediately remounted and marched off in a great hurry, leaving most of their pickets and some provisions behind them, and, what was still more, their infantry, who were in full march to join them, seeing the retreat of their horse, halted and retreated in like manner, followed for nearly ten miles by our little force. About midnight General Cunningham arrived with the remaining troops, and our strength was now 1,200 foot and 250 dragoons, with a confused rabble of about 800 Miquelets (Spanish peasants) who had enrolled themselves under the banner of Charles III. (titular King of Spain.) Next morning the enemy re-appeared, and this time in considerable force, having 4,000 regular troops commanded by General D'Asfeld, an experienced officer, and a great number of Miquelets. Brigadier Wills immediately sent an advanced party of Miquelets under Major Burston to take possession of our former posts on the hills till our troops got to their arms. General Cunningham lost no time in bringing his troops up the hill, where he found the officers who had command of the advanced party all alone, the Miquelets having deserted to a man as soon as the enemy appeared. Owing to the mountainous nature of the country, the enemy, though within musket shot, were now separated from our troops by a narrow valley. As our troops marched on the heights on one side of this valley, so the enemy appeared on the heights on the other side. A sharp musketry fire was kept up on both sides, but the situation prevented the enemy attacking us, the ascent on our side being steep. Added to this that a rising ground on our side of the valley formed a kind of natural breastwork to our men, partly protecting them from the enemy's fire. It was upon this breastwork that General Cunningham, stepping up to observe the position of the enemy, received a bullet in the groin which proved fatal next day. The command then devolved on Brigadier Wills, and had it not been for the successful imposition he had practised upon the French the previous day in regard to our numbers, our troops must have been surrounded and taken prisoners by a force nearly treble their own, for the French general had detached 600 grenadiers to attack us another way. These men took a bye-way among the mountains, unknown to our men, and suddenly appeared on our right flank, at a point where some of Lord Shannon's marines under Captain Webb were posted, driving them down the hill. Major Burston of Wills' Regiment advanced with one company of marines, and held the enemy in check until Brigadiers Wills and Palmes arrived with succour from the left flank. After an obstinate fight at close quarters the French were compelled to retire."

The enemy left about 350 killed and wounded in the above action at St. Estevan, among them being a French Colonel who commanded the detachment. Our side also suffered severely, losing about 300 men killed and wounded, including the gallant Major Burston, who received no less than thirteen bayonet wounds, from which however, he ultimately recovered and lived to do further good service to his country. The day was won, for the enemy believing that our strength was much greater than it was, and seeing their detachment routed, beat a hasty retreat.

On the 2nd April, 1706, a large army under the Duke of Anjou, who styled himself Philip V., King of Spain, appeared before Barcelona, then in possession of Charles III., and held by a small garrison of British and Spanish troops. The city seemed doomed, as a French fleet of twenty-seven sail lay off the port and kept up a strict blockade.

After Barcelona had been relieved by Admiral Leake's fleet, the British marines returned from their mountain camp in the vicinity of the lately beleaguered city to their garrisons at Gerona, Lerida, and other towns in the provinces of Catalonia and Roussillon.

On the 1st January, 1707, Wills was appointed a British Brigadier-General. As second in command of the Lerida garrison he highly distinguished himself at the two months' siege of this town by a joint Franco-Spanish force under the Duke of Orleans. The following letter[1] from Brigadier Wills to the Earl of Galway, British Commander-in-Chief in Spain, has a special interest of its own :—

"Lerida Castle,
"MY LORD, 18 Oct. 1707.

"The Enemy opened the trenches before this town the 1st inst. and the 9th, they battered the town wall with 20 pieces of cannon; the 10th they had made 2 large breaches fitt to storm but continued battering till the 12th at 6 in the evening when they made 2 attacks but were repulsed, but they made lodgment under both breaches and sapt through the stone bastion and thro' the middle wall and carried on their entrenchments to the innermost breach, which would have covered their second attack and flank'd our new work, we having defended the town to the last extremity. I spoke to the Prince of Hess to demand a capitulation for the Burgers, and told him I would stand in the breach with the troops till they had terms; but he said it was a matter for the Burgers. Then we called a Council of War and it was agreed to retire the troops to the Castle after having carried off our Cannon and ammunition to the Castle, and then the troops marcht to the upper part of the town where we now are; you may depend upon it we will dispute every foot of ground with them for I would rather see the soldiers dead than prisoners . . .

"I am, &c. &c.
"To the Earl of Galway." "CHARLES WILLS."

The garrison held out for nearly a month longer, though reduced to the greatest straits, and then capitulated on favourable terms. The troops marched out with the honours of war on 12th November, carrying two pieces of cannon and a mortar with them, and were conducted to the Earl of Galway's army, which lay encamped three leagues from thence. General Wills was, however, arrested by the Duke of Orleans, in reprisal for Brigadier-General Chiaves, a Spanish officer, taken prisoner by Sir Charles Hotham at the siege of Denia. At the same time Wills was allowed to go on his parole. This arrest seems very unjust and a breach of contract. In the summer of 1708 we find Wills in the command of 1,500 marines and a Spanish regiment, on board Sir John Leake's fleet in the Mediterranean. He had the rank of major-general from the King of Spain, and was a brigadier in the British army. His eminent services in the capture of Cagliari, the capital of Sardinia, are detailed in the *London Gazette* of October 4th, 1708, as follows :—

"Florence, September 18th.—On Thursday last Major-General Wills left this place to proceed on his way to Great Britain, after having been received at this

[1] From the copy among the "Richards' Papers" at the British Museum.

GENERAL SIR CHARLES WILLS, K.B.

Court with particular marks of distinction. He brings an account of the reduction of the city of Cagliari and the whole kingdom of Sardinia to the obedience of King Charles III. This important service was carried on under the command of that officer, who with about 2,000 foot obliged a body of 2,000 horse and another of 4,000 foot to retire before him. He pursued the latter in their retreat, and marched directly after them into Cagliari, of which city and castle he became master without the loss of one man on either side. This island abounds in corn and horses, as well as all other sorts of cattle; 20,000 sacks of corn are already shipped off for Barcelona from thence, and they offer 6,000 horses for the use of his Catholic Majesty .... Te Deums were sung at Naples for the arrival of the Queen at Barcelona and the reduction of Sardinia."

About the 15th October General Wills arrived in England. On the 1st January, 1709, Wills was promoted Major-General in the British army, and sent out to Spain again in command of reinforcements. Admiral Baker's fleet, with nine regiments of foot and one of dragoons, under the command of General Wills, sailed from Cork on September 9th, 1709, and arrived off Lisbon the first week in October. There was a design to attempt Cadiz once more, but the idea was abandoned on hearing how well prepared that strong garrison was for any assault by sea or land. The fleet proceeded to Gibraltar, and then to Barcelona, where all the troops were landed, and soon after sent into winter quarters. In the spring the Carlist army took the field. Count Staremberg commanded the Royal army, General Stanhope being second in command, and Major-Generals Carpenter, Wills, Wade, and Pepper commanded brigades. This time King Charles accompanied the army in person, and his presence stimulated the Spanish troops to fight their way to Madrid through every obstacle. British troops did not need this stimulus. General Wills was present at the decisive action of Almenara (where Stanhope led his cavalry to victory), and he took a distinguished part in the battle of Saragossa, where he commanded an infantry brigade. Colonel Thomas Harrison, then serving as adjutant-general in Spain, was sent by General Stanhope to convey the welcome news of the victory at Saragossa to Queen Anne, and Stanhope specially recommended Major-General Wills to her Majesty for promotion to the rank of Lieut.-General as a reward for "eminent services in the late action."[1] Charles III. gave Wills a commission as lieut.-general in the Spanish service and made other promotions, all "honorary and unremunerative"! On the 21st September, General Stanhope and a thousand horse entered Madrid, and a few days after Charles, "King of Spain, by the grace of the heretics," as his rival Philip jeeringly styled him, with the flower of his army made his public entry into the capital. But it was not a triumphal entry. The streets were deserted and the shops shut. Madrid had the appearance of a plague-stricken city. Nor did things improve as time went on. Castilian grandees and Castilian peasants acknowledged no monarch but Philip V., grandson of Louis the Fourteenth. The allies only possessed the ground they stood on. Food was obtained with the greatest difficulty. Money, the sinews of war, was very scarce. Great things were expected from Portugal, where an Anglo-Portuguese army was encamped near the frontier. But this relieving army came not. Neither did the expected succour from England make its appearance. Early in December the allies had to begin a retreat. The Duke of Vendôme, grandson of Henry the Fourth of

Marlborough Despatches, Vol. V., p. 168.

France, had come to the aid of Philip with a French army at his back. So popular was the cause of Philip that in a very short time Vendôme's army numbered 25,000 men. His troops, well fed, well paid, and well clothed, made such rapid marches that they came up with the left wing of the Carlist army at Brihuega on December 8th. This wing was commanded by General Stanhope, and consisted of 5,000 British troops and a Portuguese regiment. Count Staremberg, who commanded the centre of the army, had marched on to Cifuentes, five hours' march further on, as the great scarcity of food had obliged the allied army in its retreat to march in three separate divisions, some miles apart from each other. Hence the catastrophe at the little walled town of Brihuega, where Stanhope was surprised and his retreat cut off. Nothing remained but to fight it out, though the enemy were four to one. The town was invested by Vendôme's army on the 9th December. Stanhope, Carpenter, and Wills passed the night of the 8th in preparing for defence. The siege began at daybreak and lasted till seven in the evening, when the British capitulated, but not till they had lost a great number of men (600 killed and wounded), and the town was falling about their ears. "I must do that justice," says Stanhope in his despatch, "to all the general officers and to all the officers and the men that all was done by them that could be done .... Lieut.-General Wills was, during all the action, at the post which they attacked with most vigour, and which he as resolutely defended." Stanhope obtained honourable terms for his troops, but they were all made prisoners of war and marched off to Valladolid for fear of a rescue from the troops under Staremberg. Thus for a second time General Wills was made a prisoner of war, but this time he appears to have suffered a rigorous imprisonment of many months, and then returned to England, the Peace of Utrecht putting a stop to hostilities.

The next important landmark in Wills's career brings us to the Jacobite Rebellion in 1715. The Earl of Mar had raised the Pretender's standard in Scotland, and Mr. Forster, a "suspended" English M.P., had proclaimed James III. at various towns and villages in Cumberland, Westmorland, and Northumberland. Of these two "generals" we need only quote the scathing criticism of Mr. Baines the historian:—"Mar would justly have passed for the most incompetent general of the age if Forster had not proved that there was one still more incapable." When Forster was on his march to Lancaster from Kirkby Lonsdale we find Major-General Wills commanding the Royalist troops in Cheshire. On the taking of Preston by the Rebels, Wills assembled his forces first at Manchester, and then marched to Wigan, where he arrived on November 11th. He had at his disposal the cavalry regiments of Pitt, Wynne, Honeywood, Dormer, Munden, and Stanhope, and Preston's regiment of foot. He had left Colonel Newton's dragoon regiment at Manchester to check an expected rising of the disaffected in that town. At Wigan General Wills received intelligence that General George Carpenter was advancing from Durham by forced marches with about 900 cavalry, and would be ready to take the enemy in flank. Early on the morning of the 12th November Wills marched towards Preston, " a place whose natural advantages," says an able historian, in his graphic account of these events, " might have seemed to insure an obstinate resistance, did not resistance, as all history shows, depend infinitely more on the spirit of the defenders than on the strength of the ground." About one in the afternoon Wills arrived at the bridge over the Ribble, and found there about two or three hundred of the rebels' horse and foot, who, upon the approach of the Royal troops, withdrew hastily into the town, where barricades had been erected. An Horatius Cocles or a Cromwell would never have allowed King George's troops to cross that bridge without a bloody contest; and though there were seven regiments under General Wills's command, they were for the most part newly-levied men, and considerably under their strength. In addition to the Regulars, Wills had a small local force, raised by Mr. James Wood,[1] a dissenting minister. These Lancashire volunteers joined Wills before Preston. They are said to have been "partly armed with scythes, spades, and bill-hooks." It is said that when Wills found this bridge undefended he concluded the rebels were retiring from Preston preparatory to a retreat to Scotland. "General" Forster had nearly eighteen hours to prepare for the coming of the enemy, but he spent part of that time in bed, and it was entirely owing to Lord Kenmure's energy that any orders were issued for defending the town. On coming before Preston a reconnaissance was made by General Wills in person, and in consequence of his party being fired upon, and two men killed by the enemy, he ordered an immediate attack on the barricades. Preston's foot regiment made the assault, and behaved with great bravery. At the same time Wills ordered the whole town to be surrounded to the right and left by the cavalry. The rebels being well posted behind the barricades, inflicted great loss on Preston's regiment, which was commanded by Lieut.-Colonel Lord Forester, between 60 and 70 being killed and wounded in the first attack. After two barricades had been gallantly charged, and the troops repulsed with equal courage, Wills drew off his men, and all the avenues to the town being effectually secured, the cavalry were ordered to stand at their horses' heads all that night. At nine o'clock the next morning (Sunday), Lieut.-General Carpenter arrived with three dragoon regiments. As soon as the rebels perceived from the church steeple the reinforcements marching their way, they lost heart, and "General" Forster, without consulting his principal officers, sent Colonel Oxburgh to propose a capitulation. But Wills showed no disposition to treat. He said he would not enter into terms with rebels; that they had already killed many of the King's subjects, and must expect to undergo a similar fate. At last Generals Carpenter and Wills said "that if all the rebels laid down their arms and surrendered, unconditionally, they would protect them from being cut to pieces by the soldiers until further orders from the Government." When this one-sided arrangement was known in Preston, a mutiny nearly broke out. The Highlanders wished to try to cut their way through the King's troops, sword in hand. But it was too late now for such a daring enterprise, and the chiefs thought it best to yield to their fate. On Monday morning, at seven o'clock, the rebels laid down their arms, and the Royal troops, under Generals Carpenter and Wills, entered the town. A good deal of friction occurred between these two generals on this occasion, and for one particular thing. Wills was grievously disappointed at not having defeated the rebels before Carpenter's arrival; and Carpenter was equally disappointed that Wills had had all the fighting to himself, and half the glory of winning the town. Carpenter was the senior general, and this again galled Wills's proud spirit in the hour of triumph. There is a letter from Carpenter still

---

[1] *Dict. Nat. Biog.* For his services and expenses Wood received £100 from the Government.

extant, among the Townshend MSS., in which this officer accuses Wills of claiming all the honour of victory, and taking too much command on himself. That was a common charge of the envious against the successful in that age.

Let us, however, look at the form of the taunt levelled at the hero of Preston Fight. "As we were mounting to go into the town," wrote Carpenter in the letter referred to, "Mr. Wills was taking upon him great command, at which I used him very freely and was going to put him in arrest, but my Lord Carlisle and my Lord Lumley, who were present, begged me not to do it, and, indeed, at that instant it might have proved fatal to his Majesty's service, for the rebels had yet possession of their arms and the town, and Wills was likely enough to have called the troops that came with him to support him, so I did not do it." The friction between these two commanders was considerably increased by George I. promoting Wills to the rank of Lieut.-General shortly after the news of the surrender of the rebels at Preston reached London, and no notice at all being taken of Carpenter's services on this occasion. Wills was not a man to stand being "used freely" by anyone, whether his senior officer or not, and in consequence of "words" between the two, General Carpenter sent a challenge to General Wills in January, 1716. The duel was honourably compromised by the generous intervention of the Dukes of Marlborough and Montagu. But to return to Preston. Although only 1,400 prisoners were taken at Preston, there were so many leading and influential Jacobites among them, including Lords Derwentwater, Widdrington, Nithsdale, Wintoun (at whose trial General Wills gave important and damning evidence), Carnwath, Kenmure, and Charles Murray, that the insurrection, as far as England was concerned, was over. Forster was sent a prisoner to London, and made his "public entry," in company with his illustrious fellow-prisoners, on horseback, with his hands tied behind his back and his horse led by a foot-soldier. From the fact of his easy escape from prison it is not improbable that the Government connived at his flight. It is very certain they owed him a debt of gratitude for the incapacity he evinced in "defending" Preston, and from a letter written by Secretary Craggs to Lord Townshend on 24th November, 1715, it is evident Forster had a friend at Court in the matter. General Wills, however, had no friendly feeling to his late enemy, and when commanding the forces at Newcastle, in 1717, did his best to recapture Forster and other proscribed Jacobites. A letter from General Wills to his old commander, General Stanhope, concerning Jacobitism in the North, is preserved among the State Papers at the Record Office, London. The letter is as follows :—

"Newcastle, April 14th, 1717.

"SIR,

"Since my arrival here I have had several people abroad to get intelligence if the Jacobites were making any preparations, but I cannot find that they are, only that several of the rebels that made their escape are harbouring about the country, and on Friday last one of them, called Robert Bradshaw, was taken. He has made an affidavit against four merchants of this town of their drinking the Pretender's health. Three of them are taken up, and have given £2,000 bail to appear the next assizes ; the other has been out of the town for some time. This day I had an account of a Jacobite meeting at a private house. I sent Major Bland with a guard, who took the parson and 19 more at their devotions. I have them under a guard, and shall continue until I have his Majesty's further orders how I shall dispose of them. An example of these people will do a great deal of good in this country, being the people that debauches all the youth and keeps up the spirit of Jacobitism. I have sent an order to Colonel Erle, who commands Major-General Pepper's regiment at Hexham, to take up several of the rebels who I hear are lurking about the country, and I expect they will be brought in to-morrow. I have had some account that Mr. Forster was in the country, but I cannot meet with anybody that had seen him.

"I am, &c, &c,
"CHARLES WILLS."

Little remains to be told now beyond cataloguing the honours and rewards bestowed on Charles Wills for his military services. He was appointed Governor of Berwick in 1715; Colonel of the 3rd Regiment of Foot (the Buffs) 5th January, 1716; Governor of Portsmouth, 1717; Lieut.-General of the Ordnance, 22nd April, 1722; Knight of the Bath, 17th June, 1725; Colonel of the 1st Foot Guards, 26th August, 1726; General Commanding the Foot, 1739. In addition to these appointments, he was M.P. for Totnes, in Devonshire, and one of George the First's Privy Council. But, like most self-made men, Sir Charles Wills was a man of soaring ambition, and was always looking "onwards and upwards." If he had a motto it was "Excelsior."

When General George Carpenter was raised to the peerage of Ieland, as Baron Carpenter, Charles Wills thought it was time for him to have an "ermine robe" likewise. He and Carpenter had fought side by side at Saragossa and in the deadly hand-to-hand contest at Brihuega. They had both been taken prisoners, and had both undergone the hardships of a long captivity; and then they had again faced the enemy together before Preston; and had both been equally instrumental in ferreting out and committing to prison divers ill-affected Jacobites. George I. was very favourably disposed to Sir Charles Wills, and owed him a good turn for his services at Preston; but the old King was not much given to conferring peerages except on his German mistresses, whom he honoured with a free hand at the expense of the nation. Nothing was done in the matter, apparently, until the eleventh hour of this monarch's reign, when the following paragraph appeared in the 32nd Vol. of the *Political State of Great Britain* for September, 1726:—

> "About this time it was declared a patent was preparing for creating Sir Charles Wills, K.B., a Baron of Great Britain, by the style and title of Baron Preston in the County Palatine of Lancaster."

This patent was so long in coming to the birth that George I. had passed away before it was ratified, and George II. was no friend to anyone whom his father had chosen to honour.

We now come to the last ambitious "venture" of Sir Charles Wills's life. When Field-Marshal the Marquis de Montandre (a British Field-Marshal) died, in August, 1739, General Wills, as first general of the foot, aspired to the vacant *bâton*, and made so sure of getting it that the London journals announced his appointment to the marshalate. We read in the *London Daily Post*, of September 11th, 1739, this curious statement:—

> "Last Sunday the Right Hon. Sir C. Wills, K.B., Lieut.-General of the Ordnance, &c., &c., received the sacrament in St. George's Church, Hanover-square, to qualify himself to take the oaths appointed of field-marshal of all and singular his Majesty's forces, as well of horse as foot, employed or to be employed in his Majesty's service."

The *bâton*, like the "peerage," was never conferred on our ambitious general, who lived two years longer, expecting what never came, and departed this life in London, on Christmas Day, 1741, at a ripe old age.

An engraving of Sir Charles Wills, taken from a contemporary portrait, represents him as a very handsome man, with a somewhat sad and gentle cast of countenance. He does not appear to have been a popular officer, or a genial companion, and a quarrel with him only ended with life. As a soldier he was determined, inured to hardships, and though slow in generalship was a bulldog in his grip when besieging or defending. He never married, and most of his personalty, and a farm in Suffolk, were bequeathed by him to Sir Robert Rich, Bart., a future Field-Marshal. He also left £5,000 to his A.D.C., Captain Robert Rich, son of the above-named baronet.

Sir Charles Wills received a grand military funeral, and was buried in Westminster Abbey, January 2nd, 1742. The following authentic announcement appeared in *The Champion* of December 29th, 1741 :—

> "'Tis said that General Sir Charles Wills, Lieut.-General of the Ordnance, will be interred in Westminster Abbey in a pompous manner, and that the three regiments of Foot Guards, and the troops of Horse Guards, will attend the funeral procession."

CHAPTER IX

GENERAL THE RT.-HON. WM. STEUART, 1658?-1726.

THIS successful leader of men is said by Le Neve to have been descended from the Steuarts, Earls of Caithness. Be this as it may, Steuart's family were settled in Ulster before the Revolution. It is very probable that his father was the Wm. Steward (*sic*) appointed to a company in John Lord Vaughan's newly-raised Regiment of Foot in January, 1673—the Ensign to said company being the subject of this memoir.

From the poem[1] dedicated to General Steuart, in 1720, we learn that this officer served in France as a young man, and subsequently fought under the Prince of Orange in Flanders. It may, therefore, be safely affirmed that Wm. Steuart served for a short time with a British corps (probably Sir George Hamilton's) in Louis XIV.'s army. When additional forces were raised in England, in 1673, Steuart returned home and was appointed Ensign in Lord Vaughan's Regiment of Foot by Commission dated 27th January, 1673.[2] He was promoted Lieutenant 14th September following. Early in 1674, Lord Vaughan's corps was disbanded and Steuart sought service in one of the new English regiments[3] raised that year in Holland for the United Provinces. For nearly four years we have no record of Wm. Steuart; but it is apparent from the poem already mentioned that he saw much active service under the Prince of Orange and acquitted himself honourably. When there was a threatening of war between England and France, in the winter of 1677-8, Steuart again returned home and applied for a commission. He was appointed captain in Sir Charles Wheler's newly-raised infantry regiment 16th February, 1678.[4] On 17th October following, Steuart was promoted Major.[5] Wheler's, like all other British regiments raised in 1678, was disbanded early in 1679. Steuart reverted to the Dutch service.

When Edward Fitz-harris, the plotter, was brought to the bar of the King's Bench, 11th May, 1681, on a charge of high treason, this prisoner averred "he had a witness in Holland, one Major Steward (*sic*)."[6] Fitz-harris had served with Sir George Hamilton's Irish corps in France, and had been appointed Lieutenant in the Duke of Albemarle's Regiment of Foot, in England, at the same time as Steuart had joined Lord Vaughan's

---

[1] See pp. 78-9.
[2] *English Army Lists and Commission Registers*, 1661-1714. Vol. I. p. 137.
[3] Of the three English regiments raised for the Dutch Service, in 1674 two still exist in the British Army, viz., the Northumberland Fusiliers, and the 1st Batt. Royal Warwickshire Regt. The third regiment, to which presumably Wm. Steuart was appointed (then under command of Col. Disney), was disbanded at the Peace of Ryswick.
[4] *English Army Lists and Commission Registers*, 1661-1714, Vol. I. p. 211.
[5] *Ibid.* p 246.
[6] Luttrell's *Short Relation of State Affairs*, Vol. IV. p. 485.

corps; but Steuart did not attend Fitz-harris's trial,[1] for reasons that do not appear.

On the 18th May, 1683, a sanguinary duel was fought near Chelsea by Lieut-Colonel Cannon and Major Wm. Steuart, of the same regiment, the seconds being Captains Cunningham and Parker. The chronicler of this duel, writing the same day to the Duke of Albemarle at Exeter, reports that: "All is well with Major Steward (*sic*) and Captain Parker, but Cunningham is very ill wounded, and had the ill luck to come from Holland but the day before; Cannon is in the same case, but not quite so bad."[2]

Alexander Cannon[3] lived to command the Jacobite forces in Scotland after the death of Viscount Dundee at Killiecrankie; while Wm. Steuart became Commander-in-chief in Ireland in 1711.

In the summer of 1685, the English and Scots regiments in the service of Holland were recalled to England in consequence of Monmouth's Rebellion. When these six regiments landed Sedgemoor had been fought and won, so that the services of these fine British troops were not required. After two months in England they returned to Holland; but Colonel Cannon and Major Wm. Steuart were honoured by receiving appointments in James II.'s army. Cannon received the colonelcy of a dragoon regiment (the present 3rd Hussars), and Steuart was promised the first vacant company in the 1st Foot Guards. His commission was given him on 16th December, 1685.[4] All the Captains in the Foot Guards were granted the additional rank of Lieut.-Colonel in June, 1687, and Steuart's Commission describes him as "Major William Stewart" (*sic*).[5]

At the Revolution, Wm. Steuart threw in his lot with his old commander, William of Orange. In April, 1689, the colonelcies of two crack infantry regiments fell vacant by the removal from the army of Colonels Cunningham and Richards for their *lâcheté* in quitting Londonderry (which place they had been sent to relieve), then besieged by King James's Army, and returning to England with their respective regiments, saying the place could not be defended. King William appointed Lieut.-Colonel Wm. Steuart to the command of the 9th Foot, *vice* John Cunningham; and Sir George St. George was given the colonelcy of the 17th Foot in room of Solomon Richards—who was honoured at his death by being buried in the north cloister of Westminster Abbey.

In accordance with his instructions from William III., Major-General Kirke set sail for Londonderry from Liverpool on 16th May, 1689, with his own regiment (the Queen's,), Steuart's (9th), and Hanmer's (11th). The transports carried a large store of provisions, arms, and ammunition. After being driven back several times by contrary winds and obliged to shelter in Ramsey harbour, Isle of Man, Kirke's ships arrived in Lough Derry 13th June. The relieving forces found on arrival in the Lough that the besieging army were strongly entrenched on each side of

---

[1] When Fitz-harris was committed for trial, for alleged participation in the "Popish Plot," he said to the Lord Chief Justice, "I have one witness in Holland, a very material one; that I am much concerned to have for my life—his name is Steward."—(*State Trials*, Vol. VIII. p. 327). Fitz-harris was found guilty and executed.

[2] Wm. Chapman to the Duke of Albemarle, *Lord Montagu of Beaulieu's Papers*, p. 185.

[3] See notice of this officer in Vol. II. of *English Army Lists*, p. 11, note 2.

[4] *English Army Lists*, Vol. II. p. 63.

[5] *Ibid.* p. 114.

the river "with batteries of 24-pounders in the narrowest part of it."[1] A heavy boom across the river's mouth obstructed the entrance. At a council of war held by Kirke it was decided that the relief of the town by the river was too hazardous.[2] More forces were to be asked for, and then the General hoped to effect a landing and break his way through the enemy's lines. But William III. could spare no more troops, and Marshal Schomberg considered that Kirke had sufficient ships and men to relieve Derry by water. By way of harassing the Irish Army, Kirke sailed in the *Swallow* for Lough Swilly on 7th July, taking Colonel Steuart's corps with him. Protected by the *Swallow's* guns, Steuart landed with 600 men on the island of Inch and threw up works there. The following diary[3] kept by one of Steuart's officers, when serving on the island of Inch, is highly interesting as illustrative of what a few hundred determined men can do, in the immediate presence of a hostile army, when an able commander personally directs their operations.

"AN ABSTRACT OF WHAT PASSED AT THE ISLE OF INCH FROM SUNDAY, JULY 7TH, TO FRIDAY, AUGUST 2ND, [16]89.

"On the 7th of July wee sayled from Derry Lough, with a detachment of 600 men, commanded by Colonel Steward. On the 9 wee gott up with the Isle of Inch and ancored about a myle from Renfurmlin. Wee heard that the Irish people kept a great cow camp at a plaice called Tully 6 myles from Ralfermillin whereupon Colonel Steward sent thither Captain Esklin, Lieutenant Biggett, and Lieutenant Hart with 60 musketteers who were put ashore about 12 at night. The 10 in the morning Captain Richards,[4] His Majesty's Engineer, landed with an ensigne and 20 men in the island Inch, and marching about a myle came to the great strand which was then overflowed with the tyde, and having viewed the ground stacked out a redent (*sic*) work with redoubt and then sent to Colonel Steward for some field pieces, more men, and tooles. About 11 in the morning it began to grow dry and divers poor Protestants with some cattell came over to us and some of the enemy's horse came down to the opposit shore, to hinder them, whereupon Captain Richards sent to Captain Collier to come to his assistance with what men he had on board the *Greyhound* which he did very seasonably, for about 40 of the enemy's dragoons were making over to the island. We went with 30 men and met them on the midle of the strand, but after the first discharge they retired. Presently after Lieut.-Colonel St. John[5] joined us with 200 men, he having seen what passed from the tops of the hills, and happened thereupon to our succour. About 4 in the afternoon Colonel Steward came to us with tooles, 4 field pieces, and approving our designe, we fell to worke. The 11 in the morning Colonel Steward and Lieut-Colonel St. John returned from the other side of the island with their men to work

---

[1] *History of the Second Queen's Regt.* Vol. II. p. 90.
[2] *Ibid.* p. 91.
[3] Printed by the *Hist. MSS. Commission*, 12th Report, App., pt. VII. pp. 257-9.
[4] Michael Richards served in Flanders, Newfoundland, and Spain. Commanded the Artillery Train at Almanza. Chief Engineer of England 1711; Brigadier-General same year; Surveyor General of the Ordnance 1714. D. 1721.—*Ed.*
[5] See biog. notice in *English Army Lists and Commission Registers*, 1661-1714, Vol. III. p. 209.—*Ed.*

a second redoubt which wee now began. Wee brought our 4 field pieces into battery on riseing ground, and fyred now and then at the enemy's horse that apeared on the strand where they have posted 5 troopes of dragoons as if they intended to attack us, but they did not. This day a ketch was sent to Fern Lough where one Mr. Cunninghame with 40 Irish Protestants was retyred into a small island to fetch them off, and a fly boat was also sent with cattell to Derry Lough. The 12 about 2 in the afternoon 2 troopes of horse came upon the strand, and marched half way over where they halted; and there were alsoe ready drawn up on the other side 3 troopes of horse and dragoons whereupon with the help of some seamen from on board the *Greyhound* and our gunners, wee drew away our field pieces, the ground being soe advantageous as that we conveyed them to the first redoubt before the enemy could perceive us; and we kept about our guns that they might not see them till they were layed to pass, and then we shott into the body of their horse into the strand and broke them into several divisions, and soon after beat them quite off the strand to the foot of the very hills. Colonel Steward came with a party of 300 men to our assistance, and afterwards ordered the rest of our men to march from the other side of the island and to joyn us. Wee erected this night a battery between our 2 redoubts joyning it to them by 2 lines of communication. This day Colonel Steward sent 3 several messengers to endeavour to get into Derry. From the 13 to the 17 wee continued our works and put 4 canon more into the battery; wee had now formed 10 companies of new raised men and understood that [the] Major General designed to be very quickly with us to give order about supplying the Inniskilling men with arms and able officers, they being resolved to march to Derry and force the enemy to raise the siege. This afternoon Colonel Steward went over to Ralfe Emilin where Captain Esklin[1] was with his party, and ordered him to remove all the cattell and people over into Island for that the Duke of Berwick was retreated from Inniskilling and did design to attack them. The 18, the Duke of Berwick with about 1,500 horse and foot attacked our party at Ralfe Emlin who took care to barricadoe the streets and some other advantageous passages that their horse could not break in upon them. The fight lasted about 2 hours and then the enemy retired with the loss of 240 men. On our side Lieut.-Colonel Cunningham was killed and an Ensign wounded. At night we drew our party into the island. The 19 at night the Major-General arrived in Lough Sully [Swilly]. The 20 he came ashore and ordered the rest of the forces to land and encamp. In the afternoon a message came with letters from Derry advising that they were in great distress and that the boume across the river was broke, the guns drawne away, upon which he ordered with great privacy 3 ships loaded with provisions with 40 musketeers to fall down and lie by the *Swallow* at Ralfe Mullien; 2 vessels were alsoe sent away with 10 officers, viz. Colonel Osten (?), Major Tasney (?) and arms to our friends at Inniskilling. The same night the Major-General set sail for Derry Lough. From the 20 to the 24 wee were employed in finishing our work and raising 2 batteries more of 4 guns each soe that wee had now 16 pieces of cannon planted, besides 10 guns on board of 2 shipps that lay dry at low water on the strand, with detachments of 25 men on board of each. The

---

[1] Afterwards Lieut.-General Robert Echlin, Colonel of the Inniskilling Dragoons. Obliged to sell his regiment in March, 1715.—*Ed.*

enemy for several days past (?) made several motions of attacking us but upon fireing our cannons upon them always retired with loss, and by what wee understand they had more apprehension of our attacking them, than wee of theirs. Deserters of their army came daily into us, some of which said it was the French General Rose[1] himself that came upon the strand with the two troopes of horse on the 12 instant, and he received a wound in his legg and his horse in the belly by some stones a cannon bullet scattered in its fall, and that two troopers were killed. From the 25 to the 28 wee had several accounts of the successful sallies of the Protestants of Derry. The last was on Thursday 25 in which they beat the enemy quite out of their trenches and cut off almost 2 regiments, Sir Edward Vaudrey[2] being its said of the number of the slayne, with a very inconsiderable loss on the part of the besieged. Since our being here Colonel Steward hath frequently sent out partyes which have brought us many herds of cattell, soe that wee have now noe lesse than 1,000 head in this island. On the 29 about noone wee heard great shooteing as wee had done the night before. On the 30 wee had news of the successors (sic) being got into the towne, that the Irish were in a great consternation and that they had resolved to raise the siege; and in their retreat to burn and waste all before them, and that they had sent to all the considerable papists thereabouts to convey away their goods and cattell. This night wee saw several great fires towards Letterkenny which wee soposed to be villages set on fire by the enemy. The 31 by break of day several parties of dragoons were seen setting fyre to all the neighbouring villages. About 10 in the morning, Major-General Kirke returned from Derry Lough.

"August the 1st this morning about 8 of the clock severall people come over to us from Derry with the good tidings of the enemy's haveing burnt their camp the night before and raised the siege. The 2 of August, Captain Richard[s] was sent by the Major General to Derry where he found little appearance of siege by the damage done to the houses or walls, but the people had suffered extremely haveing for five weeks lived on horses, doggs, and catts, etc. They lost not during the whole siege 100 men by the sword but near 6,000 through sickness and want, and there still remained about 4,000 able fighting men in the town who abound with the spoyle of those they have killed or taken prisoners."

The forcing of the boom by H.M.S. *Mountjoy*, on 30th July, under convoy of the *Phœnix* and *Dartmouth* frigates, is an historical event known to everyone. But it is not universally known that the veteran Duke of Schomberg, Commander-in-Chief of the Forces in Ireland, had sent a peremptory order to Kirke to relieve the starving Derry garrison by river, at any cost, and without further delay.[3] After the relief of Derry, Steuart joined Schomberg's Army with his corps and took an active part in the siege of Carrickfergus, which town held out for a week and then surrendered. A novel, and probably unique, stratagem was practised by the Irish

---

[1] Lieut.-General Conrad Marquis de Rosen, a French Cavalry General, lent for the Irish Service, by Louis XIV., whom James II. had graciously honoured with the lofty title of "Marshal of Ireland."—*Ed.*

[2] Had served, in 1687, as Lieut.-Colonel of the Queen's Regt. of Horse (6th Dragoon Guards). Resigned his Comn. to Lord Preston (Secy. of State) 13 Dec. 1688, and became Master of the Horse to the Duke of Berwick. Knighted at Windsor, 29th May, 1687. Killed at the Battle of the Boyne. *See* Le Neve's *Knights*.

[3] *Nairne MSS.*, at the Bodleian Library.

garrison during this siege, which is graphically related in the pæan inscribed to Steuart in 1720.¹ All students of military history are well acquainted with Schomberg's Fabian tactics during the long, unhealthy, and trying months spent at Dundalk Camp and the good reasons for this veteran commander's protracted stay there. Those who read the confidential "Inspection Reports"² on the "Infantry reviewed at Dundalk Camp 18th to 28th October, 1689," will see at a glance how unfit some of the British regiments then were to try conclusions with an army largely composed of well-trained French troops.

Steuart served as a Brigadier³ at the Boyne, and at the commencement of the first siege of Limerick, a few weeks later, commanded the party which captured Castle Connell, "a strong place situated on the Shannon, four miles above Limerick."⁴ Steuart was wounded at the deadly and unsuccessful assault on Limerick (27th August, 1690). On this occasion three of Steuart's officers were killed and ten wounded. In the following June Steuart was one of the two Brigadiers under General Mackay who led the stormers at the taking of Athlone, and was wounded. He had command of a brigade at the battle of Aughrim, 2nd July, 1691, consisting of his own and six other British infantry regiments. Who is there who has not read of the desperate fighting that took place in the "Bloody Hollow" at Aughrim?

* * * *

In August, 1691, the second siege of Limerick, in which Steuart took an active part, resulted in the capitulation of that city. This practically left Ireland in the hands of William III.

It was only to be expected that when the excitement of war was over the soldiery should occasionally get out of hand and be guilty of disorder in various parts of Ireland. Viscount Sidney, the Lord-Lieutenant, sent Commissioners into various counties "to inquire into and regulate abuses committed by the soldiers." The fighting Earl of Galway, Lord Chief Justice Reynell, and Brigadier Wm. Steuart were sent into Meath, in June 1693,⁵ to set matters right. In the following March we find Steuart in Holland,⁶ and may conclude that he served the campaign of 1694, in Flanders, as one of the Brigadiers.

In the winter of 1694–5 it was decided to send four English regiments, of which Steuart's was one, to Cadiz to serve with Admiral Edward Russell's Fleet in the Mediterranean. Steuart⁷ was in command of the troops. France was at war with Spain as well as with Britain and Holland. The French had invaded Catalonia and seized Palamos and Rosas, which they garrisoned. The British and Dutch Fleets kept the French from making further conquests, and when Steuart and his

---

¹ See p. 79. An account of the siege of Carrickfergus is given in Samuel Macskimin's *Hist. of Carrickfergus*, 2nd edit. pp. 66–70.

² See *English Army Lists and Commission Registers*, 1661–1714, Vol. III. pp. 106–123. The "Report" on Col. Wm. Steuart's Regiment was, "Colonel good, but his officers not of the best."

³ Date of Commission not forthcoming. Millan, in his *Succession of Colonels* (1742), gives a wrong year.

⁴ Luttrell's *Short Relation of State Affairs*, Vol. II. p. 93.

⁵ Viscount Sydney to the Earl of Nottingham, 1st June, 1693. *Cal. S.P. Dom.*

⁶ London Newsletter, March, 1694. *Ibid.*

⁷ Instructions for Brigadier-General Wm. Steuart, commanding the land forces going to Cadiz: "You are to embark with your own and three other regiments of foot, and there follow such directions as you shall receive from Admiral Russell, who will appoint officers on any vacancies occurring in said regiment." 12th March, 1695. *Cal. S.P. Dom.*

infantry brigade[1] arrived at Cadiz, Russell proved himself master of the Mediterranean. The British troops were landed at Barcelona, and marched to Palamos, which they besieged on the land side while Russell bombarded that town from the sea. Palamos was too strong to be taken by a short siege, so the troops were re-embarked. Lord Macaulay tells us that "Russell spread terror along the whole shore of Provence, and kept the French fleet imprisoned in the harbour of Toulon. Fortunately for the French, Russell's fleet encountered a succession of tempests, off Provence, that drove it back to the Straits and eventually to Cadiz.[2] From thence the British squadron returned to Portsmouth in November.

Steuart was promoted Major-General 1st June, 1696. Before the close of that year he was appointed Inspector of Garrisons in Ireland.[3] This piece of preferment gave great offence to Brigadier Wm. Wolseley,[4] who had been given the post of Master-General of the Ordnance in Ireland, and considered that he had a prior right to the appointment which the King bestowed on Steuart.[5] After the Peace of Ryswick, Steuart received instructions to disband certain regiments on the Irish Establishment. On 18th July (O.S.), 1701, he was granted a yearly pension of £730 per ann. " in consideration of his good services performed unto his Majesty."[6] Steuart's strong fighting instincts prompted him to fight a duel with Captain Thomas Bellew on the Irish Half-Pay List, who had served under Steuart at the siege of Palamos.[7] Under date of 24th December, 1700, Luttrell records in his *Diary*:—"Saturday morning Major-General Steuart and Captain Bellew (whose right hands were both disabled in the late war) fought on foot with pistols; the first fired, being within two yards of the other, and shot him through the hatt; whereupon Bellew generously threw away his pistol, saying he did not desire to kill him."[8] The gallant Bellew commanded Meredyth's Regiment (37th Foot) at Blenheim[9] and retired from the Army in 1705. The Earl of Rochester writing to the Duke of Ormonde, 18th April, 1705, says:—"Colonel Bellew could not serve with any comfort in the Army, being so ill with the General [Steuart]."[10]

On 11th February, 1703, Steuart was promoted Lieut.-General. As an old guardsman, his ambition led him to ask the Duke of Ormonde to approach Marlborough on the subject of a Regiment of Guards being raised for Ireland, of which corps Steuart desired to have the command. Ormonde not only forwarded this scheme, but pointed out to Marlborough what good service Steuart had done Queen Anne in the Irish House of

---

[1] By a certificate given by Brigadier Steuart the date of embarkation is fixed as the 18th March, and the day of disembarkation, on return to England, as the 17th November. *Add. MS. Brit. Mus.* 19029.

[2] Burchett's *Naval Transactions*, p. 285.

[3] *Buccleuch Papers*, at Montague House, Vol. II. Pt. II. p. 432.

[4] *Ibid.* The Editor is responsible for the memoir of Brigadier Wolseley in the *Dict. Nat. Biog.*

[5] Wolseley to the Duke of Shrewsbury, 26th Dec. 1696.

[6] This pension was continued by Queen Anne and appears in " An account of the pensions on the Military List of Ireland," for " 31st Dec. 1713." This document is in the Editor's possession.

[7] Memorial of his war services by Col. Thos. Bellew in 1710. *Treasury Papers*, Vol. cxxxii. No. 19.

[8] Vol. IV. p. 721.

[9] *Blenheim Roll*, pp. 69–70.

[10] *Hist. MSS. Comn.* Report VII. Appx. Pt. III. p. 768.

Commons. "I must now inform your Grace," wrote Ormonde to Marlborough, 26th December, 1703, from Kilkenny, "that Lieut.-General Steuart has done all that lay in his power to serve her Majesty in the Commons. He really did good though no speaker. He has told me that your Grace would certainly be his friend . . . What he desires is that if there can be raised a regiment of guards for this Kingdom, that he may have the command of it."[1] Replying to this letter, Marlborough wrote from London to Ormonde: "As to what your Grace mentions concerning the regiment of guards for Lt.-General Steuart, upon your coming over I shall be intierly (*sic*) governed by your Grace in that matter."[2] For reasons that do not appear the desired new corps was not raised, and close on two centuries passed before a regiment of Irish Foot Guards was added to the strength of the British Army.

Steuart continued to serve on the Staff in Ireland, and was promoted General of the Foot 31st January, 1711. The same year he was appointed Commander-in-Chief in Ireland during the absence of the Duke of Ormonde and was sworn in as a Privy Councillor. On the accession of George I. Steuart was succeeded as General of the Foot by Lord Tyrawley (13th November, 1714). Rightly or wrongly, Steuart was credited by the new Government with anti-Hanoverian views, and when the Jacobite rising of 1715 loomed into sight George I. intimated to several Generals who had regiments that they must dispose of their respective colonelcies. Steuart was among the number. He sold his regiment to Col. James Campbell,[3] 27th July, 1715. Steuart passed into honourable retirement and took up his residence in Hanover Square, London. In 1720 we find him giving the munificent sum of £786 to be applied in paying for the North Tower, and the staircase therein, of All Souls College, Oxford.[4] In commemoration of Steuart's generosity, an Oxford poet[5] wrote a set of verses in honour of General Steuart, which were printed in *The Daily Journal*, of 27th April, 1721, and are as follows:—

TO THE HON^BLE GENERAL STEWART ON HIS EXCELLENCY'S
BOUNTIFUL GIFT TO ALL SOULS COLLEGE, OXFORD.

> Patron of Arts whom martial glories crown,
> Sharing of Peace and War the great renown;
> Stewart, accept the verse thy deeds demand,
> And live whilst Verse shall last, and Oxford stand.
>
> . . . .
>
> Here bards whom Heaven no nobler task ordains,
> And with sublimer fury, fires their strains;
> Numb'ring the great exploits of Ages gone,
> Shall late record the Fame which Stewart won;

---

[1] *Ibid.* p. 769.

[2] *Hist. MSS. Comn.* Report VII. Appx. Pt. III. p. 789.

[3] Afterwards Lieut.-General Sir James Campbell, K.B., who commanded the Cavalry at Fontenoy, where he lost a leg and died on the field.

[4] Entry in the Benefactors' Book, All Souls College:—"1720, Honoratissimus et excellentissimus Gulielmus Steuart arm. Dux Peditum et copiis universis in Hibernia, Regnante Anna, summo cum imperio Præfectus, ad Turrim Borealem, et ad Ascensorium ejusdem absolvendum dedit £786." Communicated by the Librarian of All Souls College.

[5] Wm. Huddesford writes from Bath, 18th Oct. 1720, to Dr. Clarke, All Souls College, Oxford, concerning verses written by him in honour of General Steuart and sends the same to Dr. Clarke for criticism.—*Leyborne-Popham Papers*, at Littlecote, printed by the *Hist. MSS. Commission*, p. 253.

Bring all his deathless actions back to light,
And paint the leader in the storm of fight;
The pressing legions join'd the field on fire,
And ranks, that where the thunder strikes expire;
Shall say, how young the Gallic coast he sought,
In thirst of war, and conquer'd as he fought;
O'er Belgic fens, shall trace his dashing course,
Through nations wasted with oppressing force;
Shall sing the people free, the tyrant fled,
And tell how Stewart fought and Nassau led;
But fairest in the future world's applause,
Shall shine his triumphs in Britannia's cause:
When fam'd Hibernia's wat'ry plains he freed,
And prostrate saw the proud invader bleed;
An ancient fortress stood well known to Fame,
And from the rocks of Fergus took its name;
Thither their force the British squadrons bend,
The trenches level, and the bastions rend;
Yet long the siege protracted they beheld,
By turns assailing and by turns repell'd;
A living wall at length their arms withstood,
And driven beasts the gaping breach renew'd;
Couch'd in the herd the warry soldier lies,
And missive death from his close ambush flies;
The squadrons shrinking at the unwarlike sight,
Now pause inglorious in the rage of flight,
'Till Stewart's voice their drooping hearts recalls,
And man and beast promiscuous carnage falls;
Pierc'd with its guard the slaughter'd fence gives way,
And Fate decides the well-disputed day;
The partial heavens in rain his march delay,
In vain the infected clime conspires his stay;
Where noisome damps the trained air o'erspread,
And strew the solitary fields with dead,
Cheerful he leads his hardy troops along,
And bribes with promis'd war the fainting throng,
Through dire contagion sweeps the drooping bands,
And half the mournful camp unpeopled stands,
He leads to battle whom diseases spare,
And conquers with the thin remains of war,
But who the glorious labour can pursue,
And set each deathless deed in open view,
The ramparts from their deep foundations broke,
The bastions burst, the tumult and the smoke,
When wounded and victorious at Athlone,
In honourable gore disdain'd he shone,
Or who can paint the terrors of the foe,
When Boyne's affrighted stream forgot to flow,
As crowding Britons stemmed the foaming tide,
And drove the Gaul from his deserted side,
Or count the marches o'er the burning plain,
When Stewart led his fearless bands in Spain?

. . . .

And now his country claims his sword no more,
Renown'd in counsels as in arms before,
Glorious retiring from tumultuous noise;
In Arts his powerful genius he employs.

The Goddess thus whom Arts and Arms obey,
Conquers alike in either diff'rent way,
Sometimes with rage she darts the pointed spear,
Anon with words she charms the willing ear,
With pleasure some comply, the rest submit with fear.

General Steuart was twice married. His first wife was Catherine Viscountess Grandison. She died insane 26th December, 1725, and was buried in the Duke of Buckingham's vault in Henry VII.'s Chapel, Westminster Abbey. According to the newspapers of the day, her funeral was conducted "in the most magnificent manner that any funeral had been performed for many years."[1] A fortnight after her burial, General Steuart got a licence from the Faculty Office to marry Elizabeth, second daughter of Sir Rowland Alston, Bart., of Odell, co. Beds., and the marriage took place shortly after. On 15th February, 1725-6, it was reported in the newspapers that General Steuart had been dangerously ill of an apoplexy, and he died on 4th June, 1726, aged 74.[2] He left no issue by either wife.[3] By his will, dated 31st May, 1726, the General left large legacies to his brother John Steuart, his nephew Colonel John Steuart, and his nieces. His nephew, Brigadier-General Wm. Steuart (who commanded the Ninth Foot at Almanza), he cut off with a shilling for his ingratitude. He bequeathed "£5,000, Irish money, to erect and endow a school for twenty poor boys in the parish of St. George, Hanover square," where he lived. General Steuart was buried with his first wife in Westminster Abbey.

[1] Col. Chester's *Westminster Abbey Registers*, p. 318, note 1.
[2] *Ibid.* The coffin plate was exposed in 1867.
[3] *Ibid.* Steuart's widow re-married Henry Rowe of Epsom, Surrey, and died 21st May 1756.

CHAPTER X.

ARCHIBALD, EARL OF FORFAR,
ACTING BRIGADIER-GENERAL AT THE BATTLE OF SHERIFFMUIR.

ARCHIBALD DOUGLAS, the only son of the first Earl of Forfar, was born 25th May, 1693. In his father's lifetime he had the courtesy title of Lord Wandell. About 1704, Queen Anne granted the latter a yearly pension of £200 *per annum* to forward his education. Like other pensions at the date in question this yearly allowance was paid irregularly. Before Queen Anne's death the second Earl of Forfar was in debt for £3,000 spent in the purchase of commissions.[1]

Lord Wandell was appointed Guidon and Captain in the Scots Troop of Horse Grenadier Guards, 6th March, 1708. In September, 1711, he purchased the majority, and fourteen months later the lieut.-colonelcy, of the Hon. Wm. Ker's Regiment of Dragoons, the present 7th Hussars. On 23rd December, 1712, Lord Wandell succeeded as 2nd Earl of Forfar.

His zeal for the Service led him in 1713 to purchase the colonelcy of a crack Infantry regiment (The Buffs) from Colonel John Selwyn for £6,000. Lord Forfar hoped to have secured this sum from his lieut.-colonelcy and troop in Ker's Dragoons; but as ill-luck would have it, this fine cavalry regiment was reduced before this nobleman had secured the purchase money from Lord Torphicken, his successor. The Dowager Lady Forfar tells us in her pathetic petition[2] to King George I. that Ker's Dragoons were broke out of their turn by Queen Anne's Ministry on account of Colonel Ker's and her son's well-known zeal for the Protestant succession. Lord Forfar, having taken over the command of Colonel Selwyn's corps, was in honour bound to pay the latter the sum agreed on. In this predicament Forfar applied to his mother and her sister, Miss Martha Lockhart. These two ladies paid off Colonel Selwyn in the course of a year or two; but "by interest, prosecution, and other expenses the original amount had increased to £7,900."[3] Hardly had this debt been wiped out before Lady Forfar and her sister had to advance further money for Lord Forfar's "equipage," when he was appointed Envoy Extraordinary to the Court of Prussia in April, 1715. Before Lord Forfar could take up his residence in Berlin his services were required at home in view of the expected Jacobite rising. His expensive outfit had to be sold, but the money realised "was exhausted by the rent of the said Earl's house in Berlin and the expense of the servants sent out there."[4] Instead of going to Berlin,

---

[1] Earl of Forfar's "Memorial" to Queen Anne in Feb., 1714.—*Treasury Papers*, Vol. 172, No. 42.
[2] Petition to the King from the Countess of Forfar, among the undated S.P. George I. at Public Record Office.
[3] *Ibid.*
[4] *Ibid.*

Lord Forfar was sent to Scotland with the Duke of Argyll, and at the battle of Sheriffmuir acted as a brigadier. In this capacity he charged at the head of Moryson's Foot, which corps suffered heavily when General Whetham's Infantry division was routed by the Earl of Mar's right wing. Forfar was wounded by a bullet in his knee and taken prisoner. The Highlanders slashed at him with their swords although he had surrendered. A letter from Stirling, written two days after the battle, says, "Lord Forfar was barbarously butchered." An interesting account of Forfar's wounds is given in the following letter [1] to Mrs. Lockhart of Lee, written from "Bothwell Castle, Nov. 16, 1715, one of the clock afternoon":—

"MADAM,

"I can, blessed be God, tell you that my Lord Forfar is alive. Upon Monday morning when we heard of an engagement, I was ordered to go to Stirling and enquire how matters in general went, and in particular how it was with his Lordship.

"All the way reports were that my Lord Forfar was kill'd and all his men cut off, till I approach'd Stirling, and then I found that my Lord was pretty sore wounded, but alive, yeat (sic) very hearty. His Lordship spoke to me as heartily as could be, and is very apprehensive that he will recover. The physicians say they have good hopes of his lordship; and thus our grief is a little lightn'd. The main thing I took care of was to be soon at Bothwel, to apprise my Lady of the true matter of fact, lest she might be kill'd with grief at the hearing an false account of his Lordship's death which, in the good providence of God, hapn'd according to my wishes, for I arriv'd here on Tuesday morning pretty early, and told her of my Lord's being alive, tho' wounded, just a little before Mr. Hamilton and another minister were desir'd to tell the melancholy news of my Lord's death, in the lest dangerous way they could think on. The true story of this engagement, as it relates to my Lord is as follows :—Upon Sunday forenoon, his Lordship having the command of three regiments, was in a marching posture, not expecting the Highlanders so near 'em as they were; whensoever then my Lord saw them, he threw from him his horse and gets his men to engage, and not long it was, till my Lord falls shot in the knee. The Highlandmen being strong in that part, viz., the mid battle, beat off our men, and did so manage as to cut off a vast deal of these regiments, that were commanded by my Lord Forfar. In this meantime my Lord was lying on the ground, and among the midst of the Highlandmen that were bearing sore upon my Lord's men, and by the following instance yowl see the merciless and most savage of the Highlanders, and at the same time the goodness of God in his providence to his Lordship. For my Lord being in the fornamed circumstances, takes out a watch to one of 'em and told him, says my Lord, 'Sir, 1 am your prisoner, pray take care of me as such, and as a reward I give you this watch,' which the Highlandman having no sooner got than he went off with himself, giving my Lord a slap in the head; his Lordship was little better treated by another to whom he had given a present of gold. At length towards the end of Sunday, another of Mar's men, the baily of Dingwell (sic), came by God's special direction, I am persuaded, and was the kindest to my Lord that could be. However, I saw my Lord at Stirling in his own lodgings, very hearty and hopefull of his recovery. And I hear since my Lord rests well, and is nothing worse. He has no fever; but was and is as sedate as can be. His Lordship has got 17 wounds, a great many of 'em after he offer'd himself prisoner; his right thumb is cut off, his left hand much hurt, as also his left arm, some cuts in his head—all of 'em making 17. My Lady went hence yesternight and was in Kilsyth all night, whence I return'd this morning. Cap. Campbell saw my Lord's surgeon yesterday morning, who said that he had very good hopes of my Lord, this

---

[1] *Analecta Scotica*, Edinburgh, 1834, Vol. I., p. 193, *et seq.*

was told me yesternight, and indeed God's being so kind to my Lord in his distrest condition, makes us hope that his life shall be precious in his sight. And, which I forgot to mention, his Lordship has got no wound in his breast, or heart, or belly, only on the forementioned places. Now, Madam, I humbly think, that we have all reason to bless God for being so kind to him in this his melancholy condition. And many fervent prayers will be a suitable exercise for everyone that has a concern in his Lordship, that God may recover him And in the meantime to be very easy contented, yea confident that it shall be so. We expect . . . . tomorrow's night. Madam, I have been so wearied with rideing ye two days and two nights begone, therefore have been so confus'd in relating the above-mentioned things, but hope you will pardon me; is all at present with my humble duty to Lee about whose ilness I am also very much concern'd, I am, Madam, your most humble servant

"RICH. HENDERSON.

"P.S.—I expect at this time my Lady is at Stirling.—
"For Madam Lockhart at Lee." [1]

Lord Forfar lingered until 8th December following, when he died. His mother records in her petition to the King that the Earl's dying request to the Duke of Argyll was "that his Majesty would allow the regiment to be sold for his mother's benefit." The Duke informed Lady Forfar "that the regiment was otherwise disposed of;[2] but his Majesty promised £4,000 should be given her. And the Earl of Orkney told her sister in his Majesty's name that another £3,000 should be given to her (Martha Lockhart)." The petition goes on to say "that only £2,500 in all had been received, and that from the sale of another commission,[3] of which £500 was deducted by the Board of General Officers to pay her son's regimental debts. That no pay as Envoy, and only a part of the usual allowance for equipage, was given to the late Earl. The Duke of Douglas got the landed estate, so that the whole fortune of petitioner's late son was exhausted, and she and her sister reduced to the greatest difficultys."

So far as Lady Forfar is concerned, there is no evidence to show that she received any bounty at the King's hand. Lord Townshend, writing to the Duke of Argyll, 3rd December, 1715, has this reference to Lord Forfar:—

"His Majesty read with very much concern what your Grace writes of the Earl of Forfar, and exprest himself with so much affection and regard to the poor Earl, that what your Grace mentions as his request for his aunt Mrs. (*sic*) Lockhart, I believe you need not doubt but it will be complyed with."[4]

The Earl of Forfar was buried in Bothwell parish church, where are monuments to the memory of his father and himself:—

"Near this Lye's the Body
of Archibald the I Earl of Forfar
Born May the 3. Anno 1653
Dyed December the 23 Anno 1712
To whose memory this Tomb was Erected
By his Constantly Loving and Afflicted Wife."

---

[1] "From a collection of original letters which belonged to Dr. Alston, Professor of Botany in the College of Edinburgh. The Earl of Forfar was Mrs. Alston's cousin."
[2] To Major-General Charles Wills.
[3] This was doubtless Lord Forfar's own Company in the Buffs.
[4] *Townshend Papers*, p. 180.

"Near this Lye's the Body
of Archibald the II Earl of Forfar
Born May the 25 Anno 1693
and Dyed December the 8 Anno 1715
To whose Dear Memory this Tomb was Erected
By his Constantly Loving and Afflicted Mother."

The arms on the first Earl's monument are Douglas impaling Lockhart :—
Argent, a heart gules, imperially crowned or, on a chief azure, 3 mullets of the field, for Douglas.

A man's heart gules, within a fetterlock sable, on a chief azure 3 boars' heads erased of the first, for Lockhart.

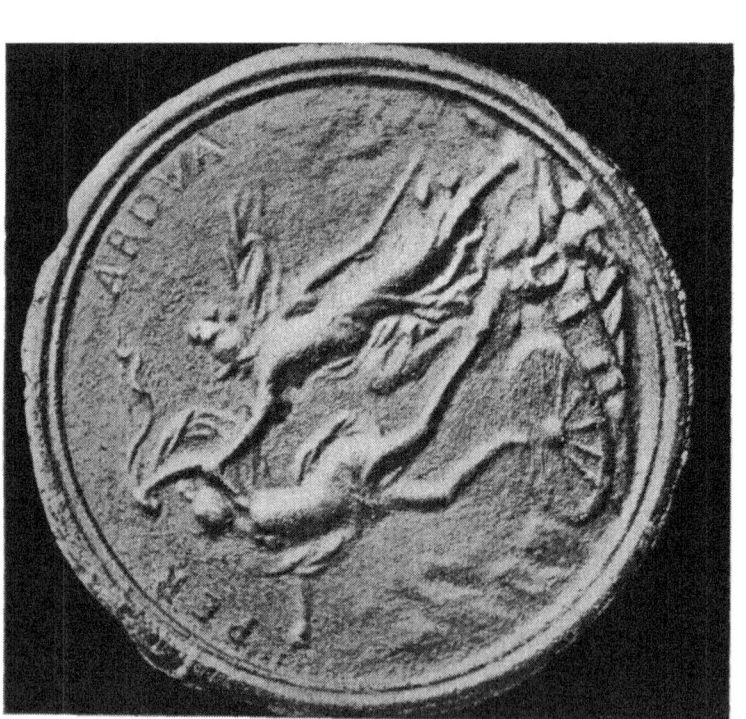

MEDAL STRUCK IN HONOUR OF CAPTAIN RICHARD MOLESWORTH, AFTERWARDS
FIELD-MARSHAL VISCOUNT MOLESWORTH.

(*See pages* 85, 86.)

CHAPTER XI.

FIELD-MARSHAL VISCOUNT MOLESWORTH.[1]

RICHARD MOLESWORTH was the second son of the first Viscount Molesworth. He was educated for the law, and sent to the Temple to finish his studies; but preferring a more active life he went to Flanders, on the outbreak of war in 1702, and served as a volunteer. Through the favour of his father's friend, the Earl of Orkney, he obtained an ensigncy in the Royal Scots, his commission being dated 14th April, 1702. At Blenheim he commanded a company of aforesaid corps. He served as A.D.C to Marlborough at Ramillies, and for some years subsequently. He was appointed Captain and Lieut.-Colonel in the Coldstream Guards, 5th May, 1707, serving at the Relief of Brussels in 1708. At the siege of Mons in 1709, he was blown up by a mine, but was little the worse for his aerial flight. He succeeded to the command of Colonel Moor's late regiment of foot, 9th June, 1710. Served in Spain with his corps, which was disbanded at the Peace of Utrecht. Appointed to the command of a newly-raised dragoon regiment in 1715. Served with the same at the capture of Preston, where he behaved with great bravery, and was wounded. Elected M.P. for Swordes, and appointed Lieut.-General of the Ordnance in Ireland, 1714. Succeeded his brother John as third Viscount in 1726; Major-General, 18th November, 1735; Lieut.-General, 2nd July 1739; General, 28th December, 1746; Master-General of the Irish Ordnance, 1st July, 1740; Governor of Guernsey, on the death of the Marquis de Montandre, 1739; Commander-in-Chief of the forces in Ireland, 1751; Field-Marshal, 29th November, 1757; F.R.S. and Governor of Kilmainham Hospital. Held at various times the Colonelcy of the Royal Inniskilling Fusiliers, the 9th Lancers, and lastly the Royal Irish Dragoons.

Viscount Molesworth died 13th October, 1758. He was twice married, and by his second wife left a son, who succeeded as fourth Viscount. Walpole, in his "Royal and Noble Authors," refers to the following military tract :—"A short course of standing rules for the Government and Conduct of an Army, designed for use in the field. With some useful observations drawn from experience, by the Right Honourable Lord Molesworth, Lieut.-General of his Majesty's Forces."

The bronze medal here represented is extremely rare, and unfortunately its present owner cannot be traced.[2] It was brought to the notice of the late John Kermack Ford, Esq., of Southsea, a well-known medal col-

---

[1] This memoir, by Charles Dalton, appeared in the *Journal of the Royal United Service Institution.*

[2] Since these lines appeared in print I was told by the late Lady Molesworth (wife of the late Rev. Viscount Molesworth) that this medal is in the Brit. Mus. collection and that a duplicate of the same is in the possession of the Molesworth family.—C.D.

lector, who obtained a photograph of the medal about 1870. The *obverse* bears the profile of Captain (afterwards Field-Marshal Viscount) Richard Molesworth, habited as a Roman warrior, with the inscription round the margin, "Riccard. Molesworth Brit. Trib. Mil." On the *reverse* a figure of Victory leading by the hand a warrior, trampling on broken artillery, with motto, "Per Ardua." The medal in question was struck in honour of Captain Molesworth, A.D.C. to Marlborough at the battle of Ramillies, having at the manifest hazard of his own life preserved that of the Duke. The incident is a well-known historical fact, but for certain reasons was hushed up at the time.

CHAPTER XII.

MEMOIR OF GEORGE KEITH, HEREDITARY EARL-MARSHAL OF SCOTLAND.

Edited by Charles Dalton, F.R.G.S.

[The following brief memoir is copied from an original MS. said to be in the handwriting of Sir Thomas Strange, Chief Justice of Madras, 1798-1816, and to have been written when a resident in Rome. Sir Thomas was son of Sir Robert Strange, the famous engraver, who was out in the '45 and for many years afterwards an exile from Britain. The MS., which appears to be a curtailed translation of M. d'Alembert's little memoir of Earl Marischal, was formerly in possession of the late Mr. Constable of Edinburgh, the well-known autograph collector, at whose sale it was bought by a dealer, from whom the present Editor acquired it. It is noticeable that Earl Marischal's share in the Jacobite descent on the West coast of Scotland, in 1719, is entirely ignored in the following memoir! It is also curious that the biographer adheres to the modern style of "Marshal" instead of Marischal.—C.D.]

This nobleman was born in the year 1687.[1] At a very early age he served under the famous Duke of Marlborough, and was made captain of the Guards by Queen Anne herself.[2] At the death of this princess, according to M. d'Alembert, he offered to proclaim the Pretender King of England at the head of his troop. This, however, the timidity of the Jacobite party would not permit, and, after having, with great honour, resigned his commission to George I., he retired into Scotland, and was one of the first who took arms in the unfortunate expedition of 1715.[3]

The Lord Marshal was strongly attached to the House of Stuart. When he proclaimed the Pretender at Edinburgh, he made him swear to restore to Scotland some of the rights of that kingdom which had been infringed by Queen Anne.

After having wandered for many months from place to place in Scotland at the risk of his life, he having been attainted, and a price having been set upon his head by the Government, he passed into Spain with some brother officers of his in the service of the Pretender, and entered into the service of that power, where Cardinal Alberoni offered him the rank of Lieut.-General. Of this he would not accept, as not thinking himself entitled to it either by his age or services, and accepted a much inferior one.

---

[1] The eldest son of Wm. Keith, ninth Earl Marshal (Marischal), who died in 1712, by Lady Mary Drummond, eldest daughter of James, fourth Earl and first Duke of Perth, Lord Chancellor of Scotland.

[2] His commission as captain and lieut.-colonel of the second or Scots troop of Horse Grenadier Guards bears date January 5, 1714.

[3] Playfair, in his *British Family Antiquity*, says that George I., being advised to remove all the Scotch nobility who were not acceptable to the Duke of Argyll, the young Earl Marischal was deprived of his military rank and emoluments at the very time that his cousin, the Earl of Mar, was dismissed from being Secretary of State. He and his brother, James Keith, joined the Earl of Mar and were attainted.

From Spain he went to Avignon, where he found his old friend and commander, the Duke of Ormonde (in the praise of whose valour, liberality, and worth all parties have ever united), who received him with open arms, and treated him as a friend rendered more dear to him than ever by the misfortunes they had undergone in the common cause.

From Avignon Lord Marshal went to Rome, where the Pretender gave him the order of the Garter, which he seldom or never wore, giving this reason for it: "Il faut renoncer sous peine de ridicule aux ornements lorsque celui, de qui on les tient, n'est pas en état de les faire respecter."

During the time of his residence at Rome, M. d'Alembert supposes that he was employed in many secret negotiations, of which, however, nothing can now be known, as he never entrusted his friends with any account of them, and thirty years before his death he burnt all his papers.

When Spain, in 1733, made war against the Emperor, Lord Marshal wrote to his Catholic Majesty to request to be employed in his service. This the King of Spain refused at first, as Lord Marshal was a Protestant, though the year before he had named him to some command against the Moors in Africa. Lord Marshal was much attached to Spain, where, as he used to say, he had many good friends, not to mention the sun, and resided chiefly in Valencia. On hearing, however, that his brother Marshal Keith [1] was wounded at the siege of Oczacow, he flew to his assistance time enough to prevent the loss of a limb, upon the amputation of which the surgeons happened at that instance to be deliberating. He followed his brother to the waters of Berage,[2] and then returned to Spain.

In 1744 the Court of France, then being at war with that of England, affected to make another attempt in favour of the Pretender, but did it so ineffectually that Lord Marshal saw through it, and endeavoured to prevail upon the prince not to be the dupe. The prince, however, did not profit by his advice, and the event was as Lord Marshal had predicted. Lord Marshal soon afterwards, on being treated with some slight by the Minister, quitted Spain and retired to Venice, where (as a man of sense and honour is always at home everywhere) he continued to amuse himself with his books, and with the conversation of men of wit and of letters. His brother, the Field-Marshal, having now quitted the service of Russia for that of Prussia, was very anxious that he should come and live with him at Berlin. To this he consented, and was, soon after, sent by the King of Prussia, the great Frederick, to the Court of France, where his lordship remained for some years, liking the nation rather better than his employment. Alas! said he, "Il faut pour ce metier une finesse que je n'ai pas et que je n'en souçie point d'avoir,"[3] and deserved the eulogium that was passed some years ago on one of our celebrated orators, when he was a short time Secretary of State, by a Minister from one of the northern courts: "J'aime beaucoup à avoir à faire avec M. F.;[4] il n'est pas chicaneur."

---

[1] The celebrated Field-Marshal James Keith, who was born in 1696. After serving some years in the Spanish army he entered the Russian service and attained the rank of General. In 1740 he entered the service of Frederick II., King of Prussia, when he became Field-Marshal. He fell at the battle of Hochkirken in 1758.

[2] Barèges, Hautes-Pyrénées.—C. D.

[3] The honest and truthful old Earl did not evidently belong to that class of ambassadors described by Sir Henry Wotton, himself an ambassador, as "good men sent abroad to tell lies for the sake of their country."—C. D.

[4] Charles James Fox.

The King of Prussia afterwards sent him as his Ambassador to Spain, whence he has been supposed to have sent[1] to that great statesman, the Earl of Chatham, the account of the family compact then settling between the two houses of Bourbon, and which, as a timid and an interested council, was treated with a studied and ill-founded contempt, to mortify a minister to whom, as Peter the Great said of Cardinal Richelieu, "sovereigns would have given one-half of their kingdoms to have governed the other half for them."

This notice then timely given, and given to such a Minister, would have secured the most splendid effects, victories, and triumphs for his country, had not the effects (*sic*) of it been impeded by a senseless and low-minded, though powerful, faction at home.

During the intervals of his embassies the King of Prussia gave him the Government of Neuchâtel, where he conducted himself in such a manner as to make himself beloved by the people of that country, who submit with impatience to be subject to a sovereign so distant from them as is the King of Prussia.

Lord Marshal's attainder being now reversed,[2] he was permitted to return into his own country, that of Scotland, where, however, he did not stay long, the coldness of the climate not being congenial to his constitution, and his habits of life having now become different from those of his countrymen. They, however, with a liberality which does them honour, would not bid against Lord Marshal when he attended in person to buy his estate.

On his return to Berlin, he lived in his usual familiarity with the King of Prussia,[3] and until ordered here;[4] he would have had the honour to have died in the arms of this great prince, had he, the king, not been obliged to join his army in Germany.

In April, 1778, he was seized with a fever which, in the course of six weeks, and after he had suffered extreme pain, carried him to the grave on May 25th in the same year.[5]

He used to say to his physician during his illness:

"Monsieur, je ne vous demande pas de me faire vivre, car vous ne pretendez point apparement m'ôter cinquante ans de mon age. Je vous prie seulement d'abréger (s'il se peut) mes maux. Après tout, je n'ai

---

[1] It is a well-known fact that the Earl Marshal, at the risk of his life and for the love of his country, he being an exile at this time, did send timely notice of the Bourbon political confederacy to Mr. Pitt. Playfair says the Earl had not left the Spanish territories thirty-six hours before the Court of Spain got notice of what he had done. In consequence of this patriotic act, George II. gave the Earl Marshal back all his lands that could be restored.

[2] An Act of Parliament was passed permitting him to inherit any other estates in Scotland. Thus he inherited the entailed estates of the Earls of Kintore on the death of the fourth Earl in 1761. He possessed that estate sixteen years, but declined taking the title of Earl of Kintore.

[3] According to Horace Walpole, the Earl Marshal owed the reversal of his attainder to Frederick the Great, whose envoy in London, Baron Knyphausen, interceded with George II. on the old exile's behalf.

[4] This is ambiguous. It would seem that he was sent to Rome on some mission, as the Stranges were residing there in 1760, and for some years after that date leading figures at the court of the Stuart exile.—C. D.

[5] He died at Potsdam, unmarried. His private fortune went to his great-nephews, Lord Elphinstone, Wm. Fullerton Elphinstone, and George Keith Elphinstone, the three grandsons of Earl Marshal's eldest sister, Lady Mary Keith, who had married, in 1711, the sixth Earl of Wigton, by whom she left at her decease, in 1721, an only daughter, Lady Clementina Fleming, heir-general of the Keiths Earl Marshal.

jamais été malade; il faut bien que j'ai ma part des misères d'humanité, et je me soumets à cet arrêt de la Nature."

Four days before he died he sent for Mr. Elliot, our Minister at the Court of Berlin, and said to him with his usual cheerfulness:

"Je vous ai fait appeler parceque je trouve plaisant qu'un ministre du Roi George reçoive les derniers soupirs d'un vieux Jacobite. D'ailleurs vous aurez peut-être quelques commissions à me donner pour Milord Chatham,[1] et comme je compte de le voir demain, ou après, je me chargerai avec plaisir de vos depêches."

Thus died Lord Marshal, who to a sound head added a most excellent heart, and who was a man of such extreme good humour that J. J. Rousseau himself, who had the honour of a very intimate acquaintance with him, and who, personally, had received very many obligations from him, had never the heart to quarrel with him.

Lord Marshal was remarkable in conversation, for telling with great point and brevity an infinite number of very entertaining stories and anecdotes. His letters were remarkably concise and elegant. To Mr. Boswell (who had the habit of making friends wherever he went) he gave the following letter (draft, as Lord Marshal called it, upon a friend near Neufchâtel):

"A Monsieur le Colonel Chaillet.
"Monsieur,
"Il vous plaira payer à M. Boswell une bonne truite du lac avec une bouteille de votre meilleur vin.
"Pour votre serviteur
"Marishall."

It seems, perhaps, superfluous to mention, in giving some account of this excellent man, that the King of Prussia presented him with the order of the Black Eagle.[2]

[1] This celebrated Minister had died about a fortnight before Lord Marshal.
[2] The foregoing memoir was contributed by me to Dr Cox's *Antiquary*, April, 1890.—C. D.

REGIMENTS ON THE BRITISH
ESTABLISHMENT, 1715.

EDITOR'S PREFACE.

The MS. Regimental List for 1715 is at the Public Record Office, London. It includes all the Regiments on the British Establishment with the exception of the old 25th Foot, the King's Own Scottish Borderers. It will be noticed that all the regiments of dragoons and foot raised in the summer of 1715 appear in this same List. The spelling of the proper names is fairly correct, but in some instances decidedly erratic. I am responsible for all the dates of officers' commissions added between square brackets. The dates in question, with a few exceptions, are taken from the imperfect MS. Army List for 1717 at the Public Record Office, and show the Army (not the Regimental) Commissions of the respective officers. Most of the names in the 1715 List have been already annotated in my series of *English Army Lists and Commission Registers*, 1661–1714, but I have thought it well to re-write the biographical notices relating to the superior officers of each regiment. Great care has been taken to revise, and sometimes add to, all my former annotations.

C. D.

REGIMENTS ON THE BRITISH ESTABLISHMENT, 1715.

LIST OF OFFICERS OF HIS MAJESTY'S FIRST TROOP OF HORSE GUARDS, WITH THE DATES OF THEIR COMMISSIONS.

[1ST LIFE GUARDS.]

NAME.	RANK.	DATE OF COMMISSION.
Duke of Montague,[1]	Capt. & Colonel	[10 May, 1715.]
Robert Dormer,[2]	1st & 2nd Lt.-Col.	—
John Blathwait,[3]	Cornet	—
John West,[4]	Guidon	11 Apr. 1715.
William Elwes,	Exempt	—
William Needham,	,,	—
William Latton,	,,	—
George Hay,	,,	—
John Julion,	Brigadier	—
Edmund Wright,	,,	—
James Macdonald,	,,	22 Oct. 1713.
William Cavell,	Sub-Brigadier	—
Thomas Smith,	,,	—
Henry Goodere,	,,	—
Richard Neale,	,,	—
Edward Whitecomb,	Chaplain	—
George Lloyd,	Adjt. & Eldest Lt.	—
John Brown,	Surgeon	—

[1] Second Duke. Lord High Constable of England at the Coronation of George I. K.G. and K.B. Served a campaign as a Volunteer under the Duke of Marlborough, whose second dau. he md. Col. of Horse 27 March, 1710. Resigned the Colonelcy of the 1st Tp. of Life Guards in 1721. Reappointed 21 June, 1737, but was removed in the following August. Master-General of the Ordnance, 1730. Col. of the 3rd Regt. of Horse (2nd D.G.) 6 May, 1740. Raised a Regt. of Ordnance on the outbreak of the '45, which corps was disbanded in 1746. This nobleman was a man of learning, and had the honour of being elected a Fellow of the Royal College of Physicians 23 Oct. 1717. D. 5 July, 1749.

[2] Son of Robert Dormer of Dorton, Bucks. Cornet in the Carabineers 10 July, 1698. Guidon and Major to the 1st Tp. of Life Guards 3 Dec. 1700. Cornet and Major 25 Aug. 1706. Lieut. and Lt.-Col. 28 Jan. 1707. Bt.-Col. 7 Feb. 1707. Col. of the Regt. aftds. known as the 6th Foot 7 Feb. 1716. He was succeeded in the command of this Corps by his bro., Brigadier-General James Dormer.

[3] Bro. to Wm. Blathwayte, the Secretary-at-War in Wm. III.'s reign. Guidon and Major 1st Tp. of Life Guards 31 Jan. 1712. Lieut. and Lt.-Col. 9 Sept. 1715. Retd. in 1749. D. in 1752.

[4] Lt. and Lt.-Col. of the 1st Tp. of Life Guards 24 Dec. 1717. Succeeded his father as 7th Baron De-La-Warr in 1723. K.B. Lord of the Bedchamber to George I. 23 June, 1725. Col. of the 1st Tp. 30 Aug. 1737. Brig.-Gen. 14 Jan. 1743. Fought at Dettingen. Maj.-Gen. 30 March, 1745. Lt.-Gen. 14 Sept. 1747. General in March, 1665. This nobleman held at different times the Governorships of New York, Tilbury Fort, and Guernsey. D. in 1766. Created Visct. Cantelupe and Earl De-La-Warr 18 March, 1761. Succeeded in his titles and colonelcy of the 1st Life Guards by his eldest son, who was a Major-General.

LIST OF OFFICERS OF HIS MAJESTY'S SECOND TROOP OF HORSE GUARDS, WITH THE DATES OF THEIR COMMISSIONS.

[2ND LIFE GUARDS.]

NAME.	RANK.	DATE OF COMMISSION.
Earl of Hertford,[1]	Captain	[8 Feb. 1714.]
Henry Cornwall,[2]	Lieutenant	[8 Dec. 1709.]
Sir Samuel Lennard,[3]	,,	[25 Oct. 1713.]
Lewis Dyves,[4]	Cornet	[,, ,,]
George Compton,	Guidon	,, ,,
James Cornuaud	Exempt	[Out in 1717.]
Samuel Weaver,	,,	[17 Feb. 1703.]
Henry Masclary,	,,	[19 July 1708.]
John Corrance,	,,	[16 June 1709.]
John Denty,	Brigadier	[18 May 1699.]
Edmund Smith,	,,	[17 Feb. 1703.]
Francis Rogers,	,,	[14 May 1705.]
George Fowke,	,,	[1 June 1705.]
Peter Hardistie,	Sub-Brigadier	[20 July 1699.]
Thomas Offley,	,,	[22 Mar. 1705.]
Thomas King,	,,	[14 May 1705.]
James Golding,	,,	[11 Sept. 1704.]
John Greenhill,	Adjutant	[14 May 1705.]
Robert Warren,	Chaplain	———
John Pawlet,	Surgeon	———

[1] Eldest surviving son of Charles Seymour, sixth Duke of Somerset. Algernon Earl of Hertford served under Marlborough at Oudenarde and Malplaquet as a Volunteer, and acted as one of his Grace's A.D.C.'s at latter battle. Col. of the regt. now known as the East Yorkshire Regt. (15th Foot) 23 Oct. 1709. Govr. of Tynemouth Castle 8 Dec. 1710. Reappointed Govr. by George I. in 1715. Govr. of Minorca 1737 Transferred to the colonelcy of the Rl. Horse Guards 6 May, 1740. Removed in Feb. 1742 to make room for the Duke of Argyll. Reinstated 10 March, 1742, on Argyll's retirement. Succeeded as 7th Duke of Somerset and sixteenth Earl of Hertford in 1748. Created, 2 Oct. 1749, Baron Warkworth and Earl of Northumberland; and the next day Baron Cockermouth and Earl of Egremont. D. without male issue 7 Feb. 1750, and his father's titles became extinct. Bd. in St. Nicholas's Chapel, Westminster Abbey.

[2] Eldest son, by a first wife of Col. Henry Cornewall, the first Colonel of the present East Norfolk Regt. (9th Foot). Guidon and Major of the 2nd Tp. of Life Guards 5 Apr. 1704. Serving as Lieut. and Lt.-Col. of above Tp. in 1740. Out of the Tp. before 1748.

[3] Appointed Capt. in the Earl of Denbigh's Dragoons 1 May, 1696. Exempt and Capt. in the 2nd Tp. of Life Guards 1 March, 1704. Guidon and Major 28 May, 1709. Cornet and Major 8 Dec. 1709. Eldest son of Sir Stephen Lennard, Bart. Succeeded his father 15 Dec. 1709. M.P. for Hythe. D. unm. 8 Oct. 1727, when the Baronetcy expired.

[4] Guidon and Major in the 2nd Tp. of Life Guards 8 Dec. 1709. Cornet and Major 25 Oct. 1713. Second Lt.-Col. of same Tp. 13 Oct. 1727. Out of the Tp. in 1733. Probably son of Capt. Lewis Dyves, who had served as a Gentleman Private in the Troop of Irish Guards in 1665. See *Irish Army Lists*, 1661–1685, p. 60, note 26.

John Duke of Montagu.

From the original of Kneller, in the Collection of
The Right Hon.ble The Earl of Egremont.

THIRD TROOP OF HORSE GUARDS.
[Disbanded 25 Dec. 1746.]

NAME.	RANK.	DATE OF COMMISSION.
Lord Newborough,[1]	Col. & Capt.	[8 Feb. 1714–5.]
Hatton Compton,[2]	Lieutenant	
John Baynes,[3]	,,	
Lewis Belleau,	Cornet	
Gabriel, Marquis de Quesne,[4]	Guidon	
Daniel Mason,	Exempts	
Adrian Metcalfe,	,,	
Henry Migett,	,,	
Philip Roberts,	,,	
Lelio Heusbergh,	Brigadier	1 June, 1710.
Joseph Neale,	,,	
Henry Sutton,	,,	
Francis Dupine,	,,	
William Kraute,	Sub-Brigadier	1 June, 1710.
William Russell,	,,	
John Slater,	,,	
Mascall Cookes,	,,	
James Edmunds,	Adjutant	
William Scrafton,	Chaplain	
Robert Gay,	Surgeon	

[1] Second son of Hugh Cholmondeley, who was created Visct. Cholmondeley of Kells, co. Meath, 29 March, 1661. Cornet to his father's Indep. Tp. of Horse, 20 June, 1685. Capt. in Lord Dover's Regt. of Horse, 1 Sept. 1685. This corps was disbanded in 1686. Capt. in the Queen Consort's Regt. of Horse (1st D.G.), 1 June, 1686. Lieut. and Lt.-Col. 1st Life Guards in 1689. Commanded the Horse Grenadiers at the battle of the Boyne and Steinkirk. Capt. and Col. of the 1st Tp. of Horse Grenadiers, 4 Oct. 1693. Brigadier of Horse, 1 June, 1697. Maj.-Gen., 9 March, 1702. Govr. of Tilbury and Gravesend, 4 May, 1702. Lt.-Gen., 1 Jan. 1704. Created Baron Newborough of Newborough, co. Wexford, 12 April, 1715, and made an English peer by the title of Baron of Newburgh, Anglesey, 10 July, 1716. Succeeded his bro. as Earl Cholmondeley, 18 Jan. 1724. General, 1 March, 1727. D. 7 May, 1733, and was succeeded by his second surviving son George.

[2] Second son of the Hon. Sir Chas. Compton (bro. to James, Earl of Northampton). Born about 1661. Cornet in the Rl. Regt. of Horse Guards, 1 July, 1685. Guidon and Major of the 3rd Tp. of Life Guards in 1691. Lieut. and Lt.-Col. 24 Jan. 1692. Saved William III. from being taken prisoner by his gallantry during the retreat from Landen in 1693, and was given a Brevet-Colonelcy, 16 Feb. 1694. Md., in 1698, his cousin Penelope Nicholas of St. Martin-in-the-Fields parish (dau. of Sir John Nicholas, K.B.). Brigadier, 9 March, 1702. Lt.-Gen., 1 Jan. 1707. Lieut.-Govr. of the Tower, 1713–1715. Retd. from the Life Guards in 1718. D. 1741.

[3] Appointed Brigadier and eldest Lt. in the King's Own Tp. of Life Guards, 28 Feb. 1683. Comn. renewed by James II. Cornet and Major, 4 Oct. 1693. Lieut. and Lt. Col. of 3rd Tp. of Life Guards, 10 July, 1694. Bt.-Colonel, 9 March, 1702. Brigdr.-Gen., 25 Dec. 1705. Maj.-Gen., 1 Jan. 1710. Probably the John Baynes of the parish of St. Margaret, Westminster, then aged 25, who had a licence, in 1684, to marry Dorothy Amherst with consent of her brother, Jeffery Amherst.

[4] Son of Abraham, Marquis du Quesne, of Bouchet, Normandy. Guidon and eldest Major of the 3rd Tp. of Life Guards, 25 Feb. 1712. Lieut. and Lt.-Col. of the 1st Tp. of Horse Grenadier Guards, 24 Dec. 1717. Commissioner of Fortifications in the English service at Port Royal, Jamaica, 1725–6. Among the *Treasury Papers* for 1740 is a Petition from "Colonel Gabriel du Quesne, formerly of the Horse Guards," to the effect that he is in an impoverished condition. He had md. Elizth., dau. of Sir Roger Bradshaigh, Bt., and widow of John Yates.

FOURTH TROOP OF HORSE GUARDS.

[*Disbanded* 25 *Dec.* 1746.]

NAME.	RANK.	DATE OF COMMISSION.
Earl of Dundonald,[1]	Captain	[6 Apr. 1714.]
Lord John Kerr,[2]	Lieutenant	16 Jan. 1709-10.
Peter Campbell,[3]	,,	31 Aug. 1711 (*sic*).
Lord George Forbes,[4]	Cornet	[16 June, 1712.]
Samuel Horsey,[5]	Guidon	31 Aug. 1711.
Daniel Charlott,	Exempt	6 Mar. 1707-8.
Richard Stacey,	,,	28 Dec. 1710.
James Gibson,	,,	[24 June, 1712.]
Charles Dilks,	,,	11 Dec. 1712.
Dunken Dee,	Brigadier	2 June, 1715.
Richard Marriott,	,,	30 June, 1710.
Thomas Kennawie,	,,	[16 Jan. 1709.]
David Campbell,	,,	10 Nov. 1714.
Henry Brightman,	Sub-Brigadier	16 Jan. 1709.
Richard Buckland,	,,	[15 Apr. 1710.]
Edward Boughton,	,,	28 Oct. 1714.
Richard Gifford,	Adjutant	5 Aug. 1714.
Robert Friend,	Chaplain	[6 Mar. 1708.]
Peter Laponge,	Surgeon	[,, ,,]

[1] Fourth Earl and one of the Representative Peers for Scotland in 1713. Sold his Comn. in April, 1719, and died 5 June, 1720. Succeeded by his son William as 5th Earl.

[2] Younger bro. to Wm. 2nd Marquis of Lothian. Cornet and Major of the Scots Tp. of Life Guards in 1702. Brigd.-Gen., 1 Jan. 1710. Colonel of the Regt. aftds. known as the 31st Foot, 8 Sept. 1715. Maj.-Gen. 5 March, 1727. D. 1 Aug. 1728.

[3] Second son of Duncan Campbell of Whitestones, Cantyre. Guidon and Major of the Scots Tp. of Life Guards, 16 Jan. 1710. Cornet and Major, 31 Aug. 1711. Col. of Horse 15 Nov. 1711. Brig.-Gen., 15 Nov. 1735. Maj.-Gen., 2 July, 1739. Lt.-Gen., 26 March, 1743. Lt.-Govr. of Portsmouth before 1747. Held the post of "First Gentleman of the Beer Buttery at the Court of St. James" (*Landed Gentry*, art. "Campbell of South Hall, co. Argyll"). D. 18 Feb. 1752.

[4] Succeeded his father as 3rd Earl of Granard in 1734. Held a Comn. in the Navy as well as in the Army. Served as a Midshipman of the *St. George* under Rooke at the capture of Gibraltar, and was A.D.C. to the Prince of Hesse Darmstadt on land. Took part in the great sea-fight off Malaga in 1704. Became heir to the Earldom of Granard by the death of his brother, Lord Forbes, who was killed at Blenheim. Served at the siege of Ostend, in 1706, under the Duke of Argyll, who procured Forbes the appointment of Brigadier in the Scots Tp. of Life Guards, of which the former was then Colonel. On 18 Nov. 1708, Forbes was advanced to be an Exempt and Captain in same Tp. He still retained his Comn. in Holt's Marines, in which he had been appointed 2nd Lieut. of Grenadiers, 24 May, 1708. Resigned his Comn. in the Marines, 16 May, 1711. Served in Spain as a Cavalry officer (Comn. dated 13 June, 1711, signed by Argyll) under Argyll, who made Forbes Lieut.-Govr. of St. Philip's, Minorca. Acted as Govr. of Minorca in 1718. Govr. of the Leeward Islands in 1729. Envoy to Russia in 1733. The Empress Anne offered Forbes the command of the Russian Navy, which he declined. At the time of his death, 16 Oct. 1765, the Earl of Granard was senior Admiral in the British Navy.

[5] Promoted Lieut. and Lt.-Colonel, 14 Sept. 1715. Out of the Tp. before 1727, in which year he applied for the Governorship of Carolina (S.P.D. George II., under date of 12 July, 1727). D. 1738.

RICHARD, EARL OF SCARBOROUGH.
From the Original in the Collection of the Earl of Scarborough.

FIRST TROOP OF HORSE GRENADIER GUARDS.

[Disbanded 25 June, 1788.]

NAME.	RANK.	DATE OF COMMISSION
Lord Lumley,[1]	Col. & Capt.	[8 Feb. 1714–15.]
Thomas Paget,[2]	Lieut.-Col.	10 Mar. 1714–15.
Robert Dent,	Major	[21 Dec. 1703.]
Thomas Wentworth,[3]	Lieutenant	[Out in 1717.
Sir Harbottle Luckyn,	,,	6 Mar. 1713–14.
Lewis des Clouseaux,	Guidon	[19 Jan. 1711.]
Simon Peacock,	Sub-Lieutenant	[15 June, 1715.]
Theodore Smith,	,,	[25 Dec. 1703.]
Robert Shirley,	Adjutant	[25 Feb. 1703.]
William Andrew,	Chaplain	9 Dec. 1708.
John Brown,	Surgeon	[1 Mar. 1694.]

[1] Richard, Visct. Lumley, second surviving son of the 1st Earl of Scarbrough. Lt.-Col. of the Queen's Regt. of Horse (1st Dn. Gds.), 27 July, 1713. He was appointed Master of the Horse and a Lord of the Bedchamber to the Prince of Wales. Served at the battle of Preston. Succeeded as 2nd Earl in 1721. Transferred to the Colonelcy of the Coldstream Guards, 18 June, 1722. Elected a Knight of the Garter in June, 1724. Attained the rank of Lt.-General, 2 July, 1739. D., unm., 29 Jan. 1740, and was succeeded by his brother Thomas as 3rd Earl.

[2] Son of the Hon. Henry Paget and grandson of Wm., 5th Baron Paget. Capt. and Lt.-Col. in the 1st Foot Guards, 5 March, 1711. Colonel of the 32nd Foot, 28 July, 1732. Transferred to the Colonelcy of the 22nd Foot, 15 Dec. 1738. Brig.-Gen., 2 July, 1739. Govr. of Minorca at the time of his death, which occurred 28 May, 1741. His only dau. and heiress, Caroline, md. Sir Nicholas Bayly, Bart., of Placenywind, co. Anglesey, and had a son, Henry Bayly, who succeeded as 9th Baron Paget in 1769.

[3] Appointed Lieut. in above Tp., 7 March, 1715. Capt. and Lt.-Col. in the 1st Foot Guards, 24 Oct. same year. Transferred to the Lt.-Colonelcy of the Royal Welsh Fusiliers, 10 Feb. 1718. Bt.-Col., 15 Dec. 1722. Col. of the 39th Foot, 15 Dec. 1732. Transferred to the 24th Foot, 27 June, 1737. Brig.-Gen., 2 July, 1739. Second in command of the troops employed in the Carthagena Expedition, 1740. Succeeded Lord Cathcart 20 Dec. 1740 as Commander-in-Chief of the Land Forces sent on aforesaid expedition, which proved a lamentable failure from incompetency, mismanagement, lack of intelligence, and malarial fever, which decimated the troops. Major-Gen. 16 Aug. 1741. Commanded a Division under Field-Marshal Wade during the campaign in Flanders, 1744. Accompanied Marshal Wade on his march to Newcastle on the breaking out of the '45. Lieut.-Gen. 5 June, 1745. Colonel of the present 5th Dragoon Guards, 22 June same year. Appointed Ambassador at Turin in 1746. D. in that city, Dec. 1747.

SECOND TROOP OF HORSE GRENADIER GUARDS.

[Disbanded 25 June, 1788.]

NAME.	RANK.	DATE OF COMMISSION.
E. de Loraine,[1]	Col. & Capt.	[1 June, 1715.]
Edmund Turnor,[2]	Lieut.-Col.	10 Feb. 1709–10.
Alexander Hubert,[3]	Major	10 Aug. 1710.
William Powlett,	Lieut. & Capt.	
Edward Hutchinson,	,, ,,	11 Jan. 1711–12.
John Duncombe,[4]	Guidon & Capt.	
Josias Hutchinson,	Sub-Lieutenant	11 Apr. 1709.
Francis Testas,	,,	
John Chaworth,	Adjutant	18 Dec. 1712.
Robert Rawlinson,	Chaplain	[11 Jan. 1715.]
Robert Bailie,	Surgeon	

[1] Lord Henry Scott, 3rd son of James, Duke of Buccleuch and Monmouth, was appointed Guidon and Major of the 2nd Tp. of Horse Grenadier Guards, 12 Feb. 1702. Col. of a newly-raised Regt. of Foot in Ireland, 5 April, 1704. Created Earl of Deloraine, 29 March, 1706. Brig.-Gen., 1 Jan. 1710. Removed from the Grenadier Guards in July, 1717. Subsequently he was made a K.B. and given the Colonelcy of the 16th Foot, from which he was transferred to the Colonelcy of the Carabineers, 9 July, 1730. Major-Gen., 1 March, 1727. D. 25 Dec. 1730. Bd. at Leadwell in Oxfordshire. Succeeded by his eldest son Francis as 2nd Earl.

[2] Only son of Edmund Turnor of Stoke Rochford, co. Lincoln, and grandson of Sir Chris. Turnor, one of the Barons of the Exchequer in 1660. Served previously as Capt. and Lt.-Col. in the Coldstream Guards. Out of the Army 4 Feb. 1722.

[3] Served previously in Col. Wm. Breton's Regt. of Foot and in the Rl. Scots Fusiliers. Promoted Lieut. and Lt.-Col. of the Scots Troop of Life Guards, 4 Feb. 1722. Serving in 1727.

[4] Appears to have been a kinsman to the Countess of Deloraine (*née* Duncombe). Ensign in the Coldstream Guards, 14 April, 1702. Capt. in the Earl of Barrymore's Regt. of Foot before 1706. Major, 22 May, 1711. Guidon and Capt. 2nd Tp. H. Grendr. Guards, 31 May, 1711, with rank of Colonel. Resigned his Comn., 24 April, 1716.

THE DUKE OF ARGYLL'S REGIMENT OF HORSE GUARDS.

[ROYAL REGIMENT OF HORSE GUARDS.]

NAME.	RANK.	DATE OF COMMISSION.
Duke of Argyll,[1]	Col. & Capt.	[13 June, 1715.]
Sir Francis Compton,[2]	1st Lieut.-Col.	[30 Apr. 1689.]
George Fielding,[3] *	2nd Lieut.-Col.	[1 Jan. 1707.]
Francis Byng,[4]	Major & Capt.	19 Feb. 1711-12.
William Marcham,†	Captain	26 Dec. 1710.
James Varey,	,,	14 Feb. 1710-11.
Andrew Percivall,	,,	22 Mar. 1710-11.
John Elwes,	,,	————
John Hawkins,	,,	————
John Wyvill,	,,	————
Giles Erle,	,,	————
Gregory Beake,	Capt.-Lieut.	23 June, 1715.
Charles Jenkinson,	Lieutenant	10 Oct. 1713.
William Caldwald,‡	,,	————
Edward Bird,§	,,	15 May, 1712.
John Gilbert,	,,	————
Henry Wroth,	,,	————
[Fras. ?] Armstrong,[5]	,,	————
[Thos.] Massingall,	,,	————
Randall Bath,	,,	————
Thomas Marcham,	Cornet	26 Feb. 1711-12.
Patee Byng,	,,	————
Robert Carey,	,,	2 Dec. 1714.
[Thos.] Taylor,	,,	————
Sir William Parsons,	,,	————
[John] Shaw,‖	,,	————
— Bartlett,	,,	————
[Fras.] Ligonier,	,,	————
[Wm.] Campbell,	,,	————
Charles Saunders,	Quartermaster	————
William Williams,	,,	————
Philip Downes,	,,	————
William Marcham,	,,	————
John Howell,	,,	18 Nov. 1708.
Robert Bond,	,,	————
John Bowles,	,,	————
[Thos.] Taylor,	,,	————
William Meggs,	,,	————
Thomas Taylor,	Adjutant	23 July, 1708.
James Richardson,	Chaplain	————
Paul Margarett,	Surgeon	————

* George Fielding to be Major, 26th June, 1705.
† William Marcham, Quartermaster, 31st October, 1706.
‡ William Caldwald, Cornet, 1st February, 1705-6.
§ Edward Bird, Cornet, 27th May, 1706.
‖ John Shaw, Quartermaster, 1st February, 1705-6.

¹ See special memoir, pp. 1–9.

² The oldest officer in George I.'s Army. Fifth son of Spencer, 2nd Earl of Northampton, by Mary, dau. of Sir Francis Beaumont, "a lady that had the resolution to behold her lord and 3 of her sons fighting at Edgehill for their Church, their King, and the Liberties of their Country" (*Historical Register*, 1716). Francis Compton is said to have seen service during the Civil War. In Feb. 1661 he was appointed Lieut. to his brother Sir Charles Compton's Tp. in the newly-raised Regt. of Horse Guards. M.P. for Warwick. On the death of his brother, Sir Charles (killed by a fall from his horse), in Nov. 1661, the King gave the vacant Tp. to Francis Compton, who was knighted 27 Dec. following. Promoted Major, 10 July, 1676. Lt.-Col., 1 July, 1685. Distinguished himself at Sedgemoor. Went over to William of Orange in Nov. 1688. Re-commissioned Lt.-Col. of the Rl. H. Gds., 30 April, 1689. Bt.-Col. 1 May, 1689. Commanded the Regt. in Flanders from May, 1689, to the spring of 1690. Fought at the Boyne and at Aughrim. Under date of 31 Oct. 1699, Luttrell records in his *Diary*: "Some days since Sir Francis Compton, 70 years old, was married to a niece of Mr. Anthony Rowe, aged 17." Sir F. Compton was made a Major-Gen. in 1704, and a Lieut.-Gen. some years later (Commission registers not forthcoming). D. 20 Dec. 1716.

³ Second son of the Rev. the Hon. John *Feilding*, D.D. (5th son of the Earl of Desmond), Canon of Salisbury, and Chaplain to William III. Appointed Capt. of the King's Tp. in the Rl. Regt. of H. Gds., 17 Jan. 1700. Major, 26 June, 1705. Bt. Lt.-Col., 1 Jan. 1707. 2nd Lieut.-Col., 19 Feb. 1712. Not in any List after 1715. D. 1738.

⁴ Brother to George, Visct. Torrington. Capt. in above corps, 5 Dec. 1700. Bt. Lt.-Col., 6 Sept. 1712. Serving in 1728. Out of the Regt. in Jan. 1734.

⁵ Served as A.D.C. to the Duke of Argyll at Sheriffmuir, and was killed. See p. 194.

GENERAL LUMLEY'S REGIMENT OF HORSE.

[1st DRAGOON GUARDS.]

NAME.	RANK.	DATE OF COMMISSION.
[Hon.] Henry Lumley,[1]	Col. & Capt.	
Thomas Panton,[Senr.][2]	Lieut.-Col.	11 Apr. 1715.
John Morey,[3]	Major & Capt.	[19 Apr. 1714.]
Christopher Billingsly,	Captain	
Galen Cope,	,,	11 Apr. 1715.
Patrick Lisle,	,,	
William Bemboe,	,,	
George Burrington,	,,	20 Mar. 1713-14.
Thomas Crowther,[4]	,,	
John Browne,	[Capt.] Lieutenant	11 Jan. 1714-15.
Morris Morgan,	[Lieutenant]	
Benjamin Bishop,	,,	
John Stone,	,,	
Francis Kingstone,	,,	
John Warren,	,,	
Charles Lawes,	,,	
Robert Wilson,	,,	
William Lancaster,	,,	
George Brabant,	Cornet	
Tomkins Wardour,	,,	
William Duckins (sic),	,,	
John Bredon,	,,	
Thomas Panton [Junr.][5]	,,	
Samuel Sewell,	,,	
John Dodsworth,	,,	
Charles Alexander,	,,	
John Deane,	,,	
[Chas.] Leaver,	Chaplain	
Claud Amyand],	Surgeon	
John Dodsworth,	Adjutant	

[1] Only brother to Richard, 1st Earl of Scarbrough. Appointed Capt. in the Queen's Regt. of Horse (now 1st D.G.), 13 June, 1685. Lt.-Col., 31 Dec. 1688. Bt.-Col., 1 Dec. 1689. Col., 10 Aug. 1692. Served with great distinction through all the wars of King William and Queen Anne. Brig.-Gen., 22 March, 1693. Maj.-Gen., 27 April, 1697. Lt.-Gen., 11 Feb. 1703. Gen. of Horse, 31 Jan. 1711. Resigned the command of his Regt. in Dec. 1717. Govr. of Jersey and an M.P. D. 18 Oct. 1722, aged 63, and was bd. in a vault under Sawbridgeworth parish church, where is a marble monument to his memory.

[2] Son of Col. Thomas Panton of the King's Troop of Life Guards, temp. Charles II. Appointed Capt. in the Queen's Regt. of Horse, 20 April, 1695. Bt.-Lt.-Col., 25 Oct. 1703. Bt.-Col., 1 July, 1706. Served at Blenheim and on Marlborough's Staff at Malplaquet, where he was wounded. Brig.-Gen., 12 Feb. 1711. Maj.-Gen., 1 May, 1730. Lt.-Gen., 5 Nov. 1735. D. 20 July, 1753. It is related of this officer's father that he was a successful gamester, and having in one night won a sum sufficient to ensure him an estate worth £1,500 a year, he never tempted fortune again, but acquired a positive aversion to both cards and dice.

[3] Appointed Capt.-Lieut. in the Queen's Regt. of Horse, 14 Feb. 1694. Capt. 1 June, 1697. Served throughout Marlborough's campaigns. Brevet-Major, 1 Jan. 1707. Sold his Comns. as Major and Captain in Feb. 1718.

⁴ This surname may be identical with the Yorkshire surname of *Crowder*. Thos. Crowther entered the Army as Lieut. in the Duke of York's Maritime Regt. of Foot, 30 March, 1681. Cornet in the Queen's Regt. of Horse, 28 July, 1685. Capt. before 1689, Major, 10 Aug. 1692. Bt.-Col., 1 Jan. 1704. Regimental Lt.-Col., 5 Aug. 1704. Commanded above Regt. at Schellenberg (after Bt.-Col. Wm. Palmer had been mortally wounded) and Blenheim. Brig.-Gen., 1 Jan. 1706. Served at Malplaquet. Maj.-Gen., 1 Jan. 1710. Left the Regt. on promotion to Maj.-Gen., but was reappointed Major to the Queen's Regt. of Horse, 27 July, 1713, and was given a Tp. in the same corps, 19 April, 1714, on resigning the Majority to Bt.-Major John Morey. D. or left the Regt. before the accession of George II.

⁵ Son of the above Col. Panton. Was "Keeper of the King's Running Horses at Newmarket," *temp.* George II., and father of the beautiful Mary, Duchess of Ancaster, who d. 1793.

LORD WINDSOR'S REGIMENT OF HORSE.

[3RD DRAGOON GUARDS.]

NAME.	RANK.	DATE OF COMMISSION.
Lord Windsor,[1]	Col. & Capt.	—
Samuel Shute,[2]	Lieut.-Col. & Capt.	—
James Eaton,[3]	Major & Capt.	—
Thomas Hull,	Captain	[24 Aug. 1707.]
Sir John Beaumont Reney,	,,	
John Pitt,[4]	,,	[24 Nov. 1711.]
Thomas Armstrong,	[Capts.] Lieutenant	[,, ,,]
Thomas Hickes,	[Lieutenant]	[24 Dec. 1708.]
William Ashby,	,,	[25 Aug. 1704.]
Ralph Anderson,	,,	
George Stevenson,	,,	
Thomas Kentish,	,,	[24 Nov. 1711.]
Thomas Baldwin,	Cornet	[25 July, 1709.]
William Ireland,	,,	
William Sing,	,,	[24 Dec. 1708.]
Michael Armstrong,	,,	[24 Oct. 1710.]
Francis Litchfield,	,,	[24 Nov. 1711.]
Benjamin Tudman,	,,	[24 Feb. 1708.]
Thomas Heskett,	Chaplain	—
George Stevenson,	Adjutant	—
Alexander Seaton,	Surgeon	[24 Dec. 1708.]

[1] Son of Thomas Windsor-Hickman, first Earl of Plymouth, by his 2nd wife, Ursula Widdington. Created Visct. Windsor, in the peerage of Ireland, 19 June, 1699, by William III. for his war services in Flanders. Joined the Army as a Cornet in the Earl of Plymouth's Regt. of Horse (3rd D.G.), 15 Oct. 1687. Lt.-Col. of same Regt., 29 May, 1690. Colonel of a newly-raised Regt. of Horse, 16 Feb. 1694. Said corps was disbanded in 1697. Brig.-Gen., 9 March, 1702. Succeeded the Earl of Macclesfield as Col. of a Regt. of Horse, 10 March, 1702. Maj.-Gen., 1 Jan. 1704. Lt.-Gen., 1 Jan. 1707. Col. of the present 3rd Dragoon Guards, 18 May, 1712. Created Baron Montjoy in the peerage of England, 31 Dec. 1711. Retd. in March, 1717. D. in June, 1738, and was succeeded in his titles by his son Herbert.

[2] Appointed Capt. in Col. Windsor's Regt. of Horse, 16 Feb. 1694. Fought at Blenheim, where he was wounded. Bt.-Major, 1 Jan. 1707. Major, 24 Aug. same year. Bt.-Col., 16 Oct. 1712. Regtal. Lt.-Col. same year. Left the Regt., 8 May, 1716. Govr. of Massachusetts, 1716–23. D. 15 April, 1742, aged 80.

[3] This officer's name is spelt "Eyton" in some Lists. Appointed Lieut. in Col. Cornelius Wood's Regt. of Horse (3rd D.G.), 1 April, 1697. Fought at Blenheim, where he served as an A.D.C. Capt., 25 Aug. 1704. Served at Ramillies and Malplaquet. Bt.-Lt.-Col. of Horse, 1 Jan. 1712. Regtal. Major same year. Lt.-Col. of above Regt., 11 Aug. 1716. D in Nov. same year.

[4] This officer left above Regt. in 1714 on appointment to a Tp. in Pepper's Dragoons (see p. 112), then on the Irish Establishment, which may account for his being included in Lord Windsor's Regt. of Horse.

LORD COBHAM'S REGIMENT OF DRAGOONS.

[1st DRAGOONS.]

NAME.	RANK.	DATE OF COMMISSION.
Richard, Lord Cobham,[1]	Colonel	[13 June 1715.]
Edward Montague,[2]	Lt.-Col. & Capt.	
George Benson [Senr.],[3]	Major & Capt.	[17 Jan. 1706.]
James Crofts,[4]	Captain	
Henry Killigrew,	,,	
John Wyvill,	,,	
Lewis Dollon,*	,,	
Peter Renouard,*	,,	6 Nov. 1712.
Thomas Rogers,	Capt.-Lieut.	,, ,,
William Kitson,	Lieutenant	[14 Mar. 1706.]
Paul Mallide,	,,	[11 Aug. 1710.]
Samuel Southouse,	,,	6 Nov. 1712.
Thomas Friend,	,,	[3 Sept. 1707.]
Ernest Schaackman,	,,	
Francis Best,	,,	[1 Dec. 1703.]
Andrew Pancier,	,,	[17 Jan. 1705.]
William Brooks,	Cornet	18 Mar. 1714–15.
Charles Dilke,	,,	30 Jan. 1711–12.
George Benson [Junr.]	,,	[28 Nov. 1710.]
William Wentworth,	,,	[25 Mar. 1702.]
Adam Sadler,	,,	
Henry Carleil,	,,	
William Brooks,	,,	[6 Nov. 1712.]
John Memuille,	,,	[11 Jan. 1715.]
Francis Duret,	Chaplain	25 July, 1708.
Thomas Stevens,	Adjutant	[10 Aug. 1710.]
Isaac Fabre.	Surgeon	

* Troop added to Ker's Dragoons. See p. 111.—ED.

[1] See special memoir in Vol. II.

[2] Brother of George Montague, 2nd Baron and 1st Earl of Halifax. Appointed Ensign in the 1st Foot Guards 10 March, 1702. Exchanged to the Royal Dragoons a year or two later. Served with the said Corps in Spain and Portugal. Gained rapid promotion. Served as Lt.-Col. at Brihuega in 1710, and was taken prisoner. Commissions not forthcoming till 1711, when Edward Montague was given a Brevet Colonelcy of Dragoons, 15 Nov. 1711. Appointed Colonel of a Regt. of Foot, 13 July, 1715. (See p. 148.) Commanded said Infantry Corps at Sheriffmuir. Brig.-Gen., 10 Nov. 1735. D. 2 Aug. 1738.

[3] Appointed Lieut. in the Rl. Dragoons, 7 Aug. 1691. Capt. in 1704. Major, 17 Jan. 1706. Served in Spain and Portugal. Bt.-Lt.-Col. of Dragoons, 6 June, 1706. Regtal. Lt.-Col., 3 Oct. 1715. Comn. renewed by George II. in 1727. Out of the Army before July, 1737.

[4] Illegitimate son of the unfortunate Duke of Monmouth by Eleanor Needham. Appointed Cornet in the Queen's Regt. of Horse, 22 Aug. 1693. Capt. in the Rl. Dragoons, 6 May, 1695. Bt.-Lt.-Col., 1 Jan. 1704. Served in Spain, and was some time A.D.C. to King Charles III. Bt.-Col., 15 May, 1706. Brig.-Gen., 12 Feb. 1711. Regtal. Major Rl. Dragoons, 3 Oct. 1715. Col. of a newly-raised Regt. of Dragoons in Ireland, 17 July, 1717. Colonel of the Regt. of Dragoons now known as the 9th Lancers, 6 July, 1719. Major-General, 11 March, 1727. He md. the daughter of Sir Thos. Taylor (after 1706), and left a daughter at his decease in March, 1732, who md. R. Wentworth Smyth-Stuart, who claimed to be Monmouth's son by the Baroness Wentworth. There is a portrait of General James Crofts at Dalkeith Palace.

THE EARL OF PORTMORE'S ROYAL REGIMENT OF DRAGOONS.

[2ND DRAGOONS.]

NAME.	RANK.	DATE OF COMMISSION
David, Earl of Portmore,[1]	Col. & Capt.	
James Campbell,[2]	Lt.-Col. & Capt.	
Charles Cathcart,[3]	Major & Capt.	
Sir Robert Hay,[4]	Captain	
Patrick Robertson,[5]	,,	
William Crawford,*	,,	
George Dunbar,*	,,	
James Livingston,*	,,	
Henry Selwyn,	,,	31 May, 1715.
Thomas Agnew,	Capt.-Lieut.	
Charles Skeen,	Lieutenant	
James Lothian,	,,	
George Armstrong,	,,	
Robert Scott,	,,	
Andrew King,	,,	
William Delavally (sic)	,,	
Alexander Auchenleck,	,,	
James Gardiner,[6]	,,	
William Lawrence,	Cornet	
Alexander Agnew,	,,	
James Kennedy,[7]	,,	
Thomas Cockran,	,,	
John Bennett,	,,	
Alexander Forbes,	,,	
George Lauder,	,,	
George Knox,	,,	
James Agnew,	,,	
James Ramsay,	Chaplain	4 May, 1714.
James Nisbitt,	Surgeon	
Robert Scott,	Adjutant	

* Troop added to Ker's Dragoons. See p. 111.—ED.

[1] Elder son of Sir Alex. Robertson, Bt., who assumed the surname of Colyear. Gained military distinction when serving with the Scots Brigade in Flanders. Was Lt.-Col. of Col. Hugh Mackay's Regt. which accompanied William III. to England in Nov. 1688. Col. of a Regt. of Scots Foot (late Wauchope's), 31 Dec. same year. Saw much service in Ireland and Flanders. Created Baron Portmore in Scotland, 1 June, 1699, and advanced to an Earldom, 13 April, 1703. Col. of the Queen's Regt. of Foot, 27 Feb. 1703. C.-in-C. in Portugal, 1710-11. Appointed Colonel of the Scots Dragoons, 21 April, 1714. Governor of Gibraltar, 7 Aug. 1713. When this fortress was besieged, in 1727, Lord Portmore was sent from England to take command of the garrison. Attained the rank of General, 31 Jan. 1711. Knight of the Thistle. D. 2 Jan. 1730. By his marriage with Catherine Sedley, Countess of Dorchester, the Earl left an only surviving son, Charles, who succeeded as 2nd Earl of Portmore.

[2] Aftds. Gen. Sir James Campbell, K.B., who was killed at Fontenoy, where he commanded the Horse. See biog. notice on p. 221, note 52.

[3] Aftds. General Baron Cathcart. See biog. notice on p. 224, note 81.

[4] Son of Sir Jas. Hay, Bt., of Limplum. Appointed Capt. in the Scots Fusiliers, 25 Oct. 1704. Transferred to the Rl. Scots Dragoons in 1706. Served at Ramillies and

Oudenarde. Bt.-Major, 1 Nov, 1711. Regtal. Major, 16 Sept. 1715. Lt.-Col. of the Rl. Scots Dragoons, 27 May, 1717. Retd. in 1742. D. at Limplum 20 Dec. 1751.

[5] Cornet in the Scots Dragoons, 31 Dec. 1692. Lieut. in 1702 Capt., 10 Jan. 1707. Fought at Blenheim, and shared in Marlborough's subsequent victories. Wounded at Sheriffmuir. It is recorded in the *Records of the Scots Greys* that prior to Sheriffmuir the Earl of Mar attempted to seduce some of the officers and men of the Greys from their allegiance, employing a lady to carry a letter to Capt. Robertson. This underhand scheme proved fruitless. Promoted Major, 27 May, 1717. Commanded 3 Tps. of the Greys at Glenshiel, 10 June, 1719.

[6] The renowned Col. James Gardiner, who fell at Preston Pans in 1745.

[7] Sixth son of Sir Thos. Kennedy, Knt., of Kirkhill, who acquired the estates of Dalquharran and Dunure in Ayrshire. Capt. in Lord Mark Kerr's Regt. (29th Foot), 20 June, 1715. Major, 15 April, 1720. Served at the defence of Gibraltar in 1727. Lt.-Col. of the Earl of Rothes's Regt. of Foot, 30 June, 1737. Wounded at Fontenoy. Col. of the Regt. aftds. known as the 43rd Light Infantry, 7 Feb. 1746. Major-Gen., 28 Jan. 1756. Lt.-Gen. in March, 1761. D. same year. *See* memoir of this officer by Charles Dalton (also Gen. Kennedy's portrait) in the *Oxfordshire Light Infantry Chronicle* for 1899.

REGIMENT OF DRAGOONS COMMANDED BY GENERAL CARPENTER.

[3RD DRAGOONS.]

NAME.	RANK.	DATE OF COMMISSION.
George Carpenter,[1]	Colonel	
Josua Guest,*[2]	Lt.-Col.	
Samuel Foley,[3]	Major	
Alexander Mullen,	Captain	23 Dec. 1712.
Alexander Read,	,,	
Thomas Browne,	,,	
George Carpenter,[4]	Capt.-Lieut.	
William Ogle,	Lieutenant	22 June, 1713.
William Smelt,	,,	20 Mar. 1712–13.
John Hoare,	,,	24 Apr. 1713.
Richard White,	,,	
Abraham Dupuy,	,,	19 Aug. 1715.
Thomas Shore,	Cornet	7 Mar. 1710–11.
John Hawksworth,	,,	12 Apr. 1712.
William Carr,	,,	22 June, 1713.
Churchill Lloyd,	,,	
Thomas Haley,	,,	
Nathaniel Carpenter,	,,	6 June, 1706.
Philip Carpenter,	Adjutant	
Francis Gore,	Chaplain	
George Chape,	Surgeon	

* Jos. Guest, Captain, 15th April, 1707.

[1] Youngest son of a Royalist officer who was wounded at Naseby. Born at Pitches Ocul, co. Hereford, 10 Feb. 1657. Page to the Earl of Montagu in his embassy to Paris in 1671. Following year joined the 3rd Tp. of Life Guards as a Gentleman Private. Appointed Quartermaster to the Earl of Manchester's Tp. in the Earl of Peterborough's newly-raised Regt. of Horse (2nd D.G.), 27 June, 1685. Cornet, 1 June, 1687. Captain in 1689. Major 18 May, 1691. Lt.-Col. 1 Jan. 1692. Served during the Irish campaign and in Flanders. Col. of the above Regt. of Dragoons, 31 Dec. 1703. Purchased said Colonelcy for 1,800 guineas. Brig.-Gen., 25 Dec. 1705. Commanded a Cavalry Brigade at Almanza, where he particularly distinguished himself and covered the retreat of the Army. Major-Gen., 10 Sept. 1708. Commanded the Cavalry at Almenara, where he was wounded. Lt.-Gen., 1 Jan. 1710. Severely wounded and taken prisoner at Brihuega in Dec. 1710, when defending the breach. Actively employed in Scotland and England during the "Fifteen," and was senior General at the taking of Preston. Governor of Minorca, 5 July, 1716. Commander-in-Chief in Scotland, 1718–19. Created Baron Carpenter, 29 May, 1719. D. 10 Feb. 1731. Bd. at Ouselbury, Hants. General Carpenter published *A Dissertation on the Manœuvres of Cavalry.*

[2] A native of Halifax, Yorkshire. Believed to have served many years in the ranks (Chester's *Westminster Abbey Registers*, p. 373). Appointed Cornet in above Regt. 24 Feb. 1704. Capt. 15 April, 1707. Served at Almanza. Lt.-Col. 22 Dec. 1713. Brig.-Gen. 24 Nov. 1735. Maj.-Gen., 31 Dec. 1742. Lt.-Gen., 27 May, 1745. Barrack-Master-General in Scotland same year. Defended Edinburgh Castle against the Rebels in 1745. D. 14 Oct. 1747, aged 85. Bd. in Westminster Abbey.

[3] Son of Dr. Samuel Foley, Bishop of Down. Appointed Capt. in above Regt. 30 June, 1710. Major, 11 May, 1712. A.D.C. to the Duke of Ormonde in Flanders. Bt.-Lt.-Col. 5 June, 1713. Serving in 1740. Retd. in 1741.

[4] Succeeded his father as 2nd Baron Carpenter. Appointed Capt.-Lieut. and Bt.-Capt. in above Regt. 22 Dec. 1712. Capt in 1st Foot Guards, 19 Aug. 1715. Second Lt.-Col. of the 1st Troop of Life Guards, 24 Jan. 1730. D. 12 July, 1749.

THE EARL OF STAIR'S REGIMENT OF DRAGOONS.
[6TH DRAGOONS.]

NAME.	RANK.	DATE OF COMMISSION
Earl of Stairs[1] (*sic*)	Colonel	[4 Mar. 1715.]
John Upton,[2]	Lt.-Col. & Capt.	23 Feb. 1709–10.
[Chas.] Otway,[3]	Major and Capt.	
Ayleway Serjeant,	Captain	[22 Apr. 1702.]
James Dumas,	,,	
August Duquery,[4]	,,	28 Aug. 1708.
Lawrence Nugent,	,,	[24 Feb. 1714.]
Montague Farrer,	Capt.-Lieut.	,, ,,
Richard Hamilton,	Lieutenant	[24 Oct. 1699.]
Gervas Sibthorpe,	,,	23 Mar. 1713–14.
Edward Loftus,	,,	[13 Oct. 1707.]
Henry Barlow,	,,	[13 Sept. 1707.]
Francis Meres,	,,	7 Mar. 1712–13.
William Kennedy,	Cornet	[Out in 1717.]
William Nugent,	,,	[13 Oct. 1707.]
James Steuart,	,,	19 Aug. 1715.
Henry Strudwicke,	,,	20 Mar. 1713–14.
Philip Gasteen,	,,	18 Jan. 1708–9.
John Hay,	,,	20 Dec. 1709.
Pascall Ducas,	Chaplain	
Robert Wigham,	Adjutant	9 Dec. 1708.
Ralph Briscoe,	Surgeon	

[1] Succeeded his father as 2nd Earl of Stair in Jan. 1707. Is said to have served at Steinkirk as a Volunteer attached to the Cameronians (*Annals of the Earls of Stair*). Appointed 2nd Lt.-Col. of the Scots Foot Guards, 12 May, 1702. Was at the storming of Venlo fort and Liége citadel. Col. of a Scots Regt. in the service of Holland, 1703. Transferred to the Cameronians, 1 Jan. 1706. Brig.-Gen., same date. Fought at Ramillies. Col. of the Scots Greys, 24 Aug. 1706. Commanded a Brigade at Oudenarde, and was sent home with despatches. Was at the taking of Lille. Maj.-Gen. 1 Jan. 1709. Present at Malplaquet. Sent as Envoy to Warsaw in the winter of 1709. Lt.-Gen., 1 Jan. 1710. Gen., 5 April, 1712. Deprived of his Regt. in Jan. 1714 for political reasons. Lt.-Gen. of the Foot in Scotland, 20 Nov. 1714. Col. of the Inniskilling Dragoons, 4 March, 1715. Envoy to Paris same year. Was again deprived of his Regt. for political reasons in April, 1734. Field-Marshal, 18 March, 1742. C.-in-C. of the British Forces on the Continent, 21 April, 1742. Nominally commanded the British and their Allies at Dettingen. Resigned his command in Sept. 1743. D.s.p. 9 May, 1747.

[2] Of Castle Upton, co. Antrim. M.P. for said county. Father of the 1st Baron Templetown. Appointed Capt. in Maj.-Gen. Steuart's Regt. of Foot, 15 July, 1697. Served with said Corps at the storming of Liége citadel and at Almanza. Lt.-Col. of Pepper's Dragoons, 12 April, 1709. Transferred to the Inniskilling Dragoons, as above. Bt.-Col., 15 Nov. 1711. Served at Sheriffmuir. Retd. 19 June, 1716.

[3] Appointed Capt. in Lord Mohun's Regt. of Foot in March, 1702. Promoted Major in Lord Slane's Regt. on the Irish Establishment before 1711 (Comn. entry not forthcoming). Placed on half-pay in 1712. Made Major of the Inniskilling Dragoons, 22 July, 1715. Served at Sheriffmuir. Lt.-Col. of Inniskilling Dragoons, 19 June, 1716. Col. of the Regt. aftds. known as the 35th Foot, 26 July, 1717. Brig.-Gen., 28 Nov. 1735. Maj.-Gen., 2 July, 1739. Retained the Colonelcy of his Regt. till his death as a full General in 1764.

[4] Appointed Capt. of an additional Tp. in above Regt., 21 Aug. 1708. Served at Sheriffmuir. Major, 19 June, 1716. The Rev. Robert Wodrow thus refers, under date of July, 1724, to this officer's death : " Towards the end of this month Major Du Cary (*sic*),

who commanded the forces in Glasgow, came back to Glasgow and dyed on the road, at the King's well. He had been ill for some time, and is much regretted. He was a French Protestant and a good soldier, and a very blameless man" (*Analecta*, Vol. III., p. 161). In the Burial Register of the High Church, Glasgow, for 1724, occurs this entry: "Augustus Dukerie, Major to the Earl of Stair's Regt. of Dragoons, buried, 15 July, 1724." His son William was buried 13 Sept. 1724.

COLONEL KERR'S REGIMENT OF DRAGOONS.

[7TH DRAGOONS.]

NAME.	RANK.	DATE OF COMMISSION.
William Kerr,[1]	Colonel	31 Jan. 1714–15.
James, Lord Torphichen,[2]	Lt.-Col.	,, ,,
Matthew Steuart,[3]	Major	,, ,,
Lewis Dollon,*	Captain	———
Peter Renouard,*	,,	———
William Crawford,†	,,	———
George Dunbar,†	,,	———
James Livingston,†	,,	31 Jan. 1714–15.
David Ogilvie,	Capt.-Lieut.	———
Alexander Auchenleck,	Lieutenant	———
William Delavale,	,,	———
James Ogilvy,	,,	———
Samuel Southouse,	,,	———
Bernard Lustau,	,,	15 June, 1715.
William Richardson,	Cornet	———
George Lawther (*sic*)	,,	———
George Knox,	,,	———
James Agnew,[4]	,,	———
[Henry] Carlisle,	,,	———
John Keat,	,,	———
James Ramsay,	Chaplain	———
William Johnson,	Adjutant	———
Patrick Telfer,	Surgeon	———

* Troop transferred from Royal Dragoons.—ED.
† Troop transferred from Scots Dragoons.—ED.

[1] The Hon. Wm. *Ker*, brother to the 1st Duke of Roxburghe. Appointed Colonel of above Regt., 10 Oct. 1709. Served in Flanders, 1710–1712. Comn. renewed, 31 Jan. 1715, the Regt. having been broke in 1714, but restored by George I. Col. Ker was wounded at Sheriffmuir, and had two horses shot. Brig.-Gen., 18 May, 1727. Governor of Blackness Castle, 19 Nov. 1723. Maj.-Gen., 10 Nov. 1735. Lt.-Gen., 2 July, 1739. M.P. for Berwick some years, and held the post of Groom of the Bedchamber to George, Prince of Wales. D., unm., 7 Jan. 1741.

[2] Seventh Baron, Capt. in Lord Mar's Foot, 1702. Appointed Lt.-Col. of Ker's Dragoons before 1713 (Comn. register not forthcoming). Served at Sheriffmuir. Retd. in June, 1720. D. 10 Aug. 1753.

[3] Lieut. in Col. Ric. Cunningham's Scots Dragoons, 7 Feb. 1695. Capt.-Lieut., 29 March, 1711. Appointed Major when the Regt was restored by George I. Comn. renewed by George II. in 1727. Out of the Regt. in 1733.

[4] One of the younger sons of Sir Andrew Agnew, Bart., of Lochnaw. Promoted Lieut., 10 May, 1718. Capt., 11 April, 1723. Major, 4 April, 1733. Serving in last-named Regt. in 1748. Out of the Army before April, 1755. D. in 1770.

GENERAL PEPPER'S REGIMENT OF DRAGOONS.

[8TH DRAGOONS.]

NAME.	RANK.	DATE OF COMMISSION.
John Pepper,[1]	Colonel & Captain	—
Thomas Erle,[2]	Lt.-Col. & Capt.	—
Abraham (sic) Bellamy,[3]	Major and Captain	—
James Pelham,	Captain	—
Edward Wills,	,,	—
[John] Pitt,[4]	,,	—
Thomas Eckhlyn,	Capt.-Lieut.	—
Christopher Zobell,	Lieutenant	—
John Hinton,	,,	—
William Kerr,	,,	—
Richard Harwood,	,,	—
Vincent Peyton,	,,	—
Robert Stevenson,	Cornet	—
Samuel Blount,	,,	—
James Johnson,	,,	—
George Pepper,	,,	—
Guy Vissouse,	,,	—
John Withers,	,,	—

[1] Appointed Capt. in the Earl of Roscommon's Regt. of Foot, in Ireland, March, 1689. Transferred in 1690 to Col. Thos. Erle's Regt. of Foot. Served throughout the Irish campaign. Appointed Capt. in Col. Henry Conyngham's newly-raised Regt. of Dragoons (the present 8th Hussars) in Feb. 1693. Promoted Major, 1 Nov. 1695. Served with his Regt. in the Peninsula during the War of the Spanish Succession. Regtal. Lt.-Colonel before 1707. Brig.-Gen., 1 Jan. 1707. Succeeded to the command of the Regt., 15 April, 1707. Commanded a Cavalry Brigade at the battle of Almanza, where he distinguished himself and gained additional honour at Saragossa (Cannon's *Records of the 8th Hussars*). Maj.-Gen., 1 Jan. 1710. Taken prisoner at Bribuega same year. Returned to England in 1712. Actively employed in England during the '15. Sold his Commission in 1719. Was aftds. a Member of Parliament, Ranger of Epping Forest and Enfield Chase. D. at Montpellier in France, 22 Dec. 1725. His present representative lives at Ballygarth Castle, Julianstown, near Drogheda.

[2] Appointed Exempt and Capt. in the 3rd Tp. of Life Guards, 12 June, 1701. Major of the Artillery Train in Spain, 31 Jan. 1708. Major of Brigadier Pepper's Dragoons, then serving in the Peninsula, 24 Dec. 1708. Served at Almenara and Saragossa. Capt. of a Tp. in said Regt., 9 Aug. 1710. Taken prisoner at Brihuega in Dec. same year. Commanded Pepper's Dragoons at Hexham in 1717 (see p. 69). Out of the Regt. in 1722. Father of Major-General Thos. Erle, Colonel of the 28th Regt. of Foot, who d. in 1777.

[3] *Adam* Bellamy. Appointed Capt. in above Regt., 13 Dec. 1706. Served in Spain during the War of the Spanish Succession. Promoted Major before 11 Jan. 1715. On 5 Feb. 1717, Sir John Hedges writes to ——— in favour of "his cousin Major Bellamy concluding the purchase of Brigadier Wm. Steuart's commission as Lt.-Col. of Col. James Campbell's Regt. of Foot" (*S.P.D.* George I., Bundle 8). Major Bellamy d. in Nov. 1718, while serving with Gen. Pepper's Regt.

[4] Youngest son of Thos. Pitt, Governor of Fort St. George, Madras, and brother to Col. Thos. Pitt, who was created Earl of Londonderry. John Pitt was appointed Cornet in Lord Berkeley's Regt. of Horse, 15 Feb. 1693. Lieut., 27 March, 1699. Fought at Blenheim. Capt.-Lieut., 24 Aug. 1707. Served at Oudenarde and Malplaquet. Capt. in Pepper's Dragoons, 1 March, 1714. Exchanged to Col. Thos. Pitt's Regt. of Horse, 20 Jan. 1716. Capt. and Lt.-Col. 1st Foot Guards, 5 June, 1717. A.D.C. to George I., 24 Oct. 1719. Governor of Bermuda, 1718-37. M.P. for Hindon, Camelford, and Old Sarum. D. 1744.

GENERAL WYNN'S REGIMENT OF DRAGOONS.

[9TH DRAGOONS.]

NAME.	RANK.	DATE OF COMMISSION.
Owen Wynn,[1]	Col. & Capt.	————
Hugh Pearson,[2]	Lt.-Col. & Capt.	————
John Dunbarr,[3]	Major & Capt.	————
Lord Leslie,[4]	Captain	————
[Andrew ?] Knox,	,,	————
Henry Smith,	,,	————
[Henry] Crawford,	Capt.-Lieut.	————
William Witherington,	Lieutenant	————
Edward Whitney,	,,	————
William Humphreys.	,,	————
Jacob Warnes,	,,	————
Gustavus Hamilton,	,,	————
Owen Wynn,	Cornet	————
William Carleton,	,,	————
Lewis Foliott,	,,	————
James Hill,	,,	————
—— Pemberton,	,,	————
Christopher Adams,	,,	————

[1] Son of Owen *Wynne* and younger brother to Brig.-Gen. James Wynne, the first Colonel of the Rl. Irish Dragoons. Owen Wynne was probably the — Wynne appointed Capt. in the Earl of Roscommon's Regt. of Foot in March, 1689. Major of the Rl. Irish Dragoons, 1 Nov. 1694. Lt.-Col. 20 July, 1695. Bt.-Col. of Dragoons, 1 Jan. 1703. Fought at Blenheim. Col. of a newly-raised Regt. of Foot, 25 March, 1705. Brig.-Gen., 1 June, 1706. Maj.-Gen. 1 Jan. 1709. Col. of the above Regt. of Dragoons (the present 9th Lancers), 22 July, 1715. Lt.-Gen. 1 March, 1727. Transferred to the Colonelcy of the 5th Horse (4th D.G.), 6 July, 1719. Col. of the Irish Dragoons, 6 Aug. 1732. D. 28 Feb. 1737.

[2] This officer was appointed Adjt.-Gen. to the British Forces in Spain, by Gen. Stanhope, 1 Aug. 1708. Lt.-Col. of Col. Robert Dalzell's Regt. of Foot, 24 Dec. 1709. Taken prisoner at Brihuega in 1710. Placed on half-pay in 1713. Lt.-Col. of above Regt. of Dragoons at its raising. D. in July, 1716. This officer may possibly have served in Col. Henry Pearson's English Regt. of Horse in the service of Portugal, *circa* 1665.

[3] This officer married Catherine Wynne, sister to Maj.-Gen. Owen Wynne. He was appointed Capt.-Lieut. of Col. Owen Wynne's newly-raised Regt. of Foot, 25 March, 1705. Captain's Commission dated same day. Major, 15 Oct. 1711. Served at the siege of Douay in 1710. Half-pay, 1713. Major of Wynne's Dragoons, 22 July, 1715. On half-pay in 1722.

[4] John, Lord Leslie, succeeded his father as 9th Earl of Rothes in 1722. Capt. and Lt.-Col. 3rd Foot Guards, 17 July, 1717. Lt.-Col. of Sir James Wood's Regt. (Scots Fusiliers) before 1727. Col. of the King's Own Borderers, 29 May, 1732—25 April, 1745. Brig.-Gen. 2 July, 1739. Fought at Dettingen. Major-Gen. 1 Jan. 1743. Lt.-Gen. 5 Aug. 1747. K.T. Commanded the Forces in Ireland, 1751. D. 1767.

BRIGADIER GORE'S REGIMENT OF DRAGOONS.

[10TH DRAGOONS.]

NAME.	RANK.	DATE OF COMMISSION.
Humphrey Gore,[1]	Col. & Capt.	——
Peter Hawker,[2]	Lt.-Col. & Capt.	——
Paston Knevet,[3]	Major & Capt.	——
[Balthazar] Guidet,[4]	Captain	——
George Treby,	,,	——
[John] Witterong,	,,	——
[Israel] Presseley,	Capt.-Lieut.	——
Henry Gore,	Lieutenant	——
John Jordan,	,,	——
Robert Blount,	,,	——
Andrew Purcell,	,,	——
Henry Courtney,	,,	——
Francis Boucher,	Cornet	——
William Prosser,	,,	——
William Stannus,	,,	——
Peter Chabane,[5]	,,	——
Thomas Hincks,	,,	——
Thomas Crawley,	,,	——

[1] Appointed Exempt and Capt. in the 2nd Troop of Life Guards in June, 1699. Lt.-Col. of Lord Cutts's newly-raised Regt. of Dragoons in 1704. Colonel of a newly-raised Regt. of Foot, 1 Feb. 1707. Served several campaigns in Spain. Brig.-Gen. 1 Jan. 1710. Fought at Almenara and Saragossa. Taken prisoner at Brihuega, where he lost all his Commissions and baggage. Raised above Regt. of Dragoons in July, 1715. Transferred to the Royal Dragoons, 12 Jan. 1723. Maj.-Gen. 6 March, 1727. Lt.-Gen. 27 Oct. 1735. Governor of Kinsale. D. 8 Aug. 1739.

[2] Of Long Parish, Co. Hants. According to the pedigree of the Hawker family in Burke's *Landed Gentry* this officer was son of Peter Hawker. He was appointed Lieut. in the Queen's Dragoons, 26 May, 1691. Capt.-Lieut. 29 March, 1694. Capt. 1 Aug. 1696. Capt. in Sir Richard Temple's newly-raised Regt. of Foot, 10 March, 1702. Major of Lord Cutts's Regt. of Dragoons in Ireland, 1704. Lt.-Col., 20 March, 1708. Served in Spain. Taken prisoner at Brihuega. Bt.-Col. 1 Jan. 1712. Lt.-Col. of Gore's Dragoons, 22 July, 1715. Left the Regt in March, 1720. Lt.-Gov. of Portsmouth at the time of his death, which occurred in 1733. *Gentleman's Magazine.*

[3] Appointed Ens. to the Colonel's Cy. in Col. Roger Elliot's newly-raised Regt. of Foot, 10 April, 1703. Lieut. 25 Dec. same year. Capt. in Col. Edmund Soame's Regt. of Foot, 25 March, 1705. Major, 10 Aug. 1709. Served in Portugal, 1708–9. Half-pay, 1713. Major of Gore's Dragoons, 22 July, 1715. Retd. on half-pay, 5 Sept. 1717. Drawing half-pay in 1722.

[4] His first Commission appears to have been as Adjt. to the Rl. Dragoons, 6 July, 1686. Major in Col. Slingsby's Horse, 8 Oct. 1688. Capt. in Rl. Regt. of Foot, 13 March, 1691. Capt. in the Earl of Essex's Dragoons, 16 Feb. 1694. Capt. in Cunningham's Dragoons (7th Hussars), 1 Oct. 1696. Serving in last-named Regt. when it was reduced in 1714. Capt. in Gore's Dragoons, 22 July, 1715. Retd. 25 Dec. 1717.

[5] Promoted Capt. 25 Aug. 1739. Major, 31 Aug. 1744. In March, 1755, a Royal Warrant signed "H. Fox" granted "the sum of 5s. per diem to Major [Peter] Chaban for the term of his natural life, on his being replaced in the 10th Dragoons by the promotion of Capt. Wm. Augustus Pitt of the same Regt. to be allowed out of the pay of the said Major Pitt, or the Major of Our said Regt., and that upon his death the Major of Our said Regt. for the time being shall receive pay conformable to the establishment." Extract from "War Office Miscellany Book," quoted in the Hon. John Fortescue's *Memoirs of the Tenth Royal Hussars*, p. 10, note.

GENERAL SIR PHILIP HONYWOOD, K.B.

BRIGADIER HONYWOOD'S REGIMENT OF DRAGOONS.
[11TH DRAGOONS.]

NAME.	RANK.	DATE OF COMMISSION.
Philip Honywood,[1]	Col. & Capt.	—
A. Hamilton,[2]	Lt.-Col. & Capt.	—
Humphrey Bland,[3]	Major & Capt.	—
John Suckling,	Captain	—
Benjamin Hauffum,	,,	—
William Robinson,	,,	—
John Maitland,	Capt.-Lieut.	—
William Lemmon,	Lieutenant	—
James Mawle,	,,	—
[James] Malkain (sic)	,,	—
Charles Steuart,	,,	—
John Matchell,	,,	—
John Campbell,	Cornet	—
William Robert Adaire,	,,	—
Charles Wheeler,	,,	—
John Burroughs,	,,	—
William Gardiner,	,,	—
[Robert] Watts,	,,	—

[1] "Second son of Charles Ludovic Honywood and brother of Robert Honywood of Charing, Kent, and Markshall, Essex" (*Historical Records of the XIth Hussars*, by Godfrey Williams, p. 366). Ensign in Col. the Hon. Jas. Stanley's Regt. 12 June, 1694. Capt. in the Royal Fusiliers, 1 April, 1696. Capt. in the Earl of Huntingdon's newly-raised Regt. of Foot, 10 March, 1702. Bt.-Major, 1 Dec. 1703. Saw service in Flanders and Spain. Col. of Col. Roger Townshend's Regt. of Foot, 27 May, 1709. Brig.-Gen. in 1710. Deprived of his Regt. same year for drinking at a dinner, in Flanders, the toast of "Damnation and confusion to the new Ministry, and to those who had any hand in turning out the old." Col. of the Regt. now known as the 11th Hussars, 22 July, 1715, which post he held until May, 1732. Commanded a Brigade at Preston in 1715, where he was wounded, and at Vigo in 1719. Transferred to the Colonelcy of the Regt. now known as the 3rd Hussars, 29 May, 1732. Commanded a Division at Dettingen. Col. of the K.D.G. 18 April, 1743. Created K.B. for his eminent services. D. 17 June, 1752, with the rank of General, and was interred at Portsmouth, of which place he was Governor at the time of his decease.

[2] "Eighth son of Wm. Hamilton of Ballyfatton, Co. Donegal" (*Records of XIth Hussars*, p. 351). Appointed 2nd Lieut. of the Grenadier Cy. in Col. Beaumont's Regt. 2 May, 1689. Served at the Boyne and in Flanders. Capt. 6 March, 1691. Major of Visct. Mountjoy's Regt. of Foot, 28 June, 1701. Commanded this Regt. at Almanza, and was taken prisoner. Lt.-Col. of Dubourgay's Foot, 8 Sept. 1711. Half-pay, 1712. Lt.-Col. of Honywood's Dragoons, 22 July, 1715. Served at Preston. Col. of the Inniskilling Fusiliers, 29 May, 1732. Brig.-Gen. 2 July, 1739. Transferred to the Colonelcy of the 14th Dragoons (present 14th Hussars), 27 June, 1737. Commanded this Regt. at Prestonpans in 1745. Maj.-Gen. 1 July, 1743. Lt.-Gen. 4 Aug. 1747. D. in Dublin 8 July, 1749.

[3] Of Blandsfort, Queen's County. This officer is said to have served several campaigns under Marlborough (Cannon's *Records 3rd Hussars*), but his earliest Commission traceable is that of Major to Col. Frederick Sibourg's Regt. of French Foot, 9 July, 1709. He was wounded at the battle of Almenara in 1710. Half-pay in 1712. Major of Honywood's Dragoons, 22 July, 1715. Recd. £100, 28 Feb. 1716, for conducting prisoners from Preston to London (*Treasury Papers*). Lt.-Col. Rl. Regt. of Horse, 26 March, 1718. Col. of the 36th Foot, 27 June, 1737. Transferred to the Colonelcy of the 13th Dragoons, 9 Jan. 1741. Col. Rl. Dragoons, 18 April, 1743. Horse shot under him at Dettingen. Fought at Fontenoy and Culloden. Brig.-Gen. 10 Jan. 1743. Maj.-Gen. 30 March, 1745. Lt.-Gen. 12 Sept. 1747. C.-in-C. in Scotland, 1747. Governor of Gibraltar, 1748-1751. Col. of the present 1st Dragoon Guards, 8 July, 1752. D. 8 May, 1763. General H. Bland was author of *Bland's Military Discipline*—a well-known eighteenth-century work.

BRIGADIER BOWLES'S REGIMENT OF DRAGOONS.
[12TH DRAGOONS.]

NAME.	RANK.	DATE OF COMMISSION.
Phineas Bowles,[1]	Col. & Capt.	———
T. Strickland,[2]	Lt.-Col. & Capt.	———
John Orfeur,[3]	Major & Capt.	———
John Pierson,	Captain	———
Giles Stevens,	,,	———
John Prideaux,	,,	———
William Wills,	Capt.-Lieut.	———
William Bourden,	Lieutenant	———
Christopher Bland,	,,	———
James Baker,	,,	———
John Johnson,	,,	———
Hugh Hilton,	,,	———
William Pomfrett,	Cornet	———
Thomas Johnson,	,,	———
Richard Hull,	,,	———
William Pierce,	,,	———
Bret Norton,	,,	———
—— Forfar,	,,	———

[1] Appointed Ensign in the Queen Dowager's Regt. of Foot, 3 Oct. 1688. Capt.-Lieut. 1 Feb. 1692. Little or nothing is known of his early career in the Army. He succeeded Col. John Caulfield in the command of an Irish Regt. of Foot, 14 July, 1705, and served with the same in Spain. Fought at Almanza, where he was taken prisoner. Returned to England same year on his parole. Rejoined his corps in Spain and fought at Saragossa. Was sent to England with the Colours captured at the last-named battle. From Col. Bowles's "Memorial" to the Treasury dated 11 July, 1711, it appears that he brought these trophies home "by the way of Italy at a very great expense for which he had received no consideration" (*S.P.D. Anne*, Bundle 20). Brig.-Gen. 12 Feb. 1711. Raised the Corps now known as the 12th Lancers in July, 1715. Transferred to the Colonelcy of the 8th Dragoons, 23 March, 1719. Appointed Quartermaster-General in Ireland, 30 May, 1720. D. 19 Nov. 1722. He left a son Phineas, who d. a Maj.-Gen. in 1739.

[2] Thos. Strickland was appointed Cornet in the Carabiniers, 25 Aug. 1704 Believed to be identical with the Thos. Strickland who was commissioned Capt. in Borr's Marines, 23 March, 1708. Resigned his Commission in Feb. 1710, but evidently was appointed Lt.-Col. to a Regt. serving in Spain, as the name of "Lt.-Col. Strickland" appears in the list of Field Officers taken prisoners at Brihuega (*English Army Lists and Commission Registers*, Vol.VI., p. 386). Lt.-Col. of Bowles's Dragoons, 22 July, 1715. D. of wounds received in a duel with Capt. Prideaux at Henley in Dec. 1715 (*Historical Register*). He probably belonged to the Irish family of this surname.

[3] Succeeded Lt.-Col. Strickland as Regtal. Lt.-Col. in Dec. 1715. "He was fifth son of William Orfeur of Highclose. Sheriff of Cumberland, 1676-7, by Elizabeth, daughter of Sir Charles Howard of Ridsdale, Co. Northumberland. He is said to have been a page to Princess (afterwards Queen) Anne. Started as Ensign in the Earl of Huntingdon's Foot (now Somersetshire L.I.), 20 June, 1685. As Capt. distinguished himself, 12 Sept. 1691, against the Irish rebels near Lismore, Co. Cork. Served with Viscount Shannon's Regt. of Marines in the Vigo Expedition, 1702. Bt.-Col. 1712. Appointed Maj. in Brig. Phineas Bowles's Regt. of Dragoons (now 12th Lancers) at its formation, 1715. Appointed Brig.-Gen. 1735. He was unmarried, and died a Major-General in 1741 in extreme old age." Communicated by Col. W. O. Cavenagh (a kinsman of Gen. Orfeur), a member of whose family possesses a very small miniature of the Duke of Cumberland (the "Butcher"), which he is said to have presented to Gen. Orfeur with these words : "I present you this miniature likeness as a token of my esteem for your valuable services to your King, to your Country, and to me ; it will provide for your succeeding generations when presented to my succeeding generations."

BRIGADIER MUNDEN'S REGIMENT OF DRAGOONS.

[13TH DRAGOONS.]

NAME.	RANK.	DATE OF COMMISSION.
Richard Munden,[1]	Col. & Capt.	———
Clement Nevill,[2]	Lt.-Col. & Capt.	———
Samuel Freeman,[3]	Major & Capt.	———
Francis Howard,	Captain	———
Lutton Lister,	,,	———
[W.] Heblethwayte,	,,	———
Henry de Grangues,[4]	Capt.-Lieut.	———
Philip Bridgman,	Lieutenant	———
Thomas Mason,	,,	———
Francis Hull,	,,	———
Henry Dawson,	,,	———
John Molyneux,	,,	———
Gerald Fitzgerald,	Cornet	———
Charles Greenwood,	,,	———
William Freeman,	,,	———
William Williamson,	,,	———
John Watson,	,,	———
Martin Obryan,	,,	———

[1] Son of Sir Richard Munden, Knt. Appointed Capt. and Lt.-Col. in the 1st Foot Guards, 22 April, 1702. In his application to Marlborough for the command of a Regt., in 1706, Col. Munden says: "Has spent a good part of his estate in the Service and had the honour to command the Battalion of Guards at Schellenberg." Lt.-Col. of Lord Lovelace's Regt. of Foot, 12 April, 1706. Col. of said Corps, 20 March, 1708. Brig.-Gen. 12 Feb. 1712. Raised the 13th Dragoons in July, 1715. Present with his Regt. at the taking of Preston. Took part in the funeral procession of the Duke of Marlborough in Aug. 1722. Left the Army in November following.

[2] Appointed Lieut. in Sir John Hanmer's Regt. of Foot, 1 Feb. 1692. Capt. 9 April, 1703. Major of Lord Lovelace's Regt. 31 Aug. 1706. Taken prisoner at Brihuega in 1710. Bt.-Col. 15 Nov. 1711. Lt.-Col. of Munden's Dragoons, 22 July, 1715. Col. of the 14th Dragoons, 9 April, 1720. Transferred to 8th Dragoons, 27 June, 1737. Removed to 6th Horse (5th D.G.), 6 May, 1740. Brig.-Gen. 5 Nov. 1735. Maj.-Gen. 2 July, 1739. Lieut.-Gen., 1 Feb. 1743. D. in Dublin, 1744. Probably son of Clement Nevill, brother to Col. Henry Smyth *alias* Nevill of Holt.

[3] Appointed Capt.-Lieut. of Sir Robert Peyton's Regt. of Foot, 28 Feb. 1689. Capt. in Dec. 1691. Exchanged to Col. Samuel Venner's Regt. of Foot. Comn. as Capt. in latter Regt. renewed in 1702. Major of Col. Nicholas Price's Regt. of Foot, 1 Sept. 1706. Half-pay in 1713. Major of Munden's Dragoons, 22 July, 1715. Present at the taking of Preston. Serving in 1717. Not in any subsequent List.

[4] On 22 July, 1707, Henry de Grangues was appointed Capt. in Baron Waleffe's French Regt. of Dragoons in the Dutch Service. This Comn. was signed by Marlborough, and appears in the War Office Comn. Book for 1712. On 14 July, 1712, De Grangues was appointed Major of Baron de Borle's Dragoons, his Comn. being signed by the Duke of Ormonde at Château Cambresis. Placed on half-pay on the English Establishment in 1713. Capt.-Lieut. of Munden's Dragoons, 22 July, 1715. Major of Sir Robt. Rich's Dragoons, with seniority in the Army from 14 July, 1712, before 1727. Lt.-Col. of the 14th Dragoons, 1 July, 1737. Col. of a newly-raised Regt. of Foot, numbered the 60th but aftds. disbanded, 21 Jan. 1741. Transferred to the Colonelcy of the 30th Foot, 24 Oct. 1742. Col. of the 9th Dragoons, 1 April, 1743. Brig.-Gen. 10 June, 1745. Col. 7th D G. 1 Nov. 1749. Maj.-Gen. 24 Sept. 1747. D. in June, 1754. Will proved at Dublin.

BRIGADIER DORMER'S REGIMENT OF DRAGOONS.

[14th DRAGOONS.]

NAME.	RANK.	DATE OF COMMISSION.
James Dormer,[1]	Col. & Capt.	———
Henry Killigrew,[2]	Lt.-Col. & Capt.	———
Sol. Rapin,[3]	Major & Capt.	———
Henry Pelham,[4]	Captain	———
William Boyle,	,,	———
Beverly Newcomin,[5]	,,	———
James Stevens,	Capt.-Lieut.	———
Henry Lasalle,	Lieutenant	———
Peter Davenport,	,,	———
Jonathan Pirke,	,,	———
Cuthbert Smith,	,,	———
James Fleming,	,,	———
Edward Stroude,	Cornet	———
Thomas Ellis,	,,	———
Thomas Delahaye,	,,	———
William Hamilton,	,,	———
William Molyneux,	,,	———
Andrew Forrester,	,,	———

[1] Son of Robert Dormer of Dorton, Bucks. Appointed Lieut. and Capt. in the 1st Foot Guards, 1 May, 1702. Capt. and Lt.-Col. 4 April, 1704. Fought at Blenheim, where he was wounded, and at Ramillies. Bt.-Col. 1 Jan. 1707. Col. of Lord Mohun's late Regt. of Foot, 1 May, 1708. Embarked for Spain in 1709. Distinguished himself at the battle of Saragossa. Present at the taking of Madrid. Taken prisoner at Brihuega in 1710. On his return to England on parole he recovered £200 from the Treasury for losses in Spain by pillage. Brig.-Gen. 12 Feb. 1711. Raised the 14th Dragoons in 1715. Served at the taking of Preston, and was slightly wounded. Succeeded his brother Robert (see p. 95) in the Colonelcy of the 6th Foot, 9 April, 1720. Maj.-Gen. 14 March, 1727. Envoy to Portugal same year. Lt.-Gen. 4 Nov. 1735. Col. of the 1st Troop of Horse Grenadier Guards, 10 Feb. 1738. Governor of Hull, 1740. D. 24 Dec. 1741.

[2] Brother to Col. Robt. Killigrew. Appointed Capt. in the Earl of Huntingdon's Regt. of Foot, 10 March, 1702. Transferred to the Rl. Dragoons in Oct. 1703. Served in Portugal and Spain. Bt.-Lt.-Col. of Dragoons, 30 Sept. 1710. Lt.-Col. of Dormer's Dragoons, 22 July, 1715. Served at Preston. Left the Regt. in Dec. 1717. On 30 Nov. 1716 a marriage licence was granted to Henry Killigrew, Esq., of St. James, Westminster, bachelor, 35, and Mrs. Frances Maria Bucknall of St. Ann, Westminster.

[3] Brother to Paul Rapin the historian. Appointed Ens. in Col. the Marquis la Caillemotte's Regt. of French Foot, 1 April, 1689. Capt. of Capt. Paul Rapin's Company in Col. Thos. Brudenell's Regt. of Foot, 18 March, 1696. Capt. in Lord Mohun's Regt. 10 March, 1702. Fought at the Boyne and in Spain. Half-pay, 1713. Major of Dormer's Dragoons, 22 July, 1715. Served at Preston. There are several letters from this officer among the uncalendared George I. S.P. for 1716. Said letters are endorsed "Col. Rapin." Is said to have d. about 1719, and to have then held the rank of Lt.-Col. See "Account of the Rapin Family" in Rapin's *Hist. of England*, Vol. I., p. ix.

[4] Second son of the 1st Baron Pelham. Raised a Troop for Dormer's Regt. and commanded it at the taking of Preston in Nov. 1715. Resigned his Commission on 3 June, 1717. Appointed Secretary-at-War in 1725. Was subsequently Paymaster-General of the Forces. First Lord of the Treasury, 1743. Chancellor of the Exchequer same year. D. 1754.

[5] Fifth son of Sir T. Newcomen, Bt., killed at the siege of Enniskillen in 1689. This veteran gave the following account of his services when applying to the Duke of Marlborough for a Troop in the New Levies of 1706: "Made an Ensign in the Lord Forbes's

Regt. in the year 1686. In 1689 he served at the battle of Killicranky as Lieut. in Colonel Hastings's Regt. and has been in Major-General Ross's Regt. of Dragoons ever since 1695." Served several campaigns under Marlborough. Is believed to have fought at Malplaquet. Capt. in Dormer's Dragoons, 22 July, 1715. Bt. Lt.-Col. in the Army, 1 Dec. 1720. Regtal. Lt.-Col. before 1727. Commission renewed by George II. D. 1731.

COLONEL NEWTON'S REGIMENT OF DRAGOONS.

[*Disbanded in Oct.* 1718.]

NAME.	RANK.	DATE OF COMMISSION.
William Newton,[1]	Col. & Capt.	——
J. Moyle,[2]	Lt.-Col. & Capt.	——
George Knightly,[3]	Major & Capt.	——
Samuel Speed,[4]	Captain	——
[Wm.] Preston,	,,	——
John Hamilton,	,,	——
Robert Maxwell,	Capt.-Lieut.	——
Thomas Carfrae,	Lieutenant	——
William Higgenson,	,,	——
John Kynaston,	,,	——
Samuel Oakley,	,,	——
Charles Keightly,	,,	——
James Halden (*sic*),	Cornet	——
Hugh MacMullan,	,,	——
Edward Rich,	,,	——
John English,	,,	——
John Penny,	,,	——
Stephen Segula,	,,	——

[1] Appointed Lieut. and Capt. in the 1st Foot Guards, 9 Nov. 1692. Wounded at the siege of Namur. Major of Sir Richard Temple's newly-raised Regt. of Foot, 13 Feb. 1702. Lt.-Col. 25 Aug. 1704. Bt.-Col. 1 Jan. 1707. Fought at Malplaquet. Col. 24 April, 1710. Half-pay, 1713. Lt.-Gov. of Chester in Feb. 1715. Raised above Regt. of Dragoons in July, 1715. When the Rebels marched into Lancashire and occupied Preston, General Wills left Col. Newton with his Dragoons at Manchester "to prevent the disaffected in that town stirring as they had promised." Accompanied his Regt. to Ireland in June, 1717. This Corps was disbanded in Oct. 1718. Col. Newton was given the Colonelcy of the 39th Foot, 28 Sept. 1722. Brig.-Gen. 4 Nov. 1727. D. 10 Nov. 1730.

[2] John Moyle was appointed Capt. in the Rl. Irish Regt. of Foot, 4 Jan. 1696. Fought at Blenheim. Lt.-Col. of Col. Roger Townshend's Regt. of Foot, 12 April, 1706. Bt.-Col. 13 April, 1707. Half-pay, 1713. Lt.-Col. of Newton's Dragoons, 22 July, 1715. Brig.-Gen. 13 March, 1727. Col. of the 36th Foot, 14 May, 1732. Maj.-Gen. 5 Nov. 1735. Removed to the 22nd Foot, 27 June, 1737. D. 3 Nov. 1738.

[3] This officer's proper name was *Keightley*, and is so given in the List of Field Officers of above Regt. in the *London Gazette* for July, 1715. He was appointed Ens. in Col. Thos. Harrison's Regt. 1 Jan. 1704. Served with this Corps in Spain, and on 28 Oct. 1709 was appointed Major of the Earl of Peterborough's Regt. of Dragoons. Taken prisoner at Brihuega in Dec. 1710. Half-pay, 1712. Serving in 1728 as Major of the Royal Scots Fusiliers. Lt.-Col. of the King's Own Regt. of Foot, 1 Feb. 1731. Commanded last-named Corps at Dettingen, where he was wounded. Again wounded at Fontenoy, and died at Ghent shortly afterwards.

[4] Appointed Capt. in Sir R. Temple's Regt. of Foot, 1 Jan. 1707. Fought at Malplaquet. Half-pay, 1713. Capt. in Newton's Dragoons, 22 July, 1715. Major of Lord Cobham's Dragoons, 25 March, 1718. Serving in 1728. D. in 1731. Probably of the same stock as John Speed the eminent cartographer, but not mentioned in the account of some of the Speed family given in the Revd. J. S. Davies's *Hist. of Southampton*.

COLONEL CHURCHILL'S REGIMENT OF DRAGOONS.*

[Disbanded in Nov. 1718.]

NAME.	RANK.	DATE OF COMMISSION.
Charles Churchill,[1]	Col. & Capt.	————
G. Bates,[2]	Lt.-Col. & Capt.	————
Hugh Drysdale,[3]	Major & Capt.	————
Richard Thomas,	Captain	————
Richard Roberts,[4]	,,	————
James Bellandine,	,,	————
Thomas Drysdale,	Capt.-Lieut.	————
Thomas Brudenall,	Lieutenant	————
John Ball,	,,	————
Andrew Ross,	,,	————
Paul George,	,,	————
Stephen Otway,	,,	————
John Girling,	Cornet	————
Richard Robinson,	,,	————
Thomas Merridan,	,,	————
— Oldfield,	,,	————
Robert Kerr,	,,	————
Francis Rainsford,	,,	————

* This Regiment was given the title of "The Prince of Wales's Own Regiment of Dragoons."—ED.

[1] Natural son of General Charles Churchill. Appointed Ens. in Prince George of Denmark's Regt. of Foot, 31 Dec. 1688. Capt. 1 Sept. 1697. Served as A.D.C. to his father at Blenheim. Capt. and Lt.-Col. in the Coldstream Guards, 25 Oct. 1704. Major of the Buffs, 3 April, 1706. Bt.-Col. 1 Jan. 1707. Col. of a Regt. of Foot (aftds. Marines), 25 March, 1709. Raised above Regt. of Dragoons in July, 1715. Removed in 1717. Appointed Col. of the Regt. now known as the 10th Hussars, 12 Jan. 1723. Attained the rank of Lt.-Gen. 2 July, 1739. D. in 1745. This officer obtained notoriety as the lover of the celebrated actress Anne Oldfield, by whom he had an illegitimate son Charles Churchill. By powerful interest the body of the above Anne Oldfield was given a resting-place in Westminster Abbey, but "the Dean and Chapter peremptorily refused permission to her paramour, General Churchill, to erect a monument to her memory."

[2] George Bates was appointed Lieut. in Col. Rowe's Regt. 12 April, 1695. Adjt. and Qr.-Mr. to Col. Thos. Brudenell's Regt. of Foot on the Irish Establishment, 28 June, 1701. Major, 1 Aug. 1707. Lt.-Col. of Col. C. Churchill's Marines, 23 Dec. 1709. Half-pay, 1714. Lt.-Col. of Churchill's Dragoons, 22 July, 1715. Lt.-Governor of Charles Fort, Kinsale, on the death of Lt.-Col. Hawley in 1724. Col. Bates d. in 1727. Will proved at Dublin same year.

[3] Son of Hugh Drysdale, D.D., Archdeacon of Ossory. Appointed Ens. in Col. Thos. Brudenell's Regt. of Foot in June, 1701. Capt. and Bt.-Major in Colonel Charles Churchill's Regt. of Marines, 23 Dec. 1709. Major of Churchill's Dragoons, 22 July, 1715. Lt.-Governor of Virginia during the latter part of George I.'s reign. D. in 1726. Will proved at Dublin.

[4] Appointed Capt. in Sir Richard Temple's Regt. of Foot, 1 April, 1706. Served for some years as a Brigade-Major in Flanders, and is believed to have been present in this capacity at Malplaquet. Half-pay, 1713. Capt. in Churchill's Dragoons, 22 July, 1715. Placed on half-pay in Nov. 1718, on reduction of above Regt. Appointed Capt. in General Evans's Dragoons before the close of George I.'s reign. Comn. renewed by George II.

COLONEL TYRRELL'S REGIMENT OF DRAGOONS.

[Disbanded in Nov. 1718.]

NAME.	RANK.	DATE OF COMMISSION
James Tyrrell,[1]	Col. & Capt.	—
J. Steuart (sic),[2]	Lt.-Col. & Capt.	—
Charles Povey,[3]	Major & Capt.	—
Ebenezer Leeds,[4]	Captain	—
William Brereton	,,	—
Thomas Lumley,	,,	—
[Robert] Hepburn,	Capt.-Lieut.	—
Charles Walker,	Lieutenant	—
William Browne,	,,	—
Peter Garrick,	,,	—
John Rushton,	,,	—
Andrew Corner,	,,	—
Lewis Downes,	Cornet	—
John Horsepool,	,,	—
Francis Horton,	,,	—
Henry Tompkins,	,,	—
Peter Temple,	,,	—
Thomas Barton,	,,	—

[1] Son and heir of James Tyrrell, who was author of a well-known *General History of England*, and grandson of Sir Timothy Tyrrell, Knt., of Oakley, Co. Bucks. Appointed Capt.-Lieut. of the Earl of Macclesfield's Regt. of Horse, 16 Feb. 1694. Soon after joining General Cadogan's Regt. of Horse was given a Bt.-Lt.-Colonelcy under date of 1 Jan. 1707. Succeeded Sir Roger Bradshaigh as Col. of a Regt. of Foot, 21 April, 1709. Half-pay, 1713. Groom of the Bedchamber to George I., 1714. Raised above Regt. of Dragoons in July, 1715. Transferred to the 17th Foot, 7 Nov. 1722. D. a Lt.-Gen. in Aug. 1742.

[2] Previous services untraced. Placed on half-pay on reduction of the Regt. in Nov. 1718. Drawing half-pay in 1722.

[3] Ensign to Capt. St. George's Indep. Cy. of Foot in Ireland, 1680. Ensign in the Irish Foot Guards, 1685. Turned out of the Irish Army by Tyrconnel. Appointed Lieut. in the 1st Foot Guards, 1 April, 1689. Additional rank of Capt. in 1691. Adjt. 20 July, 1702. Major of Lord Lovelace's Regt. of Foot, 1 Feb. 1707. Half-pay, 1712. Placed on half-pay as Major of Tyrrell's disbanded Regt. of Dragoons in 1718. Drawing half-pay in 1722.

[4] Served some years in the ranks of the Earl of Arran's Regt. of Horse (present 5th D.G.), and was appointed Lieut. in same Corps, 25 March, 1700. Served at Ramillies and Malplaquet. Bt.-Capt. 1 Jan. 1707. Capt. in Tyrrell's Dragoons, 22 July, 1715. Half-pay, 1718. Drawing half-pay in 1722. Brother to Lieut. Joseph Leeds of Lord Lovelace's Regt. of Foot in 1712.

SIR ROBERT RICH'S REGIMENT OF DRAGOONS.

[*Disbanded in Nov. 1718.*]

NAME.	RANK.	DATE OF COMMISSION.
Sir Robert Rich,[1]	Col. & Capt.	——
J. Farmer (*sic*),[2]	Lt.-Col. & Capt.	——
[Henry] Goddard,[3]	Major & Capt.	——
Anthony Lowther,[4]	Captain	——
Humphry Watson,	,,	——
John Hampden,	,,	——
[Lewis] Morton,	Capt.-Lieut.	——
[Ric.] Caulfield,	Lieutenant	——
Cholmley Rich,	,,	——
[John] Dalston,	,,	——
Thomas Mitchell,	,,	——
[Samuel] Mule (*sic*),	,,	——
[John] Dubleday,	Cornet	——
[Chas.] Stoakes,	,,	——
[Wm.] Clenahan,	,,	——
Nicholas Durell,	,,	——
— Warburton,	,,	——
John Purcell,	,,	——

[1] Of Rosehall, Suffolk. Succeeded his brother Charles as 4th Bart. Appointed Ensign in the 1st Foot Guards, 10 June, 1700. Wounded at Schellenberg as well as at Blenheim. Capt. in Brig.-Gen. Wm. Tatton's Regt. of Foot, 25 Aug. 1704. Transferred to the 1st Foot Guards as Capt. and Lt.-Col. 9 March, 1708. Bt.-Col. 24 Aug. 1709. Col. of a Regt. of Foot (late Watkins's), 1 Jan. 1710. Was taken prisoner, with other officers going to Gibraltar, by the capture of the *Hunter* frigate off Cadiz by three French privateers (Letter from Thos. Leffever to Lord Dartmouth from Lisbon, 13 Oct 1710). Raised above Regt. of Dragoons in July, 1715. Col. of the Regt. now known as the 13th Hussars, 19 Nov. 1722. Transferred to the 8th Dragoons, 23 Sept. 1725. Col. of the present 4th Hussars, 13 May, 1735. Brig.-Gen. 20 March, 1727. Maj.-Gen. 12 Nov. 1735. Lt.-Gen. 2 July, 1739. Gen. of Horse, 29 March, 1745. Field-Marshal, 28 Nov. 1757. Was an M.P. and Gov. of Chelsea Hospital. D. 1 Feb. 1768. By his will, dated 31 Oct. 1767, he desired to be buried in the vaults of St. George's, Hanover Square.

[2] John *Fermor*. Youngest son of Wm. Fermor of Welches, Sussex, by his third wife. Served as an Ensign in Brudenell's Regt. in Portugal, and temporarily lost the use of his limbs. Sent home by the Earl of Galway in 1705. Recovered his health and petitioned Marlborough for a Commission in the New Levies, 1706. Appointed Capt. in the Earl of Orrery's Regt. of Foot same year. Major, 24 June, 1707. Succeeded Col. Charles Churchill as Major of the Duke of Argyll's Regt. of Foot, 25 March, 1709. Fought at Malplaquet. Appointed Adjt.-Gen. in Spain by Argyll, 3 March, 1711. Bt.-Col. same date. Lt.-Gov. of Minorca, 28 Aug. 1711. Half-pay, 1713. Lt.-Col. of Rich's Dragoons, 22 July, 1715. M.P. for Malmesbury. D. unm. in 1722. His brother Henry Fermor was created a Bart. in 1725.

[3] Appointed Capt. of the Grenadier Cy. in the Earl of Inchiquin's Regt. of Foot in March, 1704. Major, 28 May, 1710. Bt.-Lt.-Col. 1 Jan. 1711. Half-pay as Major in 1712 Major of Rich's Dragoons, 22 July, 1715. Half-pay, 1718. Major of Crofts' Dragoons before 1727. D. in 1748. Will proved at Dublin same year.

[4] Son of John Lowther, merchant of Danzig, and nephew of 1st Viscount Lonsdale. Appointed Ensign in the Earl of Barrymore's Regt. of Foot, 27 Jan. 1706. Capt. in the Scots Fusiliers, 1 Jan. 1708. Fought at Malplaquet, where he was wounded. Comn. renewed by George I. in March, 1715. Major of Rich's Dragoons, 22 July, 1715. Capt.-Lieut. and Lt.-Col. in the Coldstream Guards, 20 Dec. 1717. Capt. and Lt.-Col. 8 July, 1721. Col. of a newly-raised Regt. of Marines, 19 Nov. 1739. Maj.-Gen. in May, 1745. D. 14 Jan. 1756, aged 59. Bd. in Westminster Abbey.

COLONEL MOLESWORTH'S REGIMENT OF DRAGOONS.

[*Disbanded in Nov. 1718.*]

NAME.	RANK.	DATE OF COMMISSION.
Richard Molesworth,[1]	Col. & Capt.	———
Robert Dancy,[2]	Lt.-Col. & Capt.	———
Edward Ridley,[3]	Major & Capt.	———
William Bellandine,[4]	Captain	———
Ant. La Mellionere,[5]	,,	———
Lord Harry Pawlet,[6]	,,	———
— Hardyman,	Capt.-Lieut.	———
Richard Thompson,	Lieutenant	———
George Malcoln,	,,	———
John Arrowsmith,	,,	———
Alexander Knapton,	,,	———
John Strawbridge,	,,	———
Benjamin Harris,	Cornet	———
— Vernon,	,,	———
James Cressett,	,,	———
Bernard Fitzpatrick,	,,	———
Sir Talbot Clarke,	,,	———
George Abell,	,,	———

[1] See special memoir of Field-Marshal Visct. Molesworth on pp. 85-86.

[2] Probably brother to Lt.-Col. Ric. *Dansey* of Sir Robt. Rich's Regt. of Foot in 1712. Does not appear in any previous List. At the taking of Preston in 1715. Placed on half-pay on reduction of the Regt. in 1718. Drawing half-pay in 1736. Retired same year.

[3] Appointed Capt. in Col. Wm. Breton's Regt. of Foot, 25 Dec. 1705. Major of Col. Ric. Molesworth's Regt. of Foot, 8 Sept. 1710. Employed as an Engineer in Catalonia, 1706; Portugal, 1707; Flanders, 1710. Half-pay as an Engineer, 1714. Major of Molesworth's Dragoons, 22 July, 1715. At the taking of Preston. Capt. and Lt.-Col. 3rd Foot Guards, 15 Jan. 1718. D. about 1730.

[4] Third son of John, 2nd Lord Bellenden and father of the 4th Duke of Roxburghe. Served as Capt. in Macartney's Regt. of Foot at Almanza, and was taken prisoner. Half-pay, 1713. Capt. in Molesworth's Dragoons, 22 July, 1715. At the taking of Preston. Capt. in the King's Regt. of Horse, 1 Aug. 1716. Major, 2 Sept. 1720. Lt.-Col. 3 April, 1733. Served at Culloden. Half-pay, 1746. Drawing half-pay, 1758.

[5] Son of Major-Gen. Isaac La Melonière. Was given an Ensign's Commission as a "child" in Col. Wm. Breton's Regt. 25 March, 1705. "Superseded by the Prince's order" (*War Office MS.* 1706). Capt. in Molesworth's Dragoons, 22 July, 1715. At the taking of Preston. Exempt and Capt. in the 2nd Troop of Life Guards, 26 Oct. 1726. Lt. and Lt.-Col. 3rd Troop of Life Guards, 15 March, 1730. Lt.-Col. Gen. Churchill's Dragoons, 9 July, 1737. Wounded at Dettingen and Fontenoy. Reduced with the Troop in 1746. Became Groom of the Chambers to the Duke of Cumberland and d. in 1761-2.

[6] Second son (by his 2nd wife) of Charles Paulet, 2nd Duke of Bolton and Lord-Lieut. of Ireland in the early part of George I.'s reign. A.D.C. to the Earl of Galway in Portugal, 1708 (?). Capt. in Molesworth's Dragoons, 22 July, 1715. At the taking of Preston. In the Regt. when it was reduced in Nov. 1718. Succeeded his brother as 4th Duke of Bolton in 1754. D. 1758.

COLONEL WILLIAM STANHOPE'S REGIMENT OF DRAGOONS.

[*Disbanded in Nov. 1718.*]

NAME.	RANK.	DATE OF COMMISSION.
William Stanhope,[1]	Col. & Capt.	——
Richard Nanfan,[2]	Lt.-Col. & Capt.	——
Richard Manning,[3]	Major & Capt.	——
David Martell,	Captain	——
James Deleuzer,	,,	——
James Gardner,	,,	——
Marcellus La Roone,[4]	Capt.-Lieut.	——
Richard Gregson,	Lieutenant	——
Matthew Swiney,	,,	——
John Leighton,	,,	——
Alexander Le Grande,	,,	——
Robert Bransby,	,,	——
Henry Durell,	Cornet	——
Paul Stephen Hewson,	,,	——
George Bernard,	,,	——
Tristram Strafford,	,,	——
[Andrew] Robinson,	,,	——
T. Wheate,	,,	——

[1] Third son of John Stanhope of Elvaston, Co. Derby. Appointed Capt. and Lt.-Col. 3rd Foot Guards, 19 June, 1710. Col. of a Regt. of Foot, 17 March, 1711. Served in Spain under the Duke of Argyll. Raised above Regt. of Dragoons in July, 1715. Was at the taking of Preston. Col. of the Regt. now known as the 13th Hussars, 20 Sept. 1725. Envoy Extraordinary to the King of Spain, 1718. Returned to England on the rupture with Spain. Ambassador at the Court of Spain, 1729. Created Baron Harrington same year, and Earl 9 Feb. 1742. Lord-Lieut. of Ireland, 1746. Brig.-Gen. 19 Nov. 1735. Maj.-Gen., 2 July, 1739. D. 1756.

[2] Appointed Capt. in Col. Thos. Farrington's newly-raised Regt. of Foot, 16 Feb. 1694. Lt.-Col. of Lord Tunbridge's Regt. of Foot, 12 April, 1706. Served with this Corps (then Humphrey Gore's) in Spain, and was at the battle of Saragossa. Half-pay, 1712. Lt.-Col. of Stanhope's Dragoons, 22 July, 1715. At the taking of Preston. Retired, 14 Jan. 1718.

[3] Appointed Lieut. in Col. Hans Hamilton's Regt. of Foot, 24 Feb. 1705. Capt. in Col. Desbordes' Regt. of Dragoons in Portugal in 1709. Major of Col. Hunt Withers's Dragoons in Portugal, 19 Sept. 1710. Placed on half-pay as Major of last-named Regt. in 1712. Major of Stanhope's Dragoons, 22 July, 1715. At the taking of Preston. Promoted Lt. Col. 14 Jan. 1718. Capt. and Lt.-Col. in 3rd Foot Guards, 14 Jan. 1719. D. at Bath in 1734.

[4] Appointed Lieut. in the 1st Batt. Royal Scots Regt. of Foot, 20 Sept. 1707. Believed to have been at the battle of Malplaquet. Taken prisoner at Brihuega in Dec. 1710, when serving as Qr.-Mr.-Gen. to Gen. Stanhope and Lieut. of Stanhope's Regt. of Dragoons. Half-pay in 1712. Capt.-Lieut. of Col. Wm. Stanhope's Dragoons, 22 July, 1715. At the taking of Preston. Half-pay on the reduction of Stanhope's Regt. same year. Appointed Capt. in Munden's Dragoons in Ireland, July, 1719. Serving as Capt. in Lt.-Gen. Wm. Ker's Dragoons in 1728.

HIS MAJESTY'S FIRST REGIMENT OF FOOT GUARDS.

NAME.	RANK.	DATE OF COMMISSION.
John, Duke of Marlborough,	Col. & Capt.	—
Henry Withers,[1]	Lt.-Col. & Capt.	—
William Tatton,[2]	1st Major & Capt.	9 Mar. 1707-8.
Richard Russell,[3]	2nd Major & Capt.	—
Andrew Wheeler,[4]	Captain	—
Thomas Ferrers,[5]	,,	—
William Lloyd,[6]	,,	—
William Barrell,[7]	,,	—
Philip Talbot (sic),[8]	,,	—
John Guise,[9]	,,	—
George Read,	,,	—
Samuel Gerrard,	,,	—
James Moyser,	,,	20th Dec. 1709.
Philip Anstruther,[10]	,,	—
Edmund Elwell,	,,	—
Joseph Ferrers,	,,	—
Alexander Montgomery,	,,	30 Mar. 1710-11.
Francis Fuller,	,,	—
Lord James Murray,[11]	,,	14 June, 1714.
Charles Frampton,	,,	—
William Blakeney,	,,	—
William Merrick,	,,	—
Josua Paul,	,,	—
John Schutz,	,,	11 Jan. 1714-15.
Thomas Sidney,	,,	—
Col. Egerton.	,,	25 Dec. 1714.
George Carpenter,	Captain	—
John Hay,	,,	—
Robert Townshend,	Capt.-Lieut.	—
David Eyton,	Lieutenant	—
Henry Brown,	,,	—
George Smith,	,,	—
Edward Colston,	,,	—
Richard Seaman,	,,	—
William Alchorne,	,,	—
John Armstrong,	,,	—
George Wilmer,	,,	—
William Bull,	,,	—
Richmond Browne,	,,	27th Apr. 1708.
Rowland Reynolds,	,,	—
Francis Rodd,	,,	—
John Fogg,	,,	—
Robert Reed,	,,	—
Thomas Bagnall,	,,	—
John Knowles,	,,	—
William Swan,	,,	—
Henry Murcott,	,,	—
Thomas Legard,	,,	—

NAME.	RANK.	DATE OF COMMISSION.
William Hetley,	Lieutenant	
Michael Margett,	,,	6th June, 1715.
Robert Brackley,	,,	
Thomas Inwood,	,,	
Robert Leighton.	,,	
James Oglethorpe,[12]	,,	21 Dec. 1713.
Hawksworth Smith,	,,	8 Dec. 1711.
John Pye,	,,	
William Sanderson,	,,	10 Apr. 1714.
John Chamberlain,	,,	
Robert Judd,	,,	
John Jodrell,	,,	
George Chudleigh,	Ensign	
John Fogg,	,,	
William Swan,	,,	
Thomas Tully,	,,	11 May, 1715.
Robert Layton,	,,	
George Sherrard,	,,	28 May, 1709.
Peregrine Jones,	,,	12 June, 1709.
Charles Colvert,	,,	27 Nov. 1709.
William Courtney,	,,	25 Mar. 1710.
Thomas Gorsuch,	,,	
Michael Rawlins,	,,	1 Nov. 1711.
Antonio Southworth,	,,	
Peter Darcey,	,,	
George Villiers Hewett,	,,	
John Girling,	,,	
Joseph Hudson,	,,	
Francis Gibson,	,,	
John Parker,	,,	
Francis Chantrell,	,,	
Edward Bettinson,	,,	
Barnaby Donston,	,,	
William Goodrick,	,,	
Edward Lutterel,	,,	23 Dec. 1713.
William Gill,	,,	
William Blakeney,	Adjutant	
Robert Townshend,	,,	
David Eyton,	Quartermaster	
Henry Brown,	,,	
Theophilus Parsons,	Solicitor	
Docr. Innis Smallwood,	Chaplain	
Archibald Harris,	Surgeon	
Charles Harris,	Surgeon's Mate	
Joshua Scaff,	,, ,,	
Roger Burrows,	Drum Major	
Thomas Morphy,	Deputy Marshal	

[1] Appointed Lieut. in the Duke of Monmouth's Regt. of Foot, 10 Feb. 1678. Sent to Tangier in 1679. Lieut. in the Tangier Regt. (2nd Foot), 2 Oct. 1683. Capt.-Lieut. 1 Oct. 1688. Bt.-Col. 1 July, 1689. Adjt.-Gen. of the Foot in Ireland, 20 Oct. 1689. Major of the Coldstream Guards, 10 Aug. 1692. Major of the 1st Foot Guards, 25 Feb. 1695. Lt.-Col. of 1st Foot Guards, 7 Dec. 1696. Brig.-Gen. 9 Feb. 1702. Maj.-General, 1 Jan.

1704. Fought at Blenheim. Lt.-Gen. 1 Jan. 1707. Saw considerable service at Tangier and in Flanders. Distinguished himself at the taking of Tournay, 1709. D. 11 Nov. 1729. Bd. in the East Cloister of Westminster Abbey, where there is a tablet inscribed to his memory.

[2] Appointed Ensign in Col. Henry Cornewall's Regt. (9th Foot), 19 June, 1685. Lieut. 1 June, 1687. Capt. in 1689. Bt.-Lt.-Col. 7 Mar. 1692. Served in Ireland and Flanders, under William III. Lt.-Col. of Col. Sam. Venner's Regt. (24th), 7 Aug. 1695. Bt.-Col. 1 Mar. 1703. Col. of last-named Regt. 25 Aug. 1704. Commanded the same at Blenheim. Sold his Colonelcy in 1708. Brig.-Gen. 1 Jan. 1707. Major of 1st Foot Guards, 9 Mar. 1708. Maj.-Gen. 1 Jan. 1710. Lt.-Col. 1st Foot Guards, 12 Oct. 1722. Lt.-Gen. 3 Mar. 1727. Col. of the Buffs, 24 Nov. 1729. D. in 1737, at which time he held the post of Governor of Tilbury Fort.

[3] Appointed Ensign to the King's Company in the 1st Foot Guards, 1 April, 1689. Capt. and Lt.-Col. 20 Aug. 1692. Served at Steinkirk in 1692, and accompanied the expedition against Brest in 1694. Bt.-Col. 19 Oct. 1704 in Portugal. Served at the defence of Barcelona in 1706. Distinguished himself at the battle of Almanza, and was granted a sum of money by Royal Warrant "in consideration of his exemplary services and conduct" (Hamilton's *Grenadier Guards*, Vol. II. p. 22). 2nd Major of the 1st Foot Guards, 9 Mar. 1708. Brig.-Gen. 1 Jan. 1710. Comns. renewed by George I. 11 Jan. 1715. 1st Major, 12 Oct. 1722. Lt.-Col. of above Regt. 24 Nov. 1729. D. in 1735 at Bath.

[4] His first commission describes him as "Andrew Wheeler *alias* Pitcairn." Appointed Ensign in 1st Foot Guards, 14 Oct. 1680. Lieut. 25 Jan. 1682. Capt. and Lt.-Col. 22 Mar. 1693. Bt.-Col. 1 Jan. 1707. Brig.-Gen. 12 Feb. 1711. Served at Malplaquet. Maj.-Gen. 9 Mar. 1727. Untraced after that date.

[5] Appointed Col. of a newly-raised Regt. of Dragoons, in Ireland, 16 Feb. 1716. *See* "Irish Establishment."

[6] Appointed Capt.-Lieut. of Prince George of Denmark's Regt. of Foot 1 Jan. 1691. Capt. 14 Sept. 1693. Bt.-Col. 1 Jan. 1707. Capt. and Lt.-Col. in 1st Foot Guards before 1709. 2nd Major 11 Oct. 1722. Under date of 2 July, 1724, the *Historical Register* records that "—Lloyd, Esq., 2nd Major in the 1st Regt. of Guards, shot himself and dyed immediately."

[7] Appointed Col. of a Regt. of Foot (late Brigadier Windsor's), 27 Sept. 1715. *See* "Irish Establishment."

[8] *Talbor* in former Lists. Appointed Capt. and Lt.-Col. in 1st Foot Guards, 25 March, 1705. Taken prisoner at Almanza. Bt.-Col. 15 Nov. 1711. Untraced after 1715.

[9] Appointed Capt. and Lt.-Col. in 1st Foot Guards, 9 April, 1706. Served at Malplaquet. Bt.-Col. 7 July, 1724. Major of the 1st Foot Guards, 20 June, 1727. Col. of the 6th Foot, 1 Nov. 1738. Brig.-Gen. 2 July, 1739. Maj.-Gen. 18 Feb. 1742. Served with distinction as a Brigadier in the Carthagena Expedition, 1740-1741. Lt.-Gen. 7 June, 1745. Gov. of Berwick. D. in 1765.

[10] Only son of Sir James Anstruther of Airdrie, N.B. Appointed Capt. and Lt.-Col. 1st Foot Guards, 1 June, 1710. Attained the rank of Lt.-Gen. and was Col. of the Cameronian Regt. from 31 Mar. 1720—Nov. 1760. Lt.-Govr. of Minorca for some years. D. s.p. Nov. 1760.

[11] Third son of the 1st Duke of Atholl. Appointed Capt.-Lieut. of the 1st Foot Guards, 19 May, 1712. Capt. of a Grenadier Cy. in above Regt. 14 June, 1714. Appointed 2nd Lt.-Col. of the Royal Regt. of Foot, 31 Mar. 1718. Out of said Regt. before 1724, when he succeeded as 2nd Duke of Atholl, K.T. D. in Jan. 1764.

[12] Youngest son of Sir Theophilus Oglethorpe. Is said to have been given an Ensign's Commission in the 1st Foot Guards by Marlborough, but the register of this appointment is not forthcoming. Lieut. and Capt. in above Regt. 21 Nov. 1713. Resigned his Commission, 23 Nov. 1715. Accompanied the Earl of Peterborough to Italy, in an official capacity, in 1717. Entered the service of the "Old Pretender" as a Secretary. In later life became famous as the Colonist of Georgia and a celebrated philanthropist. In 1737 he raised the Georgia Rangers and was appointed Colonel of the Regt. Oglethorpe was recruiting in England when the '45 broke out, and was attached with part of his corps to General Wade's Army. Brig.-Gen. 13 Feb. 1743. Maj.-Gen. 31 Mar. 1745. Lt.-Gen. 3 Sept. 1747. Gen. 22 Feb. 1765. D. 1 July, 1785.

HIS MAJESTY'S SECOND REGIMENT OF FOOT GUARDS.

NAME.	RANK.	DATE OF COMMISSION.
Lieut.-Gen. Cadogan,[1]	Col. & Capt.	
Edward Braddock,[2]	Lt.-Col. & Capt.	
Richard Holmes,[3]	Major & Capt.	
Henry Morrison,[4]	2nd Major & Capt.	
Andrew Bissett,[5]	Captain	
Lord Inchinbrook (sic),[6]	,,	
John Robinson,*	,,	7 May, 1709.
Sir Tristram Dillington,	,,	
Thomas Smith,	,,	10 Feb. 1709–10.
John Shorte,	,,	
Thomas Cæsar,	,,	12 Nov. 1713.
John Chudleigh,	,,	20 Mar. 1713–14.
John Hobart,	,,	
Charles Cadogan,[7]	,,	11 June, 1715.
Harry Pulteney,	,,	22nd July, 1715.
[William] Leigh,	,,	,, ,,
[John] Cope,†	,,	,, ,,
[John] Huske,	,,	,, ,,
John Foliott,‡	Capt.-Lieut.	12 Nov. 1713.
John Parsons,§	Lieutenant	24 Apr. 1708.
Richard Green,‖	,,	
Edward Borrett,¶	,,	
William Hanmer,	,,	13 May, 1709.
Edward Thomas,	,,	
Obadiagh Stocker,	,,	
William Price,	,,	25 Mar. 1710.
Edward Shorte,	,,	5 Apr. 1709.
Thomas Hamilton,	,,	
James Gendrault,	,,	
Thomas Serjeant,	,,	
Richard Legg,	,,	
Henry Morrison,	,,	16 Nov. 1713
John Warren,	,,	
Thomas Blount,	,,	
Henry Cox,	,,	
Edward Eaton,	,,	
[Richard] Holmes,	,,	
Peter Darcey,	,,	
Francis Wheeler,	Ensign	30 Mar. 1710.
Henry Cox,	,,	29 Aug. 1710.
James Hussey,	,,	27 June 1712.
Edward Braddock [jun.],[8]	,,	
George Bellamy,	,,	

* John Robinson, Lieutenant, 21st Mar. 1705–6.
† William (sic) Cope, Lieutenant, 25th Apr. 1706.
‡ John Foliott, Lieutenant, 2nd July, 1706.
§ Edward Borrett, Lieutenant, 20th Oct. 1706.
‖ Richard Green, Lieutenant, 8th May, 1707.
¶ John Parsons, Lieutenant, 3rd June, 1708.

The Right Honourable William Earl Cadogan Lieutenant General of His Majesty's Forces &c.

GEORGE THE FIRST'S ARMY, 1715

NAME.	RANK.	DATE OF COMMISSION.
Edward Eaton,	Ensign	
William Sotheby,	,,	
Robert Morgan,	,,	
Richard Holmes,	,,	
Gabriel Reeve,	,,	22 July, 1713.
Charles Howard,	,,	10 Aug. 1715.
Nat. Blackiston,	,,	
John King,	Chaplain	[11 Jan. 1715.]
John Folliot,	Adjutant	25 Mar. 1710.
John Parsons,	Quartermaster	
Ambrose Dickens,	Surgeon	

[1] Eldest son of Henry Cadogan, Counsellor-at-Law, of Dublin, and grandson of Major William Cadogan, Govr. of Trim, co. Meath. Served through all the wars in Flanders during the reigns of William III. and Queen Anne. He was the one man whom Marlborough delighted to honour. Succeeded the Duke of Argyll as C.-in-C. in Scotland early in 1716. Gen. 12 July, 1717. Created Baron Cadogan, 30 June, 1716, and two years later Earl Cadogan. Succeeded Marlborough as Col. of the 1st Foot Guards, 18 June, 1722, and in command of the Army. Master-General of the Ordnance, 1 July, 1722. D. without male issue, 17 July, 1726, and was succeeded in his title of Baron Cadogan by his brother Lt.-Gen. Charles Cadogan.

[2] Appointed Ensign in the Coldstream Guards, 17 June, 1682. Lieut. before Oct. 1684. Capt. and Lt.-Col. 21 March, 1689. Served in Flanders, 1694. Major and Bt.-Col. 1 Oct. 1702. Lt.-Col. of above Regt. 10 Jan. 1704. Brig.-Gen. 1 Jan. 1707. Maj.-Gen. 1 Jan. 1710. Retired 28 Sept. 1715. D. 15 June, 1725. Bd. in the Abbey Church, Bath. (See notice of his son in note 8.)

[3] Appointed 2nd Lieut. of an Independent Cy. of Grenadiers commanded by Sir Robt. Holmes, Kt., 1 Mar. 1687. This Cy. was added to Princess Anne of Denmark's Regt. of Foot before Nov. 1687. Capt.-Lieut. in the Coldstream Guards, 1 May, 1693. Capt. 8 March, 1694. Maj. and Bt.-Col. 10 Jan. 1704. Brig.-Gen. 1 Jan. 1707. Maj.-Gen. 1 Jan. 1710. Regtal. Lt.-Col. 28 Sept. 1715. Retd. in Aug. 1717. D. 7 May, 1723.

[4] Lt.-Col. Henry Moryson was appointed Col. of a Regt. of Foot (8th) in Ireland 8 Aug. 1715. See "Irish Establishment."

[5] Appointed Col. of a Regt. of Foot (30th) in Ireland, 25 Aug. 1717. See "Irish Establishment."

[6] Edward, Viscount *Hinchinbroke*, was appointed Col. of a Regt. of Foot (37th) in Ireland, 11 Dec. 1717. See "Irish Establishment."

[7] Lt.-Col. Charles (aftds. Lord) Cadogan was appointed Col. of the King's Own Regt. of Foot, 21 April, 1719. See Vol. II.

[8] Son of Maj.-Gen. Edward Braddock (see note 2). Appointed Ensign in above Regt. 10 Oct. 1710. Lieut. of Grenadiers, 1 Aug. 1716. Capt.-Lieut. and Lt.-Col. 30 Oct. 1734. Capt. and Lt.-Col. 10 Feb. 1736. 2nd Major and Bt.-Col. 2 Apl. 1743. 1st Major, 27 May, 1745. Regtal. Lt.-Col. 21 Nov. 1745. Col. of the 14th Foot, 17 Feb. 1743. Maj.-Gen. and C. in C. of the Forces sent to North America, 24 Sept. 1754. Wounded at Fort du Quesne, on the Ohio, 9 July, 1755, "of which he died the fourth day." Mackinnon's *Coldstream Guards*, Vol. II. p. 473.

HIS MAJESTY'S THIRD REGIMENT OF FOOT GUARDS.

NAME.	RANK.	DATE OF COMMISSION.
John, Earl of Dunmore,[1]	Col. & Capt.	[10 Oct. 1713.]
John Steuart (sic),[2]	Lt.-Col. & Capt.	4 Sept. 1710.
Henry Berkley,[3]	Captain	22 July, 1715.
Lord William Hay,	Major	19 Apr. 1711.
James Scott,	2nd Major	[9 June, 1713.]
Thomas Dalzell,	Captain	[Out in 1717.]
Thomas Diggs,	,,	[13 Aug. 1715.]
John Hope,	,,	3 June, 1708.
John Campbell,	,,	13 Aug. 1715.
Lord Falkland,	,,	12 Aug. 1710.
Robert Murray,	,,	4 Sept. 1710.
James St. Clair,[4]	,,	19 Dec. 1714.
[Wm.] Lord Jedburgh,[5]	,,	3 Oct. 1710.
[Wm.] Earl of Dalhousie,[6]	,,	22 Mar. 1710-11.
[George] Lord Balgony,[7]	,,	19 Apr. 1711.
Phineas Bowles,[8]	,,	[23 Mar. 1713.]
Thomas Coote,[9]	,,	20 Dec. 1714.
Thomas Young,	,,	[Out in 1717.]
John Montgomerie,	Capt.-Lieut.	[13 Aug. 1715.]
William Steuart,	Lieutenant	[1 June, 1714.]
John Scott,	,,	[3 Aug. 1715.]
William Murray,	,,	[30 Oct. 1703.]
Robert Seton,	,,	[,, ,,]
James Richardson.	,,	[Capt.-Lt. 1717.]
George Steuart,	,,	[11 Aug. 1716.]
James Murhead,	,,	[2 May, 1711.]
Alexander Macnachten,	,,	[,, ,,]
James Ogilvie,	,,	[,, ,,]
James Colquhone,	,,	[1 Mar. 1694.]
Richard Maitland,	,,	[1 Jan. 1700.]
George Foulis,	,,	[28 Nov. 1702.]
George Hepburne,	,,	[26 July, 1710.]
Neil Maccleod,	,,	[2 Nov. 1697.]
Henry Low,	,,	[30 Mar. 1713.]
Sir Charles Mylne,	,,	[18 June, 1705.]
Mat. Scroggs,	,,	22 July, 1713.
Rodrick Baine,	,,	[11 Jan. 1714.]
Charles Steuart,	Ensign	
John Davis,	,,	[24 Feb. 1714.]
William Clarke,	,,	[30 Oct. 1703.]
David (sic) Ogilvie,	,,	
Patrick Edmingston,	,,	[2 May, 1711.]
John Lowrie,	,,	[27 Sept. 1712.]
Alexander Leslie,[10]	,,	[2 Apr. 1706.]
John Scott,	,,	[1 July, 1713.]
Robert Walpole,	,,	[19 Sept. 1710.]
John Haills [Hales],	,,	[11 Jan. 1715.]
Andrew Hamilton,	,,	[13 Feb. 1705.]

NAME.	RANK.	DATE OF COMMISSION.
William Dick,[11]	Ensign	10 Dec. 1710.
Robert Montgomerie,	,,	[17 June, 1706.]
Charles Chalmers,	,,	
George Hope,	,,	19 Aug. 1715.
John Talbot,[12]	,,	
Hugh Frazer,	,,	[11 Jan. 1715.]
Edward Dauvergne,	Chaplain	14 Apr. 1713.
James Pringle,	Surgeon	
Rd. Maitland,	Adjutant	2 May, 1711.
George Steuart,	Quartermaster	

[1] Second but eldest surviving son of the 1st Earl of Dunmore. Appointed Capt. in the 1st Batt. of the Royal Regt. of Foot, 1 June, 1705. Served at Malplaquet. Succeeded as 2nd Earl of Dunmore in 1710. Col. of the 3rd Foot Guards, 10 Oct. 1713. Maj.-Gen. 14 Nov. 1735. Lt.-Gen. 2 July, 1739. Gen. 30 May, 1745. Govr. of Plymouth in 1746 with pay at the rate of £3 10s. 7¾d. per diem. D. unm. 18 Apr. 1752.

[2] Of Sorbie. Third son of the 3rd Earl of Galloway. Believed to be identical with the Capt. and Lt.-Col. John Stewart of the 1st Batt. Scots Guards who served at the siege of Namur, 1695. 1st Lt.-Col. of above Regt. 4 Sept. 1710. Brig.-Gen. same year and accompanied the 1st Batt. to Spain. Retd. 11 Nov. 1717. M.P. for Wigtownshire in the first Parliament of Great Britain and in several subsequent Parliaments. D. at Sorbie 22 Apr. 1748.

[3] Appointed Ensign in the Earl of Marlborough's Regt. of Foot (24th), 1 June, 1702. Served at Blenheim and subsequent battles in Flanders. Adjt. 24 Feb. 1708. Lieut. 25 Oct. same year. Capt. and Lt.-Col. in 3rd Foot Guards, 22 July, 1715. Appointed Col. of the King's Own Regt. of Foot, 25 Dec. 1717. Transferred to the Colonelcy of the 2nd Tp. of Horse Grenadier Guards, 21 April, 1719. Brig.-Gen. 1 Dec. 1735. D. 23 May, 1736, at Bath.

[4] Second son of Henry, 8th Baron Sinclair. Appointed Ensign in above Regt. 22 May, 1694, when still a child. Capt. in the 1st Batt. Royal Regt. of Foot, 2 Nov. 1708. Served several campaigns under Marlborough. Half-pay in 1713. Appointed Capt. and Lt.-Col. in the 3rd Foot Guards, 19 Dec. 1714. Bt.-Col. 26 June, 1722. Col. of the Regt. aftds. known as the 22nd Foot, 8 Aug. 1734. Transferred to the Royal Regt. (Royal Scots), 27 June, 1737. Brig.-Gen. 2 July, 1739. Maj.-Gen. 15 Aug. 1741. Lt.-Gen. 4 June, 1745. Gen. in 1761. He was Qr.-Mr.-Gen. in 1745 to the British forces in the Netherlands. In 1746 he commanded an Expedition sent against the French seaport of L'Orient and the peninsula of Quiberon. Subsequently sent Envoy to the Courts of Vienna and Turin in place of Lt.-Gen. Thos. Wentworth, decd. Gen. St. Clair d.s.p. at Dysart in 1761.

[5] Only son of the 2nd Marquis of Lothian. Succeeded as 3rd Marquis in 1722. Appointed Ensign in the 3rd Foot Guards, 6 March, 1708. Capt. and Lt.-Col. 3 Oct. 1710. Resigned his Commission, 4 Nov. 1718. D. in 1767.

[6] Sixth Earl. Succeeded to the title on the death of his kinsman the 5th Earl, who d. in Spain while in command of the 1st Batt. 3rd Foot Guards. Serving in 1717. Out of the Regt. before 1727. D. 8 Dec. 1739.

[7] George, Lord Balgonie, was eldest son of the 3rd Earl of Leven and 2nd Earl of Melville. Appointed Ensign in Brig-Gen. James Maitland's Regt. of Foot, 11 Mar. 1704. Capt. and Lt.-Col. in 3rd Foot Guards, 19 Apr. 1711. Resigned his Commission, 9 Sept. 1715. D. 1721, leaving a son David who succeeded as 4th Earl of Leven and 3rd Earl of Melville.

[8] Appointed Col. of the Regt. of Dragoons now known as the 12th Lancers, 23 March, 1719.—See Vol. II.

[9] Appointed Capt. and Lt.-Col. 1st Foot Guards, 21 June, 1709. Appears to have been son of Thos. Coote, of Coote Hill, Cavan, by a second marriage. Fought a duel with the Duke of Argyll in 1711, and was wounded. "Had his Company in the 1st Foot Guards taken from him, for no other reason that appeared, but his being present at the burning of the Pretender, and drinking his present Majesty's Health" (Hamilton's *History of the Grenadier Guards*, Vol. II. p. 63). Col. Coote left the Army in April, 1718.

[10] According to the MS. Army List for 1717, Alex. Leslie was appointed Ensign in the 3rd Foot Guards, 23 April, 1706. In a "List of Minors," for 1711 or 1712, young Leslie's name appears as an Ensign in said Regt. He was born about 1699 and was younger brother to George, Lord Balgonie (see note 7). Educated at Leyden. "On the eve of starting

for Holland he was ordered by his Colonel to join his Company. On the earnest representation of his father the son's attendance with his Regiment was dispensed with. Admitted a member of the Faculty of Advocates, 14 July, 1719, after he had applied to Lord Dunmore to be allowed to return home for this purpose. Shortly after his admission to the Bar he applied for permission to dispose of his Commission" (*New Scottish Peerage*). Succeeded his nephew David as 5th Earl of Leven in 1729.

[11] Great-grandson of the renowned Sir Wm. Dick of Braid. Appointed Ensign in the 3rd Foot Guards, 18 June, 1705. Served with the 1st Batt. in Spain and was promoted Lieut. and Capt. 10 Oct. 1710—his Commission being signed by General Stanhope at Madrid. Serving with same rank in 1727. "Capt. Dick settled in New York State, where he is said to have acquired some landed property. . . . He left an only child, Agnes, who, in 1747, was served heir-general of her father Wm. Dick, Capt. in the Independent Army (*sic*) of the State of New York"—*Herald and Genealogist*, Vol. VIII. p. 263.

[12] Evidently a clerical error for "Sherington Talbot," who was appointed Ensign in the 3rd Foot Guards, 23 July, 1715. See notification of his appointment on p. 188, and biog. notice.

THE EARL OF ORKNEY'S REGIMENT OF FOOT.

[1st FOOT.]

NAME.	RANK.	DATE OF COMMISSION.
George, Earl of Orkney,[1]	Colonel	
Sir James Abercrombie,[2]	1st Lt.-Col.	20 Mar. 1710–11.
Charles Cockburne,[3]	2nd Lt.-Col.	
Alexander Irwin,[4]	1st Major	
James Cunningham,[5]	2nd Major	
James Horn (sic)[6]	[Bt.] Major	
Robert Carr,	Captain	
Thomas Bruce,	,,	
Robert Hamilton,	,,	
Lord Edward Murray,[7]	,,	
George Browne,	,,	
William Brisban,	,,	
William Melvine,	,,	
James Douglas,	,,	
Alexander Ruthven,	,,	
James Erskine,	,,	
William Weir,	,,	
Lord Cumerland,	,,	
James Ballantine,	,,	
James St. Clair,[8]	,,	19 Dec. 1714.
Robert Straton,	Capt.-Lieut.	
Archibald Crawford,	Lieutenant	
Andrew Hamilton,	,,	
Andrew Skeen,	,,	
Dominick Dalton,	,,	
John Johnson,	,,	
James Straton,	,,	
Walter Innis,	,,	
James Murray,	,,	
David Grame,	,,	
Archibald Colvill,	,,	
William Innes,	,,	
Keneth McKenzie,	,,	
James Graham,	,,	
John Seymour,	,,	
James Roddam,	,,	
Patrick Steuart,	,,	
James White,	,,	
Charles Slezer,	,,	
George Inglish,	,,	
John Shaw,	,,	
John Calder,	,,	
Lord George Murray,[9]	Ensign	
John Gordon,	,,	
Charles Powlett,[10]	,,	4 Mar. 1709–10.
Arthur Balfour,	,,	

NAME.	RANK.	DATE OF COMMISSION.
Charles Gordon,	Ensign	—
John Dalyell,[11]	,,	—
Alexander Napier,	,,	—
Thomas Bruce,	,,	—
Alexander Agnew,[12]	,,	—
George Johnson,	,,	—
Archibald Cockburn,	,,	—
James Steuart,	,,	—
Richard Washington,	,,	—
William Langly,	,,	—
Rochford McNeal,	,,	—
John Watson,	,,	—
John Madgshon (*sic*)	,,	—
William Brown,	,,	—
Robert Gawen,	Adjutant	—
Thomas Parkes,	,,	—
Joseph Loveday,	Chaplain	—
Archibald Comrie,	Surgeon	—

[1] See special memoir, pp. 35–38.

[2] "Natural son of the Duke of Hamilton." (Musgrave's *Obituary*.) Appointed Ensign in the Royal Regt. 29 May, 1696. Half-pay, 1697. Capt. of an additional Cy. in above Regt. 31 May, 1701. A. D. C. to the Earl of Orkney at Blenheim, and particularly distinguished himself. Saw much service under Marlborough. Bt.-Major, 1 July, 1706. Bt.-Lt.-Col. 14 May, 1709. Capt. and Lt.-Col. in the Coldstream Guards, 1710. Sold his Commission in last-named Regt. and bought the Lt.-Colonelcy of the Royals, 20 Mar. 1711. Bt.-Col. 1 Nov. 1711. Town Major of Dunkirk, 24 Oct. 1712. Created a Bart. for his services in 1709. Retd. from the Army, 30 Mar. 1718. D.s.p. 14 Nov. 1724.

[3] Appointed 2nd Lieut. of the Grenadier Cy. in Col. Robert Hodges' Regt. (16th Foot), 31 Dec. 1688. Capt.-Lieut. 14 Mar. 1689. Capt. of the Grenadier Cy. 1 Jan. 1692. Served at Landen in 1693. Transferred to the Grenadier Cy. in the Royal Regt. 8 Mar. 1694. Bt.-Maj. 1 Mar. 1703. Wounded at Schellenberg. Bt.-Lt.-Col. 1 Jan. 1706. Served throughout Marlborough's campaigns. Commanded the 2nd Batt. of the Royal Regt. at Malplaquet. Bt.-Col. 1 Mar. 1711. 1st Lt.-Col. 30 Mar. 1718. Comn. renewed by George II. Brig.-Gen. in 1735. "Died in King Street, St. James's, suddenly, on 21 July, 1738, after eating cucumbers and drinking cyder"—*Gentleman's Mag.* 1738.

[4] Joined the Royal Regt. of Foot, 1 Oct. 1689. Adjt. to the 1st Batt. 22 May, 1694. Capt. 2 Oct. 1695. Wounded at Schellenberg, where he served as Brigade Major. 2nd Major 3 Aug. 1704. Served at Ramillies and Malplaquet. Bt.-Lt.-Col. 1 Mar. 1711. 1st Major before 1715. Serving in Ireland as Regtal. Lt.-Col. of 2nd Batt. in 1737. Appointed Col. of the 5th Foot, 27 June same year. Brig.-Gen. 1 Jan. 1743. Maj.-Gen. 24 Feb. 1744. Lt.-Govr. of Kinsale, 1744–46. Lt.-Gen. 25 Aug. 1747. D. 1752.

[5] Appointed Capt. in above Regt. 8 Mar. 1694. Wounded at Blenheim. Bt.-Maj. 1 Jan. 1706. Served at Malplaquet. Bt.-Lt.-Col. 1 Jan. 1712. 2nd Major of the Royal Regt. before 1715. Left said Regt. 1 Sept. 1718. Appointed Lt.-Govr. of Fort William same year. He attended Maj.-Gen. Wightman in the march to Glenshiel in June, 1719, and did good service against the Jacobite force (*Treasury Papers*, Vol. CCXXXV. No. 79). At the time of his death, in 1734, Col. Cunningham was Lt.-Govr. of Fort George.

[6] Bt.-Maj. James Home (or Hume) joined the Royal Regt. 1 Oct. 1689 as an Ensign. Capt.-Lieut. 1 June, 1695. Capt. 1 Aug. 1695. Served at the siege of Namur. Fought at Schellenberg, Blenheim, and other great battles under Marlborough. Bt.-Maj. 1 Jan. 1712. Regtal. 1st Major, 1 Sept. 1718. Regtal. 1st Lt.-Col. 1 July, 1737. D. about 1742.

[7] Fifth son of the 1st Marquis of Atholl. Born 28 Feb. 1669. Appointed Ensign in the Scots Guards, 13 Sept. 1687. Capt. in Col. George McGill's Regt. of Foot in 1696. Capt. in the Royal (Scots) Regt. 17 Oct. 1701. Served several campaigns under Marlborough. Deputy Lieut. for Perthshire. Govr. of Blair Castle in 1716. Serving in aforesaid Regt. 1718. Out of the Army before 1728. D. 11 Nov. 1737. Bd. in the Abbey Church, Holyrood. By the widow of Major Andrew White, Lord Edward Murray left a son John who d. 1748.—*Peerage*.

⁸ This officer's Commission as Capt. in above Regt. must be an error, as his name is given in the 3rd Foot Guards as Capt. and Lt.-Col. under same date. See p. 130 and note 4, p. 131.

⁹ Fifth son of 1st Duke of Atholl. Bn. 4 Oct. 1694. "Lord George Murray served the campaign of 1712 in Flanders as an Ensign in the Royal Regt." (communicated by the Duke of Atholl in a letter dated 24 July, 1904). His Commission as Ensign is not registered in the War Office Books; it was probably signed by the Duke of Ormonde in Flanders. "When on leave, in 1715, Lord George Murray deserted and joined Lord Mar. He was given the command of a regt. of Atholl men" (communicated by the Duke of Atholl). The subsequent career of Lord George Murray as a Jacobite leader is well known. It need only be stated here that as a soldier and leader he was immeasurably superior to any of the Georgian commanders who took the field against him during the years 1745 and 1746. He d. in North Holland on 11 Oct. 1760.

¹⁰ Charles Armand *Paulet*—an illegitimate son of the 2nd Duke of Bolton. Appointed Ensign in the Royal Regt. 4 Mar. 1710. He was then a child, and his name appears as such in "A List of Minors" for 1711, or 1712. Capt. in the Inniskilling Fusiliers on the accession of George I. Major of Lord Mark Kerr's Regt. of Foot, 12 Dec. 1717. A.D.C. to his father, the Duke of Bolton, when Lord-Lieut. of Ireland in 1717. Lt.-Col. of Brigadier Gore's Dragoons, 7 Mar. 1720. Lt.-Col. of the 1st Troop of Horse Grenadier Guards, 3 April, 1733. Col. of the 9th Regt. of Marines, 27 Dec. 1740. Half-pay, 1749. Brig.-Gen. 28 May, 1745. Maj.-Gen. 27 Sept. 1747. D. in 1751.

¹¹ Second son of Col. the Hon. Thos. Dalzell of the Scots Foot Guards. Joined the Jacobite forces in the autumn of 1715 and was taken prisoner at Preston. In a letter from James Craggs (aftds. Sec.-at-War) to Lord Townshend, dated "Preston, Nov. 23rd, 1715," occurs this passage: "My Lord Orkney has sent an express here to Mr. Wills with a letter to intercede for Lord Ch. Murray, his nephew a son of Lord Bazil Hamilton, and an officer in his own Regiment one Dalzell" (*Townshend Papers*, p. 170). It was entirely owing to Lord Orkney's intercession that Ensign John Dalzell was pardoned. He md. a dau. of Wm. Tildesley and had a son who settled in the Island of St. Christopher.

¹² One of the 21 children of Sir James Agnew, Bt. In 1724 he was a Captain on half-pay from Orkney's Regt. The *Daily Journal* of 6 May, 1724, describes a duel between the above Capt. Alex. Agnew and Major (Charles) Harrison, "brother (*sic*) to Lord Townshend," in London. Agnew ran Harrison through the body, and the latter died in a few hours. Before his end Major Harrison nobly owned that he had been the aggressor. Agnew was, therefore, not held responsible.

COLONEL KIRK'S REGIMENT OF FOOT.
[2ND FOOT.]

NAME.	RANK.	DATE OF COMMISSION.
Piercy Kirk,[1]	Col. & Capt.	19 Sept. 1710.
John Arnott,[2]	Lt.-Col. & Capt.	[15 Mar. 1712.]
John Fitzgerald,[3]	Major and Capt.	31 Oct. 1712.
Andrew De Boismorelle,	Captain	—
Robert Layton,	,,	[1 Mar. 1692.]
Roger Davis,	,,	[Out in 1717.]
Peter Heart,	,,	[6 Apr. 1706.]
John Culliford,	,,	[Out in 1717.]
John Phillips,	,,	25 Aug. 1712.
William Francks,	,,	6 Apr. 1714.
James Giles,	Capt.-Lieut.	[1 Aug. 1707.]
Dymock Lister,	Lieutenant	19 Oct. 1713.
John Dalrymple,	,,	1 Aug. 1707.
John Haylett,	,,	[2 June, 1704.]
Isaac Browne,	,,	[21 Feb. 1709.]
James Nicholls,	,,	[24 June, 1707.]
John Arthurlony (sic)	,,	[9 Feb. 1706.]
John Legg,	,,	[15 Apr. 1707.]
William Graham,[4]	,,	[16 Sept. 1710.]
Charles May,	,,	[1 Jan. 1704.]
John Slacke,	,,	[16 Feb. 1703.]
James Bradon,	Ensign	30 Sept. 1711.
John How,	,,	6 Apr. 1714.
George Arnold,	,,	25 Dec. 1713.
Samuell Chaplain,	,,	26 Apr. 1714.
John Johnson,	,,	[3 Oct. 1705.]
Henry Shepherd,	,,	13 Aug. 1708.
John Williams,	,,	[6 Sept. 1706.]
Cosby Phillips,[5]	,,	—
Samuel Hinton,	,,	13 Nov. 1710.
Francis Shaw,	Chaplain	—
William Arnott,	Adjutant	1 July, 1713.
Thomas Ross,	Quartermaster	—
Thomas Eyre,	Surgeon	—

[1] Son of Lt.-Gen. Percy Kirke. Appointed Ensign in the Duchess of York's Regt. 3 May, 1684, when only twelve months old (see "Child Commissions in the Army, 1661–1714," by Charles Dalton, printed in *Notes and Queries*, 8th Series, Vol. VIII., 30 Nov. 1895). This "Lambkin" was a captain in the Queen Dowager's Regt. (2nd Queen's) in 1689. He was for some years "housekeeper" at Whitehall Palace. Joined his Regt. as a full-blown Lt.-Col., and commanded it at Almanza, in 1707, where he and most of his officers were taken prisoners. Col. of said Regt. 19 Sept. 1710. Attained the rank of Lt.-Gen. 2 July, 1739. D. 1 Jan. 1741, "aged fifty-seven." Bd. in Westminster Abbey.

[2] John Arnot's name appears in a List of above Regt. for Jan. 1692. Promoted Capt. 1 Mar. 1696. Served in the Cadiz Expedition of 1702. Prisoner at Almanza. Bt.-Lt.-Col. 31 Feb. 1708. Served as a Paymaster-Gen. to the Forces, under Maj.-Gen. John Hill, sent to reduce Canada in 1711. Bt.-Col. 15 Nov. 1711. Of Abbotshall, near Kirkcaldy, Fife. Assumed the Baronetcy of Arnot of Arnot (see G.E.C.'s *Complete Baronetage*). Appointed Adjutant-General of Scotland, 1727. Brig.-Gen. 6 Nov. 1735. Maj.-Gen. 2 July, 1739.

Lt.-Gen. 2 Feb. 1743. "By deed dated 16 Feb. 1749-50, he disponed his Barony of Arnot in trust for his sons and three daughters." He d. 4 June, 1750, and was bd. 6 June at Trinity Church, Micklegate, York. Will proved 20 June following.

[3] This officer's services previous to his appointment as Major of above Regt. have not been ascertained. Serving in 1717. Out of the Regt. before 1727. He was probably son of Col. John Fitzgerald, who commanded an Irish Regt. of Foot at Tangier in 1663, and was for some years Lt.-Govr. of this place.

[4] Of Balliheridon, Armagh. Appointed Ensign in above Regt. 1 Sept. 1706. Taken prisoner at Almanza. Served with Gen. Hill's Expedition to Canada in 1711. Promoted Lt.-Col. of the Queen's Regt. 25 Mar. 1723. Col. of the 54th Regt. (aftds. the 43rd L.I.) 12 Aug. 1741. Transferred to the Colonelcy of the 11th Foot, 7 Feb. 1746. Brig.-Gen. 18 Apr. 1746. Accompanied the Expedition to Port L'Orient same year. D. 29 Sept. 1747. See memoir of this officer by Charles Dalton, in *The Oxfordshire Light Infantry Chronicle* for 1901.

[5] Appointed Capt. of the Grenadier Cy. in Col. Richard Philipps's newly-raised Regt. 25 Aug. 1717.

LORD FORFAR'S REGIMENT OF FOOT.

[3RD FOOT.]

NAME.	RANK.	DATE OF COMMISSION.
Archibald, Earl of Forfar,[1]	Colonel	14 Apr. 1713.
Alexander Rose,[2]	Lt.-Col. & Capt.	25 July, 1715.
Francis Williamson,[3]	Major and Capt.	,, ,,
Alexander Deane,	Captain	[3 Feb. 1705.]
Gilbert Talbot,	,,	[2 Jan. 1708.]
Nathl. Gittins,	,,	[1 May, 1708.]
John Grierson,	,,	[,, ,,]
Hugh Montgomery,	,,	[1 Oct. 1709.]
Richard Lowther,	,,	[15 Mar. 1715.]
James Bolton,	,,	24 Aug. 1715.
George Grant,	,,	,, ,,
Charles Wardlaw,	Capt.-Lieut.	[15 Mar. 1714.]
John Preston,[4]	Lieutenant	————
Samuel Wilson,	,,	[20 Apr. 1708.]
Robert Melvill,	,,	[Out in 1717.]
Thomas Seaman,	,,	[24 May, 1709.]
Benjamin Smith,	,,	[1 Oct. 1709.]
Charles Barnes,	,,	[,, ,,]
William Henry Cherette,	,,	[Out in 1717.]
William Reid,	,,	[,, ,,]
David Nairne,	,,	[,, ,,]
James Campbell,	,,	[,, ,,]
Henry Wilson,	,,	24 Aug. 1715.
Abraham Lamb,	,,	,, ,,
Charles Moone (sic)	Ensign	[1 Oct. 1709.]
William Littler,	,,	[25 Nov. 1715.]
William White,[5]	,,	————
John Strode,	,,	[Out in 1717.]
Samuel Wardlaw,	,,	[,, ,,]
Thomas Condon,	,,	[,, ,,]
William Banche (sic)[6]	,,	————
James Coult,	,,	[25 Apr. 1711.]
Richard Scott,	,,	24 Aug. 1715.
James Stone,	,,	,, ,,
John Haywood,	,,	[18 May, 1714.]
Robert Steuart,	Chaplain	[27 Feb. 1711.]
John Littler,	Adjutant	[24 Sept. 1711.]
Robert Hope,	Surgeon	[Out in 1717.]

[1] See special memoir, pp. 81-84.

[2] Possibly identical with the Capt. Alex. *Ross*, of the Earl of Orkney's Regt., who served at Blenheim and Malplaquet. Lt.-Col. Alex. Rose's Commission in the War Office Book for 1715 has this note: "This gentleman only has Major's pay." Served at the battle of Sheriffmuir. Comn. as Lt.-Col. of above Regt. renewed by George II. in 1727. Out of the Regt. before 1740.

[3] Appointed Lieut. and Capt. in the Coldstream Guards, 9 Dec. 1703. Capt. in the Buffs, 21 Apr. 1706. Served at Malplaquet. The Register of his Comn. as Major of the Buffs in

the War Office Book for 1715 has this note: "This gentleman receives only Captain's pay." Served at Sheriffmuir. Capt. and Lt.-Col. in the 1st Foot Guards, 21 Feb. 1722. Comn. renewed in 1727. Out of the Foot Guards before 1740. A certain Col. Williamson d. as Deputy-Governor of the Tower in 1747.

[4] D. in Apr. 1717.

[5] Promoted Lieut. in room of John Preston, 25 Apr. 1717. See account in the Introduction of the escape of Mr. Wm. Hay, Jacobite prisoner, from Carlisle Castle, in Mar. 1716, on the night when Ensign Wm. White was "Captain of the Guard."

[6] Ensign Wm. *Branch* was killed at Sheriffmuir. Cannon's *Records of the 3rd Buffs*, p. 166.

LIEUT.-GENERAL SEYMOUR'S REGIMENT OF FOOT.

[4TH FOOT.]

NAME.	RANK.	DATE OF COMMISSION.
William Seymour,[1]	Col. & Capt.	—
Magnus Kempenfelt,[2]	Lt.-Col. & Capt.	1 May, 1711.
William Bissett,[3]	Major & Capt.	,, ,,
Edward Purcell,[4]	Captain	—
Thomas Saville,	,,	[7 May, 1702.]
George Dumaresque,	,,	[7 July, 1702.]
John Tucker,	,,	[13 Apr. 1709.]
James Farrell,	,,	24 Mar. 1709–10.
Thomas Norcliff,	,,	30 June, 1710.
Thomas Vatchell,	,,	[23 Aug. 1711.]
Ralph Kynaston,	Capt.-Lieut.	,, ,,
Samuel Holbrook,	Lieutenant	30 June, 1710.
Richard Coren,	,,	[23 Aug. 1711.]
John Beverly,	,,	—
Henry Taaff,	,,	[17 Mar. 1709.]
John Nutt,	,,	[23 Aug. 1711.]
John Trelawny,	,,	[22 Dec. 1709.]
Samuel Anthony,	,,	26 Nov. 1713.
Richard Burchas (sic)[5]	,,	—
John Swift,	,,	[15 Nov. 1707.]
William Newton,	,,	[27 Feb. 1712.]
Francis Henry Lee,[6]	Ensign	8 Apr. 1713.
John Lillingston,	,,	12 Jan. 1712–13.
William Bush,	,,	[13 Apr. 1709.]
John Harris,	,,	30 June, 1710.
Rowland West,	,,	[23 Aug. 1711.]
Jonathan Furlong,	,,	[25 Mar. 1706.]
William Trelawny,	,,	26 Nov. 1713.
Robert King,	,,	[23 Aug. 1711.]
Maximilian Vannarsen,	,,	[Out in 1717.]
William Grills,	Chaplain	20 Aug. 1711.
John Trelawny,	Adjutant	2 May, 1712.
Richard Burcas (sic)[5]	Quartermaster	[23 Aug. 1711.]
John Beale,	Surgeon	9 Dec. 1714.

[1] Second son of Sir Edward Seymour, Bt., of Berry Pomeroy, co. Devon. Appointed 2nd Lieut. to Lord Dartmouth's own Cy. in the Rl. Fusiliers, 11 June, 1685. Capt. 1 May, 1686. Major and Lt.-Col. Coldstream Guards, 1 Jan. 1692. Regtal. Lt.-Col. of do. 10 Aug. same year. Wd. at Landen in 1693. Appointed Col. of Lord Cutts's Regt. of Foot 3 Oct. 1694. This Regt. was disbanded at the Peace of Ryswick. Col. of the Regt. aftds. known as the 24th Foot, 1 Mar. 1701. Transferred to the Queen's Own Regt. of Foot, 12 Feb. 1702. Brig.-Gen. 9 May 1702. Commanded a Brigade before Cadiz in 1702, and was wd. at Vigo. Seymour's Regt. was temporarily constituted a Regt. of Marines in 1703, and served as such on board the Fleet. Seymour was promoted Maj.-Gen. 1 Jan. 1704. Lt.-Gen. 1 Jan. 1707. He retd. in Dec. 1717, and d. 9 Feb. 1727.

[2] "Entered the Coldstream Guards as a Volunteer, 7 Oct. 1685." Appointed Qr.-Mr. to the Coldstream Guards, 1 Jan. 1689. Adjt. 1 Nov. 1690. Capt. in the Queen's Own, 1 May, 1702. Served as A.D.C. to Brig. Mathew at the taking of Vigo same year. Bt.-Maj. of

Marines 10 Jan. 1706. Regtal. Major, 30 June, 1710. Regtal. Lt.-Col. 1 May, 1711. Serving in 1717. Out of the Regt. 24 Mar. 1718. Lt.-Govr. of Jersey before 1725. He md. Anne Hunt, spinster, of St. Margaret's, Westminster (Licence dated 12 Dec. 1703). The youngest son by this marriage was Admiral Richard Kempenfelt.

[3] Serving in 1717. Out of the Regt. before 1727.

[4] Appointed Maj. of the Queen's Own Regt. 8 June, 1702. Served at Cadiz and Vigo. Regtal. Lt.-Col. 1 Mar. 1704. Appears to have sold his Lt.-Colonelcy to Kempenfelt, 1 May, 1711, as his name appears in above List as Senior Captain. Left the Regt. in May, 1716. A certain Lt.-Col. Purcell d. at Kingston-upon-Hull in 1732—*Gentleman's Magazine.*

[5] *Purchas.* Served with the Expedition to Canada, in 1711, as 1st Lieut. in above Regt. Qr.-Mr. 23 Aug. 1711. Serving in 1717.

[6] Attained the rank of Lt.-Col. in above Regt. 24 Mar. 1718. Serving as such, 1727.

GENERAL PEARCE'S REGIMENT OF FOOT.
[5TH FOOT.]

NAME.	RANK.	DATE OF COMMISSION.
Thomas Pearce,[1]	Col. & Capt.	
Peter Godby,[2]	Lt.-Col. & Capt.	10 Mar. 1707-8.
John Titchborne,[3]	Major & Capt.	
William Elrington,[4]	Captain	
Thomas Giles,	,,	28 Jan. 1707-8.
Charles Pearce,	,,	
Richard Bickerstaff,	,,	
Richard Hanmer,	,,	26 Mar. 1707.
William Vatchell,	,,	28 Apr. 1709.
Bacon Morris,	,,	
Thomas Morris,	,,	
John Morrice,	,,	24 June, 1713.
Henry Owen,	Capt.-Lieut.	
John Napper,	Lieutenant	21 May 1707.
John Elrington,	,,	21 May 1708.
John Parry,	,,	15 Aug. 1707.
Job Elrington,	,,	14 May, 1705.
Christopher Alcock,	,,	17 Dec. 1710.
Philip Barry,	,,	
Lambert Vanwell,	,,	30 Apr. 1707.
Nicholas Fenwick,	,,	
Paul Pepper,	,,	1 Dec. 1711.
William Wynne,	,,	26 May, 1712.
Francis Pyll,	,,	5 June, 1705.
John Durant Brevall,	,,	10 Nov. 1713.
Edward Hayes,	Ensign	1 Mar. 1708.
Angus Erle,	,,	29 May, 1711.
Thomas Browne,	,,	12 Oct. 1708.
Francis Offarel,	,,	20 Sept. 1707.
Henry Vatchell,	,,	1 Dec. 1711.
Peter Beakes,	,,	
Carey Godbey,	,,	17 May, 1709.
Gilbert Keene,	,,	7 Mar. 1712-13.
Butler Chancy,	,,	9 Nov. 1708.
Robert Claxton,	,,	10 Nov. 1713.
Peter Burnevell,	,,	24 June, 1710.
Samuel King,	Chaplain	
Philip Parry,	Adjutant	
John Napper,	Quartermaster	15 Aug. 1707.
Robert Hill,	Surgeon	

[1] This officer is said to have entered the Army 28 Feb. 1689, but the Register of his Comn. is not forthcoming. On 1 Apr. 1692 Pearce was appointed Capt. of the Grenadier Cy. in Lord Cutts's Regt., then serving in Flanders. Capt. of the Grenadier Cy. in the Coldstream Guards, with rank of Lt.-Col., 14 Oct. 1694. Wounded and taken prisoner on 8 July, 1695, when storming the covered way at Namur with his Company. Served in the Expedition to Cadiz in 1702, and commanded a force composed of Grenadiers at the storming of the Forts of Vigo, when he was seriously wounded by a cannon-ball. Appointed Col. of

a newly-raised Regt. of Foot, 10 Apr. 1703, from which he was removed to the corps now known as the Northumberland Fusiliers (5th Foot), 5 Feb. 1704. Brig.-Gen. 1 Jan. 1707. Served in Portugal, and highly distinguished himself at the battle of the Caya in 1709, when he was taken prisoner. On his return to England he was promoted Maj.-Gen. Govr. of Limerick in 1715. On 8 Dec. 1724, Pearce was granted an addition of 6s. 8¾d. *per diem* as a Maj.-Gen. on the Irish Establishment, "as he has distinguished himself by his vigilance and care" (*Treasury Warrant* of above date). Lt.-Gen. 5 Mar. 1727. M.P. for Melcomb Regis. Col. of the 4th D.G. 27 Sept. 1732. D. in 1739. His will, as Lt.-Gen. of the Forces, was proved at Dublin.

[2] Appointed Capt. in above Regt. 2 Apr. 1692. Served in Flanders. Major's Comn. not forthcoming. Bt.-Lt.-Col. 5 Apr. 1707. Served at the battle of the Caya in Portugal. Lt.-Col. of above Regt. 10 Mar. 1708. Serving at Gibraltar in 1712 and for some years subsequently. Out of the Regt. 25 Aug. 1722. The will of a certain Peter Godbey, Esq., was proved at Dublin in 1735.

[3] Fourth son of Sir Wm. Tichborne, Bt., of Beaulieu. Appointed 2nd Lieut. of Grenadiers in above Regt. 2 Apr. 1692. Capt. 29 Dec. 1693. Major before 1714. Sold his Comn. 28 Sept. 1715. Appointed Govr. of Charlemont, Ireland. D. in 1745.

[4] Appointed Capt.-Lieut. in above Regt, 2 Apr. 1692. Served in Flanders. Capt. 16 Feb. 1694. Bt.-Maj. 12 June, 1708. Regtal. Maj. 25 Aug. 1722. Appointed Commandant of Gibraltar 1719–1720. Lt.-Col. of above Regt. 25 Aug. 1722. Served with above Regt. at the Defence of Gibraltar in 1727. Returned to Ireland with his Corps in 1728. Not in any subsequent List.

COLONEL O'HARA'S ROYAL REGIMENT OF FUSILIERS.
[7TH FOOT.]

NAME.	RANK.	DATE OF COMMISSION.
James O'Hara,[1]	Col. & Capt.	[29 Jan. 1712–13.]
Gervas Parker,[2]	Lt.-Col. & Capt.	
Francis Rainsford,[3]	Major & Capt.	
Josua Jackson,	Captain	
Richard Baines,	,,	
James Browne,	,,	
Robert Cunningham,	,,	24 Dec. 1709.
James Flemming (*sic*)[4]	,,	[12 May, 1715.]
Pierce Griffith,	,,	18 Feb. 1709–10.
Richard Pierson,	,,	13 Mar. 1710–11.
David Barry,	,,	16 May, 1712.
Steven Petetot,	,,	14 Nov. 1712.
Robert Carthew,	Capt.-Lieut.	
George Crofts,	[1st] Lieutenant	
William Cropp,	,,	
Edward Butler,	,,	
Roger Haille,	,,	9 Oct. 1706.
Jno. Little,	,,	13 May, 1709.
John Bradshaw,	,,	
Thomas Powell,	,,	
John Cooke,	,,	
John Gunby,	,,	7 April, 1709.
Mat. Jones,	,,	20 July, 1708.
John Shireman,	,,	
Jeffery Gibbon,	,,	20 July, 1708.
Henry Crofton,	[2nd] Lieutenant	
Andrew Fitzpatrick,	,,	
John Marshall,	,,	
Joseph Dambon,	,,	
Thomas Hollyland,	,,	
Samuel Clutterbuck,	,,	
William Raudduck,	,,	14 May, 1710.
George Speke Petty,	,,	12 May, 1715.
Charles Parker,	,,	14 May, 1707.
Chichester Hamilton,	,,	
Charles Bucknall,	,,	
John Bradshaw,	Adjutant	
Thomas Rogers,	Quartermaster	
Smith Stone,	Chaplain	
[Edward] Higgins,	Surgeon	

[1] Aftds. Field-Marshal Baron Tyrawley. See special memoir in Vol. II.
[2] Appointed Ensign in Brig. Wm. Steuart's Regt. 9 Sept. 1695. Lieut. 17 May, 1697. Adjt. and Qr.-Mr. to the Rl. Fusiliers, 17 Nov. 1700. 1st Lieut. 21 Apr. 1701. Capt.-Lieut. 23 Dec. 1702. Capt. 15 Mar. 1703. Bt.-Col. 24 Dec. 1707. Accompanied his Regt. to Spain in 1705. Fought at Barcelona and Lerida. Commanded the Corps in the absence of Charles, Lord Tyrawley. Served in Minorca 1713–1714. Regtal. Lt.-Col. 11 Jan. 1715. Out of the Regt. before 4 Aug. 1722. Brig.-Gen. 14 Mar. 1727. Maj.-Gen. 6 Nov. 1735.

Lt.-Gen. 27 May, 1745. Commander-in-Chief in Ireland in 1748. In Aug. 1739 the following obituary notice appeared in the *Gentleman's Magazine:* "Gervase Parker, Esq., son to the Lieut.-General and Fort-Major of Kinsale."

[3] Eldest son of Capt. Fras. Rainsford, of the Tower of London. Served with the Rl. Fusiliers at the siege of Namur, and was wounded at the attack of the breach of Terra Nova under Lord Cutts, 20 Aug. 1695. Capt. 14 Sept. 1695. Lost an arm at the siege of Lerida in 1707. Bt.-Lt.-Col. before 1713. Major, 11 Jan. 1715. Md. Eliz. Stranwise, of Carlisle. D. a widower in 1720. Left three sons, all of whom were in the Army.—*The Genealogist*, Vol. II., p. 108.

[4] Believed to be identical with the James Fleming appointed Ensign to Viscount Mountjoy, in latter's newly-raised Regt. of Foot in Ireland, 10 Mar. 1702. 1st Lieut. in the Rl. Fusiliers, 7 Sept. 1706. Capt. 12 May, 1715. Served in Spain and Minorca; also served with his Corps on Admiral Byng's Fleet, 1718. Date of Major's Comn. not known. Lt.-Col. 4 Aug. 1722. Appointed Col. of the 36th Foot, 9 Jan. 1741. Brig.-Gen. 4 June, 1745. Served at Falkirk 17 Jan. 1746, and at the battle of Culloden same year. Maj.-Gen. 20 Sept. 1747. D. at Bath, and was bd. in Westminster Abbey, 30 Mar. 1751. The executor to his will was Lieut. John Fleming, of the Rl. Fusiliers, nephew to the testator.

BRIGADIER GROVE'S REGIMENT OF FOOT.
[10TH FOOT.]

NAME.	RANK.	DATE OF COMMISSION.
Henry Grove,[1]	Colonel & Captain	[23 June, 1715.]
Francis Columbine,[2]	Lt.-Col. & Capt.	4 Aug. 1715.
John Granville,[3]	Major & Captain	[25 Apr. 1704.]
Samuel Buller,[4]	Captain	[3 Aug. 1704.]
Charles Legg,[5]	,,	,, ,,
Richard Trevanion.[6]	,,	
Cuthbert Morland,	,,	24 Feb. 1704.
Henry Poilblanc,	,,	,, 1705.
Scipio Durour,	,,	[8 Mar. 1710.]
Manus O'Cane,	,,	15 Aug. 1710.
John Langley,	,,	[21 Sept. 1710.]
Cæsar Bonnin,	,,	[12 Jan. 1711.]
Grinvall (sic) Raleigh,	Capt.-Lieut.	25 Sept. 1712.
Henry Slingsby,	Lieutenant	[Out in 1717.]
James Scott,	,,	24 Aug. 1706.
James Littlejohn,	,,	1 May, 1709.
Robert Pujolas,	,,	[Out in 1717.]
James Cunningham,	,,	12 Jan. 1710.
Thomas Preston,	,,	3 Aug. 1704.
William Walker,	,,	[25 Sept. 1712.]
Henry Rogers,	,,	1 Jan. 1709.
Henry Sprott,[7]	,,	
Charles Tonyne,	,,	24 Jan. 1711–12.
Arthur Taylor,	Lieutenant	6 Dec. 1714.
Henry Brownjohn,[8]	,,	30 Apr. 1709.
Thomas Forth,	Ensign	11 May, 1715.
John Ramsay,	,,	[Out in 1717.]
Robert Granville,	,,	1 Jan. 1709.
August de Beez,	,,	1 Aug. 1711.
George Langley,	,,	[1 Jan. 1709.]
Edmund Titchburn,	,,	[,, ,,]
John Preston,	,,	1 Aug. 1711.
William Lyne,	,,	24 Jan. 1711–12.
Alexander Elphinston,	,,	3 Nov. 1710.
G. R. La Coudrier,	,,	26 Sept. 1712.
John Wharton,	,,	28 Sept. 1711.
Joseph Foster,	Chaplain	23 Feb. 1705.
John Cunningham,	Quartermaster	20 Apr. 1714.
David de Beez,	Surgeon	10 July, 1694.
Gustavus Hamilton,	Adjutant	20 Apr. 1714.

[1] This officer is said to have joined the Army as Ensign in Dec. 1688. He was appointed Capt.-Lieut. in the Rl. Fusiliers, 1 Aug. 1692. Capt. 20 May, 1693. Wounded at the storming of the breach of Terra Nova, Namur, 20 Aug. 1695. Major to Sir Mat. Bridges's Regt. of Foot, 2 June, 1700. Bt.-Lt.-Col. 6 May, 1703. Lt.-Col. of the Regt. known subsequently as the 10th Foot, 25 Apr. 1704. Commanded this Corps at Blenheim. Bt.-Col. 1 Jan. 1706. Wounded at Oudenarde. Taken prisoner at the siege of Ghent. Served at the siege of Tournay and the battle of Malplaquet. Brig.-Gen. 12 Feb. 1711. Col. of

above Regt. 23 June, 1715. Lt.-Govr. of Berwick, 25 June, 1715. Maj.-Gen. 8 Mar. 1727. Govr. of Dartmouth. Lt.-Gen. 31 Oct. 1735. D. 20 Nov. 1736. Bd. in Westminster Abbey.

[2] Bro. to Col. Ventris Columbine. Appointed Ensign in his brother's Regt. 1 July, 1695. Capt. 1 Mar. 1702. Lt.-Col. of Col. Heyman Rooke's Regt. of Foot, 24 Feb. 1705. Bt.-Col. 17 Feb. 1706. Half-pay, 1713. Lt.-Col. of Brigadier Grove's Regt. of Foot, 4 Aug. 1715. Brig.-Gen. 2 Mar. 1727. Maj.-Gen. 29 Oct. 1735. Col. of above Regt. 27 July, 1737. Lt.-Gen. 2 July, 1739. D. in Dec. 1746.

[3] Appointed Ensign to Sir Bevil "Greenvill," in the Earl of Bath's Regt. of Foot at its first raising. Capt.-Lieut. 20 May, 1693. Served in Flanders. Capt. 19 Apr. 1694. Bt.-Maj. 25 Oct. 1703. Reg.-Maj. 25 Apr. 1704. Fought at Blenheim and was wounded. Bt.-Lt.-Col. 4 June, 1706. Bt.-Col. 1 Nov. 1711. Served throughout Marlborough's campaigns. Left the Regt. 3 Nov. 1715. On half-pay, 1722.

[4] Appointed Ensign in above Regt. 10 Feb. 1693. Served in Flanders. Lieut. 11 Apr. 1697. Adj. in 1702. Capt. 3 Aug. 1704. Wounded at Blenheim. Served throughout Marlborough's campaigns. Bt.-Lt.-Col. 1 Jan. 1712. Out of the Regt. in 1717.

[5] Served as a Lieut. in above Regt. at Blenheim (*Blenheim Roll*, p. 45). Capt.'s Comn. dated "3 Aug. 1704." Brig.-Maj. in Flanders, 24 Dec. 1710. Served throughout Marlborough's campaigns. Bt.-Maj. 1 Jan. 1712. Appointed Capt.-Lieut. with rank of Lt.-Col. in the 3rd Regt. of Foot Guards, 25 Nov. 1717. Comn. renewed by George II. in 1727. 1st Major of said Regt. 9 July, 1736. Serving in 1740.

[6] Of Tregarthian, Cornwall. Appointed Ensign to an Independent Cy. of Foot, 22 June, 1685. Capt. in the Earl of Bath's Regt. of Foot, 20 Feb. 1688. Lt.-Govr. of Pendennis Castle, 24 Aug. 1702. Was holding this appointment at the time of the battle of Blenheim. Resigned his Comn. 23 May, 1716.

[7] "Superannuated, 25 Oct. 1715."

[8] "Dead, 15 Aug. 1716."

COLONEL MONTAGUE'S REGIMENT OF FOOT.
[11TH FOOT.]

NAME.	RANK.	DATE OF COMMISSION.
[Edward] Montague,[1]	Col. & Capt.	[13 July, 1715.]
Herbert Lawrence,[2]	Lt.-Col. & Capt.	——
Charles Irvine,[3]	Major & Capt.	——
William Carvill,	Captain	——
Richard Milborne [Sen.],	,,	——
Thomas Humble,[4]	,,	6 Dec. 1708.
John La Forey.[5]	,,	——
John Edwards,	,,	——
Richard Edwards,	,,	15 Apr. 1707.
Richard Tracey,	,,	24 June, 1715.
Henry Domergue,	,,	6 Apr. 1714.
Samuell Bernardeau,[6]	Capt.-Lieut.	——
James Francks,	Lieutenant	——
James Cord,	,,	——
Henry Downes,	,,	——
Richard Milborn,[7]	,,	——
William Hynde,	,,	——
Benjamin Snow,	,,	——
William Mortimer,[8]	,,	——
William Humphreys,	,,	——
William Horneck,	,,	——
William Weakfield,	,,	——
Thomas Stevens,	,,	24 Aug. 1715.
[Thos.] Wheler,	,,	24 Aug. 1715.
Henry Bastide,	Ensign	——
James Warren,	,,	——
Charles Hutchinson,	,,	——
Thomas Kennedy,	,,	——
Herbert Lawrence,	,,	——
Lewis La Forey,		1 Aug. 1713.
Christopher Irvine,	,,	——
Robert Browne,[9]	,,	——
Arnoldus Tulikens,[10]	,,	——
Edward Mann,	,,	24 Aug. 1715.
William Lee,	,,	24 Aug. 1715.
Paul Bachelor,	Chaplain	——
James Harrison,	Adjutant	1 Aug. 1715.
Lancelot Storey,	Quartermaster	——
Robert Brown,	Surgeon	——

[1] Promoted from Lt.-Col. of Lord Cobham's Dragoons. See biog. notice on p. 106.
[2] Probably bro. to Lt.-Col. Harry Lawrence, of the Queen's Dragoons, killed at Almanza. Appointed Ensign in the Marquis de Puizar's Regt. of Foot, 1 May, 1696. Capt. of Grenadier Cy. in Col. Roger Elliot's newly-raised Regt. of Foot, 10 Apr. 1703. Bt.-Maj. 25 May, 1706. Capt. in the Queen's Dragoons, 12 June, 1707, in room of Col. Harry Lawrence. Maj. 30 June, 1710. Lt.-Col. of Major-Gen. John Hill's Regt. (11th Foot), 11 Apr. 1712. Bt.-Col. 7 May, 1713. Served at Sheriffmuir, and was returned as "killed" (Col. Thos. Harrison's "Despatch"). This report was contradicted in the London Gazette

of 26 Nov. 1715, where it is stated that "Col. Lawrence was taken prisoner." It is recorded that the Earl of Mar sent Col. Lawrence to the Duke of Argyll a few days after the battle to sound the Duke about peace negotiations. D. in Jan. 1732, as Lt.-Col. of the 11th Foot.

[3] In *Recommendations for Commissions in the New Levies*, 1706, is the following application from this officer, who was 3rd son of Wm. Irvine, of Ballindulla: "Capt. Chas. Irvine was one of the first that appeared in arms for the Protestant interest at Inniskilling, in Ireland, where he commanded a Company of Foot. His father, then a Capt. of Horse, was killed in the Service, and two of his brothers, one a Capt. of Foot and the other a Lieut. of Horse, had the like fate. That his uncle, Sir Gerard Irvine, had the King's Commission to command 12 Troops of Horse, and this gentleman had one of them given to him instead of his company; but before they were formed into a Regiment his uncle died, so that he was advised by his friends, upon promises of preferment, to accept a lieutenancy in Sir John Hanmer's Regt. He has served in Portugal, and narrowly escaped being made prisoner when the Regt. was taken, and has been recommended by the Earl of Galway, and the other general officers there, to succeed the Major that was reported to be dead. Prays to be a Lieut.-Col. in the New Levies" (*War Office MS.*). Wounded at Almanza. Bt.-Maj. 26 Apr. 1708. Reg.-Maj. 3 July, 1708. Bt.-Lt.-Col. before 1712, in which year he accompanied his Regt. to Dunkirk, when that fortress was given up by the French. Md., in 1698, Margaret King, sister to Dr. Wm. King, Archbishop of Dublin. Retd. before 1727. D. in 1745.

[4] Killed in action at Sheriffmuir.

[5] Appointed 2nd Lieut. in Col. Henry Holt's Regt. of Marines, 15 Dec. 1705. Capt. in Col. John Hill's Regt. in 1707. Served at Sheriffmuir and Glenshiel. Capt. and Lt.-Col. in the 1st Foot Guards, 11 Dec. 1728. 2nd Maj. with rank of Col. 20 Nov. 1745. 1st Maj. 5 Oct. 1747. Col. of the 6th Regt. of Marines in 1747. Half-pay, 1748. Govr. of Pendennis Castle. His son John, Capt. R.N., was appointed Commissioner for Naval Affairs in the Leeward Islands, 1772, and created a Bart.

[6] Killed at Sheriffmuir.

[7] Do.

[8] Do.

[9] Capt.-Lieut. 12 Jan. 1740. Killed at Fontenoy, in 1745, as a Capt. in above Regt.

[10] Lieut. in above Regt. 5 Jan. 1716. Capt. 5 June, 1733. Lt.-Col. 11 Nov. 1744. D. from wounds received at Fontenoy.

COLONEL PHILLIPS'S REGIMENT OF FOOT.

[12TH FOOT.]

NAME.	RANK.	DATE OF COMMISSION.
Richard Phillips,[1]	Col. & Capt.	16 Mar. 1711–12.
John Ligonier,[2]	Lt.-Col. & Capt.	
Joseph Sawle,[3]	Major & Capt.	1 Jan. 1710–11.
Chris. Nuttal,	Captain	———
Paradine Livesay,	,,	
James Long	,,	24 June, 1708.
Nathl. Cosley,	,,	
ohn Blake,	,,	16 May, 1706.
Alexander Cosby,[4]	,,	17 Apr. 1708.
Fairfax Clements,	,,	
Patrick Livesay,	,,	
Nicholas Phynbo (sic)[5]	,,	
Benjamin Bath,	Capt.-Lieut.	———
Jacob Artsen,	Lieutenant	3 Nov. 1702.
James Smith,	,,	18 Dec. 1710.
Arthur Gambell,	,,	
James Latour,	,,	
Robert Carr,	,,	
James Mitford,	,,	5 Dec. 1704.
Edward Filmer,	,,	
Roger Danson,	,,	24 June, 1708.
Mathew Wright,	,,	16 June, 1709.
John Vivian,	,,	30 June, 1710.
John Masterson,	,,	4 Sept. 1711.
John Cossely,	,,	
Fell Tokefield,	Ensign	23 Dec. 1711.
Henry Powell,	,,	30 Mar. 1710.
Robert Milner,	,,	———
James Wright,	,,	———
John Gardner,	,,	———
George Withers,	,,	———
Charles Farmer,	,,	18 Dec. 1710.
Francis Ligonier,[6]	,,	23 Dec. 1711.
John Huntington,	,,	———
Alexander Campbell,	,,	8 Sept. 1711.
Martin Emmenes,	,,	
Charles Livesay,	Chaplain	———
Arthur Gambell,	Adjutant	———
Mat. Quin,	Surgeon	———
Mat. King,	Quartermaster	1 July, 1712.

[1] Great-grandson of Sir John Philipps, Bt., of Picton Castle, Pembrokeshire. He was probably the — Philips who served in Flanders in 1678, as a Lieut. in Lord Morpeth's Regt. of Foot. He forwarded the Prince of Orange's cause at the Revolution, and was imprisoned by the Mayor of Dartmonth for circulating the Prince's "Declaration" (*Historical Records of the 40th Regt.*, p. 496). Appointed Capt. in the Earl of Drogheda's Regt. of Foot, 8 Mar. 1689. Fought at the Boyne. "The pistols which Philipps used in this battle are in the possession of his descendant, Sir James Philipps, Bt., of Picton Castle" (*Ibid.*). Capt. in

Maj.-Gen. Kirke's Regt. of Foot in Jan. 1692 (register not forthcoming). Served in Flanders and Spain. Taken prisoner at Almanza. Bt.-Lt.-Col. 1 June, 1707. Major of Kirke's Regt. 23 July, 1707. Lt.-Col. of same Regt. 19 Sept. 1710. Col. of Livesay's late Regt. (12th Foot), 16 Mar. 1712. Raised the Regt. subsequently known as the 40th Foot, and was appointed Colonel thereof 25 Aug. 1717. Govr. of Nova Scotia, 1717–1749. Brig.-Gen. 19 Nov. 1735. Maj.-Gen. 2 July, 1739. Lt.-Gen. 28 May, 1743. Transferred to the Colonelcy of the 38th Foot, 13 Mar. 1750. D. 24 Oct. 1754, aged 90, and was bd. in Westminster Abbey.

[2] See special memoir of Field-Marshal John, Earl Ligonier, in Vol. II.

[3] Appears to have been second son of Joseph Sawle, of Penrice, Cornwall. Appointed Capt. in Livesay's Regt. 31 Jan. 1707. Major, 1 Jan. 1711. Fort-Maj. of St. Anne's Fort in Minorca, 15 Nov. 1713. Retd. in May, 1717.

[4] Brother to Brig.-Gen. Wm. Cosby, Col. of the Rl. Irish Regt. of Foot, and Govr. of New York. Appointed Capt. in Livesay's Regt. 17 Apr. 1708. Maj. of Col. Philipps's Regt. (12th Foot), 10 May, 1717. Maj. of Col. Philipp's Regt. (40th Foot), 1 Dec. 1720. Lt.-Govr. of Annapolis. Lt.-Col. of Philipps's Foot, 22 Mar. 1740. D. in Nova Scotia, 26 Dec. 1743.

[5] Appointed Lieut. in Livesay's Regt. 8 Apr. 1708. Capt. 16 June, 1709. "Capt. Fynboe, a Holsteiner," was employed as an interpreter by Admiral Norris, when sent with a British Fleet to the Baltic in 1717, being acquainted with the languages of Northern Germany (*George the First and the Northern War*, by Chance, pp. 86–7). Resigned his Comn. 25 Apr. 1716. Was given a Brevet-majority for his services to Admiral Norris. George I. gave him £300 as a "Free Gift and Royal Bounty," 25 Apr. 1718. *Treasury Accounts.*

[6] Brother to Lt.-Col. (aftds. Field-Marshal) John Ligonier. Resigned his Comn. 13 July, 1717. Joined the 8th Horse (7th D.G.) after 1720 (in which year John Ligonier was appointed Col.), and attained the rank of Major of said Corps, 1 May, 1729. Lt.-Col. 8 July, 1737. Served at Dettingen, where he was badly wounded. D. a Bt.-Col. in 1746.

COLONEL COTTON'S REGIMENT OF FOOT.
[13TH FOOT.]

NAME.	RANK.	DATE OF COMMISSION.
Stanhope Cotton,[1]	Col. & Captain	28 July, 1715.
Francis Bowes,[2]	Lt.-Col. & Capt.	—
Ferdinand Richard Hastings,[3]	Major & Capt.	—
Mark Antonio Moncall,[4]	Captain	—
John Duncomb,[5]	,,	—
John Lloyd,	,,	—
Thomas England,	,,	—
William Carleton,	,,	—
William Knypes	,,	—
Benjamin Hodder,	,,	—
Moses Moreau,	,,	—
Edmund Webb,	,,	—
Ralph Jenkins,	Capt.-Lieut.	—
Patrick Paterson,	Lieutenant	—
Isaac Bruse,	,,	—
Charles Booth,	,,	—
Robert Bullman,	,,	—
Hildebrand Jacob,	,,	—
Edward Barry,	,,	—
Charles Moncall,	,,	—
Adam Enos,	,,	—
Stephen Bateman,	,,	—
Daniel Pecquer,	,,	—
— Quinchant,	,,	—
George Walsh,	,,	24 Jan. 1712–13.
David Barry,	Ensign	—
James Charleton,	,,	—
Henry Waldron,	,,	—
Robert Fielding,	,,	—
Edward Windus,	,,	—
[Chas.] Lieving,	,,	—
Thomas Williams.	,,	—
John Hadzor,	,,	—
Jonathan Fox,	,,	—
Daniel Nicholas,	,,	—
James Barry,	,,	—
David Barry,	Chaplain	—
Matthew Draper,	Adjutant	—
John Lloyd,	Quartermaster	6 July, 1708.
John Hadzor,	Surgeon	—

[1] Appointed Capt.-Lieut. in Sir Roger Bradshaigh's Regt. of Foot at its first raising in April, 1706. Major of Col. Phineas Bowles's Regt. of Foot, 14 June, 1706. Bt.-Col. 15 Nov. 1711. Lt.-Govr. of Gibraltar same year. Col. Cotton was commissioned Capt. in Maj.-Gen. Whetham's Regt. of Foot, 20 April, 1713. Succeeded the Earl of Barrymore as Col. of the Regt. now known as the Somersetshire Light Infantry, 28 July, 1715. Believed to be the Col. Cotton who served as Staff Officer to Maj.-Gen. Wills at the siege of Preston in Nov. 1715. Commandant of Gibraltar, 1716–19. D. 7 Dec. 1725.

[2] This officer appears as Capt. of the Grenadier Company in the Earl of Barrymore's Regt. of Foot in 1706. Served with aforesaid Regt. at the battle of the Caya in 1709. Promoted Lt.-Col. 19 Aug. 1715. Commandant of Gibraltar for some months in 1719. D. or left the Regt. about 1720.

[3] Son of Brigadier Ferdinand Hastings (of the Earl of Huntingdon's family), a former Colonel of this Regt. Appointed Ens. in same Regt. 23 June, 1692. Capt. before 1702. Major, 19 Aug. 1715. Capt. and Lt.-Col. in the 1st Foot Guards, 15 June, 1716. Out of the Army before 1727.

[4] Son of Brig.-Gen. Mark Anthony Davesin de Moncal, who was Lt.-Col. of above Regt. in last reign. This Capt. Moncal appears in a "List of Minors," for 1712, as a Lieut. in the Earl of Barrymore's Regt. He left the Army before 1720.

[5] Probably son of the Major John Duncombe of the same Regt., who was preferred to the Horse Grenadier Guards, 31 May, 1711 (see p. 100). Capt. John Duncombe was appointed Capt. and Lt.-Col. in the 1st Foot Guards, 15 Oct. 1715. Col. of the 8th Regt. of Marines, 11 March, 1743. Placed on half-pay, 1748.

COLONEL HARRISON'S REGIMENT OF FOOT.

[15TH FOOT.]

NAME.	RANK.	DATE OF COMMISSION.
Henry Harrison,[1]	Col. & Capt.	8 Feb. 1714–15.
William Handasyde,[2]	Lt.-Col. & Capt.	[,, ,,]
Francis Burton,[3]	Major & Capt.	1 Jan. 1710–11.
Samuel Wishet (sic),[4]	Captain	
Richard Legg,[5]	,,	1 Feb. 1705–6.
William Haliday,	,,	21 May, 1708.
Robert Barton,	,,	24 Oct. 1708.
Walter Hamilton,	,,	[Out in 1717.]
William Howe,	,,	
John Laye,	,,	23 Apr. 1711.
Richard Talbott,	,,	1 June, 1711.
George Churchill,	,,	[Out in 1717.]
Arthur Edwards,	Capt.-Lieut.	[,, ,,]
David Bell,	Lieutenant	23 Oct. 1710.
Richard Lascelles,	,,	24 Apr. 1706.
James Whiston,	,,	24 Dec. 1706.
William Churchill,	,,	23 Oct. 1710.
Michael Brandreth,	,,	[14 Mar. 1712.]
Michael L'Abene,	,,	23 Feb. 1710–11.
Charles Crosbye,	,,	24 Oct. 1708.
John Pretty,	,,	28 Nov. 1711.
Robert Elliott,	,,	8 Mar. 1709–10.
Robert Frazier,	,,	30 Dec. 1710.
Thomas Johnson,	,,	[17 Sept. 1713.]
Alexander Abercrombie,	,,	[9 Nov. 1709.]
Goldsmith Boheme,	Ensign	1 June, 1711.
Thomas Levett,	,,	17 May, 1713.
Henry Bolt,	,,	15 July, 1711.
William Selbye,	,,	[21 Mar. 1713.]
George Sharpless,	,,	23 Feb. 1710–11.
Thomas Bowdler,	,,	[19 Aug. 1715.]
William Strachey,	,,	,, ,,
Richard Graham,	,,	15 May, 1711.
Peter Prowe,	,,	1 Mar. 1705–6.
Henry Brownjohn,	,,	10 May, 1711.
Gabriel Sediere,	,,	25 Oct. 1713.
Maximilian De l'Angle,	Chaplain	[10 Nov. 1706.]
John Whiston,	Adjutant	24 Oct. 1708.
John Bell,	Quartermaster	23 June, 1713.
Francis Faur,	Surgeon	7 July, 1702.
— La Roche,	Mate	

[1] Appointed Ens. in above Regt., 22 Feb. 1696. Lieut. and Adjt. before 1704. Wounded at Blenheim. Capt. 25 Aug. 1704. Served throughout Marlborough's campaigns. Bt.-Col. 15 Nov. 1711. Regtal. Lt.-Col. before 1715 (Commission register not forthcoming). Col. 8 Feb. 1715. Brig.-Gen. 9 Nov. 1735. Maj.-Gen. 2 July, 1739. Lt.-Gen. 5 Feb. 1743. D. in 1749.

² According to Millan's *Succession of Colonels*, 1742, Col. Wm. Handasyde obtained a Lieut.'s Commission in 1705, but the register is not to be found. On 8 Feb. 1715 he succeeded Col. Harrison as Lt.-Col. of latter's Regt. Col. Wm. Handasyde retained his post till 27 Jan. 1737, when he succeeded to the Colonelcy of the 31st Foot. He d. a Brig.-Gen. 27 Feb. 1745.

³ Appointed Capt. in Maj.-Gen. Emanuel Howe's Regt. (15th Foot), 1 March, 1705. Fought at Malplaquet. Major, 1 Jan. 1711. 1st Lt.-Col. of the 4th Tp. of Life Guards, 15 Feb. 1719. Serving in 1742. Out of the aforesaid Tp. when it was reduced in 1746. D. in 1753.

⁴ *Whitshed*. Served in Spain under Lord Galway. Appointed Capt. *en second* in Lt.-Gen. Wm. Steuart's Regt. of Foot, 13 Aug. 1708. Transferred to the Earl of Hertford's Regt. (15th Foot) about 1713. Half-pay, 1714. Restored to full-pay as Capt. in 15th Foot in Aug. 1715. Major in Lord Mountjoy's Regt. of Dragoons, 16 Feb. 1716. Major of the 8th Dragoons, 20 May, 1718. A.D.C. to the Lord-Lieutenant of Ireland. Lt.-Col. of 8th Dragoons, 2 May, 1720. Govr. of Wicklow Castle, 25 March, 1726. Col. of the 39th Foot, 28 Dec. 1740. Transferred to the Colonelcy of the 12th Dragoons, 14 June, 1743. D., as Brig.-Gen., in the spring of 1746. Will proved at Dublin.

⁵ Appointed Ens. in the Duke of Bolton's Regt. of Foot, 23 March, 1697. Lieut. in Sir Henry Belasyse's Regt. of Foot, 6 Sept. 1698. Exchanged to Col. Emanuel Howe's Regt. 10 June, 1699. Served at Blenheim. Capt. 1 Feb. 1706. Served through Marlborough's campaigns. Serving in 1717. Half-pay in 1722. Probably father of the Richard Legge of the Coldstream Guards.

LORD IRWIN'S REGIMENT OF FOOT.

[16TH FOOT.]

NAME.	RANK.	DATE OF COMMISSION.
Lord Irwin,[1]	Col. & Capt.	[11 July, 1715.]
John Cholmley,[2]	Lt.-Col. & Capt.	[,, ,,]
Michael Flemming,[3]	Major & Capt.	[1 May, 1709.]
John Reddich,[4]	Captain	
Samuel Sleigh,	,,	[1 Sept. 1699.]
William Gooch,[5]	,,	[11 Jan. 1715.]
Thomas Hoocke (sic),	,,	[28 Aug. 1704.]
John Heigham,	,,	[24 Feb. 1710.]
Shugbrough Whitney,[6]	,,	[1 Jan. 1709.]
John Smelt,	,,	4 Aug. 1715.
Thomas Fothergill,	,,	24 Aug. 1715.
William Hook,	,,	,, ,,
John Whiting,	Capt.-Lieut.	[31 Oct. 1712.]
William Mackreth,	Lieutenant	[29 June, 1705.]
John Hardie,	,,	[4 Sept. 1712.]
Garret Gaines,	,,	[1 Jan. 1709.]
Brudenel Wansborough,	,,	[1 May, 1709.]
Bartholomew Moody,	,,	[3 Nov. 1708.]
Edward Scattergood,	,,	[24 Feb. 1710.]
Richard Worthington,	,,	[24 June, 1705.]
Robert Bradford,	,,	[4 Sept. 1712.]
Robert Lawder,[7]	,,	
George Collingwood,	,,	24 Aug. 1715.
Edward Thurlow,	,,	24 Aug. 1715.
Edward Naish,	Ensign	[15 July, 1710.]
Charles Lyon,	,,	[1 May, 1709.]
James Falconer,	,,	[11 Jan. 1715.]
Henry Durell,	,,	[4 Sept. 1712.]
George Richardson,	,,	[21 Feb. 1710.]
Alexander Durham,	,,	[11 May, 1711.]
Theophilus De l'Angle,	,,	
William Adams,	,,	[15 Feb. 1711.]
Antonio Hardwelt,	,,	[25 Aug. 1704.]
John Gascoin,	,,	4 Aug. 1715.
William Scott,	,,	24 Aug. 1715.
Arthur Norcot,	,,	,, ,,
James Thwaites,	Chaplain	[24 May, 1712.]
John Whitney,	Adjutant	[7 June, 1713.]
John Smith,	Quartermaster	1 Mar. 1714.
Edmund Naish,	Surgeon	[3 Nov. 1708.]

[1] The Hon. Richard Ingram, 2nd son of Arthur, third Viscount of *Irvine*. He succeeded his elder brother as fifth Viscount, 18 May, 1714. Appointed Capt.-Lieut. in the 1st Regt. of Carabiniers (6th D.G.), 23 June, 1707. Col. of a Regt. (16th Foot), 11 July, 1715. Govr. of Hull. Transferred to the 2nd Regt. of Horse, 2 Dec. 1717. D. 10 April, 1721, of small-pox on the eve of sailing to Barbados, of which island he had been recently appointed

Govr. He md. Lady Anne Howard, 3rd dau. of Charles, 3rd Earl of Carlisle, a lady of much learning, who remarried Col. William Douglas in 1737. Lord Irvine was bd. in Westminster Abbey.

² Appointed Ens. in the 1st Foot Guards, 13 Jan. 1705. Capt. of a Grenadier Cy. in same Regt., with rank of Lt.-Col. 21 May, 1708. Lt.-Col. of a Regt. (16th Foot), 11 July, 1715. Col. of above Regt. 13 Dec. 1717. Served with said Regt. in Scotland, 1716–19. He was 2nd son of Nathaniel Cholmley (son of Sir Hugh Cholmley, Kt., Govr. of Tangier), and d. at Whitby in 1724.

³ Third son of Sir Daniel Fleming, Kt., of Rydall Hall, Westmorland. Appointed Ens. in the Hon. James Stanley's Regt. (16th Foot), 20 May, 1693. Lieut. 12 June, 1694. Capt. 25 May, 1697. Half-pay same year. Reappointed Capt. 31 May, 1701. Fought at Blenheim, where he was wounded. Bt.-Maj. 1 May, 1708. Served throughout Marlborough's campaigns. Regtal. Major, 1 May, 1709. M.P. for Westmorland. D. or left the Regt. in May, 1718.

⁴ Appointed Capt. in Col. John Carne's Regt. of Foot, 13 Oct. 1688. Capt. in Col. Hodges' Regt. (16th Foot), 31 Dec. 1688. Served at Steinkirk and Landen. Fought at Blenheim. Bt.-Lt.-Col. 1 Jan. 1706. Served throughout Marlborough's campaigns. Left the Regt. 20 June, 1717.

⁵ In the old parish church at Yarmouth is a tablet thus inscribed : "Sir Wm. Gooch, Bt., born 25 Oct. 1681. Served in Queen Anne's Wars, and married Mrs. Anne Staunton of Hampton, Middlesex. He loyally assisted quelling the Rebellion in Scotland, 1715. Lt.-Govr. of Virginia, 1727. He was the only Governor abroad against whom no inhabitant or merchant complained. Served at the siege of Carthagena, 1741. D. 15 Dec. 1751, at Bath."

⁶ Appointed Ens. in the Earl of Derby's Regt. (16th Foot), 25 Aug. 1704. Served in several campaigns under Marlborough. Lieut. 23 Dec. 1707. Capt. 1 Jan. 1709. Joined the Earl of Harrington's Dragoons (13th) as Capt. before 1728. Major, 11 June, 1733. Lt.-Col. 20 June, 1739. Served in Flanders. Wounded in an arm at Preston Pans; but supported Col. James Gardiner when mortally wounded on same disastrous field. Col. Whitney nobly fell at Falkirk a few months later.

⁷ "A Rebel" (see p. 197). Robert *Lauder* was appointed Lieut. in this Corps, 25 Dec. 1706, and was wounded at Malplaquet. Joined Mar's army in 1715.

BRIGADIER STERN'S REGIMENT OF FOOT.

[18TH FOOT.]

NAME.	RANK.	DATE OF COMMISSION.
Brigadier Stern,[1]	Col. & Capt.	18 Feb. 1711–12.
Moses Leathes,[2]	Lt.-Col. & Capt.	[,, ,,]
Frederick Lapenotier,[3]	Major	,, ,,
Peter D'Offranville,[4]	Captain	1 Jan. 1702–3.
William Leathes,[5]	,,	1 Jan. 1705–6.
Anthony Pujolas,[6]	,,	1 Nov. 1706.
Henry Wingfield,	,,	25 Mar. 1708.
Robert Parker,[7]	,,	11 Sept. 1708.
Robert Tripp,	,,	10 Aug. 1709.
John Blackney,	,,	10 Dec. 1709.
Stephen Gillman,[8]	,,	23 Mar. 1710–11.
Edward Moyle,	,,	[25 June, 1715.]
James Pinsent,	,,	20 Feb. 1711–12.
Charles Parker,	Capt.-Lieut.	[25 June, 1715.]
Joseph Young,	Lieutenant	10 Aug. 1709.
John Cherry,	,,	1 Apr. 1707.
Robert Pearson,	,,	[25 June, 1715.]
William Hopkey,	,,	23 Mar. 1710–11.
James Scott,	,,	23 May, 1710.
Thomas Carter,	,,	1 Apr. 1707.
Simon Montfort,	,,	11 Sept. 1708.
Aquilla Forster,	,,	20 Feb. 1711–12.
George Man,	,,	1 Aug. 1713.
Robert Selleoke,[9]	,,	28 Sept. 1708.
John Hamilton,	,,	23 Mar. 1710–11.
Richard Hawkins,	,,	10 Dec. 1709.
Robert Fitzsymonds,	Ensign	12 June, 1713.
Jere Messenden (sic),	,,	10 Dec. 1709.
William Clarke,	,,	23 Apr. 1713.
James Foster,	,,	8 Aug. 1711.
Alexander Agnew,	,,	1 Aug. 1713.
Edward Clements,	,,	16 Oct. 1709.
Francis Tuckey,	,,	[25 June, 1715.]
Walter Cherry,	,,	20 Feb. 1711–12.
Robert Gillman,	,,	30 June, 1711.
Benedict Blagden,	,,	23 Mar. 1710–11.
David Fowlis,	,,	15 Mar. 1711–12.
Egerton Cutler,	Chaplain	23 Dec. 1709.
Antonio Stawell,	Adjutant	1 Apr. 1713.
William Egar,	Quartermaster	22 June, 1713.
Hugh McManus.	Surgeon	10 Dec. 1710.

[1] Believed to be son of Capt. Robt. *Sterne* of the Cromwellian Army in Ireland. In 1678 this officer was serving as Ens. to Capt. John St. Leger's Independent Co. of Foot at Cork. In 1684, when the present Royal Irish Regt. of Foot was formed from certain Independent Companies in Ireland, Robert Sterne was appointed Lieut. in this Corps. Capt. 1 March, 1689. Major, 22 Dec. 1692. Lt.-Col. 21 Aug. 1695. Served at the sieges

of Limerick and Namur. Comded. his Regt. at Blenheim, Malplaquet, &c. Bt.-Col. 1 Jan. 1707. Brig.-Gen. 12 Feb. 1711. Col. of the Royal Irish Regt. 18 Feb. 1712. Appointed Govr. of the Royal Hospital, Kilmainham, in 1728. D. 1732.

[2] Probably son of Moses Leathes, the Purveyor to the fixed hospital in Ireland, 1690. Young Leathes was appointed Capt. of the Grenadier Cy. in Col. Luke Lillingston's Regt. of Foot, 22 Dec. 1694. Capt. in the Royal Irish Regt. 24 May, 1702. Wounded at Schellenberg. Bt.-Maj. 1 July, 1706. Bt.-Col. 15 Nov. 1711. Regtal. Lt.-Col. 18 Feb. 1712. Serving in 1717. Not in any subsequent List.

[3] *La Penotière.* Appointed Ens. in Prince George of Denmark's Regt. 14 Sept. 1693. Capt. in Col. Meredith's Regt. of Foot, 13 Feb. 1702. Transferred to the Royal Irish Regt. before Aug. 1704. Wounded at Blenheim. Bt.-Major, 1 July, 1706. Regtal. Major, 18 Feb. 1712. Md. Bridget, eldest dau. of the Hon. and Rev. John Feilding, D.D., youngest son of the Earl of Desmond. D., as Major of above Regt., in Jan. 1716. Capt. La Penotière, R.N., who fought at Trafalgar, brought home the despatches.

[4] Appointed Lieut. in above Regt. 7 May, 1694. Served at the siege of Namur. Capt. 1 Jan. 1703. Fought at Blenheim and subsequent battles under Marlborough. Major, 13 Jan. 1716. Serving in 1717. Not in any subsequent List.

[5] Appointed Lieut. in above Regt. 10 Feb. 1698. Capt. 1 Jan. 1706. Served at Blenheim and in Marlborough's subsequent campaigns. Resigned his Comn. to his kinsman, Lieut. Jeremiah Mussenden, 30 Nov. 1717.

[6] Appointed Ens. in the 1st Foot Guards, 1 May, 1693. 2nd Lieut. of Grenadiers, with rank of Capt., 19 April, 1697. A.D.C. to one of the General Officers at Blenheim. Capt. in the Royal Irish Regt. 1 Nov. 1706. Major, 8 June, 1720. Lt.-Col. 4 Sept. 1734. D. 24 April, 1741.

[7] Son of a Kilkenny farmer. Enlisted in Capt. Fred. Hamilton's Independent Cy. of Foot in Ireland, in Oct. 1683. This Cy. was added to Visct. Montjoy's Regt. in 1684. Turned out of the Army by Tyrconnel, when the Irish Forces were purged of all Protestant officers and soldiers. Re-enlisted, in London, in March, 1689, in Lord "Forbes's" (Royal Irish) Regt., which Corps he accompanied to Ireland the same year, and served throughout the Irish campaign. Wounded at the siege of Namur, and given an Ensigncy in the Royal Irish Regt. 16 Dec. 1695. Lieut. in 1702. Adjt. before 1706. Capt.-Lieut. 1 May, 1706. Fought at Blenheim and Ramillies. Severely wounded at the siege of Menin. Capt. of the Grenadier Cy. 11 Sept. 1708. Appointed a drill instructor in Ireland (1708), which post he held for 2 years, at the end of which time the Government gave him £200 (Capt. Robert Parker's *Memoirs*, p. 148). Resigned his Comn. in Jan. 1718, to Capt. Fred. Hamilton, a nephew of Lt.-Gen. Fred. Hamilton, who paid "a valuable consideration" for the same. *Ibid.*

[8] Appointed Ens. in above Regt. 1 Aug. 1702. Wounded at Schellenberg. Bt. to act as Lieut. in same Regt. 25 Aug. 1704. Lieut. 1 Jan. 1705. Capt. 23 March, 1711. Served throughout Marlborough's campaigns. Major, 4 Sept. 1734. Serving in 1745. Out of the Regt. before 1749.

[9] Dead on 9 Oct. 1716.

LIEUTENANT-GENERAL MEREDITH'S REGIMENT OF FOOT.
[20TH FOOT.]

NAME.	RANK.	DATE OF COMMISSION
Thomas Meredith,[1]	Col. & Capt.	———
Alexander Gay,[2]	Lt.-Col. & Capt.	———
Michael Sing (sic),[3]	Major & Capt.	———
Thomas St. Clair,[4]	Captain	———
Latham Doherty,	,,	———
Peter De la fontaine,	,,	———
John Battereau,[5]	,,	———
William Graham,	,,	———
Abraham Bickford,	,,	———
Robert Graham,	,,	———
Benjamin Jones,	,,	———
Mordecai Abbot,[6]	,,	20 Apr. 1713.
John Vickers,	Capt.-Lieut.	———
Cairnes Ash,	Lieutenant	———
Robert Hamilton,	,,	———
Thomas Newton,	,,	———
Dicksing Doherty,	,,	———
Charles Crepigny,	,,	———
Robert Johnston,	,,	———
Richard Norman,	,,	———
William Maghan,	,,	———
Andrew Creighton,	,,	———
Christopher Peard,	,,	———
Thomas James,	,,	———
James Alexander,	,,	———
Andrew Singleton,	Ensign	———
Robert Wightman,[7]	,,	———
William Cambie,	,,	20 Apr. 1713.
John Rogers,	,,	———
Francis Crane,	,,	———
William Newton,	,,	———
William Vezey,	,,	———
John Pickering,	,,	———
Michael Newton,	,,	———
Henry Abbot,	,,	———
George Eames,	,,	———
Thomas Newton,	Adjutant	———
John Heylin,	Chaplain	28 June, 1715.
Paul Craddock,	Quartermaster	———
Audley Lynn,	Surgeon	———

[1] Thomas Meredyth was appointed Capt. in the Duke of Leinster's Regt. of Horse, 23 April, 1691. Bt.-Col. 1 June, 1701. Adjt.-Gen. of the Forces in Ireland same date. Col. of a newly-raised Regt. (37th Foot) in Ireland, 13 Feb. 1702. Brig.-Gen. 1 Jan. 1704. Maj.-Gen. 1 Jan. 1707. Govr. of Tynemouth Castle, 20 Feb. 1707. Lt.-Gen. 1 Jan. 1708. Col. of the Regt. subsequently known as the 20th Foot, 4 Oct. 1714. He saw considerable service under Wm. III. and Marlborough. Was appointed Govr. of Dendermond after its capitulation in Sept. 1706, and was made Gentleman of the Horse to

the Master of the Horse in 1708 (Luttrell, Vol. VI. p. 284). Wounded at the battle of Oudenarde (*Ibid.* p. 325). M.P. for Midhurst, 1709. D. in July, 1719. He was Govr. of Londonderry at the time of his death.

[2] Appointed Adjt. to Col. Henry Rowe's Regt. of Foot, 19 April, 1694. Lieut. 23 April, 1696. Half-pay, 1698. In 1702, this officer was Lieut. in Gustavus Hamilton's Regt. (20th Foot). Served in the expedition to Cadiz, and was wounded in the attack on Guadeloupe in 1703, when serving as a Capt. Major in 1706. Lt.-Col. before 1 June, 1715. Left the Regt. 12 Nov. 1717.

[3] Previous services not ascertained. Promoted Lt.-Col. of above Regt. 12 Nov. 1717. Out of the Regt. in 1722.

[4] Appointed 2nd Lieut. of Grenadiers in above Regt. 10 Aug. 1696. Accompanied this Corps to Cadiz in 1702 as Capt. of a Cy., and on the expedition to the West Indies same year. Wounded in the attack on Guadeloupe in 1703. Left the Regt. 13 June, 1718.

[5] Appointed Qr.-Mr. to Count Paulen's Tp. in Lord Windsor's Regt. of Horse in 1702. Cornet, 1 July, 1705. Capt. in Lt.-Gen. Meredyth's Regt. (20th Foot) in June, 1715. Major, 12 Nov. 1717. Lt.-Col. 25 June, 1722. Col. of a newly-raised Regt. of Foot, 29 March, 1742. Served at the battle of Falkirk, in 1746, with this Corps, which was disbanded in 1748. D. in 1749.

[6] Appointed Capt. in above Regt. 20 April, 1713. Town Major at Gibraltar. Major of the 20th Foot, 5 April, 1723. D. in 1738. Will proved at Dublin.

[7] Probably the officer who is called "General Robert Wightman" in the *Culloden Papers*, but whose name does not appear as a General, or even as a Field Officer, in 1745, when he is said to have been at the battle of Preston Pans. *See* Wightman's Letter, dated 22 Jan. 1746, to the Lord President Forbes, among the *Culloden Papers*, pp. 266–7.

COLONEL HANDASYDE'S REGIMENT OF FOOT

[22ND FOOT.]

NAME.	RANK.	DATE OF COMMISSION.
Roger Handasyde,[1]	Col. & Capt.	3 Apr. 1712.
James Howard,[2]	Lt.-Col. & Capt.	24 Aug. 1715.
William Duncomb,[3]	Major & Capt.	24 Aug. 1715.
Robert Hume,	Captain	[1 Jan. 1703.]
William Wanless (*sic*),	,,	[18 June, 1705.]
Robert Gardner,	,,	[Out in 1717.]
Robert Lambton,	,,	3 Apr. 1712.
George Lisle,	,,	[25 July, 1709.]
William Horler,	,,	[22 Oct. 1709.]
Francis Mecheux,	,,	[Out in 1717.]
Thomas Handasyde,[4]	Capt.-Lieut.	
William Haye,	Lieutenant	
Jaspar Handasyde,	,,	
George Modd,	,,	
William Potts,	,,	[17 June, 1709.]
Mark Thurston,	,,	[22 July, 1715.]
Dugall Campbell,	,,	19 Aug. 1713.
Jere Schaak,	,,	[22 July, 1715.]
Jacob Preston,[5]	,,	
Edward Thornicroft,	,,	[21 Apr. 1709.]
Clifford Handasyde,[6]	,,	3 Apr. 1712.
John Hill,	Ensign	25 June, 1704.
Robert Maynard,	,,	[22 July, 1715.]
James Colvyn,[7]	,,	
George Hume,	,,	26 Nov. 1710.
Thomas Lisle (*sic*),	,,	[12 May, 1714.]
Thomas Wood,	,,	9 Feb. 1713–14.
Peter Schaak,	,,	[29 Sept. 1712.]
Richard Stephen Franks,	,,	[4 July, 1705.]
John Lyon (*sic*),	,,	[27 Aug. 1708.]
David Jones,	Chaplain	[22 July, 1715.]
Thomas Maynard,	Adjutant	[28 June, 1712.]
Archibald Campbell,	Surgeon	27 July, 1714.

[1] Son of Major-General Thos. Handasyde. Appointed Ensign in Col. John Gibson's Regt. of Foot, 24 Dec. 1696. Exchanged to his father's Corps (22nd Foot) about 1702, and served with the same in Jamaica. Succeeded his father as Col. 3 April, 1712. Transferred to the command of the Regt. subsequently known as the 16th Foot, 9 July, 1730. Brig.-Gen. 20 Nov. 1735. Maj.-Gen. 2 July, 1739. Lt.-Gen. 29 March, 1743. Lt.-Gov. of Fort St. Philip, Minorca. Succeeded Sir John Cope as C.-in-C. in Scotland, Oct. 1745. Superseded by General Hawley a few months later. D. 1763.

[2] Appointed Ensign in the 1st Foot Guards, 22 July, 1693. Capt.-Lt. and Qr.-Mr. in Col. Thos. Farrington's newly-raised Regt. of Foot, 16 Feb. 1694. Capt. 12 Sept. 1694. Half-pay, 28 Feb. 1698. Lieut. and Capt. 1st Foot Guards, 10 March, 1702. Served at Blenheim. Major of Col. Thos. Handasyde's Regt. (22nd Foot), in the West Indies, in 1705. Lt.-Col., 24 Aug. 1715. Left the Regt., 23 Dec. 1717.

³ Appointed Lt.-Col. of Col. Nicholas Lepell's newly-raised Regt. of Foot in Ireland, 25 March, 1705. Half-pay, 1712. Major of Handasyde's Regt. 24 Aug. 1715. Lt.-Col. of Maj.-Gen. Owen Wynne's Dragoons, 12 July, 1716. Comn. renewed by George II. in 1727.

⁴ Son of Maj.-Gen. Thos. Handasyde. Appointed Capt.-Lieut. in his father's Regt. 3 April, 1712. Lt.-Col. of Col. George Grove's Regt. (19th Foot), 5 Aug. 1715. Comn. renewed by George II. in 1727. Out of the Army in 1731.

⁵ Appointed Lieut. in Handasyde's Regt. 28 June, 1712. Half-pay, 1713. Re-appointed Lieut. in above Regt. 11 Jan. 1715. Resigned his Comn. 2 April, 1716, "rendered by wounds incapable of service" (*Add. MS.* 22264).

⁶ Appointed Lieut. in above Regt. 3 April, 1712. Left the Regt. 22 July, 1715.

⁷ D. 26 June, 1716.

MAJOR-GENERAL WHETHAM'S REGIMENT OF FOOT.

[27TH FOOT.]

NAME.	RANK.	DATE OF COMMISSION.
Thomas Whetham,[1]	Col. & Capt.	
Henry Ponsonby,[2]	Major & Capt.	
Thomas Fowkes,[3]	Captain	26 Dec. 1711.
[Chas.] Powlet,[4]	,,	
William Browne,[5]	,,	6 Nov. 1713.
George Arbuthnot,[6]	,,	26 Apr. 1714.
Henry Cope,	,,	
Jeffery Stevens,	,,	
Edmund Strudwick,	,,	7 Nov. 1713.
Thomas Blagrave,	,,	26 Dec. 1711.
James Steuart,[7]	,,	9 Feb. 1713-14.
William Upton,	Capt. Lieut.	
Henry Edmeston,	Lieutenant	
Alexander Mavitie,[8]	,,	
John Caulfield,	,,	
Richard Knight,	,,	31 Mar. 1709.
Robert Forrester,	,,	14 May, 1710.
Arthur Gore,	,,	
Edward Todd,	,,	
Chichester Fortescue,	,,	15 June, 1711.
James Fury,	,,	24 July, 1713.
Joseph Holmes,	,,	24 July, 1711.
Thomas Strudwick,	,,	20 March, 1713-14.
John Whitworth,	,,	
Thomas Smith,	Ensign	2 June, 1711.
—— Morgan,	,,	
Thomas Key,	,,	
John Browne,	,,	14 May, 1710.
Thomas Gore,	,,	14 June, 1710.
John Jones,	,,	
Leo Forrester,	,,	14 July, 1711.
John Hay,	,,	
Rupert Pratt,	,,	14 May, 1710.
Silvester Shepherd,	,,	
John Whetham,	,,	
Joseph Whetham,	Adjutant	
Charles Cotton,	Quartermaster	
John Salkeld,	Chaplain	
John Whetham,	Surgeon	

[1] Elder brother to John Whetham, whose son was the Very Rev. John Whetham, Dean of Lismore. Appointed Ens. in Sir Wm. Clifton's Regt. (15th Foot), 23 June, 1685. Capt.-Lieut., 23 Feb. 1694. Capt., 1 Aug. 1694. Whetham served with his Corps in Scotland from 1689-93, and probably was present at Killiecrankie. Maj. of Col. James Stanhope's Regt. of Foot before 1700. Col. of the Inniskilling Fusiliers, 29 Aug. 1702. Commanded the same in the West Indies, and received a Comn. "to command the troops in case of the death or absence of the Governor-in-Chief of the Leeward Islands" (5 Sept. 1702). In May, 1705, Col. Whetham took part in the expedition against Guadeloupe and in the opera-

tions against the French in that island. He remained there until sickness obliged his return to Antigua. Brig.-Gen. 1 Jan. 1707. "Commander-in-Chief of an intended Expedition," 13 May, 1709. Maj.-Gen. 1 Jan. 1710. Had a command in Catalonia, 1711–12. C.-in-C. in Scotland, 13 June, 1712. Commanded the left wing of the Royalist Army at Sheriffmuir, which wing was signally routed by the Highland levies, who were much superior in numbers. M.P. for Barnstaple, 1722. Transferred to the Colonelcy of the Regt. subsequently known as the 12th Foot, 22 March, 1725. Lt.-Gen. 2 March, 1727. Gen. 2 July, 1739. Gov. of Berwick and Holy Island, 1740. D. 28 April, 1741.

[2] Second son of the 1st Visct. Duncannon. A certain Henry Ponsonby was appointed Ens. in the Princess Anne of Denmark's Regt. of Foot, 1 May, 1693. He left that Corps before 1702; but may be identical with the Henry Ponsonby appointed Capt. in the Inniskilling Fusiliers, 25 Aug. 1705. Bt.-Lt.-Col. 1 Jan. 1712. Regtal. Maj. before 11 Jan. 1715. Lt.-Col. of above Regt. 16 Sept. 1715. Comn. renewed in 1727. Col. of the 37th Foot, 13 May, 1735. Brig.-Gen. 18 Feb. 1742. Maj.-Gen. 7 Feb. 1743. Had a command at Fontenoy, where he was killed. He md. Lady Frances Brabazon, dau. of the 5th Earl of Meath, by whom he left issue.

[3] Aftds. Lt.-Gen. Thos. Fowke, Gov. of Gibraltar. See special memoir in Vol. II.

[4] See biog. notice on p. 133, note 10.

[5] Out of the Regt. 24 Jan. 1718.

[6] Do. 12 July, 1718.

[7] Maj. 18 June, 1720. Comn. renewed in 1727.

[8] D. 17 May, 1716.

BRIGADIER STANWIX'S REGIMENT OF FOOT.

[Regiment raised in July, 1715, and disbanded in 1718.]

NAME.	RANK.	DATE OF COMMISSION.
Thomas Stanwix,[1]	Col. & Capt.	[1 Jan. 1705.]
Thomas Weld,[2]	Lt.-Col. & Capt.	[18 June, 1710.]
[Lachlan] McLean,[3]	Major & Capt.	[24 Apr. 1706.]
[John] Griffith,[4]	Captain	[22 July, 1715.]
John Hayes,	,,	12 Apr. 1706.]
Allen Browne,	,,	[13 July, 1708.]
Francis Boghert,	,,	[8 Dec. 1711.]
[Jno.] Carney,	,,	[8 July, 1710.]
George Dawson,	,,	[23 Feb. 1708-9.]
Lord Oliphant,[5]	,,	[3 Nov. 1708.]
James Holmes,	Capt. Lieut.	[12 Apr. 1706.]
Francis Jennison,	Lieutenant	[27 May, 1708.]
Robert Eaglesfield,	,,	[5 June, 1708.]
John Boteler,	,,	[29 Aug. 1707.]
John Jidoin,	,,	[16 June, 1709.]
Richard Thomas,	,,	[23 Feb. 1712.]
Robert Charge,	,,	[7 Aug. 1710.]
Gerald Elrington,	,,	[1 Aug. 1707.]
Wiltshire Castle,	,,	[1 Jan. 1711.]
Patrick Wood,	,,	[27 July, 1710.]
Donald McNeal,	,,	[Out in 1717.]
John Roose,	Ensign	[22 Apr. 1711.]
Jerome Tully,	,,	[24 June, 1710.]
John Hanning,	,,	[24 Aug. 1710.]
—— Peachy,	,,	[22 July, 1715.]
John Parker,	,,	[Out in 1717.]
Edward Sture,	,,	[23 Apr. 1711.]
Francis Martin,	,,	[10 Jan. 1709.]
[Wm.] Pudsey,	,,	[24 June, 1708.]
Thomas Gale,	,,	[22 July, 1715].

[1] This officer's surname was doubtless *Stanwigge* in olden times (see Plantagenet Harrison's *Hist. of Yorkshire*, Vol. I. pp. 492, 538). Thos. Stanwix was appointed Capt.-Lieut. in Col. Ferdinand Hastings's Regt. of Foot, 20 Jan. 1691. Capt. 19 Dec. 1692. Capt. in Col. Tidcomb's Regt. of Foot, 23 Feb. 1693. Capt. in the Earl of Arran's newly-raised Regt. of Horse, 16 Feb. 1694. Capt. in the Carabiniers, 1702. Lt.-Col. of Lord Henry Scott's newly-raised Regt. of Foot in March, 1704. Bt.-Col. 1 Jan. 1705. Lt.-Gov. of Carlisle, 5 April, 1705. Col. of a newly-raised Regt. of Foot, 12 April, 1706. Served in Portugal, and took part in the battle of the Caya, 1709. Brig.-Gen. 1 Jan. 1710. Gov. of Gibraltar, 13 Jan. 1711. Gov. of Chelsea, 24 Jan. 1715. Col. of a newly-raised Regt. of Foot, 22 July, 1715. Transferred to the Regt. subsequently known as the 30th Foot, 17 July, 1717. Removed to the 12th Foot, 25 Aug. same year. D. 14 March, 1725

[2] Appointed Lieut. of an Independent Cy. at Berwick, 26 June, 1685. Capt. in Sir Edward Hales's Regt. of Foot, 28 Aug. same year. Re-commissioned Capt. 28 Feb. 1689. Out of said Regt. in 1694. Appointed Capt. in Sir Richard Temple's newly-raised Regt. of Foot, 25 March, 1705. Served with this Corps in Flanders. Maj. 5 July, 1708. Served at Malplaquet. Lt.-Col. 24 April, 1710. Half-pay, 1713. Out of the Regt. 26 Sept. 1717.

³ Appointed Capt. in Lord Strathnaver's Regt. of Foot, 2 April, 1697. Half-pay, 1698. Capt. in Col. Wm. Evans's Regt. of Foot, 10 April, 1703. Maj. 24 April, 1706. Served at Malplaquet. Bt.-Lt.-Col. 1 Jan. 1712. Half-pay, 1713. Maj. of Stanwix's Regt. 22 July, 1715. Out of the Army in 1717.

⁴ Appointed Capt. in Visct. Molesworth's Regt. of Dragoons, 11 Aug. 1716. Retd. 25 Jan. 1718.

⁵ Patrick, 8th Lord Oliphant. A certain Patrick Oliphant was appointed Ens. in the Cameronian Regt. of Foot, 1 June, 1704, and served at Blenheim, where he was wounded. Out of said Regt. 1 Dec. 1708. This officer may have been the Hon. Patrick Oliphant who succeeded as 8th Baron in 1706. Lord Oliphant was appointed Capt. in the Rl. Regt. of Foot, 3 Nov. 1708, and is believed to have served at Malplaquet with the 1st Batt. of last-named Corps. A Scottish Representative Peer in 1710. "Sold his estate in Banffshire to James Oliphant of Gask, 14 July, 1711" (*The New Scots Peerage*, Vol. VI. p. 557). Capt. in Stanwix's Regt. 22 July, 1715. Appears to have been in this Regt. when it was disbanded in 1718. D. in London, 14 Jan. 1721.

COLONEL DUBOURGAY'S REGIMENT OF FOOT.

[Regiment raised in July, 1715, and disbanded in 1718.]

NAME.	RANK.	DATE OF COMMISSION.
Charles Dubourgay,[1]	Col. & Capt.	[1 June, 1707.]
Lord Dumbarton,[2]	Lt.-Col. & Capt.	
Edward Wolfe,[3]	Major & Capt.	
Rupert Eastland,	Captain	[12 Apr. 1706.]
William Taylor,	,,	[18 May, 1711.]
James Steuart,	,,	
Isaac Gignoux,	,,	[2 Apr. 1706.]
Humphrey Browne,	,,	[26 June, 1710.]
Daniel Tanner,	,,	[28 Apr. 1708.]
Andrew Corbett,	,,	[13 Sept. 1709.]
Hugh Jones,	Capt.-Lieut.	
John Dalbos,	Lieutenant	[2 Apr. 1706.]
Isaac Sailly,	,,	[21 Feb. 1709.]
Abraham Pinchinat,	,,	[18 May, 1711.]
Thomas Parkinson,	,,	[29 ,, ,,]
[Esth.] Shepherd,	,,	
Samuel Du Royer,	,,	[3 Jan. 1704.]
John Prince,	,,	[25 Mar. 1705.]
Charles Hutchinson,[4]	,,	
Roger Mostyn,	,,	[29 June, 1701.]
Ezekiel Jefferys,[5]	,,	
Maynard de Querin,	Ensign	[22 July, 1715.]
Charles Maidman,	,,	[24 June, 1710.]
Benjamin Harris,	,,	[Out in 1717.]
William Jameson,	,,	[15 July, 1711.]
Mark Antony Bessiere,	,,	[18 May, 1711.]
John Rouviere,	,,	[,, ,,]
Charles Rambouillet,	,,	[22 July, 1715.]
John Boitous,[6]	,,	[18 May, 1711.]
John Nappier,	,,	[22 July, 1715.]

[1] Appointed Ens. in Col. De Belcastel's Huguenot Regt. in the service of Wm. III., 4 July, 1691. Capt. in Sir George St. George's Regt. of Foot, 1 Jan. 1694. Served in Flanders and Spain. Commanded the remnant of Wightman's Regt. after Almanza with the Brevet rank of Colonel, 1 June, 1707. Col. of a French Regt. in the British Service in Spain, 10 Aug. 1709. Qr.-Mr.-Gen. in Scotland, 11 July, 1712. Comn. renewed by George I. in 1715. Col. of a newly-raised Regt. of Foot, 22 July, 1715. Said Regt. was disbanded in 1718, and Dubourgay was appointed Col. of the 32nd Foot, 28 June, 1723. Previous to this he had been appointed Lt.-Gov. of Jamaica. Brig-Gen. 11 March, 1727. D. in Edinburgh, 11 July, 1732.

[2] On 14 Oct. 1688, George, Lord Ettrick, son and heir of the Earl of Dumbarton, a child of 18 months! was commissioned Capt. in the Rl. Regt. of Foot. At the Revolution Lord Ettrick's name disappeared from the Army Lists. In 1692 the 1st Lord Dumbarton died in France, and Ettrick took up his father's forfeited title. On the accession of George I. he was appointed Lt.-Col. of Dubourgay's Regt., 22 July, 1715. Sent Ambassador to Russia in 1716 by George I., who bestowed on him an annual pension of £300. Does not appear in any subsequent list of officers. D. in France after 1749.

[3] Son of Capt. Edward Wolfe of Blood's Regt. of Foot, and father of the immortal Maj.-Gen. James Wolfe. Appointed 2nd Lieut. in Visct. Shannon's Regt. of Marines,

10 March, 1702. Maj. of Col. Wm. Newton's (late Temple's) Regt. of Foot, 24 April, 1710. Served in Flanders. Half-pay, 1713. Maj. of Dubourgay's Regt. of Foot, 22 July, 1715. Capt. and Lt.-Col. in 3rd Foot Guards, 10 July, 1717. Col. of the 1st Marine Regt. 17 Nov. 1739. Served as Adjt.-Gen. to the expedition to Carthagena in 1740-1. Brig.-Gen. 25 Feb. 1744. Maj.-Gen. 27 May, 1745. Inspector of Marines. Transferred to the Colonelcy of The King's Regt. of Foot, 25 April, 1745. Lt.-Gen. 27 Sept. 1747. D. 27 March, 1759. Bd. at Greenwich.

[4] Is said to have joined the Army in April, 1710, as a Lieut. (*Army List*, 1740). Left Dubourgay's Regt. 10 March, 1716. Appointed Capt. in Col. John Armstrong's Regt. of Foot (Royal Irish), 13 July, 1718. Serving in 1740 as senior Capt.

[5] Appointed Lieut. in Stanwix's Regt. 22 July, 1715. Transferred to Col. Clayton's Regt. about 1718. Placed on half-pay as Lieut. in last-named Corps in 1728. Drawing half-pay in 1739, then "aged 63" (*Half-Pay List*, 1739).

[6] *Boitoux.* Appointed Lieut. in Maj.-Gen. Jas. Dormer's Regt. (6th Foot), 19 Aug. 1731. Accompanied said Corps to the West Indies in 1741, and d. on active service in the spring of 1742 (*Gentleman's Mag.* 1742).

COLONEL CHUDLEIGH'S REGIMENT OF FOOT.

[34TH FOOT.]

NAME.	RANK.	DATE OF COMMISSION.
Thomas Chudleigh,[1]	Col. & Capt,	———
Thomas Whitney,[2]	Lt.-Col. & Capt.	———
Charles Douglas,[3]	Major & Capt.	———
Robert Hayes,	Captain	———
Michael More,	,,	———
Henry Skelton,[4]	,,	———
Samuel Daniels,	,,	———
Francis Mutys,	,,	———
Richard Pyott,	,,	———
Richard Doige,	,,	———
[James] Sobergues (sic)[5]	Capt.-Lieut.	———
William Hamilton,	Lieutenant	———
Timothy White,	,,	———
Walter Yard,	,,	———
John Tremaigne,	,,	———
William Hays,	,,	———
Edward Cooksey,	,,	———
Thomas Batten,	,,	———
Thomas Ford,	,,	———
—— Brereton,	,,	———
Christopher Phillips,	,,	———
Henry Stirk,	Ensign	———
John Spaddy,	,,	———
Thomas Price,	,,	———
Roger Sterne,[6]	,,	———
Thomas Kitson,	,,	———
John Brushfield,	,,	———
John Sutton,	,,	———
Thomas Parker,	,,	———
William Wickham,	,,	———

[1] Second son of Sir George Chudleigh, Bart., of Ashton. Appointed 2nd Lieut. in Col. George Villiers's Regt. of Marines, 2 Dec. 1702. Capt. in Col. Wm. Breton's Regt. of Foot, 25 March, 1705. Served at the battle of Almanza, and was taken prisoner. Bt.-Col. 15 Nov. 1711. Col. of the Regt. subsequently known as the 34th Foot, 30 Nov. 1712. Comn. renewed by George I. in Jan. 1715. D. 14 April, 1726, aged 38. He was Lt.-Gov. of Chelsea Hospital at the time of his decease. Bd. in Chelsea Hospital Cemetery.

[2] Probably son of Col. Thos. Whitney, who had commanded the Coleraine Regt. of Volunteers at the defence of Londonderry, 1689. Appointed Adjt. to Sir James Lesley's Regt. of Foot, 1 Aug. 1690. Lieut. 12 Sept. same year. Capt. 10 Feb. 1695. Bt.-Maj. 1 July, 1706. Served as an A.D.C. to one of the Generals at Blenheim. Was at Ramillies and Malplaquet. Bt.-Lt.-Col. 1 Jan. 1712. Lt.-Col. of Chudleigh's Regt. 30 Nov. 1712.

[3] Owing to the fact that there were three officers named Charles Douglas in Queen Anne's Army it is difficult to determine their respective early services. The Maj. C. Douglas of Chudleigh's Regt. was probably the Major of this name who was taken prisoner at Brihuega in Dec. 1710. On 18 Nov. 1718, Major C. Douglas was appointed Lt.-Col. of Brigadier Borr's Regt. (32nd Foot). Col. of the 5th Regt. of Marines, 21 Nov. 1739. He accompanied this Corps to the West Indies in 1740, and at the siege of Carthagena had his head taken off by a cannon-ball, 23 March, 1741. His will, dated 24 Jan. 1740, and proved 22 May, 1741,

described him as of Brentford Butts, in the parish of Hanwell, Middlesex. His widow Jacobina, executrix to the above will, was bd. in Westminster Abbey, 3 March, 1761, in the same grave with her son Lieut. William Douglas, who had died in March, 1743, aged 17.

[4] Of Braithwaite Hall, Cumberland. Appointed Capt. in Brig. Maccartney's Regt. of Foot, 20 Dec. 1708. Wounded at the siege of Douay, 1710. Half-pay, 1713. Capt. of Invalids at Portsmouth, 1714. Capt. in Chudleigh's Regt. in Jan. 1715. Sold his Company, and was appointed Capt. and Lt.-Col. 3rd Foot Guards, 8 Nov. 1718. 2nd Major, with rank of Colonel, 21 Aug. 1739. Served at Fontenoy. Col. of the 12th Foot, 28 May, 1745. Maj.-Gen. 1 June, 1745. Lt.-Gen. 18 Sept. 1747. His life is said to have been preserved in Flanders by his A.D.C., Capt. James Jones of the 3rd Foot Guards, to whom Gen. Skelton left the bulk of his property (Carter's *Historical Records of the Cameronians*). D. in April, 1757.

[5] In the Almanza Casualty Roll a — *Souberg* appears as Capt. in the composite battalion of Guards as having been taken prisoner. James Sobergues (*sic*) of Chudleigh's Foot resigned the Capt.-Lieutenancy, 3 June, 1717.

[6] Father of Laurence Sterne. See notice of Lieut. Roger Sterne in the Introduction.

SIR CHARLES HOTHAM'S REGIMENT OF FOOT.

[*Regiment raised in July, 1715, and disbanded in 1718.*]

NAME.	RANK.	DATE OF COMMISSION.
Sir Charles Hotham,[1]	Col. & Capt.	——
Fairfax Norcliff,[2]	Lt.-Col. & Capt.	——
George Green,[3]	Major & Capt.	——
Charles Hotham,	Captain	——
James Gee,[4]	,,	——
Thomas Webb,	,,	——
John Dalmas,	,,	——
[Thos.] Burroughs,	,,	——
—— Littleton,	,,	——
—— Wandesford,	,,	——
Robert Strangeways,	Capt.-Lieut.	——
John Mackelland,	Lieutenant	——
William Wains,	,,	——
William Cook,	,,	——
Jonathan Smith,	,,	——
Thomas Constable,	,,	——
James Bertet,	,,	——
William Daws,	,,	——
James Swiney,	,,	——
Thomas Hesketh,	,,	——
Bryan Mahon,	,,	——
John Moyser,	Ensign	——
James Blair,	,,	——
Richard Povey,	,,	——
Beaumont Hotham,[5]	,,	——
Thomas Sibboc (*sic*),	,,	——
James McDonald,	,,	——
John Westbrook,	,,	——
Anthony Barrell,	,,	——
[Wm. Daws],	[Adjt.]	——

[1] Eldest son of the Revd. Charles Hotham, Rector of Wigan. Succeeded to the Yorkshire baronetcy in 1691 on the death of his uncle Sir John Hotham. This officer raised an infantry corps in co. York., and was appointed Col. 25 March, 1705. Served in Portugal and Spain, and was promoted Brig.-Gen. 1 Jan. 1710. Half-pay, 1713. In July, 1715, raised a new Regt., and was appointed Col. 22 July. Some of the leading officers had served in Hotham's late Regt. On the outbreak of the '15 Hotham proceeded with his Corps to Newcastle, from whence they marched to Scotland soon after Sheriffmuir, and in Oct. 1716 were quartered at Ayr. When Hotham's Regt. was sent to Ireland, in June, 1717, Sir Charles resigned the Colonelcy and was appointed Col. of a Regt. of Dragoons (late Churchill's), which was disbanded in Nov. 1718. Sir Charles was given the Colonelcy of the 36th Foot, 7 July, 1719. M.P. for Beverley. Transferred to The King's Regt. of Foot, 3 Dec. 1720. Removed to the Colonelcy of the Rl. Dragoons, 10 April, 1721. D. 8 Jan. 1723.

[2] Eldest son of Sir Thos. *Norcliffe* of Langton, Yorkshire. Appointed Capt. of an additional Cy. in Col. Thomas Stringer's Regt. of Foot, 5 April, 1704. Maj. of Sir Charles Hotham's Regt. 19 July, 1706. Served in Spain. Promoted Lt. Col., 16 June, 1709, in which year he returned to England with Sir C. Hotham and other officers to raise recruits for last-named corps, which had dwindled to very small proportions on foreign service. When serving at Perth in 1712 he was presented with the Freedom of that City on 26 May.

Half-pay, Sept. 1712—Hotham's Corps having been disbanded at Berwick-on-Tweed by Gen. Wightman. Lt.-Col. of Hotham's newly-raised Corps, 22 July, 1715. Transferred in July, 1715, to the Lt.-Colonelcy of Hotham's Dragoons. D. 21 March, 1721. Bd. in Ripon Minster. Lt.-Col. Fairfax Norcliffe (the Editor's ancestor) was twice High Sheriff of Yorkshire, viz. in 1700 and 1715.

[3] Appointed Ens. in the Earl of Bath's Regt. of Foot, 10 Feb. 1693. Lieut. 1 Jan. 1696. Served in Flanders. Bt.-Capt. 5 April, 1704. Capt. 3 Aug. 1704. Served at Blenheim, Ramillies, and Malplaquet. As senior Capt. performed the duty of Maj. when serving with Lord North and Grey's Regt. at the forcing of the French Lines in July, 1705 (*War Office MS.*). Maj. of Col. Pocock's Regt. 1 Sept. 1710. Half-pay, 1713. Maj. of Hotham's Regt. 22 July, 1715. Serving in 1717. Believed to have been in the Regt. when disbanded in Nov. 1718.

[4] Son of Wm. Gee of Bishop Burton, co. York, by his 2nd marriage. Born in 1686. Appointed Capt. in Hotham's Regt. 1 June, 1708. Served in Spain. Half-pay, 1712. Capt. in Hotham's new Corps, 22 July, 1715. Capt. and Lt.-Col. 3rd Foot Guards, 19 June, 1715. Not in any subsequent List. Md. Constance, dau. and heir of John Moyser of Beverley.

[5] Aftds. Sir Beaumont Hotham, 7th Bart., of Scorborough, co. York. He was 2nd son of Brig.-Gen. Sir Charles Hotham, bn. 21 Feb., and bapt. at St. Margaret's, Westminster, 3 March, 1697–8. D. 1771.

COLONEL ALEXANDER'S REGIMENT OF FOOT.

[38TH FOOT.]

NAME.	RANK.	DATE OF COMMISSION.
Francis Alexander,[1]	Col. & Capt.	27 Nov. 1711.
Valentine Morris,[2]	Lt.-Col. & Capt.	[30 Mar. 1713.]
Peter Buor,[3]	Major & Capt.	,, ,,
John Marshall,	Captain	11 May, 1710.
Gervas Grills,[4]	,,	14 Nov. 1711.
Richard Carey,*	,,	9 Aug. 1709.
Philip Everard,	,,	27 Feb. 1711–12.
Henry Hughes,	,,	19 Nov. 1712.
Robert Jackson,	,,	24 Aug. 1713.
George Lucas,[5]	,,	17 July, 1714.
Richard Holland,	Capt.-Lieut.	19 Nov. 1712.
William Howard,	Lieutenant	27 Feb. 1711–12.
Eldred Mitchell,	,,	9 Feb. 1713–14.
Henry Osborne,	,,	6 Oct. 1713.
Charles Pim,[6]	,,	24 Jan. 1712–13.
Ezekiel Everest,	,,	26 June, 1708.
Edward Price,	,,	7 Mar. 1710–11.
John Simmons,	,,	6 Sept. 1712.
Alont Chancourt,	,,	14 Nov. 1711.
Mat. Aldey,[7]	,,	20 Dec. 1709.
Syer Allicock,	,,	18 May, 1714.
Francis Column (sic),	Ensign	[15 July, 1708.]
John Smith,	,,	19 Nov. 1712.
Murdoch Mackenzie,	,,	———
Henry Smith,[8]	,,	———
Charles Wrath,	,,	16 June, 1709.
Humphrey Hutchinson,	,,	———
Hertford Jones,	,,	———
Charles Alexander,	,,	———
John Morris,	,,	———
William Thorold,	Chaplain	
Thomas Chambers,	Adjutant	20 April, 1713.
Thomas Ridley,	Surgeon	———

* Deceased. Succeeded by Capt. Walsh, formerly of the Regt.

[1] Appointed Lieut. in the Duke of Bolton's 1st Regt. of Foot, 1 Jan. 1692. Adjt. 1 March, 1694. Capt. in Col. John Tidcomb's Regt. of Foot, 2 Aug. 1699. Transferred to Col. Wm. Evans's Regt. of Foot, 10 April, 1703. Maj. of Col. Wm. Breton's Regt. 25 March, 1705. Lt.-Col. of Col. James Jones's Regt. (38th Foot), 7 June, 1708. Col. of last-named Regt. 27 Nov. 1711. Saw service in the West Indies. Resigned the Colonelcy, 23 Sept. 1717. D. 24 Feb. 1723.

[2] This officer served in the West Indies during the reign of Queen Anne, but the dates of his Commissions prior to 1712 are not forthcoming. On 11 Nov. 1712, Valentine Morris was appointed Maj. of Alexander's Foot and promoted Lt.-Col. 30 March, 1713. Serving with same rank in 1740. D. about 1747. This officer's son, Valentine Morris, in a letter to Lord Dartmouth dated 26 March, 1773, says: "My father served the Crown for nearly 40 years in the Army with singular honour and reputation" (*Dartmouth MSS.*, Vol. II. p. 495).

³ Apparently belonged to a West Indian family. Lieut. Gabriel Buor served with Col. Goodwin's Regt. in the West Indies *temp.* Wm. III.; and Capt. John Otto Buor is mentioned in the West India Papers for 1710. Peter Buor was appointed Maj. in Alexander's Regt., in the room of Valentine Morris, 30 March, 1713. Out of the Regt. 9 May, 1718. Probably died in the West Indies.

⁴ Appointed Lieut. in Col. James Jones's Regt. (38th Foot), 16 June, 1709. Capt. of the Grenadier Cy. 14 Nov. 1711. Left the Regt. 29 Jan. 1718. Drawing half-pay in 1722.

⁵ Appointed Lieut. of Grenadiers in above Regt. 24 Aug. 1713. Capt. 17 July, 1714. Bt.-Lt.-Col. in the West Indies, 16 April, 1718. Regtal. Maj. 15 Dec. 1738. Lt.-Col. of above Regt. 2 April, 1743. D. at Brest in 1747, when holding the post of Lt.-Gov. of Antigua (*Gentleman's Mag.*).

⁶ Appointed Ens. in above Regt. 18 Dec. 1712. 2nd Lieut. of the Grenadier Cy. 24 Jan. 1713. Capt. 13 June, 1721. Serving with same rank in 1740.

⁷ Dead 19 Feb. 1717.

⁸ One of the ringleaders of the insurrection which broke out in Antigua in Dec. 1710, and which culminated in the murder of Col. Daniel Parke, the C.-in-C. in the Leeward Islands. Smith was sent a prisoner to England, and after many delays was tried at the King's Bench in 1714 for complicity in Col. Parke's murder. This trial was a test case, and fell through for want of sufficient evidence. See the paper on "Soldiering in the West Indies in the Reign of Queen Anne," by Charles Dalton, in the *R.U.S.I. Journal*, Jan. 1898. Untraced after 1715.

LIEUTENANT-GENERAL SANKEY'S REGIMENT OF FOOT.

[39TH FOOT.]

NAME.	RANK.	DATE OF COMMISSION.
Nicholas Sankey,[1]	Col. & Capt.	——
Thomas Townshend,[2]	Lt.-Col. & Capt.	1 Oct. 1709.
Edmund Keating,[3]	Major & Capt.	——
Nicholas Bunbury,[4]	Captain	——
Charles Sadler,	,,	——
William Smith,[5]	,,	——
Peyton Fox,	,,	——
Peter Lombard,[6]	,,	24 June, 1710.
Henry Blunt,[7]	,,	——
John Harrison,	,,	——
Lewis Ormsby,	,,	——
James Fountaine,[8]	,,	——
Roger Lort,	Capt.-Lieut.	——
Bland Summers,	Lieutenant	——
Philip Savage,	,,	——
Roger Taylor,[9]	,,	——
Standish Lee,	,,	——
William Norris,	,,	——
John Lawson,[10]	,,	——
Nathaniel Goodwin,[11]	,,	——
George Martin,	,,	7 May, 1713.
Thomas Taylor,	,,	——
Robert Loftus,	,,	——
James Swanton,[12]	,,	——
Daniel Carmichael,	,,	——
Edward Higgins,	Ensign	——
Arthur Weldon,	,,	——
Thomas Parr,	,,	6 Oct. 1713.
Henry De Ponthier,	,,	——
Richard West,	,,	——
John Hamilton,	,,	——
Peter Beaver,	,,	——
Thomas Stevens,	,,	——
Nicholas Sankey,	,,	——
John Close,	,,	——
Joseph Macknoe,	,,	——
John Mathews,	Chaplain	——
John Lawson,	Adjutant	——
Samuel Lillis,	Surgeon	——
Lewis Ormsby,	Quartermaster	——

[1] This officer appears as Capt. in a "List of Companies of Foot in Ireland, 25 June, 1682" (*Irish Army Lists*, 1661-85, p. 141). Capt. in the Irish Foot Guards before Feb. 1685 (*Ibid.*, p. 145). Turned out of the Irish Army by Tyrconnel. Succeeded John, Lord Lovelace, as Col. of a Regt. of Foot, in Ireland, 28 Sept. 1689. This Corps (called "Zancky's" in some histories) was broken in Jan. 1690, in order to recruit other Regts. (Story's *Hist. of the Wars in Ireland*). Col. Sankey was appointed Col. of Col. Ric.

Coote's Regt. (39th Foot), in Ireland, 17 March, 1703. Brig.-Gen. 1 Jan. 1704. Maj.-Gen. 1 Jan. 1707. Lt.-Gen. 1 Jan. 1710. Served in Spain and Portugal. Taken prisoner at the battle of the Caya in May, 1709 (*London Gazette*). Md., 5 Jan. 1685, Frances, dau. of Col. Marcus Trevor (created Baron Trevor and Visct. Dungannon in 1662). Gen. Sankey d.s.p. before 6 Nov. 1722. Bd. in Westminster Abbey.

[2] Appointed Capt. in Col. Lillingston's Regt. (38th Foot) in the West Indies, 14 April, 1707. Lt.-Col. of Col. Sankey's Regt. 1 Oct. 1709. Comn. renewed by George II. in 1727. Out of the Regt. before 1737.

[3] Appointed Capt. in Col. Henry Rowe's Regt. of Foot, 23 April, 1694. Capt. of the Grenadier Cy. in the Earl of Donegal's Regt. 28 June, 1701. Had Queen Anne's leave to be absent from the latter Regt. when it was sent to the West Indies in 1702. Major of Col. Ric. Coote's Regt. (39th Foot), 19 Nov. 1706. Serving in 1717. Untraced after that year.

[4] Appointed Capt. of the Grenadier Cy. in Sankey's Regt. before 1706. Served in Portugal. Bt.-Maj. 27 Nov. 1712. Serving in 1717. Untraced after that year.

[5] Dead 9 March, 1717.

[6] Do. 20 July, 1716.

[7] Do. 27 March, 1716.

[8] See notice of this officer in *The Scots Army*, 1661-88, by Charle Dalton, p. 102, note 11.

[9] Dead 3 July, 1717.

[10] Do. 2 Feb. 1717.

[11] Do. 24 Feb. 1717.

[12] Do. 13 May, 1717.

BRIGADIER GRANT'S REGIMENT OF FOOT.

[Regt. raised in July, 1715, and disbanded in 1718.]

NAME.	RANK.	DATE OF COMMISSION.
Alexander Grant,[1]	Col. & Capt.	————
[Chris.] Hibbert,[2]	Lt.-Col. & Capt.	————
[Wm.] Cecill,[3]	Major & Capt.	————
Charles Elphinstone,[4]	Captain	————
Lewis Grant,[7]	,,	————
Peregrine Lascells,[8]	,,	————
William Douglas,[5]	,,	————
James Steuart,	,,	[19 Aug. 1715.]
Lord Temple [6] (*sic*),	,,	————
—— Kennedy,	,,	————
James Dalrymple,	Capt.-Lieut.	————
Alexander Corbett,	Lieutenant	————
Alexander Comming,	,,	————
Lewis Grant,	,,	————
John Rutherford,	,,	————
James Steuart,	,,	————
James Douglas,	,,	————
David Kennedy,	,,	————
Richard Hibbert,	,,	————
John Sterling,	,,	————
—— Halshide,	,,	————
Alexander Bruce,	Ensign	————
George Brady,	,,	————
James Grant,	,,	————
Anthony Robinson,	,,	————
Alexander Bisset,	,,	————
Charles Jeffreys,	,,	————
Alexander Graham,	,,	————
Lewis Grant,	,,	[22 Aug. 1715.]
Abraham Elliott Meure,	,,	————

[1] Son and heir of Col. Ludovic Grant of Grant. Appointed Col. of a newly-raised Regt. of Foot in Scotland, 4 March, 1706. Served in Flanders, 1708–10. Taken prisoner by the French, in 1710, with some of his officers, when crossing to England from Holland, and was detained in France until an exchange of prisoners was effected. Brig.-Gen. 12 Feb. 1711. Half-pay, 1713. Govr. of Sheerness, 4 Feb. 1715. Raised a new Corps in July, 1715, and was appointed Col. Sent to Scotland with his Regt. in Aug. 1715. Grant acted as temporary Lieut.-Govr. of Edinburgh Castle when Col. James Stewart was removed in Sept. 1715. Grant also accompanied Argyll as a Volunteer when the latter marched to Leith, the citadel of which town had been seized by Brig. Mackintosh. Grant is also said to have been at Sheriffmuir, though his Regt. was in Edinburgh. M.P. for Invernessshire before and after the Union. D. at Leith, 2 March, 1720.

[2] Appointed Ens. in Col. Fred. Hamilton's Regt. 20 May, 1695. Lieut. 1 July same year. Wounded at the assault of Terra Nova, Namur, 20 Aug. 1695. Capt. of the Grenadier Cy. in Lord Paston's Regt. of Foot, 1 March, 1704. Major, 25 March, 1705. Lt.-Col. 24 Jun. 1708. Bt.-Col. 15 Nov. 1711. Half-pay, 1712. Lt.-Col. of Grant's Regt. 22 July, 1715. Further services untraced.

[3] Afterwards Lt.-Col. Wm. Cecil, Equerry to George I. See special memoir in Vol. II.

[4] Reduced with the Regt. in 1718. Drawing half-pay, 1740.

[5] A cadet of the Earl of Morton's family. A certain Wm. Douglas was appointed Ens. in the Cameronians, 1 Dec. 1708, and placed on half-pay, when serving at Ghent, 13 May, 1713. Capt. Wm. Douglas left Grant's Regt. in July, 1717, and was appointed Capt. in Wynne's Dragoons, 17 July, same year. Capt. and Lt.-Col. Coldstream Guards, 9 June, 1720. 2nd Major, 29 Dec. 1740. 1st Major, 27 April 1743. Col. of the 32nd Foot, 27 May, 1745. Brig.-Gen. 30 May, same year. Served on the Continent with the Allied Army, 1742–47. D. in Beveland from fever in Aug. 1747. His widow, Anne Viscountess Irwin, the celebrated writer and poetess (md. to Col. Wm. Douglas, 11 June, 1737), had her husband's body brought home to be buried in Sept. 1747.—*Frankland-Russell Papers* at Chequers Court.

[6] Francis, 9th Lord Sempill. Appointed Capt. in Lord Carmichael's Regt. of Dragoons, 16 April, 1711. Placed on half-pay in Ireland, 1713. Capt. in Grant's Regt. 22 July, 1715. Had a pension of £300 *per annum* from George I. (*Treasury Accounts*, 1715–16). D. 15 Aug. 1716. Succeeded by his brother John as 10th Baron.

[7] Youngest bro. to Brig. Alex. Grant. Appointed Ens. in the first Grant Regt. 6 March, 1708. Lieut. 23 July 1710. Adjt. 7 Feb. 1712. Capt. in Grant's newly-raised Regt. 22 July, 1715. Major of the Rl. Regt. of Foot, 22 Nov. 1723. Lt.-Col. of last-named Regt. 14 Aug. 1738. D. on service at Kingston, Jamaica, 11 March, 1742.

[8] In St. Mary's Church, Whitby, is a tablet thus inscribed:—

"To the Memory of
PEREGRINE LASCELLES,
General of all and Singular his MAJESTY'S
Forces who served his Country from the year 1704
In the reign of QUEEN ANNE he served in Spain
and in the Battles of
Almanara, Saragossa, and Villaviciosa
Performed the Duty of
A brave and Gallant Officer.
In the Rebellion of the Year 1715
he Served in Scotland:
and in that of 1745
after a fruitless Exertion of his Spirit and Ability
at the disgracefull rout of Preston Pans
He remained forsaken on the feild.
In all his dealings Just and disinterested,
Bountifull to his soldiers
A Father to his officers
A Man of truth and principle
In short
An HONEST MAN
He dyed March y 26th 1772 in the 88th year of his age."

COLONEL POCOCK'S REGIMENT OF FOOT.

[*Regt. raised in July, 1715, and disbanded in 1718.*]

NAME.	RANK.	DATE OF COMMISSION.
John Pocock,[1]	Col. & Capt.	————
George Whitmore,[2]	Lt.-Col. & Capt.	————
[Wm.] Maidman,[3]	Major & Capt.	————
Andrew Agnew,[4]	Captain	————
Charles Cunningham,	,,	————
Edward Molesworth,	,,	————
Francis Appleyard,	,,	————
George Massay (*sic*),	,,	————
Alexander Jacob,	,,	————
George Jackson,	,,	————
John Harris,	Capt.-Lieut.	————
Thomas Adams,	Lieutenant	————
Edward Strahan,	,,	————
Thomas Newlands,	,,	————
James Hayes,	,,	————
John Ramsay,	,,	————
John Bruce,	,,	————
Andrew Crew,	,,	————
Peter Seatler,	,,	————
Samuel Antrim,	,,	————
James Durnford,	,,	————
Christopher Wade,	Ensign	————
William Adams,	,,	————
John Watkins,	,,	————
Thomas Bowes,	,,	————
James Maidman,	,,	————
George Rossington,	,,	————
William Churchill,	,,	————
Mathew Sewell,	,,	————

[1] Appointed Ens. in Brig. Ingoldsby's Regt. of Foot, 6 Feb. 1696. Lieut. and Capt. 1st Foot Guards, 18 May, 1702. Wounded at Blenheim. Capt.-Lieut. with rank of Lt.-Col. 25 Aug. 1704. Served at Ramillies. Capt. 23 Dec. 1706. Bt.-Col. 1 Jan. 1707. Col. of a Regt. of Foot (aftds. disbanded), 15 June, 1710. Col. of a newly-raised Regt. of Foot, 22 July, 1715. Said Regt. was disbanded in 1718, and Col. Pocock was placed on half-pay. Appointed Col. of the Regt. subsequently known as the 36th Foot, 2 Dec. 1720. Transferred to the Colonelcy of The King's Regt. (8th Foot), 21 April, 1721. Brig.-Gen. 5 March, 1727. D. at his house in Leicester Fields, London, in April, 1732.

[2] Appointed Lieut. in Col. Charles Herbert's Regt. (Welsh Fusiliers), 18 Dec. 1689. Served with said Corps during the Irish campaign. Capt. in the Earl of Denbigh's Dragoons, 16 Feb. 1694. Capt. in Lord Mohun's Regt. of Foot, 10 March, 1702. Served in Spain during the War of the Spanish Succession, and as Lt.-Col. of Col. James Dormer's (late Lord Mohun's) Regt. was taken prisoner at Brihuega in Dec. 1710. Bt.-Col. 1 Jan. 1712. Half-pay. Appointed Lt.-Col. of Pocock's newly-raised Regt. of Foot, 22 July, 1715. Accompanied said Corps to Ireland in June, 1717. Capt. and Lt.-Col. 3rd Foot Guards, 5 April, 1718. Retd. 1719. A certain Col. Whitmore, M.P. for Bridgnorth, d. in 1749 ; and a dau. of Col. George Whitmore d. in 1767.—*Gentleman's Magazine.*

[3] Appointed Capt.-Lieut. of Sir Mat. Bridges's Regt. of Foot, 1 Oct. 1696. Capt. in Col. Roger Elliot's newly-raised Regt. of Foot, 10 April, 1703. Major, 25 March, 1705.

Half-pay, 1713. Major of Pocock's Regt. 22 July, 1715. Not in any subsequent List. His widow, Ann Maydman, was drawing a pension of £30 *per annum* in 1735.

[4] Eldest son of Sir James Agnew, Bt., of Lochnaw. Born in 1687. Appointed Cornet in the Rl. Scots Dragoons, 11 May, 1705. Served at Ramillies, Oudenarde, and Malplaquet. Capt. in Lord Strathnaver's Regt. of Foot, 9 Dec. 1709. Half-pay, 1713. Capt. in Pocock's Regt. 22 July, 1715. Capt. in the Rl. North British Fusiliers, 24 May, 1718. Major, 16 Jan. 1737. Lt.-Col. 2 Nov. 1739. Col. of a Regt. of Marines, 15 Aug. 1746. Half-pay, 1749. Maj.-Gen. 3 Feb. 1756. Lt.-Gen. 3 April, 1759. Govr. of Tynemouth Castle. Succeeded as 5th Bart. in 1735. D. in 1771.

COLONEL LUCAS'S REGIMENT OF FOOT.

[Regt. raised in July, 1715, and disbanded in 1718.]

NAME.	RANK.	DATE OF COMMISSION.
[Richard] Lucas,[1]	Col. & Capt.	——
George St. George,[2]	Lt.-Col. & Capt.	——
Richardson Pack,[3]	Major & Capt.	——
Anthony Hinton,[4]	Captain	——
William Hale,[5] (sic)	,,	——
Richard Henly,	,,	——
John Massay,[6] (sic)	,,	——
Walter Blount,	,,	——
Walter Manning,	,,	——
George Howard,	,,	——
John Churchill,	Capt.-Lieut.	——
Delavalle Harrison	Lieutenant	——
Solomon Tovey,	,,	——
George Robinson,	,,	——
Richard Boswell,	,,	——
—— Peterson,	,,	——
Caleb Green,	,,	——
[Wm.] Comyns,	,,	——
John Pashler,	,,	——
James Isaackson,	,,	——
Lewis Defour,	,,	——
Robert Griffith,	Ensign	——
William Castles,	,,	——
James Benningham,	,,	——
Daniel Hering,	,,	——
Bury Irwin,	,,	——
—— Graham,	,,	——
Francis Vans,	,,	——
Thomas Michaell,	,,	——

[1] Appointed Capt. in Sir Bevil Granville's Regt. of Foot, 28 April, 1697. This Cy. was reduced in 1698, and Lucas was placed on half-pay. Restored to full-pay in 1701. Major of Lord Paston's newly-raised Regt. of Foot, 1 March, 1704. Lt.-Col. 25 March, 1705. Lt.-Col. of Lord Essex's Dragoons, 29 Jan. 1708. Col. of a Regt. of Foot (late Selwyn's), 26 Feb. 1711. Half-pay, 1712. Col. of a newly-raised Regt. of Foot, 22 July, 1715. Transferred to the Colonelcy of the 38th Foot (then in the West Indies), 23 Sept. 1717. D. 25 Dec. 1729.

[2] Not in any previous or subsequent List.

[3] Appointed Capt. in Col. Nicholas Lepell's Regt. of Foot, 25 March, 1705. Served in Spain, and was taken prisoner at Brihuega in Dec. 1710. Major, 19 May, 1711. Half-pay, 1712. Major of Lucas's Regt. 22 July, 1715. Serving as Major of Col. Edward Montague's Regt. of Foot in 1728. Out of the Army before 1738.

[4] Appointed Capt. in Lord Mohun's Regt. of Foot, 1 Dec. 1706. Served in Spain. Half-pay, 1712. Capt. in Lucas's Regt. 22 July, 1715. Serving as Capt. in the Hon. Henry Ponsonby's Regt. (37th Foot) in 1737. Out of said Regt. in 1739.

[5] *Hall*. Appointed Capt.-Lieut. to Col. Wm. Delaune's Regt. in Aug. 1708. Adjt. same year. Served with said Regt. in Spain. Half-pay, 1712. Capt. in Lucas's Regt., 22 July, 1715. Untraced after 1715.

[6] Appointed Capt. in Lucas's Regt. from half-pay, 22 July, 1715. In said Regt. when it was disbanded in the winter of 1718-19. Appointed Capt. of an Independent Cy. at Hull, 3 April, 1719. Serving in 1740.

MILITARY COMMISSIONS AND NOTIFICATIONS, 1714-1718.

MEMORANDUM [FROM THE SECRETARY-AT-WAR.]

THIS List * is Extracted from the Books in the War Office which contain the Entrys of Notifications, but as the Notifications do not Express whether the Officers Displaced have had leave to Sell, a compleat List is laid before Your Lordships' House of all the Officers that have been Displaced or Dyed since His Majesties Accession to the Throne, and by whom they have been succeeded, whether by Death Displacing or Voluntary Resignation.

J. CRAGGS.

WHITEHALL,
February the 18*th*, 1717-18.

* This tabular "List" is both valuable and interesting. The original MS. was sent by the Secretary-at-War to the House of Lords at their request. It gives in a compressed and lucid form the Officers on the British Establishment who were either displaced, sold their Commissions, were killed in action, or died, since the Accession of George I. to January 1718; the names of the Regiments to which the respective Officers severally belonged, and the names of their successors with their army rank. The fourth column, containing the dates of the newly-appointed Officers' Commissions, has been added by myself, and the dates have been carefully transcribed from the early Georgian Commission Entry Books at the Public Record Office, London.—C.D.

(185)

A LIST OF SUCH OFFICERS AS HAVE BEEN DISPLACED, EITHER WITH LEAVE TO SELL OR OTHERWISE SINCE HIS MAJESTY'S ACCESSION TO THE THRONE. AS ALSO OF SUCH OFFICERS AS HAVE SUCCEEDED IN THEIR PLACES.

Add. MS. Brit. Mus. 22,264, *fol.* 129.

Names and Qualities of such Officers as have been Displaced either with Leave to Sell or otherwise.	In what Regiment.	Names and Qualities of such Officers as have Succeeded those who were Displaced, &c.	Dates of Commissions.
Qr.-Mast. Ross, resigned	Kirk's Foot	William Weston, Qr.-Mr.	[5 Oct. 1714.]
Maj.-Gen. Newton, deceased	Regiment of Foot	Lt.-Gen. Thomas Meredyth, Col.	[4 ,, ,,]
Gen. Churchill, resigned	Coldstream Regt. Foot Guards	Lt.-Gen. William Cadogan, Col.	[11 ,, ,,]
[Sam.] Parnham, deceased	4th Troop of Horse Guards	Edward Broughton	[28 ,, ,,]
	Breton's Foot	Wm. Brodie, Chaplain	[29 Nov. ,,]
Cornet Compton, preferred	Royal Horse	Robert Carey, Cornet	[2 Dec. ,,]
	Seymour's Foot	John Beale, Surgeon	[9 ,, ,,]
Lt.-Col. Dalrymple	3rd Regiment of Guards	James St. Clare, Capt.	[19 ,, ,,]
Lt.-Col. Duncan McKenzie[1]	Ditto	Lt.-Col. Thomas Coote, Capt.	[20 ,, ,,]
Lt.-Col. Hugh Owen	1st Regt. of Guards	Lt.-Col. William Egerton, Capt.	[25 ,, ,,]
[Major Walter Elliott]	[Sr. Hen. Goring]	John Beckwith, Capt.	[19 Nov. ,,]
Capt. Lassly, deceased	Breton's Foot	Thos. Killigrew, Capt.	[6 Jan. 1715.]
Lieut. Sam.? Foster	1st Regt. of Guards	Hawksworth Smith, Lieut.	[3 Feb. ,,]
Brig. Breton, deceased	Regiment of Foot	Lord Shannon, Col.	[27 Jan. ,,]
Earl of Hertford, preferred	Ditto	Henry Harrison, Col.	[8 Feb. ,,]
Lt.-Col. Harrison, preferred	Harrison's Foot	Wm. Handasyde, Lt.-Col.	[,, ,, ,,]
Lord Ashburnham[2]	1st Troop of Guards	His Grace the Duke of Montagu, Col.	[10 Mar. ,,]
Duke of Northumberland[3]	2nd Troop of Guards	The Earl of Hertford	[8 Feb. ,,]

A LIST OF OFFICERS DISPLACED, &C.—cont.

Names and Qualities of such Officers as have been Displaced either with Leave to Sell or otherwise.	In what Regiment.	Names and Qualities of such Officers as have Succeeded those who were Displaced, &c.	Dates of Commissions.
Earl of Arran [4]	3rd Troop of Guards	Lt.-Gen. Cholmondeley, Col.	[8 Feb. 1715
Lt.-Gen. Cholmondeley, pref.	1st Troop of Grendr. Guards	Lord Lumley, Col.	,, ,, ,,
William Brodie, deceased	Shannon's Foot	William Venice, Chaplain	24 Jan. ,,
Joseph Wheatley, deceased	Stearn's Foot	William Clerke, Ensign	16 Feb. ,,
	2nd Independent Company at Jamaica.	Chas. Crossley, Surgeon	7 Mar. ,,
Lt.-Col. Paget, resigned	1st Regt. of Guards	Joseph Ferrers, Capt.	,, ,, ,,
Joseph Ferrers, preferred	1st Troop of Grendr. Guards	Thos. Wentworth, Lieut.	,, ,, ,,
John Foley	1st Troop of Guards	George Hay, Exempt	3 ,, ,,
John Selwyn [5]	Forfarr's Foot	Richard Lowther, Capt.	14 ,, ,,
Capt. Lowther, preferred	Ditto	Chas. Wardlaw, Capt.-Lieut.	,, ,, ,,
Ens. Wardlaw, preferred	Ditto	Saml. Wardlaw, Ensign	,, ,, ,,
Bernard Lostau	E. of Strafford's Dragoons	Wm. Brooks, Cornet	? ,, ,,
Brig. Warring,[6] resigned	1st Troop of Grendr. Guards	Thos. Paget, Lt.-Col.	18 ,, ,,
Earl of Mareschal [7]	2nd Troop of Grendr. Guards	E. Deloraine, Col.	10 ,, ,,
Lt.-Gen. Echlyn [8]	Regiment of Dragoons	E. Stairs, Col.	4 Apr. ,,
Lord Lumley	Lumley's Horse	Brigdr. Thos. Panton, Lt.-Col.	4 Mar. ,,
Brig. Panton, preferred	Ditto	Galen Cope, Capt.	11 Apr. ,,
Conyers Darcey,[9]	1st Troop of Guards	Jno. Blathwayt, Cornet	,, ,, ,,
Jno. Blathwayt, preferred	Ditto	John West, Guidon	,, ,, ,,
Lt.-Col. Markham	1st Regiment of Guards	Thos. Sydney, Capt.	13 ,, ,,
Ens. Erle, deceased	Sutton's Foot	[Wm.] Burnet, Ensign	14 ,, ,,
	Barrymore's Foot	Wm. Charleton, Capt.	16 ,, ,,
Ens. Clare	North and Grey's Foot	Thos. Forth, Ensign	11 May ,,
Ens. Haro	1st Regiment of Guards	[Thos] Tully, Ensign	,, ,, ,,
Capt. Odiarne	Royal Fusiliers	Jas. Fleming, Capt.	12 ,, ,,

GEORGE THE FIRST'S ARMY, 1714–1718

A List of Officers Displaced, &c.—cont.

Names and Qualities of such Officers as have been Displaced either with Leave to Sell or otherwise.	In what Regiment.	Names and Qualities of such Officers as have Succeeded those who were Displaced, &c.	Dates of Commissions.
Lieut. Fleming, preferred	Royal Fusiliers	Geo. Speke Petty, Lieut.	[12 May 1715
Arthur North	1st Troop of Guards	Hen. Goodere, Sub-Brigdr.	[23 ,, ,,
Major Skeene [10]	Portmore's D.	Hen. Selwyn, Capt.	[31 ,, ,,
Thomas Fazakerly	4th Troop of Guards	Duncan Dee, Brigdr.	[2 June ,,
Capt. Greene	Meredyth's Foot	Robt. Graham, Capt.	[6 ,, ,,
Lieut. Tracy	1st Regt. of Guards	Michael Marget, Lieut.	[,, ,, ,,
Earl of Peterborow [11]	Royal Horse Guards	His Grace the Duke of Argyle, Col.	[13 ,, ,,
Earl of Strafford [12]	Royal Dragoons	Lord Cobham, Col.	[,, ,, ,,
Lt.-Col. Egerton, resigned	1st Regiment of Guards	[Ric.] Ingoldsby, Capt.	[11 ,, ,,
Col. Swan	Coldstream Guards	Lord Hinchinbroke, Capt.	[,, ,, ,,
Lieut. Graham, preferred	Meredyth's Foot	Richard Norman, Lieut.	[6 ,, ,,
Capt. Devaux, resigned	1st Troop Grendr. Guards	Simon Peacock, Sub-Lieut.	[15 ,, ,,
Ens. Allinson, deceased	Invalid Company	Walter Barlin, Ensign	[18 ,, ,,
Capt.-Lt. Knightley	Royal Horse	[Gregory] Beak, Capt.-Lieut.	[23 ,, ,,
Lord North and Grey [13]	Regiment of Foot	Brigdr. Hen. Grove, Col.	[,, ,, ,,
Capt. Ingoldsby, preferred	Stearn's Foot	Edward Moyle, Capt.	[25 ,, ,,
Edw. Moyle, preferred	Ditto	Chas. Parker, Capt.-Lt.	[,, ,, ,,
Robt. Pearson, preferred	Ditto	Fras. Tuckey, Ensign	[,, ,, ,,
Chas. Parker, preferred	Ditto	Robert Pearson, preferred	[,, ,, ,,
	Meredyth's Foot	John Heylyn, Chaplain	[28 ,, ,,
James Batson	1st Troop of Guards	Wm. Cavell, Sub-Brigdr.	[,, ,, ,,
Col. Jas. (sic) Vetch [14]	Independt. Co. of Jamaica (sic)	Thos. Phillips, Capt.	[30 ,, ,,
Brig. H. Hamilton [14]	Regt. of Foot	Lord Irwyn, Colonel	[11 July ,,
Lord Irwyn, preferred	Irwyn's Foot	Jno. Cholmondeley, Lt.-Col.	[? ,, ,,
Lt.-Col. Cholmondeley, pref.	1st Regiment of Guards	Samuel Garrard, Capt.	[,, ,, ,,

A List of Officers Displaced, &c.—cont.

Names and Qualities of such Officers as have been Displaced either with Leave to Sell or otherwise.	In what Regiment.	Names and Qualities of such Officers as have Succeeded those who were Displaced, &c.	Dates of Commissions.
Ens. Hallyburton, resigned	Shannon's Foot	James Maitland, Ensign	[15 July 1715
Ens. Smith	3rd Regiment of Guards	Sherrington Talbot,[19] Ensign	[23 ,, ,,
	Cobham's Dragoons	[Erasmus] Shorter, Capt.	[22 ,, ,,
Major Butler	Stair's Dragoons	[Charles] Otway, Major	[? 23 ,, ,,
Capt. Woodyear	Royal Horse	Giles Erle, Capt.	[23 ,, ,,
Capt. Browne	Ditto	John Wyvell, Capt.	[25 ,, ,,
	Ditto	Geo. Berkley, Cornet	
Capt. Bunbury, deceased	Meredyth's Foot	Benj. Jones, Capt.	
Capt. Lowther	Orrery's Foot	John Wynyard, Capt.	[26 ,, ,,
Earl of Barrymore[16]	Regiment of Foot	Stanhope Cotton, Col.	[28 ,, ,,
Lord Blantiere[17]	Whetham's Foot	— Powlet. Capt.	
	Coldstream Guards	Jno. Faillot (sic), Adjt.	[30 ,, ,,
Lt.-Col. Hamilton	3rd Regiment of Guards	[Henry] Berkly, Capt.	[22 ,, ,,
Lt.-Col. Boyse	Coldstream Guards	Chas. Cadogan, Capt.	[11 ,, ,,
Sir Wynwood Mowat[18]	Ditto	Jas. Gendrault, Lieut.	[30 ,, ,,
Ens. Keating	Ditto	Nath. Blackstein (sic), Ensign	
Lieut. Robt. Green	Ditto	[John] Smith, Lieut.	[23 ,, ,,
Ens. Corbet	Ditto	Robert Morgan, Ensign	[20 ,, ,,
Lt.-Col. Johnson, resigned	3rd Regiment of Guards	Thomas Diggs, Capt.	[30 ,, ,,
	Coldstream Guards	Sir Henry Heron,[23] Ensign	[20 ,, ,,
Capt. Jenkinson, preferred	Grove's Foot	Fras. Columbine, Lt.-Col.	[4 Aug. ,,
Ens. Fargeon	Lord Irwyn's Foot	John Smelt, Capt.	,, ,,
Ens. Mathews	Ditto	John Gascoin, Ensign	,, ,,
Ens. Lister	Coldstream Guards	[Hon.] Chas. Howard,[23]	[10 ,, ,,
Lord Lumley, preferred	1st Regiment of Guards	Geo. Villars Huet,[24] Ensign	
	Lumley's Horse	Wm. Cole, Capt.	[6 ,, ,,

GEORGE THE FIRST'S ARMY, 1714–1718   189

A List of Officers Displaced, &c.—cont.

Names and Qualities of such Officers as have been Displaced either with Leave to Sell or otherwise.	In what Regiment	Names and Qualities of such Officers as have Succeeded those who were Displaced, &c.	Dates of Commissions.
Lt.-Col. Whitney, preferred	Harrison's Foot	Sam. Whitshett, Capt.	
Capt. John Huske, preferred	Ditto	William Howe, Capt.	[6 Aug. 1715
Capt. Bellendine, preferred	3rd Regiment of Guards	John Scott, Lieut.	[3 ,, ,,
Capt. Henry Smith	1st Regiment of Guards	John Fogg, Lieut.	
Capt. Lamelonière	Ditto	Wm. Swan, Lieut.	[8 ,, ,,
Capt. Robinson	Ditto	Robt. Leighton, Lieut.	
Lord Cranston,[20] resigned	3rd Regiment of Guards	John Campbell, Capt.	
Jno. Campbell, preferred	Ditto	Jno. Montgomery, Capt.-Lieut.	[13 ,, ,,
Thos. Diggs, preferred	1st Troop of Guards	William Latton, Exempt	
Lieut. Wingate	Coldstream Guards	Richard Legg, Lieut.	[15 ,, ,,
Ens. Legg, preferred	Ditto	Geo. Bellamy, Ensign	
Ens. Gordon, deceased	Invalid Company	Wm. Falliot, Ensign	[16 ,, ,,
Lieut. James Stalker	Lumley's Horse	John Warren, Lieut.	[18 ,, ,,
Lieut. Calahan, deceased	Invalid Company	— Cunningham, Lieut.	
Col. Jas. Hale[21]	1st Regiment of Guards	Geo. Carpenter, Capt.	[19 ,, ,,
Lieut. Jno. Smelt, preferred	Carpenter's Dragoons	Abraham Dupuis, Lieut.	
Ens. Chalmers, resigned	3rd Regiment of Guards	Geo. Hope, Ensign	
Ens. Ash	Harrison's Foot	Thos. Bowdler, Ensign	
Ens. Mayer	Ditto	Wm. Strachey, Ensign	
	Ditto	[Thos.] Massingale, Lieut.	
	Royal Horse	Wm. Campbell, Cornet	
	Ditto	Herbert Lawrence, Ensign	
John Brown, resigned	Montagu's Foot	Jno. Pawlet, Surgeon	
Steph. De la Creuze	2nd Troop of Guards	James Stewart, Cornet	,, ,,
	Stair's Dragoons	Fras. Bowes, Lt.-Col. and Capt.	,, ,,
Major Bowes, preferred	Cotton's Foot	Ferdinando Ric. Hastings, Maj.	,, ,,
	Ditto		

A List of Officers Displaced, &c.—cont.

Names and Qualities of such Officers as have been Displaced either with Leave to Sell or otherwise.	In what Regiment.	Names and Qualities of such Officers as have Succeeded those who were Displaced, &c.	Dates of Commissions.
Capt. Hastings, preferred	Cotton's Foot	John Loyd (sic), Capt.	[19 Aug. 1715
Lieut. Loyd, preferred	Ditto	[John] Quinchant, Lieut.	,, ,,
Ens. Quinchant, preferred	Ditto	Chas. Lieving, Ensign	,, ,,
Ens. Peregrine Jones	1st Regt. of Guards	Jno. Gore, Ensign	
Major Jas. Howard, preferred	Col. Handasyde's	[Wm.] Duncombe	[24 ,,
Lieut. Stewart	Col. Dubourgay's	Roger Mostyn, Lieut.	[22 July
Lieut. Nappier	Brigdr. Stanwix's	Wiltshire Castle, Lieut.	[24 Aug.
Ens. Scott	3rd Regiment of Guards	Jno. Gordon, Ensign	[29 ,,
Capt. Thos. Morris[25]	Whitman's Foot	Jas. Fonsebran, Capt.	[8 Sept.
Lieut. Stowe, resigned	Ditto	Wm. Duckett, Lieut.	[9 ,,
Cornet Duckett, preferred	Ditto	Robert Plomer, Cornet	,, ,,
Cornet Savell, resigned	Lumley's Horse	Gregory Odiarne, Cornet	,, ,,
Lord Balgony, resigned	3rd Regiment of Guards	Geo. Howard, Capt.	,, ,,
Ens. Ramsey, preferred	Grove's Foot	Thos. Rogers, Ensign	,, ,,
Ens. Line	Ditto	Nath. Piklilton (sic), Ensign	
Robt. Dormer, preferred	1st Troop of Guards	Jno. Blathwayt, Lt.-Col.	[25 ,,
Major Blathwayt, preferred	Ditto	Jno. West, Major	,, ,,
Ens. Adams	Col. Pocock's	Henry Piketon (sic), Ensign	[12 ,,
Capt. Florance Kane	Invalid Company	[Richard] Green, Capt.	[13 ,,
Lieut. Baker	Brigdr. Bowles'	Thos. Dawes, Lieut.	,, ,,
Chas. Stewart, preferred	3rd Regiment of Guards	Chas. Murray, Ensign	[4 ,,
	Coldstream Guards	Jasper Tryce, Ensign	[14 ,,
	Ditto	Ric. Walford, Ensign	,, ,,
	Ditto	Fras. Pilliord, Ensign	,, ,,
Lord Jno. Kerr, preferred	4th Troop of Guards	Saml. Horsey, Lt.-Col.	,, ,,
Ens. Forfarr, preferred	Preston's Foot	Alex. Duroure,[26] Ensign	,, ,,

GEORGE THE FIRST'S ARMY, 1714–1718 191

A List of Officers Displaced, &c.—cont.

Names and Qualities of such Officers as have been Displaced either with Leave to Sell or otherwise.	In what Regiment.	Names and Qualities of such Officers as have Succeeded those who were Displaced, &c.	Dates of Commissions.
Ens. Forrester, preferred	Preston's Foot	Sham. Wright, Ensign	[16 Sept. 1715]
Lt.-Col. Stanhope, preferred	Whetham's Foot	Hen. Ponsonby, Lt.-Col.	,,
Major Ponsonby, preferred	Ditto	Hen. Cope, Major	,,
	Ditto	Pet. Chasseloup, Capt.	,,
Jas. Campbell, preferred	Portmore's Dragoons	Chas. Cathcart, Lt.-Col.	,,
Col. Cathcart, preferred	Ditto	Sir Robert Hay, Major	,,
Jas. Campbell	Ditto	Thos. Agnew, Capt.	,,
Lieut. Brereton	Col. Chudleigh's	Wm. Churchill, Lieut.	,,
Wm. Churchill, preferred	Col. Pocock's	Wm. Knowles, Ensign	,,
Lieut. Halshide	Brigdr. Grant's	James Urquhart, Lieut.	,,
Ens. Bruce	Ditto	Robt. Cutler, Ensign	,,
Lt.-Col. Young, resigned	3rd Regiment of Guards	Geo. Hay, Capt.	[19 ,,
Capt.-Lt. Edwards	Harrison's Foot	Mich. Brandreth, Capt.-Lieut.	[14 Aug.
Lieut. Brandreth, preferred	Ditto	Thos. Levet, Lieut.	[25 ,,
Ens. Levet, preferred	Ditto	Jno. Harris, Ensign	[20 Sept.
Capt. Price, resigned	Coldstream Guards	Jno. Wynn, Lieut.	[22 ,,
Lieut. Bransby, deceased	Sabine's Foot	Wm. Barnet, 2nd Lieut.	[26 ,,
Jno. Purcell, preferred	Sir Robert Rich's	Toby Purcell, Cornet	[22 July
Capt. Warren, resigned	Coldstream Guards	Jno. Griffith, Lieut.	[27 Sept.
Col. [Thos.] Dalyell [27]	3rd Regiment of Guards	Jno. Johnstone, Capt.	[28 Aug.
Lieut. Slingsby, resigned	Grove's Foot	William Palmer, Lieut.	[27 Sept.
Ens. Clarke, resigned	Stearn's Foot	Robert Cotter, Ensign	,,
Geo. Carpenter, preferred	Carpenter's Dragoons	Jas. Carpenter, Capt.-Lieut.	,,
Capt. Stacey, resigned	4th Troop of Guards	Duncan Dee, Exempt	[28 ,,
Maj.-Gen. Braddock	Coldstream Guards	Rich. Holmes, Lt.-Col.	,,
Maj.-Gen. Holmes, preferred	Ditto	Adolphus Oughton, 1st Major	,,

A LIST OF OFFICERS DISPLACED, &C.—cont.

Names and Qualities of such Officers as have been Displaced either with Leave to Sell or otherwise.	In what Regiment.	Names and Qualities of such Officers as have Succeeded those who were Displaced, &c.	Dates of Commissions.
Brigdr. Morrison, preferred	Coldstream Guards	Jno. Robinson, 2nd Major	[28 Sept. 1715
Ditto as Captain	Ditto	George Churchill, Capt.	,, ,,
Major Tichbourne, resigned	Pearce's Foot	Wm. Elrington, Major	,, ,,
Jas. Gibson, resigned	4th Troop of Guards	David Campbell, Exempt	,, ,,
Thos. Handasyde, preferred	Col. Handasyde's	Dugal Campbell, Capt.-Lieut.	[29 ,,
Capt. Carey, deceased	Alexander's Foot	Phillip Walsh, Capt.	1 Oct.
Capt. Cornaud, resigned	2nd Troop of Guards	Jno. Denty, Exempt	[29 Sept.
Jno. Denty, preferred	Ditto	Peter Hardistie, Brigdr.	,, ,,
Peter Hardistie, preferred	Ditto	Arthur Edwards, Sub-Brigdr.	,, ,,
[Edwd. Montagu, preferred]	Ditto	Geo. Benson, Lt.-Col.	[3 Oct.
[Geo. Benson, preferred]	Cobham's Dragoons	Jas. Crofts, Major	,, ,,
Capt. Thos. Rogers	Ditto	Andrew Pancier, Capt.-Lieut.	,, ,,
Lieut. Pancier	Ditto	Chas. Dilk, Lieut.	,, ,,
Cornet Dilk	Ditto	Thos. Stevens, Cornet	,, ,,
Cornet Sadler	Ditto	Elias Brevet, Cornet	,, ,,
Lord Blantire [28]	Whetham's Foot	Wm. Stammers, Capt.	,, ,,
Clifford Handasyde	Col. Handasyde's	Chas. Handasyde, Lieut.	[22 July
	Cotton's Foot	Jonathan Fox, Lieut.	[6 Oct.
	Ditto	Theodore Lucy, Ensign	
Col. Blakeney, resigned	1st Regiment of Guards	Mich. Margett, 2nd Adjt.	
Capt. Maitland	3rd Regiment of Guards	Wm. Clarke, 1st Adjt.	
Adjt. Maitland	Ditto	Andrew Hamilton, 2nd Adjt.	
Capt. Needham, resigned	1st Troop of Guards	Thos. Taylor, Exempt	[25 ,,
Col. Sidney, resigned	1st Regiment of Guards	[John] Duncombe, Capt.	[2 ,,
	Royal Fusiliers	Jeffrey Gibbons, Capt.-Lieut.	
Lieut. Gibbons, preferred	Ditto	— Luckin, Lieut.	

GEORGE THE FIRST'S ARMY, 1714–1718 193

A List of Officers Displaced, &c.—cont.

Names and Qualities of such Officers as have been Displaced either with Leave to Sell or otherwise.	In what Regiment.	Names and Qualities of such Officers as have Succeeded those who were Displaced, &c.	Dates of Commissions.
Major Cookman,[29] not able to do duty	Sabine's Foot	Edward Pole, Capt.	[13 Oct. 1715
Capt. Hay, preferred	1st Troop of Guards	Edmund Wright, Exempt	,, ,,
	Preston's Foot	Jno. Preston, Adjt.	,, ,,
Ens. Preston, preferred	Ditto	Gustavus Hamilton, Ensign	,, ,,
Lieut. Pierson, lunatick	Orrery's Foot	Edwd. Boyle, 2nd Lieut.	[14 ,, ,,
Hen. Le Grand, preferred	Col. Stanhope's	Peter Malet, Lieut.	,, ,,
Cornet English	Ditto	Jno. Robertson (sic), Cornet	,, ,,
Capt. Pole	Brigdr. Grant's	Jno. Robertson, Capt.	[11 ,, ,,
Lieut. Macneal, preferred	Brigdr. Stanwix's	Roger MacManus, Lieut.	[15 ,, ,,
Lieut. MacManus	Sabine's Foot	Daniel McNeal, Lieut.	,, ,,
Col. Oughton, preferred	1st Regt. of Guards	Thos. Condon, Capt.	[21 ,, ,,
Lieut. Wentworth, preferred	1st Troop Grendr. Guards	Churchill Lloyd, Lieut.	[24 ,, ,,
Col. Barrell, preferred	1st Regt. of Guards	Thos. Wentworth, Capt.	,, ,,
	Ditto	Wm. Daffy, Ensign	,, ,,
	Coldstream Guards	Wm. Burbero, Adjt.	,, ,,
Cornet Forfarr	Brigdr. Bowles's	Lord Nassau Pawlet, Cornet	,, ,,
Ens. Michael	Col. Lucas's	Jas. Brown, Ensign	,, ,,
Lieut. Sprott, superannuated	Grove's Foot	Alex. Duroure,[26] Lieut.	[25 ,, ,,
Lieut. Moreton, preferred	Fane's Foot	Alford Bataly, Lieut.	,, ,,
Lieut. Noel Marchand[30]	Ind. Company at Jamaica	Thos. Moore, Lieut.	,, ,,
Lieut. Le Grand, preferred	Col. Stanhope's	Andrew Robinson, Lieut.	[27 ,, ,,
Cornet Robinson, preferred	Ditto	Jno. Wooly, Cornet	,, ,,
Fras. Hull, preferred	Brigdr. Munden's	Jno. Watson, Lieut.	[28 ,, ,,
Cornet Watson, preferred	Ditto	Richard Henson, Cornet	,, ,,

A LIST OF OFFICERS DISPLACED, &C.—cont.

Names and Qualities of such Officers as have been Displaced either with Leave to Sell or otherwise.	In what Regiment.	Names and Qualities of such Officers as have Succeeded those who were Displaced, &c.	Dates of Commissions.
Lieut. Nazon	Pitt's Horse	Fras. Hull, Lieut.	[28 Oct. 1715
	Ditto	James Damboon, Adjt.	[1 Nov. ,,
Col. Granville	Col. Dubourgay's	[Charles] Williams, Major	[3 ,, ,,
Lieut. Hamilton, deceased	Grove's Foot	Jno. Langley, Major	
Ens. Newton, preferred	Meredyth's Foot	Wm. Newton, Lieut.	
	Ditto	Abraham Bickford, Ensign	
	1st Regt. of Guards	Rowland Reynolds, 3rd Adjt.	
Capt. Browne, resigned	Ditto	Jno. Knowles, Qr.-Mr.	
Capt. Duncombe	Cotton's Foot	Ralph Jenkins, Capt.	,, ,,
Capt. Jenkins, preferred	Ditto	Geo. Walsh, Capt.-Lieut.	,, ,,
Lieut. Walsh, preferred	Ditto	Thos. Jordaine, Lieut.	,, ,,
Ens. Pickering, resigned	Ditto	Hen. Witherhill, Ensign	
Cornet McMillen, preferred	Fane's Foot	Samuel Lowe, Cornet	[8 ,, ,,
Capt. Cole, preferred	Col. Newton's	Ric. Shuckburgh,[31] Capt.	
Ens. Pyne	Sabine's Foot	Wm. Whitmore,[32] Ensign-	
Ens. la Coudrière, resigned	Col. Pocock's	Jno. Lysons, Ensign	[15 ,, ,,
Lieut. Cunningham, preferred	Grove's Foot	Peter Mallet, Lieut.	[16 ,, ,,
Capt. Charleton, resigned	Ditto	Jas. Cunningham, Capt.	[19 ,, ,,
Lieut. Man	Cotton's Foot	Jeremiah Mussenden, Lieut.	
Ens. Mussenden, preferred	Stearn's Foot	Hugh McManus, Ensign	[18 ,, ,,
Wm. Latton, preferred	1st Troop of Guards	Jas. Batson, Brigdr.	
Thos. Condon, preferred	Forfarr's Foot	Jno. Farrer, Ensign	[23 ,, ,,
Capt. Oglethorp	1st Regt. of Guards	Robt. Hemington, Lieut.	
Lieut. Armstrong, k. at Dumbln.	Royal Horse	Jno. Bennet, Lieut.	
Doctor Freind	4th Troop of Guards	— Burscough, Chaplain	
Ens. Boheme, resigned	Harrison's Foot	David Chapean, Ensign	[19 ,, ,,

A List of Officers Displaced, &c.—cont.

Names and Qualities of such Officers as have been Displaced either with Leave to Sell or otherwise.	In what Regiment.	Names and Qualities of such Officers as have Succeeded those who were Displaced, &c.	Dates of Commissions.
Ens. Delangly, minor	Irwin's Foot	Peter Fargeon, Ensign	[5 Dec. 1715]
	Coldstream Guards	Wm. Cæsar Streng, Ensign	,,
Capt. Howard, preferred	Col. Lucas's	Philip Loyd, Capt.	,,
Jno. Menville, resigned	Cobham's Dragoons	Griffith Hatley, Cornet	,,
Chas. Loyd, preferred	Carpenter's Dragoons	Chas. Jones, Cornet	[10 ,,
[T. Strickland]	Brigdr. Bowles's	Jno. Orfeur, Lt.-Col.	,,
	Ditto	Thos. Browne, Major	,,
Lieut. Phillpott, resigned	Brigdr. Grant's	Jno. Shorthose, Lieut.	[13 ,,
Capt. Preston	Preston's Foot	Wm. Ferguson, Capt.	,,
Capt. Anstruther	Ditto	Alexr. Burnet, Capt.	,,
Capt.-Lt. Ferguson, preferred	Ditto	Fras. Graham, Capt.-Lieut.	,,
Lieut. Burnet, preferred	Ditto	Chas. Colvine, Lieut.	,,
Lieut. Elphinston	Ditto	Jas. Gordon, Lieut.	,,
Lieut. Fras. Graham	Ditto	Robt. Ross, Lieut.	,,
Ens. Erskine	Ditto	Jno. Forrester, Lieut.	,,
	Ditto	Alex. Anstruther, Ensign	,,
	Ditto	Jno. Dyer, Ensign	,,
	Ditto	Archd. Dowglass, Ensign	,,
	Ditto	Robt. Anstruther, Ensign	,,
Cornet Oldfield	Col. Churchill's	Phillip Gery, Cornet	[20 ,,
Ens. Ferguson, who has never appeared with the Regt.	Col. Lucas's	Jas. Blasford, Ensign	[28 ,,
Wm. Serafton	3rd Troop of Guards	Chas. Lamb, Chaplain	,,
Saml. Moore, deceased	Placentia	Jas. Moore, Surgeon	,,
Lieut. Walters, resigned	Sabine's Foot	Chas. Combe, 1st Lieut.	[3 Jan. 1716.]
Chas. Combe, preferred	Ditto	Roger Gower, 2nd Lieut.	,,

A List of Officers Displaced, &c.—cont.

Names and Qualities of such Officers as have been Displaced either with Leave to Sell or otherwise.	In what Regiment.	Names and Qualities of such Officers as have Succeeded those who were Displaced, &c.	Dates of Commissions.
Ens. Sydenham, resigned	Moryson's Foot	Peter Renaut, Ensign	[4 Jan. 1716
Cornet Bennet, preferred	Evans' Dragoons	Jno. Oliver, Adjt.	,, ,,
Major Hammer, killed	Portmore's Dragoons	Alex. Spittle,[33] Cornet	[5 ,, ,,
Capt. Loyd, preferred	Moryson's Foot	Leon. Loyd, Major	,, ,,
Capt. Cuttell, killed	Ditto	Chas. Stewart, Capt.	,, ,,
Capt.-Lt. Baner, killed	Ditto	Edw. Devischer, Capt.	,, ,,
Lieut. Chambers, killed	Ditto	Geo. Baanastre, Capt.-Lieut.	,, ,,
Ens. Holman, killed	Ditto	Jno. Grey, Lieut.	,, ,,
Ens. Tilbury, killed	Ditto	Jno. White, Ensign	,, ,,
Ens. Sharp, killed	Ditto	Wm. Rowland, Ensign	,, ,,
Ens. Gally, killed	Ditto	Peter Ribton, Ensign	,, ,,
Capt. Humble, killed	Montagu's Foot	Paul Pigou, Ensign	,, ,,
Capt.-Lt. Bernarden, killed	Ditto	Ric. Hartshorne, Capt.	,, ,,
Lieut. Hynde, preferred	Ditto	Wm. Hynde, Capt.-Lieut.	,, ,,
Lieut. Milbourne, killed	Ditto	Arnold Tulikens, Lieut.	,, ,,
Lieut. Mortimer, killed	Ditto	[Robt.] Grewell,[34] Lieut.	,, ,,
Ens. Tulikens, preferred	Ditto	Jas. Warren, Lieut.	,, ,,
Ens. Warren, preferred	Ditto	Lancelot Story, Ensign	,, ,,
Cornet Bursie, killed	Evans' Dragoons	Jno. Purcell, Ensign	,, ,,
Ens. Benj. Harris, preferred	Col. Dubourgay's	Rich. Symonds, Cornet	[12 ,, ,,
Major Penotier, deceased	Stearn's Foot	Sir Jno. Hamilton, Ensign	[13 ,, ,,
Dr. Livesay, resigned	Phillip's Foot	Peter D'Offrenville, Major	[20 ,, ,,
	Pitt's Horse	Chas. Ball, Chaplain	
Capt. Pitt, preferred	Maj.-Gen. Pepper's	Jno. Pitt, Capt.	[31 ,, ,,
Major Cope, resigned	Whetham's Foot	Wm. Bland, Capt.	,, ,,
		Thos. Cockrane, Capt.	,, ,,

GEORGE THE FIRST'S ARMY, 1714–1718

A LIST OF OFFICERS DISPLACED, &C.—cont.

Names and Qualities of such Officers as have been Displaced either with Leave to Sell or otherwise.	In what Regiment.	Names and Qualities of such Officers as have Succeeded those who were Displaced, &c.	Dates of Commissions.
Jno. West, preferred	1st Troop of Guards	Thos. Taylor, Guidon	[5 March 1716]
Thos. Taylor, preferred	Ditto	Daniel Leighton, Exempt	[6 Feb. ,,
Jno. Breeden, resigned	Lumley's Horse	Sam. Breeden, Cornet	——
Lieut. Bland, preferred	Pitt's Horse	Thos. Vigors, Lieut.	[24 ,, ,,
Cornet Vigors, preferred	Ditto	Jno. Eyre, Cornet	,, ,,
Lieut. Bull	1st Regt. of Guards	Thos. Tullie, Lieut.	[21 ,, ,,
Ens. Tullie, preferred	Ditto	Jos. Gronous, Ensign	,, ,,
Ens. Swann, preferred	Ditto	Gedeon Harvey, Ensign	,, ,,
Lieut. Dawes	Sir Chas. Hotham's	Martin Groundman, Lieut.	[24 ,, ,,
Lieut. Ducosne, resigned	Moryson's Foot	Thos. Launder, Lieut.	[25 ,, ,,
	Shannon's Foot	Robert Scott, Capt.	,, ,,
	Ditto	Jas. Arther, Lieut.	,, ,,
	Ditto	Jno. Sloss, Lieut.	,, ,,
	Ditto	Alex [? Fred.] Bruce, Ensign	,, ,,
Capt. Currants, resigned	2nd Troop of Guards	Edw. Whitaker, Exempt	[28 ,, ,,
Lt.-Col. Churchill	Harrison's Foot	Fras. Smith, Capt.	[6 March ,,
Fras. Shaw	Kirk's Foot	Wm. Colnet, Chaplain	,, ,,
Ens. Leighton, preferred	1st Regt. of Guards	Fras. Brerewood, Ensign	,, ,,
Capt. Bickerstaff, deceased	Pearce's Foot	Fras. Seys, Capt.	,, ,,
Ens. Clements, resigned	Stearn's Foot	Chas. Nicholson [Junr.], Ens.	[10 ,, ,,
Lieut. Lowder, rebell	Irwyn's Foot	Fras. Bushell, Lieut.	,, ,,
Ens. Rambouillet, preferred	Col. Dubourgay's	Chas. Rambouillet,[86] Lieut.	,, ,,
	Ditto	Chas. Hamilton, Ensign	,, ,,
Lieut. Yard, resigned	Col. Chudleigh's	Thos. Chudleigh, Lieut.	,, ,,
Capt. Gardiner, resigned	Col. Handasyde's	Wheeler Fletcher, Capt.	,, ,,
Cornet Ireland, resigned	Windsor's Horse	Phillip Fullerton, Cornet	[24 ,, ,,

A List of Officers Displaced, &c.—cont.

Names and Qualities of such Officers as have been Displaced either with Leave to Sell or otherwise.	In what Regiment.	Names and Qualities of such Officers as have Succeeded those who were Displaced, &c.	Dates of Commissions.
Capt. Agnew, preferred	Portmore's Dragoons	Andw. King, Capt.-Lieut.	[24 March 1716
Lieut. King, preferred	Ditto	Alexr. Forbes, Lieut.	,, ,,
	Ditto	Gilbert Geddes, Cornet	,, ,,
Lieut. Dowglass,	Plancentia (sic)	Robert Bellenden, Lieut.	
Capt. Chaworth, resigned	2nd Tooop Grendr. Guards	Hen. Brightman, Adjt.	[27 ,, ,,
Capt. Brightman, preferred	4th Troop of Guards	Bigg Ash, Sub-Brigdr.	,, ,,
Jas. Elphinstone	Grove's Foot	Wm. Bellon, Ensign	,, ,,
Capt. Robert Sanford	Egerton's Foot	Theophilus Sandford, Capt.	,, ,,
Lieut. Beverley, deceased	Seymour's Foot	[Jonathan] Furlong, Lieut.	,, ,,
Ens. Furlong, preferred	Ditto	Wm. Summer, Ensign	,, ,,
Ens. Husband, resigned	Wightman's Foot	Jno. Browne, Ensign	,, ,,
Capt. Blount, deceased	Sankey's Foot	Dan. Negus, Capt.	,, ,,
Ens. Barry	Cotton's Foot	Jno. Windus, Ensign	[2 April ,,
Lieut. Preston, rendered by wounds incapable of service	Col. Handasyde's	Wm. Geekhie, Lieut.	,, ,,
Lieut. Pudsey, resigned	Col. Pocock's	Paul Torin, Lieut.	,, ,,
Lieut. Burnet, deceased	Brigdr. Stanwix's	Jno. Rouse, Lieut.	,, ,,
Ens. Rouse, preferred	Ditto	Chas. Browne, Ensign	[10 ,, ,,
Lieut. Bransby, resigned	Col. Stanhope's	Geo. Bernard, Lieut.	,, ,,
Cornet Bernard	Ditto	Dan. Garrets, Cornet	,, ,,
Ens. Dowglass, deceased	Preston's Foot	Jno. Johnson, Ensign	,, ,,
Capt. Whitchett, preferred	Harrison's Foot	Toby Cramer, Capt.	[14 ,, ,,
Col. Davis, deceased	Kirk's Foot	Jas. Giles, Capt.	[13 ,, ,,
Capt. Giles, preferred	Ditto	Chas. May, Capt.-Lieut.	,, ,,
Lieut. May, preferred	Ditto	Ld. Wm. Beauclair,[86] Lieut.	,, ,,
Brigadier Ferrers, preferred	1st Regt. of Guards	Jas. Pelham, Capt.	[16 ,, ,,

GEORGE THE FIRST'S ARMY, 1714-1718 199

A LIST OF OFFICERS DISPLACED, &C.—cont.

Names and Qualities of such Officers as have been Displaced either with Leave to Sell or otherwise.	In what Regiment.	Names and Qualities of such Officers as have Succeeded those who were Displaced, &c.	Dates of Commissions.
Marq. Du Quesne	3rd Troop of Guards	Christr. Earnest Kain, Guidon	[16 April 1716]
Capt. Pelham, preferred	Maj.-Gen. Pepper's	Ld. Ossulstone,[87] Capt.	,, ,,
Ens. Gore	Whetham's Foot	Ric. Kent, Ensign	17 ,, ,,
Col. Duncombe, resigned	2nd Troop Grendr. Guards	Jno. White, Guidon	24 ,, ,,
Capt. Nicholas Fynboe	Phillips' Foot	Rowland Phillip, Capt.	25 ,, ,,
Lieut. Wakefield	Montagu's Foot	Miles Tomms, Lieut.	,, ,,
Lancelot Story, resigned	Ditto	Abra. Fowler, Qr.-Mr.	,, ,,
Lieut. Jacobs, resigned	Cotton's Foot	David Barry, Lieut.	,, ,,
Ens. Barry, Lieut.	Ditto	Jos. Gascoin, Ensign	,, ,,
Lieut. Patterson, resigned	Ditto	Benj. Walsh, Lieut.	8 May ,,
Col. Montagu, preferred	Cobham's Dragoons	Samuel Speed, Capt.	,, ,,
Thos. Smith, resigned	1st Troop of Guards	Ric. Parsons, Sub-Brigadier	,, ,,
Geo. Hart	Col. Lucas's	Roger Adams, Surgeon	,, ,,
Adjt. Oliver, resigned	Evans' Dragoons	Jeffry Dollard, Adjt.	10 ,, ,,
Col. Shute, preferred	Windsor's Horse	Thos. Armstrong, Capt.	9 ,, ,,
Capt.-Lt. Armstrong, preferred	Ditto	Wm. Ashby, Capt.-Lieut.	,, ,,
Lieut. Ashby, preferred	Ditto	Benj. Tudman, Lieut.	,, ,,
Cornet Tudman, preferred	Ditto	Samuel Rolle, Cornet	,, ,,
Capt. Dudley Cossby	Wightman's Foot	Thos. Cossby, Capt.	22 ,, ,,
Lieut. Mavitie, deceased	Whetham's Foot	Thos. Smith, Lieut.	17 ,, ,,
Ens. Smith, preferred	Ditto	Geo. Middleton, Ensign	,, ,,
Capt. Trevanian, resigned	Grove's Foot	Thos. White, Capt.	23 ,, ,,
Ens. Lowthorp, resigned	Egerton's Foot	Wm. Garret, Ensign	22 ,, ,,
Col. Elwell,[88] resigned	1st Regt. of Guards	Jno. Buncombe,[89] Capt.	25 ,, ,,
	Fane's Foot	Thos. Hales,[40] Lt.-Col.	,, ,,
	Lumley's Horse	Ric. Andrewes, Cornet	30 ,, ,,

A List of Officers Displaced, &c.—cont.

Names and Qualities of such Officers as have been Displaced either with Leave to Sell or otherwise.	In what Regiment.	Names and Qualities of such Officers as have Succeeded those who were Displaced, &c.	Dates of Commissions.
Col. Edw. Purcell	Seymour's Foot	Ralph Kinaston, Capt.	[31 May 1716
Capt. Kinaston, preferred	Ditto	Ric. Purchass, Capt.-Lieut.	,, ,,
Lieut. Purchass, preferred	Ditto	Wm. Trelawny, Lieut.	,, ,,
Ditto	Ditto	Edw. Williamson, Qr.-Mr.	,, ,,
Ens. Trelawny, preferred	Ditto	Chas. Jackson, Ensign	,, ,,
Ens. Gordon, exchange	Plancentia (sic)	Thos. Button, Ensign	[2 June ,,
Ens. Button, exchange	Annapolis	Alexr. Gordon, Ensign	,, ,,
Capt. Phil. Roberts, preferred	3rd Troop of Guards	Jno. Roberts, Exempt	[9 ,, ,,
Geo. Compton, resigned	2nd Troop of Guards	Philip Roberts, Guidon	,, ,,
Lieut. Cunningham, broke by a court martial	Invalid Company	[Thos.] Stewart, Lieut.	,, ,,
Jno. Knaxton	Brigdr. Grant's	Ant. Robinson, Qr.-Mr.	[2 ,, ,,
Lieut. Hutchinson, resigned	2nd Troop Grendr. Guards	Wm. Henry Cheret, Lieut.	[12 ,, ,,
Edm. Wright, preferred	1st Troop of Guards	John Montagu, Brigdr.	,, ,,
Col. Hastings, preferred	Cotton's Foot	Thos. Fowkes,[41] Major, with a Company	,, ,,
Cornet Cockrain, preferred	Portmore's Dragoons	Jno. Keir, Cornet	[14 ,, ,,
Cornet Kennedy, preferred	Ditto	Jno. Gallway, Cornet	[15 ,, ,,
Ens. Ferrys, resigned	Seymour's Foot	Thos. Tuttill, Ensign	,, ,,
Lieut. Booth, deceased	Cotton's Foot	Thos. Williams, Lieut.	,, ,,
Ens. Williams, preferred	Ditto	Frans. Cockain, Ensign	,, ,,
	Sabine's Foot	Hen. Rumsey, Capt.-Lieut.	,, ,,
Lieut. Rumsey, preferred	Ditto	Wm. Sabine, 1st Lieut.	,, ,,
Lieut. Sabine, preferred	Ditto	Jno. Chambre, 2nd Lieut.	,, ,,
	1st Regt. of Guards	Ferdinando Ric. Hastings, Capt.	,, ,,
Thos. Whitney, preferred	Col. Chudleigh's	Mich. Moore, Adjt.	,, ,,

GEORGE THE FIRST'S ARMY, 1714-1718 201

A List of Officers Displaced, &c.—cont.

Names and Qualities of such Officers as have been Displaced either with Leave to Sell or otherwise.	In what Regiment.	Names and Qualities of such Officers as have Succeeded those who were Displaced, &c.	Dates of Commissions.
Fras. Meheux, resigned	Col. Handasyde's	Fras. Leighton, Capt.	[16 June 1716
Jas. Gee, preferred	Sir Chas. Hotham's	Jno. Moyser, Capt.	[19 ,, ,,
Ens. Moyser, preferred	Ditto	Wm. Livingstoun, Ensign	,, ,,
Capt. Barry, resigned	Stair's Dragoons	Jas. Wood, Lieut., en second	,, ,,
Lt.-Col. Columbière, resigned	Royal Fusiliers	Jas. Cochrain, Capt.	,, ,,
Maj. Otway, resigned	Moryson's Foot	Chas. Hotham, Lt.-Col.	,, ,,
Col. Jno. Hope, resigned	Stair's Dragoons	Augustus Duquerry, Major	,, ,,
Col. Upton, resigned	3rd Regt. of Guards	Jas. Gee, Capt.	,, ,,
Brig. Hobard, resigned	Stair's Dragoons	Chas. Otway, Lt.-Col.	,, ,,
	2nd Regt. of Guards	[Hon.] Wm. Fitzmaurice,[42] Capt.	
Lieut. Combe, preferred	Sabine's Foot	Jno. Cross, 2nd Lieut.	[23 ,, ,,
Capt. Hotham, preferred	Sir Chas. Hotham's	Jas. Brandon, Capt.	[14 ,, ,,
Ens. Colvin, deceased	Col. Handasyde's	Merrill Riggs, Ensign	[23 ,, ,,
Robt. Thompson, resigned	Col. Molesworth's	Xopher Hargrave, Adjt.	[26 ,, ,,
Chas. Mason	Col. Tyrrell's	Geo. Turner, Surgeon	[25 ,, ,,
Lieut. Browne, resigned	1st Regt. of Guards	Jno. Nicholls, Lieut.	
Capt. Judd, resigned	Ditto	Harry Cornish, Lieut.	[26 ,, ,,
Lieut. Fury, resigned	Whetham's Foot	Richard Shelton, Lieut.	,, ,,
Lieut. Smelt	Carpenter's Dragoons	[John] Hawksworth, Lieut.	,, ,,
Cornet Hawksworth, preferred	Ditto	Geo. Cheap, Cornet	,, ,,
Cornet Shore, resigned	Ditto	Hen. Whitley, Cornet	,, ,,
Sub-Brigdr. Krant, preferred	3rd Troop of Guards	Wm. Krant, Brigdr.	[29 ,, ,,
Lieut. Marty	Ditto	Geo. Fowkes, Sub-Brigdr.	
Capt. Speed, resigned	Evans' Dragoons	[John] Cavendish, Lieut.	[26 ,, ,,
	Col. Newton's	Robt. Maxwell, Capt.	[27 ,, ,,

A List of Officers Displaced, &c.—cont.

Names and Qualities of such Officers as have been Displaced either with Leave to Sell or otherwise.	In what Regiment.	Names and Qualities of such Officers as have Succeeded those who were Displaced, &c.	Dates of Commissions.
Robert Maxwell, preferred	Col. Newton's	Thos. Carfrae, Capt.-Lieut.	[27 June 1716]
Capt. Laborde, resigned	Sir Chas. Hotham's	Peter Carew, Capt.	[19 ,, ,,
Toby Purcell, resigned	Sir Robt. Rich's	Jno. Gibson, Cornet	[13 July ,,
Capt. Ladaveze, resigned	Col. Pocock's	Peter Sadler, Capt.	[12 ,, ,,
Ens. Blair	Sir Chas. Hotham's	Arundel Strangeways [Ens.]	[,, ,,
Ens. Stone, resigned	Wills' Foot	Jno. Wilson, Ensign	[5 ,, ,,
Earl of Orrery	Regt. of Foot	Geo. Macartney, Col.	[12 ,, ,,
Paul Batchelor, exchanged	Montagu's Foot	[John] Windle, Chaplain	[,, ,,
Lieut. Plowman	Indep. Company at Jamaica	Pearce Rookwood, Lieut.	[,, ,,
[James Dumas, deceased]	Stair's Dragoons	Earl of Stairs, Capt.	[,, ,,
Major Duncombe, preferred	Col. Handasyde's	Wm. Pinfold, Major	[,, ,,
Lt.-Col. Pierson, deceased	Major-Gen. Winn's	Wm. Duncombe, Lt.-Col.	[,, ,,
Capt. Ric. Tracy	Montagu's Foot	Ric. Onslow,[44] Capt.	[14 ,, ,,
Capt. Laforey	Ditto	Wm. Brockman, Capt.	[7 ,, ,,
Lieut. Stephenson, deceased	Windsor's Horse	Wm. Synge, Lieut.	[17 ,, ,,
Capt. Lombard, deceased	Sankey's Foot	Walt. Breames, Capt.	[20 ,, ,,
[Lord Forrester]	Preston's Foot	Jno. Hope, Lt.-Col.	[19 ,, ,,
Capt. Elphinston[48]	Shannon's Foot	Jas. Dickson, Capt.	[28 ,, ,,
Lieut. Dickson, preferred	Ditto	Harry Holmes, Lieut.	[,, ,,
Ens. Vannamen, resigned	Seymour's Foot	[Edward] Williamson, Ensign	[,, ,,
Ens. Brandon, preferred	Kirk's Foot	Roger Davis, Ensign	[,, ,,
Adjt. Ross, deceased	Ditto	Jno. Williams, Adjt.	[,, ,,
Adjt. Loyd, resigned	Egerton's Foot	Mich. Wolfe, Adjt.	[,, ,,
Ens. Stephens	Sankey's Foot	Chas. Breach, Ensign	[,, ,,
Ens. Weldon	Ditto	Robt. Pigot, Ensign	[,, ,,
Ens. Higgins	Ditto	Hen. Keen, Ensign	[,, ,,

GEORGE THE FIRST'S ARMY, 1714-1718 203

A List of Officers Displaced, &c.—cont.

Names and Qualities of such Officers as have been Displaced either with Leave to Sell or otherwise.	In what Regiment.	Names and Qualities of such Officers as have Succeeded those who were Displaced, &c.	Dates of Commissions.
Ens. West -	Sankey's Foot -	Christopher Conron, Ensign -	[28 July 1716]
Lieut. Hayes, preferred -	Col. Handasyde's -	[Edward] Brereton, Lieut. -	,, ,,
Ens. Brereton -	Ditto -	Thos. Taylor, Ensign -	,, ,,
Lieut. Sadler, preferred -	Col. Pocock's -	Wm. Whitmore, Lieut. -	[18 ,, ,,
Wm. Whitmore, preferred -	Ditto -	Geo. Whitmore, Ensign -	,, ,,
Cornet Synge, preferred -	Windsor's Horse -	Wm. Nappier, Cornet -	[1 Aug. ,,
Lieut. Cox, deceased -	2nd Regt. of Guards -	Fras. Wheler, Lieut. -	,, ,,
Ens. Wheler, preferred -	Ditto -	Chas. Leslie, Ensign -	,, ,,
Lieut. Hamilton -	Ditto -	Edw. Braddock, Lieut. -	,, ,,
Sir Wm. Gordon,[45] resigned -	Shannon's Foot -	[Wm.] Spence, Capt. -	,, ,,
Ens. Ric. Walker, exchanged -	Windsor's Horse -	Jno. Haynes, Adjt. -	[8 ,, ,,
Ens. Peter Darcey, exchanged -	Coldstream Guards -	Peter Darcey, Ensign -	[1 ,, ,,
[Col. S. Shute] -	1st Regt. of Guards -	Ric. Walker, Ensign -	,, ,,
Major Eyton -	Windsor's Horse -	[Jarves] Eyton, Lt.-Col. -	[11 ,, ,,
[Sir Jno. Rayney,[46] deceased] -	Ditto -	[Thos.] Hull, Major -	,, ,,
Capt. Fowkes, preferred -	Whetham's Foot -	Wm. Ballendine, Capt. -	,, ,,
Ens. Hay, preferred -	Ditto -	Jno. Hay, Capt. -	,, ,,
Lieut. Phillips, exchanged -	O'Hara's Foot -	Thos. Scroggs, Capt. -	,, ,,
Lieut. Gamboll, exchanged -	Phillips' Foot -	Arth. Gamboll, Lieut. -	,, ,,
Lord Frankland,[47] resigned -	3rd Regt. of Guards -	[Edward] Phillips, Lieut. -	,, ,,
Lieut. Hamilton, resigned -	Harrison's Foot -	Geo. Stewart, Capt. -	,, ,,
Ens. Milner, deceased -	Wihtman's Foot (sic) -	Jno. Howe, Capt. -	,, ,,
Lieut. Gunby, deceased -	O'Hara's Foot -	Jno. Wightman, Ensign -	,, ,,
Capt. Griffith, preferred -	Brigdr. Stanwix's -	Jno. Supple, Lieut. -	,, ,,
Wm. Ballendine, preferred -	Col. Molesworth's -	Fras. Billingsly, Capt. -	,, ,,
		[John] Griffith, Capt. -	,, ,,

204   GEORGE THE FIRST'S ARMY, 1714–1718

A LIST OF OFFICERS DISPLACED, &C.—cont.

Names and Qualities of such Officers as have been Displaced either with Leave to Sell or otherwise.	In what Regiment.	Names and Qualities of such Officers as have Succeeded those who were Displaced, &c.	Dates of Commissions.
Lieut. Hutton, deceased	McCartney's Foot	Jas. Martin, 1st Lieut.	[12 Aug. 1716
Capt. Phillips, deceased	Indep. Company, Placentia	Paul Mascarene,[48] Capt.	[15 ,, ,,
Lord Semple (sic), deceased	Brigdr. Grant's	Lord [Frederick] Howard, Capt.	[29 ,, ,,
Capt. Campbell, preferred	4th Troop of Guards	Isaac Ash, Brigdr.	[15 ,, ,,
Lieut. BrownJohn(sic),deceased	Grove's Foot	Thos. Jeckyll, Lieut.	[24 ,, Sept.
Lieut. Moncall	Cotton's Foot	Jas. Charlton, Lieut.	[,, ,,
Major Hastings, preferred	Ditto	Geo. Walsh, Capt.	[,, ,,
Capt.-Lt. Walsh, preferred	Ditto	David Barry, Capt.-Lieut.	[15 ,, ,,
	McCartney's Foot	Robert Catherwood, 2nd Lieut.	[,, ,,
Lieut. Cornwall	Sabine's Foot	Jno. Braithwayt, 2nd Lieut.	[24 ,, ,,
Lieut. Moore, exchanged	Indep. Company at Jamaica	Mark Delaunay, Lieut.	[,, ,,
Capt.-Lt. Hardiman	Col. Molesworth's	Andrew Doyle, Capt.-Lieut.	[15 ,, ,,
Ens. McKenzie, deceased	Brigdr. Grant's	Hugh Grant, Ensign	[2 Oct. ,,
Lieut. Dickstone (sic),preferred	Shannon's Foot	Fras. Molsey, Lieut.	[,, ,,
Capt. Cockram, preferred	4th Troop of Guards	Geo. Harrison, Sub-Brigdr.	[,, ,,
	Wills' Foot	Jno. Supple, Lieut.	[,, ,,
	Ditto	[James] Barnes, Lieut.	[,, ,,
Capt. Stewart, preferred	3rd Regt. of Guards	Peter Fargeon, Lieut.	[6 ,, ,,
Lieut. Sellocke, deceased	Stearne's Foot	Jno. Keefe, Lieut.	[9 ,, ,,
Capt. Kane, deceased	Grove's Foot	Hen. Cary, Capt.	[11 ,, ,,
Lieut. Vigers, resigned	Pitt's Horse	Phillip Tench, Lieut.	[13 ,, ,,
Chaplain Coucher, deceased	Evans' Dragoons	Jno. Mason, Chaplain	[10 Nov. ,,
Geo. Loyd, deceased	1st Troop of Guards	Ric. Neal, Brigdr.	[17 ,, ,,
Ric. Neal, preferred	Ditto	Wm. Robinson, Sub-Brigdr.	[,, ,,
Lieut. Smith, deceased	1st Regt. of Guards	Geo. Chudleigh, Lieut.	[,, ,,
Geo. Chudleigh, preferred	Ditto	Jno. Bickerstaff, Ensign	[,, ,,

GEORGE THE FIRST'S ARMY, 1714–1718

A LIST OF OFFICERS DISPLACED, &C.—cont.

Names and Qualities of such Officers as have been Displaced either with Leave to Sell or otherwise.	In what Regiment.	Names and Qualities of such Officers as have Succeeded those who were Displaced, &c.	Dates of Commissions.
Col. Eyton, deceased	Windsor's Horse	Jno. Ligonier, Lt.-Col.	[22 Nov. 1716]
Col. Ligonier, preferred	Phillips' Foot	Lord Hinchinbroke, Lt.-Col.	[,, ,, ,,]
Col. Pultney	Coldstream Guards	Jno. Folliot, Capt.	[23 ,, ,,]
Capt. Folliot, preferred	Ditto	Lord Herbert, Capt.-Lieut.	[,, ,, ,,]
Lieut. Barry, preferred	Cotton's Foot	Thos. Lister, Lieut.	[24 ,, ,,]
Lieut. Serjeant, resigned	Coldstream Guards	Jno. Sawbridge, Lieut.	[,, ,, ,,]
Ens. Bruce,[49] old and infirm	Wightman's Foot	Christr. Hopton, Ensign	[30 ,, ,,]
Cornet Rice, deceased	Col. Tyrrell's	Fairfax Wallis, Cornet	[,, ,, ,,]
Lieut. Davenport, preferred	Brigdr. Dormer's	Josiah Patterson, Lieut.	[,, ,, ,,]
Capt. Stone, deceased	Grove's Foot	Thos. Holland, Capt.	[6 Dec. ,,]
Lieut. Supple, provided for	O'Hara's Foot	[Roger] McManus, Lieut.	[22 Nov. ,,]
Ens. Fargeon, preferred	Irwyn's Foot	Geo. Welburne, Ensign	[8 Dec. ,,]
Cornet Cavendish, preferred	Evans' Dragoons	Robt. Joderell, Cornet	[11 ,, ,,]
Dr. Smallwood, deceased	4 Indep. Companies at New York	Thos. Braine,[50] Surgeon	[7 ,, ,,]
Lieut. Churchill, exchanged	1st Regt. of Guards	Robt. Cox, Chaplain	
Ens. Bowdler, exchanged	Harrison's Foot	Simon Loftus, Lieut.	[15 ,, ,,]
Lieut. Doherty	Ditto	Ric. Aplin, Ensign	[,, ,, ,,]
Adjt. Eaglesfield	Meredyth's Foot	Cromwell Ward, Lieut.	[17 ,, ,,]
Cornet Strafford, deceased	Brigdr. Stanwix's	Stanwix Ross, Adjt.	[,, ,, ,,]
Thomas Walton	Col. Stanhope's	Jno. Fras. Duvernet, Cornet	[1 Jan. 1717]
Lieut. Kentish, broke	Col. Chudleigh's	Randall Churchill, Qr.-Mr.	
Cornet Baldwin, preferred	Windsor's Horse	Thos. Baldwin, Lieut.	[8 ,, ,,]
Adjt. Haynes made Qr.-Mr.	Ditto	Wm. FitzThomas, Cornet	[,, ,, ,,]
Lieut. Jeffreys	Ditto	Jno. Seaward, Adjt.	[,, ,, ,,]
	Seymour's Foot	Thos. Moore, Lieut.	[,, ,, ,,]
Ens. Huntingdon, deceased	Phillips' Foot	Danl. Cooke, Ensign	[12 ,, ,,]

A List of Officers Displaced, &c.—cont.

Names and Qualities of such Officers as have been Displaced either with Leave to Sell or otherwise.	In what Regiment.	Names and Qualities of such Officers as have Succeeded those who were Displaced, &c.	Dates of Commissions.
Ens. Graham -	Col. Lucas's	Ric. Lucas, Ensign -	[1 Feb. 1717
Fras. Smith, deceased	Harrison's Foot	Edwd. Richbell, Capt.	[2 ,, ,,
Capt. Melvin, deceased	Orkney's Foot	Jno. McQueen, Capt.	[25 Jan. ,,
Lieut. Lawson, deceased	Sankie's Foot	Phillip Dunbar, Lieut.	[2 Feb. ,,
Lieut. Gore -	Whetham's Foot	Jno. Hoare, Lieut.	[11 ,, ,,
Capt. Elves -	1st Troop of Guards	Jno. Montagu, Exempt	,, ,,
Jno. Montagu, preferred	Ditto	Jonathan Driver, Brigdr.	,, ,,
— Goodere -	Ditto	John Elwes, Sub-Brigdr.	,, ,,
Lieut. Campbell -	Wills' Foot	Wm. Littler,[51] Lieut.	[25 Nov. 1716.
Ens. Littler, preferred	Ditto	Jonathan Moubray, Ensign	,, ,,
Capt. Kennedy, preferred	Brigdr. Grant's	Alex. Corbett, Capt.	[11 Feb. 1717.
Lieut. Corbett, preferred	Ditto	Abr. Mure, Lieut. -	,, ,,
Ens. Mure, preferred	Ditto	— Pollock, Ensign -	,, ,,
Earl of Portmore -	Regt. of Dragoons	Jas. Campbell,[52] Col.	[15 ,, ,,
Ens. Arnold, resigned	Kirk's Foot -	Edm. Wiseman, Ensign	[25 Oct. 1716.
Lieut. Arthur, deceased	Shannon's Foot	Wm. Randall, Capt.-Lieut.	[19 Feb. 1717.
Lieut. Aldey, deceased	Alexander's Foot	Murdoch McKenzie, Lieut.	,, ,,
Ens. Mackenzie, preferred	Ditto	Jas. Gamble, Ensign	,, ,,
Lieut. Holbroke, deceased	Seymour's Foot	Ric. Wennan, Lieut.	—
Capt. Doherty, resigned	Meredyth's Foot	Hen. Clayton, Capt.	[28 ,, ,,
Capt. Sadlier, resigned	Sankie's Foot -	Wm. Hoare, Capt.	[2 Mar. ,,
Ens. Davis, resigned	3rd Regt. of Guards	Wm. Lister, Ensign -	,, ,,
Capt. Alchorne, resigned	1st Regt. of Guards	Chas. Rambouillet, Lieut.	,, ,,
Ens. Browne, resigned	Fane's Foot -	Thos. Povey, Ensign	,, ,,
Major Wyvill, preferred	Cobham's Dragoons	Jno. Thayer, Capt. -	,, ,,
Ens. Wightman, resigned	Wightman's Foot	Math. Bateman, Ensign	,, ,,

GEORGE THE FIRST'S ARMY, 1714-1718

A List of Officers Displaced, &c.—cont.

Names and Qualities of such Officers as have been Displaced either with Leave to Sell or otherwise.	In what Regiment.	Names and Qualities of such Officers as have Succeeded those who were Displaced, &c.	Dates of Commissions.
Capt. Smith, resigned	Wightman's Foot	Edwd. Tyrrell, Capt.	[2 Mar. 1717
Capt. Tyrrell, preferred	Ditto	Jno. Browne, Capt.-Lieut.	,, ,,
Lieut. Browne, preferred	Ditto	[John] Dunmury⁵⁸ (sic), Lieut.	,, ,,
Ens. Dummery (sic), preferred	Ditto	Florand D'Auteville, Ensign	,, ,,
Jno. Spittle, resigned	Col. Pocock's	Wm. Cheselden, Surgeon-	,, ,,
Lieut. Rambouillet, preferred	Col. Dubourgay's	Amls. Guerrin, Lieut.	,, ,,
Duke of Argyle	Royal Horse	Marqs. of Winchester, Col.	[8 ,, ,,
Lieut. Sodon, deceased	Pitt's Horse	Phillip Smith, Lieut.	[9 ,, ,,
Cornet Smith, preferred	Ditto	Ric. Otway, Cornet	,, ,,
Capt. Smith, deceased	Sankie's Foot	Roger Lort, Capt.	,, ,,
Col. Diggs, resigned	3rd Regt. of Guards	Jno. Darby, Capt.	,, ,,
Theod. Smith, resigned	1st Troop of Grendr. Guards	Justinian Logan, Sub-Lieut.	,, ,,
Ens. Povey	Sir Chas. Hotham's	Duncan Bell, Ensign	,, ,,
	Whetham's Foot	Alex. Bruce, Ensign	[11 ,, ,,
Lieut. Mallet, resigned	Grove's Foot	Goodwin Moreton, Lieut.	[9 ,, ,,
Cornet Kennedy, resigned	Stair's Dragoons	Robt. Wigham, Cornet	,, ,,
Capt. Hawkins	Royal Horse	Robt. Carey, Capt.	[14 ,, ,,
Saml. Horsey, preferred	4th Troop of Guards	Jas. Garth, Guidon	,, ,,
Edwd. Boughton, resigned	Ditto	Jno. Seguin, Sub-Brigdr.	,, ,,
Lieut. Maitland, resigned	Shannon's Foot	Jas. Fargason (sic)	[9 ,, ,,
Ens. Ferguson, preferred	Ditto	Chas. Macky, Ensign.	,, ,,
Lieut. Hay, resigned	Macartney's Foot	Jno. Williams, 1st Lieut.	,, ,,
Ens. Honnywood, deceased	Kirk's Foot	Wm. Degg, Ensign	[14 ,, ,,
Chaplain Mathews	Sankie's Foot	Fras. De Trefontaine, Chaplain	,, ,,
Lord Windsor	Regt. of Horse	Geo. Wade, Col.	[19 ,, ,,
Maj.-Gen. Wade, preferred	Regt. of Foot	Hen. Hawley, Col.	,, ,,

A List of Officers Displaced, &c.—cont.

Names and Qualities of such Officers as have been Displaced either with Leave to Sell or otherwise.	In what Regiment.	Names and Qualities of such Officers as have Succeeded those who were Displaced, &c.	Dates of Commissions.
Col. Hawley, preferred	Evans' Dragoons	Thos. Howard,[54] Lt.-Col.	[19 Mar. 1717
Capt.-Lt. Lort, preferred	Sankie's Foot	Wm. Norris, Capt.-Lieut.	[26 ,, ,,
Lieut. Cherrat, preferred	Wills' Foot	Jno. Hayward, Lieut.	[21 ,, ,,
Ens. Hayward, preferred	Ditto	— Williams, Ensign	[,, ,,
Robt. Hope	Ditto	— Crawford, Surgeon	[,, ,,
Adjt. Lawson, deceased	Sankie's Foot	Roger Lort, Adjt.	[4 Apr. ,,
Capt. Talbot, resigned	Harrison's Foot	Roger Comberbach, Capt.	[,, ,,
Ens. Beak, resigned	Pearce's Foot	Jno. Tichburne, Ensign	[16 ,, ,,
Cornet Eyre, resigned	Pitt's Horse	Thos. Dunning, Cornet	[9 Mar. ,,
Lieut. Norris, preferred	Sankie's Foot	Arthur Balfour, Lieut.	[6 Apr. ,,
Cornet ——, deceased	Royal Horse	Fras. Emelie, Cornet	[18 ,, ,,
Capt. Stacey, resigned	4th Troop of Guards	Jno. Faverall, Brigdr.	[20 ,, ,,
Capt. McKenzie, to pay his debts to ye Regt.	Macartney's Foot	Wm. Innis, Capt.	[15 March ,,
Cornet Stewart, resigned	Stair's Dragoons	Wm. Bradshaw, Cornet	[22 Apr. ,,
Lieut. McManus	Brigdr. Stanwix's	Jno. St. Johns, Lieut.	[20 ,, ,,
Capt. Wynn, resigned	Coldstream Guards	Nath. Blackstone, Lieut.	[,, ,,
Ens. Blackstone, resigned	Ditto	Thos. Venner, Ensign	[,, ,,
Ens. Bradock, resigned	Ditto	Thos. Corbett, Ensign	[,, ,,
Ens. Corbett, preferred	Ditto	Jno. Hodges, Ensign	[,, ,,
Ens. Shappard (sic), deceased	Kirk's Foot	Wm. Wightman, Ensign	[24 ,, ,,
Lieut. Aldey, deceased	Alexander's Foot	Robt. Browne, Lieut.	
Lieut. Goodwyn, deceased	Sankie's Foot	Hugh Edgar, Lieut.	[24 ,, ,,
Ens. Hinton, resigned	Kirk's Foot	Jas. Franck, Ensign	[23 ,, ,,
Lieut. Hay, resigned	Macartney's Foot	Wm. Bennet Silvester, 1st Lieut.	[25 ,, ,,
Lieut. Preston, deceased	Wills' Foot	Wm. White, Lieut.	[,, ,,

GEORGE THE FIRST'S ARMY, 1714-1718

A List of Officers Displaced, &c.—cont.

Names and Qualities of such Officers as have been Displaced either with Leave to sell or otherwise.	In what Regiment.	Names and Qualities of such Officers as have Succeeded those who were Displaced, &c.	Dates of Commissions.
Ens. White, preferred	Wills' Foot	Nath. Smith, Ensign	[25 April 1717
Lieut. Hopkey, resigned	Ditto	Chas. Wills, Ensign	,, ,,
Ens. Blagden, preferred	Stearne's Foot	Benedict Blagden, Lieut.	,, ,,
Jno. Ball	Ditto	[Park] Pepper,[55] Ensign	,, ,,
Lieut. Stewart	Col. Pocock's	Thos. Adams, Qr.-Mr.	,, ,,
Cornet Gardner	Brigdr. Honywood's	Wm. Gardner, Lieut.	[26 ,, ,,
Ens. Macqueen, deceased	Ditto	Alexr. Stewart, Cornet	,, ,,
Lieut. Butter, deceased	Invalid Company	[John] Stephens, Ensign	
Ens. Martin, preferred	Brigdr. Stanwix's	—— Martin, Lieut.	
Maj. Sawle, resigned	Ditto	Thos. Nesbit, Ensign	
Ens. Maitland, resigned for want of health	Phillips' Foot	Alexr. Cossby, Major	[10 May ,,
Alexr. Cossby, preferred	Shannon's Foot	Wm. Prothero, Ensign	,, ,,
Ens. Montgomery, resigned	Phillips' Foot	Wm. Moore, Capt.	,, ,,
Lieut. Hubard,[56] resgd. by reason of wounds and infirmitys	3rd Regt. of Guards	Geo. Vier [Weir], Ensign	,, ,,
Lieut. Swanton, deceased	Moryson's Foot	Sam. Parker,[57] Lieut.	[13 ,, ,,
Ens. Close, preferred	Sankie's Foot	[John] Close, Lieut.	,, ,,
Qr.-Mr. Stewart, resigned	Ditto	Wm. Stewart, Ensign	[13 ,, ,,
Ens. Ferguson, resigned	3rd Regt. of Guards	Ric. Maitland, Qr.-Mr.	,, ,,
Capt.-Lieut. Rawleigh, resigned	Preston's Foot	Thos. Lesslie, Ensign	[21 ,, ,,
Capt. Cawlfield, deceased	Grove's Foot	Arthur Taylor, Capt.-Lieut.	[25 ,, ,,
Lieut. Ledgerd, resigned	Cy. at Annapolis	Jno. Doucet,[58] Capt.	[27 ,, ,,
Lieut. Healy, deceased	1st Regt. of Guards	Edwd. Lutterell, Lieut.	,, ,,
Wm. Dawes	Sabine's Foot	Thos. Hodges, 1st Lieut.	,, ,,
	Sir Chas. Hotham's	Thos. Tiboe, Adjt.	,, ,,

A List of Officers Displaced, &c.—cont.

Names and Qualities of such Officers as have been Displaced either with Leave to Sell or otherwise.	In what Regiment.	Names and Qualities of such Officers as have Succeeded those who were Displaced, &c.	Dates of Commissions.
Owen Wynne	Maj.-Gen. Wynn's	Phil. Cox, Adjt.	[27 May 1717]
Lieut. Butler, deceased	Brigdr. Stanwix's	[Wm.] Pudsay, Lieut.	
Ens. Tully, preferred	Ditto	Tulley, Lieut.	
Fras. Jenison	Ditto	Stanwix Ross, Ensign	
Capt. Pelham	Brigdr. Dormer's	Jno. Bridges, Qr.-Mr.	[3 June ,,
——Stepens (*sic*), preferred	Ditto	Jas. Stevens, Capt.	,,
Lieut. Lasalle, preferred	Ditto	Hen. Lasalle, Capt.-Lt.	,,
Cornet Stroud, preferred	Ditto	Edwd. Stroud, Lieut.	,,
Jas. Sauberge	Col. Chudleigh's	[Wm.] Ross, Cornet	,,
Lieut. Walton	Ditto	[Thos.] Walton, Capt.-Lieut.	,,
Wm. Hamilton	Brigdr. Dormer's	Thos. Rice,[59] Lieut.	,,
Chaplain Richardson	Royal Horse	Geo. Thornborough, Adjt.	[6 ,,
Lieut. Mackleod, resigned	3rd Regt. of Guards	Jno. Bailey, Chaplain	[3 ,,
Ens. Clark	Ditto	Wm. Clark, Lieut.	
Mr. Briscoe, resigned	Stair's Dragoons	Robt. Biggar, Ensign	[6 ,,
Col. Cathcart,[81] resigned	Campbell's Dragoons	Wm. Hamilton, Surgeon	[27 May ,,
Sir Robt. Hay, preferred	Ditto	Sir Robt. Hay, Lt.-Col.	,,
Col. Cathcart's Troop	Ditto	Capt. Robinson, Major	,,
Ens. Lutterel, preferred	1st Regt. of Guards	Wm. Eriskine, Capt.	
Major Lawson, resigned	Preston's Foot	Robt. Greenway, Ensign	[12 ,,
Major Lawson's Company	Ditto	Robt. Ferguson,[60] Major	,,
Ens. Greenwood	Fane's Foot	Peter Halket, Capt.	[15 ,,
Lieut. Trotter, resigned for want of health	Ditto	Robt. Wilmot, Ensign	
Ens. Cousins, preferred	Ditto	[John] Cousins, Lieut.	[18 ,,
		Jno. Boudler, Ensign	,,

GEORGE THE FIRST'S ARMY, 1714–1718   211

A List of Officers Displaced, &c.—cont.

Names and Qualities of such Officers as have been Displaced either with Leave to Sell or otherwise.	In what Regiment.	Names and Qualities of such Officers as have Succeeded those who were Displaced, &c.	Dates of Commissions.
Capt. Levisys (sic), resigned	Phillips' Foot	Alexr. Campbell, Capt.	[25 April 1717]
Ens. Campbell, preferred	Ditto	Jno. Pearce, Ensign	,, ,,
Capt. Redish	Irwyn's Foot	Chas. Howard, Capt.	[20 June ,,
Maj. Marchand, deceased	Royal Horse	Geo. Feilding, Capt.	[23 ,, ,,
Lieut. Taylor, deceased	Sankie's Foot	Peter Dumas, Lieut.	[3 July ,,
Ens. Lascells, resigned	Moryson's Foot	Chas. Chambers, Ensign	,, ,,
Adjt. Parry, resigned	Pearce's Foot	Chas Pearce, Adjt.	,, ,,
Lieut. Parry, resigned	Ditto	Thos. White, Lieut.	,, ,,
Ens. Chanterel, resigned	1st Regt. of Guards	Jno. Lee, Ensign	,, ,,
Capt. Gouch, resigned	Irwyn's Foot	Wm. Morden, Capt.	,, ,,
Lieut. Furlong, resigned	Seymour's Foot	Wm. Williams, Lieut.	,, ,,
Ens. Morgan, resigned	Whetham's Foot	Wm. Rutherford, Ensign	,, ,,
	Royal Horse	Jno. Varey,[61] Capt.	
Capt. Campbell, deceased	4th Troop of Guards	[Robert] Read, Exempt	[12 ,, ,,
Lieut. Pyle	Pearce's Foot	Jas. Ormsby, Lieut.	,, ,,
Lord Delorraine	2nd Troop Gren. Guards	Lord Forrester, Col.	[17 ,, ,,
Col. Montgomery	3rd Regt. of Guards	Lord Leslie, Capt.-Lieut.	,, ,,
Lt.-Col. Campbell	Ditto	Lord Fredk. Howard, Capt.	,, ,,
Ens. Jones, Minor	Alexander's Foot	[Wm.] George, Ensign	,, ,,
Lieut. Bateman, resigned	Cotton's Foot	Daniel Nicholas, Lieut.	,, ,,
Ens. Nicholas, preferred	Ditto	Robt. Gregg, Ensign	,, ,,
Col. Churchill	Regt. of Dragoons	Sir Chas. Hotham, Col.	,, ,,
Capt. Mason, resigned	4th Troop of Guards	Chas. Walker, Exempt.	[19 ,, ,,
Ens. ——, deceased	Phillips' Foot	Jno. Horseman, Ensign	[22 ,, ,,
Col. Armstrong,[62] preferred	1st Regt. of Guards	Geo. Sherrard, Lieut.	,, ,,
Ens. Sherrard, preferred	Ditto	Humph. Fish, Ensign	,, ,,

o 2

A LIST OF OFFICERS DISPLACED, &C.—cont.

Names and Qualities of such Officers as have been Displaced either with Leave to Sell or otherwise.	In what Regiment.	Names and Qualities of such Officers as have Succeeded those who were Displaced, &c.	Dates of Commissions.
Lt.-Col. Otway, resigned	Stair's Dragoons	Alexr. Montgomery,[68] Lt.-Col.	[26 July 1717]
Lt.-Col. Montgomery, preferred	1st Regt. of Guards	Jno. Pitt, Lt.-Col.	[?5 ,, ,,
Lieut. Hunt, resigned	Coldstream Guards	Hen. Hildeyard,[64] Lieut.	[19 July ,,
Ens. Howard, preferred	Ditto	[Edward] Rich, Ensign	,, ,,
Maj. Finny, resigned	Fane's Foot	[James] Butler, Major	[27 ,, ,,
Capt. Butler, preferred	Ditto	[John] Pickering, Capt.	,, ,,
Lieut. Modds	Handasyde's	Ric. Ellis, Lieut.	,, ,,
Lieut. Jaspr. Handasyde	Ditto	Thos. Wood, Lieut.	,, ,,
Ens. Wood	Handasyde's	Chas. Parkington, Ensign	,, ,,
Ens. Pickering, preferred	Fane's Foot	Hen. Lee, Lieut.	,, ,,
Ens. Briscoe, resigned	Wightman's Foot	Benj. Clayton, Ensign	1 Aug. ,,
Capt. Read, preferred	1st Regt. of Guards	Geo. Macartney,[65] Lieut.	—
Ens. Keyes, resigned	Whetham's Foot	Thos. Hopley, Ensign	[5 ,, ,,
Qr.-Mr. Williams, who by reason of his age could not do the duty	Royal Horse	Hen. Miget,[66] Qr.-Mr.	,, ,,
Brigdr. Crofts, preferred	Cobham's Dragoons	Humph. Bland, Major	,, ,,
Maj.-Gen. Holmes, resigned	Coldstream Guards	Adolphus Oughton, Lt.-Col.	[12 ,, ,,
Col. Oughton, preferred	Ditto	Jno. Robinson, 1st Major	,, ,,
Col. Robinson, preferred	Ditto	Sir Tristan Dillington, 2nd Major	,, ,,
Lord Herbert, preferred	Ditto	[Henry] Lord Herbert, Capt.	,, ,,
Capt. Hanmer, preferred	Ditto	Wm. Hanmer, Capt.-Lieut.	,, ,,
Lieut. McNeal, preferred	Sabine's Foot	Martin Maden, Lieut.	,, ,,
Lieut. Johnston, preferred	Ditto	Alexr. Johnson 1st Lieut.	,, ,,
		Chas. Eaton, 2nd Lieut.	,, ,,

GEORGE THE FIRST'S ARMY, 1714–1718 213

A List of Officers Displaced, &c.—cont.

Names and Qualities of such Officers as have been Displaced either with Leave to Sell or otherwise.	In what Regiment.	Names and Qualities of such Officers as have Succeeded those who were Displaced, &c	Dates of Commissions.
Lieut. Dupuys, resigned	Carpenter's Dragoons	Hen. Briscoe, Lieut.	[12 Aug. 1717]
Arthur Gamble, resigned	Phillips' Foot	[Edmund] Phillips, Adjt.	[13 ,, ,,]
Ens. Ligonier, resigned	Ditto	Wm. Bath, Ensign	[,, ,, ,,]
Robt. Baillie, resigned	2nd Troop Gren. Guards	Hosea Figuel, Surgeon	[12 ,, ,,]
Lieut. Shelton, deceased	Whetham's Foot	Ruper (sic) Pratt, Lieut.	[,, ,, ,,]
Ens. Pratt, preferred	Ditto	Ric. Brewer, Ensign	[19 ,, ,,]
Col. Phillips	Regt. of Foot	Brigdr. Stanwix, Col.	[25 ,, ,,]
Brigdr. Bisset, preferred	Coldstream Guards	Jno. Huske, Capt.	[17 ,, ,,]
Maj. Bland, preferred	Honywood's	Jno. Suckling, Major	[,, ,, ,,]
Capt. Moryson, resigned	Ditto	Ric. Tracey,[67] Capt.	[,, ,, ,,]
Capt. Farmer,[68] incapable of further service by reason of his wounds received at Dumblain	Coldstream Guards	Sam. Needham, Lieut.	[21 ,, ,,]
Lieut. Phil. Dunbar, exchange	Evans' Dragoons	Pet. Renovard, Lieut.	[17 ,, ,,]
Lieut. Wansbrough, exchange	Sankie's Foot	Brudenel Wansbrough, Lieut	[,, ,, ,,]
Major Loyd, resigned	Irwyn's Foot	Phil. Dunbar, Lieut.	[,, ,, ,,]
	Moryson's Foot	Abr. Devischer, Major without a company	[,, ,, ,,]
[Capt. Lloyd]	Moryson's Foot	Hen. Moryson, Capt.	[21 ,, ,,]
Capt.-Lt. Randall, deceased	Shannon's Foot	Jas. Hamilton, Capt.-Lt.	[27 ,, ,,]
Lieut. Hamilton, preferred	Ditto	Jas. Abercombie (sic) Lieut.	[,, ,, ,,]
Capt. Metcalfe, resigned	3rd Troop of Guards	Jno. Mohun, Exempt	[2 Sept. ,,]
Capt. Jno. Pitt, resigned	Pitt's Horse	Phil. Tench, Capt.	[29 Aug. ,,]
Lieut. Tench, preferred	Ditto	[Robert] Cornwall, Lieut.	[,, ,, ,,]
Capt. Cheslup, resigned	Whetham's Foot	Wm. Upton, Capt.	[,, ,, ,,]

A List of Officers Displaced, &c.—cont.

Names and Qualities of such Officers as have been Displaced either with Leave to Sell or otherwise.	In what Regiment.	Names and Qualities of such Officers as have Succeeded those who were Displaced, &c.	Dates of Commissions.
Wm. Upton, preferred	Whetham's Foot	Jno. Petit,[69] Capt.-Lt.	[29 Aug. 1717
Governour Pitt	Indep. Cy. at Jamaica	Sir Nicholas Laws,[70] Capt.	[25 ,, ,,
Capt. Morrice, resigned	Pearce's Foot	Hen. Owen, Capt.	[26 ,, ,,
Capt.-Lt. Owen, preferred	Ditto	[John] Napper, Capt.-Lt.	[26 ,, ,,
Adjt. Stawell, resigned by reason of sickness	Stearn's Foot	Ric. Hawkins, Adjt.	[5 Sept. ,,
Major Knyvett	Gore's	Thos. Croasdale, Major	[7 ,, ,,
Capt. Kennauvie, resigned	4th Troop of Guards	Nath. Southen, Brigdr	[7 ,, ,,
Lt.-Col. Middleton [72]	Shannon's Foot	[John] Grace,[71] Lt.-Col.	[17 July ,,
Lieut. Napper, preferred	Pearce's Foot	Thos. Montgomery, Lieut.	[26 Aug. ,,
Jno. Ducross, resigned	Evans' Dragoons	David Williamson, Surgeon	[10 Sept. ,,
Ens. Phillips, resigned	Kirk's Foot	Jas. Giles, Ensign	[4 ,, ,,
Ens. Lyons, resigned	Grove's Foot	Leonard Robinson	[8 ,, ,,
Ens. Aiton, resigned	Preston's Foot	Jas. Ereskine, Ensign	
Ens. George, preferred	Alexander's Foot	Wm. Hopkey, Ensign	[9 ,, ,,
Lt. Bayne, resigned	3rd Regt. of Guards	Patrick Edmington, Lieut	
Ens. Edmington, preferred	Ditto	Thos. Dalbyn, Ensign	
Ens. Warlow, resigned	Wills' Foot	Thos. Masters, Ensign	[13 ,, ,,
Ens. Anstruther, deceased	Preston's Foot	Jno. Murray, Ensign	
Col. Alexander	Regt. of Foot	Ric. Lucas, Col.	[23 ,, ,,
Ld. Hinchinbroke, preferred	Stanwix's Foot	Thos. Welde, Lt.-Col.	[26 ,, ,,
Capt. Fox, resigned	Sankie's Foot	Wm. Campbell, Capt.	
Doctor Sharpe [73]	Indep. Cy. at New York	Robt. Jenny, Chaplain	[1 Oct. ,,
Doctor Andrew, resigned	1st Troop of Guards	n o. Paris, Chaplain	
Major Grace, preferred	Shannon's Foot	Robt. Walkinshaw, Major	[9 ,, ,,
Robt. Walkinshaw, preferred	Ditto	Jas. Hamilton, Capt.	

GEORGE THE FIRST'S ARMY, 1714–1718   215

A List of Officers Displaced, &c.—cont.

Names and Qualities of such Officers as have been Displaced either with Leave to Sell or otherwise.	In what Regiment.	Names and Qualities of such Officers as have Succeeded those who were Displaced, &c.	Dates of Commissions.
Capt. Hamilton, preferred	Shannon's Foot	Robt. Dowglass, Capt.-Lt.	[9 Oct. 1717]
Lieut. Hamilton, preferred	Ditto	Chas. Maitland, Lieut	,, ,,
Ensign Maitland, preferred	Ditto	Jas. Hamilton, Ensign	,, ,,
Adjt. Gregson	Stanhope's	Mathew Swinny, Adjt.	,, ,,
Capt. Griffith Jones, exchange	Sabine's Foot	Edw. Pole, Capt.	[12 ,, ,,
Ens. Gore, broke	1st Regt. of Guards	Ld. Harry Beauclerk,[74] Ensign	,, ,,
Cornet ——, deceased	Evans' Dragoons	Ld. Chas. Fitzroy,[75] Cornet	[18 ,, ,,
Lieut. Mawle, preferred	Honywood's	Wm. Robt. Adair,[76] Lieut.	,, ,,
Cornet Adair, preferred	Ditto	Sam. Hinton, Cornet	,, ,,
Lieut. Strawbridge, resigned	Molesworth's	Thos. Vernon, Lieut.	[23 ,, ,,
Cornet Vernon, preferred	Ditto	Steph. Cotton, Cornet	,, ,,
Capt. Armstrong, resigned	Wade's Horse	[James] Carpenter, Capt.	,, ,,
Lt.-Col. Howard, preferred	Evans' Dragoons	[Charles] La Noe,[77] Lt.-Col.	,, ,,
Major La Noe, preferred	Ditto	Jno. Folliot, Major	,, ,,
Cornet Symonds, resigned	Ditto	[John] Lewis, Cornet	[24 ,, ,,
Capt. Shorter, resigned	Cobham's Dragoons	James Maule, Capt.	[18 ,, ,,
Lieut. Keefe, resigned	Stearn's Foot	Fras Tuckey, Lieut.	[23 ,, ,,
Ens. Tuckey, preferred	Ditto	Roger Cary, Ensign	,, ,,
Lieut. Seaton, resigned	3rd Regt. of Guards	Geo. Ogilvie, Lieut.	,, ,,
Ens. Ogilvie, preferred	Ditto	Sam. Lovet, Ensign.	,, ,,
Lieut. Vivion (sic), deceased	Stanwix's Foot	[John] Gardiner, Lieut.	[19 ,, ,,
Ens. Gardiner, preferred	Ditto	Hen. Soule, Ensign	,, ,,
Ens. Bateman, resigned	Wightman's Foot	Chas. Ellis, Ensign	[26 ,, ,,
Capt. Bonnin, resigned	Grove's Foot	Robt. Pujolas, Capt.	[31 ,, ,,
——, deceased	Handasyde's	[Thos.] King, Lieut.	
Capt.-Lt. Carpenter, preferred	Carpenter's Dragoons	Wm. Ogle, Capt.-Lt.	[6 Nov.

216   GEORGE THE FIRST'S ARMY, 1714–1718

A LIST OF OFFICERS DISPLACED, &C.—cont.

Names and Qualities of such Officers as have been Displaced either with Leave to Sell or otherwise.	In what Regiment.	Names and Qualities of such Officers as have Succeeded those who were Displaced, &c.	Dates of Commissions.
Lieut. Ogle, preferred	Carpenter's Dragoons	Wm. Karr, Lieut.	[6 Nov. 1717]
Cornet Karr, preferred	Ditto	Jno. Gwyn, Cornet	[13 ,, ,,
Ens. Hopley	Whetham's Foot	Ric. Kellet, Ensign	[6 ,, ,,
Lieut. Pujolas, preferred	Grove's Foot	[James] Hide Hatch, Lieut.	[18 ,, ,,
Lieut. Fitz Patrick, deceased	O'Hara's Foot	Ric. Burchett, Lieut.	[6 ,, ,,
Brigdr. Stewart	3rd Regt. of Guards	Lord Wm. Hay, Lt.-Col.	
Lord Wm. Hay, preferred	Ditto	James Scott, 1st Major	
Col. Scott, preferred	Ditto	Robt. Murray, 2nd Major	
[John Stewart]	Ditto	Adam Williamson,[78] Capt.	[18 ,, ,,
Chaplain Stoughton, deceased	Bowles's	Benj. Woodroffe, Chaplain	
Chas. Legg, preferred	Grove's Foot	Jeffrey Prendergast, Capt.	[25 ,, ,,
Lord Leslie, preferred	3rd Regt of Guards	Chas. Legg, Capt.-Lieut.	
Col. Hay, deceased	Ditto	Lord Leslie, Capt.	[30 ,, ,,
Capt. Leathes	Stearn's Foot	Jeremiah Mussendon, Capt.	
Lieut. Mussenden, preferred	Ditto	Jas. Adair, Lieut.	
Chas. Crossby, resigned by reason of indisposition	Independent Company at Jamaica	Robert Irwin, Surgeon	[4 Dec. ,,
Ambrose Dickens, resigned	Coldstream Guards	Jno. Harris, Junr. Surgeon	[13 ,, ,,
Lieut. Walker	Tyrrell's	Daniel Tomkins, Lieut.	
Cornet Tomkins, preferred	Ditto	Jenkin Leyson, Cornet	
Col. Fane	Regt. of Foot	Lord Hinchinbroke. Col.	[11 ,, ,,
Lord Lumley	1st Troop Gren. Guards	Jno. Fane,[79] Col.	
Gen. Lumley	Regt. of Horse	Lord Irwyn, Col.	[13 ,, ,,
Lt.-Col. Cholmley, preferred	Cholmley's Foot	Wm. Robinson, [Lt.]-Col.	
Ens. Gronous	1st Regt. of Guards	Wm. Burton, Ensign	[26 ,, ,,
Lieut. Carmichael, resigned	Sankie's Foot	Joseph Macnoe, Lieut.	[2 ,, ,,

A List of Officers Displaced, &c.—cont.

Names and Qualities of such Officers as have been Displaced either with Leave to Sell or otherwise.	In what Regiment.	Names and Qualities of such Officers as have Succeeded those who were Displaced, &c.	Dates of Commissions.
Lt.-Col. Gay - - -	Meredyth's Foot -	Mich. Synge, Lt.-Col. -	[12 Nov. 1717]
Major Synge, preferred -	Ditto -	Jno. Battereau, Major -	,, ,,
	Ditto -	Adam Enos, Capt. -	,, ,,
Lieut. Bellendine - -	Hinchinbroke's Foot	Jno. Pollock, Lieut. -	—
Ens. Gill - - -	1st. Regt. of Guards	Chas. Russell, Ensign -	[17 Dec.
Lt.-Col. Howard - -	Handasyde's -	Wm. Pinfold, Lt.-Col. -	23 ,,
Wm. Pinfold, preferred -	Ditto -	Jasper Tryce, Major -	,, ,,
Sir Talbot Clarke, resigned	Molesworth's -	Jno. Buckmaster, Cornet	25 ,,
Major Guyditt (sic), resigned	Gore's -	Phil. Gery, Capt. -	,, ,,
Col. Nanfan - -	Stanhope's -	Ric. Manning, Lt.-Col. -	[14 Jan. 1718]
Ric. Manning, preferred -	Ditto -	Jas. Gardner,[80] Major -	,, ,,
Capt. Gardner, preferred -	Ditto -	Marcell Laroon, Capt. -	,, ,,
Lieut. Leighton, preferred	Ditto -	Jno. Wooly, Lieut. -	,, ,,
Cornet Wooly, preferred -	Ditto -	Wm. Brathwayt, Cornet -	,, ,,
Major Ridley, preferred -	Molesworth's -	Andrew Doyle, Major -	[15 ,,
Capt. Griffith, resigned -	Ditto -	[Robt.] Thompson, Capt. -	[25 ,,

[1] "Second son of Colin Mackenzie second of Kincraig" (*Military Hist. of Perthshire*, p. 45). Capt. of an Indep. Cy. in the Highlands, 12 April, 1704. Capt. and Lt.-Col. 3rd Foot Guards same year. Bt.-Col. of Foot, 15 Nov. 1711. This officer is said to have served as a Cadet in Dumbarton's Regt. at Sedgemoor (*Military Hist. of Perthshire*, p. 45). He commanded a Highland Cy. in Inverness-shire during the greater part of Queen Anne's reign. D. on Christmas Day, 1723.

[2] John, 3rd Baron. Appointed Capt. and Col. of 1st Troop of Life Guards, 7 July, 1713. Had previously commanded a Regt. of Horse on the Irish Establishment, which corps was disbanded in 1713. Created Earl of Ashburnham, 14 May, 1730. D. 1737.

[3] George Fitzroy, natural son of Charles II, by Barbara Villiers. Created Earl of Northumberland in 1674 and Duke eight years later, was first appointed Col. of the 2nd Life Guards Troop by James II. Removed by Wm. III. in 1689. Col. of the Rl. Horse Guards in 1703. Transferred to the Second Troop of Guards, 4 Jan. 1712. D. a Lt.-Gen. 1716, when his titles expired.

[4] Resigned on account of his brother James, Duke of Ormonde, being impeached for high treason. Chancellor of Oxford University in 1715. D. 1721.

[5] Served at Malplaquet as Capt. in the First Foot Guards. Eldest son of Maj.-Gen. Wm. Selwyn, Gov. of Jamaica. Appointed Col. of a Regt. of Foot, *vice* Delaune, in 1709. Sold said Regt. 26 Feb. 1711, and bought the Colonelcy of the 3rd Buffs from the Duke of Argyll for £7,000. Greatly distinguished himself at the siege of Douay, where he was severely wounded. Sold the Colonelcy of the Buffs to the Earl of Forfar in April, 1713, for £6,000, but retained his Cy. in said Regt. till March 1715, as named on p. 186. He was father of the famous wit, George Augustus Selwyn.

[6] Brig.-Gen. Richard Waring was appointed Col. of the 7th Regt. of Horse, 15 Feb. 1715. See Irish Establishment.

[7] See special memoir, pp. 87–90.

[8] Third son of Robert Echlyn, of Ardquin, Co. Down. Succeeded to the command of the Inniskilling Dragoons, 30 Dec. 1691. Was obliged to sell the Colonelcy on account of his Jacobite proclivities. Subsequently joined the Earl of Mar's standard. Was sent to help Huntly and Seaforth to reduce Inverness (*Stuart Papers*). Gen. Echlyn's brother, Henry, was created a baronet of Ireland in 1721.

[9] Appointed Cornet and Maj. 28 Jan. 1706. Probably son of Sir Conyers Darcy, Master of the Horse to George I.

[10] George *Skene* was appointed Cornet in the Rl. Scots Dragoons, 28 Feb. 1694. Lt. 4 May, 1702. Served at Blenheim. Capt. 16 Jan. 1707. Fought at Ramillies and Malplaquet. Bt.-Major before 1715. Acted as Agent for the Earl of Stair in London for some years. See letter from Maj. Skene to Lord Stair, dated "London, 18 April, 1718," in Graham's *Annals of the Viscount and 1st and 2nd Earls of Stair*, Vol. II. Appx. p. 381.

[11] Charles Mordaunt, 3rd Earl of Peterborough and 1st Earl of Monmouth, was appointed Ambassador to the Italian States in the summer of 1715.

[12] Thomas Wentworth, Earl of Strafford, a distinguished soldier and diplomatist, was grand-nephew of the famous Earl of Strafford. He was included in the impeachment by Parliament of Lords Oxford and Bolingbroke. D. 1739.

[13] Wm. North, 6th Baron North and 2nd Lord Grey. Appointed Capt. and Lt.-Col. in the 1st Foot Guards, 14 Feb. 1702. Col. of the Regt. subsequently known as the 10th Foot, 15 Jan. 1703. Commanded said Corps at Blenheim and had his right hand shot off. Brig.-Gen. 1 June, 1706. Maj.-Gen. 1 Jan. 1709. Lt.-Gen. 1 Jan. 1710. Gov. of Portsmouth 5 Sept. 1712. D. s.p. in 1734.

[14] Col. *Samuel* Vetch, Gov. of Placentia. The Indep. Cy. was in Newfoundland and not in Jamaica, as stated in the text. See biog. notice of this officer in *English Army Lists and Commission Registers*, 1661–1714, Vol. VI. p. 192, note 20.

[15] Hans Hamilton joined the Army as Ens. in Col. A. Douglas's Regt. of Foot, 15 Oct. 1688. Capt.-Lieut. 31 Dec. 1688. Capt. 21 Feb. 1689. Lt.-Col. 1 Feb. 1697. Bt.-Col. before Aug. 1704, when he commanded Lord Derby's Regt. (16th Foot) at Schellenberg, where he was wounded. Col. of the Regt. aftds. known as the 34th Foot, 1 Feb. 1706. Served as 2nd Maj.-Gen. in Spain under Lord Peterborough. Transferred to the Colonelcy of his old corps (16th Foot), 23 June, 1713. Sold his Comn. on date named in text. D. in 1721.

[16] James, 4th Earl. Purchased the Colonelcy of 13th Foot, 15 March, 1702. As a Maj.-Gen. distinguished himself at the battle of the Caya, in Portugal, and was taken prisoner. Lt.-Gen. 1710. D. 15 Jan. 1747, at Castle Lyons, where is a splendid monument to his memory.

[17] Robert Stewart, second son of Alex. 5th Lord *Blantyre*. Succeeded his brother as 7th Baron, 23 June, 1713. On 14 May, 1713, Robert Stewart was appointed Fort.-Maj. of Fort St. Philip in Minorca, where his corps was then serving. D. 17 Nov. 1743, and was succeeded by his son Walter.

[18] Appointed Ens. in the Coldstream Guards, 19 Aug. 1707. Of Inglistoun, N.B. Lt. and Capt. 11 July 1712. First Adjt. from 16 Nov. 1713 to 29 July, 1715, when he retired. Granted a pension of £100 per ann. by George I.

[19] Third son of Dr. Wm. Talbot, successively Bishop of Oxford, Salisbury, and Durham. Born 1699. Capt. in Col. Wm. Egerton's Regt. (20th Foot), 12 May, 1726. Exchanged as Capt. to Col. Fras. Columbine's Regt. (10th Foot), 25 Dec. 1728. Lt.-Col. of Gen. Dalzell's Regt. in the West Indies (38th Foot), 5 Feb. 1747. While serving with his Regt. at Antigua Col. S. Talbot md. his third wife Charlotte, dau. of Thomas Freeman, of Antigua, by whom he had a dau. " Indiana," who md. in 1774 Lewis Garland, Esq. of Michaelstown, Essex (see Burke's *Landed Gentry*). Col. S. Talbot was appointed Col. of the 74th Foot, 25 April, 1758, and transferred to Colonelcy of the 43rd Foot, 24 March, 1761. Removed to the 38th Foot, 12 April, 1662. D. a Maj.-Gen. in Nov. 1766. In the old Army Lists he is wrongly styled the "Hon. Sherington Talbot."

[20] William, 5th Lord *Cranstoun*. Had been appointed Capt. and Lt.-Col., 4 May 1709. Md. Lady Jane Kerr, 2nd dau. of 2nd Marquis of Lothian. D. in 1727.

[21] Had been appointed Capt. and Lt.-Col. by George I. in Jan. 1715.

[22] Son of Sir Charles Heron, Bt. of Chipchase. Lt. 3 Oct. 1728. Left the Army in 1741. D. in 1749.

[23] Second son of Charles, 3rd Earl of Carlisle. Lt.-Gov. of Carlisle 1725. A.D.C. to the King, 1734. As Maj.-Gen. commanded a Brigade at Dettingen and Fontenoy. Recd. four wounds at latter battle. Commanded the British Infantry at Val and Roucoux. K.B. 1749. Gov. successively of Inverness, Fort George, and Fort Augustus. Col. of 19th Foot, 1738-1748. This Corps having green facings was called "Howard's Greens" to distinguish it from the 3rd Foot, then commanded by Lt.-Gen. Thos. Howard—"Howard's Buffs." The Hon. Charles Howard was M.P. for Carlisle and a Deputy Chamberlain to George II. D. at Bath, 25 Aug. 1765.

[24] Possibly a kinsman of George, Viscount *Hewett*. Not in any subsequent List.

[25] This veteran officer had served many years in the Regt. subsequently known as the 17th Foot, and took part in the siege of Namur and other campaigns. Resided near Carlisle. His grandson, Capt. Charles Morris, joined the 70th Foot in 1779 as Ens. and served with this corps during the American War of Independence. Subsequently served in the 2nd Life Guards. He was a poet of no mean order and a well-known convivial character in his day.

[26] Younger son of Francis Duroure, a refugee French officer in Ireland. Appointed Lieut. in Brigadier Henry Grove's Regt. of Foot, 25 Oct. 1715. Capt. in same corps, 11 Jan. 1722. Maj. of Col. Douglas's newly-raised Regt. of Marines, 8 Dec. 1739. Served with said corps in the Carthagena Expedition. Lt.-Col. of Wentworth's Regt. (24th Foot), 7 April 1741. Col. 38th Foot, 27 Feb. 1751. Transferred to the King's Own, 12 May, 1756. Attained the rank of Lt.-Gen. 6 Dec. 1760. He was Capt. of St. Mawe's Castle, Cornwall. D. at Toulouse 2 Jan. 1765, aged 73. His elder brother, Scipio, Adjt.-Gen. of the British Forces, d. of wounds recd. at Fontenoy. Gen. Alex. Duroure was bd. in Westminster Abbey, where is a monument in the Cloisters to the memory of the aforesaid brother.

[27] Third son of Sir John *Dalzell*, of Glenae, Bt. Had served over 20 years in the Scots Guards and was given a Bt.-Colonelcy, 15 Nov. 1711. His brother, Capt. James Dalzell, and his son John joined the Earl of Mar's standard in 1715, which perhaps accounted for the father leaving the Army. D. in 1743.

[28] Evidently a false entry, as Lord Blantyre's retirement is noted on p. 192. See note 17.

[29] Henry Cookman was appointed Ens. in Col. John Courthope's newly-raised Regt. of Foot, 23 April, 1694. Capt. in Brig. Tiffin's Regt. (27th Inniskillings), 27th April, 1696. Half-pay 1698. Capt. in the Rl. Welsh Fusiliers, 20 Aug. 1701. Wounded at Blenheim, Bt.-Maj. 1 Jan. 1706.

[30] This officer had a chequered career. As an Ens. in Col. Hill's Regt. (11th Foot) he fought at Almanza and was taken prisoner. In 1711 he was in the West Indies, where he acted as an Engineer. Cashiered by Court Martial, 8 Nov. 1712. Pardoned in 1713. Appointed Lieut. of an Indep. Cy. in Jamaica, 7 June 1714. Engineer at Vigo in 1719. Half-pay same year. Capt. of an Invalid Cy. at Hull, 23 June, 1721. Held this post till his death in 1745.

[31] Appears to have been a son, by 2nd marriage, of Sir Chas. Shuckburgh, 2nd Bart. of Shuckburgh, Co. Warwick. Appointed Capt. in the Carabiniers, 14 April, 1718. Maj. 11 July, 1737. Lt.-Col. 12 July, 1743. D. about 1746.

[32] Probably a son of Col. George Whitmore, of same Regt. On 13 May, 1735, Wm. Whitmore was appointed Capt. in the 2nd Queen's Regt. of Foot. Major, 20 April, 1743. Capt. and Lt.-Col. in the 3rd Foot Guards, 1 May, 1745. Col. of the 53rd Regt. at its first raising, 25 Dec. 1755. Major-Gen. 23 Jan. 1758. Lt.-Gen. 15 Dec. 1750. D. in 1771.

[33] Had previously served as Qr.-Mr. to Major Chas. Cathcart's Troop in same Regt. Lieut. 27 Mar. 1721. This officer was present at a *fracas* which took place at the Black Bull Inn, Jedburgh, on 9 Aug. 1726, when Sir Gilbert Eliott of Stobs killed Col. James Stewart of Stewartfield. At the inquiry which took place before the Justices of the Peace, Lieut. Spittle, of the Royal North British Dragoons, was sworn, "and stated that both the parties had been at a Head Court for determining the list of voters for the year. The Lieut. described how Col. Stewart had thrown a glass of wine at Sir Gilbert Eliott, which struck that gentleman in the face, and immediately after Sir Gilbert rose, and the deponent saw him draw his sword and run it into the Colonel's body, while he was sitting in his chair" (*Rulewater and its People*, by George Tancred, late Capt. Scots Greys, p. 26). Lieut. Spittle was serving in 1728, but out of the Army before 1740.

[34] *Granville*. Killed in action at Glenshiel, June, 1719.—Earl Stanhope to Secretary Methuen, from Hanover, 3 July, 1719.

[35] Ensign in Col. Dubourgay's newly-raised Regt. of Foot, 22 July, 1715. Lt. and Capt. 1st Foot Guards, 2 March, 1717. Capt. and Lt.-Col. 1 Sept. 1742. Retired 12 Apr. 1743. D. 1747.

[36] *Beauclerk*. Second son of the 1st Duke of St. Albans and grandfather of the 4th Duke. Appointed Capt. in the 1st Regt. of Horse (K.D.G.), 8 June, 1721. Serving in 1728. D. in 1733. Bd. in Westminster Abbey.

[37] Charles Bennet, 3rd Lord Ossulston, succeeded his father as 2nd Earl of Tankerville in 1722. Left the Army before 1720. He was created a K.T. and d. in 1753.

[38] Second son of Sir John *Elwill*, Bt. by his 2nd mge. Appointed Capt. and Lt.-Col. in 1st Foot Guards, 10 Nov. 1710. Succeeded his bro. Sir John Elwill as 3rd Bt. in Sept. 1727. "Filled for several years the office of Comptroller of Excise" (Burke's *Extinct Baronetage*). Md. Anne, dau. of Wm. Speke of Beauchamp, co. Somerset. D. 2 Nov. 1740, and was succeeded by his son John.

[39] At first sight this officer's surname may be taken for a clerical error; but this is not the case. John Buncombe served for 26 years as Capt. and Lt.-Col. in 1st Foot Guards, and retd. 22 April, 1742. In Millan's *Succession of Colonels*, 1742, Cols. John Duncombe and John Buncombe come next each other in the List.

[40] Appointed Col. of a Regt. of Foot on the Irish Establishment, 11 Dec. 1717. Said corps was disbanded in 1718. Half-pay same year. D. from a fall out hunting, 8 Aug. 1729.

[41] *Fowke*. Son of Capt. Thomas Fowke, of Col. Nich. Lepell's Regt. of Foot, and grandson of John Fowke, of Stepney. Thos. Fowke, Junr. was an Ensign to his father, Capt. Thos. Fowke, in Lepell's Regt. in 1707. On 30 June of said year an exchange took place between father and son—Capt. Fowke being appointed Ensign in his son's place while Ensign Fowke succeeded to his father's Company! The Commission Registers notifying this exchange are given in *English Army Lists and Commission Registers*, 1661-1714, Vol. VI. p. 243, and bear interesting testimony to the method which a father adopted to secure advancement in the Army for his son. Capt. Thos. Fowke, finding himself in failing health, resigned his Company in Lepell's Regt. to his son, Ensign Thos. Fowke, and, *mirabile dictu*, stepped into his son's shoes and did duty as Ensign, while the son succeeded his father in command of the Company! In less than a year ex-Capt. Fowke died. His unselfish foresight had put his son over the heads of many older officers and given him the needed start in life. Capt. Fowke served with his Regt. in Spain during the latter part of the Spanish Succession War, and exchanged to the Inniskilling Regt. of Foot, also in Spain, 26 Dec. 1711. His Comn. in last-named Corps was renewed by George I. in 1715. Appointed Major of the Regt. now known as the Somerset Light Infantry in 1716. Preferred to the Lt.-Colonelcy of the 7th Dragoons, 25 June, 1720. Raised the Regt. afterwards known as the 43rd Light Infantry in Jan. 1741. Transferred to the Colonelcy of the 2nd Queen's Regt. of Foot, 13 Aug. 1741. Brigdr.-Gen. 1 June, 1745. Served as 2nd in command at the battle of Preston Pans. Was a Major-Gen. on the Staff in Flanders in 1748. Appointed Governor of Gibraltar in 1754. For an error of judgment in refusing to send troops from Gibraltar to the relief of Port Mahon when besieged by the French fleet, in 1756, Fowke was recalled, tried by a Court Martial, and cashiered for practically the same offence which lost Admiral Byng his head. The strong feeling in Fowke's favour induced George III. to restore this unfortunate General to his former rank in the Army, and he was appointed Maj.-Gen. in Ireland, 2 Aug. 1761. He d. a Lt.-Gen. at Bath in 1765. The present Sir Frederick Fowke, Bt. of Lowesby, co. Leicester, is the representative of Lt.-Gen. Thos. Fowke.

[42] Served in Queen Anne's reign as Lt.-Col. of Lord Slane's Regt. of Foot in Ireland, which corps was disbanded after the peace of Utrecht. Succeeded his father as 2nd Earl of Kerry in 1741. Retd. from the Coldstream Guards in Jan. 1718. D. in 1747.

[43] The Hon. Arthur Elphinstone. Half bro. to John, 5th Baron Balmerinoch. Appointed Capt. in Maitland's Regt. (25th Foot), 27 March, 1714. Served with his corps at Sheriffmuir. "Hearing the Pretender had landed at Peterhead on 22 Dec. following, he took

leave of the officers of the Regiment, told them he had resigned his commission, and immediately set off for Perth, where he joined the Pretender, who had arrived there" (Higgins's *Records of the King's Own Borderers*, pp. 31–2). Joined the Chevalier in France early in 1716 and paid £500 for a Cy. in the French service (*Stuart Papers*, Vol. III. p. 164). Joined Prince Charles Edward's standard in 1745. Succeeded his half-bro. as 6th Baron Balmerinoch in Jan. 1746. Fought at Culloden and was taken prisoner. Sent to the Tower, tried, and executed, 18 Aug. 1746.

[44] Second son of — Onslow (son of Sir Arthur Onslow, Bt.), Commissioner of Excise. Appointed Capt.-Lieut. and Lt.-Col. 1st Foot Guards, 7 July, 1724. Capt. in do. 9 March, 1727. Col. 39th Foot, 1 Nov. 1731. Transferred to the 8th (King's) Foot, 6 June, 1739. Maj.-Gen. 1 July, 1743. Removed to the 1st Tp. of Horse Grenadier Guards two years later. Lt.-Gen. 6 Aug. 1747. Governor of Plymouth, 1759. D. in 1770. His second son, Richard, was created a Bt. in 1797.

[45] Appointed Capt.-Lieut. of the Earl of Leven's Regt. (25th Foot), 29 Aug. 1689. Capt. of the Grenadier Cy. 26 Feb. 1690 Bt.-Lt.-Col. 1 May, 1705, with precedency from 1 March, 1703. Created a Bt. of Nova Scotia, 29 July, 1706. Younger son of Wm. Gordon of Earlston, co. Kirkcudbright, who fell at the battle of Bothwell Bridge. Appointed Lt.-Govr. of Fort William, 12 Sept. 1711. D.s.p. in Dec. 1718, when the baronetcy passed to his elder bro. Alexander, according to the limitation of the patent.

[46] *Rayney*. Fourth Bt. of Wrotham, Kent. Cornet in the Carabiniers, 24 March, 1708. Capt. in General Wood's Regt. of Horse (3rd D. G.), 23 April, 1709. Fought at Oudenarde and Malplaquet.

[47] Lucius Henry Cary, sixth Visct. Falkland. Appointed Lt.-Col. *en second* of Col. Bowles's Foot in Spain, 5 March, 1708. Capt. and Lt.-Col. 3rd Foot Guards, 22 Aug. 1710. Served as A.D.C. to Gen. James Stanhope during the campaign of 1710 in Spain, and was honourably mentioned in Stanhope's despatch announcing the victory at Almenara. Taken prisoner at Brihuega same year. D. 1730.

[48] See biog. notice in *English Army Lists and Commission Registers*, 1661–1714, Vol. VI. p. 286, note 2.

[49] Served in Brigadier Blood's Regt. (17th Foot) at Almanza and was taken prisoner. Comn. as Ensign renewed by George I. in 1715. Probably accompanied his corps from Ireland to Scotland in the autumn of 1715 and was present at Sheriffmuir.

[50] A contemporary copy of this officer's commission is among the *S.P.D. George I.* at the Public Record Office, and is as follows :—

"GEORGE P.C.R.

"George, Prince of Wales, &c., Guardian of the Kingdom of Great Britain and his Majesty's Lieutenant within the same, to Thomas Braine, surgeon, greeting. We do in his Majesty's name constitute and appoint you to be surgeon to his Majesty's four Independent Companys of Foot in his Majesty's Province of New York in America. You are therefore carefully and diligently to discharge the duty of surgeon by doing and performing all and all manner of things thereunto belonging and you are to observe and follow such orders and directions as you shall receive from Brigadier Robert Hunter, his Majesty's Captain General of the said Province, or any other your superior officer according to the rules and Discipline of Warr. Given at the Court of St. James the seventh day of December 1716 in the third year of his Majesty's reign.

"By his Royal Highness's command.

"P. METHUEN.

"Entd. with the Secy. at Warr. Rd. Arnold."

[51] In 1709, Sergt. Wm. Littler of Col. Godfrey's Regt. (16th Foot) was promoted to an Ensigncy in Prince George of Denmark's Regt. (3rd Foot) for the following signal act of bravery. "When the besieging Army appeared before Lille, in 1708, the French outguards retired, and Sergt. Littler of the 16th Foot swam across the river with a hatchet, and cut the fastening which held up a drawbridge to enable a party to pass the stream, for which act of gallantry he was rewarded with a commission as ensign in Prince George of Denmark's Regt." (Millner's *Journal of Marches, Battles, and Sieges*). Lieut. and Capt. in the 1st Foot Guards, 26 Dec. 1726. Capt.-Lieut. and Lt.-Col. 27 Dec. 1738. Capt. and Lt.-Col. 26 April, 1740. D. 26 March, 1742. See article on "Commissions from the British Ranks," by Charles Dalton, in the *Rl.U.S. Institution Journal*, Feb. 1900.

[52] Of Lawers. Youngest son of James, 2nd Earl of Loudoun. Appointed Capt. in the Rl. Scots Fusiliers, 25 Feb. 1702. Fought at Blenheim. Lt.-Col. of the Rl. Scots Dragoons, 24 Aug. 1706. Commanded said corps at Oudenarde and Malplaquet. Bt.-Col. 1 Nov. 1711. Transferred from the Colonelcy of the 9th Foot to the Scots Greys, 15 Feb. 1717. Brigdr.-Gen. 15 Nov. 1735. Maj.-Gen. 2 July 1739. Lt.-Gen. 18 Feb. 1742. Created K.B. directly after Dettingen for his conspicuous gallantry in that

battle. Commanded the British Horse at Fontenoy, where he lost a leg and d. shortly afterwards.

⁵³ *Dumaresq.* Served in same corps at Almanza and was taken prisoner. Present at Sheriffmuir. Capt. 5 July, 1735. Serving in Minorca, 1740.

⁵⁴ Nephew to Francis, 5th Lord Howard of Effingham. He was of Great Bookham, Surrey. Bapt. there in 1684. Believed to be identical with the —— Howard who was appointed Ens. in Col. Wm. Evans's newly-raised Regt. of Foot, 10 Apr. 1703. According to the *Records of the 3rd Foot* (Cannon's), Thos. Howard saw service under Marlborough. Taken prisoner at Brihuega in 1710. Bt.-Col. 15 Nov. 1711. From the Lt.-Colonelcy of Gen. Evans's Dragoons, Howard was appointed Col. of the 24th Foot, 10 Sept. 1717. Transferred to the 3rd Foot in 1737. Commanded a Brigade in Germany in 1743. Resigned the Colonelcy to his son George (aftds. F. M. Sir George Howard, K.B.) in 1749. D. a Lt.-Gen. 31 March, 1753. Bd. at Great Bookham.

⁵⁵ Eldest son of Gilbert Pepper of Dublin by his 2nd wife, who was dau. of Col. Daniel Parke, Gov. and C.-in-C. of the Leeward and Caribbee Islands, assassinated in 1710. Parke Pepper was appointed Maj. of the 49th Foot, 29 May, 1753. Lt.-Col. of said corps a few years later. D. in 1777. Will proved at Dublin.

⁵⁶ Edward *Hobart*, appointed 1st Lieut. of Grenadiers in the King's (8th) Regt. of Foot, 24 Mar. 1705. Served as Ens. in same corps at Blenheim. Fought at Malplaquet and Sheriffmuir.

⁵⁷ Called "Palmer" in the Comn. Entry Book, 1717–18, at the Public Record Office.

⁵⁸ Appointed 2nd Lieut. in Col. Edward Fox's Regt. of Marines, 10 Mar. 1702. 1st Lieut. 23 Dec. same year. Capt. in Col. Godfrey's Regt. (16th Foot), 1 May, 1709. Served at Malplaquet. Lt.-Govr. of Annapolis, 25 May, 1717. There are several letters from this officer in Vol. II. of the *Nova Scotia Archives*, edited by A. M. Macmechan, 1908.

⁵⁹ Called "Price" in the Comn. Entry Book for 1717–18 at the Public Record Office.

⁶⁰ Nephew to Brig. James Ferguson, Col. of the Cameronians. Among the undated S.P. temp. George I. at the Public Record Office is the following petition, which is so badly spelt in the original that it is thought advisable to give it in correct orthography:—

"Memorial of Lt.-Col. Robert Ferguson, of Col. Anstruther's Regt. [the Cameronians] to the Hon Charles Delafay one of his Majesty's Principal Secretaries of State.

"Sheweth that I have served nigh thirty-seven years in the Army in all stations faithfully, in Flanders both King William's wars and Queen Anne's, was in all the battles, and most of the sieges and received several wounds, particularly at Blenheim, when there was no life expected for me, which with the many severe fatigues in my long service and age have brought me to that pass that I find myself incapable of undergoing and enduring these fatigues any more, nor to serve his Sacred Majesty with the wonted vigour as usual. . . . After the affair at Preston, where I was much exposed, I was obliged to purchase the majority or dispose ; and the year following for the same reason to purchase the Lt.-Colonelcy of Col. Hope at a very high price, and brought thereby a heavy load of debt upon me, that I have not been able to clear myself hitherto having a young small family and my wife in a very sickly deplorable condition at the present.

" For the above reasons I earnestly beseech you for God's sake to use your utmost endeavours that I may have leave to dispose [of my commission] that may pay my just debts and retire and serve my God in my old age, and endeavour to cherish my poor distressed family the best way I can, which will much contribute to ease my present troubles ; and if that cannot be granted that his Majesty would be graciously pleased to confer some small Government upon me either in Britain, or Ireland, which with my Lt.-Colonel's pay would in a short time, if God please to spare me, clear me of my debts, but alas ! it is grievous to me when I think that my poor family must be left beggars, and if possible would rather incline to have leave to dispose, and I am conscious that my family and self shall never forget the obligations but always earnestly pray for your welfare."

Col. R. Ferguson appears as Lt.-Col. of Anstruther's Regt. in 1730 List. Dead in Dec. 1738.

⁶¹ Not in any subsequent List. James Varey was a Capt. of some years' standing in same corps.

⁶² This is a manifest error. There was no "Colonel" Armstrong in the 1st Foot Guards at the date in question.

⁶³ Had served previously in the 1st Foot Guards, having exchanged from 3rd Foot Guards in 1711. Comn. as Lt.-Col. of the Inniskilling Dragoons renewed by George II. Out of the Regt. 1730.

⁶⁴ Possibly 4th son of Sir Christopher Hildyard, Bt. who d. in 1723.

⁶⁵ Believed to have been son of Lt.-Gen. George Maccartney. Appointed Capt. in Gen. Wm. Evans's Dragoons, 10 Feb. 1722. Serving in said corps in 1740.

⁶⁶ Promoted Cornet 12 May, 1726. Lieut. 18 July, 1707. Served at Fontenoy as Capt.-Lt. of the Royal Horse Guards, and was wounded.

⁶⁷ Served previously as Capt. in Visct. Mountjoy's Regt. of Dragoons on the Irish Establishment. Capt. in the 3rd Regt. of Horse (2nd D. G.), 25 July, 1722. Comn. renewed by George II. Out before 1740.

⁶⁸ *Fermor.* See p. 122, note 2.

⁶⁹ John Peter Petit was eldest son of Brigadier Isaac Petit, Chief Engineer in Minorca. Appointed Capt. in the Royal Irish Regt. of Foot, 8 June, 1720. Served on board the Fleet in 1718-19. Got permission from the King to return to Minorca in Sept. 1719, to be instructed as an Engineer by his father (Stanhope to Secretary-at-War, from Hanover, 5 Sept. 1719). Resigned his post as Sub-Engineer, 13 Mar. 1722. Comn. as Capt. in the 11th Foot renewed by George II. Out of the Army before 1740. D. at Little Aston, Staffordshire, in June, 1737.

⁷⁰ This knight was Governor of Jamaica and d. there in 1731.

⁷¹ Appointed Cornet in Lord Denbigh's Regt. of Dragoons, 16 Feb. 1694. 2nd Lieut. of Grenadiers in Lord Huntingdon's Regt. 10 Mar. 1702. Capt. 4 Feb. 1704. Major of Major-Gen. Maitland's Regt. (25th), 30 Apr. 1711. Bt.-Lt.-Col. 1 Jan. 1712. Served at Sheriffmuir.

⁷² Of Seaton, Co. Aberdeen. Fifth son of George Middleton, D.D., Minister of Glamis, who was nephew to John, Earl of Middleton. Capt. in the Duke of Argyll's Regt. (3rd Foot), 24 May, 1709. Lt.-Col. of Maitland's Regt. 18 Mar. 1711. Bt.-Col. 15 Nov. 1711. Served at Sheriffmuir. Col. of his old Corps (25th), 17 June, 1721. Transferred to the 13th Foot, 29 May, 1732. Brig.-Gen. 13 Nov. 1735. D. 4 May, 1739. Was M.P. for Aberdeen burghs. Gov. of Holy Island, and Dep.-Gov. of Tynemouth Castle.

⁷³ Dr. John Sharp was appointed "Chaplain to the Forts and Forces at New York," 14 Apr. 1712. He was a learned divine, and in 1717 published in London a booklet entitled *The Charter of the Kingdom of Christ Explained,* &c.

⁷⁴ Fourth son of the 1st Duke of St. Albans. Born 1701. Appointed Capt. in the Earl of Londonderry's Regt. (3rd Foot), 14 Oct. 1727. Capt. and Lt.-Col. 1st Foot Guards, 13 May, 1735. Col. 48th Foot, 14 Mar. 1743. Exchanged to 31st Foot, 22 Apr. 1745. Returned 8 May, 1749. D. 1761.

⁷⁵ Second son of Charles, Duke of Cleveland and Southampton, by his 2nd wife. D. at Paris, 10 Aug. 1723, aged 21. Bd. in Westminster Abbey.

⁷⁶ Comn. renewed by George II. Serving as Lieut. in same corps, 1745. Believed to be the Wm. Robert Adair of Ballymena, Co. Antrim, "a Capt. of Horse," who d. 19 Apr. 1762, and was ancestor of Sir Hugh Adair, 3rd Bart. of Flixton Hall, Suffolk. See Major G. T. Williams's *Hist. Records of the XIth Hussars,* Appx. III. p. 319.

⁷⁷ Appointed Major of the Earl of Essex's Regt. of Dragoons (4th Dragoons), 4 May, 1711. Bt.-Lt.-Col. 1 Jan. 1712. Col. of the 36th Foot, 21 Apr. 1721. Transferred to the 8th King's Regt. of Foot, 8 May 1739. D. in Dec. 1738.

⁷⁸ This distinguished officer was probably son of Surgeon Adam Williamson, of Brigadier Meredyth's Regt. (37th Foot), who was at the battle of Blenheim. On 12 May, 1706, Adam Williamson was appointed Lieut. in Meredyth's Regt. and served several campaigns with said corps. Placed on half-pay as Capt. in Brigd. Primrose's Regt. in 1713. Capt. in Brigd. Sutton's Regt. 29 Aug. 1715. A.D.C. to Lt.-Gen. Cadogan in Holland same year. Under date of 14 Nov. 1715, appeared this notice in the *London Gazette:* "Whitehall, Nov. 14. On the 12th inst. in the evening arrived Capt. Williamson Aid de Camp to Lt.-Gen. Cadogan with the Treaty of Barrier, signed at Antwerp on the 5th inst. o. s." Adjt.-Gen. to the Forces with rank of Col. in Feb. 1722. Brigd.-Gen. 2 July, 1739. Maj.-Gen. 14 Aug. 1741. Lt.-Gen. 3 July, 1745. D. in 1748.

⁷⁹ The Hon. John Fane succeeded as 7th Earl of Westmorland in June, 1736. The previous year he had been created Baron Catherlough in the peerage of Ireland. Appointed Capt. in Gen. Cadogan's Regt. of Horse, 24 Mar. 1709. Served at Malplaquet. Commandant at Chester during the '15. Col. of the 37th Foot, 23 Aug. 1715. Transferred to the 1st Tp. of Life Guards, 4 July, 1733. Resigned said post, 1737. Maj.-Gen. 16 Nov. 1735. Lt.-Gen. 2 July, 1739. D. in Aug. 1762.

⁸⁰ Younger son of Lt. Patrick Gardiner of the Earl of Derby's Regt. (16th Foot) by Mary Hodge (or Hodges) dau. of Col. Robert Hodge of aforesaid Regt. killed at Steinkirk. Lt. Patrick Gardiner was of Torwood Head, Linlithgowshire, and fought at Blenheim. James Gardiner, according to the memoir by R. Doddridge, was born in 1689, and joined one of the Scots Regts. in the service of Holland at the age of fourteen. He served at Ramillies (*ibid.*). Gardiner's first Comn. in the British Army, that can be traced, is that of Lt. to an additional troop in the Royal North British Dragoons (Scots Greys), which Comn. bears date 24 Feb. 1708. Fought at Oudenarde and Malplaquet. His name occurs in an original undated MS. list of the "North British Dragoons" for 1712 or 1713

(See *English Army Lists and Comm. Registers*, 1661-1714, Vol. VI. p. 34). This bears out the assertion that Gardiner served some years in the "Greys," which his biographer in the *Dict. of Nat. Biog.* throws doubt upon. On the formation of Col. Wm. Stanhope's Regt. of Dragoons in July, 1715, Gardiner was appointed Capt. in said Corps, and served with it at the taking of Preston. Appointed Master of the Horse, in 1716, to the Earl of Stair, the Ambassador to France. Took part in Lord Stair's splendid entry into Paris in Feb. 1719. Major of Stanhope's Dragoons, 14 Jan. 1718. Half-pay same year, Major of the Earl of Stair's Inniskilling Dragoons, 20 July, 1724. Lt.-Col. 24 Jan. 1730. Col. of the Regt. now known as the 13th Hussars, 18 Apr. 1743. Served in Flanders. Killed at the battle of Preston Pans in 1745. This officer's sudden transition from a dissolute to an extremely religious life when living in Paris, 1719, has been justly utilised by several writers as a moral to adorn a tale. Col. Gardiner was buried in Tranent Church at the north-west corner. By his wife, Lady Frances Erskine, daughter of the 4th Earl of Buchan, he left several children.

[81] Son of Alan, 7th Lord Cathcart, whom he succeeded in 1732. Appointed Capt. in Col. George Maccartney's newly-raised Regt. of Scots Foot, 29 Jan. 1704. Transferred to the Royal Scots Dragoons, 24 Aug. 1706. Served at Ramillies and Oudenarde. Major, 24 Mar. 1709. Lt.-Col. 16 Sept. 1715. Commanded a squadron of the Scots Greys at Sheriffmuir. Cathcart's decisive charge contributed greatly to Argyll's defeat of the left wing of the rebel army. Col. of the 9th Foot, 15 Feb. 1717. Removed to 31st Foot, 13 Aug. 1728. Col. 7th Horse, 7 Aug. 1733. Brig.-Gen. 27 Nov. 1735. Maj.-Gen. 2 July, 1739. C.-in-C. of the British Forces in the West Indies, 1740. D. of dysentery at the Island of St. Christopher, 20 Dec. 1740.

The Right Hon.ble Charles Lord Cathcart.
one of ye Sixteen Peers for Scotland, Major Gen.l of his Maj.tys Forces, Colonel of ye Regiment of Carabineers

NON-REGIMENTAL COMMISSIONS, 1714-1719

BRITISH ESTABLISHMENT

GEORGE R.
1714–15

Mem.—*The names of Officers given below have been mostly annotated in English Army Lists and Commission Registers, 1661–1714.*

John, Duke of Marlborough¹ to be Capt.-Gen. of Our Land Forces	Westminster, 4 Sept. 1714.		*a*
Do. to be Colonel of Our [First] Regt. of Foot Guards	St. James's, 26 ,,	,,	*a*
Thomas Erle, Esq. to be Governor and Captain of Southampton [and Portsmouth] (*Renewed Comn.*)	,, 27 ,,	,,	*a*
Ben Waide to be Surgeon to the town of Kingston-upon-Hull (*Renewed Comn.*)	,, 29 ,,	,,	*a*
John, Duke of Marlborough to be Master-General of the Ordnance	,, 1 Oct.	,,	*g*
General Thos. Erle to be Lieut.-Gen. of do.	,, ,, ,,	,,	*g*
George Wade, Esq. to be Major-Gen. of Our Forces as well Horse as Foot	,, 3 ,,	,,	*a*
Sir Samuel Garth to be Physician-General of Our Land Forces	,, 15 ,,	,,	*a*
John Jones, Esq. to be Lieut.-Governor of Hull and rank as Colonel of Foot	,, 16 ,,	,,	*a*
Frederick Hamilton, Esq. to be Lieut.-Gen. over all Our Forces as well Horse as Foot	,, 2 Nov.	,,	*a*
Joseph Sabine, Esq. to be Major-Gen. of do. (*Renewed Comn.*)	,, 4 ,,	,,	*a*
Richard Fiddis to be Chaplain to Our Town and Garrison of Kingston-upon-Hull (*Renewed Comn.*)	,, 2 Dec.	,,	*a*
Colonel John Armstrong to be Chief Engineer (Warrant signed by the Duke of Marlborough)	,, 9 ,,	,,	*g*
[George Earl of Orkney to be Governor of Virginia	,, 17 ,,	,,	]

NON-REGIMENTAL COMMISSIONS

(*Commissions renewed* 11 *January*, 1715 *a*).

Nicholas Roope to be Captain and Governor of Dartmouth Castle and Blockhouse.
John Joynes to be Surgeon at Tilbury Fort.
John Phillips, clerk, to be Chaplain at Plymouth.
William Hawkins to be do. at the Tower of London.
Richard Trevanion to be Lieut.-Governor of Pendennis Castle.

George Cholmondly to be Captain and Governor of the Fort and Blockhouse of West Tilbury with the entrenchments and fortifications thereof and also of Our Town of Gravesend.

John Johnson, clerk, to be Chaplain at West Tilbury.

Charles Trelawny to be Captain and Governor of Plymouth and Capt.-General of Our Royal Cittadel there and all the fortresses thereof, St. Nicholas Island and of the castles and forts therein.

John Trelawny to be Town [and Fort] Major of Plymouth.

Jacob Prosser, clerk, to be Chaplain at Portsmouth.

Robert Heart (*sic*) to be Surgeon at do.

Colonel Thomas Collier[2] to be Lieut.-Governor of the Island of Jersey and of the forts and garrisons therein.

John Baptist Sorsoleil, clerk, to be Chaplain of do.

Giles Spicer[3] to be Lieut.-Governor of Our Island of Guernsey.

John Bonnamy, clerk, to be Chaplain of the Island of Guernsey. (*Renewed Comn.*).

Robert Dalzell to be Town Major of Portsmouth. (*Renewed Comn.*).

Do. to be Brig.-General].

William Smith, M.D. to be Physician of Our Town and Garrison of Portsmouth. (*Renewed Comn.*)

Thomas King[4] to be Lieut.-Governor of Sheerness. (*Do.*)

George Winsley to be Fort Major of do. (*Renewed Comn.*)

John Wren, clerk, to be Chaplain of do.

Searle Spranger to be Surgeon of do. (*Renewed Comn.*)

Fitzmorris Gifford to be Town Major of Berwick-upon-Tweed. (*Do.*)

Mathew Draper to be Lieut.-Governor of Landguard Fort. (*Do.*)

Francis Hamond to be Governor of above Fort. (*Do.*)

John Armstrong, Esq. to be Quarter-master General of all Our Forces in Our Service and to rank as Colonel of Foot. (*Renewed Comn.*) - - - - - St. James's, 13 Jan. 1715.*a*

Thomas Lascelles, Esq. to be Deputy Quartermaster-General and rank as Lieut.-Col. (*Renewed Comn.*) - - - - - ,, ,, ,, ,, *a*

Metcalf Graham, Esq. to be Adjutant-General and rank as Colonel of Horse. (*Renewed Comn.*) - - - - - - - ,, ,, ,, ,, *a*

David Crawford, Esq. to be Commissary-General of the Musters. (*Renewed Comn.*) ,, ,, ,, ,, *a*

eph Mason,[5] Esq. to be Major of Our Tower of London - - - - ,, 18 ,, ,, *a*

Samuel Vetch, Esq. to be Governor of Nova Scotia and of Our Town and Garrison of Annapolis Royal. (*Renewed Comn.*) - ,, 20 ,, ,, *a*

John Middleton, Esq. to be Lieut.-Governor of Tynemouth Castle - - - - ,, 28 ,, ,, *a*

Thomas Murphy[6] to be Barrack-Master of Our Barracks in the Savoy - - - ,, 1 Feb. ,, *a*

John, Duke of Argyll to be General and Commander-in-Chief of all and singular Our Troops and Forces which we have sent or shall hereafter send from time to time into Spain. (*Renewed Comn.*) - - ,, 21 ,, ,, *a*

Francis (*sic*) Hazelwood⁷ to be Chaplain to
the garrison at Berwick-upon-Tweed - St. James's, 14 Mar. 1715.*a*

(*Commissions Renewed 23 March*, 1715.)

Henry Morryson, Esq. to be Brig.-Gen. of all Our Forces as well Horse as Foot	- St. James's, 23 Mar. 1715.*a*				
Henry Lumley, Esq. to be General of Our Horse	,,	,,	,,	,,	*a*
Thomas Erle, Esq. to be do. of Our Foot	,,	,,	,,	,,	*a*
Robert Sterne, Esq. to be Brig.-Gen. of all Our Forces as well Horse as Foot	,,	,,	,,	,,	*a*
Charles, Earl of Orrery to be Major-Gen. of all Our Forces as well Horse as Foot	,,	,,	,,	,,	*a*
Thomas, Lord Visct. Windsor to be Lieut.-Gen. of do.	,,	,,	,,	,,	*a*
Henry Grove, Esq. to be Brig.-Gen. of do.	,,	,,	,,	,,	*a*
Robert Nappier, Esq. to be do. of do.	,,	,,	,,	,,	*a*
Robert Hunter, Esq. to be do. of do.	,,	,,	,,	,,	*a*
Owen Wynne, Esq. to be Major-Gen. of do.	,,	,,	,,	,,	*a*
William, Lord Visct. Mountjoy to be Lieut.-Gen. of do.	,,	,,	,,	,,	*a*
Thomas Panton, Esq. to be Brig.-Gen. of do.	,,	,,	,,	,,	*a*
Lord John Kerr, to be do. of all Our Forces employed or to be employed in Our Service	,,	,,	,,	,,	*a*
John Hill, Esq. to be Major-Gen. of all Our Forces as well Horse as Foot	,,	,,	,,	,,	*a*
Nicholas Sankie (*sic*), Esq. to be Lieut.-Gen. of do.	,,	,,	,,	,,	*a*
Sir Charles Hotham, Bt. to be Brig.-Gen. of do.	,,	,,	,,	,,	*a*
Heyman Rooke, Esq. to be Major-Gen. of do.	,,	,,	,,	,,	*a*
Thomas Whetham, Esq. to be do. of do.	,,	,,	,,	,,	*a*
Thomas Ferrers, Esq. to be Brig.-Gen. of do.	,,	,,	,,	,,	*a*
David Creighton, Esq. to be do. of do.	,,	,,	,,	,,	*a*
[Phineas] Bowles, Esq. to be do. of do.	,,	,,	,,	,,	*a*
Richard, Lord Cobham to be Lieut.-Gen. of do.	,,	,,	,,	,,	*a*
Richard Waring, Esq. to be Brig.-Gen. of do.	,,	,,	,,	,,	*a*
William Tatton, Esq. to be Major-Gen. of do.	,,	,,	,,	,,	*a*
Patrick Mead, Esq. to be Brig.-Gen. of do.	,,	,,	,,	,,	*a*
Joseph Wightman, Esq. to be Major-Gen. of do.	,,	,,	,,	,,	*a*
Richard Russell, Esq. to be Brig.-Gen. of do.	,,	,,	,,	,,	*a*
Philip Honywood, Esq. to be do. of do.	,,	,,	,,	,,	*a*
Henry, Earl de Lorraine to be do. of do.	,,	,,	,,	,,	*a*
Harry Mordaunt, Esq. to be Lieut.-Gen. of do.	,,	,,	,,	,,	*a*
Charles Wills, Esq. to be Major-Gen. of do.	,,	,,	,,	,,	*a*
Gilbert Primrose, Esq. to be do. of do	,,	,,	,,	,,	*a*
Richard Sutton, Esq. to be Brig.-Gen. of do.	,,	,,	,,	,,	*a*
John Baynes, Esq. to be Major-Gen. of do.	,,	,,	,,	,,	*a*
Robert Maugridge to be Drum-Major-Gen. of Our Forces. (*Renewed Comn*.)	,,	15 June	,,	*a*	

Thomas Sydenham to be Secretary to the General of Our Horse and the General of Our Foot in England - - - -	St. James's,	25 June	1715	a
Thomas Brouncker,[8] Esq. to be Captain of a Company of Foot in the Regt. raised or to be raised in Our Town of Portsmouth for Our Service - - - - -	,,	,, ,,	,,	a
George Watkins, Esq. to be Deputy Governor of Southsea Castle - - - -	,,	29 ,,	,,	a
William Mathew, Esq.[9] to be Lieut.-Govr. of Nevis, in room of Daniel Smith - -	,,	30 ,,	,,	
Robert Wilson, Esq. to be Lieut.-Govr. of Jersey and of the forts and garrisons therein whereof General Henry Lumley is Governor - - - - -	,,	4 July	,,	a
John Garret to be Chaplain to the garrison at Kingston-upon-Hull - - - -	,,	22 ,,	,,	a
Edward Hall, Esq. to be Captain of Tinmouth (sic) in Northumberland in the absence of the Governor and Lieut.-Govr. thereof - - - - - -	,,	27 Sept.	,,	a
William Burroughs,[10] Esq. to be Commissary-Gen. of Stores and Provisions to the Forces belonging to the States General which We have now taken into Our Service - - - - - -	,,	1 Nov.	,,	a
Robert Lowther,[11] Esq. to be Capt.-Gen. of Barbados and the Caribbee Islands, etc.	,,	,, ,,	,,	n
Edward, Lord Hinchinbrook to be Our Aide-de-Camp - - - - - -	,,	25 Dec.	,,	a
Lewis Barton to be Town Adjutant of Portsmouth and Surveyor of the Fortifications of Our said town - - - -	,,	,, ,,	,,	a
[Lord Archibald Hamilton to be Governor of Jamaica. (Renewed Comn.) - -	——		,,]	

APPOINTMENTS NOTIFIED IN THE *LONDON GAZETTE*, 1715.

Brig.-Gen. Thos. Stanwix to be Governor of Chelsea - - - - - -	St. James's,	24 Jan.	1715.	
Colonel Thos. Chudleigh to be Lieut.-Governor of do. - - - - -	,,	,, ,,	,,	
Colonel Samuel Vetch to be Governor of Placentia and of the Town and Garrison of Annapolis - - - - -	,,	28 ,,	,,	
Alex. Inglis, Esq., to be Chirurgeon-General to His Majesty's Forces - - -	,,	,, ,,	,,	

Benjamin Teale, Esq., to be Apothecary-General to His Majesty's Forces	St. James's	28 Jan. 1715.
Earl of Hertford to be Governor of Tynemouth Castle	,,	4 Feb. ,,
Earl of Carlisle to be do. of Carlisle	,,	,, ,, ,,
Brig.-Gen. Thos. Stanwix to be Lieut.-Governor of do.	,,	,, ,, ,,
Major-Gen. Charles Wills to be Governor of Berwick-upon-Tweed	,,	,, ,, ,,
Col. Wm. Dobyns to be Lieut.-Governor of do.	,,	,, ,, ,,
Wm. Thompson, Esq., to be Governor of Scarborough Castle	,,	,, ,, ,,
Brig.-Gen. [Richard] Sutton to be do. of Kingston-upon-Hull	,,	,, ,, ,,
Multon Lambard, Esq., to be Lieut.-Governor of Tilbury Fort and Gravesend	,,	,, ,, ,,
Nicholas Forster to be Town Major of do.	,,	,, ,, ,,
Sir John Gibson, Knt., to be Lieut.-Governor of Portsmouth	,,	,, ,, ,,
Brig.-Gen. Alex. Grant to be Governor of Sheerness	,,	,, ,, ,,
John Redstone, Esq., to be Governor of the Isle of Wight	,,	,, ,, ,,
John Leigh, Esq., to be Governor of Yarmouth Castle in above Island	,,	,, ,, ,,
Ant. Morgan, Esq., to be Governor of Cowes Castle	,,	,, ,, ,,
Henry Hooke, Esq., to be Lieut.-Governor of Plymouth	,,	,, ,, ,,
Sydney Godolphin, Esq., to be Governor of the Scilly Isles	,,	,, ,, ,,
Colonel [Wm.] Newton to be do. of Chester	,,	,, ,, ,,
Robert Doyley,[12] Esq., to be Deputy to the Lieut.-Governor of the Tower	,,	,, ,, ,,
Edward Byam,[13] Esq., to be Lieut.-Governor of Antigua	,,	,, ,, ,,
George Hay, Esq., to be do. of Monserrat (sic)	,,	,, ,, ,,
Wm. Mathew, Esq., to be Lieut.-Governor of St. Christopher	,,	,, ,, ,,
John Webb, Esq., to be Captain and Commander of Upnor Castle	,,	14 Mar. ,,
Thos. Byde, Esq., to be Judge-Advocate-General of His Majesty's Forces	,,	22 April ,,
Major Thos. Talmash to be Lieut.-Governor of Monserrat	,,	20 May ,,
Lord Irwin to be Governor of Kingston-upon-Hull	,,	29 July ,,
Hatton Compton,[14] Esq., to be Lieut.-Governor of the Tower Hamlets	,,	,, ,, ,,
General Wm. Cadogan to be Captain and Governor of the Isle of Wight	,,	31 ,, ,,

The Rt.-Hon. Frederick Hamilton[15] to be Lieut.-Gen. of His Majesty's Forces	St. James's	7 Oct. 1715.
Charles, Earl of Carlisle,[16] to be Constable of the Tower	,,	10 ,, ,,
Charles Wills, Esq., to be Lieut.-Gen. of His Majesty's Forces	,,	18 Nov. ,,

COMPANIES OF INVALIDS.

(Commissions dated at St. James's 11 January, 1715.a)
Mem.—*The officers named below had served in the late reign.*

SHEERNESS.

John Mowatt, Capt.
John Walker, Lieut.
James Mereweather, Ensign.

GREENWICH.

John Bristow, Capt.
Kilby Essington, Lieut.
Jeremiah Mapp, Ensign.

LANDGUARD FORT.

Mat. Draper, Capt.
John Macmahon, Lieut.
Garret Murphy, Ensign.

TILBURY.

George Bruce, Capt.
John Simpson, Lieut.
———, Ensign.

DOVER.

John Carwarden, Capt.
John Satterthwaite, Lieut.
Gideon Litetre (*sic*), Ensign.

CHESTER.

Alex. Churchill, Capt.
Henry Jackson, Lieut.
John Moore, Ensign.

TYNEMOUTH CASTLE.

Richard Betsworth, Capt.
Andrew Hay, Lieut.
———, Ensign.

[John Lewis] De La Béné, Capt.
———, Lieut.
John Stevens, Ensign.

Tilbury Fort.

Henry Gunn, Capt.
——, Lieut.
John Tessur, Ensign.

Hampton Court.

Robert D'Oyley, Capt.
Edward Doughty, Lieut.
John McQuin, Ensign.

Windsor Castle.

Florence Kane, Capt.
Francis Benson, Lieut.
Wm. Alison, Ensign.

TWELVE COMPANIES OF INVALIDS FOR PORTSMOUTH.

Mem.—*Names preceded by a cross denote that the Officers in question received Commissions in the Regiment of Invalids formed in March, 1719.*

†George Wyndram, Lt.-Col., Capt.	2 Aug. 1715.	a
†Hugh Plucknet, Capt.-Lieut.	,, ,,	,, a
Do. Adjutant	,, ,,	,, a
†Wm. Proby, Capt.	,, ,,	,, a
John Sledall, Lieut.	3 Sept. ,,	a
Bryan Carigan, Ensign	,, ,,	,, a
Major George Wandesford, Capt.	2 Aug. ,,	a
†John Ledsom, Lieut.	[,, ,, ,,	]a
George Faunt, Ensign	,, ,,	,, a
Thos. Hyde, Capt.	,, ,,	,, a
Arthur Moseley, Lieut.	,, ,,	,, a
George Cockle, Ensign	,, ,,	,, a
†Gwyn Vaughan, Capt.	,, ,,	,, a
Richard Devenish, Lieut.	,, ,,	,, a
Sydney Wandesford, Ensign	,, ,,	,, a
Richard Evans, Capt.	,, ,,	,, a
Joseph Elliott, Lieut.	,, ,,	,, a
Mathew Magee, Ensign	,, ,,	,, a
George Gibbon, Capt.	,, ,,	,, a
——, Lieut.	,, ,,	,, a
†Alex. Frazer, Ensign	,, ,,	,, a
Major Alex. Hardine, Capt.	,, ,,	,, a
Samuel Sturton, Lieut.	,, ,,	,, a
Robt. Rutherford, Ensign	,, ,,	,, a
Multon Lambert, Capt.	,, ,,	,, a
Israel Frank, Lieut.	,, ,,	,, a
Edmund Cardiff, Ensign	,, ,,	,, a

†Gilbert Symonds, Capt.	2 Aug. 1715	a
Wm. Ross, Lieut.	,, ,, ,,	a
John Percivall, Ensign	,, ,, ,,	a
George Watkins, Capt.	,, ,, ,,	a
Richard Burchett, Lieut.	,, ,, ,,	a
Daniel Gilligan, Ensign	,, ,, ,,	a
Luke Spicer, Capt.	,, ,, ,,	a
Alex. Macdonald, Lieut.	,, ,, ,,	a
†Edward Symms, Ensign	,, ,, ,,	a

SUPPLEMENTARY COMMISSIONS.

†Alex. Littlejohn to be Surgeon to the ten Companies of Invalids at Portsmouth	St. James's, 15 Aug. 1715.	a
†Alex. Frazer to be Lieut. to Captain George Gibbon's Company of Invalids at Portsmouth	,, 15 Sept. ,,	a
Peter Gardner to be Ensign to above Company	,, 16 ,, ,,	a

TWO COMPANIES OF INVALIDS AT PLYMOUTH.

John Crosbie, Capt.	13 Aug. 1715.	a
Wm. McCullock, Lieut.	,, ,, ,,	a
Kenneth Fraser, Ensign	,, ,, ,,	a
Andrew Johnston, Capt.	,, ,, ,,	a
John Hope, Lieut.	,, ,, ,,	a
John Horsman, Ensign	,, ,, ,,	a

COMPANY OF INVALIDS AT FALMOUTH.

James McCormick, Capt.	13 Aug. 1715.	a
Edward Murray, Lieut.	,, ,, ,,	a
John Screwton, Ensign	,, ,, ,,	a

COMPANY OF INVALIDS AT PENDENNIS.

†Richard Jones, Capt.	13 Aug. 1715.	a
James Bix, Lieut.	,, ,, ,,	a
Rice Edwards, Ensign	,, ,, ,,	a

SUPPLEMENTARY COMMISSIONS.

Charles Forman, Esq., to be Agent to four Companies of Invalids	St. James's, 13 Aug. 1715.	a
John Mulcaster, Esq., to be do. [in place of Forman]	,, 5 Nov. ,,	a

ESTABLISHMENT FOR CHELSEA HOSPITAL, 1715.

Brig.-General Thos. Stanwix to be Governor	St. James's,	13 Jan.	1715.	*a*
Richard Betsworth, Esq., to be First Major (*Renewed Comn.*) - - - -	,,	19 April	,,	*a*
Major Florence Kane to be Second Major (*Renewed Comn.*) - - - -	,,	,,	,,	*a*
Robert English, Esq., to be Comptroller (*Renewed Comn.*) - - - -	,,	,,	,,	*a*
Dr. Emanuel Langford to be First Chaplain (*Renewed Comn.*) - - - -	,,	,,	,,	*a*
Alex. Inglis to be Surgeon - - -	,,	,,	,,	*a*
Isaac Garnier to be Apothecary (*Renewed Comn.*) - - - - - -	,,	,,	,,	*a*
Dr. John Smart to be Physician - - -	,,	23	,,	*a*

SCOTS ESTABLISHMENT.

1714.

John, Duke of Argyll to be General of Our Foot in Scotland (*Renewed Comn.*)	St. James's, 25 Sept.	1714.	*a*
John, Earl of Stair to be Lieut.-General of do. in do. - - - - - -	,, 20 Nov.	,,	*a*

1715.

Thos. Whetham, Esq., to be General and Commander-in-chief in Scotland in the absence of John, Duke of Argyll and John, Earl of Stair - - - - - -	,,	13 Jan. 1715.	*a*
Major-General Joseph Wightman to be General and Commander-in-Chief in Scotland in the absence of the Duke of Argyll, the Earl of Stair, and Maj.-Gen. Thos. Whetham - - -	,,	28 ,, ,,	*m*
James, Earl of Hyndford to be Brig.-General of all Our Forces as well Horse as Foot (*Renewed Comn.*) - -	,,	23 Mar. ,,	*a*
Charles Dubourgay, Esq., to be Quartermaster-General in Scotland (*Renewed Comn.*) - - - - - -	,,	20 Aug. ,,	*a*
Robert Monrow [17] (*sic*), Esq., to be Governor of Our Castle and Fort of Inverness and of all the military works and fortifications thereunto belonging - - -	,,	,, ,,	*a*
John, Earl of Sutherland [18] to be Lieut.-General of all Our Forces as well Horse as Foot -	,,	16 Nov. ,,	*a*

SCOTS ESTABLISHMENT.

EDINBURGH CASTLE.

George, Earl of Orkney, Governor and Capt. of a Company	————	1714 a
James Stewart, Esq., Lieut.-Governor	St. James's, 11 Jan.	1715. a
Francis Lindsay, Lieut. of Lord Orkney's Company	,, ,, ,,	,, a
James Smith, Ens. of do.	,, ,, ,,	,, a
Wm. Dunlop, Chaplain to the garrison	,, ,, ,,	,, a
Alex. Kerr do. do. do.	,, 13 Apr.	,, a
Surgeon John Knox, Surgeon to do.	,, 1 June	,, a

STIRLING CASTLE.

Sir James Campbell of Arkindlesse (*sic*), Lieut.-Governor	St. James's, 11 Jan.	1715. a
[Major] Wm. Holburn, Lieut. of a Company	,, ,, ,,	,, a
Charles Craigengelt, Ensign of do.	,, ,, ,,	,, a
Sir James Campbell of Arkindlesse to be Capt. of the Company in garrison at do.	,, 13 Apr.	,, a
Colin Campbell to be Ensign to the above Cy.	,, 16 Aug.	,, a

DUMBARTON CASTLE.

[Wm. Earl of Glencairn, Governor	————	1714]
Do. Capt. of a Company	St. James's, 11 Jan.	1715. a
Wm. Campbell, Lieut. of do.	,, ,, ,,	,, a

FORT WILLIAM.

[Lieut-General James Maitland, Governor]
[Sir Wm. Gordon, Bt., Lieut.-Governor - - St. James's, 12 Sept. 1711]

THREE INDEPENDENT COMPANIES IN THE HIGHLANDS.

Mem.—*The names and dates given between brackets do not appear in the Commission Entry Book, 1714–1716, at the Public Record Office, London; but are to be found in the Lists given in "A Military History of Perthshire," pp. 46, 47.*

[Lt.-Col.] Alex. Campbell [of Fonab], Capt.	21 Jan. 1715. a
Colin Fairfull, 1st Lieut.	,, ,, ,, a
Colin Campbell 2nd Lieut.	,, ,, ,, a

[Lt.-Col. Wm. Grant, Capt. - - - - 21 Jan. 1715.]
[Colin Campbell of Skipnish, 1st Lieut. - - „ „ „]
Archibald Forbes, 2nd Lieut.- - - - 10 Aug. „ *a*

[Lt.-Col. Robert Munro, Capt. - - - 9 „ 1714.]
[John Campbell of Carrick, 1st Lieut. - - „ „ „]
[Alex. Fraser of Culduthel, 2nd Lieut. - - „ „ „]

COMPANY OF GUNNERS OF THE FIELD TRAIN ESTABLISHED AT EDINBURGH CASTLE.[1]

April, 1715. *g*

Capt. John Slezer, Commander, at - - - £100 per annum.
Capt. Theodore Dury, Engineer of North
   Britain, at - - - - - - £127 15*s*. per annum.
David Livingston, Lieut. in above Company at- £91 5*s*. per annum.
Alex. Campbell, Commissary, at - - - do. do.
[Gerald Napier, do. of the horses]
        1 Corporal.
        9 Paid Gunners.
        6 Practitioner do.
        6 Bombardiers.
        1 Petardier (Colt Tichborne).
        2 Miners.

James Campbell, Storekeeper at Edinburgh Castle.
James Robb, do. at do.
James Gibson, Gunsmith at do.
Robert Forrest, Storekeeper at Stirling Castle.
John Doun, Deputy Storekeeper at do.
Donkin Kerr, Storekeeper at do.
Alex. Muir, do. at Fort William.
James Browne, Smith at do.
Walter Galloway, Wheelwright at do.

GIBRALTAR.

1714–1715.

GOVERNOR.

David, Earl of Portmore (*Renewed Comn.*), St. James's, 28 Oct. 1714.*a*

LIEUT.-GOVERNOR.

Col. Ralph Congreve (*Renewed Comn.*), St. James's, 14 Mar. 1715.*a*

---

[1] A full account of the Scots Artillery Company, by Charles Dalton, is printed in the *R. A. Institution Proceedings* for Dec. 1895.

TOWN ADJUTANT.

Hugh Montgomery (*Renewed Comn.*), St. James's, 11 Jan. 1715.

SURGEON.

James Penman, St. James's, 14 Nov. 1715.*a*

COMMISSARY OF STORES AND PROVISIONS.

Thos. Medlycott, St. James's, 19 July 1715.*a*

MINORCA.
1714–1715.

GOVERNOR.

John, Duke of Argyll, to be Governor of Minorca and Port Mahon (*Renewed Comn.*), St. James's, 29 Sept. 1714.*a*

LIEUT.-GOVERNOR.

Col. Richard Kane (*Renewed Comn.*), St. James's, 14 Mar. 1715.*m*

SURGEON AT FORT ST. PHILIP.

Colin Campbell (*Renewed Comn.*), St. James's, 11 Jan. 1715.*a*

SURGEON'S MATE AT FORT ST. PHILIP.

James Scott, St. James's, 4 July 1715.*a*

SURGEON'S MATE AT FORT ST. ANNE.

John Rotrou, St. James's, 4 July 1715.*a*

COMMISSARY-GENERAL OF STORES.

[Giles Earle (*Renewed Comn.*),——1715].

ARTILLERY OFFICERS AT GIBRALTAR.
1715.*g*

CHIEF ENGINEER.
Major John Hanway.

SUB-ENGINEER.
Jonas Moore.

CAPTAIN OF THE GUNNERS AND MATROSSES.
Christopher Briscoe.

HIS LIEUT.
Samuel Little.

STOREKEEPER AND PAYMASTER
Thos. Musgrave, Esq.

BARRACK-MASTER.
James Bargus.

FIREWORKER.
John Forbes.

ARTILLERY OFFICERS AT PORT MAHON.[a]
1715.

CHIEF ENGINEER.
Brigadier-General Peter Durand.

SUB-ENGINEER.
James More.

FIRE-MASTER AND MASTER-GUNNER.
Leonard Jackson.

STOREKEEPER AND PAYMASTER.
John Partridge.

BARRACK-MASTER.
Wm. Lewis.

GARRISON AT ANNAPOLIS ROYAL, NOVA SCOTIA.

Commissions renewed at St. James's, 8 Apr. 1715.a

Mem.—*These four Companies formed the nucleus of Col. Richard Philipps's Regt. of Foot in Aug. 1717.*

COMPANIES.

Christopher Aldridge, Capt.
John Jephson, Lieut.
Thos. Button, Ensign.

Laurence Armstrong, Capt.
James Campbell, Lieut.
John Keating, Ensign.

[a] *Dickson MSS.* printed in *R. A. Proceedings*, Vol. xxviii, p. 439.

Thos. Caulfield, Capt.
Joseph Bennett, Lieut.
James Erskine, Ensign.

John Williams, Capt.
Edward Broadstreet, Lieut.
Thos. [*sic*] Hamilton, Ensign.

GOVERNOR.
Col. Samuel Vetch.

CHAPLAIN.
John Harrison.

FORT MAJOR.
Fras. Spelman.

COMMISSARY OF STORES.
Peter Capon.

SURGEON.
Wm. Skeen.

SUPPLEMENTARY COMMISSION.

Wm. Sherriff to be Commissary of Stores of War, in the room of Peter Capon, St. James's, 16 July, 1715.*a*

ARTILLERY OFFICERS AT ANNAPOLIS ROYAL, 1715. *g*

ENGINEER.
George Vane.

STOREKEEPER AND PAYMASTER.
Humphry Hutchinson.

MASTER-GUNNER.
John Burgess.

INDEPENDENT COMPANIES OF FOOT AT PLACENTIA IN NEWFOUNDLAND.

Mem.—*These four Companies were incorporated in August, 1717, into Col. Richard Philipps's newly-raised Regt. of Foot.*

John Stanhope to be Captain in place of
   [Thos.] Phillips - - - - - St. James's, 15 Mar. 1715 *a*
   Henry Davis, Lieut. -   ,,   8 April ,, *a*
   Timothy Gully, Ensign - - -   ,,   ,,   ,,   *a*
[Robt. Handy to be Capt.-Lieut. of Col. Fras. Nicholson's Company]
   Alex. Douglas, Lieut. -   ,,   ,,   ,,   ,,   *a*
   Angus Nicholson, Ensign - - - ,,   ,,   ,,   ,,   *a*
[Col. Samuel Vetch, Capt.]
   Francis Fox, Lieut. -   ,,   ,,   ,,   ,,   *a*
   Thos. Pickstock, Ensign - - -   ,,   ,,   ,,   ,,   *a*
[Col. John Moody, Captain]
   Robt. Harvey, Lieut. -   ,,   ,,   ,,   ,,   *a*
   Philip Buckhurst, Ensign - - -   ,,   ,,   ,,   ,,   *a*

OFFICERS OF THE PLACENTIA GARRISON.

[Col.] John Moody to be Governor - - St. James's, 3 Feb. 1715 *a*
Jacob Rice to be Chaplain of the said garrison   ,,   8 April ,, *a*
Robert Balendine to be Town Major - -   ,,   ,,   ,,   ,,   *a*
Samuel Moore to be Surgeon - - -   ,,   ,,   ,,   ,,   *a*
Benjamin Whichcott to be Commissary of
   Stores - - - - - - -   ,,   ,,   ,,   ,,   *a*

COL. FRAS. NICHOLSON'S COMPANY AT PLACENTIA.

Alex. Gordon to be Ensign - - - St. James's, 1 Aug. 1715 *a*
Thos. Phillips, to be Captain of a Company
   lately commanded by Col. Sam. Vetch -   ,,   30 June   ,,   *a*

ARTILLERY OFFICERS AT PLACENTIA.

1715.*g*

ENGINEER.

Wm. Horneck.

MASTER-GUNNER AND STOREKEEPER.

John Huxford (*sic*).

INDEPENDENT COMPANIES IN THE PROVINCE OF NEW YORK.

Commissions dated at St. James's, 21 Jan. 1715.a

Robert Hunter, [19] Capt.
Samuel Symms, 1st Lieut.
John Riggs, 2nd Lieut.
Archibald Kennedy, 3rd Lieut.

James Weems, Capt.
John Pinhorne, 1st Lieut.
Henry Holland, 2nd Lieut.
John Scott, 3rd Lieut.

Peter Mathew, Capt.
Thos. Garland, 1st Lieut.
Fletcher Mathew, 2nd Lieut.
Charles Oliver, 3rd Lieut.

Richard Ingoldsby, Capt.
John Collins, 1st Lieut.
Philip Schuyler, 2nd Lieut.
Charles Huddy, 3rd Lieut.

ADJT. TO THE ABOVE FOUR COMPANIES.

Archibald Kennedy, 28 Jan. 1715.a

ADDITIONAL APPOINTMENTS TO THE COMPANIES IN THE PROVINCE OF NEW YORK

Hugh Monro to be Lieut. to Capt. Peter Mathew's Independent Company at Albany. St. James's, 14 June 1715. a
James (sic) Riggs to be Lieut. to Capt. James Weems' Independent Company - ,, 29 ,, ,, a
Alex. Blackhall to be Lieut. to Capt. Ric. Ingoldsby's Company - - - - ,, 14 July ,, a

---

INDEPENDENT COMPANIES IN JAMAICA.
1715.

Joseph Delaunay to be Capt. of that Independent Company whereof [Robert] Rookwood, Esq. was Capt. in Our Island of Jamaica - - - - - - - St. James's, 1 June 1715.a

Lord Archibald Hamilton [20] to be Capt. of that Independent Company in Jamaica whereof you yourself were late Capt. (*Renewed Comn.*) - - - - St. James's 2 Sept. 1715. *a*

[Noel Marchand [21] to be 2nd Lieut. to Capt. Rookwood's Independent Company in Jamaica. (*Renewed Comn.*) - - - 1715.]

INDEPENDENT COMPANY IN BERMUDA.

Benjamin Bennett, Esq.[22] to be Capt. of the Independent Company in Bermuda in place of Henry Pulleyn - - - - St. James's, 12 Mar. 1715. *a*
Robert Bigland, to be Lieut. to above Company ,, 16 July ,, *a*
Walter Mitchell, to be Ensign to do. - - ,, ,, ,, ,, *a*

---

[1] The day on which news of Queen Anne's death reached Hanover, George I., by writ of Privy Seal, appointed Marlborough Capt.-Gen. This date was $\frac{6}{17}$ Aug. 1714. Letters Patent were issued at Westminster on the date given in the text.

[2] Served at Steinkirk as Lt.-Col. of the Prince of Hesse Darmstadt's Regt. (6th Foot), and in 1695 was appointed Lt.-Gov. of Jersey. On 9 Aug. 1717 there appears in *Treasury Accounts*, under the head of "Rewards for Service," this item :—"To Mary Collier widow of Col. Thos. Collier, late Lt.-Gov. of Jersey, being as well to reimburse the charges as to reward the service of her said late husband being ordered, upon His Majesty's Accession to the throne, to get intelligence of the preparations suspected to be then making in France for a descent on this Kingdom, £80."—*Record Office MS.*

[3] Giles Spicer obtained his first Commission in the reign of Charles II., being appointed Ens. in the Duke of York's Maritime Regt. Transferred to an Ensigncy in the 1st Foot Guards, 17 April, 1680. Lieut., 26 Jan. 1685. Capt.-Lieut. to Col. John Berkeley's Regt. of Dragoons, 17 July, 1688. Capt., 31 Dec. 1688. Major, 31 March, 1690. Served in Scotland same year. Lt.-Col. 1 Aug. 1692. Fought at Steinkirk. Resigned his Comn. in the Cavalry 30 May, 1696. Appointed Waggon-Master-General to Marlborough's Army about 1702, and served in that capacity at Blenheim (See Dalton's *Blenheim Roll*, p. 2), and subsequent campaigns. Lt.-Gov. of Guernsey, 10 April, 1711. Among the undated *S.P. George I.*, at the Public Record Office is a petition from Charles Cornelius Donovan, on the Half Pay List, "in behalf of the distressed children of the late Col. Spicer, Lt.-Gov. of Guernsey, who died after 56 years' service, leaving nothing for their subsistence." Petitioner was Col. Spicer's son-in-law.

[4] Appointed Ens. in the Holland Regt. (3rd Foot), 13 Jan. 1678. Capt. in the Earl of Huntingdon's Regt. (13th Foot), 25 Sept. 1688. Capt. and Lt.-Col. Coldstream Guards, 31 Dec. 1688. Depy.-Gov. of the Tower, 11 March, 1689. Exchanged to the 1st Foot Guards, 1 May, 1689. Lt.-Gov. of Sheerness, 1 Dec. 1690. Bt.-Col., 29 Sept. 1706. Serving in 1st Foot Guards in 1709. Out of said Regt. before 1715. D. about 1725. His will, which is in the Editor's possession, bears date 3 June, 1725. The testator bequeaths to Mrs. Margaret Saville *alias* Smith, "all that my capital mansion house called Dollycorsline, and all those my messuages, cottages, farms, lands, tenements, rents, and hereditaments in the county of Montgomery and Merioneth in Wales, which I purchased from the executors and heirs of the Right Honourable Roger, late Earl of Castlemain, in the Kingdom of Ireland." After the decease of the said Mrs. Margaret Saville, "then to my daughter Mary King." The testator desired to be buried "decently and without pomp in the new Chappel in Westminster as near as may be to my late daughter Elizabeth King."

[5] Appointed Capt. in Brigadier Wills's Marines, 5 April, 1709. Had served for six years previously in said corps. Half-pay in 1713.

[6] This appears to be the first Barrack-Master's Comn. on the English Establishment.

[7] Held the post of Chaplain at Hull till July, 1715. A certain Thomas Hazelwood had served as Chaplain to Maj.-Gen. Evans's Regt. in the reign of Queen Anne, and was placed on half-pay in 1713.

⁸ Appears to have been son of Christopher Brouncker, of Portsmouth, by Catherine Gilbourne, his wife. The said Christopher was kinsman to the last Lord Brouncker. Thos. Brouncker, of Portsmouth, md. Mary, dau. of Peter Bridger, of St. Michael, Cornhill. Marriage Licence dated 1 June, 1695. The Company referred to in T. Brouncker's Commission was never formed apparently.

⁹ Governor Mathew's appointment is referred to in *Treasury Papers* under date of 30 June, 1715. He was son of Col. Wm. Mathew, who was knighted by Queen Anne 23 March, 1704, on being appointed Gov. of the Leeward Islands. His father d. 4 Dec. 1704. Wm. Mathew was appointed subsequently Lt.-Gen. of the Leeward Islands, and held this post until his death in Sept. 1752, as recorded in the *Gentleman's Magazine*.

¹⁰ Acted as Commissary-General to the Dutch troops in Scotland in 1716. His name appears in the *Treasury Papers* for that year.

¹¹ Nephew of Henry, 3rd Visct. Lonsdale. Appointed Keeper of Ordnance Stores in the Tower at a salary of £400 per ann. in Sept. 1708. Govr. of Barbados in 1710. His rule in his West Indian Government was not appreciated by the Barbadians, who petitioned for his recall. Returned to England in April, 1714. Reappointed Gov. of Barbados in 1715. Recalled about 1719. Md. Catherine, dau. of Sir Joseph Pennington, which lady's mother was the Hon. Margaret Lowther, dau. of the 1st Visct. Lonsdale. Special interest attaches to the fact that Govr. Robert Lowther's daughter, the beautiful Eleanor Lowther, was General Wolfe's *fiancée*, and the hero of Quebec wore her miniature during his last Canadian campaign. The miniature in question is now in the possession of Lord Barnard.

¹² Fifth son of Sir John D'Oyley, Bt., of Chiselhampton, Co. Oxford. Appointed Major of the Tower of London, July, 1702. Capt. of an Invalid Cy. at the Tower, 10 May, 1711. Capt. of an Invalid Cy. at Hampton Court in 1715 (see p. 233). D'Oyley acted as Lieut. of the Tower during the incarceration of the Scottish peers. On the formation of Col. Edmund Fielding's Regt. of Invalids in March, 1719, Major R. D'Oyley was appointed a Capt. therein.

¹³ Brigadier-General Edward Byam was brother to Col. Willoughby Byam (mortally wounded at the taking of St. Kitts, 1690). Held the Government of Antigua from 1715–1741, when he died.—*Herald and Genealogist*, Vol. I., p. 378.

¹⁴ See biog. notice on p. 97, note 2. On 21 Sept. 1715, this officer wrote as follows to Lord Townshend from the Tower: "My Lord, this morning at 6 o'clock I received an order from the Privy Council, and since that I have the honour of another letter from your Lordship, both directing without loss of time my regulating the Militia of the Tower Hamlets to be in readiness to march whenever His Majesty's service shall require ; this is to acquaint your Lordship that there is no Horse belonging to the Tower Hamlets, but two very strong Regiments of Foot ; and [they] are ready to march when his Majesty pleases. I am, &c., H. Compton."

[P.S.] "This morning early gave orders for the searching for, and seizing of Papists, Jacobites, and Non-Jurors, according to orders."—*Townshend Papers*, p. 162.

¹⁵ See register of his Commission as Lt.-Gen. on p. 227. It may be that he was re-commissioned on being appointed a Privy Councillor.

¹⁶ Succeeded the Earl of Northampton as Constable. Charles Howard, 3rd Earl of Carlisle, was appointed Govr. of Carlisle 3 March, 1693. Present at the surrender of Preston in Nov. 1715. First Lord of the Treasury for a short time and Constable of Windsor Castle. D. at Bath 1 May, 1738. Bd. in the mausoleum at Castle Howard, Yorkshire.

¹⁷ Son and heir of Sir Robert Munro, of Foulis, Bt., who was Sheriff of Ross and Cromarty. Capt. Robert Munro served under Marlborough, and was a Capt. in the Royal Regt. of Foot in 1710. (Comn. not forthcoming). Succeeded in June, 1716, as Govr. of Inverness and Capt. of an Independent Company, by Simon, Lord Lovat. When the Independent Companies of the Black Watch in the Highlands were formed into a Regiment in Oct. 1739, the Lieut.-Colonelcy of said Corps was bestowed on Sir Robert Munro of Foulis. This gallant officer commanded the Black Watch at Fontenoy. " Sir Robert had obtained leave of the Duke of Cumberland to allow the Highlanders to fight in their own way. According to the usage of his countrymen, he ordered the whole regiment to clap to the ground on receiving the French fire. Instantly after its discharge the men sprang up, and coming close to the enemy, poured in their shot upon them to the certain destruction of multitudes, and drove them precipitately back through their own lines ; then retreating, drew up again, and attacked a second time after the same manner. Those attacks they repeated several times on the same day, to the surprise of the whole army. Sir Robert was everywhere with his regiment, notwithstanding his great corpulency; and when in the trenches he was hauled out by the legs and arms by his own men, but it was to be observed that when he commanded the whole regiment to clap to the ground, he alone himself stood upright, with the colours behind him, ready to receive the fire of

the enemy, and this because, as he said, though he could easily lie down, his great bulk would not suffer him to rise up quickly" (Doddridge's *Life of Colonel James Gardiner*). For his services at Fontenoy Sir Robert Munro was appointed Colonel of the 37th Foot, 17 June, 1745. He commanded this Corps at the battle of Falkirk, where he was killed His body was honourably interred in Falkirk churchyard by direction of the Earl of Cromartie and the Macdonalds.

[18] As Lord Strathnaver, was appointed Col. of a newly-raised Regt. in Scotland, 19 April, 1689. Col. of a new Regt. in 1693. Served with said corps in Flanders from 1694 to the Peace of Ryswick. Succeeded as 15th Earl of Sutherland in 1703. Knight of the Thistle. In *Memoirs of the Life of Lord Lovat*, published in London, 1746, there is the following reference to the Earl of Sutherland's activity against the Jacobites in the autumn of 1715 : " Much about this time the Earl of Sutherland had drawn together a body of 1,800 in the shire of Ross, intending to prevent Lord Seaforth from joining the main army of the rebels at Perth : Seaforth understanding this, and finding himself 4,000 strong, marched directly to give the Earl battle ; but the Earl being so much inferior in number, retreated to Sutherland, as well to save his men as to draw Seaforth further north and divert him for some time from joining the rebels at Perth ; but his Lordship contented himself with ravaging the country and went strait (*sic*) to Perth, where he remained till after the defeat of the rebels at Dumblain." Lord Sutherland subsequently marched against Seaforth's forces. Their leader submitted himself and his followers to the King's mercy. The Earl of Sutherland was thrice married and was succeeded by his grandson, William, Lord Strathnaver.

[19] Son of James Hunter, of the Hunterston family (Paterson's *Hist. of Ayr and Wigtown* Vol. III., p. 354). Appointed Aide-Major to Lord Cardross's Dragoons, 19 April, 1689. Capt. in the Rl. Scots Dragoons 28 Feb. 1694. Brigade-Major to the Dragoons in Flanders, 28 May, 1695. Major of the Rl. Irish Dragoons, 23 April, 1698. Bt.-Lt.-Col. 1 Jan. 1703. Fought at Blenheim and Ramillies. Bt.-Col. 1 Jan. 1706. Appointed Govr. of Virginia in 1708. Taken prisoner by the French on his way to America, but was soon afterwards exchanged for the Bishop of Quebec, then a prisoner in the hands of the English. (Luttrell's *Diary*, Vol. VI., p. 336). Govr. of New York in 1709. Brig.-Gen. 12 Feb. 1711. Maj.-Gen. 10 March, 1727. Govr. of Jamaica, 20 June, 1729. D. in Jamaica, 31 March, 1734. There is a memoir of Gen. Hunter in the *Dict. Nat. Biog.*, but his early services and comns., as given above, are omitted from said memoir. His wife was a dau. of Sir Thos. Orby, Bt., of Burton Petwardine, Lincolnshire, and relict of Lord John Hay, 2nd son of the Marquess of Tweeddale.

[20] Seventh son of Wm., Duke of Hamilton (so created) and Anne, Duchess of Hamilton, in her own right. Appointed Govr. of Jamaica, in room of Maj.-Gen. Thos. Handasyde, 15 July, 1710. Capt. of an Indep. Cy. in Jamaica, 7 June, 1714. This and Capt. Robert Rookwood's Companies were formed from soldiers of Col. Roger Handasyde's Regt. (22nd Foot), who volunteered for service in Jamaica when Col. Handasyde's corps left that Island in May, 1714. These Companies formed the nucleus of the 49th Foot in 1743.

[21] See p. 219, note 30.

[22] Appointed Capt. in the 1st Marine Regt. 21 July, 1693. Capt. in Col. Thos. Brudenell's Regt. of Marines, 19 July, 1698. Govr. of Bermuda, 2 May, 1701. Succeeded as Govr. by Capt. Henry Pulleyne in 1713.

LIST OF THE GENERAL OFFICERS UPON THE ESTABLISHMENT OF GUARDS AND GARRISONS FOR THE YEAR 1716.*

GENERALS.

	Allowance per annum.
Thos. Erle	£1,200
Henry Lumley	do.
Duke of Argyll to the day of his dismission	do.

LIEUT.-GENERALS.

Henry Withers	£970
Lord Cadogan	do.
George Carpenter	do.
Lord Cobham	do.
Earl of Stair	do.
Charles Wills	do.

MAJOR-GENERALS.

William Tatton	£485
Joseph Sabine	do.
William Evans	do.
John Pepper	do.
Joseph Wightman	do.
George Wade	do.

BRIGADIERS.

John Stewart	£365
Wm. (sic) Russell[1]	do.
Andrew Bissett	do.
Thomas Stanwix	do.
Sir Charles Hotham	do.
Humphry Gore	do.
Philip Honywood	do.
Phineas Bowles	do.
George Preston	do.
Thomas Panton	do.
James Dormer	do.

* *Treasury Papers*, Vol. CXCVIII, No. 12.

NON-REGIMENTAL COMMISSIONS.
1716.

John Gumley [2] to be Deputy Commissary of the Musters of all Our Forces and Armies which at any time hereafter shall be raised or maintained in Our Pay, Service, or Entertainment in Our Kingdom of Great Britain and the Islands and Territories thereunto belonging	St. James's, 23 April 1716.	*a*
George, Lord Forbes to be Lieut.-Govr. of Fort St. Philip in Minorca	,, 19 June ,,	*a*
Henry Grove, Esq. to be Our Lieut.-Govr. of Berwick-upon-Tweed	,, 25 ,, ,,	*a*
Lieut.-Gen. George Carpenter to be Governor of Minorca and the Town and Garrison of Port Mahon, etc.	,, 5 July ,,	*a*
Thomas Pitt, Esq. to be Governor of Jamaica	,, 6 ,, ,,	*m*
George Maccartney,[3] Esq. to be Lieut.-Gen. of all His Majesty's Forces as well Horse as Foot	,, 12 ,, ,,	*a*
Robert Napier to be Surgeon's Mate at Fort St. Anne, Minorca	Hampton Ct., 28 ,, ,,	*a*
John Hay to be Captain of the Ports (*sic*) of Fort St. Philip, Minorca	,, ,, ,, ,,	*a*
Hunt Withers, Esq. to be Brig.-Gen. of all His Majesty's Forces as well Horse as Foot	St. James's, 8 Dec. ,,	*a*

INDEPENDENT COMPANIES OF INVALIDS.
COMMISSIONS, 1716–18.

Kingsmill Eyre, Esq. to be Agent to the four Companies of Invalids whereof John Mulcaster was late agent	St. James's, 4 Jan. 1716.	*a*
Thomas Merriman to be Ensign to Lieut.-Col. George Winram's Company of Invalids doing duty in Jersey	,, 6 Mar. ,,	*a*
George Cockle to be Lieutenant to Captain Luke Spicer's Company of Invalids doing duty in Jersey	,, 8 ,, ,,	*a*
John Perkins to be Ensign to Captain Thomas Hyde's Company of Invalids at Jersey	Hampton Ct., 28 July ,,	*a*
Jeffrey Saunders, Esq. to be Capt.-Lieut. of that Company in the 12 Companies of Invalids whereof Lieut.-Col. George Wyndram (*sic*) is Captain	St. James's, 9 Mar. 1717.	*a*

Jeffrey Saunders, Esq. to be Adjt. of the 12 Companies of Invalids - - -	St. James's, 9 Mar. 1717.	*a*
Hugh Plucknet, Esq. to be Captain of that Company of Invalids at Upnor Castle whereof Captain Mat. Draper, decd. was late Captain - - - -	,, ,, ,, ,,	*a*
George Phillbridge to be Ensign to Captain George Watkins' Company of Invalids in room of Ensign Stephens (*sic*) - -	,, 2 May ,,	*a*

SCOTS ESTABLISHMENT.
1716.

James Trail to be Ensign to the Company in garrison at Stirling Castle - -	St. James's, 25 Feb. 1716.	*a*
Simon, Lord Lovatt[4] (*sic*) to be Governor of Our Castle and Fort of Inverness and of all the military works and fortifications thereunto belonging - - -	,, 8 June ,,	*a*
Do. to be Captain of an Independent Company of Foot in the Highlands of North Britain in the room of Captain Robert Monro - - - - - -	,, ,, ,, ,,	*a*
Alex. Gordon to be sole Deputy Commissary of the Musters in Scotland - -	,, 9 ,, ,,	*a*
George, Lord Carpenter to be Commander-in-Chief in Scotland - - - -	,, 6 July ,,	*m*
James Johnson to be Lieutenant to Lord William Hay's Company in garrison at Blackness Castle - - - -	,, 17 ,, ,,	*a*
[Lord William Hay to be Governor of Blackness Fort and Captain of a Company -	——— 1716 ?]	

NON-REGIMENTAL COMMISSIONS.
1717.

Robert Lawson to be Adjutant to Chelsea Hospital - - - - -	St. James's, 19 Feb. 1717.	*a*
George (*sic*) Vaughan,[5] Esq. to be Our Lieut.-Governor of Landguard Fort whereof [Fras.] Hamon[d] is Governor -	,, 8 Mar. ,,	*a*
James Brett, Esq. to be Comptroller of Chelsea Hospital - - - -	,, 14 ,, ,,	*a*
James Craggs,[6] Junr., Esq. to be Secretary at War - - - - - -	,, 13 April ,,	*b*
John Dowcett, Esq. to be Lieut.-Governor of Annapolis Royal in America - -	,, 25 May ,,	*b*

George Smith,[7] clerk, to be Chaplain-Gen. of Our Land Forces - - - - - St. James's, 24 June 1717. *b*
Thomas Maynard, Esq. to be Commissary-Gen. of Our Stores of War and Provisions for Our Forces in Minorca in room of Giles Erle, Esq. - - - - - - „ 12 July „ *b*
William, Lord Cadogan to be General of all Our Forces as well Horse as Foot - „ „ „ „ *b*
Lieut.-Gen. Henry Withers to be Governor of Sheerness - - - - - „ 17 „ „ *b*
John Lewis de la Bene,[8] Esq. to be Lieut.-Governor of Tynemouth Castle in room of John Middleton, Esq. - - - - „ „ „ „ *b*
Colonel James O'Hara[9] to be Our A.D.C. in room of Brigdr.-Gen. James Crofts - -Hampton Ct., 17 Aug. „ *b*
John Cholmley, Esq. to be our A.D.C. - - „ „ „ „ *b*
Peter Capone, Esq. to be Commissary of Our Stores of War and Provisions at Annapolis Royal - - - - - „ 24 „ „ *b*
Martin Purcell, Esq. to be Lieut.-Governor of Placentia in the room of John Moody „ 25 „ „ *b*
Lieut.-Col. Peter Hawker to be Lieut.-Governor of Portsmouth in the room of Sir John Gibson, Kt. decd. - - - „ 1 Nov. „ *b*
Mordecai Abbot, Esq. to be Town Major of Gibraltar - - - - - „ 18 „ „ *b*
John Webb,[10] Esq. to be Governor of Upnor Castle together with the two Batteries or Sconces call'd James and Middleton Batteries near adjacent thereunto and of such soldiers as shall from time to time be entertain'd there for the defence of the same - - - - - „ 25 Dec. „ *b*
Gerard Russell,[11] Esq. to be Governor of Our Fort and Batteries at Yarmouth, Norfolk - - - - - - „ „ „ „ *b*
Do. to be Governor of Our Town of Yarmouth in Norfolk - - - - - „ „ „ „ *b*

SCOTS ESTABLISHMENT, 1717–1718.

John, Earl of Rothes to be Captain of Our Company of Foot in garrison at Stirling Castle - - - - - - St. James's, 25 Feb. 1717.*a*
John Blacketer[18] (*sic*), Esq., to be Lieut.-Governor of above castle - - - „ „ „ „ *a*
Archd. Hay of Tarvet to be Lieutenant of that Company of Foot in Stirling Castle, whereof John, Earl of Rothes is Captain and Governor - - - - - „ 30 Mar. „ *a*

1718.

James Le Blanc to be Lieut. to Our Company in garrison in Edinburgh Castle whereof George, Earl of Orkney is Constable and Governor, and also to be Fort Major of Our said Castle - - - Kensington, 23 May 1718.*b*

James Cunningham,[14] Esq., to be Lieut.-Governor of Our Foot called Fort William in Scotland in the room of Sir Wm. Gordon, Bt., deceased - - St. James's 12 Dec. ,, *b*

1719.

[Sir Robert Pollock,[15] Bt., to be Governor of Fort William - - - - - - ,, 12 Jan. 1719.]

INDEPENDENT COMPANIES IN JAMAICA, 1716–18.

Thomas Pitt, Senr., Esq., to be Captain of that Independent Company in Jamaica whereof the Lord Archibald Campbell [Hamilton] was late Captain - - - St. James's, 25 June 1716.*a*

John Butcher to be Lieut. of the Independent Company in Jamaica commanded by Sir Nicholas Lawes, Kt., the Governor - ,, 25 Feb. 1717.*b*

Sir Nicholas Lawes,[16] Kt., to be Captain of the Independent Company in Jamaica whereof Governor Pitt was Captain - ,, 25 Aug. ,, *b*

Edward Rookwood to be Lieut. of that Independent Company of Foot doing duty at Jamaica [whereof Joseph Delaunay is Captain] - - - - - - ,, 20 Nov. 1718.*b*

INDEPENDENT COMPANY IN THE BAHAMAS.

1717.

Woodes Rogers,[17] Esq., to be Captain of that Independent Company of Foot which We have appointed to do duty in Our Bahama Islands in America - - - - - Hampton Ct., 6 Nov. 1717.*b*

Robt. Beauchamp[18] to be 1st Lieut. to above Company - - - - -St. James's, 23 Oct. (*sic*) ,, *b*

Thos. Mathews to be 2nd Lieut. to do. - ,, 25 Dec. ,, *b*
Thos. Ockold to be 3rd Lieut. to do. - ,, ,, ,, ,, *b*
James Briett to be Surgeon to do. - - ,, ,, ,, ,, *b*

NON-REGIMENTAL COMMISSIONS.
1718.

Daniel Cabrol to be Surgeon's Mate to Fort St. Anne in Minorca - - - -	St. James's, 18 Jan. 1718.	b
Wm. Salter to be Commissary of the Musters of all Our Forces in the Bahamas - -	,, 7 Mar. ,,	b
Colonel —— Russel to be Governor of Dartmouth in room of Nicholas Roope - -	,, 14 ,, ,,	n
The Lord Castlecomer [19] to be Secretary at War in room of James Craggs, Junr. -	,, ,, ,, ,,	n
Thos. Micklethwaite,[20] Esq., to be Lieut.-Gen. of the Ordnance in room of General Erle - - - - - - -	,, 18 ,, ,,	n
Lieut.-Gen. George Maccartney to be Governor of Berwick in room of Lieut.-Gen. Wills -	,, ,, ,, ,,	n
Lord Cadogan to be General of the Foot in room of General Erle - - - -	,, ,, ,, ,,	n
Lieut.-Gen. Charles Wills to be Governor of Portsmouth in room of Erle - - -	,, ,, ,, ,,	n
Thos. Moore, Esq., to be Comptroller of Chelsea Hospital - - - - -	,, 24 ,, ,,	b
George Lucas, Esq., to be Lieut.-Col. of His Majesty's Forces in the [West India] Islands under my command and that you take post accordingly, signed by Lord Arch. Hamilton at Antigua - -	,, 16 Apr. ,,	a
Lieut.-Gen. C. Wills to be Lieut.-Gen. of the Ordnance - - - - - -	,, 22 ,, ,,	n
Bacon Morris, Esq., to be Our Lieut.-Governor of Landguard Fort, whereof Francis Haman (*sic*), Esq., is Governor-	Kensington, 29 ,, ,,	b
Wm. Sherriff, Esq., to be Commissary of the Musters of all Our Forces at Annapolis Royal - - - - - - -	,, 4 May ,,	b
Do. to be Deputy-Judge-Advocate of Our Force at Annapolis Royal - - -	,, ,, ,, ,,	b
Elijah Impey,[22] Esq., to be Secretary and Register (*sic*) to the Commissioners for the Government of Chelsea Hospital -	,, 12 ,, ,,	b
Kingsmill Eyre,[23] Esq., to be do. [in place of Elijah Impey whose commission was cancelled] - - - - - -	,, 20 ,, ,,	b
Combe Winsley,[24] Esq., to be Fort Major of Our Fort and Garrison of Sheerness, whereof Lieut.-Gen. Henry Withers is Governor - - - - - -	,, 27 ,, ,,	b
—— Charnock, Esq., to be Judge-Advocate of Placentia - - - - -	,, 25 Aug. ,,	n
John Vincent, Esq., to be Fort-Major of Fort St. Philip's in Our island of Minorca -	Hampton Ct., 17 Sept. ,,	b

Lewis Petit,[25] Esq., to be Lieut.-Governor of Fort St. Philip's in Minorca, and in the absence of Our Governor and Lieut.-Governor of Our said Island to command in Chief Our whole Island of Minorca, etc. - - - - - - - - St. James's, 18 Nov. 1718.*b*

George Gibbon,[26] Esq., to be Lieut.-Governor of Our Town of Portsmouth and of Our Royal Cittadell there, and of all forts, fortresses, and fortifications thereunto belonging - - - - - - ,, 3 Dec. ,, *b*

INDEPENDENT COMPANIES IN THE PROVINCE OF NEW YORK.

1718.

Charles Huddy to be Third (*sic*) Lieut. of Our Independent Company of Foot doing duty in Our Province of New York in America, commanded by Colonel Richard Ingoldsby - - - - - - St. James's, 27 May 1718.*b*

John Riggs, Esq., to be Captain of the Independent Company of Foot doing duty at New York, whereof Peter Mathews, Esq., deceased, was late Captain - - - - - - - ,, 19 Dec. ,, *b*

George Ogilvie to be [2nd ?] Lieut. to that Independent Company of Foot at New York commanded by Robert Hunter, Esq., the Governor of the Province - - - ,, ,, ,, ,, *b*

1719.

GEORGE R.

George, etc., to Our trusty and well-beloved Dr. Thomas Gibson,[27] greeting. We reposing especial trust in your experience, prudence, and ability, do by these presents constitute and appoint you to be Physician-General of Our Land Forces raised and to be raised for Our service. You are therefore carefully and diligently to discharge the duty of Physician-General by doing and performing all, and all manner of things thereunto belonging. And you are to observe and follow such orders and directions from time to time as you shall receive from Us or any other your superior officer according to the rules and discipline of war. Given at Our Court at St. James's the twenty-third day of January 1718–19 in the fifth year of Our Reign. By His Majesty's commands.

J. CRAGGS.

War Office Commission Book, 1718-23.

¹ Richard Russell. See p. 127, note 3.

² John Gumley, of Isleworth, was a wealthy glass-manufacturer and army contractor. He owed his appointment in the text to Wm. Pulteney, Secretary-at-War, afterwards the celebrated statesman, who married Gumley's daughter about 20 Dec. 1714. This lady, who was 17 when she married Pulteney, aftds. Countess of Bath, d. in Sept. 1758 and was buried at St. Martin-in-the-Fields, Mdx. ; but after the Earl of Bath's decease, in 1764, her body was removed to her husband's vault in Westminster Abbey, where several of her children were buried.

³ This officer has been handed down to posterity, rightly or wrongly, as the murderer of James, Duke of Hamilton, having, it was averred, stabbed the Duke as he lay wounded on the ground after the latter's duel with Lord Mohun, who was killed. About the 1st of June, 1716, Gen. Maccartney sent the following petition (*S.P. Dom. Geo. I.*) to the King :—

"Your Petitioner, in custody of the Marshal of the King's Bench Prison, dos stand indicted for the murther of James, Duke of Hamilton and Brandon, to which indictment having pleaded Not Guilty, by order of the Honble. the Judges of the Court of King's Bench, I am to putt myself upon Tryall by my Country on Wednesday the sixth day of this Inst. That in the month of December, 1712, a Bill of Indictment was preferred and found by the then Grand Jury of Middlesex for the murther of Charles, Lord Mohun, which indictment being then presented to Tryall against Col. James Hamilton in order thereby your Petitioner's name was therein and necessarily inserted though not intended to be prosecuted with effect. And in regard that Lady Mohun is not only pleased to declare, but does likewise request and pray your Majesty that my plea of Not Guilty may be confessed by your Majesty's Attorney Generall, Your Petitioner therefore most humbly prays your Majesty's pleasure may be signified that your Majesty's Attorney Generall do confess my plea of not guilty. And your Petitioner shall ever pray, &c.

"GEORGE MACCARTNEY."

The upshot of this petition was that Gen. Maccartney was released. George I. restored him to his former position in the army as a Lieut.-General, and bestowed on him the Colonelcy of the Rl. Scots Fusiliers. In the following year Maccartney was appointed Govr. of Berwick. Govr. of Portsmouth 15 April, 1719. In 1727 this officer was transferred to the 7th Horse (6th D. G.) He d. in July, 1730.

⁴ The two Commissions given to Lord Lovat are now among the Stuart Papers at Windsor Castle. As Simon Fraser, Yr. of Beaufort, this nobleman served as 1st Lieut. of the Grendr. Cy. in Lord John Murray's Scots Regt. in 1695. He was tried and outlawed for several heinous offences in 1701. Took the side of the Government in the '15. For his services he was pardoned and received a gift of the forfeited life-rent of the Lovat estates, and assumed the title of 10th Lord Lovat, which was confirmed to him in 1730 by the Court of Session. He went to Court in June, 1716, and in a letter to President Forbes of 21 June writes :—" I have my two Commissions in my pocket ; and the Prince told me last night he was glad they were exped[it]ed " (*Culloden Papers*, p. 56). Above Indep. Company was reduced with the two others in 1717 ; but in April, 1725, George I. ordered six new Companies to be raised for the Highlands—one of which was bestowed on Simon, Lord Lovat. This nobleman, after changing sides on several notable occasions, joined in the '45, and was beheaded on Tower Hill in 1747.

⁵ Gwyn Vaughan served as Lieut. *en second* in Col. Bowles's Regt. of Foot, 1708-1712. Half-pay, 1712. Capt. of an Invalid Company in Jan. 1715. He was son of Wm. Gwyn Vaughan of Trebarrial (Major Leslie's *Hist. of Landguard Fort*, p. 114). Held this post till 29 April, 1718. Capt.'in Col. Fielding's Regt. of Invalids, 11 March, 1719. He was subsequently one of the fourteen Commissioners of Customs for Great Britain (*Ibid.*). D. 1758.

⁶ Only son of James Craggs, one of the Postmasters-General. Born in 1686. On 16 Mar. 1718 was appointed a Privy Councillor and one of the Principal Secretaries of State. D. of small-pox, 16 Feb. 1721, and was bd. in General Monk's vault, Westminster Abbey.

⁷ Not identified with the Rev. George Smith, Chaplain to Col. Fane's Regt. (37th Foot) in 1715.

⁸ Appointed Capt. in the Earl of Argyll's Regt. of Foot, 6 April, 1693. Capt. in Sir Richard Temple's Regt. of Foot in 1702. Bt.-Major, 1 July, 1706. Served at Malplaquet and in subsequent campaigns under Marlborough. Bt. Lt.-Col. 1 Jan. 1712. Capt. of an Invalid Company at Tynemouth in Jan. 1715. Untraced after 1717.

⁹ Aftds. Field-Marshal Lord Tyrawley. See special Memoir in Vol. II.

¹⁰ Served as Capt. in Col. Borr's Regt. of Marines from 1706-1710. Govr. of Upnor Castle, 16 Feb. 1711, and Capt. of a Cy. in said garrison same date. See renewed Comn. on

p. 231. Recommissioned with increased powers, 25 Dec. 1717, as given in the text. Held this post till his death in 1733. Called "Major John Webb" in his obituary notice in the *Gentleman's Mag.*

[11] Had served in the late reign as Capt. in Sir Robert Rich's Regt. of Foot, and was placed on half-pay in 1713. He appears to have been a descendant of Sir Wm. Russell, Bt., Treasurer to the Navy, temp. Charles I., who md. a Miss Gerard-Gerard Russell. Governor of Yarmouth. D. 1744.

[12] Eighth Earl. Commanded a Troop of Gentlemen Volunteers at Sheriffmuir in Argyll's Army. D. in 1722, and was succeeded by his son, Lord Leslie. See p. 113, note 4.

[13] Fifth son of John *Blackader* the elder, a Scotch divine. Born in the parish of Glencairn, co. Dumfries, 14 Sept. 1664. Appointed Lieut. in the Cameronians at the raising of this corps in April, 1689. Capt. 14 Jan. 1693. Served in all the battles and engagements in which his Regt. took part in Flanders. Wounded at Blenheim. Promoted Major in Dec. 1705. Lt.-Col. in Oct. 1709. Sold his Commission after the taking of Bouchain in 1711. Commanded a corps of Glasgow Volunteers during the '15. Held the appointment of Lieut.-Gov. of Stirling Castle till his death, 31 Aug. 1729. Bd. in the West Church, Stirling. He left a valuable MS. which was printed many years afterwards, and is known as *The Life and Diary of Lt.-Colonel John Blackader.*

[14] See p. 134, note 5. In his memorial to the Lords of the Treasury, *circa* 1723, Cunningham speaks of his "34 years' service." He goes on to say "he has neither spared his person, purse, nor credit. His attendance on Major-General Wightman at Glenshiel was by the Major-General's orders. Petitioner commanded a detachment of 340 men from the regiments of Wightman, Montague, and Cholmley for enquiring into the murder of 12 men of Wightman's by the Camerons." *Treasury Papers,* Vol. CCXXXV. No. 79.

[15] Sir Robert Pollock of that Ilk represented Renfrewshire in Parliament. He had served in the late reign as Lt.-Col. and Bt.-Col. of the Earl of Hyndford's Regt. of Dragoons. In 1719 £50 was granted to Sir Robt. Pollock, Govr. of Fort William, for Intelligence. *Treasury Papers,* Vol. CCXLIV. No. 39.

[16] D. in Jamaica, 1731. *Gentleman's Mag.*

[17] On 24 Jan. 1705, a marriage licence was granted to "Woodes Rogers of the city of Bristol, merchant, bachelor, about 25, and Mrs. Sarah Whetstone, spinster, 18, with consent of her father, the Hon. Rear-Admiral Wm. Whetstone, of St. Paul, Covent Garden, Middlesex, Esq. at St. Mary Magdalen, Old Fish St. London." Mr. Woodes Rogers d. as Gov. of the Bahamas in 1732. *Gentleman's Mag.*

[18] Possibly the Cornet Robert Beauchamp of the Duke of Schomberg's Regt. of Horse (7th D.G.) who had served in several of Marlborough's campaigns.

[19] Christopher Wandesford, 2nd Viscount Castlecomer in the Peerage of Ireland. In 1714 he had sat for Ripon. Privy Councillor to George I. same year, and Gov. of Kilkenny. Died 23 June, 1719, and was succeeded as 3rd Viscount by his only son Christopher.

[20] Had been "Treasurer of the transports" in Queen Anne's reign. D. of apoplexy, 28 March, 1718. *Historical Register.*

[21] Appointed Lieut. *en second* in Brigdr. Joseph Wightman's Regt. of Foot, 5 March, 1708. Capt. in Brigdr. Thos. Pearce's Regt. of Foot, 17 Aug. 1710. Gov. of Landguard Fort, 23 Sept. 1719. Held this post till his death in 1744. Major Leslie's *Hist. of Landguard Fort.*

[22] There is a note attached to this entry as follows :—"This Commission was suppressed the 20 May, 1718, by another granted by his Majesty to Kingsmill Eyre, Esq."

[23] Younger son of Sir Samuel Eyre, Knt. of Newhouse and Chilhampton, Wilts. On 26 July, 1721, a marriage licence was granted to "Kingsmill Eyre, Esq., of Chelsea, Mdx. bachelor, 38, and Mary Ann Lefever, of St. James, Westminster, spinster, 21." D. in 1743 while holding the post named in the text.

[24] Doubtless son of Capt. George Winsley, who had been Fort Major at Sheerness since 1691.

[25] Of the Norman family of Petit des Etans, which had long been settled near Caen. Came to England at the Revocation of the Edict of Nantes. Is said to have been appointed to the Artillery Train in Ireland, 1691 (*Dict. Nat. Biog.*). Served with the Descent Train, 1693. Appointed an Engineer on the English Estabt. in 1697. One of the Engineers to the Peace Train of 1698. Served with the Portuguese Train, 1703–1704. Taken prisoner, but exchanged soon after. Accompanied the Ordnance Train to Gibraltar in 1705. Appointed Capt. in Brigdr. Joseph Wightman's Regt. of Foot when serving in Spain. Distinguished himself at the capture and defence of Barcelona in 1705–1706. With the Train at Almanza. Defended Tortosa. Taken prisoner when Tortosa capitulated. Was exchanged and served at the taking of Port Mahon in 1708. Given the rank of a Brigadier in the Spanish service

by Charles III. Appointed Lieut.-Governor of Port Mahon and Chief Engineer. Sent to Scotland in 1715 as Chief Engineer (*List of R.E. Officers*). Returned to Minorca in 1716 as Chief Engineer. D. at Naples, 24 May, 1720.

[26] Served as a Lieut. in Col. Wm. Breton's Regt. of Foot at Almanza and was taken prisoner. Capt.-Lieut. 16 June, 1709. Half-pay in 1712. Captain of an Invalid Company at Portsmouth, 2 Aug. 1715.

[27] Author of *The Anatomy*. Uncle to Dr. Edmund Gibson, Bishop of London, 1723–1748. He md. secondly Anna Cromwell, 6th dau. of Richard Cromwell the Protector. This lady was the only one of the Protector Richard's children " born in the purple." Dr. Thos. Gibson d. in Bedford Row, Holborn, 16 July, 1722. He left no issue. His wife survived him till 7 Dec. 1727. She and her husband are buried in the graveyard at the back of the Foundling Hospital, where is a handsome altar monument with marble tablets and inscriptions to both ; also the Gibson arms impaling those of Cromwell.

SUPPLEMENTARY COMMISSIONS IN REGIMENTS ON THE BRITISH ESTABLISHMENT, 1715–1719

FIRST TROOP OF LIFE GUARDS.

[The Hon.] John West¹ to be Lieut. and rank as eldest Lt.-Colonel	St. James's, 24 Dec. 1717.	b
Daniel Leighton,² Esq. to be Guidon and rank as eldest Major	,, ,, ,, ,,	b
Thomas Taylor, Esq. to be Cornet and do.	,, ,, ,, ,,	b
Alex. Davis, Esq. to be Exempt and rank as eldest Capt.	,, 25 ,, ,,	b
John Williamson to be Marshal of Our Four Troops of Horse Guards	,, 12 Feb. 1717-18.	b
Richard Parsons to be Brigadier and eldest Lieut.	Kensington, 23 July, 1718.	b
Esme Clarke³ to be Sub-Brigadier and eldest Cornet	,, ,, ,, ,,	b

¹ See p. 95, note 4.

² Eldest son, by 2nd wife, of Sir Edward Leighton, Bt. of Watlesborough, Co. Salop. Born in 1694. Exempt and Capt. in above Troop, 6 Feb. 1715. Lt.-Col. of Sir Robert Rich's Dragoons, 30 June, 1737. Serving in 1746. Out in 1749. D. in 1765. His son, Capt. Herbert Leighton, was Equerry to Frederick, Prince of Wales.

³ This officer had probably served some years in the ranks of the Life Guards. His father, Mr. Wm. Clark, had been "Page of the back-stairs," to Charles II's Queen, and had d. in 1682. In his will, Wm. Clark names his sons "Esme and Thomas." Esme Clark was promoted Brig. and eldest Lieut. 19 May, 1720. Serving with same rank in 1740.

SECOND TROOP OF LIFE GUARDS.

Gerrard Leighton¹ to be Sub-Brigadier and eldest Cornet in Our 2nd Troop of Horse Guards	St. James's, 8 Nov. 1718.	b
Arthur Edwards² to be Brigadier and eldest Lieut.	,, ,, ,, ,,	b
Henry Lambe to be Chaplain	,, ,, ,, ,,	b

¹ *Gerard* Leighton was youngest brother to Lt.-Col. Daniel Leighton of the 1st Troop. Appointed Capt. in Col. Roger Handasyde's Regt. (22nd Foot), 15 Aug. 1722. Serving in 1730.

² Promoted Exempt and Capt. 16 May, 1720. Second Major, 21 May, 1733. D. about 1743.

THIRD TROOP OF LIFE GUARDS.

Algernoon Coot[1] (*sic*) Esq. to be Guidon and eldest Major of Our 3rd Troop of Horse Guards and to rank as eldest Major	St. James's, 24 Dec. 1717.	*b*
Christopher Kien[2] (*sic*), Esq. to be Cornet and eldest Major [in the room of the Marquis du Quesne] and to rank as eldest Major	,, ,, ,, ,,	*b*
James Kilner to be Chaplain	Kensington, 26 June, 1718.	*b*
James Edmunds to be Brigadier and eldest Lieut.	St. James's, 21 Nov. ,,	*b*
George Berty (*sic*) to be Brigadier and eldest Lieut.	,, ,, ,, ,,	*b*
John Slater to be Adjutant and Lieut.	,, ,, ,, ,,	*b*
Philip Gayner to be Sub-Brigadier and eldest Cornet	,, ,, ,, ,,	*b*
Christopher Ernest Kien[2] (*sic*), Esq. to be Lieut. and Lt.-Col. and to rank as eldest Lt.-Col.	,, 22 ,, ,,	*b*
John Mohun,[3] Esq. to be Guidon and Major and to rank as eldest Major	,, ,, ,, ,,	*b*
Algernon Coot,[1] Esq. to be Cornet and Major and to rank as do.	,, ,, ,, ,,	*b*
John Shaw, Esq. to be Exempt and eldest Capt.	,, 21 Jan. 1718–19.	*c*
John Chamberlain to be Brigadier and Lieut.	,, 27 ,, ,,	*c*

[1] Younger son of Charles, 3rd Earl of Mountrath. Born 1689. Cornet and Major in above Troop, 21 Nov. 1718. Succeeded his elder brother as 6th Earl, 27 March, 1720. Left the Troop about that year. D. 27 Aug. 1744. Bd. in Westminster Abbey.

[2] Lieut. and Lt.-Col. of above Troop, 21 Nov. 1718. Serving the year the above Troop was disbanded, 1746.

[3] Promoted Lieut. and Lt.-Col. 28 May, 1725. D. in London, 1731.

FOURTH [SCOTS] TROOP OF LIFE GUARDS.

Clement Hilgrove[1] to be Sub-Brigadier and eldest Cornet of Our 4th Troop of Horse Guards - - - - - - St. James's, 25 Jan. 1717-18.*b*

James Garth,[2] Esq. to be Cornet and eldest Major and to rank as eldest Major of Horse - - - - - - Kensington, 12 June, 1718.*b*

James Frontine,[3] Esq., to be Guidon and eldest Major and to rank as eldest Major of do. ,, ,, ,, ,, *b*

[1] Brig. and eldest Lieut. 24 May, 1723. Exempt and Capt. 25 Dec. 1738. Served at Dettingen. Wounded at Fontenoy. Placed on half-pay in 1746 when above Troop was disbanded. Drawing half-pay in 1769 as noted in the *Army List* for said year.

[2] In 1712 this officer was a "minor" in Brig. Hans Hamilton's Regt. of Foot with the rank of Lieut. He d. in 1731 as Major of above Troop and was bd. in Westminster Abbey. In the "Funeral Book" his name is entered as "Thomas Garth, Esq." (*Westminster Abbey Registers*.) He was brother to Sir Samuel Garth, knt. Physician-General to the Army.

[3] Out of the Troop in 1721.

FIRST TROOP OF HORSE GRENADIER GUARDS.

Gabriel, Marquis du Quesne[1] to be Lieut. and Lt.-Colonel of Our 1st Troop of Horse Grenadier Guards and to rank as eldest Lt.-Col. of Horse - - - - St. James's, 24 Dec. 1717.*b*

Wm. Godolphin,[2] Esq. to be Major of do. and rank as eldest Major - - - - ,, 2 Jan. 1717-18.*b*

—— Brownjohn to be Adjt. and rank as Lieut. [in room of Robert Shirley] - - - ,, 8 Nov. 1718.*b*

Robert Shirley to be Sub-Lieut. and rank as eldest Lieut. - - - - - - ,, ,, ,, ,, *b*

Wm. Lloyd, Esq. to be Lieut. and rank as eldest Captain - - - - - ,, 29 ,, ,, *b*

[1] See p. 97, note 4.
[2] Comn. renewed by George II. Out of the Troop before 1740.

ROYAL REGIMENT OF HORSE [GUARDS.]

Wm. Megs[1] (sic) to be Qr.-Mr. to the Duke of Argyll's own Troop	St. James's, 3 June, 1715.	c
Thos. Taylor[2] to be Cornet to Capt. Fras. Byng	,, 23 ,, ,,	a
Do. to be Qr.-Mr. to Capt. Rupert Browne	,, ,, ,, ,,	a
John Shaw[3] to be do. to Capt. James Varey	,, ,, ,, ,,	a
Henry Wroth[4] to be Lieut. to Capt. John Hawkins	,, ,, ,, ,,	c
George Berkeley[5] to be Cornet to the Colonel	,, 25 July ,,	a
Pattee Byng[6] to be Capt. in room of Giles Earl (sic)	Hampton Ct. 25 Aug. 1716.	a
George Byng[7] to be Cornet in room of Pattee Byng	,, ,, ,, ,,	a
Edward Bearcroft[8] to be Cornet to Col. Fielding	Kensington, 15 May, 1718.	b
Sir James Chamberlain[9] to be Cornet to Capt. Patty (sic) Byng	,, ,, ,, ,,	b
Alex. Small to be Surgeon	,, 20 ,, ,,	b
Thos. Marcham[10] to be Lieut. to Capt. Patty Byng	,, 9 July ,,	b

[1] *Meggs*. His obituary notice in the *Gentleman's Mag.* for 1733 describes him as "Quarter-Master to the Duke of Bolton's Regiment."

[2] "Receives only Quarter-Master's pay" (note in the MS.). Promoted Lieut. 14 Jan. 1721. Serving as senior Lieut. in 1740.

[3] Out of the Regt. before 1728.

[4] Serving as Lieut. in the Earl of Deloraine's Foot in 1730.

[5] The Hon. George Berkeley, brother to the 3rd Earl of Berkeley. Not in any subsequent List. D. in 1746 as Master of St. Katherine's Hospital, near the Tower.

[6] Eldest son of Adml. Visct. Torrington. Succeeded as 2nd Viscount in 1733. Was for some time Paymaster-General in Ireland. Capt. of the Yeomen of the Guard. D.s.p. 23 Jan. 1747.

[7] Succeeded his brother Pattee as 3rd Viscount. Col. of the 4th Marines, 1744. Attained the rank of Maj.-Gen. 19 Sept. 1745. Col. 48th Foot, 24 July, 1749. D. in 1750.

[8] Not in any subsequent List.

[9] Sir James *Chamberlayne*, Bt. of Wickham. Co. Oxford. Capt. Rl. Regt. of Horse Guards, 20 Jan. 1731. Commanded a squadron of his corps at Dettingen. Fought at Fontenoy. Major, 27 May, 1745. Serving in 1749. Out before 1757. D. 23 Dec. 1776, and was succeeded in the baronetcy by his brother.

[10] Cornet, 26 Feb. 1712. Capt. 18 July, 1737. His obituary notice in the *Gentleman's Mag.* for 1755 describes him as "Capt. of the Royal Blues."

THE KING'S OWN REGIMENT OF HORSE.
[1st DRAGOON GUARDS.]

John Browne,¹ Esq. to be Capt. in Gen. Lumley's Regt. of Horse	St. James's, 11 Jan. 1715.*a*
Tomkins Wardour,² Esq. to be Capt.-Lieut. [in room of Browne]	,, ,, ,, ,, *a*
Christopher Billings to be Cornet	,, ,, ,, ,, *a*
Viscount Irwyn (*sic*)³ to be Col. and Capt. of a Troop	,, 13 Dec. 1717.*a*
Timothy Carr to be Cornet to Major Morey, in Viscount Irwyn's Regt. of Horse	,, 10 Feb. 1718.*b*
Patrick Lisle, Esq. to be Major and Capt. of a Troop	,, 14 ,, ,, *b*
Thos. Hunt, Esq. to be Capt. of that Troop whereof Major John Morey was Capt.	,, 28 ,, ,, *b*
Humphrey Bland,⁴ Esq. to be Lt.-Col. of Our own Regt. of Horse, commanded by Viscount Irwyn	,, ,, ,, ,, *b*
George Brabant to be Lieut. to Capt. George Burrington	,, ,, ,, ,, *b*
Wm. Watson to be Cornet to the Colonel's own Troop	,, ,, ,, ,, *b*
Wm. Walton (*sic*)⁵ to be Lieut. to Capt. Wm. Benbow	,, 1 Nov. ,, *b*
Timothy Carr to be Lieut. to Capt. Galen Cope	,, ,, ,, ,, *b*
Richard Manning to be Cornet to the Colonel's own Troop	,, ,, ,, ,, *b*
Samuel Strudwick to be Cornet to Capt. Thos. Hunt	,, ,, ,, ,, *b*
Wm. Duckett⁶ to be Adjutant	,, ,, ,, ,, *b*
Francis Lambert to be Lieut to Capt. Cole	,, 2 Jan. 1719.*b*
John Chamberlain to be Lieut. to Capt. Thos. Hunt.	,, ,, ,, ,, *b*
Cuthbert Wightman to be Cornet to Capt. Wm. Benbow	,, 13 ,, ,, *b*

¹ Appointed Cornet in above Regt. 5 Aug. 1704. Served at Malplaquet and other campaigns under Marlborough. Capt.-Lieut. 11 June, 1715. Lt.-Col. of Gen. Wm. Evans's Dragoons, 7 May, 1721. Transferred to the Lt.-Colonelcy of his old Corps, 30 June, 1737. Bt.-Col. 10 May, 1742. Commanded this Corps at Dettingen and Fontenoy. Major-Gen. 26 March, 1754.

² Son of Wm. Wardour of Whitney Court, Co. Hereford. Cornet in above Regt. 24 Oct. 1707. Served at Malplaquet. Appointed Guidon and Major of the 2nd Troop of Horse, 13 Oct. 1728. Lt.-Col. 21 May, 1733. Col. of the 41st Foot, 1 April, 1743. D. 13 Feb. 1752, aged 64. Bd. in Westminster Abbey.

³ See biog. notice on p. 156, note 1.

⁴ See do. on p. 115, note 3.

⁵ Serving in 1730 as Capt.-Lieut. of the 6th Regt. of Horse. Not in any subsequent List.

⁶ This officer's name is wrongly given as "Duckins" in the MS. *Army List* for 1715. (See p. 103). Wm. Ducket (or Duckett) was appointed Cornet in above Regt. 22 Aug. 1712.

Major 2nd Troop Horse Grendr. Guards, 9 June, 1721. Lt.-Col. of said Troop, 15 Mar. 1729. Serving in 1740. Retd. in Jan. 1741. M.P. for Calne 1727, 1734, 1737-9. Younger son of Wm. Duckett of Hartham, Wilts, and brother to George Duckett the poet and author. The *London Magazine* for 1739 records that "Col. Wm. Duckett, M.P. for Calne, voted for the Convention with Spain." He d. 12 Dec. 1749 and was bd. in the north transept of Petersham Church, Surrey, where is a tablet to his memory. His widow, *née* Turberville, d. 3 Feb. 1780, aged 80, and was bd. in same Church.—*Memoirs of the Family of Duckett,* by Sir George Duckett, Bt.

MAJOR-GENERAL WADE'S REGIMENT OF HORSE.
[3RD DRAGOON GUARDS.]

Collis Ray[1] to be Cornet to Capt. Balladine's Troop in Major-General Wade's Regt. of Horse	St. James's, 13 Mar. 1717-18.*b*
Michael Armstrong[2] to be Lieut. to Lieut.-Col. [John] Ligonier	„ „ „ „ *b*
Wm. Wade[3] to be Cornet to Major Hull	„ „ „ „ *b*

[1] Collis *Rea*. Comn. renewed by George II.

[2] Served as a Qr.-Mr. in above Regt. at Oudenarde and Malplaquet. Cornet, 10 Oct. 1709. Capt. 10 Apr. 1733. Is said to have fought at Culloden. Third son of Robert Armstrong of Ballyard, King's County, and father of General Bigoe Armstrong. The death of a certain Michael Armstrong, Esq., at Chelsea, is recorded in the *Gentleman's Mag.* for 1757.

[3] Belonged to the family of Field-Marshal Wade. Capt. in above Regt. 20 Feb. 1719. Major, 3 Apr. 1733. Served at Culloden. His silver medal for that battle is still in the possession of his representative.

THE ROYAL DRAGOONS.*

John Memville[1] to be Cornet to that Troop whereof Edward Montagu, Esq., is Capt. in the Earl of Strafford's Regt. of Dragoons	St. James's, 11 Jan. 1715.*a*
Patrick Maxwell[2] to be Cornet *en second* in Lord Cobham's Dragoons	„ 22 Aug. „ *a*
Samuel Speed,[3] Esq. to be Major to Our Royal Regt. of Dragoons commanded by Visct. Cobham and to be Capt. of a Troop	„ 26 Mar. 1718.*b*
James Griffith,[4] Esq. to be Capt. in the room of Major Humphry Bland	„ „ „ „ *b*

* Served in Lancashire in 1715, and was present at the surrender of Preston.

[1] Resigned his Commission in Dec. 1715.

[2] It appears from the memorial to the Treasury of Lieut. Mat. Sempill of Ker's Dragoons, that the King only granted Commissions *en second* to seven officers in 1715. The reason for these appointments is not stated. Patrick Maxwell appears in no subsequent List.

[3] See p. 119, note 4.

[4] Not in any subsequent List.

ROYAL NORTH BRITISH DRAGOONS.*

[ROYAL SCOTS GREYS.]

John Campbell to be Lieut. in Our Royal Regt. of North British Dragoons commanded by the Earl of Portmore	St. James's, 22 Aug. 1715.*a*
Sir Thos. Hay¹ to be Cornet to Capt. — in do.	Kensington, 1 June, 1718.*b*
James Ross² to be Cornet to Capt. Henry Selwyn in do.	Hampton Court, 17 Sept. ,, *b*

* Served at Sheriffmuir.
¹ Second Bart. of Alderstone. Capt. 11 June, 1720. Major 6 Feb. 1741. Lt.-Col. 27 May, 1742. Commanded the Greys at Dettingen and Fontenoy. Retd. in May, 1745. D. 1750.—*Gentleman's Mag.*
² Promoted Capt. 21 Mar. 1723. Serving in 1740.

THE KING'S OWN REGIMENT OF DRAGOONS.*

[3RD HUSSARS.]

Francis Scott¹ to be Lieut. *en second* in Lt.-General Carpenter's Regt. of Dragoons	St. James's, 22 Aug. 1715.*a*
Henry Whitley² to be Adjt.	Hampton Court, 7 Sept. 1718.*b*
Alex Baird,³ Esq. to be Cornet to Col. Alex. Reade's Troop	,, ,, 8 Oct. ,, *b*

* Served at Sheriffmuir.
¹ Served previously as Lieut. in Col. the Hon. W. Ker's Dragoons. One of the seven officers to whom the King granted Commissions *en second* (See p. 267, note 3). Not in any subsequent List.
² Cornet, 16 June, 1716. Lieut. 16 Jan. 1721. Comn. renewed by George II. Capt. 12 June, 1743. Served at Dettingen and Fontenoy. Attained the rank of Major-General 13 Aug. 1761. Col. of the 9th Dragoons, 6 Apr. 1759. D. as Lt.-General in Jan. 1771.—*Gentleman's Mag.*
³ Not in any subsequent List. Believed to be younger son to Sir John Baird, a Lord of Session, who was created a Bart. in 1695. Alex. Baird d. in 1743.

THE EARL OF STAIR'S DRAGOONS.*
[6TH INNISKILLING DRAGOONS.]

David Makgill¹ to be Cornet *en second* in the Earl of Stair's Dragoons	St. James's, 26 Sept. 1715.*a*
James Montgomery² to be Cornet to the Earl of Stair's Troop	,, 14 Feb. 1717–18.*b*
Montagu Farrer,³ Esq. to be Capt. in room of Capt. Serjeant	Kensington, 19 Apr. 1718.*b*
Alex. Auchinleck,⁴ Esq. to be Capt.-Lieut. [in room of Montagu Farrer]	,, ,, ,, ,, *b*
Wm. Nugent⁵ to be Lieut. to Lt.-Col. Montgomery's Troop	St. James's, 3 Jan. 1718–19.*b*
Philip Gasteen⁶ to be Lieut. to Major Duquery's Troop	,, ,, ,, ,, *b*
Wm. Hamilton⁷ to be Cornet to do.	,, ,, ,, ,, *b*
Patrick Agnew⁸ to be do. to Lt.-Col. Montgomery	,, ,, ,, ,, *b*

* Served at Sheriffmuir.

¹ Not in any subsequent List. Served previously in Col. the Hon. W. Ker's Dragoons, which Corps was temporarily broken in 1714.

² Probably son of Lt.-Col. Alex. Montgomery of above Regt. Not in any subsequent List.

³ Attained the rank of Major of above Regt. 15 Aug. 1734. Serving with same rank in 1742. Believed to have served at Dettingen and to have retd. soon afterwards. D. at Carlisle in 1763 aged 84.—*Gentleman's Mag.*

⁴ Promoted Capt. 25 Dec. 1725. On half-pay in 1739.

⁵ Serving with same rank in 1740.

⁶ Out of the Regt. before 1727.

⁷ Lieut. 8 Apr. 1721. Serving in 1730. On half-pay in 1739.

⁸ One of the 21 children of Sir James Agnew, Bt., of Lochnaw, by Lady Mary Montgomerie dau. of Alex. 8th Earl of Eglinton. Patrick Agnew was educated for the law; but finding there was too much competition in the legal profession for him to make a living in that line of life, he turned his attention, by his father's advice, to the Army. The Earl of Stair being Sir James Agnew's near neighbour, and friend, was asked by the baronet to let his son purchase a cornetcy in his lordship's regiment (Agnew to Lord Stair, 31 Jan. 1718), and the commission given in the text was the result. Patrick Agnew was promoted Lieut. 31 May, 1727. Serving as Lieut. with same Corps in the Flanders campaigns of 1742–1745.

THE PRINCESS OF WALES'S OWN ROYAL REGIMENT OF DRAGOONS.*

[7TH HUSSARS.]

[The Hon.] Wm. Kerr¹ (*sic*) to be Colonel of Our most dear daughter Wilhelmina Princess of Wales's Own Royal Regt. of Dragoons, and to be Capt. of a Troop - - - - -	St. James's, 1 Aug. 1715.*a*
Wm. Johnston² to be Cornet *en second* in above Regt. - - - -	,, 22 ,, ,, *a*
[Mathew Sempill³ to be do. do. -	,, ,, ,, ,,]
Wm. Kirby to be Qr.-Mr. to Capt. Lewis Dollon's Troop [*Comn. signed by Col. Kerr*] - - - -	London, 7 Sept. ,, *a*
Wm. Johnston² to be Cornet to Capt. Peter Renovard's Troop - - -	St. James's, 15 June, 1716.*a*
Benjamin Rider to be Cornet to the Colonel's own Troop - - -	Hampton Court, 14 Aug. 1717.*b*
James Agnew⁴ to be Lieut. to Capt. George Dunbar's Troop - - -	Kensington, 10 May, 1718.*b*
George Knox to be do. to Capt. Lewis Dollon's Troop - - - -	,, ,, ,, ,, *b*
Henry Bateman Parkins to be Cornet to Capt. James Livingston - - -	,, ,, ,, ,, *b*
Peter Malet to be Cornet to Capt. George Dunbar - - - - -	,, ,, ,, ,, *b*

* "Broke" in Ireland early in 1714. Restored by George I., 3 Feb. 1715, in a letter to Wm. Pulteney, Secretary at War. Three Troops were taken from the Rl. North British Dragoons, and two from the Royal Dragoons, as noted on pp. 106, 111. The Colonel was re-com-missioned on 1 Aug. 1715 in consequence of the new title of "Princess of Wales's Own Royal Regt. of Dragoons" being bestowed. This Corps served at Sheriffmuir.

¹ The Hon. Wm. Ker, younger son of the 3rd Earl of Roxburghe and brother to the 1st Duke of Roxburghe. Col. of above Regt. 10 Oct. 1709. Served under Marlborough and Ormonde. Had two horses shot under him at Sheriffmuir. Brig.-Gen. 18 May, 1727. Maj.-Gen. 10 Nov. 1735. Lt.-Gen. 2 July, 1739. Was M.P. for Berwick for some years, and held the post of Groom of the Bed-chamber to George, Prince of Wales. D. unm. 7 Jan. 1741.

² Had been Cornet in the Regt. before it was broke. Cornet to Capt. Renovard's Troop, 15 June, 1716.

³ Appointed Cornet in above Regt. 1 Mar. 1695. Lieut. 29 Mar. 1711. Broke with the Regt. in 1714. From his Memorial to the Treasury in 1721 (?) it appears that he had served 28 years as a commissioned officer in Col. Kerr's Regt., and on 22 Aug. 1715 was "one of the seven officers to whom the King granted Commissions *en second*, but had received no pay since the date of said Commission" (*Treasury Papers*, vol. ccxxxiii, no. 3). Further services untraced.

⁴ See biog. on p. 111, note 4.

MAJOR-GENERAL PEPPER'S REGIMENT OF DRAGOONS.*

[8TH HUSSARS.]

Alex. Stewart[1] to be Cornet *en second*	St. James's,	26 Sept. 1715.*a*
Thos. Sheffield Austin[2] to be Cornet	,,	28 July, 1716.*i*
Samuel Whitshed,[3] Esq. to be Major and Capt. of a Troop in room of Adam Bellamy decd.	,,	20 Nov. 1718.*j*

* "Broke" in 1714. Restored by George I. in 1715.
[1] Had served as a Cornet in the Hon. W. Ker's Dragoons before the reduction of said Corps in 1714. Services untraced after 1715.
[2] Capt. in same Regt. 5 June, 1726. Serving in 1740. He was second son of Sir Robert Austen, Bt., of Bexley. Succeeded to the baronetcy on the death of his brother Sir Robert in 1743. D. s.p. about 1758.—Burke's *Extinct Baronetage*.
[3] See biog. notice on p. 154, note 4.

MAJOR-GENERAL OWEN WYNNE'S REGIMENT OF DRAGOONS.*

[9TH LANCERS.]

Francis Rannells[1] to be Qr.-Mr. to Capt. Henry Smith	London, 22 July, 1715.*a*
John Langlands[2] to be Cornet *en second*	St. James's, 22 Aug. ,, *a*
Owen Wynne[3] to be Lieut. to Capt. —— Knox	,, 25 Dec. ,, *a*
John Folliott to be Cornet to Capt. [Henry] Smith	,, ,, ,, ,, *a*
Thos. Cox to be Qr.-Mr. to Lord Leslie's Troop	London, 8 Feb. 1715–16.*a*

Regiment sent to Ireland, 25 June 1717.

Wm. Douglas,[4] Esq., to be Capt. in room of Lord Leslie	St. James's, 17 July 1717.*j*
John Carmichael[5] to be Cornet in room of Wm. Carleton	,, 2 Dec. ,, *j*
Wm. Carleton[6] to be Lieut. to Capt. Wm. Douglas in room of Wm. Whittington, decd.	,, ,, ,, ,, *j*
Anthony Morgan to be Cornet to Major-Gen. Wynne's Troop in room of John Carmichael	,, 21 ,, ,, *j*
Charles Howard,[7] Esq. to be Capt. in room of Henry Smyth	,, 16 Apr. 1718.*j*

---

* Served under General Wills at the taking of Preston.

[1] *Reynolds.* Cornet in May 1719. Lieut. in 1727. Serving in 1745.

[2] Had served as Cornet in the Hon. W. Ker's Regt. of Dragoons before said Corps was reduced in 1714. Drawing half-pay in 1722.

[3] Son of Lewis Wynne and nephew to Maj.-Gen. Owen Wynne. Served as Ensign and Lieut. in his uncle's Regt. of Foot from 1705–1713, when he was placed on half-pay. Capt.-Lieut. 12 July, 1737. Succeeded to the family property of Hazlewood, Co. Sligo. (See Burke's *Landed Gentry.*) Attained the rank of Lt.-Col. of the 9th Dragoons, 9 April, 1756.

[4] See biog. notice on p. 179, note 5.

[5] Appointed Major of the Earl of Harrington's Dragoons, 22 Nov. 1720. Serving in 1730.

[6] Serving as senior Lieut. in same Regt. 1740. A certain Wm. Carleton's death is notified in the *Gentleman's Mag.* for 1771, aged 78.

[7] The Hon. Charles Howard. See biog. notice on p. 219, note 23.

BRIGADIER-GENERAL HUMPHRY GORE'S REGIMENT OF DRAGOONS.

[10TH HUSSARS.]

Wm. Graham to be Qr.-Mr. to Capt. Paston Knyvett - - - - - - -	—— 27 July, 1715.	a
Nicholas Stevenson to be Qr.-Mr. to Capt. George Treby - - - - - -	London, 2 Aug. ,,	a
Wm. Howard to be Qr.-Mr. to Capt. —— -	,, 18 ,, ,,	a
Michael Higginson to be do. to Capt. Wittewrong - - - - - -	,, ,, ,, ,,	a
Richard Bridell to be do. to do. - - -	,, 9 Mar. 1716–7.	a
Peter Bradshaw[1] to be Lieut. to Capt. [George] Treby - - - - -	St. James's 2 July ,,	a
Godfrey Shipway[2] to be Cornet to Capt. John Wittewrong - - - -	,, 1 Nov. 1718.	b
Samuel Woodward,[3] Esq. to be Capt. of a Troop - - - - - - -	,, 12 Dec. ,,	b

[1] This officer has been identified by the compiler of the *Memoirs of the Tenth Hussars* as Peter *Bradshaigh*, who was a Lieut. on half-pay from Col. Wm. Stanhope's Dragoons in 1714 (*Half-Pay Army List*, 1714). Exchanged to half-pay 19 Aug. 1726.

[2] From half-pay Ensign in Maj.-Gen. Rooke's Regt. Lieut. in Churchill's (late Gore's) Dragoons, 24 Feb. 1728. Not in any subsequent List.

[3] From half-pay Col. Maurice Nassau's Regt. of Dragoons. Out of the Regt. 12 July, 1723.

BRIGADIER-GENERAL PHILIP HONEYWOOD'S REGIMENT OF DRAGOONS.*

[11TH HUSSARS.]

John Maitland¹ Esq. to be Captain of that Troop in Brigadier Philip Honeywood's Regt. of Dragoons whereof Wm. Robinson was late Captain	St. James's, 18 Dec. 1717.	*b*
Wm. Leman,² Esq. to be Capt.-Lieut.	,, ,, ,, ,,	*b*
Robert Watts³ to be Lieut. to Capt. Richard Tracey	,, ,, ,, ,,	*b*
Richard Reynolds⁴ to be Cornet to Capt. John Maitland	,, 25 Feb. 1717–18.	*b*
Jeremiah Easthope⁵ to be Cornet to Capt. Richard Tracey	Kensington, 14 May 1718.	*b*
Peter (*sic*) Wheeler⁶ to be Lieut. to Capt. John Maitland	,, 15 ,, ,,	*b*

* Served at Preston. See *Historical Records of the XI Hussars* by Capt. Godfrey Williams.

¹ Served in Borr's Marines in late reign as 2nd and 1st Lieut. Major in Lord Mark Kerr's Dragoons (11th), 31 May, 1732. Serving as Major in 1745. Out of the Army before 1749.

² Capt. 3 May, 1720. Served in the late reign as Ensign and Lieut. in Col. Roger Townshend's Regt. Half-pay 1712. Serving in same Regt. in 1745.

³ Serving as Lieut. in the 2nd Regt. of Horse in 1728. Capt. 19 May, 1736. Serving in 1740.

⁴ Called "Reynell" in subsequent Lists. Lieut. 4 Feb. 1722. Serving in 1740 as Lieut. in the 6th Horse.

⁵ Not in any subsequent List.

⁶ Commission renewed by George II., but Christian name not given. Probably "Peter" is a clerical error for Charles Wheeler.

BRIGADIER-GENERAL PHINEAS BOWLES'S REGIMENT OF DRAGOONS.*

[12TH LANCERS.]

Roger Moore to be Qr.-Mr. to Capt. John Peirson	London, 1 Aug. 1715.*a*
Edgar Tipping to be do. to Lt.-Col. Thos. Strickland	,, 1 ,, ,, *a*
Joseph Harris to be do. to Capt. [John] Prideaux	,, 1 ,, ,, *a*
Alex. Shand to be do. to Lt.-Col. Orfeur	,, 20 June 1717.*a*
Richard Honeywood¹ to be Cornet to Capt. Peirson	St. James's, 12 Mar. 1717–18.*b*
Wm. Burton² to be Cornet to Capt. ——	Kensington, 3 July 1718.*b*
Abraham Desmar³ to be Cornet to Capt. John Prideaux	Hampton Ct., 22 Aug. ,, *b*
John Dalston⁴ to be Cornet to Major Thos. Brown in room of Wm. Bourden (*sic*), preferred	,, 6 Dec. ,, *j*

* This Corps was not employed against the Jacobites in 1715. It was sent to Ireland in Oct. 1718, where it remained for seventy-five years.

¹ Out of the Regt. before 1728. Of Marks Hall, Essex. D. 1758. He was uncle to Col. Philip Honeywood of Howgill Castle, Westmorland.—*Gentleman's Mag.*

² Commission renewed by George II. Out of the Regt. before 1736.

³ *Idem.*

⁴ This officer had served as Lieut. in the Marquis de Montandre's Portuguese Regt. of Foot in 1709. Lieut. in Sir Robert Rich's Dragoons, 22 July, 1715. Said Corps was disbanded in 1718. Promoted Major of Bowles's Dragoons, 14 July, 1720. Out of the Army before 1727. He was younger son of Sir John Dalston, Bt., of Dalston, Cumberland.

BRIGADIER-GENERAL RICHARD MUNDEN'S REGIMENT OF DRAGOONS.*

[13TH HUSSARS.]

John Houghton to be Adjutant	St. James's, 22 July 1715.	*a*
Charles Lambert to be Qr.-Mr. to Capt. Hebblethwait's Troop	London, 5 Aug. ,,	*a*
Richard Henson to be do. to Lt.-Col. Clement Nevill's do.	,, ,, ,, ,,	*a*
Jonathan Cochran to be do. to Brigadier Munden's own do.	,, ,, ,, ,,	*a*
Wm. Ellis to be do. to Capt. Fras. Howard's Troop	,, ,, ,, ,,	*a*
John Price to be do. to Capt. Lutton Lister's do.	,, ,, ,, ,,	*a*
Richard Parry to be do. to Lt.-Col. (*sic*) Freeman's do.	,, ,, ,, ,,	*a*
Robt. Wrench to be do. to Col. Clement Nevill's do.	,, 25 Apr. 1716.	*a*
Thos. Wildey to be do. to Capt. Lutton Lister's do.	,, 3 Aug. 1718.	*b*

* Served at Preston under Gen. Wills. Regt. sent to Ireland in Oct. 1718.

BRIGADIER-GENERAL JAMES DORMER'S REGIMENT OF DRAGOONS.*

[14TH HUSSARS.]

Caleb Harbert¹ (sic) to be Surgeon	22 July 1715.*j*
[Peter] Pickering² to be Chaplain	,, ,, ,, *j*
William Hamilton³ to be Cornet [and Adjutant]	,, ,, ,, *j*

Regt. sent to Ireland in May, 1717.

Robert Bettesworth⁴ to be Cornet to Capt. Beverly Newcomen in room of Andrew Forrester	Dublin Castle, 14 Aug. 1717.*j*
William Boyle,⁵ Esq., to be Major in room of Major Solomon Rapin and Captain of a Troop	,, 13 Sept. ,, *j*
Peter Morin,⁶ Esq., to be Captain in room of Major Boyle	,, ,, ,, ,, *j*
William Boyle,⁵ Esq., to be Lt.-Col. and Captain of a Troop in room of Lt.-Col. Harry Killigrew	,, 21 Dec. ,, *j*

---

* Served at Preston. See Col. H. B. Hamilton's *Hist. of the XIV. Hussars.*

¹ Served at Blenheim as Surgeon's Mate to Visct. Howe's Regt. of Foot. Surgeon to Lord Mohun's Regt. 5 April, 1708. Untraced after 1715.

² Serving as Chaplain in 1729.—*Records.*

³ Promoted Lieut. 20 Aug. 1720. Comn. renewed by George II. Serving in 1736 with same rank. Out of the Regt. before 1740.

⁴ On half-pay in 1722.

⁵ Appointed Cornet in the Duke of Schomberg's Regt. of Horse 1 May, 1694. Bt.-Capt. 6 April, 1708. Fought at Oudenarde and Malplaquet. There is a duplicate of this officer's commission as Major, dated "20 Aug. 1717," but the words "and Capt. of a Troop" are omitted. Lt.-Col. of Dormer's Dragoons, 21 Dec. 1717. Out of the Regt. 1 Dec. 1720. Younger son of the Hon. Henry Boyle. Col. Wm. Boyle md. the only dau. of Sir Samuel Garth, Bart. M.D., who was Physician-General to the Army.

⁶ Appointed Lieut. in Col. John Gibson's Regt. of Foot, 20 Jan. 1698. Re-appointed Lieut. in Col. Gibson's newly-raised Regt. of Foot (28th), 10th Mar. 1702. Taken prisoner at Almanza, where he was wounded. Capt. 24 July, 1707. Comn. as Capt. in Windsor's (late Gibson's) Regt. renewed by George I. in 1715. Out of Dormer's Regt. before 1730.

COLONEL WM. NEWTON'S REGIMENT OF DRAGOONS.*

Wm. Mason to be Surgeon - - - -	St. James's, 22 July 1715.	*a*
James Rouse¹ to be Qr.-Mr. to Capt. Samuel Speed - - - - -	London, 23 ,, ,,	*a*
Wm. Wyndham to be do. to Lt.-Col. John Moyle - - - - - - -	,, ,, ,, ,,	*a*
John Robertson² to be Cornet to Capt. William Preston - - - - -	,, 15 Oct. ,,	*j*
Samuel Lowe³ to be do. to Capt. John Hamilton - - - - - -	,, 8 Nov. ,,	*j*
Thomas Carfrae⁴ to be Capt. - - -	,, 27 June 1716.	*j*
John Penny⁵ to be Lieut. to Capt. Wm. Preston - - - - - - -	St. James's, 22 Jan. 1717.	*j*
John Nossiter⁶ to be Cornet to Capt. Richard Maxwell - - - - -	,, ,, ,, ,,	*j*

Regt. sent to Ireland, 25 June, 1717.

Thos. Carfrae to be Adjutant - - -	St. James's, 5 July, 1717.	*j*
Justin Macarty⁷ to be Cornet to Capt. —— in room of James Haldane - - -	Dublin, 2 Jan. 1717-18.	*j*
James Kirk⁸ to be Cornet to Capt. —— in room of Sir T. Pennington, Bt. - -	[,,] 24 ,, ,,	*j*

Quarter-Masters reduced with the Regt. in 1718, and placed on half-pay.

John Gillespey.*o*
M. Ant. Bernardon.*o*
Wm. Banks.*o*

---

* This corps was left by General Wills at Manchester when the Jacobite forces entered Lancashire early in Nov. 1715, "to prevent the disaffected in that town from stirring as they had promised." (Lord Townshend to the Duke of Argyll, 15 Nov. 1715.) The Regt. was sent to Scotland early in 1716.
  ¹ Half-pay on the reduction of the Regt. in 1718. Drawing half-pay in 1739.
  ² Cornet in Stanhope's Dragoons in Oct., 1718.
  ³ Reduced with the Regt. Drawing half-pay in 1739.
  ⁴ Appointed Ensign in Sir Richard Temple's Regt. 25 Mar. 1709. Served at Malplaquet. Lieut. in Newton's Dragoons, 22 July, 1715. On half-pay 1722.
  ⁵ Apointed Lieut. in Sir R. Temple's Regt. 25 Apr. 1713. Reduced with Newton's Dragoons. Drawing half-pay in 1739.
  ⁶ Reduced with the Regt. Drawing half-pay in 1739.
  ⁷ Not in any subsequent Lists.
  ⁸ *Ibid.*

THE PRINCE OF WALES'S OWN ROYAL REGIMENT OF DRAGOONS COMMANDED BY COLONEL CHARLES CHURCHILL.*

Thos. Bates[1] to be Surgeon	St. James's, 22 July 1715.	a
Cornet John Girling[2] to be Adjutant	,, ,, ,, ,,	a
Wm. Marston to be Chaplain	,, ,, ,, ,,	e
Brigdr.-General Sir Charles Hotham,[3] Bt. to be Colonel of the Prince of Wales's Own Royal Regt. of Dragoons whereof Col. Chas. Churchill was late Colonel and to be Capt. of a Troop in said Regt.	,, 17 ,, 1717.	b

Quarter-Masters reduced with the Regt. in 1718 and placed on half-pay.

John Wale.o
John Butler.o

* This corps served under General Carpenter in Northumberland and marched with him to Preston, Lancashire, in pursuit of the rebels. A Royal warrant of 8 March, 1716, granted £600 to "Col. Charles Churchill as Colonel of Our most dear son, George Augustus, Prince of Wales's Own Regt. of Dragoons, in consideration of their losses by horses killed and disabled, and other extraordinary expenses in their long and continued marches, in a very rigorous season, in pursuit of the rebels who were taken prisoners at Preston." Quoted in *Memoirs of the Tenth Royal Hussars* by the Hon. John Fortescue, p. 9.

[1] Placed on half-pay in 1726. Drawing half-pay in 1739.
[2] Placed on half-pay on the reduction of the Regt. in 1718. Drawing half-pay in 1739.
[3] See biog. notice on p. 172, note 1.

COLONEL JAMES TYRRELL'S REGIMENT OF DRAGOONS.

Philip Rice[1] to be Cornet to Col. James Tyrrell	St. James's,	7 May 1716 a
Robert Hepburne,[2] Esq. to be Capt. of that Troop whereof Thomas Lumley, Esq. was late Capt. in Col. James Tyrrell's Regt. of Dragoons	,,	7 Dec. 1717. b
Peter Garrick,[3] Esq. to be Capt.-Lieut.	,,	,, ,, ,, b
Stephen de la Creuse[4] to be Lieut. to Capt. ——	,,	,, ,, ,, b

Quarter-Master reduced with the Regt. in 1718 and placed on half-pay.

John Herring.*o*

[1] Dead 30 Nov. 1716.

[2] Appointed Lieut. in Col. James Tyrrell's Regt. of Foot 5 July, 1712. Half-pay, 1713. Capt.-Lieut. in Tyrrell's Dragoons 22 July, 1715. Half-pay 1718. Capt. in Lord Mark Kerr's Regt. of Dragoons 13 May, 1735. Serving in 1745.

[3] Son of a Huguenot refugee from Bordeaux. The name was originally *Garric*. Peter Garrick was appointed Lieut. in Tyrrell's Regt. of Foot 3 Nov. 1708. Half-pay in 1713. Lieut. in Tyrrell's Dragoons 22 July, 1715. Half-pay 1718. Capt. in Major-Gen. Kirke's Regt. (2nd Foot) 26 Dec. 1726. Md. Arabella dau. of the Rev. — Clough, Vicar-Choral of Lichfield Cathedral, 13 Nov. 1707. Their second son and third child was David Garrick the famous comedian. Capt. Peter Garrick's will was dated 13 Jan. 1736-7 and proved in April following. (*Westminster Abbey Registers.*)

[4] Appointed Cornet in the Inniskilling Dragoons 7 March, 1713. Resigned his Cornetcy 19 Aug. 1715. Half-pay from Tyrrell's Dragoons 1718. Drawing half-pay in 1739.

SIR ROBERT RICH'S REGIMENT OF DRAGOONS.

Edward Uvedale to be Surgeon	St. James's, 22 July, 1715.	*a*
Cornet John Dubleday¹ to be Adjt.	,, ,, , ,,	*a*

Regt. sent to Ireland 25 June, 1717.

Brigdr.-General James Crofts² to be Colonel of Our Regt. of Dragoons lately commanded by Sir Robert Rich, Bt. and to be Capt. of a Troop in do.	[St. James's] 17 July, 1717.	*j*
Lewis Morton,³ Esq. to be Capt. in room of Ant. Lowther	,, 20 Dec.	*j*
Samuel Meulh (*sic*), Esq. to be Capt.-Lieut.	,, ,, ,,	*j*
John Carmichael⁴ to be Lieut. to Capt. Lewis Morton in room of Samuel Meuhl	,, 21 ,, ,,	*j*
James Gould,⁵ Esq. to be Capt. in room of Lewis Morton	,, 26 Aug. 1718.	*j*
Benjamin Griffith, Chaplain, to be Chaplain to above Regt. in room of Stephen Ashton, superseded	,, 18 Sept. ,,	*j*

Quarter-Masters reduced with the Regt. in 1718 and placed on half-pay.

Maurice Brackhill.*o*
Thomas Barton.*o*

---

¹ Called "Henry Doubleday" in the "Gradation List, 1728." Serving as Lieut. in Gore's Dragoons in 1730.
² See biog. notice on p. 106, note 4.
³ Second son of Matthew Ducie Moreton (created Baron Ducie) of Moreton, Staffs. This officer's full name was "Rowland Lewis Ducie Moreton." Capt. and Lt.-Col. 3rd Foot Guards 2 May 1739. Appointed Col. of the 6th Marines 22 Nov. 1739. D. in April, 1741, on board a transport in Carthagena harbour.
⁴ See p. 269, note 5.
⁵ Reduced with the Regt. in 1718. Drawing half-pay in 1739.

COLONEL RICHARD MOLESWORTH'S REGIMENT OF DRAGOONS.*

Daniel Gervais[1] to be Qr.-Mr. to Capt. De la Meloniere	London, 25 July, 1715.*a*
Joseph Gronous,[2] Esq. to be Capt. of that Troop whereof Major Ridley was late Capt. in Col. Molesworth's Regt. of Dragoons	St. James's, 8 Feb. 1718 *b*
George Malcolm,[3] Esq. to be Capt.-Lieut.	,, ,, ,, ,, *b*
Benjamin Harris[4] to be Lieut. to Capt. ——	,, ,, ,, ,, *b*
George Abell[5] to be Cornet to Captain [Richard] Thompson	,, 11 ,, ,, *b*
John Armfield[6] to be Cornet to Capt. La Meloniere	,, ,, ,, ,, *b*
Chris. Hargrave[7] to be Cornet to Capt. ——	Kensington, 20 May ,, *b*

Quarter-Masters reduced with the Regt. in 1718 and placed on half-pay.

William Bulkley.*o*
James Quiggen.*o*

---

* This corps was at the surrender of Preston in Nov. 1715.
[1] Reduced with the Regt. Drawing half-pay in 1739.
[2] Not in any subsequent List.
[3] Reduced with the Regt. Drawing half-pay in 1722.
[4] *Ibid.*   [5] *Ibid.*   [6] *Ibid.*
[7] *Ibid.*

COLONEL WM. STANHOPE'S REGIMENT OF DRAGOONS.*

John Hepburn¹ to be Surgeon	St. James's, 22 July, 1715.	*a*
Richard Gregson² to be Adjt.	,, ,, ,, ,,	*a*
Thos. Cummins to be Qr.-Mr. to Major Richard Manning	London, 5 Aug. ,,	*a*
Darby Murphy to be do. to Capt. Jas. Gardner (*sic*)	,, ,, ,, ,,	*a*
Daniel Gerritt³ (*sic*) to be do. to Capt. Jas. Deleuze	,, ,, ,, ,,	*a*
Wm. Forrest to be do. to Capt. David Martell	,, ,, ,, ,,	*a*
Wm. Wallis to be do. to the Colonel's own Troop	,, 19 ,, ,,	*a*
Fras. Gumbleton to be do. to Capt. ——	,, ,, ,, ,,	*a*
George Stanhope⁴ to be Cornet to the Colonel's Troop	St. James's, 23 June 1716.	*a*
John Leighton,⁵ Esq. to be Capt.-Lieut.	,, 14 Jan. 1718	*b*
George Armitage⁶ to be Cornet to that Troop whereof —— is Capt. in above Regt.	Hampton Ct. 2 Oct. ,,	*b*

Quarter-Master reduced with the Regt. in 1718 and placed on half-pay.

Wm. Stubbins.*o*

---

* Served at Preston in 1715. Sent to Scotland early in 1716.

¹ Surgeon to the Marquis de Montandre's Regt. of Foot 13 Dec. 1709. Half-pay 1718. Drawing half-pay in 1739.

² Resigned the Adjutancy 9 Oct. 1717. Drawing half-pay in 1722.

³ *Garrett.* Reduced with the Regt. Drawing half-pay in 1739.

⁴ Reduced with the Regt.

⁵ Do. Attained the rank of Lt.-Col. 28 Nov. 1739 and appointed to the 2nd Regt. of Marines. Drawing half-pay in 1749.

⁶ Reduced with the Regt.

OFFICERS OF THE ENGLISH TRAIN OF ARTILLERY.

MAY 13, 1715.g

CAPTAINS.

Edmund Williamson.
Wm. Bousfield.[1]

FIRST LIEUTS.

Ralph Wood.
George Bredenstein.

SECOND LIEUTS.

George Spencer.
Roger Colborne.

FIRE-WORKERS.

Zach. Smith.
Thos. Heydon.
James Finny.

ENGINEERS.

John Hanway.
Albert Borgard.[2]
Lewis Petitt.[3]
Thos. Lascelles.[4]
Wm. Horneck.

SUB-ENGINEERS.

Francis Hawkins.[5]
John Barker.
John Selioke.
Benjamin Withall.

GENTLEMEN OF THE ORDNANCE.

Chris. Briscoe.[6]
Wm. Holford.
John Palmer.
Thos. Musgrave.
Thos. White.
John Alderne.

---

[1] In 1689 this officer was appointed a Gunner to the Artillery detachment sent to the relief of Londonderry in the spring of this year. Served as a Bombardier in the Irish Train during the campaign of 1690-1 and was at the Boyne, Aughrim, sieges of Galway and Limerick. Fought at Landen as a 2nd Lieut. in the Flanders Train and was at the bombardment of Dieppe and Havre de Grace. Appointed Capt. in the Peace Train of 1698. Served at Ramillies and Oudenarde. Major, 1 Aug. 1719. Served at the attack and capture of Vigo same year. Appointed Major of the Royal Artillery in 1727. D. at Greenwich 4 Dec. 1736.

² See p. 284, note 1.
³ See p. 254, note 25.
⁴ Served at Blenheim, where he was wounded, and in subsequent campaigns in Flanders. Dep.-Qr.-Mr.-Gen. 22 Dec. 1712. Placed on half-pay as Capt. in Major-Gen. Owen Wynne's Regt. of Foot in 1713. Commissioner for demolishing the Dunkirk fortifications in Sept. 1713. Recd. £3 *per diem* whilst employed at Dunkirk. On the death of Major-Gen. Armstrong in 1742, Col. Lascelles was appointed Surv.-Gen. and Chief Engineer of Great Britain. Col. in the Army 13 March, 1743. Held his appointments until 1750, when he retired on account of his advanced age. D. in 1751 aged 81.—*Gentleman's Mag.*
⁵ Served as an Engineer officer at Blenheim and subsequently in Spain, Newfoundland, and Jamaica. Placed on half-pay as Major in 1715.
⁶ Gentleman of the Ordnance in the Peace Train of 1698. Served as Adjutant to the Train of Artillery at Blenheim. Was recommended by Brig. Blood for the command of the Artillery Train in Portugal (*War Office MS.*). Capt. of a Company of Artillery in Flanders, 1710. Capt. of do. at Gibraltar before 1717. Serving in last-named garrison in 1720.

LIEUT.-GENERAL ALBERT BORGARD.

ARTILLERY TRAIN FOR SERVICE IN SCOTLAND,
Nov. 1715.g *

COLONEL.
Albert Borgard.[1]

CAPTAINS.
Zach. Smith.
James Richards.

LIEUTS.
James Deal.
Godfry Franks.

GENTLEMEN OF THE ORDNANCE.
Jonathan Lewis.
Anthony Brown.

FIRE-WORKERS.
Thos. Bassett.
Abraham Carpenter.
John Melledge.
George Michaelson.

SURGEON.
John Pawlett.

ASSISTANT SURGEON.
Samuel Marshall.

COMMISSARY OF STORES AND PAYMASTER.
H. Hutcheson.

CLERK.
Joseph Burton.

CHIEF ENGINEER.
Lewis Petit.

---

* The King's Warrant to the Master-Gen. of the Ordnance for sending a Train to Scotland was signed 27 Nov. 1715 (*Cleaveland R.A. Notes*). Owing to stormy weather and adverse winds the English Train did not arrive at Leith until 26 Jan. 1716. Col. Borgard received orders "to send the vessells with the Artillery to a place called Innerkeithen till further orders and to march with all the officers and artillery people from Edinburgh to Stirling" (*Col. Borgard's Diary*). They found that Argyll had already obtained ten pieces of cannon and four mortars with their carriages and ammunition from Berwick. "I was ordered," writes Col. Borgard, "by his Grace to take upon me the command of fifteen pieces of cannon ordered from Edinburgh, &c. for field service, which [artillery] was in such confusion as cannot be expressed; part of which Artillery I brought so far as the town of Dundee, where I was ordered to bring the Train back again to Edinburgh by water." The Edinburgh Train which Borgard found in such a deplorable state of confusion was the "Scottish Artillery Train" (see p. 237). Argyll was in great need of gunners to work his own guns and those brought from Berwick (Dr. Campbell's *Life of Argyll*, p. 248). It appears that some of Borgard's gunners marched with Argyll's forces to Perth (*Ibid.*); also two or three of the officers belonging to the English Train, viz., Chief Engineer Petit, and Jonathan Lewis—Gentleman of the Ordnance—who was sent to Inver-

ness in the spring of 1716. As for the rest of the English Train, with guns and stores, Col. Borgard received orders in March, 1716, from General Cadogan, who had succeeded Argyll as C.-in-C. in Scotland, "to send the vessells with the Artillery back again to London [from Leith] and the Train people to march from thence." *Ibid.*

[1] This distinguished officer, the first Colonel Commandant of the Royal Regt. of Artillery, was a Dane by birth and belonged to an ancient family. The following summary of his war services and Commissions taken from Borgard's own *Diary*, is given in the last edition of Kane's *List of Officers of the Royal Regt. of Artillery, 1716-1899* :—

"BATTLES

Year	Place	Nation	Notes
1676	Oeland	Danish	Naval engagement in the Baltic.
"	Halmstadt	"	
"	Lund	"	
1677	Ronneburgh	"	
"	Odderval	"	
1678	Wittan	"	
1683	Vienna	Polish	
1685	Grau	Hungarian	
1688	Budjack	Polish	
1689	Nuys	Prussian	
1691	Salankamen	Hungarian	
1692	Steenkirk	British	
1693	Landen	"	
1705	Brozas	"	
1707	Almanza	"	
1710	Almanara	"	
"	Saragossa	"	Severely wounded in four places.
"	Villa Viciosa	"	do. in left leg.

"SIEGES.

Year	Place	Nation	Notes
1675	Wismar	Danish	
1676	Helsingborg	"	
"	Landskroom	"	
"	Christianstadt	"	
1677	Marstrand	"	
1685	Neuchausel	Hungarian	
1686	Buda	"	
1688	Kamince Podolsky	Polish	
1689	Keyserswaert	Prussian	
"	Bonn	"	
"	Mentz	"	
1692	Namur	French	
1694	Huy	British	
1695	Namur	"	
1702	Fort St. Catherine, Cadiz	"	
"	Fort Matagorda	"	
"	Fort Durand, Vigo	"	
1705	Valencia d'Alcantar	"	
1706	Ciudad Rodrigo	"	Left arm shattered.
"	Alcantara	"	Wounded in left breast.
1708	Fort St. Philip, Minorca	"	
1709	Villa Nova	"	
"	Balaguer	"	
1719	Vigo	"	

"Commissions and appointments held by Lieut.-Gen. Borgard, who d. 7 Feb. 1751, aged 92:—
Firemaster (Artillery) 1693, signed by Lord Sidney.
Capt. and Adjt. (Artillery) 1695, signed by Lord Romney.
Engineer, 27 March, 1698, signed by Lord Romney.
Commander of Allied Artillery in Spain and Portugal, 1703.
Chief Firemaster of England, 9 Aug. 1712, signed by Lord Rivers.
Assistant Surveyor of Ordnance, 25 April, 1718, signed by George I.
Brigadier-General, 1 March, 1726, signed by George I."

The Rt Honble Thomas Erle Esqr Lieutenant General of Her Majesty's Forces and Ordnance Governor of Portsmouth and One of Her Majesty's most Honble Privy Council &c.

ORDNANCE LIST.

8 March, 1715.g

John, Duke of Marlborough, Master-General.
Thomas Erle,[1] Esq., Lieut.-General of the Ordnance.
Wm. Bridges,[2] Esq., Surveyor-General.
Chris. Musgrave,[3] Esq., Clerk.
Dixie Windsor,[4] Esq., Keeper of his Majesty's Stores of Ordnance.
Richard King,[5] Esq., Clerk of the Deliveries of Ordnance Stores.
Chas. Eversfield,[6] Esq., Treasurer and Paymaster.
James Craggs,[7] Esq., Secretary.
Col. Michael Richards,[8] Chief Engineer.
Talbot Edwards,[9] 2nd Engineer.
Col. Christian Lilly,[10] 3rd do.
Peter Carle and James Moore, Esqs., to travel into foreign parts, perfect themselves in the art of fortifications and mathematicks as may render them capable to serve his Majesty as Engineers, at £100 each per annum.
Thos. Phillips. Esq., Engineer.
Col. James Pendlebury, Master-Gunner of Great Britain, to exercise scholars to shoot in great ordnance at £190 per annum.
Richard Leake ⎱
Wm. Bousfield ⎬ Mates to the Master-Gunner at £45 10s. per annum each.
John Baxter ⎰
Major Jonas Watson,[11] Bombardier, at £13 8s. 4d. per annum.
Col. H. Hopke,[12] Comptroller of Fireworks.
Col. Albert Borgard, Chief Firemaster.
John Baxter, mate to Col. Borgard.
Capt. Chas. Ball, Waggon-Master.

---

[1] Second son of Thomas Erle and grandson of Sir Walter Erle, Knt., a distinguished Cavalier officer. Held the rank of Major in the Dorsetshire Militia at the Revolution and was one of the first officers to join the Prince of Orange. Served at the Boyne and at the first siege of Limerick. Col. of a Regt. (19th Foot) 1 Jan. 1691. Greatly distinguished himself at the battle of Aughrim, where he was twice taken prisoner, but was rescued by his own men. Fought at Steinkirk and at Landen. At latter battle he left a sick bed in order to take part in the engagement, and was wounded. Brig.-Gen. 22 March, 1693. Gov. of Portsmouth, 1 July, 1694. Major-Gen. 1 June, 1696. Lt.-Gen. 11 Feb. 1703. Commanded a division at the Battle of Almanza. Commanded an expedition against the coast of France in 1708 (Comn. as C.-in-C. dated 25 June, 1708). Sold the Colonelcy of his Regt. to Col. George Freake 23 March, 1709. Promoted General 31 Jan. 1711. Recommissioned Gov. of Portsmouth by George I and appointed Gen. of the Foot. Md. Elizabeth, 2nd dau. of Sir Wm. Wyndham, and d. at his seat at Charborough, Dorset, 23 July, 1720. Bd. in Charborough Church, where is a monument thus inscribed:—

> "In this vault are interred the remains of THOMAS ERLE, General and commanding of the Foot, and one of the Lords Justices in Ireland, Governor of Portsmouth and Lieut.-General of the Ordnance, and one of the Privy Council in England. He raised a Regiment in this County at the Revolution which he carried over to Ireland with him. And they signalized themselves both at the Battle of the Boyne and Aughrim and afterwards served with great honour both in Flanders and Spain (sic) during the reign of Queen Anne. He died in the year 1720."

² Succeeded by Brigdr. Michael Richards in 1715.
³ Succeeded by Edward Ashe in 1715.
⁴ Brother to Visct. Montjoy (so created).   D. 20 Oct. 1743.
⁵ Col. Richard King, the Engineer officer of this name.   D. in 1767.
⁶ Succeeded by Lt.-Gen. Harry Mordaunt in 1715.
⁷ See biog. notice on p. 253, note 6.
⁸ See biog. notice on p. 73, note 4.
⁹ Appointed 2nd Engineer of England in 1710.   D. at the Tower in 1719.
¹⁰ D. a Brig.-Gen. in Jamaica, 1738.
¹¹ Killed at the siege of Carthagena in 1741.
¹² *Hopkey*. D. in 1734 as Brig.-Gen.

TWO COMPANIES OF ARTILLERY.

Raised by Royal Warrant 26 May, 1716.*

[ROYAL REGIMENT OF ARTILLERY.]

1st COMPANY.

James Richards,[1] Capt.
Thomas Hughes,[2] 1st Lieut.
George Aikenhead,[3] 2nd Lieut.
Joseph Egerton,[4] 3rd Lieut. } Lieut.
Jonathan Lewis,[5] 4th Lieut. } Fire-workers.
3 Sergeants.
3 Corporals.
3 Bombardiers.
30 Gunners.
50 Mattrosses.

2nd COMPANY.

Thomas Pattison,[6] Capt.
Thomas Holman,[7] 1st Lieut.
James Deal,[8] 2nd Lieut.
John Roope,[9] 3rd Lieut. } Lieut.
John Brooks,[10] 4th Lieut. } Fire-workers.
3 Sergeants.
3 Corporals.
3 Bombardiers.
30 Gunners.
50 Mattrosses.

---

* The King's Warrant and the Establishment for the two Companies of Artillery are printed in *Notes on the Early History of the Royal Regt. of Artillery* by Col. Cleaveland.

[1] Served as Adjt. to the Artillery Train at Almenara, Saragossa, and Villa Viciosa in 1710.

[2] Was a Fire-worker on board one of the bomb vessels in the Cadiz expedition of 1702. Capt. 10 Dec. 1718. Served at Gibraltar during the siege of 1727. D. in 1737.

[3] Believed to have served with the Artillery Train in Flanders, 1709. Gentleman of the Ordnance, 1710. Half-pay as Qr.-Mr. to the Flanders Train, 1715. 1st Lieut. 10 Dec. 1718. D. in 1730.

[4] 2nd Lieut. 10 Dec. 1718. This appointment was for the Port Mahon establishment.—Kane's *R.A. List*, p. 1.

[5] Served at Saragossa and Villa Viciosa as a Gentleman of the Ordnance. Sent to Scotland with Col. Borgard's Train in Dec. 1715, and was detached on service at Inverness in 1716. 2nd Lieut. 30 Dec. 1718. Went with the expedition to Vigo in 1719. 1st Lieut. 24 Nov. 1719. Capt.-Lieut. 1 April, 1725. Capt. 1 Feb. 1734. Major 1 Sept. 1741. Succeeded to the command of the R.A. before Carthagena in 1741, on the death of Col. Watson, and "appointed himself a Lt.-Col. until the pleasure of his Majesty was known." 2nd in command of the R.A. in Flanders in 1744. Served at Fontenoy. Retd. on full pay in Jan. 1748. D. in 1751.

[6] An Artillery Cadet in 1706. Gentleman of the Ordnance in Spain 1708–1710. At the capture of Minorca, 1708, and at the siege of Balaguer and Villa Nova in 1709. Served the campaign of 1710 in Spain. Half-pay as Capt. in 1714. Major R.A. 1 Jan. 1737. Lt.-Col. 18 May, 1742. Served in Minorca 1725–1738. Commanded the R.A. at Dettingen and Fontenoy. Retd. full pay 9 March, 1748. D. in 1753.—Kane's *R.A. List*.

[7] Gunner in 1680. Master-Gunner of the Artillery detachment sent to the relief of Londonderry in May, 1689. 2nd Lieut. of the Flanders Train in 1693. Served several

campaigns under William III. 1st Lieut. of the Peace Train in 1698. Served at Blenheim as a Fire-worker. Half-pay in 1715. Capt.-Lieut. 1 Oct. 1721. Killed at the defence of Gibraltar, 5 March, 1721.

[8] Bridge-Master to the Artillery Train in Flanders about 1709. 1st Lieut. 24 Nov. 1719. Capt.-Lieut. 1 Oct. 1721. Capt. 1 April, 1725. " Superanuated, living with rank of Lt.-Col. in 1748."—Kane's *R.A. List*.

[9] Sent out to Newfoundland as an Engineer about 1704. Took an active part in the defence of St. John's. Taken prisoner by the French in 1705. His account of the taking of St. John's is extant and has been printed in Prowse's *History of Newfoundland*, 2nd Edit., pp. 263–264. Served subsequently as a Gentleman of the Ordnance to the Artillery Train in Spain, and was granted half-pay as Lieut. in 1714. D. in 1719.

[10] 2nd Lieut. 30 Dec. 1718. " This appointment was for Port Mahon " (Kane's *R.A. List*). Further services untraced.

THE FIRST REGIMENT OF FOOT GUARDS.

[THE GRENADIER GUARDS.]

Joseph Palmer[1] to be Ens. to Capt. Fras. Fuller	St. James's, 13 April 1715.	*a*
Francis Brerewood[2] to be do. to Capt. Chas. Frampton	,, 6 Mar. ,,	*a*
Richard Waller[3] to be do. to Col. Talbot's Company	Hampton Ct. 1 Aug. ,,	*a*
John Bickerstaff,[4] Esq. to be Lieut. of Major-Gen. Wm. Tatton's Company and to rank as Capt.	St. James's, 10 Dec. 1717.	*b*
Jonathan Hoo Keate[5] to be Ens. to Col. Reade's Company	,, ,, ,, ,,	*b*
Charles Calvert,[6] Esq. to be Lieut. to Lt.-Col. Wm. Blakeney and to rank as Capt.	,, 4 Jan. 1718.	*b*
Timothy Gully,[7] Esq. to be do. to Lt.-Col. Hastings and to rank as Capt.	,, 5 ,, ,,	*b*
Edward Carr[8] to be Ens. to above Company	,, 22 ,, ,,	*b*
John Hoare (*sic*), Esq.[9] to be Capt. in the room of Lt.-Col. Wentworth and to rank as Lt.-Col.	,, 10 Feb. ,,	*b*
Henry Jansen[10] to be Ens. to Lt.-Col. Howe and to rank as Capt.	,, 13 Mar. ,,	*b*
John Montagu, Esq. to be Capt. in the room of Lt.-Col. Ferrers and to rank as Lt.-Col.	,, ,, ,, ,,	*b*
Francis Henry Lee,[11] Esq. to be Capt. of the Grenadier Company whereof Lord James Murray was late Capt. in Our 1st Foot Guards and to rank as Lt.-Col.	,, 24 ,, ,,	*b*
Richard Peirson,[12] Esq. to be Capt. in the room of Lt.-Col. Wm. Blakeney and to rank as Lt.-Col.	,, 3 Apr. ,,	*b*
Sir John Buckworth,[13] Bt. to be Lieut. to Lt.-Col. Pitt and to rank as Capt.	Kensington, 25 ,, ,,	*b*
Henry Metford to be Ens. to Lt.-Col. Lee	,, 12 June ,,	*b*
John Rawlinson, Esq., to be Lieut. to Lt.-Col. Gerrard and to rank as Capt.	,, 23 July ,,	*b*
Edward Carr,[8] Esq. to be Lieut. to Lt.-Col. John Duncombe and to rank as Capt.	St. James's, 19 Dec. ,,	*b*
Charles Dobson to be Ens. to Lt.-Col. Ferd. Richard Hastings	,, ,, ,, ,,	*b*
Gideon Harvey,[14] Esq. to be Lieut. to Lt.-Col. Philip Anstruther	,, 13 Jan. 1719.	*b*

[1] Out of the Regt. before 1727.
[2] Do.
[3] Do.
[4] Ens. in above Regt. 1 Nov. 1716. Out before 1727.

[5] Out of the Regt. before 1727. 2nd son of Sir Gilbert Hoo Keate, Bt.

[6] Out of the Regt. before 1727.

[7] Comn. renewed by George II. D. in 1731.

[8] Lieut. and Capt. 19 Dec. 1718. Capt. and Lt.-Col. 7 Feb. 1741. Second Major, 27 April, 1749. First Major in 1753. Lt.-Col. of 1st Foot Guards, 30 Sept. 1758. Col. 50th Foot, 5 May, 1760. D. a Lt.-Gen. in Sept. 1764.

[9] Called Howe in "Nominal Roll of Officers" given in Sir W Hamilton's *Hist. of the Grenadier Guards.* Out of the Regt. before 1727.

[10] Lieut. and Capt. 12 May, 1720. Serving in 1730.

[11] Appointed Ens. in the Queen's Regt. (4th Foot)— 8 April, 1712. Serving as Capt. and Lt.-Col. in the 1st Foot Guards in 1728.

[12] *Pierson.* Appointed Ens. in the 1st Foot Guards, 10 March, 1702. Wounded at Schellenberg (*Records*). Lieut. and Capt. 22 June, 1709. Served throughout Marlborough's campaigns. Capt. in the Rl. Fusiliers 30 March, 1711. Retd. 22 April, 1742. D. 3 Jan. 1743, at York, and left directions that his body should lie in state 40 days! *Gentlemen's Mag.*

[13] Son of Sir John Buckworth, Bt. of Sheen, Surrey. Left the Guards before 1727. D. 3 Jan. 1759, aged 54, and was bd. in the dormitory of Eton College Chapel.

[14] Killed at Fontenoy, where he served as Lieut. and Capt. in above Regt.

COLDSTREAM GUARDS.

Lord Hinchinbrook[1] to be Capt. and to rank as Lt.-Col.	St. James's	11 June 1715.	a
Nathaniel Blakiston[2] to be Ens. to Col. Smith	„	20 July „	a
Henry Pulteney,[3] Esq., to be Capt. of a company added to the Coldstream Guards and to rank as Lt.-Col.	„	22 „ „	a
Sir Harry Heron,[4] Bt. to be Ens. to Lt.-Col. Pulteney	„	28 „ „	a
John Price[5] to be Ens. to Lt.-Col. Wm. Leigh	„	15 „ „	a
Edward Rich[6] to be Ens. to the Colonel's Company	„	19 „ 1717.	b
Wm. Lord Bury[7] to be Capt. [of Grenadiers] in the room of John Haske and to rank as Lt.-Col.	Hampton Ct.	25 Aug. „	b
George Furness[8] to be Ens. to Lt.-Col. George Churchill	St. James's,	19 Dec. „	b
Wm. Hanmer,[9] Esq. to be Capt. of that Company whereof Lord Henry Herbert was late Capt. and to rank as Lt.-Col.	„	20 „ „	b
Henry Vachell[10] to be Ens. to the Colonel's Company	„	3 Jan. 1718.	b
George Chudleigh,[11] Esq. to be Capt. in room of Lt.-Col. Fitzmaurice and to rank as Lt.-Col.	„	„ „ „	b
Wm. Caesar Strang,[12] Esq. to be Lieut. to Lt.-Col. Adolphus Oughton and to rank as Capt.	„	1 Feb. „	b
Thos. Hockenhull[13] to be Ens. to Lt.-Col. Cope in Our 2nd Regt. of Foot Guards commanded by Lord Cadogan	„	24 Mar. „	b
Robert Williamson[14] to be Ens. to Lt.-Col. John Chudleigh	Kensington,	15 May „	b

[1] See list of Evans's Dragoons, under "Regts. on the Irish Establishment, 1715," note 3.
[2] Ens. 20 July, 1715. Resigned in Feb. 1723. *Records.*
[3] From 2nd Foot Guards. Had served at Almanza, where he was taken prisoner. 2nd son of Col. Wm. Pulteney and younger brother of Wm. Earl of Bath. Col. 13th Foot, 5 July, 1739. Attained the rank of General, 22 Feb. 1765. D. 28 Oct. 1767. Bd. in Westminster Abbey.
[4] See p. 219, note 22.
[5] "Dead in Nov. 1720." *Records.*
[6] Out 3 Jan. 1718. Served previously as Cornet in Col. Newton's Dragoons.
[7] Succeeded as 2nd Earl of Albemarle, 30 May, 1718. K.G.; A.D.C. to the King, 31 March, 1727. Col. 29th Foot, 1731-3. Transferred to 3rd Troop of Horse Guards, 8 May, 1733-4. Served at Dettingen. Lieut. and Gov.-Gen. of Virginia in Sept. 1737. Returned to the Coldstream Guards as Col. 5 Oct. 1744. Wounded at Fontenoy. Fought at Culloden. D. at Paris, 22 Dec. 1754. Mackinnon's *Coldstream Guards*, p. 477.
[8] Lieut. and Capt. 25 Nov. 1720. Capt. in 2nd Regt. of Horse, 11 Sept. 1721. Serving as senior Capt. in 1740. D. 1741.

[9] Scion of the old Flintshire family of this name. Appointed Lieut. of Grenadiers in above Regt. 13 May, 1709. Served at Malplaquet on 10 May, 1717. He recd. £155 odd (in addition to the £100 before paid him) " to recompense his own care, and trouble, and expence in conducting Count Gyllenberg to the Castle of Plymouth and returning from thence" (*Treasury Accounts—Revenue Quarterly*). On 25 Dec. 1740 Lt.-Col. Hanmer was appointed Col. of a newly-raised Regt of Marines. D. in Sept. 1741.

[10] " Dead in Oct. 1732." *Records.*

[11] Ens. 1st Foot Guards, 8 March, 1703. Wounded at Malplaquet. Lieut. and Capt. in 1716. D. 4 Sept. 1739 leaving a son John, who succeeded as 6th Bart. of Ashton, Co. Devon.

[12] Ens. 5 Dec. 1715. "Resigned in May, 1723." *Records.*

[13] "Dead in Oct. 1732." *Ibid.*

[14] Lieut. and Capt. 10 April, 1733. "Promoted to Capt. of a Company of Invalids at Plymouth, 5 March, 1746." *Ibid.*

THE THIRD FOOT GUARDS

[THE SCOTS GUARDS.]

Andrew Hamilton,[1] Esq. to be Lieut. to Lt.-Col. —— and to rank as Capt. of Foot - - - - - - -	St. James's,	12 Jan.	1718.	b
—— Hume,[2] to be Ens. to Lt.-Col. —— -	,,	15	,,	b
[George] Whitmore,[3] Esq. to be Capt. in the room of Lt.-Col. Coote, and to rank as Lt.-Col. - - - -	,,	5 Apr.	,,	b
Charles Ingram[4] to be Ens. to Lord Fred Howard - - - - - -	,,	16 ,,	,,	b
Henry Bennett[5] to be Ens. to Capt. ——	Kensington,	25 ,,	,,	b
Wm. Lister,[6] Esq. to be Lieut. to Lt.-Col. —— and to rank as Capt. - - -	,,	,, ,,	,,	b
Edward Mathews[7] to be Ens. to Lt.-Col. Toby Cramer - - - - -	,,	9 July	,,	b
John Braithwaite[8] to be Ens. to Lt.-Col. James Gee - - - - -	Hampton Court,	19 Aug.	,,	b
Henry Skelton,[9] Esq. to be Capt. in the room of Lord Jedburgh, and to rank as Lt.-Col. - - - - -	St. James's,	4 Nov.	,,	b

[1] Served previously as 2nd Adjt. Out of the Regt. before 1727.

[2] Untraced.

[3] See biog. notice on p. 180, note 2.

[4] Promoted Capt. and Lt.-Col. 5 July, 1737. Major and Col. 3 Apr. 1743. Adjt.-Gen. in England. D. in 1748. *Gentleman's Mag.*

[5] Not in any subsequent List.

[6] Ensign 2 May, 1717. Capt. and Lt.-Col. 4 May, 1740. Serving in 1746. D. at Twickenham in 1774. *Gentleman's Mag.*

[7] Out before 1727.

[8] Belonged to the old Westmorland family of this name. Born in 1696. Became "Governor of the African Company's factories on the south coast of Africa, and was killed on board the Baltic merchantman in an engagement off Sicily in 1740 with a Spanish privateer" (Burke's *Extinct Baronetage*). His only son, a Major-General in the Army, was created a Bart. in 1802.

[9] Of Braithwaite Hall, Westmorland. Appointed Capt. in Brigadier George Maccartney's Regt. of Foot, 20 Dec. 1708. Wounded at the siege of Douay in 1710. Half-pay in 1713. Capt. of Invalids at Portsmouth, in 1714. Capt. in Col. Thos. Chudleigh's Regt. of Foot in 1715. Sold his Cy. on being appointed to the 3rd Foot Guards. Major and Col. last-named corps 21 Aug. 1739. Col. of 12th Foot, 28 May, 1745. Served at Fontenoy. Maj.-Gen. 1 June, 1745. Lt.-Gen. 18 Sept. 1747. His life is said to have been preserved in Flanders by his A.D.C., Capt. James Jones of the 3rd Foot Guards, to whom General Skelton left the bulk of his property (Carter's *Historical Records of the Cameronians*). D. in Apr. 1757.

THE ROYAL [SCOTS] REGIMENT OF FOOT.

Regt. sent to Ireland in March, 1715.

Wm. Rawlins[1] to be Quarter-Master	St. James's, 23 Aug. 1714.	*a*
Wm. Crawford[2] to be Ens. to Capt. James Hamilton	,, 22 Oct. ,,	*a*
Isaac Hamon[3] to be Capt.	,, 19 July 1715.	*a*
Paul Rycaut[4] to be Lieut. to Capt. Wm. Brisbane	,, 1 Oct. ,,	*a*
John Holborne[5] to be Ens. in room of Lord George Murray	28 Nov. ,,	*a*
Alex. Brodie[6] to be Ens. to Capt. Wm. Brisbane	11 Feb. 171$\frac{5}{6}$.	*a*
[Edwd.] Momby[7] to be Lieut. to Lord Cumberland (*sic*)	11 June 1716.	*i*
Robert Gawne[8] to be Lieut. to Capt. Robt. Hamilton	,, ,, ,,	*i*
Gilbert Browne[9] to be Adjt.	15 ,, ,,	*i*
John McQueen,[10] Esq., to be Capt. in room of Wm. Melvin (*sic*), decd.	25 Jan. 171$\frac{6}{7}$.	*j*
Claud Fraser[11] to be Ens. to Lord Edward Murray in room of George Johnston	21 Nov. 1717.	*j*
Chas. Cockburne,[12] Esq., to be 1st Lt.-Colonel and Capt. of a Cy.	30 Mar. 1718	
Lord James Murray[13] to be 2nd Lt.-Colonel in room of Sir James Abercrombie [and Capt. of a Cy.]	31 ,, ,,	*j*
James Hamilton,[14] Esq. to be Capt. in room of James Ballendine	6 June ,,	*j*
James Home,[15] Esq. to be Major and Capt. of a Cy. in the room of James Cunningham	1 Sept. ,,	*j*
John Ramsay,[16] Esq. to be Capt. in room of James Home	,, ,, ,,	*j*

[1] The date of this officer's commission proves that it was signed by the Lords Justices as the King did not arrive in England until Sept. A certain Wm. Rawlings was on half-pay in 1722.

[2] Promoted Lieut. 4 Apr. 1734. Serving in Ireland in 1740.

[3] Appointed 2nd Lieut. in the Royal Scots Fusiliers, 1 May, 1709. Served at Malplaquet. Major of the Royal Regt. of Foot, 10 July, 1737. Lt.-Col. Queen's Regt. of Foot, 1 April, 1743. Out of said Regt. in 1746. The will of a certain Isaac Hamon was proved at Dublin in 1755.

[4] Capt. 2 March, 1719. Serving in Ireland in 1740 as senior Capt. in above Regt.

[5] Scion of the Menstrie family. Appointment not forthcoming in any of the Commission Entry Books, but given in a Scottish Gazette and communicated by the Duke of Atholl in a letter to Mr. Dalton dated 24 July, 1904. John Holborne appears as an Ensign in Lord Orkney's Regt. in the MS. *Gradation List*, 1730, at the Public Record Office; but the date of his Ensigncy is given therein as "1 Oct. 1715."

[6] Not in any subsequent List of this Regt.

[7] Serving as Lieut. in Ireland in 1736.

[8] Capt. 14 Aug. 1738. Serving in 1740. This officer joined the Royal Scots (2nd Batt.), 4 April, 1707, and served several campaigns in Flanders.

[9] Untraced.

[10] Appointed Ens. in above Regt. 22 May, 1694. Lieut. 23 June, 1704. Wounded at Schellenberg. Served several subsequent campaigns under Marlborough. Serving as Capt. in Ireland in 1736. Out before 1740.

¹¹ Lieut. 11 July, 1722. Serving in 1740. His will as "Claud Fraser of Gracedieu, Liberty of Waterford, Esq.," was proved at Dublin in 1749.
¹² See p. 134, note 3.
¹³ See p.127, note 11.
¹⁴ Joined the 2nd Batt. of the Royal Scots, 1 Sept. 1708, and served with same in Flanders. Untraced after 1718.
¹⁵ See p. 134, note 6.
¹⁶ Probably the John Ramsay appointed Ens. to the Indep. Cy. in Edinburgh Castle, in 1712. Major of the Royal Scots, 14 Aug. 1738. Lt.-Col. 12 March, 1742. Serving in 1749. Out before 1753.

THE PRINCESS OF WALES'S OWN REGIMENT OF FOOT.

[2ND FOOT,—THE QUEEN'S REGIMENT.]

John Arnot¹ to be Ens. to Capt. Edward Daniell's Company in Our Most Dear Daughter Wilhelmina Carolina, Princess of Wales's Own Regt. of Foot commanded by Col. Piercy Kirke	St. James's, 26 Sept. 1715.	a
Edmund Wiseman² to be Ens. to Capt. Fitzgerald	„ 14 Feb. 1717.	b
Wm. Hickman³ to be Ens. to Col. John Arnot	Kensington, 3 July 1718.	b
Benjamin Rudyard,⁴ Esq., to be Capt.	St. James's, 26 Sept. „	b

¹ Capt. Lieut. 7 Nov. 1739. Capt. in Col. Laforey's Marines about 1747. Son of Sir John Arnot, Adjt.-General of Scotland, who was sometime Lt.-Col. of above Regt. (See p. 136, note 2). Capt. Arnot took up the title of Bart. after his father's death in 1750.
² Son of Sir Edmund Wiseman, Knt. Serving as Ens. in General Whetham's Regt. (12th Foot), in 1730. D. in 1741. Burke's *Baronetage*.
³ Capt.-Lieut. of Gen. Sabine's Regt. of Welsh Fusiliers, 22 Dec. 1722. Capt. 23 March, 1731. Served at Fontenoy, and was wounded. Lt.-Col. of above Regt. 16 Feb. 1748.
⁴ From Capt. half-pay. Major, 27 July, 1745. Serving in 1749.

THE EARL OF FORFAR'S REGIMENT OF FOOT.*

[3RD FOOT,—THE BUFFS.]

Francis Williamson,[1] Esq. to be Major of the Earl of Forfar's Regt. of Foot, and Capt. of a Company - - - - St. James's, 25 July 1715.*a*
"This gentleman receives only Captain's pay."
Alex. Rose,[2] Esq. to be Lt.-Colonel of aforesaid Regt. and Capt. of a Company - St. James's, 25 July 1715.*a*
"And this gentleman only Major's pay."
James Bolton,[3] Esq. to be Captain [of an additional Company] - - - - St. James's, 24 Aug. 1715,*a*
George Grant,[4] Esq. to be do. [of an additional Company] - - - - ,, ,, ,, ,, *a*
Henry Wilson to be Lieut. to Capt. James Bolton - - - - - - ,, ,, ,, ,, *a*
Abraham Lamb to be do. to Capt. George Grant - - - - - - ,, ,, ,, ,, *a*
John Haywood to be Ens. to Capt. James Bolton - - - - - - ,, ,, ,, ,, *a*
Samuel Stone to be do. to Capt. George Grant ,, ,, ,, ,, *a*
Charles Slezer[5] to be Qr.-Mr. to above Regt. ,, ,, ,, ,, *a*
Wm. Smith to be Ens. to Capt. Thos. White in Lt.-General Charles Wills's Regt. of Foot - - - - - - - ,, 25 Apr. 1717.*b*
Nathaniel Smith[6] to be Qr.-Mr. - - - ,, 28 Jan. 1718.*b*
Wm. Pownell (*sic*),[7] Esq. to be Capt.-Lieut. - ,, 5 Mar. ,, *b*
Edmund Quarles[8] to be Lieut. to Capt. John Grievson - - - - - - - ,, 9 Jan. 1719.*b*

---

* Served at Sheriffmuir.

[1] See p. 138, note 3.

[2] See p. 138, note 2.

[3] Appointed Ens. in above Regt. 14 Sept. 1693. Fought at Blenheim, where he was wounded. Lieut. 25 Aug. 1704. Served in several campaigns under Marlborough. Capt. 16 June, 1719. Half-pay, 1713. Serving as Capt. in 1730. Out before 1740.

[4] Capt. in Col. Alex. Grant's Regt. of Scots Foot, 18 Aug. 1707. Capt. in Col. John Selwyn's Regt. 18 March, 1711. Half-pay, 1713. Serving as Capt. in Col. Harrison's Regt. (15th Foot) in 1730. Capt. of an Independent Cy. in the Highlands, 24 March, 1733. Major of the Black Watch, 25 Oct. 1739. Was for a time Gov. of Fort St. George. 3rd surviving son of Ludovic Grant, of Grant. D. 1755. *Gentleman's Mag.*

[5] Appointed Ens. in the 2nd Batt. Royal Scots, 1 Sept. 1708. Believed to have served at Malplaquet. Second son of Capt. John Slezer of the Artillery Company in Scotland. See biog. notice of this family in *English Army Lists and Commission Registers*, 1661–1714, Vol. V. p. 227, note 2.

[6] Promoted Lieut. in above Regt. 9 Nov. 1723. Serving in 1730. Out before 1740. D. as Lt.-Gov. of Chelsea Hospital in 1773. *Gentleman's Mag.*

[7] Wm. Pownall of Barnton, in Cheshire, to which property he succeeded on the death of his father Thomas Pownall. He d. 1731. Burke's *Commoners.*

[8] Second Lieut. in Brigadier Wills's Marines, 21 Nov. 1707. Half-pay, 1713. Re-commissioned 2nd Lieut. in Wills's Regt. of Foot, 25 March, 1715. First Lieut. of Grenadiers in Stanwix's Foot, 14 Aug. 1717. Capt.-Lieut. in the Earl of Londonderry's Regt. of Foot, 5 Nov. 1736. D. about 1742.

THE KING'S OWN REGIMENT OF FOOT.

[4TH FOOT,—THE KING'S OWN ROYAL LANCASTER REGIMENT.]

Thos. Goddard,[1] Esq. to be Capt. of a Company [added to above Regt.]	St. James's,	26 Sept. 1715.	*a*
Magnus Kempenfelt[2] to be Ens. to Capt. James Duff	,,	,, ,,	,, *c*
Richard Purchass[3] to be Qr.-Mr.	,,	25 Dec.	,, *a*
Henry Berkeley,[4] Esq. to be Colonel of the Regt. of Foot whereof Lt.-General Wm. Seymour was late Colonel, and to be Capt. of a Company.	,,	,, ,,	,, *a*
John Mercer,[5] to be Ens. to Capt. —— Vachell	,,	27 Jan. 1718.	*b*
Sir Charles Mylne,[6] Knt. to be Capt. of that Company whereof Jas. Duff was late Capt.	,,	1 Apr. ,,	*b*
Joseph Richardson[7] to be Ens. to Capt.——	,,	5 ,, ,,	*b*
John Trelawny,[8] Esq. to be Capt. in the room of Thos. Vachell	Hampton Court,	28 Aug. ,,	*b*
Charles Jackson,[9] to be Lieut. to Capt. Dumaresq	,,	,, ,,	,, *b*
James Monteith,[10] to be Ens. to Capt. James Farrell	,,	,, ,,	,, *b*

[1] Second Lieut. in above Regt. 20 June, 1704. 1st Lieut. 2 Jan. 1706. Held the post of Qr.-Mr. previous to Jan. 1708. Capt. before 1714, in which year his name appears on the half-pay list. D. at Portsmouth, 1732. *Gentleman's Mag.*

[2] See p. 140, note 2.

[3] See p. 141, note 5.

[4] See p. 131, note 3.

[5] Cornet in the Royal Regt. of Horse Guards, 22 April, 1727. Lieut. 9 July, 1739. Serving in 1740.

[6] Second Lieut. in the Scots Foot Guards, 18 June, 1705. Serving in Lord Cadogan's Regt. (4th Foot), in 1728. Out before 1740.

[7] Serving in above Regt. with same rank, in 1728. Out before 1740.

[8] Adjt. 2 May, 1712. Serving as Capt. in above Regt. in 1728. Out before 1740.

[9] Out of Regt. before 1728.

[10] Do.

MAJOR-GENERAL THOMAS PEARCE'S REGIMENT OF FOOT.*

[5TH FOOT,—NORTHUMBERLAND FUSILIERS.]

Charles Vachell to be Ens. to Capt. Chas. Pearce	St. James's, 3 Jan. 1718.	b
Patrick McAva to be do. to Capt. Henry Owen	,, 18 Mar. ,,	b
Mathew Rathbone to be do. to Capt. ——	Kensington, 9 June ,,	b
Wm. Ellis to be Surgeon	Hampton Ct., 2 Oct. ,,	b
Ralph Urwin to be Ens. to Capt. Henry Owen	,, ,, ,, ,,	b
—— Bullock to be do. to Capt. ——	St. James's, 1 Nov. ,,	b
Augustus Earle to be Lieut. to Col. Peter Godby	,, ,, ,, ,,	b
Henry Collopp to be do. to Capt. Wm. Vachell	,, 15 ,, ,,	b

* Pearce's Regt. went to Gibraltar in 1712 and remained there fifteen years. On their return home, in 1728, Pearce's were sent to Ireland, and of the eight officers named above only two, viz. Ralph Urwin (promoted Lieut. 24 Nov. 1722) and Surgeon Ellis returned with this Regt.

THE ROYAL FUSILIERS.*

[7TH FOOT,—ROYAL FUSILIERS.]

Joseph Dambon to be [2nd] Lieut. to Capt. Piers Griffiths	St. James's, 11 Jan. 1715.	b
Abraham Meure to be Lieut. to Capt. ——	Kensington, 19 Apr. 1718.	b
Bryan Janson to be Lieut. to Captain Stephen Petitot	,, 15 May ,,	b
Jeffrey Gibbons, Esq. to be Capt. in the room of Richard Peirson	,, ,, ,, ,,	b
John Bradshaw, Esq. to be Capt.-Lieut.	,, ,, ,, ,,	b
Guy Johnson to be [1st] Lieut. to the Company of Grenadiers whereof —— is Capt.	Hampton Ct., 9 Aug. ,,	b
John Perier to be [2nd ?] Lieut. to Capt. Robt. Cunningham in room of Henry Crofton	,, 6 Feb. 1718-9.	j

* Serving in Minorca on the accession of George I. In the summer of 1718 embarked on board Admiral Byng's fleet as Marines and sailed for Sicily to co-operate with the Imperial forces against the Spaniards. Believed to have served on board Byng's fleet in the naval battle off Messina. Returned home in May, 1719. None of the seven officers named above were serving in the Royal Fusiliers in 1728.

BRIGADIER-GENERAL HENRY GROVE'S REGIMENT OF FOOT.*

[10TH FOOT,—LINCOLNSHIRE REGIMENT].

John Wharton to be Lieut. to Capt. Henry Poilblanc - - - - - -	St. James's, 28 Dec. 1717.	b
Alex. Boisragon to be Ens. to Capt. Jeffrey Prendergast - - - - - -	,, ,, ,, ,,	b
Goodwin Moreton to be Lieut. to Capt. ——	,, 4 Jan. 1718.	b
Giles Peacock, Esq. to be Capt. of that Company whereof Jeffrey Prendergast was late Capt. - - - - -	,, 28 Feb. ,,	b
Wilmot Vaughan to be Ensign to Captain [Col.] Columbine - - - - -	,, 5 Mar. ,,	b
Charles Beaumont to be Qr.-Mr. - - -	,, 3 Apr. ,,	b
John Trepsack to be Chaplain - - -	,, 12 Nov. ,,	b

* At the Peace of Utrecht this corps remained in Flanders and was quartered at Ghent and Nieuport till after the Barrier Treaty was concluded, late in 1715, when it returned home. Only two of the officers named above were serving in same corps in 1728, viz. Goodwin Moreton and Alex. Boisragon. Moreton was promoted Capt. 7 Nov. 1739. Boisragon was still an Ensign in 1728 and out of the Regt. before 1740.

MAJOR-GENERAL JOHN HILL'S REGIMENT OF FOOT.*

[11TH FOOT,—DEVONSHIRE REGIMENT.]

Thos. Goddard[1] to be Ens. to Major Ervin (*sic*)	St. James's, 14 June 1715.	*a*
Richard Tracey (*sic*),[2] Esq. to be Capt. in the room of Thos. Harrison	,, 24 ,, ,,	*a*
[Edward Montague,[3] Esq. to be Colonel in the room of Major-Gen. John Hill	,, 13 July ,,	]
Henry Domergue,[4] Esq. to be Capt. [of an additional Company]	,, 24 Aug. ,,	*a*
Thos. Wheeler[5] to be Lieut. to Capt. Domergue	,, ,, ,, ,,	*a*
[Henry Downes,[6] Esq., to be Capt. of an additional Company	,, ,, ,, ,,	]
Edward Man[7] to be Ens. to Capt. Henry Spence [Downes]	,, ,, ,, ,,	*a*
Wm. Lee[8] to be Ens. to Capt. Domergue	,, ,, ,, ,,	*a*
John Henry Bastide[9] to be Lieut. to Capt. Henry Downes	,, 25 Feb. 1717.	*b*
John Dalgardno[10] to be Ens. to Capt. John Edwards	,, ,, ,, ,,	*b*
Wm. Bever to be Ens. to Capt. Hartshorne	Kensington, 10 May 1718.	*b*
Charles Fonjuliane[11] to be Ens. to do.	,, 22 July ,,	*b*
George Munroe[12] to be Lieut. to Capt. Henry Downes	Hampton Ct., 19 Aug. ,,	*b*

* Served at Sheriffmuir and had several officers killed. See p. 196.

[1] Ensign to Col. Lawrence's Cy. in above Regt. 24 June, 1714. Sub-Brigadier and Cornet in the 4th Troop of Life Guards, 23 Nov. 1720. Brigdr. and Lieut. 15 Feb. 1739. Exempt and Capt. 10 May, 1740. Major, 13 Oct. 1741. Troop disbanded in 1746 and the officers placed on half-pay with an additional allowance.

[2] Lieut. and Capt. 1st. Foot Guards, 24 April, 1712. Capt. in 11th Dragoons, 1716. Capt. in Visct. Mountjoy's Regt. of Foot on the Irish Establishment, 20 April, 1717. Capt. in 3rd Horse, 25 July, 1722. Serving in 1730. Appears to have been eldest son of the Hon. Robert *Tracy* (son of 2nd Visct. Tracy) and to have predeceased his father in 1734.

[3] See biog. notice on p. 106, note 2.

[4] From half-pay. Not in any subsequent List.

[5] On half-pay in 1722.

[6] Killed in action at Glenshiel in June, 1719.

[7] Out before 1727.

[8] Promoted Lieut. 13 Aug. 1722. Serving as Lieut. in 1740.

[9] Serving as Lieut. in 1740.   [10] *Ibid.*

[11] Lieut. 7 Feb. 1740.

[12] Comn. renewed in 1727. Out before 1740. A certain Lieut. Munro of Duroure's (12th) Foot was killed at Dettingen.

BRIGADIER-GENERAL STANWIX'S [LATE PHILIPPS'S] REGIMENT OF FOOT.*

[12TH FOOT,—SUFFOLK REGIMENT.]

John Cunningham to be Ens. to Capt. —— in room of Daniel Coot (sic)	Kensington, 25 Apr. 1718.	b
Henry Barrett to be Lieut. to Capt Alex. Cosby	„ 2 July „	b
Charles Hutchinson, Esq. to be Capt. in room of [Major Joseph] Sawle	„ 9 „ „	b
Edmund Harris to be Lieut. to Captain ——	Hampton Ct., 23 Oct. „	b
John Hayes, Esq. to be Capt. in room of [John] Blake	St. James's, 13 Jan. 1719.	b
Alex. Bisset to be Ens. to Capt. John Hayes	„ 29 „ „	c

* Serving in Minorca on the accession of George I. and for some years subsequently. Said to have served as Marines on board Sir George Byng's fleet in 1718. Of the above six officers only two, viz. Capt. John Hayes and Ensign Alex. Bisset, were serving in this corps in 1728. Both these officers were out before 1740. Chas. Hutchinson was senior Capt. in Gen. Armstrong's Regt. (18th Foot) in 1740; and Henry Barrett was senior Lieut. in Armstrong's the same year.

THE EARL OF BARRYMORE'S REGIMENT OF FOOT.*

[13TH FOOT,—SOMERSETSHIRE LIGHT INFANTRY.]

Peter (sic) Fielding to be Ens. to Capt. Mark Ant. Moncal in the Earl of Barrymore's Regt. of Foot	St. James's, 14 Sept. 1714.	a
Christopher Legard to be Lieut. to Capt. ——	„ 4 Jan. 1718.	b
Richard Stone to be Qr.-Mr.	„ „ „ „	b
Theophilus Lucy to be Adjt.	„ 28 Feb. „	b
Edward Scott to be Ens. to Capt. ——	„ „ „ „	b
Merril Riggs to be Ens. to Capt. —— in room of Ensign Masters	Kensington, 12 May, „	b
Alex. Jacob, Esq. to be Capt. in room of George Walsh	St. James's, 1 Dec. „	b
Theophilus Lucy, Esq. to be Capt. in room of Thos. England	„ 23 Jan. 1718-9.	c

* Serving at Gibraltar on the accession of George I. and for some years subsequently. Of the above seven officers only three, viz. Ensigns Robert Fielding and Edward Scott, also Lieut. Christopher Legard, were serving in this corps in 1728, the first-named with a Lieut's. commission dated 8 Dec. 1726. Legard was still a Lieut. in the Regt. in 1740, and Scott was a Lieut. with a commission dated 14 Sept. 1730.

COLONEL HENRY HARRISON'S REGIMENT OF FOOT.*

[15TH FOOT,—EAST YORKSHIRE REGIMENT.]

Wm. Tracey (sic),¹ Esq. to be Capt. in the room of Tobias Cramer	St. James's,	25 Dec. 1717.			b
James Whiston,² Esq. to be Capt. in the room of John Hoare (sic)	,,	17 Feb. 1718.			b
Henry Brownjohn³ to be Lieut. to Capt. Barton	,,	,,	,,	,,	b
Robt. Streeter to be Ens. to Col. Henry Harrison	,,	,,	,,	,,	b
Charles Crosbie⁵ to be Adjt.	,,	,,	,,	,,	b
John Pretty,⁶ Esq. to be Capt. in room of Robt. Barton	Hampton Ct.	19 Aug.		,,	b
Wm. Selby⁷ to be Lieut. to Capt. Wm. Tracey	,,	,,		,,	b
John Bell⁸ to be Ens. to Capt. [Lt.-Col]. Wm. Handasyde	,,	,,	,,	,,	b
Robt. Frazer,⁹ Esq. to be Capt.-Lieut.	,,	17 Sept.		,,	b
John Harris¹⁰ to be Lieut. to Capt. John Pretty	,,	,,	,,	,,	b
John Wildbraham¹¹ to be Ens. to Capt. Wm. Tracey	,,	,,	,,	,,	b

* One of the regiments left in Flanders after the Peace of Utrecht, which returned home after the signing of the Barrier Treaty at the end of 1715. Serving in the west of Scotland in 1719. A detachment of 200 men from this corps took part in the action at Glenshiel in June, 1719.

¹ Not in any subsequent List. Possibly the eldest son, by a first wife, of the 5th Visct. Tracy, which son predeceased his father.

² Appointed Adjt. to above Regt. 24 Oct. 1708. Served at Malplaquet. Out of the Army before 1728.

³ Served in Lord North and Grey's Regt. as Lieut. and Adjt. in Queen Anne's reign. Untraced after 1718.

⁴ Untraced.

⁵ Lieut. in above Regt. 24 Oct. 1708. Served at Malplaquet. Capt. in the Royal Scots Dragoons, 25 Dec. 1726. Major, 14 July, 1737. Lieut.-Col. of the Regt. afterwards known as the 43rd Foot, 29 Jan. 1741. Md. first Miss Warburton, sister to Jane, Duchess of Argyll. Retd. 3 Feb. 1757.

⁶ Lieut. in above Regt. 20 Mar. 1711. Serving in 1728. Out in 1740.

⁷ Capt. 12 Jan. 1740. Killed at the siege of Carthagena in 1741.

⁸ Ensign 24 Oct. 1708. Served at Malplaquet. Qr.-Mr. 23 June, 1713. Re-appointed Ensign as given in the text. Lieut. 26 Dec. 1726. Capt. 13 Mar. 1741. Served at Carthagena. Major, 25 April, 1743. Serving in 1748. Out of the Regt. before 1754.

⁹ Lieut. 30 Dec. 1710. Capt. 7 Mar. 1724. Serving in 1728. Out before 1740.

¹⁰ Out before 1728.

¹¹ Wilbraham. Lieut. 7 Mar. 1723. Out before 1740.

VISCOUNT IRWIN'S REGIMENT OF FOOT.*

[16TH FOOT,—BEDFORDSHIRE REGIMENT.]

Thos. Fothergill,¹ Esq. to be Capt. [of an additional Company]	St. James's, 24 Aug. 1715.	a
Wm. Hook,² Esq. to be do. [of do.]	,, ,, ,, ,,	a
Edward Thurloe,³ to be Lieut. to Capt. Fothergill	,, ,, ,, ,,	a
Arthur Norcot⁴ (sic) to be Ens. to do.	,, ,, ,, ,,	a
George Collingwood⁵ to be Lieut. to Capt. Hook	,, ,, ,, ,,	a
Wm. Scott⁶ to be Ens. to do.	,, ,, ,, ,,	a
John Smith⁷ to be Qr.-Mr.	,, ,, ,, ,,	a
John Cholmley,⁸ Esq. to be Col. of Our Regt. of Foot lately commanded by Viscount Irwin and Capt. of a Company	,, 13 Dec. 1717.	b
Wm. Robinson,¹¹ Esq. to be Lt.-Col. in the room of Lt.-Col. Cholmley	,, ,, ,, ,,	b
Chas. Weddell,⁹ Esq. to be Capt of that Company whereof the Col. was late Capt.	,, 28 ,, ,,	b
Wm. Scot⁶ to be Ens. to Capt. Chas. Weddell	Kensington, 10 May 1718.	b
Samuel Sleigh,¹⁰ Esq. to be Major	Hampton Ct. 8 Oct. ,,	b
Wm. Robinson,¹¹ Esq. to be Capt. of that Company whereof Michael Flemming (sic) was late Capt.	,, ,, ,, ,,	b

* Sent to Scotland in 1716. Under date of 21 April, 1716, Charles Farcasone (sic) writes to the Duke of Mar : " The detachment gone out from Inverlockie towards the Isles consists of 600 men and is commanded by Col. Clayton and Lt.-Col. Cholmondly of Irvin's Regt." *Stuart Papers.*

¹ Lieut. 26 April, 1706. Served several campaigns in Flanders. Capt. 10 Nov. 1713. Half-pay 1714. Untraced after 1717.

² Ensign, 1 June, 1702. Wounded at Blenheim. Lieut. 25 Aug. 1704. Major, 30 Sept. 1730. Lt.-Col. of the Cameronians, 15 Dec. 1738. Out of the Army before 1748. D. 1762.

³ Ens. 30 Nov. 1712. Half-pay, 1713. Capt. 4 Nov. 1736. Serving in 1740.

⁴ *Northcote.* In the "Gradation List" for 1730, this officer is said to have been appointed Ensign in the Army, 1 May, 1709. Out of the Army before 1740.

⁵ Ens. 1 May, 1709. Served at Malplaquet. Half-pay, 1713. Capt. 12 Sept. 1734. Serving in 1740.

⁶ Lieut. 5 Nov. 1736. Serving in 1740.

⁷ Had served as Qr.-Mr. in Queen Anne's reign.

⁸ See biog. notice on p. 157, note 2.

⁹ Serving in above Regt. in 1730. Out before 1740.

¹⁰ Major S. Sleigh joined above Regt. in 1693. Wounded at Blenheim, where he served as Capt. Bt.-Maj. 1 Jan. 1712. Serving in 1730. Out before 1740.

¹¹ From Capt. in Honeywood's Dragoons. Appointed Colonel of a newly-raised Regt. of Marines, 18 Nov. 1739. D. at Port Royal, Jamaica, in 1741, when in command of said Regt. which was almost entirely decimated by an epidemic.

THE ROYAL REGIMENT OF FOOT OF IRELAND.*

[18TH FOOT,—ROYAL IRISH REGIMENT.]

Wm. Cosby,[1] Esq. to be Col. of Our Royal Regt. of Foot of Ireland in room of Robert Stearne, Esq. and to be Capt. of a Company - - - - -	St. James's,	24 Dec. 1717.	b
Frederick Hamilton[2] [Junr.], Esq. to be Capt. in the room of [Robert] Parker - -	,,	15 Jan. 1718.	b
James Pincent[3] (sic), Esq. to be Capt. en second - - - - - -	Kensington,	20 May ,,	b
Hugh McManus to be Lieut. to Capt. Henry Wingfield - - - - -	,,	,, ,, ,,	b
Wm. Smith to be Ens. to Capt. Moses Leathes	,,	,, ,, ,,	b
John Williams to be Ens. to the Colonel's Company - - - - -	Kensington,	23 July ,,	b
Charles Nicholson to be Lieut. to Capt.——	St. James's,	2 Jan. 1719.	b
Francis Ingoldsby to be Ens. to Capt.——	,,	,, ,, ,,	b
Peregrine Lascelles,[4] Esq. to be Capt. in the room of [Jeremiah] Mussenden - -	——?	14 ,, ,,	b

* Embarked for Minorca in 1718.

[1] Appointed Cornet in Cadogan's Regt. of Horse, 25 Aug. 1704, and served several campaigns in Flanders with said Corps. Served as A.D.C. to Gen. Stanhope during the Spanish campaign of 1710, and was sent with despatches from Brihuega to Marshal Count Staremberg in Dec. 1710, with intelligence of the attack by the French on aforesaid town. Brig.-Gen. 30 Nov. 1735. Youngest son of Alex. Cosby of Stradbally Hall, Queen's County. Gov. of New York and the Jerseys. D. 10 March, 1736.

[2] Nephew of Lt.-Gen. Frederick Hamilton, a former Col. of above Regt. Out of the Army before 1740.

[3] James *Pinsent* was a Capt. in above Regt. on the Accession of George I., and it does not appear why he was given a Commission *en second* in 1718. It may be that he had retired, but on the Regt. going abroad in said year he was allowed temporarily to take the place of an officer employed elsewhere.

[4] Appointed Adjt. to Lord Lovelace's Regt. of Foot, 12 April, 1706. Capt. 13 July, 1708. Half-pay from Col. Wm. Stanhope's Foot in 1712. Capt. in Grant's Foot in 1715 (p. 178). Serving as Capt. in Gen. Churchill's Dragoons in 1728. Capt.-Lieut. 1st Foot Guards, 11 June, 1731. Capt. and Lt.-Col. 5 June, 1733. Col. of a newly-raised Regt. of Foot (47th), 13 March, 1743. Maj.-Gen. 27 March, 1754. Lt.-Gen. 16 Jan. 1758. D. in 1772, aged 88. See copy of the inscription on the tablet erected to his memory, in Whitby parish Church, on p. 179, note 8.

LIEUT.-GENERAL MEREDYTH'S REGIMENT OF FOOT.*

[20TH FOOT,—LANCASHIRE FUSILIERS.]

John Price¹ to be Ens. to Capt. Abbot	St. James's, 14 April, 1718.	b
Thos. Tuthill to be do. to the Colonel's Company	,, 29 ,, ,,	b
Francis Rousseliere² to be do. to Capt. Mordecai Abbot	Kensington, 10 May, ,,	b
Thos. Nesbit to be do. to do.	,, 9 June, ,,	b
Richard Perdue,³ Esq. to be Capt. in room of Thos. St. Clair	,, 13 ,, ,,	b

* Serving at Gibraltar during all George I.'s reign.
¹ Capt. 28 Aug. 1737. Serving in 1740.
² Capt. 31 Aug. 1739. Serving in 1740.
³ Serving in 1730. Out before 1740.

COLONEL ROGER HANDASYDE'S REGIMENT OF FOOT.

[22ND FOOT,—CHESHIRE REGIMENT.]

Wm. Dodd[1] to be Lieut. to Major Howard's Company in Col. Handasyde's Regt. at St. Jago de la Vega [Jamaica]	St. James's, 2 Dec. 1714.	a
Peter Schaak[2] to be Ens. to Capt. Robt. Lambert	,, 23 July, 1715.	a
Edward Walsh,[3] Esq. to be Capt. [of an additional Company]	,, ,, ,, ,,	a
Hyde Howard to be Lieut. to Capt. Edward Walsh	,, ,, ,, ,,	a
Edward Brewerton to be Ens. to do.	,, ,, ,, ,,	a
Daniel Houghton,[4] Esq. to be Capt. [of an additional Company]	,, ,, ,, ,,	a
John Odgers to be Lieut. to Capt. Houghton	,, ,, ,, ,,	a
Richard Brady[5] to be Ens. to do.	,, ,, ,, ,,	a
Edward Pinson to be Qr.-Mr.	,, 25 Dec. ,,	a
Peter La Chapelle[6] to be Ens. to Capt. ——	,, 1 March 1718.	b
Richard Richmond to be do. to Capt. ——	,, 3 April, ,,	b
Richard Francks to be Lieut. to Capt. ——	,, ,, ,, ,,	b
Wm. Gee[7] to be Ens. to Capt. ——	Kensington, 29 ,, ,,	b
Dugal Campbell, Esq. to be Capt. in room of Robt. Lambton	,, 9 July ,,	b
Archibald Campbell[8] to be Ens. to Major Pinfold	Hampton Ct. 20 Aug. ,,	b
Francis Leighton,[9] Esq. to be Capt. in room of Wm. Wamless	St. James's, 1 Nov. ,,	b

[1] Was Lieut. of one of the two Companies which remained in Jamaica when this Regt. was recalled home in 1714. Dodd was serving as senior Lieut. of his Company in Jamaica, 1740.

[2] Ensign 29 Dec. 1712. Lieut. 25 March, 1723. Serving in 1727.

[3] Served in the Royal Irish Regt. as Ensign at Schellenberg, where he was wounded. Lieut. before 1708. Out of Handasyde's Regt. before 1727.

[4] Lieut. in Bowles's Regt. of Foot 13 May, 1709. Half-pay, 1713. Capt.-Lieut. and Lt.-Col. 1st Foot Guards 12 Oct. 1722. Capt. and Lt.-Col. 7 July, 1724. Raised the 45th Foot, now known as the Sherwood Foresters, and was appointed Col. 11 Jan. 1741. Brig.-Gen. 5 June, 1745. Resigned his Colonelcy same month. D. 12 Sept. 1747. Was probably father of Daniel Houghton, the well-known African explorer.

[5] Lieut. 6 Dec. 1731. Serving in 1740.

[6] Lieut. 19 Oct. 1732. Serving in 1740.

[7] Attained the rank of Lt.-Col. of 20th Foot 29 May, 1742. Commanded said Corps at Dettingen and Fontenoy. Killed in last-named battle. He belonged to the family of Gee of Bishop Burton, East Yorkshire.

[8] Capt.-Lieut. 12 Aug. 1736. Serving in 1740.

[9] Second son of Sir Edward Leighton, Bt. by his 2nd wife. Attained the rank of Lieut.-Gen. and was Col. of the 32nd Foot from 1 Dec. 1747 until his death in June 1773.

LIST OF VISCOUNT SHANNON'S REGIMENT OF FOOT.*
[25TH FOOT,—KING'S OWN SCOTTISH BORDERERS.]

[From the MS. Army List for 1717 at the Public Record Office, London. This List of Lord Shannon's Regt. is noted as "certified by Lord Shannon, 3 Sept. 1717."]

CAPTS.	LIEUTS.	ENSIGNS.
Richard, Vt. Shannon,[1] Col. 26 Jan. 1715.	Jas. Hamilton, Capt.-Lieut. 27 Aug. 1717.	Jas. Maxwell, 11 Mar. 1704.
John Grace,[2] Lt.-Col. 17 July 1717	Robt. Douglas, 9 Mar. 1705.	Chas. Maitland, 10 Dec. 1710.
[Major's Cy. vacant]	Richard Maitland, 9 Mar. 1706.	Jno. Maitland, 17 May 1714.
Robt. Walkinshaw, 4 May 1711.	Chas. Maitland, 8 June 1708.	Fred. Bruce,[5] 25 Feb. 1716.
Pat. Ronald, 15 May 1711.	Alex. Moncreif, 24 June 1712.	Chas. Wilkie, 27 July 1711.
Jas. Biggar,[3] 18 Oct. 1711.	Abr. Satyr, 10 Apr. 1712.	Robt. Middleton, 10 Feb. 17$\frac{12}{13}$.
Thos. Killigrew, 6 Jan. 17$\frac{14}{15}$.	David Laurence, 20 Mar. 1714.	Henry Stapleton, 11 Dec. 1712.
Alcomb Milbanke,[4] 24 Aug. 1715.	Alex. Biggar, 3 May 1715.	Wm. Gordon, 3 May 1715.
Jno. Broughton, 24 Aug. 1715.	Jno. Sloss (*sic*), 25 Feb. 1716.	Jas. Maitland, 15 July 1715.
Robt. Scott, 25 Feb. 1716.	Harry Holmes, 28 July 1716.	Chas. Mackay, 9 Mar. 171$\frac{6}{7}$.
Jas. Dixon, 28 July 1716.	Fras. Mosely, 2 Oct. 1716.	Wm. Prothero, 10 May 1717.
Wm. Spens, 1 Aug. 1716.	Jas. Farquarson, 9 Mar. 1717 [? 1st Lieut.]	
[Gr. C. ?]	Jas. Abercromby, 27 Aug. 1717. [? 2nd Lieut.]	

CHAPLAIN.
Wm. Venice,
24 Jan. 1714/5.

ADJT.
Jeremiah Bossingo,
25 July 1695.

QR.-MR.
Jas. Hamilton,
25 Aug. 1715.

SURGEON.
Wm. Murray,
1 Aug. 1712.

SUPPLEMENTARY COMMISSIONS.

Patrick (sic) Haldane,[6] Esq., to be Capt. of that Company whereof [Thos.] Killigrew was late Capt. in Visct. Shannon's Regt.	St. James's, 24 Dec. 1717.	b
Delaval Denton[7] to be Lieut. to Capt. James Haldane	,, 14 Feb. 1718.	b
Sir John Wederburn[8] (sic) to be Ens. to Capt. Broughton	Hampton Ct. 10 Sept. ,,	b

* Served at Sheriffmuir.

[1] Son of the Hon. Richard Boyle and grandson of Francis Boyle 1st. Visct. Shannon. Born in 1674. Is said to have served at the Boyne as a Volunteer. Accompanied the Duke of Ormonde to Flanders and fought at Landen in 1693. Served three successive campaigns under William III. in Flanders. Appointed Guidon and Major of the 2nd Troop of Horse Guards 1 Feb. 1696. Succeeded his grandfather as Visct. Shannon before 12 Feb. 1702, when he was appointed Colonel of a newly-raised Regt. of Marines. Served in the Cadiz expedition of 1702, and commanded the British Grenadiers at the storming of the Spanish forts at Vigo. Was present at the taking of Barcelona in 1705. Lt.-Gen. 1 Jan. 1709. Col. of the 25th Foot in 1715. Lt.-Gen. on the Staff in Ireland, 1716. Com.-in-Chief in Ireland 17 Oct. 1720. Comn. as C.-in-C. renewed by George II. in 1727. Col. of the Carabiniers, 17 June, 1721. Col. of 4th Troop of Guards, 9 March 1727. Govr. of Portsmouth in room of the Duke of Argyll in 1737. Appointed a Field-Marshal in 1739, and d. 20 Dec. 1740. Bd. in the parish church of Walton-on-Thames, where is a sumptuous monument to his memory sculptured by Roubillac.

[2] See p. 223, note 71.

[3] Capt. in above Regt. 18 Oct. 1711. Promoted Major 19 July, 1732. Lt.-Col. of the 37th Foot 27 March, 1742. Believed to have served with the 37th at Dettingen. Dead in Feb. 1746.

[4] According to Burke's *Baronetage* this officer was Acclom Milbanke, 6th son of Sir Ralph Milbanke, Bt. Further services untraced.

[5] Capt.-Lieut. 1 March 1739. Believed to have served at Fontenoy.

[6] *James Haldane.* Appointed Cornet in Col. Wm. Newton's Regt. of Dragoons 22 July 1715. Present with said Corps at the surrender of Preston in Nov. 1715. Major of the 4th (Scots) Troop of Guards 5 July 1735. Lt.-Col. of Brigadier Guise's Regt. (6th Foot) 13 Oct. 1741. Accompanied said Regt. same month from Greenock to the West Indies and commanded this Corps on active service. D. at sea on return with the troops in Dec. 1742. He was 3rd son of John Haldane of Gleneagles who was M.P. for Perth.

[7] From Lieut. in the Royal Irish Dragoons. D. in 1720. Will proved at Dublin.

[8] Son of Sir Alex. Wedderburne, Bt. D.s.p. in 1722.

MAJOR-GENERAL WHETHAM'S REGIMENT OF FOOT.*

[27TH FOOT,—1ST BATTALION ROYAL INNISKILLING FUSILIERS.]

Francis Billingsley,[1] Esq., to be Capt. in the room of Wm. Brown	St. James's, 24 Jan. 1718.	b
Lewis Gwin[2] (sic) Esq., to be Capt. in the room of George Arbuthnot	Kensington, 12 July ,,	b

* It is stated in *Records and Badges of the British Army* (Edit. 1900) that above Regt. served in Scotland during the rebellion of 1715-16. This statement is not borne out by facts. The Royal Inniskilling Fusiliers were certainly not with Argyll at Sheriffmuir, though their Colonel—Maj.-Gen. Whetham—was; and in a "List of the Troops in Scotland, Oct. 1716," among the *Stuart Papers* at Windsor Castle, the Corps in question is conspicuous by its absence.

[1] Out of the Regt. before 1727.

[2] From Lieut. in Col. Richard Lucas's Regt. of Foot. Serving as senior Capt. in 1740. D. 1761. Will proved at Dublin same year.

MONUMENT TO FIELD-MARSHAL VISCOUNT SHANNON IN THE PARISH CHURCH, WALTON-ON-THAMES.

STATUE OF FIELD-MARSHAL VISCOUNT SHANNON ON HIS MONUMENT
IN THE PARISH CHURCH, WALTON-ON-THAMES.

COLONEL THOMAS CHUDLEIGH'S REGIMENT OF FOOT.
[34TH,—1ST BATTALION, THE BORDER REGIMENT OF FOOT.]

Alex. Grant,[1] Esq., to be Capt [of an additional Company] - - - - - St. James's, 26 Sept. 1715. *a*
Abraham Devisher [2] (*sic*), Esq., to be do.[of do.] ,, ,, ,, *a*
Wm. Rendall to be Lieut. to Capt. Devisher ,, ,, ,, *a*
Michael Studholme [3] to be Ens. to do. - ,, ,, ,, *a*
Thos. Collet to be do. to Capt. Alex. Grant ,, ,, ,, *a*
Thos. Watson [4] to be Lieut. to do. - - ,, ,, ,, *a*

Regt. sent to Ireland in June, 1717.

John Hely,[5] Esq., to be Capt. in the room of Henry Skelton — 1 Oct. 1717. *j*
George Gumley to be Ens. to Col. Thos. Chudleigh's own Cy. in room of John Sutton — 13 Feb. 1717–8. *j*
Maurice Powell [6] to be Surgeon (*sic*) in room of Philip Broome, superseded - - — 14 Mar. ,, *j*
John Tremayne [7] to be Adjt. in room of Michael Moore - - - - — 22 April ,, *j*
Wm. Hays, Esq., to be Capt.-Lieut. in room of Thos. Walton, decd. - - - — 29 Sept. ,, *j*
Thos. Chudleigh to be Lieut. to Capt. Robt. Hays - - - - - - - — , ,, *j*
Michael Brandreth,[8] Esq., to be Major in room of Charles Douglas preferred, and Capt of a Cy. - - - - - - - — 18 Nov. ,, *j*
John Edgar to be Surgeon in room of Thos. Whitney - - - - - — 31 Jan. 1718–9. *j*
John Cunningham to Lieut. to Capt. Michael Moore in room of John Tremayne, decd. — 26 Feb. ,, *j*
Thos. Chudleigh to be Adjt. in room of Tremayne - - - - - - - — ,, ,, *j*

[1] On half-pay in 1722.

[2] Lieut. in above Regt. before 1713, in which year his name appears as one of the officers reduced in Brigdr. Hamilton's Regt. stationed at Newport. Believed to have been nearly related to Capt. Edmund De Fisher of Gen. Webb's Regt. (8th Foot), in which Corps he was subsequently appointed Major (see p. 213). On 6 Apr. 1720 was appointed Lt.-Col. of last-named Corps (The King's). Col. Devisher d. in London 25 Oct. 1736. He was a brother officer, when in Chudleigh's Regt., of Ensign Roger Sterne, and was a kind benefactor and friend of the hapless Sterne family. Indeed, one of Roger Sterne's children was called "Devischer," but d. an infant.—Lawrence Sterne's *Fragment of Autobiography.*

[3] Lieut. 9 June, 1723. Serving in 1730.

[4] Called "Walton" in another entry. D. as Capt.-Lieut. in Sept. 1718.

[5] Commission renewed by George II. in 1727. Lt.-Col. of 34th Foot 15 Dec. 1738. D. in 1741.—*Gentleman's Mag.*

[6] According to the *Army List*, 1740, Maurice Powell's Commission as *Ensign* was dated 6 March, 1718, and it is very probable that the word "Surgeon" in the entry given in the text ought to read "Ensign." This officer was appointed Major of 34th Foot 15 Dec. 1738, and Lt.-Col. 12 Aug. 1741 *vice* Hely. Col. Powell fell at the battle of Falkirk in 1746.

[7] D. in Feb. 1719.

[8] Comn. renewed by George II. in 1727. D. in London 1731.—*Gentleman's Mag.*

COLONEL FRANCIS ALEXANDER'S REGIMENT OF FOOT.*

[38TH FOOT,—1ST BATTALION, SOUTH STAFFORDSHIRE REGIMENT.]

Col. Richard Lucas¹ to be Col. and Capt. of a Cy. in room of Francis Alexander	— 23 Sept.	1717. *b*
James Blachford² to be Lieut. to Capt. [Henry] Hughes	St. James's, 9 Nov. ,,	*b*
Hugh Plucknet,³ Esq. to be Capt. in the room of —— Jackson, deceased	,, 15 ,, ,,	*b*
Lewis Charlott⁴ to be Ens. to Lt.-Col. Val. Morris	,, 28 Dec. ,,	*b*
Thos. Watts,⁵ Esq. to be Capt. in room of Geyrvess (*sic*) Gryles	,, 29 Jan.	1718.*b*
Richard Lucas⁶ to be Ens. to Capt. ——	,, 8 Mar. ,,	*b*
Alex. Hardine,⁷ Esq. to be Major and Capt. of a Company	Kensington, 9 May ,,	*b*
Wm. Howard,⁸ Esq. to be Capt.-Lieut.	Hampton Ct., 8 Oct. ,,	*b*
Wm. Withrington⁹ to be Lieut. to Capt. ——	St. James's, 1 Nov. ,,	*b*
Roger Adams to be Surgeon	,, 8 ,, ,,	*b*
Orlando Billingsly to be Ens. to [Lt.-Col. Valentine] Morris	,, 19 Dec. ,,	*b*

* Embarked for the West Indies in 1706, where it remained for nearly sixty years.
¹ See notice on p. 182, note 1.
² The will of "James Blachford of the Duke of Marlborough's Regt. of Foot" was proved at Dublin in 1750. *Index to Prerogative Wills of Ireland.*
³ Appointed Capt.-Lieut. of Lieut.-Col. George Windram's Company of Invalids at Portsmouth, 2 Aug. 1715. Capt. in Col. Edmund Fielding's Regt. of Invalids, 11 Mar. 1719. Lieut.-Governor of Landguard Fort, 1719-30. Serving as Capt. in Col. Henry Grove's Regt. (10th Foot) in 1730. Out of said Regt. before 1740.
⁴ Not in any subsequent List.
⁵ *Ibid.*
⁶ Probably a child and son of Col. Richard Lucas.
⁷ Appointed Capt.-Lieut. of Sir Charles Hotham's newly-raised Regt. of Foot, 25 Mar. 1705. Served at Alicante during the long siege of this town by the French in 1709. Major 21 Feb. 1709. Half-pay, 1713. D. in the West Indies before 1720. There is a monument to his widow, Agnes Hardine, in Westminster Abbey. She d. 8 Aug. 1720.
⁸ Promoted from Lieut. in same Regt. Not in any subsequent List.
⁹ Widdrington. Promoted Capt. 23 Dec. 1738. Serving in 1740.

LIEUT.-GENERAL SANKEY'S REGIMENT OF FOOT.*

[39TH FOOT,—1ST BATTALION, DORSETSHIRE REGIMENT.]

Peter Beaver[1] to be Lieut. to Capt. Daniel Negus	St. James's, 6 Feb. 1718.	b
Thos. Trenchard[2] to be Ens. to Capt. Breton	,, ,, ,, ,,	b
Arthur Davis[3] to be Ens. to Capt. James Townshend	,, 8 ,, ,,	b
Thomas Forth[4] to be Ens. to Capt. Walter Breams	,, 28 ,, ,,	b
[Peter Petit[5] to be Lieut. to Capt. ———	,, 12 Mar. ,,	]
John Lloyd to be Ensign to Capt. Wm. Campbell	,, 3 Apr. ,,	b
Lewis Ormsby, Esq. to be Adjt.	Kensington, 3 June ,,	b
Roger Lort[6] to be Qr.-Mr.	,, ,, ,, ,,	b

* One of the four Regts. sent to Minorca on board Admiral Byng's fleet in 1718.

[1] Promoted Capt. 12 May, 1731. Serving in 1740.

[2] Appears to have been elder son of Col. Thos. Trenchard of Wolverton, co. Dorset. Out of the Regt. before 1727.

[3] Out before 1727.

[4] Serving as Capt. in Col. Chas. Otway's (35th Foot) in 1725. Out 6 May, 1726.

[5] In a "List of Officers of Engineers on the New Establishment, 1716–1757" (printed in *List of Officers of the Corps of Royal Engineers*, p. 3), Peter Petit is stated to have been appointed a Practitioner Engineer on 1 Oct. 1717 and Lieut. in Sankey's Regt. 12 March, 1718. Capt. in the Rl. Irish Regt. 15 Feb. 1721. Resigned in Sept. 1726. D. in London, Sept. 1768.

[6] Serving as Capt. in Col. Chas. Otway's Regt. of Foot (35th) in 1725. Out before 1740.

COLONEL RICHARD PHILIPPS'S REGIMENT OF FOOT.*

[40TH FOOT,—1ST BATTALION, THE PRINCE OF WALES'S VOLUNTEERS.]

The Commissions were dated at Hampton Court, 25 Aug. 1717.b

CAPTS.	LIEUTS.	ENSIGNS.
Ric. Philipps,¹ Col.	———	John Morgan.
Martin Purcell,² Lt.-Col.	———	Thos. Button.
Laurence Armstrong,³ Major.	Jas. Campbell.	John Keating.
Paul Mascarine.⁴		
Chris. Aldridge.⁵	John Jeppson.	[Philip Buckhurst.]
John Dowcett.⁶	Francis Fox.	Jas. Erskine.
Cosby Philipps, Grendrs.	Reynell Nugent, 1st Lieut. ⎫ ——— 2nd Lieut. ⎬	———
Robt. Handy.	Robt. Bellenden.	Thos. Pickstock.
John Williams.	Edw. Broadstreet (*sic*)	Otho Hamilton.⁷
John Blower.		
John Stanhope.	———	Thos. Mathews.

CHAPLAIN.
Simon Paget.

QUARTERMASTER.
Richard Hughes.

SURGEON.
John Calhoune.

SUPPLEMENTARY COMMISSIONS.

Hubert Marshall to be Ens. to Capt. ——— in Col. Richard Phillipps's (*sic*) Regt. - - St. James's, 25 Dec. 1717.*b*

1718.

Peregrine Fury⁸ to be Ens. to Capt. ——— in above Regt. in place of Ens. Buckhurst - ,, 10 Mar. 1718.*b*

Joseph Bennett, Esq., to be Capt. in room of John Williams in above Regt. - - Kensington, 15 May ,, *b*

Wm. Moor, Esq. to be Capt. of that Company whereof Cosby Phillipps was late Capt. in do. - - - - - - ,, 6 July ,, *b*

Otho Hamilton⁷ to be Lieut. to Capt. Wm. Moor in do. - - - - - - - ,, 9 Aug. ,, *b*

Richard Sawle to be Ens. to Capt. Joseph Bennett in do. - - - - - - Hampton Ct. 15 ,, ,, *b*

Richard Bull to be Lieut. to Capt. John Stanhope in do. - - - - · - - ,, 2 Oct. ,, *b*

* Formed from the Independent Companies in garrison at Annapolis (Nova Scotia) and Placentia (Newfoundland). The head quarters of the Regt. was at Annapolis. An excellent *Historical Records of the* 40*th Regt.* by Capt. Smythies was published in 1894.

[1] See biog. notice on p. 150, note 1.

[2] From half-pay Major of Sir Daniel Carroll's Regt. of Dragoons. Untraced after June, 1719, when his name appears as an absentee officer of Col. Philipps's Regt. given in the *London Gazette* (No. 5756) and ordered to leave Great Britain and return to his Regt.

[3] Served at Oudenarde and Malplaquet. Shipwrecked in the St. Lawrence when serving with Brig. John Hill's ill-fated expedition. Capt. of an Independent Company at Annapolis, 16 Oct. 1712. Lieut.-Col. of Philipps's Regt. 1 Dec. 1720. Lieut.-Gov. of Nova Scotia in 1725. D. by his own hand 7 Dec. 1739. See Capt. Smythies' *Records*.

[4] Jean Paul Mascarine came of a Huguenot family. Born in 1685. Through the influence of M. Rapin de Thoyras, the well-known English historian, a retired British officer, young Mascarine obtained an Ensign's Commission in Col. La Barthe's Huguenot Regt. 2 Apr. 1706. Embarked for New England in 1709 to take part in an intended expedition to Canada. Was a *protégé* of Col. Fras. Nicholson and Col. Sam. Vetch. Capt. in Col. William Walton's New England Regt. 1 Apr. 1710, and served at the siege of Port Royal in Sept. 1710. Promoted Bt.-Major by Gen. Nicholson, 13 Oct. 1710. His subsequent services at Annapolis, when that place was besieged by the French in 1744, are matters of Canadian history. Regimental Lieut.-Col. 27 Dec. 1742. Bt.-Col. 1 June, 1750. Sold his Commission in 1751. Maj.-Gen. 22 Jan. 1758. D. in Jan. 1760

[5] Serving as Capt. in 1740.

[6] Capt. in Col. Godfrey's Regt. of Foot, 1 May, 1709. Served at Malplaquet. Capt. of an Independent Company at Annapolis in 1715.

[7] Lieut. 9 Aug. 1718. Capt. 3 Sept. 1739. Major, 30 Jan. 1746. Lieut.-Gov. of Placentia with £182 *per annum* before 1758. D. in 1770.—*Gentleman's Mag.*

[8] Ensign in Lieut.-Gen. Maccartney's Regt. 25 Aug. 1711. Said Commission was signed by Brigr. John Hill on board the *Windsor* in the River St. Lawrence. Placed on half-pay in 1713. Appointed Secretary to Chelsea Hospital, but in what year does not appear. D. 1759.—*Gentleman's Mag.*

BRIGADIER-GENERAL STANWIX'S REGIMENT OF FOOT.

[Disbanded in Nov. 1718.]

[Philip Pennington, Esq. to be Capt. of an additional Cy.	St. James's, 26 Sept. 1715.]	
Christopher Russell¹ to be Lieut. to Capt. Philip Pennington	,, ,, ,, ,,	*a*
Wm. Shewen, Esq., to be Capt. [of an additional Company]	,, ,, ,, ,,	*a*
Charles Fell to be Ens. to Capt. Wm. Shewen	,, ,, ,, ,,	*a*
Francis Jennison to be Qr.-Mr.	,, 25 Dec. ,,	*a*
—— Brown to be Ens. to [the Col.'s Cy.]	,, 2 Apr. 1716.	*e*
Edward Stillingfleet to be Ens. to Capt. ——	St. James's, 11 June 1717.	*b*

Regiment sent to Ireland, 25 June, 1717.

John Armstrong,² Esq. to be Col. of Our Regt. of Foot lately commanded by Thomas Stanwix, Esq. and to be Capt. of a Company	St. James's, 17 July 1717.	*b*
John Williams to be Ens. to the Colonel's Cy. in room of Ensign Brown, decd.	— 14 Aug. ,,	*j*
Sir Robert Montgomery³ to be Lieut.-Col. and to be Capt. of a Company	Hampton Ct., 26 Sept. ,,	*j*
Nathaniel Jackson⁴ to be Adjt. in room of [Lieut.] Robert Eaglesfield	— 12 Dec. ,,	*j*
Thos. Columbine to be Ens. to Col. John Armstrong's Company	— 8 Mar. 1717-8.	*j*
Robert Meares to be Chaplain in room of Jonathan Smedley superseded	— 26 Aug. 1718.	*j*

¹ Placed on half-pay on reduction of the Regt. "Provided for in Ireland in 1729." *Half-pay List*, 1739.

² Eldest son of Robert Armstrong of Ballyard, King's County. Born 31 Mar. 1674. This distinguished engineer served on Marlborough's staff at Blenheim and was A.D.C. to the Duke at Oudenarde. Also held for some years the post of A.Q.M.G. in Flanders. Greatly distinguished himself at the battle of Wynendale when conducting a convoy of 700 wagons from Ostend to Menin. A.D.C. to Marlborough at Malplaquet. Served at the sieges of Menin and Bouchain (mentioned in despatches). Chief Commissioner for the demolition of the fortifications at Dunkirk. Qr.-Mr.-Gen. of the Forces, 22 Dec. 1712. Chief Engineer, with rank of Col. 9 Dec. 1714. Held likewise the post of Surveyor-General of the Ordnance, Deputy Lieut.-Gen. of the Ordnance, Col. of the Rl. Irish Regt. of Foot (13 May, 1735—15 April, 1742). He was promoted Maj.-Gen. 2 July, 1739. D. at the Tower of London, 1742, and was buried within the graveyard of the church within the Tower, where there is an inscription to his memory.

³ Third Bt. of Skelmorlie. Appointed Lt.-Col. of Lord Strathnaver's Regt. of Foot 25 Dec. 1709. Half-pay 1713. Mentioned in a Scottish news-letter of 27 Jan. 1716 as being sent from Burntisland with a detachment from the garrison to harry the rebels. Placed on half-pay when Armstrong's Corps was reduced. Drawing half-pay in 1722. Is said in the *Extinct Baronetage* to have been Governor of a garrison in Ireland and to have died in 1731.

⁴ Half-pay on reduction of the Regt. Drawing half-pay in 1739.

SIR CHARLES HOTHAM'S REGIMENT OF FOOT.*

[Francis Savill to be Capt. of an additional Cy. - St. James's, 26 Sept. 1715.]
Peter Foucault¹ to be Lieut. to Capt. Fras. Savill - ,, ,, ,, ,, a
William Crosby to be Ens. to do. - ,, ,, ,, ,, a
[Josias Laborde, Esq. to be Capt. of an additional Cy. - ,, ,, ,, ,,]
Timothy Quinn to be Lieut. to Capt. Laborde - ,, ,, ,, ,, a
Robert Sterling to be Ensign to do. - ,, ,, ,, ,, a
James Burton to be Quarter-Master - ,, 25 Dec. ,, a

Regiment sent to Ireland, 25 June, 1717.

Thomas Ferrers,² Esq. to be Colonel of Sir Charles Hotham's late Regt. of Foot and Capt. of a Company - St. James's, 17 July, 1717. b
Edward Browne, Esq. to be Capt. in room of Thomas Burrowes in Brigadier Thomas Ferrers's Regt. of Foot in Ireland - ,, 20 Aug. ,, j
John Cunningham to be Lieut. to Capt. Peter Carew in room of Lieut. Jonathan Smith, decd. - ,, 9 Jan. 1717-8. j

---

* Disbanded in Nov. 1718 and the officers placed on half-pay.
¹ Drawing half-pay in 1739.
² See "List of Brig. Ferrers's Regt. of Foot on the Irish Establishment for Feb. 1716" in Vol. II. and note on this officer.

BRIGADIER-GENERAL ALEXANDER GRANT'S REGIMENT OF FOOT.*

[Disbanded in Nov. 1718].

James Grant to be Surgeon	St. James's, 22 July, 1715.	a
John Rutherford to be Adjt.	,, ,, ,, ,,	a
Edward Massey, Esq., to be Capt. [of an additional Company]	,, 26 Sept. ,,	a
John Severn to be Ens. to Capt. Edward Massey	,, ,, ,, ,,	a
Edward Pole, Esq. to be Captain [of an additional Company]	,, ,, ,, ,,	a
William Gough to be Lieut. to Capt. Pole	,, ,, ,, ,,	a
George Mackenzie to be Ens. to do.	,, ,, ,, ,,	a
Philip Chapman to be Captain	,, 29 ,, ,,	a

Regiment sent to Ireland, 25 June, 1717.

[Maurice] Nassau,[1] Esq. to be Col. of Our Regt. of Foot lately commanded by Brig.-Gen. Alexander Grant and to be Capt. of a Company	St. James's, 17 July 1717.	b & j
Daniel McNeal[2] Esq. to be Capt. in room of Wm. Douglas	,, ,, ,, ,,	a
John Rutherford[3] to be Adjt. in room of John Rutherford (*sic*)	,, 1 Nov. ,,	j
John Grant to be Ens. to Capt. [Major] Wm. Cecil in room of James Grant	,, 1 Jan. 1717-8.	j
Leonard Burgh to be Ens. to Capt. Wm. Douglas (*sic*) in room of Ant. Robinson	,, 7 July 1718	

* Joined the Duke of Argyll in Scotland after Sheriffmuir and marched north with the Royal Army in Jan. 1716.

[1] Kinsman to Major-Gen. the Earl of Rochford. Generally called Count Maurice Nassau. Appointed Ens. to the Queen's Company in the 1st Foot Guards 10 March, 1702. Fought at Blenheim. Capt. in Brig.-Gen. Wm. Tatton's Regt. 25 Aug. 1704. Served at Ramillies. Lieut.-Col. *en second* of Visct. Mountjoy's Regt. of Foot in Spain 5 March, 1708. Lieut.-Col. of William Watkins's Regt. of Foot 16 March, 1709. Col. of a Regt. of Foot 12 Dec. 1711. Col. of a Regt. on the Irish Establishment 16 Feb. 1716, which Corps was disbanded in 1717. Half-pay 1718. D. in 1722.

[2] *McNeil* served previously as 2nd Lieut. of Col. Wm. Grant's Independent Company in the Highlands (disbanded in 1717). Drawing half-pay in 1722. A certain Daniel McNeil, Esq., of Coleraine, Co. Derry, d. in 1765, and his will was proved at Dublin.

[3] Drawing half-pay in 1739.

COLONEL CHARLES DUBOURGAY'S REGIMENT OF FOOT.

[Disbanded in Nov. 1718.]

Toby Norris, Esq. to be Captain [of an additional Company]	St. James's, 26 Sept. 1715.	*a*
Thos. Wise to be Lieut. to Capt. Toby Norris	,, ,, ,, ,,	*a*
Richard Nugent to be Ensign to do.	,, ,, ,, ,,	*a*
[Thos. Lascelles[1] to be Capt. of an additional Cy.	,, ,, ,, ,,]	
Thos. Lewis to be Ensign to Capt. Thos. Lascelles	,, ,, ,, ,,	*a*
Peter Bouys (*sic*) to be Qr.-Mr.	,, 25 Dec. ,,	*a*

Regiment sent to Ireland, 25 June, 1717.

Thos. Williams[2] to be Lieut. to Capt. —— in room of Lieut. Parkinson	St. James's, 3 July 1717.	*b*
Hugh Jones, Esq. to be Capt. in room of James Stewart	,, 2 Jan. 1717-8.	*j*
Wm. Maidman,[3] Esq. to be Capt.-Lieut. in room of Hugh Jones	,, ,, ,, ,,	*j*

[1] Believed to be identical with Lieut.-Col. Thos. Lascelles who was an Engineer to the English train of Artillery in May, 1715. See biog. notice on p. 282, note 4.

[2] Reduced with the Regt. Drawing half-pay in 1739.

[3] Appointed Lieut. in Major-Gen. Wm. Evans's Dragoons 2 Jan. 1719. Out of the Army before 1730.

COLONEL JOHN POCOCK'S REGIMENT OF FOOT.*

Thomas Bruce[1] to be Adjt.	St. James's, 22 July 1715.	a
— Spittle to be Surgeon	,, ,, ,, ,,	a
John Broughton[2] to be Chaplain	,, ,, ,, ,,	a
Francis Pierson,[3] Esq., to be Capt. [of an additional Company]	,, 26 Sept. ,,	a
John Parslow to be Ens. to Capt. Pierson	,, ,, ,, ,,	a
Edmund Waring to be Lieut. to do.	,, ,, ,, ,,	a
Abel Rotolph Ladeveze,[4] Esq., to be Capt. [of an additional Company]	,, ,, ,, ,,	a
Hugh Pudsay[5] to be Lieut. to Capt. Ladeveze	,, ,, ,, ,,	a
John Ball to be Qr.-Mr.	,, 29 Mar. 1716.	a

Regiment sent to Ireland, 25 June, 1717.

George Marly to be Chaplain in room of Doctor Broughton	— 24 Oct. 1717.	j
— Guerin to be Adjt. in room of Thos. Adams	— 28 Nov. ,,	j
Henry Smyth,[6] Esq., to be Lt.-Colonel in room of George Whitmore and Capt. of a Cy.	— 25 Mar. 1717-8.	j
Mathew Sewell[7] to be Lieut. to Capt. Chas. Cunningham in room of John Ramsay	— 9 May 1718.	j
Robert Waller to be Ens. to do. in room of Mat. Sewell	— ,, ,, ,,	j
John Bathe[8] to be Ens. to Capt. Appleyard in room of Thos. St. John	— 3 July ,,	j
John Mead[9] to be Ens. to Capt. Edward Molesworth in room of Wm. Adams	— 4 ,, ,,	j
Edward Newton to be Ens. to Capt. —— in room of William, Lord Wallingford	— 1 Oct. ,,	j

* Disbanded in Nov. 1718.
[1] Out before 1717.
[2] D.D. Out 24 Oct. 1717.
[3] Capt. in the Earl of Pembroke's Regt. of Foot on the Irish Establishment, 25 April 1711. Major in Bisset's Regt. (30th Foot), 27 Sept. 1732. Lieut.-Col. 35th Foot, 8 Jan. 1740. Retd. 1 June, 1745.
[4] From half-pay as Capt. *en second* in Maj.-Gen. Gorges's reduced Regt. of Foot.
[5] Probably son of Hugh Pudsey who was Wagon-Master-Gen. to the Forces in Flanders, 1711. Lieut. Hugh *Pudsey* was drawing half-pay in 1722.
[6] Believed to be identical with the "Henry Smith" serving as Capt. and Lieut.-Col. in the 3rd Foot Guards in 1727.
[7] Attained the rank of Lieut.-Col. to the 67th Foot, 4 Oct. 1745. This newly-raised corps was reduced in 1748. Lieut.-Col. Sewell was appointed Capt. of an Invalid Company at Pendenis, 24 July, 1754. Living in 1758.
[8] Drawing Ensign's half-pay in 1739.
[9] *Ibid.*

COLONEL RICHARD LUCAS'S REGIMENT OF FOOT.

[Disbanded in 1719.]

Lewis Gwin to be Lieut. to Capt. Wm. Hall	St. James's,	13 Sept.	1715.	*a*
Wm. Comyns to be Lieut. to Capt. Walter Blunt	,,	22 ,,	,,	*a*
Lacon Wm. Oliver to be Lieut. to Capt. Richard White	,,	26 ,,	,,	*a*
Myles Parker to be Ens. [to do.] [	,,],	,,	,,	*a*
John Mohun,¹ Esq., to be Capt. [of an additional Company]	,,	,,	,,	*a*
Richard White,² Esq., to be do. [of do.]	,,	,,	,,	*a*
John Prendergast to be Lieut. to Capt. John Mohun	,,	,, Oct.	,,	*a*
James Browne³ to be Ens.	,,	25 Oct.	,,	*j*
Edward Hill to be Qr.-Mr.	,,	25 Dec.	,,	*a*
Roger Adams to be Surgeon	,,	8 May	1716.	*j*

Regiment sent to Ireland, 25 June, 1717.

Edward, Lord Hinchinbroke,⁴ to be Colonel in room of Richard Lucas and Capt. of a Cy.	—	23 Sept. 1717.	*b*
John Boswell, Esq., to be Capt. in Lord Hinchinbroke's Regt. in Ireland in room of John Mohun	—	23 Nov. ,,	*j*
Bury Irwin⁵ to be Lieut. to Capt. J. Boswell in room of Boswell	—	,, ,, ,,	*j*
— Irwin⁶ to be Ens. to Capt. —— in room of Bury Irwin	—	,, ,, ,,	*j*
Thomas Hales,⁷ Esq., to be Colonel of that Regt. of Foot whereof Edward, Lord Hinchinbroke, was late Col. and to be Capt. of a Cy.	—	11 Dec. ,,	*j*
Harry Gardiner to be Lieut to Capt. John Massey in room of Lewis Gwin	—	2 June 1718.	*j*
Wm. Coleman to be Lieut. to Capt. Richard White in room of George Robinson decd.	—	25 Mar. 1718-9.	*j*

---

¹ Capt. in the Earl of Barrymore's Regt. 27 April, 1707. Served with said Regt. in the Peninsula. Exchanged to Wills's Marines in 1709. Half-pay, 1713. Left the Regt. 23 Nov. 1717.

² Probably the officer of this name appointed Capt. in Col. Bowles's Regt. of Foot, 16 Mar. 1710. Reduced with Col. Hales's Regt. in 1719.

³ Drawing half-pay in 1739.

⁴ Appointed Col. of 37th Foot, 11 Dec. 1717. See biog. notice on p. 331, note 3.

⁵ Drawing half-pay in 1739.

⁶ Called "Ensign Burrow Erwin" in *Half-Pay List*, 1739.

⁷ Killed by a fall when hunting, 8 Aug. 1729.

Edward Lord Hinchingbrooke.

G. Kneller S R. Imp. et Angl. Eques Aur. pinx: Sold by I. Smith at ye Lyon & Crown in Russel Street Covent Garden.

(See page 331.)

REGIMENTS ON THE IRISH ESTABLISHMENT, 1715.

EDITOR'S PREFACE.

The following Lists are given in the MS. Commission Entry Book, 1709–1716, at the Public Record Office, Dublin. But many of the supplementary commission registers (notably those for Col. Pitt's Regt. of Horse after the arrival of said Corps in England, July, 1715) are extracted from the English Commission Book, 1714–1716, at the Public Record Office, London. The dates of officers' commissions given between square brackets are added by the Editor. The dates so given under the respective heads of "Clayton's Regt.," "Wightman's Regt.," "The Scots Fusiliers," "Preston's Regt.," and "Disney's Regt." are taken from the MS. Army List for 1717 at the Public Record Office, London. All the other dates between brackets are copied from the Commission Entry Books at Dublin.

C. D.

COLONEL THOMAS PITT'S REGIMENT OF HORSE.*
[2ND DRAGOON GUARDS.]

Commissions Renewed by George I., 1st June, 1715.

CAPTAINS.	LIEUTENANTS.	CORNETS.	QUARTER-MASTERS.
Thomas Pitt, Colonel [9 Feb. 1714–15].	—	—	—
—— Lt.-Col.	—	—	—
Richard Whitworth, Major.	—	Robert Cornwall.	—
[Thos.] Ligoe.	Nicholas Hutchinson [20 Novr. 1714].	Philip Smith.	—
George Walker	—	William Boyle [8 Jany. 1713–14].	Nicholas Lawless [20 Novr. 1714].
Francis Naizon.	—	—	Nicholas French [?] [20 Novr. 1714].

* Imperfect List. See p. 326.

COLONEL THOMAS PITT'S REGIMENT OF HORSE.

Pitt's Regt. embarked for England 20 July, 1715, and the Officers' Commissions were renewed by George I., 1st Aug. 1715, on the Regt. being styled "H.R.H. The Princess of Wales's Own Regt. of Horse."

Thomas Pitt,[1] Esq., to be Colonel and Capt. of a Troop - - - - - - - St. James's, 1 Aug., 1715.
James Otway,[2] Esq., to be Lt.-Colonel and Capt. of a Troop - - - - ,, ,, ,,
Richard Whitworth,[3] Esq., to be Major and Capt. of a Troop - - - - - ,, ,, ,,
George Walker, Esq., to be Capt. in do. - - ,, ,, ,,
Francis Naizon, Esq., to be do. - - - ,, ,, ,,
James Dambon, Esq., to be do. in room of [Thos.] Ligoe - - - - - - ,, ,, ,,
Nicholas Hutchinson to be Lieut. [to Capt. Dambon] - - - - - - - ,, ,, ,,
Peter Naizon, Esq., to be Capt.-Lieut. - - ,, ,, ,,
[Philip Smith to be Cornet to Capt. Dambon ,, ,, ,,]
Anthony Rankin to be Lieut. to Lt.-Col. Otway - - - - - - - - ,, ,, ,,
Daniel Soden to be Lieut. to Major Whitworth ,, ,, ,,
[Robert Cornwall to be Cornet to do. - - ,, ,, ,,]
William Bland to be Lieut. to Capt. George Walker - - - - - - - - ,, ,, ,,
Oliver Pocklington to be Chaplain - - ,, ,, ,,
Alex. Stevenson to be Cornet to Capt. ——— - [,, ,, ,,]
Isaac Lenoir to be Cornet to Lt.-Col. Otway - ,, ,, ,,
Charles James Otway to be Cornet to Capt. [Fras.] Naizon] - - - - - ,, ,, ,,
Chris. Lowe to be Cornet to Capt. ——— - ,, ,, ,,

[1] Second son of Thos. Pitt, Gov. of Fort St. George. Created Baron Londonderry 3 June, 1719, and Earl of Londonderry in 1726. Gov. of Jamaica, 6 July, 1716. Capt.-Gen. of the Leeward Islands in 1726. D. at St. Kitts, 12 Sept. 1729.

[2] Appointed Ens. in Col. Ric. Brewer's Regt. 20 Feb. 1692. Capt. in Col. Thos. Farrington's Regt. 22 Nov. 1694. Re-commissioned Capt. in Farrington's newly-raised Regt. (29th Foot) 10 March, 1702. Major of Harvey's Horse (2nd D.G.) before 1713. Promoted Lt.-Col. of said Corps, 28 May, 1713. Col. of the 9th Foot, 7 Jan. 1718. D. 23 Dec. 1725.

[3] Son of Richard Whitworth of Adbaston, Co. Stafford, and bro. to Charles, Baron Whitworth, the celebrated diplomatist. Cornet in the Earl of Macclesfield's Regt. of Horse, 8 Feb. 1702. Capt. in Harvey's Horse (2nd D.G.), 2 Jan. 1711. Major, 28 May, 1713. Brigade-Major to several Cavalry Regts. in Ireland 25 Nov. 1715. Lt.-Colonel, 1 Jan. 1718. Held this post until Feb. 1750, about which time he probably died.

THE PRINCE OF WALES'S OWN REGIMENT OF HORSE.
[4TH DRAGOON GUARDS.]

Commissions renewed by George I., 1st June, 1715.

CAPTAINS.	LIEUTENANTS.	CORNETS.
Sherington Davenport,[1] Colonel.*	No troop.	
Thomas Hatton, Lieutenant-Colonel.	David Renovard, Captain-Lieutenant.	Anan Lambert.
Charles Chibbalds, Major.	Delaval Denton.	James Butler.
John Fielding.	Samuel Coppin.	Samuel Ogle [23 July 1715].
Richard Allen.	Francis Hurry.	George Byng.
James Carr.	Peter Agar [1 May 1714].	Price Hartstonge.
Richard Stuart.	William Baldwin.	Earl of Roscommon.

CHAPLAIN.
William Hallifax, D.D.

SURGEON.
Hannibal Hall.

SUPPLEMENTARY COMMISSIONS.

John Leicester to be Lieut. in room of Samuel Coppin	23 July, 1715	*h*
David Renovard, Esq., to be Major in room of Major Chas. Chibbalds, and Capt. of a Troop	30 ,, ,,	*h*
John Leicester, Esq., to be Capt.-Lieut. in room of David Renovard	23 Aug. ,,	*h*

* NOTE.—"This officer's Commission as Colonel directed him to obey the orders of His Royal Highness the Prince of Wales, as well as those of his superior officers."

[1] Appointed Ens. in Sir E. Hales's Regt. 24 Aug. 1685. Adjt. of the Queen Dowager's Regt. of Horse 25 Feb. 1687. Cornet in do. 1 Dec. 1688. Served several campaigns in Flanders under William III. and was appointed Brigade-Major to the Light Horse, 7 May, 1694. Capt. and Lt.-Col. 1st Troop of Life Guards, 3 Dec. 1700. Bt.-Col. of Horse, 11 March, 1702. Major-Gen. 1 Jan. 1710. Col. of the 6th Horse (4th D.G.), 9 Feb. 1715. D. in Ireland as Maj.-Gen. 5 July, 1719. He was elder son of Henry Davenport by Eliz. dau. of Sherington Davenport.

MAJOR-GENERAL GEORGE KELLUM'S REGIMENT OF HORSE.
[5TH DRAGOON GUARDS.]

Commissions renewed by George I., 1st June, 1715.

CAPTAINS.	LIEUTENANTS.	CORNETS.
Major-General George Kellum,[1] Colonel.	Daniel Crespin, Captain Lieutenant.	Adam Cardonnel.
Brigadier-Genl. Robert Napier,[2] Lieut.-Col.	Henry Demaris [29 April 1714].	Maurice Bocland.
William Hall, Major [10 Feb. 1715].	William Portal.	William Henry Burrows.
Washington, Lord Tamworth[3] [20 April 1714].	John Pope.	Daniel Paule.
Metcalf Graham.	Thomas Rawdon.	John Waller.
Charles Cadogan.	Walter Pendergrass.	Richard Reynolds [23 Feb. 1713-14]

CHAPLAIN.
Peter Gaty Gojac.

SURGEON.
Daniel Cabrol.

SUPPLEMENTARY COMMISSIONS.

John Waller, Esq., to be Captain in the room of Charles Cadogan	St. James's, 1 June, 1715.	*i*
Daniel Paul, Esq., to be Captain	,, 8 Nov. ,,	*i*
Wm. Farrer to be Cornet to Col. Metcalf Graham	,, 25 ,, ,,	*i*
Thos. Tennison[4] to be Cornet to Major Wm. Hall	,, 28 ,, ,,	*h*

[1] Joined the Army as Cornet to the Duke of Shrewsbury's Indep. Tp. of Horse, 20 June, 1685. This Tp. was soon aftds. incorporated into the present 5th D.G. Capt. 31 Dec. 1688. Major, 1 Jan. 1692. Lt.-Col. 26 June, 1701. Bt.-Col. 27 June, 1703. Brig.-Gen. 1 Jan. 1707. Served at Malplaquet. Maj.-Gen. 1 Jan. 1710. Lt.-Gen. 5 Apr. 1712. Col. of above Corps, 22 Dec. 1712. D. 2 Oct. 1732.

[2] Called "Napper" in some Lists and "Nappier" in others. Appointed Capt. in Col. John Coy's Regt. of Horse (5th D.G.), 20 Jan. 1692. Major, 14 Apr. 1702. Bt.-Lt.-Col. 25 Aug. 1704. Fought at Blenheim at the forcing of the French lines, 1705, and subsequent battles under Marlborough. Brig.-Gen. 12 Feb. 1711. Col. of above Regt. 27 May, 1717. Maj.-Gen. 12 Mar. 1727. D. as Lt.-Gen. 10 Nov. 1739.

[3] Succeeded his father as 2nd Earl Ferrers, 25 Dec. 1717. Capt. in above Regt. 20 Apr. 1714. Left the Army, 26 March, 1717. D. 4 Apr. 1729.

[4] Promoted Lieut. 10 Nov. 1719. Serving as senior Lieut. in same Regt. 1740. A scion of the Irish family of this name, and kinsman to Dr. Thos. Tenison, Archbishop of Canterbury, who d. 1715.

BRIGADIER-GENERAL RICHARD WARING'S REGIMENT OF CARABINIERS.

[THE CARABINIERS.]

Commissions renewed by George I., 1st June, 1715.

CAPTAINS.	LIEUTENANTS.	CORNETS.
Brigadier-General Richard Waring,[1] Col.	No Troop.	
John Peter, Lieutenant-Colonel.	Thomas Scaife, Captain-Lieutenant.	Richard Blackwell [1st Decr. 1713].
George Robinson, Major.	James Harrison.	Henry Gordon.
William Gwyn.	William Finley.	Charles Tassell.
John Allen.	Charles Lancaster.	Philip Chenevix.
Richard Edmonds.	Philip Peck.	Sir Astley Beaumont.
Charles Echlin.[2]	John Lovick.	Euseby Strafford [3] (*sic*)

CHAPLAIN.
William Wells.

SURGEON.
William Stone.

---

[1] Appointed Lieut. in the Earl of Danby's Volunteer Regt. of Dragoons, 16 July, 1690. Lieut. and Capt. of the Grenadier Tp. of 2nd Troop of Life Guards, 30 Nov. 1691. Major of the 1st Troop of Horse Grenadier Guards, 25 Feb. 1703. Lt.-Col. of do. 25 Dec. 1703. Bt.-Col. same year. Brig.-Gen. 12 Feb. 1711. Col. of the Carabiniers, 15 Feb. 1715. He belonged to the family of Waring of Waringstown, Co. Down, and served with his Troop at Steinkirk. An interesting letter from this officer to John Ellis, Esq., giving an account of the losses suffered by his Troop at Steinkirk, is printed in the Appendix to Vol. VI. of *English Army Lists and Commission Registers*, 1661–1714, p. 394. Gen. Waring retired in June, 1721. D. 8 Dec. 1737.

[2] Left the Regt. 24 July, 1718. In his will, proved at Dublin in 1754, he is described as of "Ardquin, Co. Down, Esq."

[3] Second son of Edward *Stratford*, of Great Belan, Co. Kildare. Left the Regt. 22 May 1718. Settled at Corbally, Queen's County. D. in 1753. Will proved at Dublin. His younger brother, John, was created Earl of Aldborough.

MAJOR-GENERAL CHARLES SYBOURG'S REGIMENT OF HORSE.

[7TH DRAGOON GUARDS.]

Commissions renewed by George I., 1st June, 1715.

CAPTAINS.	LIEUTENANTS.	CORNETS.
Major-General Charles Sybourg,[1] Colonel.	Francis Law, Captain-Lieutenant.	
William Bray, Lieutenant-Colonel.	George Bennett.	Thomas Baynton.
Robert Norton, Major.	Samuel Pope [23rd Feb. 1714–15].	Richard Prescott[2] [22 Feb. 1714–15].
Stephen Palmes.	Erasmus Shorter.	John Briggs.
Molineux Robinson.	John Floyer.	Ben. Colson.
Claudius Testefolle.	John Seagram.	John, Lord Bellew,[3] Baron of Duleek [6 Feby. 1713–14].

CHAPLAIN.
Josias Sandby.

SURGEON.
Ben. Ecles.

---

[1] Is said to have been an illegitimate son of Meinhardt, Duke of Schomberg. Major of above Regt. 1 May, 1694. Lt.-Col. 1 March, 1703. Bt.-Col. 1 Jan. 1704. Commanded his Corps at Schellenberg, Blenheim, and Ramillies. Brig.-Gen. 1 Jan. 1707. Commanded a Brigade at Oudenarde. Maj.-Gen. 1 Jan. 1710. Col. of a Regt. of Foot (late Orrery's), 8 Dec. 1710. Col. of his former Regt. (7th D.G.), 12 Oct. 1713. Sold his Colonelcy, 1720. Gov. of Fort William, in Scotland, Apr. 1725. Is said to have amassed a fortune of £80,000. D. 25 Jan. 1733, and was bd. in Westminster Abbey.

[2] Served previously as Ens. in Brig.-Gen. Tatton's Regt. (24th Foot). Lieut. in Sybourg's Regt. 21 Jan. 1716. Capt. 15 Dec. 1738. Of North Clonmore, Co. Tipperary. D. 1747.

[3] Fourth Lord Bellew. Succeeded his father in 1714. Bn. 1702. Md. 1st in 1731, Lady Anne Maxwell, dau. of Wm. Earl of Nithsdale. Lord Bellew d. in 1770 without male heirs, and his title expired.

MAJOR-GENERAL WILLIAM EVANS'S REGIMENT OF DRAGOONS.

[4TH HUSSARS.]

Commissions renewed by George I., 1st June 1715.

CAPTAINS.	LIEUTENANTS.	CORNETS.
Major-General William Evans,[1] Colonel.	Edward Hawley, Captain-Lieutenant.	
Henry Hawley,[2] Lieutenant-Colonel.	Thomas Bickerton.	Charles Lukyn.
Charles Lanoe, Major.	John Olivier.	John Cavendish.
John Farrar.	Richard Close [22 Sept. 1714].	John Baynton.
Berkeley Sidney Knox.	Ben. Martyr.	Walter Philips.
Lord Hinchinbroke.[3]	George Colley.	John Curfie.

CHAPLAIN.
Robert Coucher.

SURGEON.
John Ducros.

SUPPLEMENTARY COMMISSIONS.

Nathaniel Halhed[4] to be Cornet to the Colonel's Troops - - - - - - -	St. James's, 6 April 1715.	h
Edward Hill, Esq. to be Capt. in room of Lord Hinchinbroke - - - - -	„ 11 June „	h
Thomas Bickerton, Junr. to be Lieut. to Lt.-Col. Henry Hawley - - - -	„ 23 Aug. „	h

Regt. embarked for Scotland in the autumn of 1715.

---

[1] Appointed Lieut. in the 1st Foot Guards, 3 Oct. 1690. Served at Landen, and was twice wounded at the siege of Namur. Capt.-Lieut. 15 July, 1695. Capt. of Grenadiers, 1 Aug. 1695. Col. of a newly-raised Regt. of Foot, 10 Apr. 1703. Brig.-Gen. 1 Jan. 1707. Maj.-Gen. 1 Jan. 1710. Col. of a Regt. of Dragoons (4th), 24 Oct. 1713. Fought at Sheriffmuir, and was slightly wounded. Accompanied Argyll in his march to Aberdeen early in 1716. Lt.-Gen. 6 March, 1727. Transferred to the Colonelcy of the present 2nd D.G. 6 Aug. 1733. Gen. 2 July, 1739. D. 29 Jan. 1740.

[2] Aftds. Lt.-Gen. Henry Hawley, Col. of the Royal Dragoons and Gov. of Portsmouth, who d. 24 March, 1759. He was severely wounded at Sheriffmuir. Served at Dettingen and Fontenoy. Commanded the Royalist Forces at Falkirk in 1746, and was defeated. A full account of "General Hawley's Parentage," by Charles Dalton, is given in *Notes and Queries*, 8th series, Vol. IX.

[3] Son of Edward Montagu, 3rd Earl of Sandwich. Capt. and Lt.-Col. Coldstream Guards, 11 June, 1715. Appointed A.D.C. to George I. 25 Dec. same year. Lt.-Col. of 12th Foot, 22 Nov. 1716. Col. of a Regt. of Foot (disbanded in 1718), 23 Sept. 1717. Transferred to 37th Foot, 11 Dec. same year. In Nov. 1718, Visct. Hinchinbroke fought a duel in the piazza of Covent Garden with Capt. Campbell; the former was slightly wounded and the latter dangerously (*Historical Register*). Lord Hinchinbroke md. a dau. of Alex. Popham, Esq., of Littlecote, and d. in 1722, leaving a son who succeeded as 4th Earl of Sandwich in 1729.

[4] Lieut. 8 May, 1722. Drawing half-pay from Ker's Dragoons in 1739.

LIEUTENANT-GENERAL ROSS'S REGIMENT OF DRAGOONS.
[ROYAL IRISH DRAGOONS.]

Commissions renewed by George I., 1st June 1715.

CAPTAINS.	LIEUTENANTS.	CORNETS.
Lieut.-General Charles Ross,[1] Colonel.	Charles Betty, Captain-Lieutenant.	Jeremiah Balfour.
John Hill,[2] Lieutenant-Colonel.	James Poe.	William Higgins.
Richard Gore, Major.	Edward Hamilton.	James Welsh.
Robert Drury.	John Shelston.	Ant. Cope [1st Feb. 1713–34].
John Usher.	William Ross.	Charles, Lord Murray[4] (*sic*).
William Cope [1st Feb. 1713–14].	Michael Parker.	Charles Gilmore.
John Johnston.	Henry Villiers.	William Gilmore.
George Ross.	Edward Hill.[3]	Richard Johnson.
Wrottesley Betton.	George McKean.	William Robertson.

CHAPLAIN.
James Fleming.

SURGEON.
James Scott.

SUPPLEMENTARY COMMISSIONS.

Gustavus Hamilton, Esq. to be Capt. in room of Robert Drury	17 Aug. 1715.	*h*
Sir William Johnston[5] to be Capt. in room of John Johnston	27 „ „	*h*
Thos. Sidney,[6] Esq. to be Colonel of His Majesty's Regt. of Dragoons of Ireland whereof Charles Ross, Esq. was late Colonel and to be Capt. of a Troop in do.	5 Oct. „	*i*
Richard Johnston to be Lieut. to Capt. George Ross	25 „ „	*i*
John Knox to be Cornet to Capt. John Usher [in room of Lord, Charles Murray]	23 Dec. „	*i*

[1] Of Balnagowan. Son of the 11th Baron Ross. Cornet in the King's Regt. of Scots Horse, 5 Nov. 1685. Capt. in Col. Jas. Wynne's Regt. of Inniskilling Dragoons before July, 1689. Lt.-Col. of last-named Regt. before 1694. Bt.-Col. 16 Feb. 1694. Regimental Col. 16 July, 1695. Brig.-Gen. 9 March, 1702. Maj.-Gen. 1 Jan. 1704. Served at Blenheim and in Marlborough's subsequent campaigns. Lt.-Gen. 1 Jan. 1707. Col.-General of all the Dragoon Forces, 1 May, 1711. Gen. 1 Jan. 1712. On 8 Oct. 1715, was removed from the command of his Regt., but was reappointed 1 Feb. 1729. D. at Bath 5 Aug. 1732. Bd. at Fearn in Ross-shire.

² Appointed Capt. in above Regt. 6 Nov. 1694. Major of said Corps, 24 Apr. 1707. Bt.-Lt.-Col. 1 Jan. 1707. Served throughout Marlborough's campaigns. Bt.-Col. 1 Nov. 1711. John Hill, of Culmore (ancestor of the baronets Hill of Londonderry), writes on 9 June, 1716, to Dr. Wm. King, D.D., Archbishop of Dublin- "I was acquainted with your Grace in my younger years at Dungannon, Dublin, and Londonderry." (*A Great Archbishop of Dublin*, 1650-1729). Out of the Regt. in Sept. 1719.

³ Appointed Capt. in Gen. Evans's Dragoons, 11 June, 1719. On half-pay in 1722.

⁴ Fourth son of the 1st Duke of Atholl. The following account of Lord Charles Murray is given in Burke's *Peerage*—" Charles, a Cornet of Horse, joined the Chevalier in 1715, and had the command of a regiment. After the surrender of Preston, his lordship, being amongst the prisoners, was tried by a court-martial as a deserter, and sentenced to be shot; but he was reprieved and d.s.p. in 1720."

⁵ Bro. to Sir John Johnston, of Westerhall, to whose baronetcy he succeeded in 1711.

⁶ Bro. to Joscelin, 7th Earl of Leicester. Appointed Capt. in Col. James Rivers's Regt. (6th Foot), 1 Jan. 1704. Capt. and Lt.-Col. 1st Foot Guards, 25 March, 1705. Obliged to sell his Comn. for £1,000 in April, 1714, by Queen Anne's Govt. to make way for a Roman Catholic officer named Markham. Col. Sydney d. 27 Jan. 1729.

BRIGADIER-GENERAL THOMAS HARRISON'S REGIMENT OF FOOT.

[6TH FOOT.]

Commissions renewed by George I., 1st June 1715.

CAPTAINS.	LIEUTENANTS.	ENSIGNS.
Brigadier-Genl. Thomas Harrison,[1] Colonel.	Solomon White, Capt.-Lt. [20 May 1714].	Henry Price.
John Ramsey, Lieutenant-Colonel.	William Campbell.	Robert Buggin.
Charles, Harrison,[2] Major.	No Company.	—
William Maule [29 May 1715].	William Beaufort.	Bingham Harrington.
Thomas Collier.[3]	Elias Landy.	Charles Nelson [26 March 1715].
Philip Brydal.	Arthur Brereton.	—
Ratcliffe Brodley.	Abraham Hunt.	John Clark.
Philip Babington [23 May 1715].	John Beaumont.	John Tottershall.
John Murray [26 March 1715].	James McGee.	James Duval.
Edward Columbine.	Samuel Reynolds.	Henry Hartigan.
Philip Bearde, Grendr. Cy.	Peter Petit, 1st Lieut. [20 May 1713]. Richard Miller, 2nd Lieutenant.	

CHAPLAIN.
Robert Cocking.

ADJUTANT.
Arthur Brereton.

SURGEON.
Richard Miller.

SUPPLEMENTARY COMMISSIONS.

Major Chas. Harrison to be Capt. of that Cy. whf. Col. Thos. Collier decd. was late Capt. St. James's, 29 June 1715. *h*

Nathaniel Michel[4] to be Ensign - - - „ 7 July „ *h*

---

[1] Nearly related, either by marriage or half blood, to Lord Townshend, the Sec. of State. Appointed Capt. and Lt.-Col. in the 1st Foot Guards, 10 March, 1705. Bt.-Col. 1 Jan. 1707. Adjt.-Gen. in Spain, 29 June, 1708. Col. of the Regt. subsequently known

as the 6th Foot, 14 June, 1708. Commanded this Corp at Saragossa, and was sent home with dispatches. Adjt.-Gen. in Scotland, 1715, and served at Sheriffmuir. Wrote an account of the battle, which is printed in Dr. John Campbell's *Life of the Duke of Argyll* (pp. 192–5). Sent to London with the news of Argyll's victory, and received £500 from George I. and was also knighted. Sold his Colonelcy in March, 1716. Not styled Brigadier in any other List.

² Brother to Col. T. Harrison. Appointed Capt.-Lieut. of Col. John Hill's Regt. 7 Feb. 1708. Capt. of the Port at Dunkirk, 27 June, 1712. On half-pay before 1722. See account of this officer's duel with Capt. Alex. Agnew on p. 135, note 12. Major Harrison was mortally wounded and d. in a few hours. According to the *Daily Journal* of 6 May, 1724, the combatants had a dispute upon Bishop Burnet's *Hist. of His Own Time*. Major Harrison is called "brother to Lord Townshend" in aforesaid newspaper.

³ See p. 243, note 2.

⁴ Major of above Regt. 19 Jan. 1740.

LIEUTENANT-GENERAL JOHN RICHMOND WEBB'S REGIMENT OF FOOT.

[THE KING'S.]

Commissions renewed by George I., 11th January 1715.

CAPTAINS.	LIEUTENANTS.	ENSIGNS.
Lieutenant-General J.R. Webb,[1] Colonel.	John Brozier,[4] Captain-Lieutenant.	John Gally.[6]
Anthony Colombier, Lieutenant-Colonel.	John Chambers.[5]	William Sharp.[7]
Peter Hamers,[2] Major.	John Turner.	Charles Tilbury.[8]
Benjamin Cuttle.[3]	Richard Kenny.	John Holman.[9]
John Farcy.	Peter De Cosne.	John Cowley.
James Beschefer.	Thomas Redwood.	Samuel Howe.
William Congreve.	Peter Ribton.	Thomas Sydenham.
Borelace Webb.	Theophilus Nicholls.	John Young.
Leonard Lloyd.	Conductor Ball.	Christopher Russell.
Arthur Usher, Grendr. Cy.	Edward Hobart, 1st Lieut.	
	John Smith,[10] 2nd Lieut.	

CHAPLAIN.
Thomas White.

ADJUTANT.
William Boyd.

SURGEON.
James Chambers.

SUPPLEMENTARY COMMISSIONS.

Henry Moryson,[11] Esq. to be Colonel in room of John Richmond Webb and to be Capt. of a Cy. - - - - - - St. James's, 5 Aug. 1715.*a*

Regt. embarked for Scotland in Oct. 1715.

John Vezian to be Qr.-Mr. - - - - St. James's, 25 Dec. ,, *a*

---

[1] See reference to this distinguished officer in the Introductory chapter.
[2] Served as Capt. in above Regt. at Blenheim and subsequent campaigns in Flanders. Killed at Sheriffmuir.
[3] Joined above Regt. as Ensign in 1689. Fought at Blenheim and subsequent campaigns. Killed at Sheriffmuir.
[4] Wounded at Schellenberg and at Blenheim. Fought at Malplaquet. Killed at Sheriffmuir.

[5] Killed at Sheriffmuir
[6] Do.
[7] Do.
[8] Do.
[9] Wounded and taken prisoner at Sheriffmuir. Died of his wounds while in the enemy's hands. *Records of the King's Regt.*
[10] D. in Aug. 1718.
[11] Appointed Lieut. in the Coldstream Guards, 31 Dec. 1688. Taken prisoner at the siege of Namur in July, 1695 (*Records*). Bt.-Col. 19 Oct. 1704. Brig.-Gen. 1 Jan. 1710. Second Major to the Coldstream Guards, 5 Apr. 1711. Commanded a Brigade at Sheriffmuir. D. at his house near Hampton Court, 16 Oct. 1720.

LIEUTENANT-GENERAL WILLIAM STEUART'S REGIMENT OF FOOT.

[9TH FOOT.]

Commissions renewed by George I., 1st June, 1715.

CAPTAINS.	LIEUTENANTS.	ENSIGNS.
Lieut.-General William Steuart,[1] Col.	Michael Doyne, Captain-Lieutenant [22 Feb. 1713–14].	Benjamin Darby [19 March, 1713–14].
William Steuart,[2] Lieutenant-Colonel.	Mark Kerr.	Thomas Cardiffe [9 April, 1714].
Verney Lloyd, Major. [1st May, 1715].	John Irwin.	George Cuningham.
Colonel Fiennes Twisleton.	John Castillion.	John Montgomery.
Richard O'Farrel.[3]	Thomas Constable.	William Dingly.
John Ashe.	Jeremiah Jack.	Nicholas Romaine.
Henry Dabsac.	Robert Howard.	Thomas Bolton.
Joseph Shewbridge [6th August, 1714].	Richard Dickinson.	Nathaniel Wilcox.
Thomas Hussey.	Robert Crookshanks [17 March, 1713–14].	Steuart Nugent.
John Filbridge, Grendr. Cy.	Rowley Godfrey, 1st Lieut.	
	James Steuart, 2nd Lieut.	

CHAPLAIN.
Benjamin Gregory.

ADJUTANT.
Robert Crookshanks.

SURGEON.
Robert Neilson.

SUPPLEMENTARY COMMISSIONS.

James Campbell,[4] Esq. to be Colonel in the room of Wm. Steuart and to be Capt. of a Cy. - - - - - - - St. James's, 27 July, 1715. *a*

Henry Le Grand, Esq. to be Capt. in the room of Col. Fiennes Twisleton - - - „ 10 Oct. „ *h*

---

[1] See special memoir, pp. 71–80.

[2] Nephew to Gen. Wm. Steuart. Appointed Capt. in his uncle's Regt. in Ireland, 1689. Bt.-Major, 28 July, 1691. Wounded at the first siege of Limerick on 27 Aug. 1690, when the city was unsuccessfully stormed. Commanded the above Corps at Almanza. Taken prisoner a few days after that battle at Alcira. Brig.-Gen. 12 Feb. 1711. He was of "Ballylaune." Md. the Hon. Mary Villiers, dau. of the 4th Visct. Grandison and d. 10 Nov. 1736. M.I. in Bath Abbey.

[3] Promoted Major, 8 Aug. 1717. Lt.-Col. 20 Dec. 1722. Col. of the 22nd Foot, 12 Aug. 1741. Served as a Brigadier in the Expedition to Port L'Orient in 1746. Maj.-Gen. 24 March, 1754. D. in 1757.

[4] See biog. notice on p. 221, note 52.

COLONEL JASPER CLAYTON'S REGIMENT OF FOOT.

[14TH FOOT.]

Commissions renewed by George I., 1st June, 1715.

CAPTAINS.	LIEUTENANTS.	ENSIGNS.
Jasper Clayton,[1] Colonel.	Edmund Wright, Captain-Lieutenant [15 Sept. 1713].	Richard Sinnot [14 April, 1714].
Charles Kendal,[2] Lieutenant-Colonel [15 April, 1707].	Henry Nevill [1 Nov. 1711].	William Brabazon.
Charles Otway,[3] Major.	George Moncriefe.	Nicholas West [1st June, 1715].
Matthew Lafitte [1 June, 1714].	Edward Gibson.	Benjamin Carson [7 Aug. 1711].
Stanley Monk [28 Jan. 1713–14].	George Heighington [1 June, 1715].	John Scrivener.
Thomas Harrison [5 Dec. 1710].	James Ramsey [1 Sept. 1706].	Philip Lloyd.
William Barlow [5 Jan. 1712].	Charles Standish [10 April 1714].	George Ward [1 March, 1706].
Anthony Welsh [30 April, 1707].	Dennis King [19 Sept. 1713].	William Jones [28 Sept. 1714].
Thomas Hayles.	Ralph Hansard [20 Sept. 1714].	Thomas Bray [2 July, 1709].
William Jones, Grendr. Cy.	William Cormack, 1st Lieut. [1 Oct. 1696].	
	Benjamin Green, 2nd Lieut. [1 March, 1706].	

CHAPLAIN.
John Orfeur.

ADJUTANT.
Edmund Wright
[2 April, 1714].

SURGEON.
Patrick Miller.

SUPPLEMENTARY COMMISSIONS.

John Reading,[4] Esq. to be Major in room of Charles Otway - - - - 12 Aug. 1715.*h*

Regt. embarked for Scotland in Oct. 1715.

David Stevenson to be Qr.-Mr. - - - St. James's, 25 Dec. ,, *a*

[1] Appointed Capt. in Steuart's Regt. (9th Foot), 23 Apr. 1696. Lt.-Col. of the Hon. James Stanley's Regt. 20 March, 1705. Transferred to Col. Hill's Regt. (11th Foot) as Lt.-Col. 20 Apr. 1706. Bt.-Col. 1 March, 1707. Col. of Regt. of Foot (afterwards disbanded), 8 Dec. 1710. Gov. of Dunkirk, 24 Oct. 1712. Served several campaigns under Marlborough, and fought at Almanza. Col. of 14th Foot, 15 June, 1713. Fought at Sheriffmuir. Was actively employed in the Western Highlands during the years 1716-1719. Served at Glenshiel in June, 1719. Attained the rank of Lt.-General, 2 July, 1739, and was killed at Dettingen, where he commanded a division.

[2] Son of Nicholas Kendal, merchant. Lieut. in above Regt. 28 Feb. 1689. Qr.-Mr. 24 Sept. same year. Capt. 1 Aug. 1693. Served at the battle of Landen and at the siege of Namur. Major before 1706. Lt.-Col. 15 Apr. 1707. Saw much service in Scotland, 1715-1717. Left the Regt. in 1718.

[3] See biog. notice on p. 110, note 3.

[4] Served as Capt. in Col. Wade's Regt. (33rd Foot) at Almanza. Was wounded and taken prisoner. Bt.-Major, 1 Jan. 1712. Town Major of Limerick, 14 Feb. 1716. Lt.-Col. of Clayton's Regt. 14 Feb. 1718. Possibly identical with John Reading, Esq. of Clonegown, King's County, whose will was proved at Dublin in 1747.

MAJOR-GENERAL WIGHTMAN'S REGIMENT OF FOOT.
[17TH FOOT.]

Commissions renewed by George I., 1st June, 1715.

CAPTAINS.	LIEUTENANTS.	ENSIGNS.
Major-General Joseph Wightman.[1] Colonel [20 Aug. 1707].	Edward Tyrrell, Captain-Lieutenant [20 March, 1714].	Henry Briscoe [Out in 1717].
Oliver Brooke,[2] Lieutenant-Colonel [23 Nov. 1709].	Richard Radley [Out in 1717].	Gregory Milner [Out in 1717].
Chris. Russell,[3] Major [23 Nov. 1709].	Roger Pedley [4 July, 1707].	William Hubbald [Out in 1717].
Andrew Pope [22 June, 1713, Capt. of Foot].	Robert Mountford [25 April, 1706].	James Marquis [24 June, 1707].
John Smith [Out in 1717].	Edward Martin [20 Oct. 1704].	Edward Crofts [30 April, 1711.
Thomas Morris[4] [Out in 1717].	John Beaumont [28 June, 1712].	John Dumaresq [12 June, 1705]
William Lloyd [24 June, 1705, Capt. of Foot].	Francis Paynton [15 April, 1707].	Thomas Morris[7] [20 March, 1710].
Edward St. George [15 April, 1703].	John Rivason [22 June, 1703].	Andrew Booth [31 Oct. 1711].
Dudley Cosby.[5]	William Ingram [4 March, 1704].	William Bruce [Out in 1717].
Loftus Cosby,[6] Grendr. Cy. [15 April, 1707].	John Brown, 1st Lieut. [12 June, 1705]. William Cobb, 2nd Lieut. [31 Jan. 1711].	

CHAPLAIN.
Francis Alexander Hirondel.
[7 July, 1707].

ADJUTANT.
James Grigg.
[1 Jan. 1704.]

SURGEON.
Andrew Vimcelle.
[6 Nov. 1702.]

Regt. embarked for Scotland in Oct. 1715.

Chris. Forster to be Qr.-Mr. - - - - St. James's, 25 Dec. 1715.*a*

[1] See special memoir, pp. 48–54.

[2] Appointed Lieut. in Sir George St. George's Regt. of Foot, 1 Jan. 1692. Capt.-Lieut. 1 Jan. 1694. Capt. 20 Aug. 1695. Served at the siege of Namur. Fought at Almanza. Major, 19 Aug. 1707. Lt.-Col. 23 Nov. 1709. Serving as Lt.-Col. in 1739. D. same year. *Gentleman's Mag.*

[3] This officer was commissioned Ensign in above Regt. (17th Foot) 29 Sept. 1688. Served in Flanders, Portugal, Spain, and during the '15 in Scotland. Attained the rank of Regtal. Lt.-Col. 5 June, 1722. His eleven Commissions are in the possession of his representative, Col. Christopher Russell, late R.E., and are enumerated in Vol. VI. of *English Army Lists and Comn. Registers*, p. 90. Lt.-Col. Chris. Russell d. at Ciudadela, Minorca, 29 Oct. 1729, where he was Lt.-Governor.

[4] See biog. notice on p. 219, note 25.

[5] Of Stradbally Hall, Queen's County. Fought at Almanza, where he was taken prisoner. Left the Regt. 22 May, 1716. Was M.P. for Queen's County. D. 24 May, 1729.

[6] Fought at Almanza, where he was taken prisoner. D. at Marseilles, 3 Jan. 1726. *Landed Gentry*.

[7] Father of Capt. Chas. Morris of the 2nd Life Guards, who is referred to in note on the Morris family, p. 219, note 25.

BRIGADIER-GENERAL RICHARD SUTTON'S REGIMENT OF FOOT.

[19TH FOOT.]

Commissions renewed by George I., 11th January, 1714-15.

CAPTAINS.	LIEUTENANTS.	ENSIGNS.
Brigadier-General Richard Sutton,[1] Col.	Samuel Norman, Captain-Lieutenant.	Joseph Green.
[George Grove],[2] Lieut.-Col.		
Richard Hawley,[3] Major.	Thomas Piercy.	Thomas Browne.
Thomas Woodhouse.	William Mercer.	Robert Moore.
Richard Stone.	John Massy.	Joseph Furness.
James Phillips.	Michael Legg.	
John Furness.	Matthew Waller.	William Barton.
	John Whiting.	Edward Rawson.
William Leigh.	Thomas Clift (*sic*).	
Thomas Pratt, Grendr. Cy.	Charles Mainwaring, 1st Lieut. (?)	
	Sir Warren Crosby (*sic*). 2nd Lieut. (?)	
Joseph Stisted [11 Jan. 1714-15].	Mons. Simons.	

ADJUTANT.
Mons. Simons.

SURGEON.
Peter Toussaint.

SUPPLEMENTARY COMMISSIONS.

Randolph Baron to be Ens. to Capt. (*sic*) Geo. Grove - - - - - - -	St. James's, 24 March, 1715.*i*	
Wm. Rousby to be do. to Capt. Richard Stone	,, 24 April, 1715.*a & i*	
Edward Browne, Esq. to be Capt. in room of Thos. Pratt - - - - - -	,, 14 May, 1715.*i*	
Thos. Handasyde,[4] Esq. to be Lt.-Colonel of Col. George Grove's Regt. of Foot [late Sutton's] and Capt. of a Company - -	,, 5 Aug. ,,	*a*
George Grove,[2] Esq. to be Colonel in room of Richard Sutton and to be Capt. of a Cy.	,, ,, ,,	*h*
Leming Richardson to be Ens. to Major Richard Hawley - - - - - -	,, 8 ,, ,,	*h*
Adam Williamson,[5] Esq. to be Capt. in room of Wm. Leigh - - - - - -	,, 29 ,, ,,	*h*

[1] See special memoir, pp. 55–58.
[2] Appointed Ens. in Col. Fitzpatrick's Regt. 21 May, 1692. 2nd Lieut. in the Rl. Fusiliers, 25 Aug. 1693. Served in Flanders and at Cadiz. Capt. in Col. Wm. Evans's Regt. of Foot, 10 Apr. 1703. Col. of the 19th Foot, 5 Aug. 1715. D. from the effects of a fall from his horse, 13 Oct. 1729.
[3] Younger son of Henry Hawley of Brentford. Mentioned in his father's will. Ens. in Erle's Regt. 7 March, 1692. Lieut. 13 Aug. 1695. Capt. 21 Jan. 1703. Major, 10 June, 1710. Commission renewed by George II. Serving as Major in 1740. Not in any List after that year.
[4] See biog. notice on p. 163, note 4.
[5] See biog. notice on p. 223, note 78.

THE EARL OF ORRERY'S REGIMENT OF SCOTCH FUZILIERS.
[ROYAL SCOTS FUSILIERS.]

Commissions renewed by George I., 1st March 1715.

CAPTAINS.	1ST LIEUTENANTS.	2ND LIEUTENANTS.
Charles, Earl of Orrery,[1] Colonel.	Mongo Mathie, Captain-Lieutenant [23 April, 1712].	William Ross [18 March, 1709].
William Murray,[2] Lieutenant-Colonel [24 Sept. 1708].	Robert Paterson [18 March, 1709].	Robert Herries [18 March, 1709].
James Montresor,[3] Major. [1 Oct. 1709].	Charles Swan [18 March, 1709].	Henry Russell [1 Oct. 1709].
John Douglas [24 Aug 1706].	George Skene [1 Oct. 1709].	Thomas Pierson.
George Home[4] [24 Dec. 1706].	Lewis Dick [18 March, 1709].	James Graham [1 Jan. 1708].
Robert Urquhart [16 March, 1708].	William Row [24 Aug. 1704].	Charles Clarke [23 June, 1710].
Alexander Abercrombie [3 Sept. 1709].	Philip Basset [8 June, 1711].	James Cuming [18 March, 1709].
William McHenry, Grendr. Cy. [Out in 1717].	David Braymer [24 June, 1707].	Isaac Hamond [Out in 1717].
James Ogilvie [Out in 1717].	William Nodding [24 Oct. 1710].	Laurence Drummond [26 Oct. 1710].
Anthony Lowther [Out in 1717].	Francis Skene [18 March, 1709].	James Murray [24 Nov. 1710].

CHAPLAIN.
Robert Middleton.

ADJUTANT.
Mongo Mathie.

SURGEON.
John Craig.

NOTE.—"I, George Skene, Lieutenant and Agent for the Regiment of Scotch Fuziliers commanded by the Right Honourable the Earl of Orrery, do certify that the above are the names of the several officers in the said Regiment, and that their several Commissions are as I believe and to the best of my knowledge dated as above.
"(Signed) GEORGE SKENE."

SUPPLEMENTARY COMMISSIONS.

Regt. embarked for Scotland in the summer of 1715.

Arman [d] du Perron to be 2nd Lieut. to Capt. Wm. Machandry's Company of Grenadiers	St. James's,	1 Aug.	1715.	*a*
Walter Christie, Esq. to be Capt [of an additional Company] in the North British Fuziliers	,,	24 ,,	,,	*a*
Thos. Donne, Esq. to be do. [of do.]	,,	,, ,,	,,	*a*
Andrew Hay to be 1st Lieut. to Capt. Christie	,,	,, ,,	,,	*a*
Roger Hutton to be do. to Capt. Thos. Doune	,,	,, ,,	,,	*a*
Wm. Warlock to be 2nd Lieut. to Capt. W. Christie	,,	,, ,,	,,	*a*
Thos. Michelson to be do. to Capt. Thos. Donne	,,	,, ,,	,,	*a*
Robert Pattison to be Qr.-Mr.	,,	,, ,,	,,	*a*

[1] Second son of Roger, 2nd Earl of Orrery. Succeeded his bro. as 4th Earl in 1703. Col. of a newly-raised Regt. of Foot in Ireland, 1 March, 1704. Removed to another corps (aftds. disbanded), 24 Feb. 1707. Brig.-Gen. 1 Jan. 1709. Served at Malplaquet and greatly distinguished himself. Maj.-Gen. 17 Aug. 1710. Appointed Envoy to the States of Brabant and Flanders. Col. of the North British Fusiliers, 8 Dec. 1710. Served under the Duke of Ormonde in 1712. A Lord of the Bedchamber to George I. 1714. Resigned his Colonelcy in July, 1716. Sent to the Tower on a charge of high treason in 1722; but no crime was proved against him. D. 8 Aug. 1731.

[2] Younger bro. to Sir Jas. Murray, Bt. of Clermont. Appointed Capt. in above Regt. 14 Sept. 1693. Major, 15 Aug. 1706. Lt.-Col. 24 Sept. 1708. Commanded above Regt. at Malplaquet and at Sheriffmuir. D. or left the Army in Apr. 1718.

[3] Son of Jacques de Trésor, a Huguenot refugee (Burke's *Landed Gentry*). Appointed Ens. in Col. John Hales's Regt. 26 Feb. 1691. Transferred to the Scots Foot Guards, 1 Sept. 1691. Lieut. and Capt. 22 May, 1694. Capt. in the Scots Fusiliers, 25 Feb. 1702. Fought at Blenheim. Major, 1 Oct. 1709. Wounded at Malplaquet. Lt.-Gov. of Fort William, in Scotland, at the time of his death, 29 Jan. 1724, aged 56.

[4] Called "Hume" in previous lists. Served at Malplaquet. In the above list of the Earl of Orrery's Regt. given in the Irish Comn. Book, 1709–1716, Capt. Home is noted as "afterwards Sir George Home." Untraced after 1717.

THE PRINCE OF WALES'S OWN REGIMENT OF ROYAL WELSH FUZILIERS.

[ROYAL WELSH FUSILIERS.]

Commissions renewed by George I., 1st June, 1715.

CAPTAINS.	1ST LIEUTENANTS.	2ND LIEUTENANTS.
Major-General Joseph Sabine,[1] Colonel.	John Pennefather, Captain-Lieutenant.	John Sabine.
Arthur Brett,[2] Lieutenant-Colonel.	John Heley [20 April 1714].	Molineux Robinson.
Thomas Vincent,[3] Major.	Charles Walters.	Alexander Johnson.
Henry Cookman.[4]	William Armstrong.	William Sabine.
Southwell Pigott.	Nicholas Kelly.	Charles Combe.
Ralph Whitfield.	James Gordon.[6]	Joseph Matthew Pennefather.
James Bissell.	Henry Hickman.	— Cornwall.
William Cole.	Richard Dunbar.	Thomas Bolton.
Newsham Peers.[5]	Malachi Hawtayne.	Robert Bransby.
Griffith Jones, [Grendr. Cy.]	Henry Rumsey.	James Carey.

ADJUTANT.
Peter Hewet.

SURGEON.
Thomas White.

SUPPLEMENTARY COMMISSIONS.

Peter Hewet to be Adjt.	St. James's, 1 June, 1715.	*a*
Wm. Hawtayne to be Chaplain	„ 23 July „	*a*

Regt. embarked for England in the autumn of 1715.

Edward Thetford, Esq. to be Capt. [of an additional Company]	St. James's, 26 Sept. „	*a*
John Powell, Esq. to be do. [of do.]	„ „ „	*a*
Wm. Gale to be 1st Lieut. to Capt. Thetford	„ „ „	*a*
Edward Stannard to be 2nd Lieut. to do.	„ „ „	*a*
John Weldon to be do. to Capt. Powell	„ „ „	*a*

---

[1] Grandson of Avery Sabine, Alderman of Canterbury. Appointed Capt.-Lieut. of Sir H. Ingoldsby's Regt. 8 March, 1689. Capt. of the Grendr. Cy. same year. Major of Col. Herbert's Regt. (23rd Foot), 13 July, 1691. Served in the Irish campaign that year. Lt.-Col. 6 June, 1695. Bt.-Col. 1 Jan. 1703. Wounded at Schellenberg, where he commanded the Regt. Col. of the Welsh Fusiliers, 1 Apr. 1705. Brig.-Gen. 1 Jan. 1707. Distinguished himself at Ramillies and Oudenarde. Maj.-Gen. 1 Jan. 1710. Lt.-Gen. 4 March, 1727. Gen. 2 July, 1730. Appointed Gov. of Gibraltar in 1730, and d. there

24 Oct. 1739. Gen. Sabine purchased the estate of Tewin, in Herts, 1715, and was interred in Tewin Church, 1739. "George I. twice visited Tewin House, near Hertford, the property of General Sabine, who had spent £40,000 on building and furnishing it, inspecting the fine marble hall and staircase, the collection of pictures and fine frescoes." *The First George in England and Hanover*, by Lewis Melville, Vol. II., p. 10.

[2] Capt. in above Regt. 2 Apr. 1705. Wounded at Malplaquet. Major, 24 Dec. 1711. Bt.-Col. 15 Nov. same year. Out of the Regt. 10 Feb. 1718.

[3] Appointed 2nd Lieut. in Brigadier Ric. Ingoldsby's Regt. (23rd Foot), 31 May, 1701. Lieut. with power to act as Capt. 24 June, 1706. Capt. 24 Nov. 1708. Wounded at Malplaquet. Bt.-Lt.-Col. 1 Jan. 1712. Not in any List after 1715.

[4] See p. 219, note 29. Superannuated, 13 Oct. 1715.

[5] 2nd Lieut. in above Regt. 25 Apr. 1706. 1st. Lieut. 24 June, 1707. Wounded at Malplaquet. Lt.-Col. 22 Dec. 1722. Succeeded Gen. Sabine as Col. of the Regt. 23 Nov. 1739. D. of wounds recd. at the battle of Dettingen.

[6] Younger son of the 5th Visct. Kenmure by his 3rd wife. *New Scottish Peerage*.

MAJOR-GENERAL GILBERT PRIMROSE'S REGIMENT OF FOOT.
[24TH FOOT.]

Commissions renewed by George I., 1st June, 1715.

CAPTAINS.	LIEUTENANTS.	ENSIGNS.
Major-General Gilbert Primrose,[1] Col.	John Douglas, Captain-Lieutenant.	Samuel Needham.
Patrick Meade,[2] Lieutenant-Colonel.	John Parr.	Abel Warren [1 Oct. 1714].
Thomas Pollexfen,[3] Major.	John Ballard.	John Gordon.
Charles Mitford.	Timothy Thomas.	William Congreve.
Richard Harwood.	James Maxwell.	James Gabriel Maturin.
Philip Bragg.	John Gardiner.	Ralph Lisle.
Benjamin Drake.	Henry Berkeley.	John Scott.
Verney Lloyd.[4]	Julius Cæsar Parkes.	Charles Milson.
Gilbert Primrose.	Christopher Geary.	William Widdington [1 Nov. 1714.]
Thomas Albritton, Grendr. Cy.	Samuel Furnes, 1st Lieut.	
	Michael Swift, 2nd Lieut.	

CHAPLAIN.
Peter Maturin.

ADJUTANT.
James Maxwell.

SURGEON.
Samuel Mungan.

SUPPLEMENTARY COMMISSIONS.

Hector Hammon[5] (*sic*) to be Capt.	St. James's,	20 May, 1715	*a*
Samuel Needham to be Lieut. to Capt. Hammon	[Dublin]	30 Nov. ,,	*i*
Thomas Sinnott to be Ens. to the Colonel's Cy.	,,	5 Dec. ,,	*i*
Benjamin Larwood,[6] Esq., to be Capt.	,,	19 ,, ,,	*i*
Courthope Meade to be Ens. to Lt.-Col. Thos. Pollexfen	,,	20 ,, ,,	*i*
Wm. Bissell to be Qr.-Mr.	St. James's,	25 ,, ,,	*a*

[1] Third son of Sir Archibald Primrose, Bt. a Lord of Session. Lieut in the King's Foot Guards, 1 Sept. 1680. Adjt. 19 March, 1686. Capt. and Lt.-Col. 21 March, 1692.

Bt.-Col. 1 March, 1703. Wounded at Schellenberg, where he commanded the Battalion. 2nd Major, 24 March, 1705. Brig.-Gen. 1 Jan. 1707. Col. of the 24th Foot, 9 March, 1708. Maj.-Gen. 1 Jan. 1710. Retd. in Sept. 1717. D. 1731.

[2] Third son of Lt.-Col. Wm. Meade, of Ballintubby, co. Cork. Capt. in above Regt. at its first raising, 8 March, 1689. Served in Ireland and on board the Fleet. Major, 18 Oct. 1695. Lt.-Col. of the 24th Foot, 25 Aug. 1704. Commanded this Corps at Blenheim Bt.-Col. 1 Jan. 1706. Served at Ramillies. Fought at Malplaquet. Brig.-Gen. 12 Feb. 1711. D. in 1732. Will dated 9 Apr. 1726. Proved 30 June, 1732.

[3] Capt. in above Regt. 20 March, 1694. Bt.-Major 1 Jan. 1706. Bt.-Lt.-Col. 1 Jan. 1712. Wounded at Blenheim. Served in several subsequent campaigns in Flanders. Serving in Ireland with the brevet rank of Col. in 1724.

[4] Capt. Verney Lloyd was appointed Major of Steuart's Regt. of Foot, 1 May, 1715 (see p. 338), and is wrongly given in the above List. He was succeeded as Capt. by Hector Hamon on 20 May, 1715, whose Commission is quoted in the text.

[5] Appointed Ensign in Col. Toby Caulfield's Regt. of Foot in Ireland, 7 Apr. 1708. Capt. in Primrose's Regt. 20 May, 1715. Major, 3 Nov. 1735. D. in 1741. Will proved at Dublin.

[6] Called "Peter" Larwood in English Comn. Entry Book, 1714–1716. Further services untraced.

BRIGADIER-GENERAL GEORGE PRESTON'S REGIMENT OF FOOT.

[THE CAMERONIANS.]

Commissions renewed by George I., 1st June, 1715.

CAPTAINS.

Brigadier General
  George Preston,[1]
    Col.
  [1 Jan. 1706].
George, Lord Forrester,[2]
    Lieut. Colonel.
James Lawson,[3]
    Major.
William Drummond.

Alexander Ogilvie
  [28 Aug. 1711].
Robert Preston.[4]

Wadham Spragge
  [25 Aug. 1704].
Robert Ferguson[5]
  [1 Aug. 1706].
William Anstruther.

William St. Clair,
    Grendr. Cy.
  [3 May, 1711].

LIEUTENANTS.

William Ferguson,
    Captain-Lieutenant
  [29 Apr. 1713].
Alexander Burnett
  [7 Oct. 1709].
James Simpson
  [1 June, 1704].
Robert Pringle
  [1 Sept. 1707].
William Russell
  [1 Oct. 1709].
William Dyer
  [10 Jan. 1706].
William Elphinstone.

Francis Graham
  [1 Aug. 1706].
John Colville
  [19 June, 1710].
Robert Barkly (*sic*)
    (1st Lieut.)

John Blair (2nd Lieut.)
  [28 Aug. 1711].

ENSIGNS.

James Ferguson.

Andrew Forrester.

Francis Scott
  [1 Dec. 1708].
Charles Colville
  [19 June 1710].
John Ayton
  [30 Apr. 1711].
David Ayton.

Richard Harris
  [20 Aug. 1711].
Robert Ross
  [1 Oct. 1709].
James Gordon
  [25 Aug. 1704].

CHAPLAIN.

Samuel Holliday[6]
  [1 Dec. 1708].

ADJUTANT.

John Gilchrist
  [1 June, 1715].

SURGEON.

Alexander Arthur [Senr.]
  [1 Aug. 1796].

Returned from Ireland to England in the summer of 1715.

SUPPLEMENTARY COMMISSIONS.

Hugh Simple (sic), Esq., to be Capt. [of an additional Company]	St. James's, 26 Sept. 1715.		a
John Dalrymple, Esq., to be Capt. [of do.]	,,	,,	,, a
George Bayly to be Lieut. to Capt. Dalrymple	,,	,,	,, a

[1] Younger son of Sir George Preston, Bt. of Valleyfield, Co. Perth. Appointed Capt. in the Scots Dragoons, 8 Sept. 1692. Bt.-Lt.-Col. 1 Aug. 1702. Regtal. Major, 1 Apr. 1704. Lt.-Col. same year. Bt.-Col. 1 Jan. 1706. Sold his Lt.-Colonelcy same year. Col. of the Cameronians, 24 Aug. 1706. Fought at Blenheim. Wounded at Ramillies. Commanded his Corps at Malplaquet. Brig.-Gen. 12 Feb. 1711. Gov. of Nieuport, 19 May, 1713. Lt.-Gen. 2 July, 1739. He succeeded Col. James Stewart as Deputy Governor of Edinburgh Castle in the autumn of 1715. On the outbreak of the '45, Lt.-Gen. Preston, then in his 86th year, proceeded at once to Edinburgh and held the Castle for the King until the insurrection was over. The Government thought it necessary to despatch Lt.-General Guest to Edinburgh to take over the supreme command, but it is generally believed that had it not been for Preston's strength of character, and his unceasing vigilance, General Guest would have surrendered the Castle to the Stuart forces after Preston Pans. It is recorded of Gen. Preston that "every two hours a party of soldiers wheeled him in an armchair round the guards that he might personally see if all were on the alert" (Grant's *Memoirs of the Castle of Edinburgh*, p. 171). This splendid old veteran d. on 7 July, 1748, aged 88.

[2] Son of Wm. Baillie, 3rd Lord Forrester. Cornet in the Rl. North Brit. Dragoons, 1 Jan. 1707. Served at Oudenarde and Malplaquet. Out of the Cavalry before 1711. Bt.-Col. of Foot, 15 Nov. 1711. Commanded the Cameronians at the attack and capture of Preston in Nov. 1715, and was wounded. Succeeded Lt.-General Wills in command of the 30th Foot, 5 Jan. 1716. Transferred to the Colonelcy of the 2nd Tp. of Horse Grenadier Guards, 17 Jan. 1717. Removed to the 4th Tp. of Life Guards (Scots Troop), 21 April 1719. D. 17 Feb. 1727.

[3] Ensign in above Regt. 1 Apr. 1691. Lieut. 7 May, 1694. Capt. 1 June, 1704. Wounded at Schellenberg, also at Blenheim. Fought at Malplaquet. Major in 1711. Bt.-Lt.-Col. 1 Jan. 1712. Wounded at the attack on Preston in Nov. 1715. Sold his Majority, 12 June, 1717, to Capt. Robt. Ferguson of same corps.

[4] It is recorded in Rapin's *Hist. of England* that this officer was captured in the attack on Preston, in Nov. 1715, and that his life was gallantly saved by a Jacobite officer. Vol. IV. p. 451.

[5] See biog. notice on p. 222, note 60.

[6] Samuel *Haliday*. Served with above Regt. in Flanders. On half-pay in 1722.

BRIGADIER-GENERAL ANDREWS WINDSOR'S REGIMENT OF FOOT.

[28TH FOOT.]

Commissions renewed by George I. 1 June 1715.

CAPTAINS.	LIEUTENANTS.	ENSIGNS.
Brigadier-General Andrews Windsor[1] Col.	Henry Serau, Captain-Lieutenant.	Thomas Tonge.
William Davidson,[2] Lieutenant-Colonel.	Charles Gignone.	Daniel Lewis.
Huntington Manning,[3] Major.	Richard Cranley.	Dennis Sullivan.
George Nodes.	George Coates.	John Moore.
Stephen Downes [28 Decr. 1713].	Robert Fleming [8 April 1714].	William Davidson.
Peter Morin.	Henry Pym.	Thomas Fitz Thomas.
Valentine Crome.	Robert Turnbull.	Marmaduke Soul.
Lewis Liermont.	William Taylor.	Alexander Johnson.
James Gibson.	John Raphson.	Henry Cossard.
John Champfleury, Grendr. Cy.	Scott Floyer, 1st Lieut.	
	Joseph Capell, 2nd Lieut. [27 April 1714].	

CHAPLAIN.

Henry Breary.

ADJUTANT.

William Davidson.

SURGEON.

Alexander Johnson.

SUPPLEMENTARY COMMISSIONS.

Wm. Barrell,[4] Esq., to be Colonel in room of
    Andrews Windsor, and Capt. of a Cy. - St. James's, 27 Sept. 1715 *a*
William Graham to be Surgeon - - - —   5 Dec. ,, *i*

---

[1] Youngest bro. to Thos. Viscount Windsor. Appointed Cornet in the Rl. Regt. of Horse Guards, 20 Feb. 1698. Capt. and Lt.-Col. 1st Foot Guards, 15 Jan. 1702. Fought at Blenheim. Bt.-Col. 1 Jan. 1706. Served at Ramillies. Wounded at Malplaquet. Col. of the 28th Foot, 1 Oct. 1709. Brig.-Gen. 12 Feb. 1711. Retd. in Sept. 1715.

² Appointed Capt. of the Grendr. Cy. in Col. John Gibson's Regt. 28 Feb. 1695. Taken prisoner at Almanza, where he served as Bt.-Lt.-Col. Regtal. Lt.-Col. 21 Sept. 1710. D. or left the Regt. in Dec. 1718.

³ Appointed Ens. in the 1st Foot Guards, 30 Apr. 1702. Lt.-Col. of Sir C. Hotham's Regt. 21 Feb. 1709. Bt.-Lt.-Col. same date. Served with said Corps in Spain. Major of 28th Foot, 21 Sept. 1710. Adjt.-Gen. of all his Majesty's Forces in Ireland, 28 Jan. 1717.

⁴ Appointed Lieut. and Capt. 1st Foot Guards, 27 Mar. 1698. 1st Lieut. of Grendr. Cy. in 1702. Adjt. before 1704. Fought at Blenheim. Capt. and Lt.-Col. 5 Jan. 1705. Bt.-Col. 1 Jan. 1707. Served throughout Marlborough's campaigns. Brig.-Gen. 7 Mar. 1727. Col. 22nd Foot, 25 Aug. 1730. Transferred to 4th Foot, 8 Aug. 1734. Maj.-Gen. 1 Nov. 1735. Lt.-Gen. 2 July, 1739. Gov. of Pendennis Castle. D. 8 Aug. 1749. Bd. in Westminster Abbey, where is a monument to his memory, which was erected by his only son and executor, Savage Barrell. The inscription thereon describes Gen. Barrell as "of an ancient Herefordshire family."

LORD MARK KERR'S REGIMENT OF FOOT.

[29TH FOOT.]

Commissions renewed by George I., 1 June 1715.

CAPTAINS.	LIEUTENANTS.	ENSIGNS.
Lord Mark Kerr,[1] Colonel.	No Company.	
Charles Cracherode,[2] Lieutenant Colonel.	Joseph King.	Mark Hollingworth.
Benjamin Columbine,[3] Major.	John Pitman.	Henry Debrose.
	Ebenezer Darby.	
Robert Minzies.	Alexander Man, Captain-Lieutenant.	Howell Herd.
John Greenwood.	David Henderson.	John Dally.
Peter Bonafous.	Thomas Peirson.	William Shenton
Reuben Caillaud.	Henry Staughton.	Daniel Caillaud [24 Novr. 1713].
John Brooke.	Henry Symes.	William Ash.
David Paine.	John Charlton [24 Novr. 1713].	Henry Melling.
Hugh Montgomery [24 Novr. 1713].	Richard Mallen.	Francis Salisbury.
John Miller, Grendr. Cy.	James Steuart, 1st Lieut.	
	Jonathan Young, 2nd Lieut.	

CHAPLAIN.

Henry Bland.

ADJUTANT.

Andrew Charlton
[24 Novr. 1713.]

SURGEON.

Bartholomew Black.

SUPPLEMENTARY COMMISSIONS.

James Kennedy,[4] Esq., to be Capt. in room of Robert Miniz (*sic*) - - - - - - -	29 June 1715	*i*
Lord Mark Kerr to be Capt. of that Cy. whf. Peter Bonafous was late Capt. in above Regt. - - -	10 Aug. ,,	*h*
James Kerr, Esq., to be Capt.-Lieut. - - - -	30 Nov. ,,	*i*
Wm. Lake to be Lieut. to Capt. Ruben Caulfield (*sic*) -	,, ,,	*i*

[1] Fourth son of Robert 1st Marquess of Lothian. Appointed Capt. in Lord Jedburgh's Regt. of Dragoons, 15 Apr. 1697. Lt.-Col. of Col. Geo. Maccartney's Regt. of Foot, 29 Jan. 1704. Served in Flanders. Col. of a newly-raised Regt. of Foot in Scotland, 29 May 1706. Commanded his Corps at Almanza and was wounded. Brig.-Gen. 12 Feb. 1711. Col. 29th Foot, 7 Oct. 1712. Gov. of Carrickfergus and Belfast in 1716; also C.O. of all His Majesty's Forces in the counties of Down and Antrim. Comded. an Infantry Brigade in the Expedition to Vigo, 1719. Maj.-Gen. 10 Mar. 1727. Lt.-Gen. 1 Nov. 1735. Gov. of Guernsey in 1740. Gen. in 1743. At the time of the battle of Preston Pans, Lord Mark Kerr was Gov. of Berwick. It is recorded that when Gen. "Johnny" Cope arrived in hot haste at the gates of Berwick, after his defeat by Prince Charlie, Lord Mark dryly remarked to the fugitive: "You are the first general who ever brought the first news of his own defeat!" Lord Mark Kerr d. 2 Feb. 1752, and was bd. in Kensington Church. At the time of his death he was Colonel of the 11th Dragoons.

[2] Appointed Lieut. in Col. John Hales's Regt. of Foot 12 March 1688. Capt. 1 Nov. 1689. Capt. in Col. Farrington's Regt. of Foot. 16 Feb. 1694. Lt.-Col. of 29th Foot 23 Nov. 1710. Retd. in Jan. 1717. See anecdote of Mordaunt Cracherode on p. 49.

[3] Appointed Cornet in Leveson's Horse (2nd D.G.), 1 July, 1698. Capt. in Farrington's Foot (29th) in 1703. Major 23 Nov. 1710. Lt.-Col. 28 Jan. 1717. Retd. following Dec. He was of Morely, co. Antrim. Md. Mary dau. of Edward Harrison, of same county, by Joanna dau. of Dr. Jeremy Taylor, Bishop of Dromore. By this lady Col. Columbine had one dau. who md. in 1736 Sir Edward Hales, Bt. Mrs. Columbine md. secondly Sir Cecil Wray, 11th Bart. of Glentworth, co. Lincoln, formerly a Captain in above Regt. By this marriage Sir Cecil Wray had no issue. See *Hist. of the Wrays of Glentworth*, by Charles Dalton, F.R.G.S., Vol. II., p. 153.

[4] See biog. notice on p. 108, note 7.

MAJOR-GENERAL CHARLES WILLS'S REGIMENT OF FOOT.
[30TH FOOT.]

Commissions renewed by George I., 25 March 1715.

CAPTAINS.	1ST LIEUTENANTS.	2ND LIEUTENANTS.
Major General Charles Wills,[1] Colonel.	William Davison, Captain-Lieutenant.	Henry Aylmer.
Richard Cobham,[2] Lieutenant-Colonel.	Richard Lethat.	Edmund Quarles.
David Ward, Major.		John Hobart.
John Saunders, Grendr. Cy.	John Roper.	
Charles Williams.	Rothwell Stow.	Charles Rainsford.
Walter Palliser.[3]	John Thompson.	Patrick Aylmer.
Hugh Palliser.[4]	Thomas Dawes.	Ventris Scott.
Charles Davison.	Thomas Newdigate.	Edmund Martin.
Michael Midford.	Thomas Burston.	Tiddeman Roberts.
William Scott.	William Cooke.	William Pritchard.
	Henry Long.	Benjamin Sladden.

CHAPLAIN.
Alexander Innes.

ADJUTANT.
James Baker.

SURGEON.
David Hall.

NOTE.—"These are to certify that the above-said Officers' Commissions in Lieut. (*sic*) General Wills's Regiment to the best of my knowledge bear date the 25th March, 1715.

"(Signed) RICHARD COBHAM."

SUPPLEMENTARY COMMISSIONS.

James Baker to be [2nd?] Lieut. to Capt. Walter Palliser 13 Sept. 1715 *i*
Edward Wolfe, Esq., to be Major and Capt. of
    a Cy. - - - - - - - St. James's, 1 Nov. „ *a*

---

[1] See special memoir, pp. 59–70.

[2] Appointed Lieut. in the Duke of Bolton's Regt. of Foot, 30 Dec. 1689. Served in the West Indies. Capt. in Col. E. Dutton Colt's Regt. of Marines, 19 July, 1698. Major of Col. Fox's Marines, 26 June, 1703. Lt.-Col. 21 May, 1706. Half-pay, 1713. Lt.-Col. of Wills's Regt. of Foot, 25 Mar. 1715. D. or retd. in July, 1717.

[3] Appointed Lieut. in Prince George of Denmark's Regt. of Foot, 14 Sept. 1693. Capt. in Col. Saunderson's Foot, 15 May, 1697. Placed on h.p. as Capt. in Wills's Marines in Dec. 1713. Re-commissioned Capt. in Wills's Foot, 25 Mar. 1715. Left the Regt. 25 Aug. 1717. Of this officer Col. W. O. Cavenagh, who is nearly related to the Pallisers, writes: "Col. Walter Palliser was bro. to Col. Thos. Palliser of Portobello, co. Wexford, Capt. John Palliser, and Capt. Hugh Palliser. He was of North Deighton, Yorkshire, and md. Eliz. dau. of Samuel Sterne. This lady was aunt to Laurence Sterne the author."

[4] Of North Deighton, Yorkshire. Youngest son of John Palliser of Newby Wiske, Yorkshire. "He was shot through both cheeks at the battle of Almanza. He md. Mary dau. of Humphrey Robinson of Thicket Priory, Yorkshire, and was father of Admiral Sir Hugh Palliser, Bt." Communicated by Col. W. O. Cavenagh.

SIR HENRY GORING'S REGIMENT OF FOOT.

[31ST FOOT.]

Commissions renewed by George I., 1 June 1715.

CAPTAINS.	LIEUTENANTS.	ENSIGNS.
Sir Henry Goring,[1] Colonel.	Alexander Wilson, Captain-Lieutenant.	John Pierson.
George Blakeney,[2] Lieutenant-Colonel.	William Risdall.	Thomas Webb.
Richard Prater, Major.	Thomas Daracote.	Charles Whittick.
Roger Flower [25 April 1714].	Ant. Ladeveze.[4]	Adam Elliot [1 Nov. 1713].
John Beckwith [19 Nov. 1714].		John Blakeney.
Cutts Hassan.	Abraham Ardesoife.	Charles Millet.
Fleetwood Watkins.	Edward Thompson.	Arthur Swift.
Rupert Handcock.	Peter Haviland.	Joseph Harding.
John Busby, Grendr. Cy.	Edward O'Bryen, 1st Lieut.	
	Lionel Seaman, 2nd Lieut.	

CHAPLAIN.
John Phillips.

ADJUTANT.
Ant. Ladeveze.[4]

SURGEON.
William Scott.

SUPPLEMENTARY COMMISSIONS.

Lord John Kerr[3] to be Colonel of Our Regt. of Foot lately commanded by Sir Harry Goring, Bt. and to be Capt. of a Cy.	St. James's, 8 Sept. 1715.*a*	
Alex. Wilson, Esq. to be Capt. of Grenadiers in room of John Busby	,, ,, ,,	*i*
Robert Blakeney to be Ens. to Capt. Wilson	,, ,, ,,	*i*
Wm. Spicer to be Ens. to Capt. Roger Flower	,, 1 Nov. ,,	*i*
John Plummer to be Ens. to Capt. Cutts Hassan	,, ,, ,,	*i*
John Blackney to be Lieut. to Capt. John Busby's [late] Cy. of Grenadiers	,, 23 ,, ,,	*i*

[1] Of Highden, Sussex. Succeeded his half-bro. Sir Charles Goring as 3rd Bart. in 1714. Appointed Capt. in Col. Edmund Soame's Regt. of Foot, 25 Mar. 1705. Transferred to Masham's Foot, 30 Apr. 1707. Col. of a Regt. of Marines (31st Foot), 1 Mar. 1711. Half-pay, 1713. Reappointed Col. on the restoration of above Regt. in 1715. Obliged to sell his Comn. in Sept. 1715, being in league with the Jacobites. Arrested in 1722 on suspicion. D. 1732.

[2] Younger son of Wm. Blakeney of Mount Blakeney near Kilmallock, and uncle to the distinguished General Wm., Lord Blakeney. Appointed Qr.-Mr. to Sir John Guise's Regt. of Foot, 12 Nov. 1688. Lieut. in Col. John Foulkes's Regt. of Foot, 15 Mar. 1690. Capt. 5 Aug. 1691. Transferred to Col. Wm. Northcote's Regt. of Foot, 14 Jan. 1695. Capt. in Col. George Villiers's Regt. of Marines, 10 Mar. 1702. Bt.-Major, 8 Mar. 1703. Served at Cadiz in 1702 and at the taking of Vigo. At the siege of Toulon in 1707 and at the capture of Cagliari in 1708. Half-pay in 1713. Resigned his Comn. in Apr. 1718 to his nephew Wm. Blakeney.

[3] Younger bro. to Wm. 2nd Marquess of Lothian. Appointed Cornet and Major of the Scots Troop of Life Guards, 25 Aug. 1702. Lt. and Lt.-Col. 6 Jan. 1709. Col. of 31st Foot, 8 Sept. 1715. Maj.-Gen. 5 Mar. 1727. Held this Colonelcy until his death on 1st Aug. 1728.

[4] Major of above Regt. 29 May, 1732. Promoted Lieut.-Col. 22 Jan. 1741. Out of the Army before 1746. D. 1771. Will proved at Dublin same year.

BRIGADIER-GENERAL JACOB BORR'S REGIMENT OF FOOT.
[32ND FOOT.]

Commissions renewed by George I., 25 March 1715.

CAPTAINS.	1ST LIEUTENANTS.	2ND LIEUTENANTS.
Brigadier-General Jacob Borr,[1] Colonel.	George Gordon, Captain-Lieutenant.	Anthony Kendall.
George Burston,[2] Lieutenant-Colonel.	Thomas Fitz-gerald.	George Wray.
Robert Kemp, Major.	Francis Sullivan.	Thomas Hoysted.
Humphrey Cory.[3]	John Hollingworth.	Gamaliel Capel.
William Lee.	John Greenall.	John Cox.
Richard Mullins.	James Fade.	Edward Bilton.
Peter Colborn.	John Roper.	William Vanse.
Bernard Dennet.	— Butler.	[Philip] Cradock.
Thomas Norton.	John Goodwyn.	John Cranwell.
Stephen Sanderson.	Richard Harris.	Peter Margaret.

CHAPLAIN.
Thomas Hesketh.

ADJUTANT.
James Nowland.

SURGEON.
Henry Hill.

NOTE.—" I do hereby certify that the above Officers' Commissions bear date 25 Mch. 1715, except Lt. Butler's and Lieut. Cradock's, which bear date the 25th June 1715.
" (Signed)   GEORGE BURSTON."

SUPPLEMENTARY COMMISSION.
Robert Brudenell to be 2nd Lieut. to Lt.-Col. George Burston 30 Nov. 1715.*i*

[1] Appointed Capt. in Col. Collingwood's Regt. of Foot, 1 Aug. 1692. Saw service in the West Indies. Succeeded to the command of Col. Fox's Regt. of Marines on the death of that officer at Gibraltar, 29 Oct. 1704. Served as Qr.-Mr.-Gen. to Earl Rivers from 5 June, 1706. Brig.-Gen. 1 Jan. 1713. Half-pay in 1710. Re-commissioned Col. of above Regt. 25 Mar. 1715. D. in 1723.

[2] Son of an Irish clergyman and bro. to Dr. Daniel Burston, Dean of Waterford. "Educated at Dublin College. Trailed a pike under Capt. Baskerville in the Royal Regt. of Foot of Ireland, in 1677, and three years afterwards purchased an Ensigncy for £200 in Capt. Trevor Floyd's Company in Col. Fairfax's Regt. . . . Joined the Prince of Orange at Honiton (Nov. 1688) and entered himself a volunteer in Col. Talmash's Regt. In March following was made Lieut. to Col. Fairfax in Lord Castleton's Regt. Served all through King William's War and at Namur. Half-pay after Ryswick. Made eldest Captain in Lord Shannon's Marines in 1702. Was a Bt.-Major at the action at St. Estevan in Spain, where he received 13 wounds. Left for dead on the field. Served at the siege and relief of Barcelona; also at the siege of Lerida in 1707. Brevet of Col. of Foot signed by the Earl of Galway, in Spain, 10 July, 1707. Lt.-Col. of Wills's Marines, 26 Apr. 1708. Lt.-Col. of Borr's Regt. of Foot, 25 Mar. 1715. Retd. 4 Nov. 1718." See *Case of Colonel Burston*, printed in London, 1720.

[3] Served at Cadiz, Vigo, and Gibraltar as Capt. in Col. Fox's Marines. By a strange chance he was present at the battle of Almanza and taken prisoner. Left the Regt. as Major.

MAJOR-GENERAL GEORGE WADE'S REGIMENT OF FOOT.
[33RD FOOT.]

Commissions renewed by George I., 25 March 1715.

CAPTAINS.	LIEUTENANTS.	ENSIGNS.
Major-General George Wade,[1] Colonel.	John Nicholas, Capt.-Lt. [1 April 1714].	William Sommer.
Thomas Howard,[2] Lieutenant-Colonel.	Henry Lacey.	John Martin.
John Archer,[3] Major.	Alexander La Milliere.	Arnold James Breams.
Oliver Wheeler.	John Gore.	Peter Reynolds.
John Reading.[4]	Joseph Clifford.	Charles Donnell.
John Hauteclaire.	James Herle.	Anderson Saunders [18 March 1713].
Richard Chalmer Cobb.	Christopher Williams.	Peter Belbese [1 April 1714].
Henry Graham.	John Mallet.	Thomas Lacey.
John Owen.[5]	Thomas Kerr.	Edward Polhill.
Christopher Clapham, Grendr. Cy.	John Bedford, 1st Lieut.	
	Philip Brydal, 2nd Lieut.	

CHAPLAIN.
William Denny.

ADJUTANT.
Christopher Williams.

SURGEON.
Peter Daulhat
[28 Oct. 1713].

NOTE.—" I do hereby certify that the above Officers' Commissions bear date the 25th March 1715.
"(Signed) J. ARCHER."

SUPPLEMENTARY COMMISSIONS.

John Ecles (*sic*) to be 2nd Lieut. to Capt. Christopher Clapham's Grenadier Company St. James's, 1 June 1715.*a*
John Mallet, Esqr. to be Capt. in room of John Owen - - - - - - — 13 ,, ,, *i*
Wm. Wade to be Ens. to Major-General Wade's Cy. - - - - - - — 25 ,, ,, *i*
John Baker to be Chaplain - - - - — 12 Dec. ,, *i*

---

[1] See special memoir of Field-Marshal George Wade in Vol. II.
[2] See biog. notice on p. 222, note 54.
[3] Appointed Capt. in above Regt. 24 Dec. 1707. Major, 25 Mar. 1715. Lt.-Col. 19 Mar. 1717. Out of the Regt. before 1730.
[4] See notice on p. 340, note 4.
[5] Out of the Regt. 13 June 1715.

LIEUTENANT-GENERAL RICHARD GORGES'S REGIMENT OF FOOT.

[35TH FOOT.]

Commissions renewed by George I. in June 1715.

CAPTAINS.	LIEUTENANTS.	ENSIGNS.
Lieutenant-General Richard Gorges,[1] Col.	Thomas Gardiner, Captain-Lieutenant.	Cornelius O'Brien.
David Dunbar,[2] Lieut.-Col. [27 June 1715].	Oliver Arthur.	Stephen Deane.
Philip Dunbar,[3] Major [27 June 1715].	Saul Bruce.	Richard Hankinson.
— Maxwell [27 June 1715].	Seymour Wroughton.	Thomas Dunbar.
Richard Willoughby.	Andrew Willoughby.	Patrick Gentleman.[5]
Thomas Cudmore.	James Tyre.	John Wardlour (*sic*).
John Anthony Berniere.	William Ings.	George Vickers.
Abel Dalley.	Sampson Christian.	St. Lawrence Burford.
John Wichalse.	William Wright.	Herbert Love.
William Rice, Grendr. Cy.	Edward Warren, 1st Lieut.	
	Richard Codd, 2nd Lieut.	

CHAPLAIN.
Henry Mathews
[3 June 1714].

ADJUTANT.
Richard Codd.

SURGEON.
John Johnson.

SUPPLEMENTARY COMMISSIONS.

Edward Warren,[4] Esq. to be Capt. in room of Richard Willoughby - - - -	—	25 Nov. 1715.	*i*
Thos. Bamber to be Ens. to above Cy. - -	—	,, ,,	*i*
Charles Ward to be Ens. to Lt.-Col. David Dunbar - - - - - - -	—	,, ,,	*i*
Richard Hankinson to be Lieut. to Major Philip Dunbar - - - - - -	—	,, ,,	*i*
— Sandford to be 1st Lieut. to Capt. Wm. Rice's Grenadier Cy. - - - - -	—	, ,,	*i*
Toby Purcell, Esq. to be Capt. in the room of Thomas Cudmore - - - - -	St. James's,	,, ,,	*a*

[1] Eldest son and heir of Dr. Robert Gorges of Kilbrew, Co. Meath, by Jane dau. of Sir Arthur Loftus, knt., and sister of Adam, Visct. Lisburne. Capt. of the Grendr. Cy. in Lord Lisburne's Regt. 8 Mar. 1689. Served throughout the Irish campaign, 1690–1691. Adjt.-Gen. of the Forces in Ireland, 23 Apr. 1697. Bt.-Col. 2 Mar. 1699. Col. of a newly-raised Regt. of Foot, 10 Apr. 1703. Served under Peterborough in Spain as Adjt.-Gen. Col. of 35th Foot, 15 Apr. 1706. Maj.-Gen. 1 Jan. 1707. Lt.-Gen. 1 Jan. 1710. D. 12 April 1728.

[2] Served as Capt. in above Regt. at Almanza, where he was wounded and taken prisoner. Left the Regt. 10 July 1718.

[3] Appointed Lieut. in Col. Edward Jones's Regt. in Ireland, 2 Nov. 1710. Half-pay, 1713. Capt. in Gorges's Foot, 1st June 1715. Out of the Regt. before 1718.

[4] Served at Almanza as a Lieut. Wounded and taken prisoner there. Left the Regt. in May 1718.

[5] Appointed Ensign in above Regt. in April, 1707. Capt. 25 April, 1736. Serving in 1740.

COLONEL HENRY DISNEY'S REGIMENT OF FOOT.
[36TH FOOT.]

Commissions renewed by George I., 1st June 1715.

CAPTAINS.	LIEUTENANTS.	ENSIGNS.
Robert Innes,[1] Lieutenant-Colonel [24 June 1707].	Dudley Acland.	
William Hargrave,[2] Major. [28 Jan. 1710].	William Skeyne [25 June 1707].	John Hargrave [15 Feb. 1711].
Fitzherbert Tempest [30 April 1711].	William Joyce [10 Sept. 1712].	John Hope [14 Feb. 1711].
John Lloyd.	Robert Clark [5 April 1715].	Samuel Cutts [9 Sept. 1712].
Arthur Whitmore [15 April 1707].	James Sell [10 Sept. 1712].	Edward Whitmore[4] [13 March 1711].
Francis Fleming.	Francis Scott [25 Dec. 1709].	Charles Barton.
John Grant.	William Tonge [24 June 1712].	Eresey Nicholls (*sic*) [10 Sept. 1712].
John Sterling.	James Hurst [5 April 1707].	Hugh Murray [10 Sept. 1712]
	Roger Irwyn [28 Jan. 1710].	James Collins.
Colonel Henry Disney,[3] Capt. of Gren. Cy.	John Dancer, Capt.-Lieutenant. Michael Edwards, 2nd Lieut. [10 Sept. 1712].	

CHAPLAIN.
John Harris.

ADJUTANT.
Richard Lloyd.

SURGEON.
Dudley Acland.

SUPPLEMENTARY COMMISSIONS.

Lewis Adeane to be Ens. to Lt.-Col. Robert Innes	— 5 June 1715.*h*	
Wm. Egerton,[5] Esq. to be Colonel in the room of Col. Henry Disney and to be Capt. of a Company	St. James's, 25 July ,,	*a*
Embarked for Scotland in October 1715.		
George Holland to be Qr.-Mr.	St. James's, 25 Dec. ,,	*a*

[1] Appointed Lieut. in Lord Charlemont's Regt. (36th), 28 June 1701. Served in the Expedition to Cadiz and in the West Indies. Bt.-Lt.-Col. 24 June 1707. Lt.-Col. of above Regt. 28 Jan. 1710. Served with General Hill's expedition to Canada in 1711. Bt.-Col. 15 Nov. 1711. Served at Sheriffmuir. Left the Regt. 16 Apr. 1718.

[2] Ensign in Lord Charlemont's Regt. 23 Apr. 1694. Served at Cadiz in 1702; also in the West Indies. Major, 28 Jan. 1710. Present at Sheriffmuir. Lt.-Col. 16 Apr. 1718. Col. 31st Foot, 1 Jan. 1730. Transferred to the 9th Foot in 1737 and to the Rl. Fusiliers, 27 Aug. 1739. D. a Lieut.-Gen. 21 Jan. 1751. Bd. in Westminster Abbey. His monumental inscription records that he had been Governor of Gibraltar.

[3] This officer's real name was *Desaulnais*, but he Anglicised it to Disney. Ens. in the 1st Foot Guards, 1 Mar. 1694. Lieut. and Capt. 15 Feb. 1703. Served at Blenheim as an A.D.C. Capt. and Lt.-Col. 1st Foot Guards, 11 Mar. 1708. Col. of 36th Foot, 23 Oct. 1710. Served with the expedition to Canada in 1711. Sold his Colonelcy 25 July 1715. Col. 29th Foot, 25 Dec. 1725. D. 21 Nov. 1731. Bd. in the cloisters of Westminster Abbey, where there is a tablet to his memory.

[4] Attained the rank of Col. of the 22nd Foot, 11 July, 1757. He served at the 2nd capture of Louisburg, in 1758, under Wolfe, as a local Brig.-Gen. and was appointed Gov. of that place. Drowned at Plymouth, near Boston, New England, 11 Dec. 1761. Appears to have been son of Capt. Arthur Whitmore of same regt. The latter was of York, and in his will, proved 16 Feb. 172½, names a son "Edward," and refers to "my effects which chiefly consist of Army arrears due from Government." *Herald and Genealogist*, Vol. VI. p. 682.

[5] Capt. and Lt.-Col. 1st Foot Guards, 25 Dec. 1714. Served at Sheriffmuir and saw subsequent service in Scotland, 1716-1719. Transferred to the 20th Foot, 6 July, 1719. D. 15 July, 1732. He was bro. to the 4th Earl of Bridgewater (created a Duke in 1720) and to Dr. Henry Egerton, Bishop of Hereford.

COLONEL WILLIAM WINDRESS'S REGIMENT OF FOOT.
[37TH FOOT.]

Commissions renewed by George I., 1st June 1715.

CAPTAINS.	LIEUTENANTS.	ENSIGNS.
William Windress,[1] Colonel.	Charles Jones.	William Wye.
John Fane,[2] Lieutenant-Colonel.	Henry Ballenden (*sic*).	Thomas Dowset.
Philip Finney, Major.	William Gee.	John Scourrier.
Patrick Maxwell.	Thomas Timpson.	George Bell.
Raphael Walsh.	Richard Parsons.	John Pickering.
Anthony Ligoniere.	George Trotter.	Henry Merriden.
William Graves.	John Chilcot.	Thomas Brady.
Henry Redknap.	Thomas Jones.	Edmond Browne.
John Southby.	John Nangle.	Walter James Greenwood.
James Butler, Grendr. Cy.	Churchill Hastings, 1st Lieut.	
	John Savile Gooderich,[3] (*sic*) 2nd Lieut.	

CHAPLAIN,
George Smith.

ADJUTANT.
John Chilcot.

SURGEON.
Thomas Bell.

SUPPLEMENTARY COMMISSIONS.

John Fane,[2] Esq. to be Col. of Our Regt. of Foot whereof Wm. Windress was late Col. and to be Capt. of a Company	St. James's, 23 Aug. 1715.	*a*
Edward Hall, Esq. to be Capt. [of an additional Company]	„ 26 Sept. „	*a*
James De Hays to be Lieut. to Capt. Hall	„ „ „	*a*
Samuel Watts to be Ens. to do.	„ „ „	*a*
[Richard Dyer to be Capt. of an additional Company	„ „ „	]
John Cowper to be Ens. to Capt. Richard Dyer	„ „ „	*a*
Henry Harman Van Deck to be Qr.-Mr.	„ 25 Dec. „	*a*

[1] Appointed Ens. in the Coldstream Guards, 1 Jan. 1692. Lieut. and Capt. 2 Nov. 1702. Lt.-Col. of Gen. Meredyth's Regt. (37th Foot), 9 Mar. 1705. Bt.-Col. 1 Jan. 1707. Commanded this Corps at Malplaquet. Regtal. Col. 1 May, 1710. D. in Aug. 1715.

[2] See Biog. notice on p. 222, note 79.

[3] 4th son of Sir John *Goodricke*, Bt. Bapt. at Normanton, 16 Jan. 1689-90. Capt. in Col. Roger Handasyde's Regt. in 1717. Md. same year, at Chester, Adeliza dau. of George Herbert, Esq. and had 2 daus. the elder of whom was sempstress to George III. Capt J. S. Goodricke d. in London and was bd. at St. James's, Westminster, 20 Feb. 1721. *Hist. of the Goodrickes.*

HIS MAJESTY'S TRAIN OF ARTILLERY IN IRELAND, 1716

A LIST OF THE PRINCIPALL AND INFERIOR OFFICERS, GUNNERS, AND MATTROSSES BELONGING TO HIS MAJESTIE'S TRAINE OF ARTILLERY IN IRELAND.*

[1716]

Garrisons.	Persons' Names.	Employments.	Pay ℣ Annum.		
			£	s.	d.
Dublin	W^{m.} Ld. Visco^{t.} Mountjoy[1]	Master Generall	500	0	0
,,	Richard Molsworth[2]	Lieutenant	300	0	0
,,	James Wybault[3]	Major	200	0	0
,,	George Houghton	Comptroller	200	0	0
,,	Hector Pain	Clerke	100	0	0
,,	Thomas Burgh[4]	1st ⎫	300	0	0
,,	John Corniele[5]	2nd ⎬ Engineers	182	10	0
,,	Arthur Gore[6]	3rd ⎭	146	0	0
,,	Arthur Stewart[7]	⎫ Gent. of ye Ordnce at £73 each.	146	0	0
,,	Robert Leeson	⎭			
,,	Brent Smith[8]	Storekeeper	100	0	0
,,	Johnathan Keat[9]	Chirurgeon	91	5	0
,,	Francis Cocksedge[10]	Paymaster	45	12	6
,,	John Logan	⎫ Firemasters at £73 each	146	0	0
,,	James Stewart	⎭			
,,	George Alston	⎫ Bombardiers at £36 10s. each	73	0	0
,,	John Wattson	⎭			
,,	James Willson	Armouror	73	0	0
,,	Jacob Barrion	Assistant Armouror	36	10	0
,,	Roger Mulligan	⎫			
,,	Thomas Guest	⎬ Assistant Arm^{rs.} at £36 10s. each.	109	10	0
,,	Robert Baker	⎭			
,,	Phillip Bowne	Wheelwright at	36	10	0
,,	Joseph Merrfield	Waggon Maker at	36	10	0
,,	Robert Greenway	Smith at	36	10	0
,,	Peter Vandeluier	Harness Maker at	36	10	0
,,	Jacob Fenner	Master Gunner at	50	0	0
,,	Hugh Clements	Mast^{r.} Gunner's Mate at	25	0	0
,,	David Hubert	⎫			
,,	Peter Pouchin				
,,	John Deane				
,,	Edmond Marsden	⎬ 7 Gunners at £18 5s. each	127	15	0
,,	John Roberts				
,,	Sankey Bourgoine				
,,	Anthony Lasseur	⎭			
,,	Thomas Pitts	⎫			
,,	David Bowne				
,,	William Darby	⎬ 5 Gunners more at £18 5s. each.	91	5	0
,,	Hugh Fleming				
,,	William Morris	⎭			

A LIST OF THE PRINCIPALL AND INFERIOR OFFICERS, ETC.—*cont.*

Garrisons.	Persons' Names.	Employments.	Pay ⅌ Annum.		
			£	s.	d.
Dublin	James Peticrew				
,,	John Stephens				
,,	Timothy Tuman				
,,	Henry Skamon				
,,	John Davis				
,,	John Whitehead	12 Mattrosses at £13 13s. 9d. each.	164	5	0
,,	Thomas Potts				
,,	Jown Newell				
,,	William Small				
,,	Daniell Flaherty				
,,	William Newgent (*sic*)				
,,	John Logan				
Charlemont	William Lewis	Storekeeper at	18	5	0
,,	William Emerson	Mattrosse at	13	13	9
Londonderry	Michaell Hewettson	Storekeeper at	40	0	0
,,	Stephen Husbands	2 Gunners at £18 5s. each	36	10	0
,,	William Downing				
,,	John Wright	2 Mattrosses at £13 13s. 9d. each.	27	7	6
,,	Simon Dogherty				
Kinsale	John Love	Storekeeper	40	0	0
,,	Edward Brinn	Master Gunner	36	10	0
,,	Cuthbert Quinn				
,,	John Lezier				
,,	Robert Hart				
,,	Moses Stowards	8 Gunners at £18 5s. each	146	0	0
,,	Patrick Farrell				
,,	John Thompson				
,,	John Wiltshire				
,,	Andrew Pember				
,,	William McDaniell				
,,	James Stowards	4 Mattrosses at £13 13s. 9d. each.	54	15	0
,,	John Crawford				
,,	Mathew Dowdall				
Athlone	Edward Thomas	Gunner at	18	5	0
,,	Barth. Madden	Mattrosse at	13	13	9
Gallway	Jeffry Cooke	Storekeeper at	40	0	0
,,	William Swetnam				
,,	Francis Morris	3 Gunners at £18 5s. each	54	15	0
,,	Robert Cooke				
,,	John Scott	2 Mattrosses at £13 13s. 9d. each.	27	7	6
,,	David Murray				
Duncannon	Abraham Sandoz [11]	Storekeeper at	40	0	0
,,	Adam Jenkins	Mastr. Gunner at	36	10	0

A List of the Principall and Inferior Officers, etc.—cont.

Garrisons.	Persons' Names.	Employments.	Pay ⅌ Annum.
			£ s. d.
Duncannon	Nicholas Chapman -	} 2 Gunners at £18 5s. each -	36 10 0
,,	Thomas Lattimore -		
,,	James Hannah -	} 2 Mattrosses at £13 13s. 9d. each.	27 7 6
,,	James Kerney -		
Waterford	Abraham Sandoz [12] -	Storekeeper at - - -	10 0 0
,,	Ralph Vaughan -	Storekeeper at - - -	40 0 0
Limrick	Gilbert Buxton -	} 4 Gunners at £18 5s. each -	73 0 0
,,	Thomas Boyce -		
,,	George Robinson -		
,,	John Parker -		
,,	William Curtis -	} 2 Mattrosses at £13 13s. 9d. each.	27 7 6
,,	George Peasley -		
Carrickfergus	David Morrison -	Storekeeper at - - -	40 0 0
,,	Joseph Davis -	Gunner at - - -	18 5 0
,,	John Lloyd -	Mattrosse at - - -	13 13 9
			£4,283 8 9

Contingencies.

For Postage of Letters & provideing Fire, Candles, & Stationary Ware for yᵉ use of yeᵉ Ordnance Office, and for Rent of Storehouses in Out Garrisons, Hooping and provideing Casks for Powder & Small Ball; For transmitting Stores from one Garrison to another as the Service Requires, Painting Gun Carriages & divers other Necessarys, Six hundred and Sixty Pounds ⅌ Annum. 660 0 0

£4,943 8 9

---

* This list is taken from the *Stowe MS.* 446, fo. 25, at the Brit. Mus. It appears to be unique, as no similar list could be found at the Record Office in Dublin. The date is undoubtedly 1716, as the Commission of Rodolph Cornielle as 2nd Engineer was renewed by George I. 1st June 1715; and on 15th June, 1716, John Cornielle succeeded to said post. And whereas the total cost of the Irish Ordnance Train amounted to £4,943 8s. 9d. in 1716, it was £4,979 18s. 9d. in 1717 (*Artillery Establishment*, 1717, Dublin Record Office), the extra sum of £36 10s. in 1717 being accounted for by the appointment of a "Clerk to the Surveyor and Controller of the Office at £36 10s. per annum." *Ibid.*

[1] Eldest son of Sir Wm. Stewart, 1st Visct. Mountjoy. Succeeded to the title on the death of his father at the battle of Steinkirk in 1692. Lieut.-General in the Army and Col. of a Regt. of Dragoons raised in Ireland in Feb. 1716 and disbanded the following year. D. in London, 10 Jan. 1727.

[2] Aftds. 3rd Viscount Molesworth. *See* special memoir, pp. 85-86.

³ Served some years as a subaltern in the Royal Fusiliers, and was present with this Corps at Cadiz and the taking of Vigo in 1702. He had been employed as an Engineer by King William III. in 1697 (*English Army Lists and Commission Registers*, 1661–1714, Vol. IV., p. 171). Appointed Third Engineer in Ireland, 1703. Author of a book on "Gunnery." Comn. as Major renewed by Geo. II. D. in 1728.

⁴ Appointed Capt. in the Royal Regt. of Foot, 1 Aug. 1692. Served at Steinkirk, Landen, and the siege of Namur. Appointed Third Engineer of Ireland in 1697. Attained the rank of Chief Engineer and Surveyor-General of Ireland. D. 18 Dec. 1730. Was M.P. for Naas at the time of his death.

⁵ Succeeded his father, Rodolph Cornielle, as Second Engineer of Ireland, 15 Sept. 1716. This comn. was signed by George I.

⁶ D. or retd. in Dec. 1717.

⁷ Succeeded as Third Engineer of Ireland, 20 Dec. 1717. Believed to be 4th son of the 1st Visct. Mountjoy, according to Burke's *Extinct Peerage*. D. in 1723.

⁸ A certain Brent Smith was appointed Lieut. in Col. Ric. Brewer's Regt. of Foot, 1 Nov. 1694.

⁹ Appointed Surgeon-General to the British Forces in Portugal, 1 Oct. 1703. Placed on half-pay in 1712. Comn. renewed by George II. in 1727.

¹⁰ A certain Fras. Cocksedge had been appointed Lieut. in Brigadier Owen Wynne's Regt. of Foot, 24 July 1708. Out of said Regt. in 1713.

¹¹ Was subsequently granted a pension on the Irish Establishment of £45 12s. 6d. per ann., and was living on the accession of George II. This officer's son, Abraham Sandoz, was appointed Ensign in Visct. Mountjoy's Regt. of Foot, 28 June, 1701.

¹² *See* note 11.

INDEX

A

Abbot, Hen., 160.
........., Mordecai, 160, 249.
Abell, Geo., 123, 279.
Abercrombie, Alex. (Hen. Harrison's Regt.), 154.
........., Alex. (Lord Orrery's Regt.), 345.
........., Jas., 213, 307.
........., Sir Jas., 133.
Acland, Dudley, 364 bis.
Adair, Jas., 216.
Adair, Adaire, Wm. Robt., 115, 215.
Adams, Chris., 113.
........., Rog., 199, 310, 319.
........., Thos., 180, 209.
........., Wm. (Lord Irwin's Regt.), 156.
........., Wm. (Pocock's Regt.), 180.
Adeane, Lewis, 364.
Agar, Peter, 327.
Agnew, Cornet Alex., 107, 111.
........., Ensign Alex., 134, 158.
........., And., 180.
........., Jas., 107, 111, 267.
........., Pat., 266.
........., Thos., 107, 191.
Aikenhead, Geo., 287.
Albritton, Thos., 349.
Alchorne, Wm., 125.
Alcock, Chris., 142.
Alderne, John, 281.
Aldey, Mat., 174.
Aldridge, Chris., 239, 312.
Alexander, Cornet Chas., 103.
........., Ensign Chas., 174.
........., Fras., 174.
........., Jas., 160.
Alison, Wm., 233.
Allen, John, 329.
........., Ric., 327.
Allicock, Syer, 174.
Alston, Geo., 369.
Amyand, Claud, 103.
Anderson, Ralph, 105.
Andrew, Wm., 99.
Andrewes, Andrews, Ric., 199.
Anstruther, Phil., 125.
........., Robt., 195.
........., Wm. 351.
Anthony, Sam., 140.
Antrim, Sam., 180.
Aplin, Ric., 205.
Appleyard, Fras., 180.

Arbuthnot, Geo., 164.
Archer, John, 361.
Ardesoife, Abr., 358.
Argyll, John Campbell, 2nd Duke of, Letter of to Wm. Stewart, M.P., 10; Memoir of, 1–9; Regt. of, 101, 187; Comns. to, 228, 235, 238, 246.
Armfield, John, 279.
Armitage, Geo., 280.
Armstrong, Fras., 101, 194.
........., Geo., 107.
........., John, 125, 211, 227, 228, 314.
........., Laurence, 239, 312.
........., Mich., 105, 264.
........., Thos., 105, 199 bis.
........., Wm., 347.
Arnold, Geo., 136.
Arnot, Col. John, 136.
........., Ensign John, 295.
........., Wm., 136.
Arnott. See Arnot
Arran, Chas. Butler, Earl of, 186.
Arrowsmith, John, 123.
Arther. See infra.
Arthur, Alex., 351.
........., Jas., 197.
........., Oliver, 352.
Arthurlony. See Ochterlony.
Artsen, Jacob, 150.
Ash, Bigg, 198.
........., Cairnes, 160.
........., Isaac, 204.
........., Wm., 355.
Ashburnham, John, Lord, 185.
Ashby, Wm., 105, 199 bis.
Ashe, John, 338.
Auchenleck, Alex., 107, 111, 266.
Austin, Thos. Sheffield, 268.
Aylmer, Henry, 357.
........., Pat., 357.
Ayton, David, 351.
........., John, 351.

B

Baanastre. See Banastre.
Babington, Philip, 334.
Bachelor, Paul, 148.
Bagnall, Thos., 125.
Bailey, John, 210.
Bailie, Robt., 100.

INDEX

Baine, Roderick, 130.
Baines, Ric., 144.
Baird, Alex., 265.
Baker, Jas. (Bowles's Regt.), 116.
........., Jas. (Wills's Regt.), 357 *bis*.
........., John, 361.
........., Robt., 369.
Baldwin, Thos., 105, 205.
........., Wm., 327.
Balendine. *See* Bellenden.
Balfour, Arthur, 133, 208.
........., Jeremiah, 332.
Balgony, George Leslie, Lord, 130, 190.
Ball, Chas. (Chaplain), 196.
........., Chas. (Waggon Master), 285.
........., Conductor, 336.
........., John, 120.
........., Qr.-Mr. John, 318.
Ballantine, Jas., 133.
Ballard, John, 349.
Ballenden (*sic*), Robt., 366.
Bamber, Thos., 362.
Banastre, Geo., 196.
Banche. *See* Branch.
Banks, Wm., 275.
Barclay, Robt., 351.
Bargus, Jas., 239.
Barker, John, 281.
Barkly. *See* Barclay.
Barlin, Walt., 187.
Barlow, Hen., 110.
........., Wm., 339.
Barnes, Chas., 138.
........., Jas., 204.
Barnet, Wm., 191.
Baron, Randolph, 343.
Barrell, Anthony, 172.
........., Wm., 125, 193, 353.
Barrett, Hen., 301.
Barrion, Jacob, 369.
Barry, Capt. David, 144.
........., Ensign David, 152, 199, 204.
........., Chaplain David, 152.
........., Edw., 152.
........., Jas., 152.
........., Philip, 142.
Barrymore, Ric. Barry, 4th Earl of, 188.
Bartlett, (—), 101.
Barton, Chas., 364.
........., Lewis, 230.
........., Robt., 154.
........., Thos., 121, 278.
........., Wm., 343.
Basset, Philip, 345.
........., Jos., 283.
Bastide, Capt. Hen., 148.
........., Lieut. John Hen., 300.
Bataly, Alford, 193.
Bateman, Math., 206.
........., Stephen, 152.

Bates, G[eorge], 120.
........., Thos., 276.
Bath, Ben., 150.
........., Randall, 101.
........., Wm., 213.
Bathe, John, 318.
Batson, Jas., 194.
Batten, Thos., 170.
Battereau, John, 160, 217.
Baxter, John, 285 *bis*.
Bayly, Geo., 352.
Baynes, John, 97, 229.
Baynton, John, 331.
........., Thos., 330.
Beake, Gregory, 101, 187.
........., Peter, 142.
Beakes. *See* Beake.
Beale, John, 140, 185.
Bearcroft, Edw., 262.
Bearde, Philip, 334.
Beauchamp, Robt., 250.
Beauclair. *See infra*.
Beauclerk, Lord Harry, 215.
........., Lord Wm., 198.
Beaufort, Wm., 334.
Beaumont, Sir Astley, 329.
........., Chas., 299.
........., John (Thos. Harrison's Regt.), 334.
........., John (Wightman's Regt.), 341.
Beaver, Peter, 176, 311.
Beckwith, John, 185, 358.
Belbese, Peter, 361.
Bell, David, 154.
........., Duncan, 207.
........., Geo., 366.
........., John, 154, 302.
........., Thos., 366.
Bellamy, Abr., 112.
........., Geo., 128, 189.
Bellandine. *See* Bellenden.
Belleau, Louis, 97.
Bellenden, Robt., 198, 241, 312.
........., Jas., 120.
........., Wm., 123, 203 *bis*.
Bellew, John, Lord, of Duleek, 330.
Bellon, Wm., 198.
Bemboe, Wm., 103.
Béné. *See* De La Béné.
Bennet, Geo. } *See infra*.
........., John }
Bennett, Ben., 213.
........., Geo., 330.
........., Hen., 293.
........., John, 107, 194.
........., Jos., 240, 312.
Benningham. *See* Bermingham.
Benson, Geo. [senr.], 106, 192 *bis*.
........., Geo. [junr.], 106.
Berkeley, Geo., 188.
........., Col. Hen., 130, 188, **297**.

INDEX

Berkeley—*cont.*
........., Lieut. Hen., 349.
Berkley, Berkly. *See supra.*
Bermingham, Jas., 182.
Bernard, Geo., 124, 198.
Bernardeau, Sam., 148.
Bernardon. M. Ant., 275.
Bernière, John Anthony, 362.
Bertet, Jas., 172.
Bertie, Geo., 260.
Berty. *See supra.*
Beschefer, Jas., 336.
Bessière, Mark Ant., 168.
Best, Fras., 106.
Betsworth, Ric., 232, 235.
Bettesworth, Robt., 274.
Bettinson, Edw., 126.
Betton, Wriothesley, Wrottesley, 332.
Betty, Chas., 332.
Bever, Wm., 300.
Beverly, John, 140.
Bickerstaff, John, 204, 289.
........., Ric., 142.
Bickerton, Thos., 331.
........., Thos., Jun., 331.
Bickford, Abr., 160, 194.
Biggar, Alex., 307.
........., Jas., 307.
........., Robt., 210.
Bigland, Robt., 243.
Billings, Chris., 263.
Billingsley, Chris., 103.
........., Fras., 203, 308.
........., Orlando, 310.
Billingsly. *See supra.*
Bilton, Edward, 360.
Bird, Edward, 101 *bis.*
Bishop, Ben., 103.
Bissell, Jas., 347.
.... Wm., 349.
Bisset, Alex., 178, 301.
........., And., 128, 246.
........., Wm., 140.
Bix, Jas., 234.
Blachford, Jas., 310.
Black, Bartl., 355.
Blackader, John, 249.
Blacketer. *See* Blackader.
Blackhall, Alex., 242.
Blackiston. *See* Blakiston.
Blackney. *See* Blakeney.
Blackstein, Blackstone. *See* Blakiston.
Blackwell, Ric., 329.
Blagden, Benedict, 158, 209.
Blagrave, Thos., 164.
Blair, Jas., 172.
........., John, 351.
Blake, John, 150.
Blakeney, Geo., 358.
........., Capt. John, 158.

Blakeney—*cont.*
........., Lieut. John, 358 *bis.*
.... Robt., 358.
........., Wm., 125, 126.
Blakiston, Nat., 129, 188, 208, 291.
Bland, Chris., 116.
........., Hen., 355.
........., Humph., 115, 212, 263.
........., Wm., 196, 326.
Blantyre, Robt. Stewart, 7th Lord, 188, 192.
Blasford, Jas., 195.
Blathwait. *See infra.*
Blathwayt, John, 95, 186 *bis*, 190 *bis.*
Blount, Robt., 114.
........., Sam., 112.
........., Thos., 128.
........., Walt., 182.
Blower, John, 312.
Blunt, Hen., 176.
Bocland, Maurice, 328.
Boghert, Fras., 166.
Boheme, Goldsmith, 154.
Boisragon, Alex., 299.
Boitoux, John, 168.
Bolt, Hen., 154.
Bolton, Jas., 138, 296.
........., Thos. (Steuart's Regt.), 338.
........., Thos. (Welsh Fusiliers), 347.
Bonafous, Peter, 355.
Bond, Robt., 101.
Bonnamy, John, 228.
Bonnin, Cæsar, 146.
Booth, And., 341.
........., Chas.. 152.
Borgard, Albert, 281, 283, 285.
Borr, Jacob, 360.
Borrett, Edw., 128 *bis.*
Bossingo, Jeremiah, 307.
Bosswell. *See* Boswell.
Boswell, John, 319.
........., Ric., 182.
Boteler, John, 166.
Boucher, Fras., 114.
Boudler, John, 210.
Boughton, Edward, 98.
Bourden, Wm., 116.
Bourgoine, Sankey, 369.
Bousfield, Wm., 281, 285.
Bouys, Pet., 317.
Bowdler, Thos., 154, 189.
Bowes, Fras., 152, 189 *bis.*
........., Thos., 180.
Bowles, John, 101.
.... Phineas [sen.], 116, 229, 246.
........., Phineas [jun.], 130.
Bowne, David, 369.
........., Philip, 369.
Boyce, Thos., 371.
Boyd, Wm., 336.
Boyle, Edw., 193.

Boyle—*cont*.
........., Wm., 118, 274 *bis*, 325.
Brabant, Geo., 103, 263.
Brabazon, Wm., 339.
Brackhill, Maurice, 278.
Brackley, Robt., 126.
Braddock, Edw. [sen.], 128, 191.
........., Edw. [jun.], 128, 203.
Bradford, Robt., 156.
Bradon, Jas., 136.
Bradshaw, John, 144, 298.
........., Pet., 270.
........., Wm., 208.
Brady, Geo., 178.
........., Ric., 306.
........., Thos., 366.
Bragg, Philip, 349.
Braine, Thos., 205.
Braithwaite, Braithwayt, John, 204, 293.
Branch, Wm., 138.
Brandon, Jas., 201.
Brandreth, Michael, 154, 191 *bis*, 309.
Bransby, Robt. (Stanhope's Dragoons), 124.
........., Robt. (Welsh Fusiliers), 347.
Brathwayt, Wm., 217.
Bray, Thos., 339.
........., Wm., 330.
Braymer, David, 345.
Breach, Chas., 202.
Breames Walt., 202.
Breams, Arnold Jas., 361.
Breary, Hen., 353.
Bredenstein, Geo., 281.
Bredon, John, 103.
Breeden, Sam., 197.
Brereton, (—), 170.
........., Arth., 334 *bis*.
........., Edw., 203.
........., Wm., 121.
Brerewood, Fras., 197, 289.
Breton, Wm., 185.
Brett, Arth., 347.
........., Jas., 248.
Brevall, John Durant, 142.
Brevet, Elias, 192.
Brewer, Ric., 213.
Brewerton, Edw., 306.
Bridell, Ric., 270.
Bridges, John, 210.
........., Wm., 285.
Bridgman, Philip, 117.
Briett, Jas., 250.
Briggs, John, 330.
Brightman, Hen., 98, 198.
Brinn, Edw., 370.
Brisbane, Wm., 133.
Briscoe, Chris., 238, 281.
........., Hen. (Carpenter's Dragoons), 213.
........., Hen. (Wightman's Regt.), 341.
........., Ralph, 110.

Bristow, John, 232.
Broadstreet, Edw., 240, 312.
Brockman, Wm., 202.
Brodie, Alex., 294.
........., Wm., 185.
Brodley, Ratcliffe, 334.
Brook, John, 355.
Brooke, Oliver, 341.
Brooks, John, 287.
........., Wm., 106 *bis*, 186.
Broughton, Edw., 185.
........., Capt. John, 307.
........., Chaplain John, 318.
Brouncker, Thos., 230.
Brown, (—), 314.
........., Ant., 283.
........., Hen., 125, 126.
........., Jas., 193.
........., Surgeon John, 95, 99.
........., Lieut. John, 341.
........., Robt., 148.
........., Wm., 134.
Browne, Allen, 166.
........., Chas., 198.
........., Edmund, 366.
........., Edward, 343.
........., Geo., 133.
........., Gilbert, 294.
........., Humphry, 168.
........., Isaac, 136.
........., Jas., 319.
........., Jas. (Smith), 237.
........., Jas. (Royal Fusiliers), 144.
........., John (Wightman's Foot), 198, 207.
........., John (Cobham's Horse), 103, 263.
........., John (Whetham's Foot), 164.
........., Richmond, 125.
........., Robt., 148, 208.
........., Capt. Thos., 109, 195.
........., Ensign Thos., 343.
........., Wm. (Tyrrell's Dragoons), 121.
........., Wm. (Whetham's Foot), 164.
Brownjohn, (—), 261.
........., Lieut. Hen., 146, 302.
........., Ensign Hen., 154.
Brozier, John, 336.
Bruce, Alex. (Grant's Regt.), 178.
........., Alex. (Shannon's Regt.), 197.
........., Alex. (Whetham's Regt.), 207.
........., Fred., 307.
........., George, 232.
........., John, 180.
........., Saul, 362.
........., Adjt. Thos., 318.
........., Capt. Thos., 133.
........., Ens. Thos., 134.
........., Will., 205, 341.
Brudenell, Robt., 360.
........., Thos., 120.
Bruse, Isaac, 152.

INDEX

Brushfield, John, 170.
Brydal, Capt. Phil., 334.
........., Lieut. Phil., 364.
Buckhurst, Phil., 241, 312.
Buckland, Ric., 98.
Buckmaster, John, 217.
Bucknall, Chas., 144.
Buckworth, Sir John, Bt., 289.
Buggin, Robt., 334.
Bulkley, Wm., 279.
Bull, Ric., 312.
........., Wm., 125.
Buller, Sam., 146.
Bullman, Robt., 152.
Bullock, (—), 298.
Bunbury, Nich., 176.
Buncombe, John, 199.
Buor, Peter, 174.
Burbero, Wm., 193.
Burcas, Burchas, Ric. See Purchas.
Burchett, Ric., 216, 234.
Burford, St. Lawrence, 362.
Burgess, John, 240.
Burgh, Leonard, 315.
........., Thos., 369.
Burnet, (—). See Burnet, Wm.
........., Alex., 195.
........., Wm., 186.
Burnett, Alex., 351.
Burnevell, Peter, 142.
Burrington, Geo., 103.
Burroughs, (—). See Burroughs, Thos.
........., John, 115.
........., Thos., 172.
........., Wm., 230.
Burrows, Rog., 126.
........., Wm. Hen., 328.
Burscough, (—), 194.
Burston, Geo., 360.
........., Thos., 357.
Burton, Fras., 154.
........., Jos., 283.
........., Wm. (1st Foot Guards), 216.
........., Wm. (Honywood's Dragoons), 272.
Bury, Wm. Keppel, Viscount, 291.
Busby, John, 358.
Bush, Wm., 140.
Bushell, Fras., 197.
Butcher, John, 250.
Butler, (—), 360.
........., (—), 188.
........., Edw., 144.
........., Capt. Jas., 366.
........., Major Jas., 212.
........., Cornet Jas., 327.
........., John, 276.
Button, Thos., 200, 239, 312.
Buxton, Gilbert, 371.
Byam, Edward, 231.
Byde, Thos., 231.

Byng, Fras., 101.
........., Geo., 262, 327.
........., Patee, Pattee, 101, 262.

C

Cabrol, Dan., 251, 328.
Cadogan, Chas., 128, 188, 328.
........., Wm., Earl of. See infra.
........., Gen. Wm., 128, 185, 231, 246, 249, 251.
Caesar, Thos., 128.
Caillaud, Dan., 355.
........., Reuben, 355.
Calder, John, 133.
Caldwald. See infra.
Caldwell, Wm., 101 bis.
Calhoune, John, 312.
Calvert, Chas., 126, 289.
Cambie, Wm., 160.
Campbell, (—), 101.
........., Alex., 150, 211.
........., Alex., of Fonab, 236.
........., Arch., 162, 306.
........., Lieut. Colin, 236.
........., Ensign Colin, 236.
........., Lieut. Colin, of Skipnish, 237.
........., Surgeon Colin, 238.
........., David, 98, 192.
........., Dugal, 162, 192, 306.
........., James (Storekeeper), 237.
........., James (Indep. Cy.), 239, 312.
........., Sir James, of Ardkinglas, 236 bis.
........., James (Lord Forfar's Regt.), 138.
........., Col. the Hon. James (Lord Portmore's Regt.), 107, 191, 206, 338.
........., James (Commissary), 237.
........., Cornet John, 115.
........., Capt. John, 130, 189 bis.
........., Lieut. John, 265.
........., John, of Carrick, 237.
........., Peter, 98.
........., Wm. (Horse Guards), 101, 189.
........., Wm. (Sankey's Regt.), 214.
........., Wm. (Indep. Cy.), 236.
........., Wm. (Thos. Harrison's Regt.), 334.
Capel, Gamaliel, 360.
........., Jos., 353.
Capell. See supra.
Capon, Peter, 240, 249.
Cardiff, Edm., 223.
Cardiffe, Thos., 338.
Cardonnel, Adam, 328.
Carew, Peter, 202.
Carey, Jas., 347.
........., Ric., 171.
........., Robt., 101, 185, 207.

Carfrae, Thos., 119, 202, **275** *bis*.
Carigan, Bryan, 233.
Carle, Peter, 285.
Carleil. *See* Carlisle.
Carleton, Cornet Wm., 113, 269.
........., Capt. Wm., 152.
Carlisle, (—). *See* Carlisle, Hen.
........., Hen., 106, 111.
........., Chas. Howard, 3rd Earl of, 231, 232.
Carmichael, Dan., 176.
........., John, 269, 278.
Carney, (—). *See* Carney, John.
........., John, 166.
Carpenter, Abr., 283.
........., General Geo., 109, 246, 247, 248.
........., Capt. Geo., 109, 125, 189, 191.
........., Jas., 191, 215.
........., Nat., 109.
........., Philip, 109.
Carr, Edw., 289 *bis*.
........., Jas., 327.
........., Robt. *See* Kerr.
........., Robt., 150.
........., Timothy, 263 *bis*.
........., Wm., 109, 216.
Carson, Ben., 339.
Carter, Thos., 158.
Carthew, Robt., 144.
Carvill, Wm., 148.
Carwarden, John, 232.
Cary, Hen., 204.
........., Rog., 215.
Castillion, John, 338.
Castle, Wiltshire, 166, 190.
Castlecomer, Chris. Wandesford, 2nd Visct., 251.
Castles, Wm., 182.
Cathcart, [Hon.] Chas., 107, 191 *bis*, 210.
Catherwood, Robt., 204.
Caulfield, (—). *See* Caulfield, Ric.
........., John, 164.
........., Ric., 122.
........., Thos., 240.
Cavell, Wm., 95, 187.
Cavendish, John, 201, 331.
Cecil, (—). *See* Cecil, Wm.
........., Wm., 178.
Chabane, Peter, 114.
Chalmers, Chas., 131.
Chamberlain, Sir Jas., 262.
........., John (1st Foot Guards), 123.
........., John (2nd Life Guards), 260.
........., John (King's Regt. of Horse), 263.
Chambers, Chas., 211.
........., Jas., 336.
........., John, 336.
........., Thos., 174.
Chambre, John, 200.
Champfleury, John, 353.

Chancey, Butler, 142.
Chancourt, Al., 174.
Chantrell, Fras., 126.
Chape. *See* Cheap.
Chapeau, David, 194.
Chaplain, Sam., 136.
Chapman, Nich., 371.
........., Phil., 316.
Charge, Robt., 166.
Charleton, Jas., 152, 204.
........., Wm., 186.
Charlott, Dan., 98.
........., Lewis, 310.
Charlton, And., 355.
........., John, 355.
Charnock, (—), 251.
Chasseloup, Peter, 191.
Chaworth, John, 100.
Cheap, Geo., 109, 201.
Chenevix, Phil., 329.
Cheret. *See infra*.
Cherette, Wm. Hen., 138, 200.
Cherry, John, 158.
........., Walt., 158.
Cheselden, Wm., 207.
Chibbalds, Chas., 327.
Chilcot, John, 366 *bis*.
Cholmley, John, 156, 187 *bis*, 249, 303.
Cholmondeley, George, 186 *bis*, 228.
........., Lt.-Col. *See* Cholmley, John.
Cholmondly. *See* Cholmondeley.
Christian, Sampson, 362.
Christie, Walt., 346.
Chudleigh, Geo., 126, 204, 291.
........., John, 128.
........., Adjt. Thos., 197, 309 *bis*.
........., Col. Thos., 170, 230.
Churchill, Alex., 232.
........., Col. Chas., 120.
........., Gen. Chas., 185.
........., George, 154, 192.
........., John, 182.
........., Randal, 205.
........., Wm. (Harrison's Regt.), 154.
........., Wm. (Pocock's Regt.), 180, 191 *bis*.
Clapham, Chris., 361.
Clark, John, 334.
........., Robt., 364.
........., Wm. *See* Clarke.
Clarke, Chas., 345.
........., Esme, 259.
........., Sir Talbot, 123, 217.
........., Wm. (3rd Foot Guards), 130, 192, 210.
........., Wm. (Sterne's Foot), 158, 186.
Claxton, Robt., 142.
Clayton, Benj., 212.
........., Hen., 206.
........., Jasper, 339.
Clements, Edw., 158.

Clements—*cont*
........, Fairfax, 150.
........, Hugh, 369.
Clenahan, (—). *See* Clenahan, Wm.
........, Wm., 122.
Clifford, Jos., 361.
Clift, Thos. (*sic*), 343.
Close, John, 176, 209.
........, Ric., 331.
Clutterbuck, Sam., 144.
Coates, Geo., 353.
Cobb, Ric. Chalmer, 361.
........, Wm., 341.
Cobham, Sir Ric. Temple, Visct., 106, 187, 229, 246.
........, Ric., 357.
Cochrain, Jas., 201.
Cochran, Jonathan, 273.
........, Thos. *See* Cochrane.
Cochrane, Thos., 107.
Cockain, Fras., 200.
Cockburn, Arch., 134.
........, Chas., 133, 294.
Cocking, Robt., 334.
Cockle, Geo., 233, 247.
Cockrane, Thos., 196.
Cocksedge, Fras., 369.
Codd, Ric., 362 *bis*.
Colborn, Peter, 360.
........, Roger, 281.
Cole, Wm. (Lumley's Regt.), 188.
........, Wm. (Welsh Fusiliers), 347.
Coleman, Wm., 319.
Collet, Thos., 309.
Colley, Geo., 331.
Collier, Thos., 228, 334.
Collingwood, Geo., 156, 303.
Collins, Jas., 364.
........, John, 242.
Collop, Hen., 298.
Colnet, Wm., 197.
Colquhoun, Jas., 130.
Colson, Ben., 330.
Colston, Edw., 125.
Columbier, Columbière, Ant., 201, 336.
Columbine, Ben., 355.
........, Edward, 334.
........, Fras., 146, 188.
........, Thos., 314.
Column, Fras., 174.
Colvert. *See* Calvert.
Colvill, Arch., 133.
........, Chas. *See infra.*
Colville, Chas., 351.
........, John, 133, 351.
Colvine, Chas., 195.
Colvyn, Jas., 162.
Combe, Chas., 195 *bis*, 347.
Comberbach, Rog., 208.
Comming. *See* Cumming.

Compton, Sir Fras., 101.
........, Geo., 96.
........, Hatton, 97, 231.
Comrie, Arch., 134.
Comyns, (—). *See* Comyns, Wm.
........, Wm., 182.
Condon, Thos., 138, 193.
Congreve, Ralph, 237.
........, Capt. Wm., 336.
........, Ensign Wm., 349.
Conron, Chris., 203.
Constable, Thos. (Hotham's Regt.), 172.
........, Thos. (Steuart's Regt.), 338.
Cook, Wm., 172.
Cooke, Dan., 205.
........, Jeffry, 370.
........, John, 144.
........, Robt., 370.
........, Wm., 357.
Cookes, Mascall, 97.
Cookman, Hen., 193, 347.
Cooksey, Edw., 170.
Coot. *See* Coote.
Coote, Algernon, 260 *bis*.
........, Thos., 130, 185.
Cope, (—). *See* Cope, John.
........, Anthony, 332.
........, John, 128.
........, Galen, 103, 186.
........, Hen., 164, 191.
........, Wm., 332.
Coppin, Sam., 327.
Corbett, Alex., 178, 206.
........, And., 168.
........, Thos., 208.
Cord, Jas., 148.
Coren, Ric., 140.
Cormack, Wm., 339.
Corneille, John, 369.
Corner, And., 121.
Cornewall, Hen., 96.
........, Robt., 213, 325, 326.
Cornicle. *See* Corneille.
Cornish, Harry, 201.
Cornuaud, Jas., 96.
Cornwall, (—), 347.
Corrance, John, 96.
Cory, Humphrey, 360.
Cosby, Alex., 150, 209.
........, Dudley, 199, 341.
........, Loftus, 341.
........, Thos., 199.
........, Wm., 304.
Cosley, Nat., 150.
Cossard, Hen., 353.
Cossby. *See* Cosby.
Cossely, John, 150.
Cotter, Robt., 191.
Cotton, Chas., 164.
........, Stanhope, 152, 188.

Cotton—*cont.*
........., Steph., 215.
Coucher, Robt., 331.
Coult, Jas., 138.
Courtney, Hen., 114.
........., Wm., 126.
Cousins, John, 210.
Cowley, John, 336.
Cowper, John, 366.
Cox, Hen., 128 *bis.*
........., John, 360.
........., Phil., 210.
........., Robt., 205.
........., Thos., 269.
Cracherode, Chas., 355.
Craddock, Paul, 160.
Cradock, (—). *See* Cradock, Phil.
........., Phil., 360.
Craggs, James, junr., 248, 285.
Craig, John, 345.
Craigengelt, Chas., 236.
Cramer, Toby, 198.
Crane, Fras., 160.
Cranley, Ric., 353.
Cranston, Wm., Lord, 189.
Cranwell, John, 360.
Crawford, (—). *See* Crawford, Henry.
........., (—), 208.
........., Arch., 133.
........., David, 228.
........., Hen., 113.
........., John, 370.
........., Capt. Wm., 107, 111.
........., Ensign Wm., 294.
Crawley, Thos., 114.
Creighton, And., 160.
........., David, 229.
Crepigny, Chas., 160.
Crespin, Dan., 328.
Cressett, Jas., 123.
Creuse. *See* De La Creuse.
Crew, And., 180.
Croasdale, Thos., 214.
Crofton, Hen., 144.
Crofts, Edw., 341.
........., Geo., 144.
........., Jas., 106, 192, 278.
Crome, Valentine, 353.
Crookshanks, Robt., 338 *bis.*
Cropp, Wm., 144.
Crosbie, Chas., 154, 302.
........., John, 234.
........., Sir Warren, Bt., 343.
Crosby, Chas. *See* Crosbie.
........., Sir Warren. *See* Crosbie.
........., Wm., 314.
Cross, John, 201.
Crossley, Chas., 186.
Crowther, Thos., 103.
Cudmore, Thos., 362

Culliford, John, 136.
Cumerland, Colin Lindsay, Lord, 133.
Cuming, Jas., 345.
Cumming, Alex., 178.
Cummins, Thos., 280.
Cuningham, Geo., 333.
Cunningham, (—), 189.
........., Chas., 180.
........., Major Jas., 133, 250.
........., Lieut. Jas., 146, 194 *bis.*
........., Qr.-Mr. John, 146.
........., Ensign John, 301.
........., Lieut. John, 309, 314.
........., Robt., 144.
Curfie, John, 331.
Curtis, Wm., 371.
Cutler, Egerton, 158.
........., Robt., 191.
Cuttle, Ben., 336.
Cutts, Sam., 364.

D

Dabsac, Hen., 338.
Daffy, Wm., 193.
Dalbos, John, 168.
Dalbyn, Thos., 214.
Dalgardno, John, 300.
Dalhousie, Wm. Ramsay, 6th Earl of, 130.
Dalley, Abel, 362.
Dally, John, 355.
Dalmas, John, 172.
Dalrymple, Jas., 178.
........., John (Kirke's Regt.), 136.
........., John (Preston's Regt.), 352.
Dalston, (—). *See* Dalston, John.
........., John, 122, 272.
Dalton, Dominick, 133.
Dalyell, John. *See* Dalzell.
Dalzell, John, 130.
........., Robt., 228 *bis.*
........., [The Hon.] Thos., 134, 191.
Dambon, Jas., 194, 326.
........., Jos., 144, 298.
Dancer, John, 364.
Dancy, Robt., 123.
Daniels, Sam., 170.
Danson, Rog., 150.
Daracote, Thos., 353.
Darby, Ben., 338.
........., Ebenezer, 355.
........., John, 207.
........., Wm., 369.
Darcy, Conyers, 186.
........., Peter, 126, 128, 203
Darcey. *See* Darcy.
Daulhat, Pet., 361.

INDEX

D'Auteville, Florand, 207.
Dauvergne, Edw., 131.
Davenport, Peter, 118.
........., Sherington, 327.
Davidson, Lt.-Col. Wm., 353.
........., Adjt. Wm., 353 bis.
Davis, Alex., 259.
........., Arth., 311.
........., Hen., 241.
........., John (Gunner), 370.
........., John (3rd Foot Guards), 130.
........., Jos., 371.
........., Rog., 136, 202.
Davison, Chas., 357.
........., Wm., 357.
Dawes, Thos. (Bowles's Regt.), 190.
........., Thos. (Wills's Regt.), 357.
Daws, Wm., 172 bis.
Dawson, Geo., 166.
........., Hen., 117.
Deal, Jas., 283, 287.
Deane, Alex., 138.
........., Cornet John, 103.
........., Gunner John, 369.
........., Stephen, 362.
De Beez, August., 146.
........., David, 146.
De Boismorelle, Andr., 136.
Debrose, Hen., 355.
Deck. *See* Van Deck.
De Cosne, Pet., 336.
Dee, Duncan, 98, 187, 191.
........., Dunkan. *See supra.*
Defour, Lewis, 182.
Degg, Wm., 207.
De Grangues, Hen., 117.
De Guerin, Maynard, 168.
Dehays, Jas., 366.
De La Béné, John Lewis, 232, 249.
........., Michael, 154.
De La Coudrière, G. R., 146.
De La Creuse, Stephen, 189, 277.
De la Fontaine, Pet., 160.
Delahaye, Thos., 118.
De L'Angle, Max, 154.
........., Theoph., 156.
Delaunay, Joseph, 242.
........., Mark, 204.
Delaval, Wm., 107, 111.
Delavale, Delavally. *See* Delaval
Deleuzer, Jas., 124.
Deloraine, Henry Scott, Earl of, 100, 186, 229.
De Lorraine, Hen., Earl. *See supra.*
Demaris, Hen., 328.
Dennet, Bernard, 360.
Denny, Wm., 361.
Dent, Robt., 99.
Denton, Delaval, 308, 327.
Denty, John, 96, 192.

De Quesne. *See* Du Quesne.
De Ponthier, Hen., 176.
Des Clouseaux, Lewis, 99.
Desmar, Abr., 272.
De Trefontaine, Fras., 207.
Devenish, Ric., 233.
Devischer, Abr., 213, 309.
........., Edw., 196.
Devisher. *See supra.*
Dick, Lewis, 345.
........., Wm., 131.
Dickins, Ambrose, 129, 216.
Dickinson, Ric., 338.
Dickson, Jas., 202.
Diggs, Thos., 130, 188.
Dilk, Dilke, Dilks, Chas., 98, 106, 192 bis.
Dillington, Sir Tristram, Bt., 123, 212.
Dingly, Wm., 338.
Disney, Hen., 364.
Dixon, John, 307.
Dobson, Chas., 289.
Dobyns, Wm., 231.
Dodd, Wm., 306.
Dodsworth, John, 103 bis.
D'Offranville, Peter, 158, 196.
Dogherty, Simon, 370.
Doherty, Dicksing (*sic*), 160.
........., Latham, 160.
Doige, Ric., 170.
Dollard, Jeffry, 199.
Dollon, Lewis, 106, 111.
Domergue, Hen., 148, 300.
Donne, Thos., 346.
Donnell, Chas, 361.
Donston, Barnaby, 126.
Dormer, Jas., 118, 246.
........., Robt., 95.
Doucet, Doucett, John, 209, 248, 312.
Doughty, Edw., 233.
Douglas, Alex., 241.
........., Arch., 195.
........., Col. Chas., memoir of, 17–34.
........., Lt.-Col. Chas., 170.
........., Jas. (Orkney's Regt.), 133.
........., Jas. (Grant's Regt.), 178.
........., John (Primrose's Regt.), 349.
........., John (Orrery's Regt.), 345.
........., Robt., 215, 307.
........., Wm., 178, 269.
Doun, John, 237.
Dowcet. *See* Doucet.
Dowdall, Mathew, 370.
Dowglass. *See* Douglas.
Downes, Hen., 148, 300.
........., Lewis, 121.
........., Philip, 101.
........., Stephen, 353.
Downing, Wm., 370.
Dowset, Thos., 366.
Doyle, And., 204, 217.

D'Oyley, Doyley, Robt., 231, 233.
Doyne, Michael, 338.
Drake, Ben., 349.
Draper, Mat., 152, 228, 232.
Driver, Jonathan, 206.
Drummond, Lawrence, 345.
........., Wm., 351.
Drury, Robt., 332.
........., Theodore, 237.
Drysdale, Hugh, 120.
........., Thos., 120.
Dubleday, (—). See infra.
........., John, 122, 278.
Dubourgay, Chas., 168, 235.
Ducas, Pascall, 110.
Duckett, Wm., 103, 190 bis, 263.
Duckins. See Duckett.
Ducros, John, 331.
Dumaresq. See infra.
Dumaresque, Geo., 140.
........., John, 207 bis, 341.
Dumas, Jas., 110.
........., Pet., 211.
Dumbarton, Geo. Douglas, 2nd Earl of, 168.
Dummery. See Dumaresq.
Dunbar, David, 362.
........., George, 107, 111.
........., Philip (Sankey's Regt.), 206, 213.
........., Philip (George's Regt.), 362.
........., Ric., 347.
........., Thos., 362.
Dunbarr, Geo. See Dunbar.
........., John, 113.
Duncomb, John (Guidon and Capt.), 100.
........., Capt. John, 152, 192.
........., Wm. See Duncombe.
Duncombe (—). See infra.
.... Wm., 162, 190, 202.
Dundonald, John Cochrane, 4th Earl of, 98.
Dunlop, Wm., 235.
Dunmore, John Murray, 2nd Earl of, 130
Dunmuresq. See Dumaresq.
Dunning, Thos., 208.
Duperron, Armand, 346.
Dupine, Fras., 97.
Dupuis, Dupuy, Abr., 109, 189.
Duquerry, Augustus, 110, 201.
Duquery, August. See supra.
Du Quesne, Gabriel, Marquis, 97, 261.
Durand, Pet., 239.
Durell, Cornet Hen., 124.
........., Ens. Hen., 156.
........., Nich., 122.
Duret, Fras., 106.
Durham, Alex., 156.
Durnford, Jas., 180.
Duroure, Alex., 190, 193.
........., Scipio, 146.
Du Royer, Sam., 168.
Duval, Jas., 334.

Duvernet, John Fras., 205.
Dyer, John, 195.
........., Ric., 366
........., Wm., 351.
Dyves, Lewis, 96.

E

Eaglesfield, Robt., 166.
Eames, Geo., 160.
Earle, Augustus, 298.
........., Giles. See Erle.
Easthope, Jeremiah, 271.
Eastland, Rupert, 168.
Eaton, Chas., 212.
........., Edw., 128, 129.
........., Jas., 105, 203 bis.
Echlin. See Echlyn.
Echlyn, Chas., 329.
........., Capt. Thos., 112.
........., Lt.-Gen. Thos., 186.
Ecles, Ben., 330.
........., John, 361.
Edgar, Hugh, 208.
........., John, 309.
Edmeston, Hen., 164.
Edmingston, Edmington, Pat., 130, 214.
Edmonds, Ric., 329.
Edmunds, Jas., 97, 260.
........., Ric. See Edmonds.
Edwards, Arth. (Harrison's Regt.), 154.
........., Arth. (2nd Life Guards), 192, 259.
........., John, 148.
........., Michael, 364.
........., Ric., 148, 234.
........., Talbot, 285.
Egar, Wm., 158.
Egerton, Jos., 287.
........., [Hon.] Wm., 125, 187, 364.
Elliot, Adam, 358.
........., Major Walt., 185.
Elliott, Jos., 233.
........., Robt., 154.
Ellis, Chas., 215.
........., Ric., 212.
........., Thos., 118.
........., Qr.-Mr. Wm., 273.
........., Surgeon Wm., 298.
Elphinston, Alex. (Grove's Regt.), 146.
........., Chas., 178.
Elphinstone, [Hon.] Arthur, 202.
........., Wm., 351.
Elrington, Gerald, 166.
........., Job, 142.
........., John, 142.
........., Wm., 142, 192.
Elwell, Elwill, Edmund, 125, 199.

INDEX

Elwes, John, 101, 206.
........., Wm., 95.
Emerson, Wm., 370.
Emmenes, Martin, 150.
Emslie, Fras., 208.
England, Thos., 152.
English, John, 119.
........., Robt., 235.
Enos, Adam, 152, 217.
Ereskine, Eriskine. *See* Erskine.
Erle, Angus, 142.
........., Giles, 101, 188, 238.
........., Gen. Thos., 227 *bis*, 229, 246, 285.
........., Lt.-Col. Thos., 112.
Erskine, Jas. (Preston's Regt.), 214.
........., Jas. (Orkney's Regt.), 133.
........., Jas. (Philipps's Regt.), 312.
........., Wm. 210.
Essington, Kilby, 232.
Evans, Ric., 233.
........., Wm. 246, 331.
Everard, Phil., 174.
Everest, Ezekiel, 174.
Eversfield, Chas., 285.
Eyre, John, 197.
........., Kingsmill, 247, 251.
........., Thos., 136.
Eyton, David, 125, 126.
........., Jas. *See* Eaton.

F

Fabre, Isaac, 106.
Fade, Jas., 360.
Faillot. *See* Folliot.
Fairfull, Colin, 236.
Falconer, Jas., 156.
Falkland, Lucius Henry Cary, 6th Viscount, 130.
Falliot, Wm., 189.
Fane, [The Hon.] John, 216, 366 *bis*.
Farcy, John, 336.
Fargason. *See* Ferguson.
Fargeon, Pet., 195, 204.
Farmer, Chas., 150.
........., J[ohn]. *See* Fermor.
Farquharson, Jas., 307.
Farrar, John, 331.
Farrell, Jas., 140.
........., Pat., 370.
Farrer, John, 194.
........., Montagu, 110, 266.
........., Wm., 328.
Faunt, Geo., 233.
Faur, Fras., 154.
Faverall, John, 208.

Fazakerley, Thos., 187.
Feilding, George, 101 *bis*, 211.
Fell, Chas., 314.
Fenner, Jacob, 369.
Fenwick, Nich., 142.
Ferguson, (—), 195.
........., Jas. (Preston's Foot), 351.
........., Jas. (Shannon's Regt.), 207.
........., Robt., 210, 351.
........., Wm., 195 *bis*, 351.
Fermor, John, 122, 213.
Ferrer. *See* Farrar.
Ferrers, Jos., 125, 186 *bis*.
........., Thos., 125.
Fiddis, Ric., 227.
Fielding, Geo. *See* Feilding.
........., John, 327.
........., Pet. *See* Fielding, Robt.
........., Robt., 152, 301.
Figuel, Hosea, 213.
Filbridge, John, 338.
Filmer, Edw., 150.
Finboe, Nich., 150, 199
Finley, Wm., 329.
Finney, Philip, 366.
Finny, Jas., 281.
Fish, Humph., 211.
Fitzgerald, Gerald, 117.
........., John, 135.
........., Thos., 360.
Fitzmaurice, [Hon.] Wm., 201.
Fitzpatrick, And., 144, 216.
........., Bernard, 123.
Fitzroy, Lord Chas., 215.
Fitz Simons, Fitzsymonds, Robt., 158.
Fitz Thomas, Thos., 353.
........., Wm., 201, 205.
Flaherty, Dan., 370.
Fleming, Fras., 364.
........., Hugh, 369.
........., Lieut. Jas., 118, 186.
........., Capt. Jas., 144.
........., Chaplain Jas., 332.
........., Michael, 156.
........., Robt., 353.
Flemming. *See* Fleming.
Fletcher, Wheeler, 197.
Flower, Rog., 358.
Floyer, John, 330.
........., Scott, 353.
Fogg, Lieut. John, 125.
........., Ensign John, 126, 189.
Foley, Sam., 109.
Foliott, John. *See* Folliot.
........., Lewis, 113.
Folliot, Folliott, Col. John, 128 *bis*, 129, 188, 205, 215.
........., Cornet John, 269.
Fonjuliane, Chas., 300.
Fonsebran, Jas., 190.

Forbes, Alex., 107, 198.
........., Arch., 237.
........., George, Lord, 98, 247.
........., John, 239.
Ford, Thos., 170.
Forfar, (—), 116.
........., Archd. Douglas, 2nd Earl of, memoir of, 81–84.
........., Regt. of, 138.
Forman, Chas., 234.
Forrest, Robt., 237.
........., Wm., 280.
Forrester, Andrew, 118, 351.
........., George Baillie, 4th Lord, 202, 211, 351.
........., John, 195.
........., Leo, 164.
........., Robt. 164.
Forster, Aquila, 158.
........., Chris., 341.
Fortescue, Chichester, 164.
Forth, Thos., 146, 186, 311.
Foster, Jas., 158.
........., Jos., 146.
Fothergill, Thos., 156, 303.
Foucault, Pet., 314.
Foulis, David, 158.
........., Geo., 130.
Fountaine, Jas., 176.
Fourness. *See* Furness.
Fowke, Geo., 96, 201.
........., Thos., 164, 200.
Fowkes. *See* Fowke.
Fowler, Abr., 199.
Fowlis. *See* Foulis.
Fox, Fras., 241, 312.
........., Jonathan, 152, 192.
........., Peyton, 176.
Frampton, Chas., 125.
Franck or Francks, Jas. (Montague's Regt.), 148.
........., Jas. (Kirke's Regt.), 208.
........., Ric., 306.
........., Wm., 136.
Frank, Israel, 233.
Franks, Godfrey, 283.
........., Ric. Steph., 162.
Fraser, Alex., of Culduthel, 237.
........., Claud, 294.
........., Hugh, 131.
........., Kenneth, 234.
Frazer, Alex., 233, 234.
........., Robt., 154, 302.
Frazier. *See* Frazer.
Freeman, Sam., 117.
........., Wm., 117.
French, Nich., 325.
Friend, Robt., 98.
........., Thos., 106.
Frontine, Jas., 261.
Fuller, Fras., 125.

Fullerton, Philip, 197.
Furlong, Jonathan, 140, 198 *bis*.
Furnes. *See* Furness.
Furness, Geo., 291.
........., John, 343.
........., Jos., 343.
........., Sam, 349.
Fury, Jas., 164.
........., Peregrine, 312.
Fynboe. *See* Finboe.

G

Gaines, Garret, 156.
Gale, Thos., 166.
........., Wm., 347.
Galloway, Walter, 237.
Gallway, John, 200.
Gally, John, 336.
Gambell, Arthur, 150 *bis*, 203.
Gamble, Jas., 206.
Gamboll. *See* Gambell.
Gardiner, Harry, 319.
........., Jas., 107, 124, 217.
........., John (Stanwix's Regt.), 215.
........., John (Primrose's Regt.), 349.
.... Thos., 362.
........., Wm, *See* Gardner, Wm.
Gardner, Jas. *See* Gardiner, Jas.
........., John, 150.
........., Peter, 234.
.... Robt., 162.
........., Wm., 115, 209.
Garland, Thos., 242.
Garnier, Isaac, 235.
Garrard, Sam., 187.
Garret, Dan., 198, 280.
........., John, 230.
........., Wm., 199.
Garrick, Pet., 121, 277.
Garth, Jas., 207, 261.
........., Sir Sam., Bart., M.D., 227.
Gascoin, John, 156, 188.
........., Jos., 199.
Gasteen, Philip, 110, 266.
Gawen, Robt. *See* Gawne.
Gawne, Robt., 134, 294.
Gay, Alex., 160, 217.
........., Robt., 97.
Gayner, Philip, 260.
Geary, Christopher, 349.
Geddes, Gilbert, 198.
Gee, Jas., 172, 201.
........., Wm. (Handasyde's Regt.), 306.
........., Wm. (Windress's Regt.), 366.
Geekhie, Wm., 198.
Gendrault, Jas., 128, 188.
Gentleman, Pat., 362.

INDEX

George, Paul, 120.
........., Wm., 211.
Gerrard, Sam., 125.
Gerrit, Gerritt. *See* Garret.
Gervais, Dan., 279.
Gery, Philip, 195, 217.
Gibbon, Geo., 233, 252.
........., Jeffrey. *See* Gibbons.
Gibbons, Fras., 126 (Gibson).
........., Jeffery, Jeffry, Jeffrey, 144, 192 *bis*, 298.
Gibson, Edw., 339.
........., Fras. *See* Gibbons.
........., Jas. (4th Tp. of Life Guards), 98.
........., Jas. (Windsor's Foot), 353.
........., Jas. (Gunsmith), 237.
........., Sir John, Knt., 231.
........., John (Rich's Dragoons), 202.
........., Thos., M.D., 252.
Gifford, Fitzmorris, 228.
........., Ric., 98.
Gignone, Chas., 353.
Gignoux, Isaac, 168.
Gilbert, John, 101.
Gilchrist, John, 351.
Giles, Jas., 136, 198, 214.
........., Thos., 142.
Gill, Wm., 126.
Gillespey, John, 275.
Gilligan, Dan., 234.
Gillman, Robt., 158.
........., Stephen, 158.
Gilmore, Chas., 332.
........., William, 332.
Girling, Cornet John, 120, 276.
........., John (1st Foot Guards), 126.
Gittins, Nat., 138.
Glencairn, Wm. Cunningham, 12th Earl of, 236 *bis*.
Godby, Carey, 142.
........., Peter, 142.
Goddard, (—), 122.
........., Hen., 122.
........., Thos. [sen.], 297.
........., Thos. [jun.], 300.
Godfrey, Rowley, 338.
Godolphin, Sydney, 231.
........., Wm., 261.
Gojac, Peter Gaty, 328.
Golding, Jas., 96.
Gooch, Wm., 156.
Goodere, Hen., 95, 187.
Gooderiche. *See infra*.
Goodricke, John Savile, 366.
........., Wm., 126.
Goodwin, Nat., 176.
Goodwyn, John, 360.
Gordon, Alex. (Indep. Cy.), 200, 241.
........., Alex. (Commissary), 248.
........., Chas., 133.

Gordon—*cont*.
........., Geo., 360.
........., Hen., 329.
........., Jas. (Preston's Regt.), 195, 351.
........., Jas. (Welsh Fusiliers), 347.
........., John (Orkney's Regt.), 133.
........., John (3rd Foot Guards), 190.
........., John (Primrose's Regt.), 349.
........., Sir Wm., Bt., 203, 236.
........., Ensign Wm., 307.
Gore, Arth. (Whetham's Regt.), 164.
........., Arth. (3rd Engineer), 369.
........., Fras., 109.
........., Hen., 114.
........., Humphry, 114, 246.
........., John (1st Foot Guards), 190.
........., John (Wade's Regt.), 361.
........., Ric., 332.
........., Thos., 164.
Gorges, Ric., 361.
Goring, Sir Hen., Bt., 358.
Gorsuch, Thos., 126.
Gough, Wm., 316.
Gould, Jas., 278.
Gower, Roger, 195.
Grace, John, 214, 307.
Graham (—), 182.
........., Alex., 178.
........., David, 133.
........., Fras., 195, 351.
........., Hen., 361.
........., Jas. (Orkney's Regt.), 133.
........., Jas. (Lord Orrery's Regt.), 345.
........., Metcalf, 228, 328.
........., Ric., 154.
........., Robt., 160, 187 *bis*.
........., Wm. (Kirke's Regt.), 136.
........., Wm. (Meredith's Regt.), 160.
........., Wm. (Gore's Dragoons), 270.
........., Wm. (Windsor's Foot), 353.
Grame. *See* Graham.
Grant, Alex., 178, 231, 309.
........., Geo., 138, 296.
........., Hugh, 204.
........., Jas., 178.
........., John (Grant's Regt.), 316.
........., John (Disney's Regt.), 364.
........., Ensign John, 316.
........., Capt. Lewis, 178.
........., Lieut. Lewis, 178.
........., Ensign Lewis, 178.
........., Wm., 237.
Granville, John, 146, 194.
........., Robt., 146, 196 (Grewell).
Graves, Wm., 366.
Green, Ben., 339.
........., Caleb, 182.
........., Geo., 172.
........., Jos., 343.
........., Ric. (2nd Foot Guards), 128 *bis*, 190.

Green—*cont.*
........., Ric. (Invalid Company), 190.
Greenall, John, 360.
Greenhill, John, 96.
Greenway, Robt. (1st Foot Guards), 210.
........., Robt. (Smith), 369.
Greenwood, Chas., 117.
........., John, 355.
........., Walt. Jas., 366.
Gregg, Robt., 211.
Gregory, Ben., 338.
Gregson, Ric., 124, 280.
Grewell. *See* Granville, Robt.
Grey, John, 196.
Grierson, John, 138.
Griffith, Ben., 278.
........., Jas., 264.
........., Capt. John, 166, 203.
........., Lieut. John, 191.
........., Pierce, 144.
........., Robt., 182.
Grigg, Jas., 341.
Grills, Gervas, 174.
........., Wm., 140.
Gronous, Jos., 197, 279.
Groundman, Martin, 197.
Grove, Geo., 343 *bis.*
........., Hen., 187, 229, 247.
Guerin (—), 318.
Guerrin, Amls., 207.
Guest, Joshua, 109 *bis.*
........., Thos., 369.
Guidet, Balthazar, 114, 217.
Guise, John, 125.
Gully, Timothy, 241, 289.
Gumbleton, Fras., 280.
Gumley, Geo., 309.
........., John, 247.
Gunby, John, 144.
Gunn, Hen., 233.
Gwin, Lewis, 308, 319.
Gwyn, John, 216.
........., Wm., 329.

H

Hadzor, John, 152 *bis.*
Haille. *See* Hale.
Haills. *See* Hales.
Haldane, Jas., 119, 308.
........., Patrick. *See supra*, Jas.
Halden. *See* Haldane.
Hale, Jas., 189.
........., Roger, 144.
........., Wm. *See* Hall.
Hales, John, 130.
........., Thos., 199, 319.

Haley, Thos., 109.
Halhed, Nathl., 331.
Haliday, Sam., 351.
........., Wm., 154.
Halket, Pet., 210.
Hall, David, 357.
........., Edw. (Capt. of Tynemouth Castle), 230.
........., Edw. (Windsor's Regt.), 366.
........., Hannibal, 327.
........., Wm. (Lucas's Regt.), 182.
........., Wm. (Kellum's Regt.), 328.
Hallifax, Wm., 327
Halshide (—), 178.
Halyburton, Thos., 188.
Hamers, Pet., 336.
Hamilton, Ensign and Adjt., Andrew, 130, 192.
........., Lieut. Andrew, 133, 293.
........., Arch., 115.
........., Lord Archibald, 230, 243.
........., Chas., 197.
........., Chichester, 144.
........., Edw., 332.
........., Fred., 227, 232.
........., Fred., junr., 304.
........., Adjt. Gustavus, 146.
........., Capt. Gustavus, 332.
........., Lieut. Gustavus, 113.
........., Ensign Gustavus, 193.
........., Hans, 187.
........., Capt. Jas., 213, 214, 307 *bis.*
........., Ensign Jas., 215.
........., Jas. (Royal Regt. of Foot), 294.
........., Capt. John, 119.
........., Lieut. John, 158.
........., Ensign John, 176.
........., Sir John, 196.
........., Otho, 128, 212 *bis.*
........., Ric., 110.
........., Capt. Robt., 133.
........., Lieut. Robt., 160.
........., Thos. (Coldstream Guards), 128.
........., Thos. (*sic*). *See* Hamilton Otho.
........., Walt., 154.
........., Cornet Wm., 118, 266, 274.
........., Lieut. Wm., 170.
........., Surgeon Wm., 210.
Hammond, Fras. *See* Hamond
Hamon, Hector, 349.
........., Isaac, 294, 345.
Hamond, Fras., 228.
........., Isaac. *See* Hamon.
Hampden, John, 122.
Handasyde, Chas., 192.
........., Clifford, 162, 192.
........., Jasper, 162.
........., Rog., 162.
........., Thos., 162, 343.
........., Wm., 154, 185.

INDEX

Handcock, Rupert, 358.
Handy, Robt., 241, 312.
Hankinson, Ric., 362 *bis*.
Hanmer, Ric., 142.
........., Wm., 128, 212, 291.
Hannah, Jas., 371.
Hanning, John, 166.
Hansard, Ralph, 339.
Hanway, John, 238, 281.
Harbert (*sic*), Caleb, 274.
Hardie, John, 156.
Hardine, Alex., 233, 310.
Harding, Jos., 358.
Hardistie, Pet., 96, 192.
Hardwelt, Ant., 156.
Hardyman (—), 123.
Hargrave, Chris., 201, 279.
........., John, 364.
........., Wm., 364.
Harrington, Bingham, 334.
Harris, Arch., 126.
........., Cornet Ben., 123, 279.
........., Ensign Ben., 168.
........., Chas., 126.
........., Edmund, 301.
........., John (Disney's Regt.), 364.
........., John (Harrison's Foot), 191, 302.
........., John (Seymour's Regt.), 140.
........., John (Pocock's Regt.), 180.
........., John, junr. (Coldstream Guards), 216.
........., Jos., 272.
........., Ric. (Preston's Regt.), 351.
........., Ric. (Wills's Regt.), 360.
Harrison, Chas. 334 *bis*.
........., Delaval, 182.
........., Geo., 204.
........., Hen., 154, 185 *bis*.
........., Jas. (The Carabiniers), 329.
........., Jas. (Montague's Regt.), 148.
........., Chaplain John, 240.
........., Capt. John, 176.
........., Brig.-Gen. Thos., 334.
........., Capt. Thos., 339.
Hart, Peter, 136.
........., Robt. (Gunner), 370.
........., Robt. (Surgeon), 228.
Hartigan, Hen., 334.
Hartshorne, Ric., 196.
Hartstonge, Price, 327.
Harvey, Gedeon, Gideon, 197, 289.
........., Robt., 241.
Harwood, Ric., 112, 349.
Hassan, Cutts, 358.
Hastings, Churchill, 366.
........., Ferd. Ric., 152, 189, 190, 200.
Hatch, Jas. Hide, 216.
Hatley, Griffith, 195.
Hatton, Thos., 327.
Hauteclaire, John, 361.

Haviland, Pet., 358.
Hawker, Pet., 214, 249.
Hawkins, Fras., 281.
........., John, 101.
........., Ric., 158, 214.
........., Wm., 227.
Hawksworth, John, 109, 201.
Hawley, Edw., 331.
........., Col. Hen., 207, 331.
........., Ric., 343.
Hawtayne, Malachi, 347.
........., Wm., 347.
Hay, And. (Invalid Cy.), 232.
........., And. (Lord Orrery's Regt.), 346.
........., Arch., 249.
........., Geo. (Lt.-Gov. of Montserrat), 231.
........., Capt. Geo., 95, 186, 191.
........., Chaplain John, 247.
........., Cornet John, 110.
........., Capt. John (1st Foot Guards), 125.
........., Ensign John, 164, 203.
........., Sir Robt., 107, 191, 210.
........., Sir Thos., 265.
........., Wm. *See* Haye.
........., Lord Wm., 130, 216, 248.
Haye, Wm., 162.
Hayes, Edw., 142.
........., Jas., 180.
........., John, 166, 301.
........., Robt., 170.
........., Wm., 170, 309.
Hayles, Thos., 339.
Haylett, John, 136.
Haynes, John, 203.
Hays. *See* Hayes.
Hayward, Haywood, John, 138, 208, 296.
Hazelwood, Fras. (*sic*), 229.
Heart. *See* Hart.
Hebelthwayte (—), 117.
........., W., 117.
Heigham, John, 156.
Heighington, Geo., 339.
Heley, John, 347.
Hely, John, 309.
Hemington, Robt., 194.
Henderson, David, 355.
Henley, Ric., 182.
Henly. *See* Henley.
Henson, Ric., 193, 273.
Hepburn (—). *See* Hepburne, Robt.
........., Geo., 130.
........., John, 280.
Hepburne, Robt., 121, 277.
Herbert, Lord. *See infra*.
........., Hen., Lord, 205, 212.
Herd, Howell, 353.
Hering, Dan., 182.
Herle, Jas., 361.
Heron, Sir Harry, Sir Henry, 188, 291.
Herries, Robt., 345.

B B 2

Herring, John, 277.
Hertford, Algernon Seymour, Earl of, 96, 185 bis, 231.
Hesketh, Chaplain Thos., 105, 360.
........., Lieut. Thos., 172.
Heskett. See Hesketh.
Hetley, Wm., 126.
Heusbergh, Lelio, 97.
Hewet, Pet., 347 bis.
Hewett, Geo. Villiers, 126, 188.
Hewettson, Michael, 370.
Hewson, Paul. Steph., 124.
Heydon, Thos., 281.
Heylin, Heylyn, John, 160, 187.
Hibbert (—). See Hibbert, Chris.
........., Chris., 178.
........., Ric., 178.
Hickes, Thos., 105.
Hickman, Hen., 347.
........., Wm., 295.
Higgenson, Wm., 119.
Higgins (—). See Surgeon Edward.
........., Surgeon Edward, 142.
........., Ensign Edward, 176.
........., Wm., 332.
Higginson, Michael, 270.
Hildeyard. See infra.
Hildyard, Hen., 212.
Hilgrove, Clement, 261.
Hill, Qr.-Mr. Edw., 319.
........., Capt. Edw., 331, 332.
........., Hen., 360.
........., Jas. 113.
........., Maj.-Gen. John, 229.
........., John (Handasyde's Regt.), 162.
........., Col. John (Ross's Dragoons), 332.
........., Robt., 142.
Hilton, Hugh, 116.
Hinchinbroke, Edward Montagu, Lord, 128, 187, 205, 216, 230, 291, 319, 331.
Hinchinbrook. See supra.
Hincks, Thos., 114.
Hinton, Ant., 182.
........., John, 112.
........., Sam., 136, 215.
Hirondel, Fras. Alex., 341.
Hoare, John (Carpenter's Dragoons), 109.
........., John (Whetham's Foot), 206.
.... John (First Foot Guards). See Howe.
........., Wm., 206.
Hobart, Edward, 209 (Hubard), 336.
........., John (Wills's Regt.), 357.
........., John (Coldstream Guards), 128.
Hockenhull, Thos., 291.
Hodder, Ben., 152.
Hodges, John, 208.
........., Thos., 209.
Holborne, John, 294.
Holbrook, Sam., 140.

Holburn, Wm., 236.
Holford, Wm., 281.
Holland, Geo., 364.
........., Hen., 242.
........., Ric., 174.
........., Thos., 205.
Holliday. See Haliday.
Hollingworth, John, 360.
........., Mark, 355.
Hollyland, Thos., 144.
Holman, John, 336.
........., Thos., 287.
Holmes (—). See Holmes, Ensign Ric.
........., Harry, 202, 307.
........., Jas., 166.
........., Jos., 164.
........., Maj.-Gen. Ric., 128, 191 bis.
........., Ensign Ric., 128, 129.
Home, Geo., 345.
........., Jas., 133, 294.
Honeywood, Ric., 272.
Honywood, Phil., 115, 229, 246.
Hook. See infra.
Hooke, Hen., 231.
........., Thos., 156.
........., Wm., 156, 303.
Hope, Geo., 131, 189.
........., John (Disney's Regt.), 364.
........., Lt.-Col. John, 130, 202.
........., John (Invalid Cy.), 234.
........., Robt., 138.
Hopke. See Hopkey.
Hopkey, H[enry], 285.
........., Wm., 158, 214.
Hopley, Thos., 212.
Hopton, Chris., 205.
Horler, Wm., 162.
Horne. See Hume, Jas.
Horneck, Wm., 148, 241, 281.
Horseman, John, 211, 234.
Horsepool, John, 121.
Horsey, Sam., 98, 190, 207.
Horton, Fras., 121.
Hotham, Beaumont, 172.
........., Chas., 172, 201.
........., Sir Chas., 172, 211, 229, 246, 276.
Houghton, Dan., 306.
........., Geo., 369.
........., John, 273.
How. See Howe.
Howard, Chas., [Hon.] Chas., 129, 188, 211, 269.
........., Fras., 117.
........., Lord Fred., 204, 211.
........., Geo. (Lucas's Regt.), 182.
........., Geo. (3rd Foot Guards), 190.
........., Hyde, 306.
........., Jas., 162, 190.
........., Robt., 338.
........., Thos., 208, 361.

INDEX

Howard—cont.
........., Wm. (Bowles's Regt.), 270.
........., Wm. (Alexander's Regt.), 174, 310.
Howe, John, 136, 203.
........., John (First Foot Guards), 289. (Hoare.)
........., Sam., 336.
........., Wm., 154, 189.
Howell, John, 101.
Hoysted, Thos., 360.
Hubard (—), Lieut. See Hobart, Edw.
Hubbald, Wm., 341.
Hubert, Alex., 100.
........., David, 369.
Huddy, Chas., 242, 252.
Hudson, Jos., 126.
Huet, Geo. Villiers. See Hewett.
Huffum, Ben., 115.
Hughes, Hen., 174.
........., Ric., 312.
........., Thos., 287.
Hull, Fras., 194.
........., Ric., 116.
........., Thos., 105, 203.
Humble, Thos., 148.
Hume (—), 293.
........., Geo., 162.
........., Jas., 133, 294.
........., Robt., 162.
Humphreys, Wm. (Wynne's Dragoons), 113.
........., Wm. (Montague's Foot), 148.
Hunt, Abr., 334.
........., Thos., 263.
Hunter, Robt., 229, 242.
Huntington, John, 150.
Hurry, Fras., 327.
Hurst, Jas., 364.
Husbands, Steph., 370.
Huske (—). See infra.
........., John, 128, 213.
Hussey, Jas., 128.
........., Thos., 338.
Hutcheson, H. See Hutchinson.
Hutchinson, Ensign Chas., 148.
........., Lieut. Chas., 168.
........., Capt. Chas., 301.
........., Edward, 100.
........., H., 283.
........., Humphry, 174, 240.
........., Josias, 100.
........., Nicholas, 325, 326.
Hutton, Roger, 346.
Huxford (sic), John, 241.
Hyde, Thos., 233.
Hynde, Wm., 148, 196 bis.
Hyndford, Jas. Carmichael, Earl of, 235.

I

Impey, Elijah, 251.
Inglis, Alex., 230, 235.
........., Geo., 133.
Inglish. See Inglis.
Ingoldsby, Fras., 304.
........., Ric., 242.
........., [Ric.], 187 bis.
Ingram, Chas., 293.
........., Wm., 341.
Ings, Wm., 362.
Innes, Alex., 357.
........., Robt., 364.
........., Walter, 133.
........., Wm. (Rl. Regt. of Foot), 133.
........., Wm. (Maccartney's Regt.), 208.
Innis. See Innes.
Inwood, Thos., 126.
Ireland, Wm., 105.
Irvine, Chas., 148.
........., Chris., 148.
Irwin, (—), 319.
........., Alex., 133.
........., Bury, 182, 319.
........., John, 338.
........., Ric. Ingram, 5th Visct., 156, 187 bis, 216, 231, 263.
........., Robt., 216.
Irwyn, Lord. See Irwin, Ric.
........., Roger, 364.
Isaackson, Jas., 182.

J

Jack, Jeremiah, 338.
Jackson, Chas., 200, 297.
........., Geo., 180.
........., Hen., 232.
........., Joshua, 144.
........., Leonard, 239.
........., Nat., 314.
........., Robt., 174.
Jacob, Alex., 180, 301.
........., Hildebrand, 152.
James, Thos., 160.
Jameson, Wm., 168.
Jansen, Hen., 289.
Janson, Bryan, 298.
Jeckyll, Thos., 204.
Jedburgh, Wm. Kerr, Lord, 130.
Jefferys (or Jeffreys), Chas., 178.
........., Ezekiel, 168.
Jenkins, Adam, 370.
........., Ralph, 152, 194 bis.
Jenkinson, Chas., 101.
Jennison, Fras., 166, 314.
Jenny, Robt., 214.

Jephson, John, 239.
Jeppson, John, 312.
Jidoin (*sic*), John, 166.
Joderell, Robt., 205.
Jodrell, John, 126.
Johnson, Alex. (Welsh Fusiliers), 212, 347.
........., Alex. (Windsor's Regt.), 351.
........., Alex. (Surgeon), 351.
........., Geo. *See* Johnston.
........., Guy, 298.
........., [Jas.]. *See* Johnstone.
........., Jas. (Indep. Cy.). *See* Johnston, Jas.
........., Jas., 112.
........., John (Kirke's Regt.), 136.
........., John (Bowles's Dragoons), 116.
........., John (Preston's Foot), 198.
........., John (Orkney's Regt.), 133.
........., John (Chaplain), 228.
........., John (Surgeon), 362.
........., Ric. *See* Johnston, Ric.
........., Thos. (Bowles's Dragoons), 116.
........., Thos. (Harrison's Foot), 154.
........., Wm., 111.
Johnston, Alex. *See* Johnson.
........., And., 234.
........., Geo., 134.
........., Jas., 248.
........., John, 332.
........., Ric., 332 *bis*.
........., Robt., 160.
........., Wm., 267 *bis*.
........., Sir Wm., 332.
Johnstone, Lt.-Col. Jas., 188.
........., John, 191.
Jones, Ben., 160, 188.
........., Chas. (Windress's Regt.), 366.
........., Chas. (Carpenter's Regt.), 195.
........., Dav., 162.
........., Griffith, 347.
........., Hertford, 174.
........., Hugh, 168, 317.
........., Col. John, 227.
........., Ens. John, 164.
........., Mat., 144.
........., Peregrine, 126.
........., Ric., 234.
........., Thos., 366.
........., Capt. Wm., 339.
........., Ensign Wm., 339.
Jordain, John. *See* Jordan.
........., Thos., 194.
Jordan, John, 114.
Joyce, Wm., 364.
Joynes, John, 227.
Judd, Robt., 126.
Julion, John, 95.

K

Kain (*sic*). *See* Kien.
Kane, Florence, 190, 233, 235.
........., Ric., 238.
Karr, Wm. *See* Carr.
Keat, John, 111.
........., Jonathan, 369.
Keate, Jonathan Hoo, 289.
Keating, Edmund, 176.
........., John, 239, 312.
Keefe, John, 204.
Keen, Hen., 201.
Keene, Gilbert, 142.
Keightley, Chas., 119.
........., George, 119.
Keir, John, 200.
Kellet, Ric., 216.
Kellum, Geo., 328.
Kelly, Nic., 347.
Kemp, Robt., 360.
Kempenfelt, Magnus, 140, 297.
Kendal, Chas., 339.
Kendall, Ant., 360.
Kennawie, Thos., 98.
Kennedy (—), 178.
........., Archd., 242 *bis*.
........., David, 178.
........., Jas., 107, 355.
........., Thos., 148.
........., Wm., 110.
Kenny, Ric., 336.
Kent, Ric., 199.
Kentish, Thos., 105.
Ker, [Hon.] William (brother to the Duke of Roxburghe), 111, 267.
Kerny, Jas., 371.
Kerr, Alex., 236.
........., Donkin, 237.
........., Jas., 355.
........., Lord John, 98, 190, 229, 358.
........., Lord Mark, 355 *bis*.
........., Lieut. Mark, 338.
........., Cornet Robt., 120.
........., Capt. Robt., 133.
........., Thos., 361.
........., Wm. *See* Ker, Hon. Wm.
........., Wm., 112.
Key, Thos., 164.
Kien, Chris., Christopher Ernst, 199, 260 *bis*.
Killegrew, Thos., 185.
Killigrew, Capt. Henry, 106.
........., Lt.-Col. Henry, 118.
........., Thos., 307.
Kilner, Jas., 260.
Kinaston. *See* Kynaston.
King, And., 107, 198.
........., Dennis, 339.
........., John, 129.
........., Jos., 355.

King—*cont*.
  ...., Mathew, 150.
  ...., Ric., 285.
  ...., Robt., 140.
  ...., Sam., 142.
  ...., Lt.-Col. Thos., 228.
  ...., Lieut. Thos., 215.
Kingstone, Fras., 103.
Kirby, Wm., 267.
Kirk, Jas., 275.
  ...., Piercy, 136.
Kitson, Thos., 170.
  ...., Wm., 106.
Knapton, Alex., 123.
Knevet, Paston, 114.
Knight, Ric., 164.
Knightley, Ric., 187.
Knightly, Geo. *See* Keightley, George.
Knowles, John, 125, 194.
  ...., Wm., 191.
Knox (—). *See* Knox, Andrew.
  ...., And. [?], 113.
  ...., Berkeley Sidney, 331.
  ...., Geo., 107, 111, 267.
  ...., Surgeon John, 236.
  ...., Cornet John, 332.
Knypes, Wm., 152.
Krant. *See infra*.
Kraut, Kraute, Wm., 97, 201.
Kynaston, John, 119.
  ...., Ralph, 200.

L

L'Abene. *See* De La Béné.
Laborde, Josias, 315.
Lacey, Hen., 361.
  ...., Thos., 361.
La Chapelle, Pet., 306.
La Coudrière. *See* De La Coudrière.
Ladeveze, Abel Rotolph, 318.
  ...., Ant., 358 *bis*.
Lafitte, Matthew, 339.
La Forey, Laforey, John, 148.
  ...., Lewis, 148.
Lake, Wm., 355.
Lamb, Abr., 138, 296.
  ...., Chas., 195.
Lambard, Multon, 231, 238.
Lambe, Hen., 259.
Lambert, Anan., 327.
  ...., Chas., 273.
  ...., Fras., 263.
  ...., Multon. *See* Lambard.
Lambton, Robt., 162.
La Mellonière, Ant., 123.
La Millière, Alex., 361.

Lancaster, Chas., 329.
  ...., Wm., 103.
Landy, Elias, 334.
Langford, Emmanuel, 235.
Langlands, John, 269.
Langley, Geo., 146.
  ...., John, 146, 194.
  ...., Wm., 134.
La Noe, Chas., 215, 331.
La Penotièr[e], Fred., 158.
Laponge, Peter, 93.
Laroon, Marcell; La Roon, Marcellus, 124, 217.
Larwood, Ben., 349.
  .... Peter (*sic*), 349, note 6.
Lasalle, Hen., 118, 210.
Lascelles, Peregrine, 178, 304.
  ...., Ric., 154.
  ...., Thos., 228, 281, 317.
Lasseur, Ant., 369.
Latour, Jas., 150.
Lattimore, Thos., 371.
Latton, Wm., 95, 189.
Lauder, Geo., 107, 111.
  ...., Robt., 156, 197.
Launder, Thos., 197.
Laurence, David, 307.
  ...., Herb. *See* Lawrence.
Law, Fras., 330.
Lawder, Robt. *See* Lauder.
Lawes, Chas., 103.
  .... Sir Nich. *See* Laws.
Lawless, Nich., 325.
Lawrence, Herb. [sen.], 148.
  ...., Herb. [jun.], 148, 189.
  ...., Wm., 107.
Laws, Sir Nich., 214, 250.
Lawson, Geo., 166.
  ...., Jas., 351.
  ...., John, 176 *bis*.
  ...., Robt., 248.
Laye, John, 154.
Layton, Ens. Robt. *See* Leighton.
  ...., Capt. Robt., 136.
Leake, Ric., 285.
Leathes, Moses, 158.
  ...., Wm., 158.
Leaver, (—). *See* Leaver, Chas.
  ...., Chas., 103.
Le Blanc, Jas., 250.
Ledsom, John, 233.
Lee, Fras. Hen., 140, 289.
  ...., Hen., 212.
  ...., John, 211.
  ...., Standish, 176.
  ...., Wm. (Montague's Regt.), 148, 300.
  ...., Wm. (Borr's Regt.), 360.
Leeds, Ebenezer, 121.
Leeson, Robt., 369.
Legard, Chris., 301.

Legard—*cont.*
........, Thos., 125.
Legg, Chas., 146, 216.
........, John, 136.
........, Mich., 343.
........, Ens. Ric., 128, 189.
........, Capt. Ric., 154.
Le Grand, Alex., 124.
........, Henry, 338.
Leicester, John, 327 *bis.*
Leigh, (—). *See* Leigh, Wm.
........, John, 231.
........, Wm. (Coldstream Guards), 128.
........, Wm. (Sutton's Regt.), 343.
Leighton, Dan, 197, 259.
........, Fras., 201, 306.
........, Gerrard, 259.
........, John, 124, 280.
.... Robt., 126.
Leman, Wm., 115, 271.
Lemmon. *See* Leman.
Lennard, Sir Sam., 96.
Lenoir, Isaac, 326.
Leslie, Alex., 130.
........, [Hon.] Chas., 203.
........, John, Lord, 113, 211, 216.
Lesslie, Thos., 209.
Letetre, Gideon (*sic*), 232.
Lethat, Ric., 357.
Levet, Levett, Thos., 154, 191
Lewis, Dan., 353.
........, John, 215.
........, Jonathan, 283, 287.
........, Thos., 317.
........, Wm. (Barrack Master), 239.
........, Wm. (Storekeeper), 370.
Leyson, Jenkin, 216.
Lezier, John, 370.
Liermont, Lewis, 353.
Lieving, Chas., 190.
Ligoe, (—), 325.
Ligonier, (—). *See* Ligonier, Fras.
........, Fras., 150.
........, John, 150, 205 *bis.*
Ligonière, Ant., 366.
Lillingston, John, 140.
Lillis, Sam., 176.
Lilly, Christian, 285.
Lindsay, Fras., 236.
Lisle, Geo., 162.
........, Pat., 103, 263.
........, Ralph, 349.
........, Thos., 162.
Lister, Dymock, 136.
........, Lutton, 117.
........, Thos., 205.
........, Wm., 206, 293.
Litchfield, Fras., 105.
Litetre. *See* Letetre.
Little, John, 144.

Little—*cont.*
........, Sam., 239.
Littlejohn, Alex., 234.
........, Jas., 146.
Littler, John, 138.
........, Wm., 138, 206 *bis.*
Littleton, (—), 172.
Livesay, Chas., 150.
........, Paradine, 150.
........, Pat., 150.
Livingston, David, 237.
........, Jas., 107, 111.
Livingstoun, Wm., 201.
Lloyd, Churchill, 109, 193.
........, Geo., 97.
........, John (Mattross), 371.
........, John (Sankey's Regt.), 311
........, John (Disney's Regt.), 364.
........, John (Cotton's Regt.), 152.
........, John (Cotton's Regt.), 152, 190 *bis.*
........, Leonard, 196 *bis*, 336.
........, Capt. Phil., 195.
........, Ensign Phil., 339.
........, Ric., 364.
........, Verney, 338, 349.
........, Wm. (Horse Gren Guards), 261.
........, Wm. (1st Foot Guards), 125.
........, Wm. (Wightman's Regt.), 341.
Loftus, Edward, 110.
........, Robt., 176.
........, Simon, 205.
Logan, John (Firemaster), 369.
........, John (Mattross), 370.
........, Justinian, 207.
Lombard, Peter, 176.
Long, Hen., 357.
........, Jas., 150.
Lorraine, Hen., Earl de. *See* Deloraine.
Lort, Rog., 176, 207, 208, 311.
Lostau, Bernard, 111.
Lothian, Jas., 107.
Lovat, Simon Fraser, Lord, 248 *bis.*
Love, Herb., 362.
........, John, 370.
Loveday, Jos., 134.
Lovet, Sam., 215.
Lovick, John, 329.
Low, Hen., 130.
Lowe, Chris., 326.
........, Sam., 194, 275.
Lowrie, John, 130.
Lowther, Ant., 122, 345.
........, Ric., 138, 186.
........, Robt., 230.
Loyd. *See* Lloyd.
Lucas, Geo., 174, 251.
........, Col. Ric., 182, 214.
........, Ens. Ric., 206, 310.
Luckin, (—), 192.
Luckyn, Sir Harbottle, 99.

INDEX

Lucy, Theod., 192.
........., Theoph., 301 *bis*.
Lukyn, Chas., 331.
Lumley, Henry, 103, 229, 246.
........., Richard, Viscount, 99, 186.
........., Thos., 121.
Lumly, John, 121.
Lustau. *See* Lostau.
Lutterel, Lutterell. *See infra.*
Luttrell, Edw., 126, 209.
Lyne, Wm., 146.
Lynn, Audley, 160.
Lyon, Chas., 156.
........., John, 162.
Lysons, John, 194.

M

McAra, Pat., 298.
Macartney, Geo. *See* Maccartney.
Macarty, Justin, 275.
Maccartney, Lt.-Gen., Geo., 202, 247, 251.
........., Capt. Geo., 212.
McCormick, Jas., 234.
MacCulloch, Wm., 234.
McDaniell, Wm., 370.
Macdonald, Alex., 234.
........., Jas., 172.
McGee, Jas., 334.
McHenry, Wm., 345.
Mackay, Chas., 207, 307.
McKean, Geo., 332.
Mackelland, John, 172.
Mackenzie, Geo., 316.
McKenzie, Lt.-Col. Duncan, 185.
........., Kenneth, 133.
........., Murdoch, 174, 206.
Mackreth, Wm., 156.
Macky. *See* Mackay.
Maclean (—). *See infra.*
........., Lachlan, 166.
Macleod, Neil, 130.
Macmahon, John, 232.
MacManus, McManus, Hugh, 158, 194, 304.
........., Roger, 193, 205.
MacMullan, Hugh, 119.
Macnachten, Alex., 130.
McNeal, Dan., 193, 316.
MacNeal, Donald, 166.
........., Rochford, 134.
Macnoe, Jos., 176, 216.
McQueen, John, 206, 294.
McQuin, John, 233.
Madden, Barth., 370.
Maden, Martin, 212.
Madgshou, John, 134.
Magee, Mat., 233.
Maghan, Wm., 160

Mahon, Bryan, 172.
Maidman (—). *See* Maidman, Wm.
........., Chas., 168.
........., Jas., 180.
........., Wm., 180, 317.
Mainwaring, Chas., 343.
Maitland, Lieut. Chas., 215, 307.
........., Ensign Chas., 307.
........., Ensign Jas., 188, 307.
........., Lt.-Gen. Jas., 236.
........., John (Honywood's Regt.), 115, 271.
........., John (Lord Shannon's Regt.), 307.
........., Capt. Ric., 130, 131, 209.
........., Lieut. Ric., 307.
Makgill, Dav., 266.
Malcolm, Geo., 123, 279.
Malet, Pet., 193, 194, 267.
Malkain (—). *See infra.*
........., Jas., 115.
Mallen, Ric., 355.
Mallet, John, 361 *bis*.
Mallide, Paul, 106.
Man, Alex., 355.
........., Edw. *See* Mann, Edw.
........., Geo., 158.
Mann, Edw., 148, 300.
Manning, Huntington, 353.
........., Ric., 124, 217, 263.
........., Walt., 182.
Mapp, Jeremiah, 232.
Marcham, Thos., 101, 262.
........., Wm. [sen.], 101 *bis*.
........., Wm. [jun.], 101.
Marchand, Noel, 243.
Margaret, Peter, 360.
Margarett, Paul, 101.
Marget, Margett, Mich., 126, 187, 192.
Marischal, Geo. Keith, 10th Earl, memoir of, 87-90.
........., Regt. of referred to, 192.
Markham, Thos., 186.
Marlborough, John Churchill, Duke of, 125, 227 *ter.*, 285.
Marly, Geo., 318.
Marquis, Jas., 341.
Marriott, Ric., 98.
Marsden, Edmond, 369.
Marshall, Hubert, 312.
........., Lieut. John, 144.
........., Capt. John, 174.
........., Sam., 283.
Marston, Wm., 276.
Martell, David, 124.
Martin (—), 209.
........., Edmund, 357
........., Edw., 341.
........., Fras., 166.
........., Geo., 176.
........., Jas., 204.
........., John, 361.

Martyr, Ben., 331.
Mascarene. *See infra.*
Mascarine, Paul, 204, 312.
Masclary, Hen., 96.
Mason, Dan., 97.
........., John, 204.
........., Jos., 228.
........., Thos., 117.
........., Wm., 275.
Massay, Massey. *See* Massy.
Massingall, Thos., 101, 189.
Massy, Edw., 316.
........., Geo., 180.
........., John (Lucas's Regt.), 182.
........., John (Sutton's Regt.), 343.
Masters, Thos., 214.
Masterson, John, 150.
Matchell, John, 115.
Mathew, Fletcher, 242.
........., Pet., 242.
........., Wm., 230, 231.
Mathews, Edw., 293.
........., Hen., 362.
........., John, 176.
........., Thos., 250, 312.
Mathie, Mongo, 345 *bis*.
Matthews, Hen. *See* Mathews.
Maturin, Jas. Gabriel, 349.
........., Pet., 349.
Maugridge, Robt., 229.
Maule, Jas., 115, 215.
........., Wm., 334.
Mavitie, Alex., 164.
Mawle. *See* Maule.
Maxwell (—), 362.
........., Jas. (Lord Shannon's Regt.), 307.
........., Jas. (Primrose's Regt.), 349.
........., Pat. (Rl. Dragoons), 264.
........., Pat. (Windress's Regt.), 366.
........., Robt., 119, 201.
May, Chas., 136, 198 *bis*.
Maynard, Robt., 162.
........., Thos., 162, 249.
Mead, John, 318.
........., Pat. *See* Meade.
Meade, Courthope, 349.
........., Pat., 229, 349.
Meares, Robt., 314.
Mecheux, Meheux, Fras., 162, 201.
Medlycott, Thos., 238.
Meggs, Wm., 101, 262.
Megs. *See* Meggs.
Melledge, John, 283.
Melling, Hen., 355.
Melvill, Chas.,
Melville, Robt., 138.
........., Wm., 133.
Melvine. *See* Melville.
Memville, John, 106, 264.
Mercer, John, 297.

Mercer—*cont.*
........., Wm., 343.
Meredith, Meredyth, Thos., 160, 185.
Meres, Fras., 110.
Mereweather, Jas., 232.
Merrfield, Jos., 369.
Merrick, Wm., 125.
Merridan, Hen., 366.
........., Thos., 120.
Merriden. *See supra.*
Merriman, Thos., 247.
Messenden. *See* Mussenden.
Metcalfe, Adrian, 97.
Metford, Hen., 289.
Meuhl, Sam., 122, 278.
Meure, Abr. Elliott, 178, 298.
Michaell, Thos., 182.
Michaelson, Geo., 283.
Michel, Nat., 334.
Michelson, Thos., 346.
Micklethwaite, Thos., 251.
Middleton (—), Lt.-Col., 214.
........., Geo., 199.
........., John, 228, 231.
........., Chaplain Robt., 345.
........., Ensign Robt., 307.
Midford, Mich., 357.
Miget, Migett, Hen., 97, 212.
Milbanke, Alcomb, 307.
Milborne, Ric. [sen.], 148.
........., Ric. [jun.], 148.
Miller, John, 355.
........., Pat., 339.
........., Ric., 334 *bis*.
Millet, Chas., 358.
Milner, Gregory, 341.
........., Robt., 150.
Milson, Chas., 349.
Minzies, Robt., 355.
Mitchell, Eldred, 174.
........., Thos., 122.
........., Walt., 243.
Mitford, Chas., 349.
........., Jas., 150.
Modd, Geo., 162.
Mohun, John, 213, 260.
Molesworth, Edw., 180.
.... Ric. (aftds. 3rd Viscount), memoir of, 85, 86 ; Regt. of, 123, 369.
Molsey. *See* Moseley, Fras.
Molsworth. *See supra* Molesworth.
Molyneux, John, 117.
........., Wm., 118.
Momby, Edw., 294.
Moncall, Chas., 152.
........., Mark Antony, 152.
Moncrief, Alex., 307.
Moncriefe, Geo., 339.
Monk, Stanley, 339.
Monro, Hugh, 242.

INDEX

Monrow. *See* Munro.
Montagu, John, 200, 206, 289.
Montague (—). *See* Montague, Edw.
........., Edw., 106, 148, 192, 300.
........., John, Duke of, 95, 185.
Montandre, Marquis de (aftds. a British Field-Marshal), memoir of, 39-47.
Monteith, Jas., 297.
Montfort, Simon, 158.
Montgomerie, John. *See* Montgomery.
........., Robt., 131.
Montgomery, Alex., 125, 212.
........., Hugh, 138, 238, 355.
........., Jas., 266.
........., John, 189, 338.
........., Sir Robt., 314.
........., Thos., 214.
Montjoy. *See* Mountjoy.
Montrevor, Jas., 345.
Moody, Bart., 156.
........., John, 241 *bis*.
Moone, Chas., 138.
Moor, Wm., 312.
Moore, Jas., 195.
........., Jas. (Sub-Engineer), 285.
........., John, 232, 353.
........., Jonas, 238.
........., Michael, 200.
........., Robt., 343.
........., Rog., 272.
........., Sam., 241.
........., Thos. (Comptroller at Chelsea), 251.
........., Thos. (Indep. Cy.), 193.
........., Thos. (Seymour's Regt.), 206.
........., Wm., 209.
Mordaunt, Harry, 229.
Morden, Wm., 211.
More, Jas., 239.
........., Michael, 170.
Moreau, Moses, 152.
Moreton, Goodwin, 207, 299.
Morey, John, 103.
Morgan (—), 164.
........., Ant., 231, 269.
........., John, 312.
........., Maurice, 103.
........., Morris. *See supra*.
........., Robt., 129, 188.
Morin, Pet., 274, 353.
Morland, Cuthbert, 146.
Morphy, Thos., 126.
Morrice, John, 142.
Morris, Bacon, 142, 251.
........., Fras., 370.
........., John, 174.
........., Thos., 142, 190, 341 *bis*.
........., Valentine, 174.
........., Wm., 369.
Morrison, Dav., 371.
........., Hen. *See* Moryson.

Mortimer, Wm., 148.
Morton (—). *See infra*.
........., Lewis Ducie, 122, 278.
Moryson, Brig.-Gen. Hen., 128, 213, 229, 336.
........., Capt. Hen., 128.
Moseley, Art., 233.
........., Fras., 204, 307.
Mosely. *See supra*.
Mostyn, Rog., 168, 190.
Moubray, Jonathan, 206.
Mountford, Robt., 341.
Mountjoy, Wm. Stewart, Visct., 229, 369.
Mowatt, John, 232.
........., Sir Winwood, Bt., 188.
Moyle, Edw., 158, 187.
........., J——., 119.
Moyser, Jas., 125.
........., John, 172, 201.
Muir, Alex., 237.
Muirhead, Jas., 130.
Mulcaster, John, 234.
Mule. *See* Meuhl.
Mullen, Alex., 109.
Mulligan, Rog., 369.
Mullins, Ric., 360.
Munden, Ric., 117.
Mungan, Sam., 349.
Munro, Robt., 235, 237.
Munroe, Geo., 300.
Murcott, Hen., 125.
Mure, Abr., 206.
Murhead. *See* Muirhead.
Murphy, Darby, 280.
........., Garret, 232.
........., Thos., 228.
Murray, Chas., 190.
........., Lord Charles, 332.
........., Dav., 370.
........., Edw., 234.
........., Lord Edward, 133.
........., Lord George, 133.
........., Hugh, 364.
........., Jas. (Royal Regt.), 133.
........., Jas. (Scots Fusiliers), 345.
........., Lord James, 125, 294.
........., John (Preston's Regt.), 214.
........., John (Thos. Harrison's Regt.), 334.
........., Robt., 130, 216.
........., Wm. (Scots Fusiliers), 345.
........., Wm. (Lord Shannon's Regt.), 307.
........., Wm. (3rd Foot Guards), 130.
Musgrave, Chris., 285.
........., Thos., 239, 281.
Mussenden, Jeremiah, 158, 194 *bis*, 216.
Mutys, Fras., 170.
Mylne, Sir Chas., 130, 297.

N

Nairne, Dav., 138.
Naish, Edmund, 156.
........., Edw., 156.
Naizon, Fras., 325, 326.
........., Pet., 326.
Nanfan, Ric., 124.
Nangle, John, 366.
Napier, Alex., 134.
........., Gerald, 237.
........., Robt. (Surgeon), 247.
........., Robt. (Brig.-Gen.), 229, 328.
Napper, John, 142 *bis*, 214.
Nappier, John, 168.
........., Robt. *See* Napier.
........., Wm., 203.
Nassau, (—). *See infra.*
........., Maurice, 316.
........., Morris. *See supra.*
Neal. *See* Neale.
Neale, Jos., 97.
........., Ric., 95, 204.
Needham, Sam., 213, 349 *bis.*
........., Wm., 95.
Negus, Dan., 198.
Neilson, Robt., 338.
Nelson, Chas., 334.
Nesbit, Nesbitt, Thos., 209, 305.
Nevill, Clement, 117.
........., Hen., 339.
Newborough, George Cholmondeley, Lord, 97.
Newcomen, Newcomin, Beverley, 118.
Newdigate, Thos., 357.
Newell, John, 370.
Newgent. *See* Nugent.
Newlands, Thos., 180.
Newton, Edw., 318.
........., Maj.-Gen. [John], 185.
........., Mich., 160.
........., Thos., 160 *bis.*
........., Col. Wm., 119, 231.
........., Lieut. Wm., 140, 194.
........., Ensign Wm., 160.
Nicholas, Dan., 152, 211.
........., John, 361.
Nicholls, Eresey, 364.
........., Jas., 136.
........., John, 201.
........., Theoph., 336.
Nicholson, Angus, 241.
........., Chas., 304.
........., Chas., junr., 197.
Nisbett, Nisbitt, Jas., 107.
Nodding, Wm., 345.
Nodes, Geo., 353.
Norcliff. *See* Norcliffe.
Norcliffe, Fairfax, 172.
........., Thos., 140.
Norcot. *See* Northcote.
Norman, Ric., 160, 187.
........., Sam., 343.
Norris, Toby, 317.
........., Wm., 176, 208.
North, Wm., Lord North and Grey, 187.
Northcote, Arth., 156, 303.
Northumberland, George Fitzroy, Duke of, 185.
Norton, Bret, 116.
........., Robt., 330.
........., Thos., 360.
Nossiter, John, 275.
Nowland, Jas., 360.
Nugent, Lawrence, 110.
........., Reynell, 312.
........., Ric., 317.
........., Steuart, 338.
........., Wm. (Stair's Dragoons), 110, 266.
........., Wm. (Irish Train), 370.
Nutt, John, 140.
Nuttal, Chris., 150.

O

Oakley, Sam., 119.
O'Brien, Cornelius, 362.
........., Edw., 358.
........., Martin, 117.
Obryan, O'Bryen. *See* O'Brien
O'Cane, Manus, 146.
Ochterlony, Arthur, 136. (Arthurlony.)
Ockold, Thos., 250.
Odgers, John, 306.
Odiarne, Gregory, 190.
O'Farrel, Fras., 142.
........., Ric., 338.
Offarel. *See* O'Farrel.
Offley, Thos., 96.
Ogilvie, Alex., 351.
........., David (3rd Foot Guards), 130.
........., David (Ker's Dragoons), 111.
........., Geo. (Indep. Cy.), 252.
........., Geo. (3rd Foot Guards), 215.
........., Jas. (Scots Fusiliers), 345.
........., Jas. (3rd Foot Guards), 130.
Ogilvy, Jas., 111.
Ogle, Sam., 327.
........., Wm., 109, 215.
Oglethorpe, Jas., 126.
O'Hara, [Hon.] Jas., 144, 249.
Oldfield, (—), 120, 195.
Oliphant, Patrick, 8th Lord, 166.
Oliver, Chas., 242.
........., John, 196.
........., Lacon Wm., 319.
Olivier, John, 331.

INDEX

Onslow, Ric., 202.
Orfeur, Col. John, 116, 195.
........., Chaplain John, 339.
Orkney, Geo. Hamilton, Earl of, memoir of, 35-38 ; Regt. of, 133 ; Comns. to, 227, 236.
Ormsby, Jas., 211.
........., Lewis, 176 *bis*, 311.
Orrery, Chas. Boyle, Earl of, 229, 345.
Osborne, Hen., 174.
Ossulston, Charles Bennet, 3rd Lord, 199.
Otway, (—). *See* Otway, Chas.
........., Chas., 110, 188, 201, 339.
........., Chas. Jas., 326.
........., Jas., 326.
........., Ric., 207.
........., Steph., 120.
Oughton, Adolphus, 191, 193, 212.
Owen, Hen., 142, 214.
........., Hugh, 185.
........., John, 361.

P

Pack, Richardson, 182.
Paget, Simon, 312.
........., Thos., 99, 186.
Pain, Hector, 369.
Paine, Dav., 355.
Palliser, Hugh, 357.
........., Walt., 357.
Palmer, John, 281.
........., Jos., 289.
........., Wm., 191.
Palmes, Steph., 330.
Pancier, And., 106, 192.
Panton, Thos. [sen.], 103, 186, 229, 246.
........., ... [jun.], 103.
Paris, John, 214.
Parker, Chas. (Royal Fusiliers), 144.
........., Chas. (Sterne's Regt.), 158, 187.
........., Gervas, 144.
........., John (Stanwix's Regt.), 166.
........., John (1st Foot Guards), 126.
........., John (Gunner), 371.
........., Mich., 332.
........., Myles, 319.
........., Robt., 158.
........., Sam., 209.
........., Thos., 170.
Parkes, Julius Caesar, 349.
........., Thos., 134.
Parkington, Chas., 212.
Parkins, Hen. Bateman, 267.
Parkinson, Thos., 168.
Parr, John, 349.
........., Thos., 176.

Parry, John, 142.
........., Phil., 142.
........., Ric., 273.
Parslow, John, 318.
Parsons, John, 128, 129.
........., Ric. (1st Life Guards), 199, 259.
........., Ric. (Windress's Foot), 366.
........., Theoph., 126.
........., Sir Wm., 101.
Partridge, John, 239.
Pashler, John, 182.
Paterson, Pat., 152.
........., Robt., 345.
Patterson, Josiah, 205.
Pattison, Robt., 346.
........., Thos., 287.
Paul, Paule, Dan., 328 *bis*.
Paul, Josua, 125.
Paulet, Chas. Armand, 133, 164, 188.
........., Lord Harry, 123.
........., Lord Nassau, 193.
Pawlet, Lord Harry. *See* Paulet.
........., John, 96, 189, 283.
........., Lord Nassau. *See* Paulet.
Paynton, Fras., 341.
Peachy, (—), 166.
Peacock, Giles, 299.
........., Simon, 99, 187.
Pearce, Chas., 142, 211.
........., John, 211.
........., Thos., 142.
Peard, Chris., 160.
Pearson, Hugh, 113.
........., Robt., 158, 187.
Peasley, Geo., 371.
Peck, Phil., 329.
Pecquer, Dan., 152.
Pedley, Rog., 341.
Peers, Newsham, 347.
Peirson, Fras., 318.
........., Ric. *See* Pierson.
........., Thos., 355.
Pelham, Hen., 118.
........., Jas., 112, 198.
Pember, And., 370.
Pemberton, (—), 113.
Pendergrass, Walt., 328.
Pendlebury, Jas., 285.
Penefather. *See* Pennefather.
Penman, Jas., 238.
Pennefather, John, 347.
........., Jos. Mathew, 347.
Pennington, Phil., 314.
Penny, John, 119, 275.
Pepper, Geo., 112.
........., John, 112, 246.
........., Park, 209.
........., Paul, 142.
Percivall, And., 101.
........., John, 234.

Perdue, Ric., 305.
Perier, John, 298.
Perkins, John, 247.
Perron, Arman[d] du. *See* Du Perron.
Peter, John, 329.
Peterborough, Chas. Mordaunt, Earl of, 187.
Peterson (—), 182.
Petetot, Steven, 144.
Peticrew, Jas., 370.
Petit, John, 214.
........., Lewis, 252, 281, 283.
........., Pet., 311, 334.
Petty, Geo. Speke, 144.
Peyton, Vincent, 112.
Philipps, Cosby, 136, 312.
........., Richard, 150, 312.
Philips, Cosby. *See* Philipps.
........., Walt., 331.
Phillbridge, Geo., 248.
Phillip, Rowland, 199.
Phillips, Chris., 170.
........., Cosby. *See* Philipps.
........., Edmund, 213.
........., Edw., 203.
........., Jas., 343.
........., Capt. John, 136.
........., Chaplain John, 227.
........., Chaplain John, 358.
........., Ric. *See* Philipps.
........., Thos. (Indep. Cy.), 187, 241.
........., Thos. (Engineer), 285.
Phynbo. *See* Finboe.
Pickering (—). *See infra* John.
........., John, 160, 212, 366.
........., Pet., 274.
Pickstock, Thos., 241, 312.
Pierce, Wm., 116.
Piercy, Thos., 343.
Pierson, Capt. John, 116.
........., Ensign John, 358.
........., Ric., 144, 289.
........., Thos., 345.
Pigot, Robt., 202.
Pigott, Southwell, 347.
Pigou, Paul, 196.
Piketon, Hen., 190.
Piklilton. *See* Pilkington.
Pilkington, Nat., 190.
Pilliord, Fras., 190.
Pim, Chas., 174.
Pincent. *See* Pinsent.
Pinchinat, Abr., 168.
Pinfold, Wm., 202, 217.
Pinhorne, John, 242.
Pinsent, Jas., 158, 304.
Pinson, Edw., 306.
Pirke, Jonathan, 118.
Pitman, John, 355.
Pitt (—). *See* Pitt, John.
........., John, 105, 112, 196, 212.

Pitt—*cont.*
........., Thos. (aftds. Earl of Londonderry), 247, 250, 325, 326.
Pitts, Thos., 369.
Plomer, Robt., 190.
Plucknet, Hugh; Plukenet, Hugh, 233 *bis*, 248, 310.
Plummer, John, 358.
Pocklington, Oliver, 326.
Pocock, John, 180.
Poe, Jas., 332.
Poilblanc, Hen., 146.
Pole, Edw., 193, 215, 316.
Polhill, Edw., 361.
Pollexfen, Thos., 349.
Pollock (—) (Grant's Regt.), 206.
........., John (Lord Hinchinbroke's Regt.), 217.
........., Sir Robt., 250.
Pomfrett, Wm., 116.
Ponsonby [Hon.] Hen., 164, 191.
Ponthier, Henry De. *See* De Ponthier.
Pope, And., 341.
........., John, 328.
........., Sam., 330.
Portal, Wm., 328.
Portmore, David Colyear, Earl of, 107, 237.
Potts, Thos., 370.
........., Wm., 162.
Pouchin, Pet., 369.
Povey, Chas., 121.
........., Ric., 172.
........., Thos., 206.
Powell, Hen., 150.
........., John, 347.
........., Maurice, 309.
........., Thos., 144.
Powlet *or* Powlett (—). *See* Paulet, Chas. Armand.
Powlett, Chas. *See* Paulet, Chas. Armand.
........., Wm., 100.
Pownall, Wm., 296.
Pownell. *See* Pownall.
Prater, Ric., 358.
Pratt, Rupert, 164, 213.
........., Thos., 343.
Prendergast, Jeffrey, 216.
........., John, 319.
Prescott, Ric., 330.
Presseley (—). *See infra*.
........., Israel, 114.
Preston (—). *See* Preston, Wm.
........., Geo., 246, 351.
........., Jacob, 162.
........., John (Lord Forfar's Regt.), 138.
........., John (Preston's Regt.), 193 *bis*.
........., John (Henry Grove's Regt.), 146.
........., Robt., 351.
........., Thos., 146.
........., Wm., 119.

INDEX

Pretty, John, 154, 302.
Price, Edw., 174.
........., Hen., 334.
........., John (Munden's Dragoons), 273.
........., John (Coldstream Guards), 291.
........., John (Meredyth's Regt.), 305.
........., Thos., 170.
........., Wm., 128.
Prideaux, John, 116.
Primrose, Major-Gen. Gilbert, 229.
........., Capt. Gilbert, 349.
Prince, John, 168.
Pringle, Jas., 131.
........., Robt., 351.
Pritchard, Wm., 357.
Proby, Wm., 233.
Prosser, Jacob, 228.
........., Wm., 114.
Prothero, Wm., 209, 307.
Prowe, Pet., 154.
Pudsay, Hugh, 318.
........., Wm., 166, 210.
Pudsey. *See supra.*
Pujolas, Ant., 158.
........., Robt., 146, 215.
Pulteney, Harry, Hen., 128, 291.
........., Wm., Secretary-at-War, Letter from, xxiii.
Purcell, And., 114.
........., Edw., 140.
........., John (Rich's Dragoons), 122.
........., John (Montague's Regt.), 196.
........., Martin, 249, 312.
........., Toby, 191, 362.
Purchas, Purchass, Ric., 140 *bis*, 200, 297.
Pye, John, 126.
Pyll, Fras., 142.
Pym, Hen., 353.
Pyott, Ric., 170.

Q

Quarles, Edmund, 296, 357.
Quesne. *See* Du Quesne.
Quiggen, Jas., 279.
Quin, Mat., 150.
Quinchant (—), 152.
........., John, 190 *bis*.
Quinn, Cuthbert, 370.
........., Timothy, 315.

R

Radley, Ric., 341.
Rainsford, Chas., 357.
........., Cornet Fras., 120.
........., Major Fras., 144.
Raleigh, Granville, 146.
........., Grinvall. *See supra.*

Rambouillet, Chas., 168, 197, 206.
Ramsay, Jas. (Chaplain), 107, 111.
........., Ensign John (Henry Grove's Regt.), 146.
........., Lieut. John (Pocock's Regt.), 180.
........., Capt. John (Royal Regt.), 294.
Ramsey, Jas., 339.
........., John, 334.
Randall, Wm., 206.
Rankin, Ant., 326.
Rannells, Fras., 269.
Raphson, John, 353.
Rapin, Solomon, 118.
Rathbone, Mathew, 298.
Raudduck. *See* Rudduck.
Rawdon, Thos., 328.
Rawlins, Mich., 126.
........., Wm., 294.
Rawlinson, John, 289.
........., Robt., 100.
Rawson, Edw., 343.
Ray, Collis, 264.
Rayney, Sir John Beaumont, Bt., 105, 203.
Read (—). *See* Read, Robt.
........., Alex., 109.
........., Geo., 125.
........., Robt., 211.
Reading, John, 339, 361.
Reddich, John, 156.
Redknap, Hen., 366.
Redstone, John, 231.
Redwood, Thos., 336.
Reed, Robt., 125.
Reeve, Gabriel, 129.
Reid, Wm., 138.
Renaut, Pet., 196.
Rendall, Wm., 309.
Reney. *See* Rayney.
Renovard, Dav., 327 *bis*.
........., Pet., 106, 111, 213.
Reynolds, Pet., 361.
........., Ric., 271, 328.
........., Rowland, 125, 194.
........., Sam., 334.
Ribton, Pet., 196, 336.
Rice, Jacob, 241.
........., Philip, 277.
........., Thos., 210.
........., Wm., 362.
Rich, Cholmley, 122.
........., Edw., 119, 212, 291.
........., Sir Robt., Bt., 122.
Richards, Jas., 283, 287.
........., Michael, 285.
Richardson, Geo., 156.
........., Chaplain Jas., 101.
........., Lieut. Jas., 130.
........., Jos., 297.
........., Leming, 343.
........., Wm., 111.

Richbell, Edw., 206.
Richmond, Ric., 306.
Rider, Ben., 267.
Ridley, Edw., 123.
........., Thos., 174.
Riggs, Jas. (*sic*), 242.
........., John, 242, 252.
........., Merrill, 201, 301.
Risdall, Wm., 358.
Rivason, John, 341.
Robb, Jas., 237.
Roberts, John (3rd Life Guards), 200.
........., John (Irish Train), 369.
........., Philip, 97, 200.
........., Ric., 120.
........., Tiddeman, 357.
Robertson, John (Capt.), 193.
........., ... (Cornet), 193, 275.
........., Pat., 107.
........., Wm., 332.
Robinson (—). *See* Robinson, And.
........., ... Capt., 210.
........., And., 124, 193.
........., Ant., 178, 200.
........., Geo. (Lucas's Regt.), 182.
........., Geo. (The Carabiniers), 329.
........., Geo. (Irish Train), 371.
........., John, 128, 192, 212.
........., Leonard, 214.
........., Molineux, 330, 347.
........., Ric., 120.
........., Wm. (Honywood's Dragoons), 115, 216, 303.
........., Wm. (1st Life Guards), 204.
Rodd, Fras., 125.
Roddam, Jas., 133.
Rogers, Fras., 96.
........., Hen., 146.
........., John, 160.
........., Capt. Thos., 106.
........., Qr.-Mr. Thos., 144.
........., Ensign Thos., 190.
........., Woodes, 250.
Rolle, Sam., 199.
Romaine, Nic., 338.
Ronald, Pat., 307.
Rooke, Heyman, 229.
Rookwood, Edw., 250.
........., Pearce, 202.
Roope, John, 287.
........., Nich., 227.
Roose, John, 166.
Roper, John, 357, 360.
Roscommon, Robert Dillon, 7th Earl of, 327.
Rose, Alex., 138, 296.
Ross, And., 120.
........., Chas., 332.
........., Geo., 332.
........., Jas., 265.
........., Robt., 195, 351.

Ross—*cont.*
........., Stanwix, 205, 210.
........., Thos., 136.
........., Wm. (Dormer's Dragoons), 210, 345.
........., Wm. (Invalid Cy.), 234.
........., Wm. (Rl. Irish Dragoons), 332.
........., Wm. (Scots Fusiliers), 345.
Rossington, Geo., 180.
Rothes, John Leslie, 6th Earl of, 249.
Rotrou, John, 238.
Rousby, Wm., 343.
Rouse, Jas., 275.
........., John, 198.
Rousselière, Fras., 305.
Rouvière, John, 168.
Row, Wm., 345.
Rowland, Wm., 196.
Royer, Sam. Du. *See* Du Royer.
Rudduck, Wm., 144.
Rudyard, Ben., 295.
Rumsey, Hen., 200, 347.
Rushton, John, 121.
Russel, (—), 251.
Russell, Chas., 217.
........., Chris. (Stanwix's Regt.), 314.
........., Chris. (Wightman's Regt.), 341.
........., Chris. (Moryson's Regt.), 336.
........., Gerard, 249 *bis*.
........., Hen., 345.
........., Ric., 125, 229, 246.
........., Wm. (Preston's Regt.), 351.
........., Wm. (3rd Life Guards), 97.
........., Wm. *See also* Ric.
Rutherford, Lieut. John; Adjt. John, 178, 316 *bis*.
........., Robt., 233.
........., Wm., 211.
Ruthven, Alex., 133.
Rycaut, Paul, 294.

S

Sabine, John, 347.
........., Jos., 227, 246, 347.
........., Wm., 200, 347.
Sadler, Adam, 106.
........., Chas., 176.
........., Pet., 202.
Sailly, Isaac, 168.
St. Clair, Jas., 130, 133, 185.
........., Thos., 160.
........., Wm., 351.
St. Clare. *See* St. Clair.
St. George, Edw., 341.
........., Geo., 182.
St. John, John, 208.
St. Johns. *See* St. John.

INDEX

Salisbury, Fras., 355.
Salkeld, John, 164.
Salter, Wm., 251.
Sandby, Josias, 330.
Sanderson, Steph., 360.
........, Wm., 126.
Sandford, (—), 362.
........, Theoph., 198.
Sandoz, Abr. [sen.], 370.
........, Abr. [jun.], 371.
Sankey, Col. Nicholas, 176, 229.
........, Ensign Nicholas, 176.
Sankie. *See* Sankey.
Satterthwaite, John, 232.
Satyr, Abr., 307.
Saunders, Anderson, 361.
........, Chas., 101.
........, Jeffrey, 247, 248.
........, John, 357.
Savage, Phil., 176.
Savill, Fras., 315.
Saville, Thos., 140.
Sawbridge, John, 205.
Sawle, Jos., 150.
........, Ric., 312.
Scaff, Josh., 126.
Scaife, Thos., 329.
Scattergood, Edw., 156.
Schaack. *See* Schaak.
Schaackman, Ern., 106.
Schaak, Jeremiah, 162.
........, Pet., 162, 306.
Schutz, John, 125.
Schuyler, Phil., 242.
Scot, Wm., 303.
Scott, Edw., 301.
........, Fras. (The King's Dragoons), 265.
........, Fras. (Preston's Regt.), 351.
........, Fras. (Disney's Regt.), 364.
........, Jas. (Sterne's Regt.), 158.
........, Jas. (3rd Foot Guards), 130, 216.
........, Jas. (Grove's Regt.), 146.
........, Jas. (Surgeon's Mate), 238.
........, Jas. (Surgeon), 332.
........, John, 130 *bis*, 189.
........, John (Indep. Cy.), 242.
........, John (Primrose's Regt.), 349.
........, John (Irish Train), 370.
........, Ric., 138.
........, Robt., 107 *bis*, 197, 307.
........, Ventris, 357.
........, Wm. (Irwin's Regt.), 156, 303.
........, Wm. (Wills's Regt.), 357.
........, Wm. (Goring's Regt.), 358.
Scourrier, John, 366.
Scrafton, Wm., 97.
Screwton, John, 234.
Scrivener, John, 339.
Scroggs, Mat., 130.
........, Thos., 203.

Seagram, John, 330.
Seaman, Lionel, 358.
........, Ric., 125.
........, Thos., 138.
Seatler, Pet., 180.
Seaton, Alex., 105.
Seaward, John, 205.
Sedière, Gabriel, 154.
Seguin, John, 207.
Segula, Steph., 119.
Selby, Selbye, Wm., 154, 302.
Selioke, John, 281.
........, Robt., 158.
Sell, Jas., 364.
Selleoke. *See* Selioke.
Selwyn, Hen., 107, 187.
........, John, 186.
Sempill, Fras., 9th Lord, 178.
........, Hugh (aftds. 11th Lord), 352.
........, Mat., 267.
Semple, Lord. *See* Sempill.
Serau, Hen., 353.
Serjeant, Ayleway, 110.
........, Thos., 128.
Seton, Robt., 130.
Severn, John, 316.
Sewell, Mat., 180, 318.
........, Sam., 103.
Seymour, John, 133.
........, Wm., 140.
Seys, Fras., 197.
Shand, Alex., 272.
Shannon, Ric. Boyle, 2nd Viscount, 185, 307.
Sharp, John, 214.
........, Wm., 336.
Sharpe. *See* Sharp.
Sharpless, Geo., 154.
Shaw, (—), 101.
........, Fras., 136.
........, John (The Royal Regt.), 133.
........, [John], 101.
........, John (Rl. Horse Guards), 262.
........, John (3rd Life Guards), 260.
Shelston, John, 332.
Shelton, Ric., 201.
Shenton, Wm., 355.
Shepherd, Esth., 168.
........, Hen., 136.
........, Silvester, 164.
Sheriffe, Wm. *See* Sherriff.
Sherrard, Geo., 126, 211.
Sherriff, Wm., 240, 251 *bis*.
Shewbridge, Jos., 338.
Shewen, Wm., 314.
Shipway, Godfrey, 270.
Shireman, John, 144.
Shirley, Robt., 99, 261.
Shore, Thos., 109.
Shorte, Edw., 128.
........, John, 128.

Shorter, Erasmus, 188, 330.
Shorthose, John, 195.
Shuckburgh, Ric., 194.
Shute, Sam., 105.
Sibboc, Thos., 172.
Sibthorpe, Gervas, 110.
Sidney, Thos., 125, 332.
Silliock. *See* Selioke, John.
Silvester, Wm. Bennet, 208.
Simmons, John, 174.
Simons, Mons., 343 *bis*.
Simple. *See* Sempill.
Simpson, Jas., 351.
........., John, 232.
Sing. *See* Synge.
Singleton, And., 160.
Sinnet. *See* Sinnot.
Sinnot, Ric., 339.
........., Thos., 349.
Skamon, Hen., 370.
Skeen. *See* Skene.
Skelton, Hen., 170, 293.
Skene, And., 133.
........., Chas., 107.
........., Fras., 345.
........., Lieut. Geo., 345.
........., Major Geo., 187.
........., Wm., 240.
Skeyne, Wm., 364.
Slacke, John, 136.
Sladden, Ben., 357.
Slater, John, 97, 260.
Sledall, John, 233.
Sleigh, Sam., 156, 303.
Slezer, Chas., 133, 296.
........., John, 237.
Slingsby, Hen., 146.
Sloss, John, 197, 307.
Small, Alex., 262.
........., Wm., 370.
Smallwood, Docr. Innis, 126.
Smart, John, 235.
Smelt, John, 156, 188.
........., Wm., 109.
Smith, Ben., 138.
........., Brent, 369.
........., Cuthbert, 118.
........., Edmund, 96.
........., Fras., 197.
........., Geo. (1st Foot Guards), 125.
........., Geo. (Chaplain), 249, 366.
........., Hawkworth, 126, 185.
........., Hen. (Wynne's Dragoons), 113.
........., Hen. (Alexander's Regt.), 174.
........., Jas., 150, 236.
........., John (Webb's Regt.), 336.
........., John (Wightman's Regt.), 341.
........., John (Alexander's Regt.), 174.
........., John (Lord Irwin's Regt.), 156, 303.
........., [John] (Coldstream Guards), 138.

Smith—*cont*.
........., Jonathan, 172.
........., Nat., 209, 296.
........., Philip, 207, 325, 326.
........., Theodore, 99.
........., Thos. (Whetham's Regt.), 164, 199.
........., Thos. (1st Life Guards), 95.
........., Thos. (Coldstream Guards), 128.
........., Wm. (Meredyth's Regt.), 176.
........., Wm. (M.D. at Portsmouth), 228.
........., Wm. (Lord Forfar's Regt.), 296.
........., Wm. (Rl. Irish Regt.), 304.
........., Zach., 281, 283.
Smyth, Hen., 318.
Snow, Ben., 148.
Sobergues, Jas., 170, 210.
Soden, Dan., 326.
Sommer, Wm., 361.
Sorsoleil, John Baptist, 228.
Sotheby, Wm., 129.
Soul, Marmaduke, 353.
Soule, Hen., 215.
Southby, John, 366.
Southen, Nat., 214.
Southose, Sam., 106, 111.
Southworth, Antonio, 126.
Spaddy, John, 170.
Speed, Sam., 119, 199, 264.
Speke, Geo., 187.
Spelman, Fras., 240.
Spence. *See* Spens.
Spencer, Geo., 281.
Spens, Wm., 203, 305.
Spicer, Giles, 228.
........., Luke, 234.
........., Wm., 358.
Spittle, (—), 318.
........., Alex., 196.
Spragge, Wadham, 351.
Spranger, Searle, 228.
Sprott, Hen., 146.
Stacey, Ric., 98.
Stainwix, Thos. *See* Stanwix.
Stair, John Dalrymple, 2nd Earl of, 110, 186, 202, 235, 246.
Stairs. *See* Stair.
Stammers, Wm., 192.
Standish, Chas., 339.
Stanhope, Geo., 280.
........., John, 241, 312.
........., Wm., 124.
Stannard, Edw., 347.
Stannus, Wm., 114.
Stanwix, Thos., 166, 213, 230, 231, 235, 246.
Stapleton, Hen., 307.
Staughton, Hen., 355.
Stawell, Ant., 158.
Stephens, (—). *See infra* John (Invalid Cy.).
........., John (Invalid Cy.), 209, 232.
........., John (Irish Train), 370.

Sterling, John (Grant's Regt.), 178.
........., John (Disney's Regt.), 364.
........., Robt., 315.
Stern. See Sterne.
Sterne, Ric., 158.
........., Robt., 229.
........., Rog., 170.
Steuart. See also Stewart.
........., 1st Lieut. Jas., 355.
........., 2nd Lieut. Jas., 338.
........., Genl. Wm., memoir of, 71–80.
........., ... Regt. of, 338.
........., ... Verses on, 78.
........., Lt.-Col. Wm., 338.
Stevens, Giles, 116.
........., Jas., 118, 210.
........., Jeffery, 164.
........., John, 232.
........., Thos. (Lord Cobham's Dragoons), 106, 192.
........., Thos. (Montague's Regt.), 148.
........., Thos. (Sankey's Regt.), 176.
Stevenson, Alex., 326.
........., Dav., 339.
........., Geo., 105 bis.
........., Nich., 270.
........., Robt., 112.
Stewart, Alex., 209, 268.
........., Arth., 369.
........., Chas. (Moryson's Foot), 196.
........., Chas. (Honywood's Dragoons), 115.
........., Chas. (3rd Foot Guards), 130.
........., Geo., 130, 131, 203.
........., J——, 121.
........., Jas. (Lord Stair's Dragoons), 110, 189.
........., Jas. (Lord Orkney's Regt.), 134, 236.
........., Jas. (Whetham's Regt.), 164.
........., Jas. (Dubourgay's Regt.), 168.
........., Jas. (Grant's Regt.), 178 bis.
........., Jas. (Firemaster), 369.
........., John, 130, 246.
........., Matt., 111.
........., Pat., 133.
........., Robt., 138.
........., Thos., 200.
........., Wm. (3rd Foot Guards), 130.
........., Wm. (Sankey's Regt.), 209.
Stillingfleet, Edw., 314.
Stirk, Hen., 170.
Stisted, Jos., 343.
Stoakes [Chas.], 122.
Stocker, Obadiah, 128.
Stone, Jas., 138.
........., John, 103.
........., Ric. (Captain), 343.
........., Ric. (Quarter-Master), 301.
........., Sam., 296.
........., Smith, 144.
........., Wm., 329.

Storey, Story, Lancelot, 148, 196.
Stow, Rothwell, 357.
Stowards, Jas., 370.
........., Moses, 370.
Strachey, Wm., 154, 189.
Stratford, Euseby. See Stratford, Euseby.
........., Thos. Wentworth, Earl of, 187.
........., Tristram, 124, 205.
Strahan, Edw., 180.
Strang, Wm. Caesar, 195, 291.
Strangeways. See infra.
Strangways, Arundel, 202.
........., Robt., 172.
Stratford, Euseby, 329 (Strafford).
Straton, Jas., 133.
........., Robt., 133.
Strawbridge, John, 123.
Streeter, Robt., 302.
Strickland, T——, 116.
Strode, Edw., 118, 210.
........., John, 138.
Stroud, Stroude, Edw. See supra.
Strudwick, Edmund, 164.
........., Hen., 110.
........., Sam., 263.
........., Thos., 164.
Strudwicke. See supra.
Stuart, Ric., 327.
Stubbins, Wm., 280.
Studholme, Mark, 309.
Sture, Edw., 166.
Sturton, Sam., 233.
Suckling, John, 115, 213.
Sullivan, Dennis, 353.
........., Fras., 360.
Summers, Bland, 176.
Supple, John (O'Hara's Foot), 203.
........., John (Wills's Foot), 204.
Sutherland, John, 15th Earl of, 235.
Sutton, Hen., 97.
........., John, 170.
........., Ric., memoir of, 55–58.
........., ... Comns. to, 229, 231.
........., ..., Regt. of, 343.
Swan, Chas., 345.
........., Col. [Cornelius], 187.
........., Lieut. Wm., 125, 189.
........., Ensign Wm., 126.
Swanton, Jas., 176.
Swetnam, Wm., 370.
Swift, Arth., 358.
........., John, 140.
........., Mich., 349.
Swiney, Jas., 172.
........., Matth., 124, 215.
Swinny. See supra.
Sybourg, Chas., 330.
Sydenham, Thos., 230, 336.
Sydney, Thos., 186.
Symes, Hen., 355.

Symms, Edw., 234.
........., Sam., 242.
Symonds, Gilb., 234.
........., Ric., 196.
Synge, Mich., 160, 217.
........., Wm., 105, 202.

T

Taaff, Hen., 140.
Talbor, Phil., 125.
Talbot, Gilbert, 138.
........., John. *See* Talbot, Sherington.
........., Ric. *See* Talbott, Ric.
........., Sherington, 131, 188.
Talbott, Ric., 154.
Talmash, Thos., 231.
Tamworth, Washington, Lord, 328.
Tanner, Dan., 168.
Tassell, Chas., 329.
Tattershall, John, 334.
Tatton, Wm., 125, 229, 246.
Taylor (—). *See* Taylor, Thos. (Horse Guards).
........., Arth., 146, 209.
........., Roger, 176.
........., Thos. (Horse Guards), 101 *bis*, 192, 262 *bis*.
........., Thos. (Sankey's Regt.), 176.
........., Thos. (First Troop of Guards), 197, 259.
........., Thos. (Handasyde's), 203.
........., Wm. (Dubourgay's Regt.), 168.
........., Wm. (Windsor's Regt.), 353.
Teale, Ben., 230.
Telfer, Pat., 111.
Tempest, Fitzherbert, 364.
Temple, Pet., 121.
Tench, Phillip, 204, 213.
Tennison, Thos., 328.
Tessur, John, 233.
Testas, Fras., 100.
Testefolle, Claudius, 330.
Tharlow, Edw., 156.
Thayer, John, 206.
Thetford, Edw., 347.
Thomas, Edw. (Coldstream Guards), 128.
........., Edw. (Irish Train), 370.
........., Ric. (Churchill's Dragoons), 120.
........., Ric. (Stanwix's Regt.), 166.
........., Tim., 349.
Thompson, Edw., 358.
........., John (Wills's Regt.), 357.
........., John (Irish Train), 370.
........., Ric., 123.
........., Robt., 217.
........., Wm., 231.
Thornborough, Geo., 210.
Thornicraft, Edw., 162.
Thorold, Wm., 174.

Thurloe, Edw., 303.
Thurston, Mark, 162.
Thwaites, Jas., 156.
Tiboe, Thos., 209.
Tichborne, Colt., 237.
........., Edm., 146.
........., John, 142, 208.
Tichburne. *See supra*.
Tilbury, Chas., 336.
Timpson, Thos., 366.
Tipping, Edgar, 272.
Titchborne. *See* Tichborne.
Todd, Edw., 164.
Tokefield, Fell, 150.
Tomkins, Dan., 216.
Tomms, Miles, 199.
Tompkins, Hen., 121.
Tonge, Thos., 353.
........., Wm., 364.
Tonyne, Chas., 146.
Torin, Paul, 198.
Torphichen, Jas. Sandilands, Lord, 111.
Tottershall. *See* Tattershall.
Toussaint, Pet., 343.
Tovey, Solomon, 182.
Townshend, Robt., 125, 126.
........., Thos., 176.
Tracey. *See* Tracy.
Tracy, Ric., 148, 213, 300.
........., Wm., 302.
Trail, Jas., 248.
Treby, Geo., 114.
Trelawny, Chas., 228.
........., John, 140 *bis*, 228, 297.
........., Wm., 140, 200.
Tremaigne, Tremayne, John, 170, 309.
Trenchard, Thos., 311.
Trepsack, John, 299.
Trevanion, Ric., 146, 227.
Tripp, Robt., 158.
Trotter, Geo., 366.
Tryce, Jasper, 190, 217.
Tucker, John, 140.
Tuckey, Fras., 158, 187, 215.
Tudman, Ben., 105, 199.
Tulikens, Arnoldus, 148, 196.
Tulley (—), 210.
Tullie, Thos., 197.
Tully, Jerome, 166.
........., Thos., [Thos.], 126, 186.
Tuman, Tim., 370.
Turnbull, Robt., 353.
Turner, Geo., 201.
........., John, 336.
Turnor, Edmund, 100.
Tuthill, Thos., 200, 305.
Twisleton, Fiennes, 338.
Tyre, Jas., 362.
Tyrrell, Edw., 207, 341.
........., Jas., 121.

INDEX

U

Upton, John, 110.
........, Wm., 164, 213.
Urquhart, Jas., 191.
........, Robt., 345.
Urwin, Ralph, 298.
Usher, Arth., 336.
........, John, 332.
Uvedale, Edw., 278.

V

Vachell, Chas., 298.
........, Hen., 142, 291.
........, Thos., 140.
........, Wm., 142.
Van Deck, Hen. Harman, 366.
Vandeleur, Pet., 369.
Vandeluier, Pet. *See supra.*
Vane, Geo., 240.
Vannamen, Max., 140.
Vans, Fras., 182.
Vanse, Wm., 360.
Vanwell, Lambert, 142.
Varey, Jas., 101.
........, John, 211.
Vatchell. *See* Vachell.
Vaughan, Geo. *See infra* Gwyn.
........, Gwyn, 233, 248.
........, Ralph, 371.
........, Wilmot, 299.
Venice, Wm., 186, 307.
Venner, Thos., 208.
Vernon (—), 123.
........, Thos., 215.
Vetch, Col. James. *See infra,* Sam.
........, Col. Sam., 187, 228, 230, 240, 241.
Vezey, Wm., 160.
Vezian, John, 336.
Vickers, Geo., 362.
........, John, 160.
Vier [Weir], Geo., 209.
Vigors, Thos., 197.
Villiers, Hen., 332.
Vimcelle, And., 341.
Vincent, John, 251.
........, Thos., 347.
Vissouse, Guy, 112.
Vivian, John, 150.

W

Wade, Chris., 180.
........, Geo., 207, 227, 246, 361.
........, Wm., 264, 361.
Waide, Ben., 227.
Wains, Wm., 172.
Wakefield, Wm., 148.
Waldron, Hen., 152.

Wale, John, 276.
Walford, Ric., 190.
Walker, Chas., 121, 211.
........, Geo., 325, 326.
........, John, 232.
........, Ric., 203.
........, Wm., 146.
Walkinshaw, Robt., 214, 307.
Waller, John, 328 *bis.*
........, Matth., 343.
........, Ric., 289.
........, Robt., 318.
Wallis, Fairfax, 205.
........, Wm., 280.
Walpole, Robt., 130.
Walsh (—), 174.
........, Ben., 199.
........, Edw., 306.
........, Geo., 152, 194, 204.
........, Phillip, 192.
........, Raphael, 366.
Walters, Chas., 347.
Walton, Thos., 210.
........, Wm., 263.
Wandesford (—), 172.
........, Geo., 233.
........, Syd., 233.
Wanless (*or* Wamless), Wm., 162.
Wansborough, Brudenel, 156, 213.
Wansbrough. *See* Wansborough.
Warburton (—), 122.
Ward, Chas., 362.
........, Cromwell, 205.
........, David, 357.
........, Geo., 339.
Wardlaw, Chas., 138, 186.
........, Sam., 138, 186.
Wardlour, John, 362.
Wardour, Tomkins, 103.
Waring, Edmund, 318.
........, Ric., 186, 229, 329.
Warlock, Wm., 346.
Warnes, Jacob, 113.
Warren, Abel, 349.
........, Edw., 362 *bis.*
........, Jas., 148, 196.
........, John (Lumley's Horse), 103, 189.
........, John (2nd Foot Guards), 128.
........, Robt., 96.
Warring. *See* Waring.
Washington, Ric., 134.
Watkins, Fleetwood, 358.
........, Geo., 230, 234.
........, John, 180.
Watson, Humph., 122.
........, Cornet John, 117, 193.
........, Ensign John, 134.
........, Jonas, 285.
........, Thos., 309.
........, Wm., 263.

INDEX

Watts (—), Robt., 115, 271.
........., Sam., 366.
........., Thos., 310.
Wattson, John, 369.
Weakfield. *See* Wakefield.
Weaver, Sam., 96.
Webb, Borelace, 336.
........., Edm., 152.
........., John, 231, 249.
........., John Richmond, 336.
........., Capt. Thos., 172.
........., Ensign Thos., 358.
Weddell, Chas., 303.
Wedderburne, Sir John, 308.
Wederburn. *See* Wedderburne.
Weems, Jas., 242.
Weir, Geo., 209. *See also* Vier (*sic*).
........., Wm., 133.
Welburne, Geo., 205.
Weld, Thos., 166, 214.
Welde. *See* Weld.
Weldon, Arth., 176.
........., John, 347.
Wells, Wm., 329.
Welsh, Anthony, 339.
........., Jas., 332.
Wenman, Ric., 206.
Wentworth, Thos., 99, 186, 193.
........., Wm., 106.
West, John, 95, 186, 190, 259.
........., Nich., 339.
........., Ric., 176.
........., Rowland, 140.
Westbrook, John, 172.
Weston, Wm., 185.
Wharton, John, 146, 299.
Wheate, T——, 124.
Wheeler, And., 125.
........., Chas., 115.
........., Fras. *See* Wheler.
........., Oliver, 361.
........., Pet. (*sic*), 271.
........., Thos., 300.
Wheler (—). *See* Wheler, Thos.
........., Fras., 128, 203.
........., Thos., 148.
Whetham, Surgeon John, 164.
........., John, 164.
........., Ensign Jos., 164.
........., Thos., 164, 229, 235.
Whichcott, Ben., 241.
Whiston, Jas., 154, 302.
........., John, 154.
Whitaker, Edw., 197.
White, Jas., 133.
........., John (Tp. Gren. Gds.), 199.
........., John (Moryson's Regt.), 196.
........., Ric. (Carpenter's Dragoons), 109.
........., Ric. (Lucas's Regt.), 319.
........., Solomon, 334.

White—*cont.*
........., Thos. (Grove's Regt.), 199.
........., Thos. (Pearce's Regt.), 211.
........., Thos. (Artillery Train), 281.
........., Thos. (Webb's Regt.), 336.
........., Thos. (Welsh Fusiliers), 347.
........., Timothy, 170.
........., Wm., 138, 208.
Whitecomb, Edw., 95.
Whitehead, John, 370.
Whitfield, Ralph, 347.
Whiting, John, 156, 343.
Whitley, Hen., 201, 265.
Whitmore (—). *See* Whitmore, Geo.
........., Arth., 364.
........., Edw., 364.
........., Geo., 180, 203, 293.
........., Wm., 194, 203.
Whitney, Edw., 113.
........., John, 156.
........., Shugbrough, 156.
........., Thos., 170.
Whitshed, Sam., 154, 189, 268.
Whitshett. *See supra*.
Whittick, Chas., 358.
Whitworth, John, 164.
........., Ric., 325, 326.
Wichalse, John, 362.
Wickham, Wm., 170.
Widdington, Wm., 349.
Widdrington, Wm., 310.
Wigham, Robt., 110, 207.
Wightman, Cuthb., 263.
........., John, 203.
........., Major-General Jos., memoir of, 48-54.
........., ..., Comns. to, 229, 235, 246.
........., ..., Regt. of, 341.
........., Robt., 160.
........., Wm., 208.
Wilbraham, John, 302.
Wilcox, Nat., 338.
Wildbraham. *See* Wilbraham.
Wildey, Thos., 273.
Wilkie, Chas., 307.
Williams (—), 208.
........., Chas. (Dubourgay's Regt.), 194.
........., Chas. (Wills's Regt.), 357.
........., Chris., 361 *bis*.
........., John (Kirke's Regt.), 136, 202.
........., John (Maccartney's Regt.), 207.
........., John (Indep. Cy.), 240, 312.
........., John (Rl. Irish Regt.), 304.
........., John (Armstrong's Regt.), 314.
........., Thos. (Cotton's Regt.), 152, 200.
........., Thos. (Dubourgay's Regt.), 317.
........., Wm. (Rl. Horse Guards), 101.
........., Wm. (Seymour's Regt.), 211.
Williamson, Adam, 216, 343.
........., Dav., 214.
........., Edm., 281.

Williamson—*cont.*
........., Edw., 200, 202.
........., Fras., 138, 296.
........., John, 259.
........., Robt., 291.
........., Wm., 117.
Willoughby, And., 362.
........., Ric., 362.
Wills, Gen. Sir Chas., K.B., memoir of, 59-70.
........., ..., Regt. of, 357.
........., ..., Comns. to, 229, 231, 232, 246, 251.
........., Ensign Chas., 209.
........., Edward, 112.
........., Wm., 116.
Willson, Jas., 369.
Wilmer, Geo., 125.
Wilmot, Robt., 210.
Wilson, Alex., 358 *bis*.
........., Hen., 138, 296.
........., John, 202.
........., Robt., 103, 230.
........., Sam., 138.
Wiltshire, John, 370.
Winchester, Marqs. of (Charles Paulet), 207.
Windle, John, 202.
Windress, Wm., 366.
Windsor, Andrews, 353.
........., Dixie, 285.
........., Thos., Lord Visct., 105, 229.
Windus, Edw., 152.
........., John, 198.
Wingate (—), 189.
Wingfield, Hen., 158.
Winsley, Combe, 251.
........., Geo., 228.
Winyard. *See* Wynyard.
Wise, Thos., 317.
Wiseman, Edm., 206, 295.
Wishet. *See* Whitshed.
Withall, Ben., 281.
Witherhill, Hen., 194.
Witherington, Wm., 113.
Withers, Geo., 150.
........., Hen., 125, 246, 249.
........., Hunt, 247.
........., John, 112.
Withrington, Wm., 310, 349. (Widdington, Widdrington).

Witterong. *See infra.*
Wittewrong, John, 114.
Wolfe, Edw., 168, 357.
........., Mich., 202.
Wood, Jas., 201.
.... Pat., 166.
.... Ralph, 281.
.... Thos., 162, 212.
Woodhouse, Thos., 343.
Woodroffe, Ben., 216.
Woodward, Sam., 270.
Wooly, John, 193, 217.
Worthington, Ric., 156.
Wrath, Chas., 174.
Wray, Geo., 360.
Wren, John, 228.
Wrench, Robt., 273.
Wright, Edmund, 95, 193, 339 *bis*.
........., Jas., 150.
........., John, 370.
........., Mat., 150.
........., Sham (*sic*), 191.
........., Wm., 362.
Wroth, Hen., 101, 262.
Wroughton, Seymour, 362.
Wybault, Jas., 369.
Wye, Wm., 366.
Wyndham, Wm., 275.
Wyndram, Geo., 233.
Wynn, John, 191.
Wynne, Col. Owen, 113, 229, 269.
........., Cornet Owen, 113.
........., Wm., 142.
Wynyard, John, 188.
Wyvell, Wyvill, John, 101, 106, 188.

Y

Yard, Walt., 170.
Young, John, 336.
........., Jonathan, 355.
........., Jos., 158.
........., Thos., 130, 191.

Z

Zobell, Chris., 112.

www.ingramcontent.com/pod-product-compliance
Lightning Source LLC
Chambersburg PA
CBHW060452300426
44113CB00016B/2569